The
Critical Surf Studies
Reader

The
Critical Surf Studies
Reader / DEXTER ZAVALZA HOUGH-SNEE

AND ALEXANDER SOTELO EASTMAN, EDITORS

Duke University Press   Durham and London   2017

Cover designed by Heather Hensley; interior designed by Courtney Leigh Baker
Typeset in Garamond Premier Pro by Westchester Publishing Services

Library of Congress Cataloging-in-Publication Data
Names: Hough-Snee, Dexter Zavalza, editor. | Sotelo Eastman, Alexander, [date] editor.
Title: The critical surf studies reader / Dexter Zavalza Hough-Snee and Alexander Sotelo
Eastman, editors.
Description: Durham : Duke University Press, 2017. | Includes bibliographical references
and index. | Description based on print version record and CIP data provided by
publisher; resource not viewed.
Identifiers: LCCN 2017015437 (print)
LCCN 2017018130 (ebook)
ISBN 9780822372820 (ebook)
ISBN 9780822369578 (hardcover)
ISBN 9780822369721 (pbk.)
Subjects: LCSH: Surfing. | Surfing—Social aspects.
Classification: LCC GV839.5 (ebook) | LCC GV839.5 .C75 2017 (print) |
DDC 797.3/2—dc23
LC record available at https://lccn.loc.gov/2017015437

Cover art: RooM the Agency/Alamy Stock Photo.

Contents

List of Abbreviations

AAU   American Athletic Union

ALAS   Asociación latinoamericana de surfistas profesionales [Latin American Association of Surfing Professionals] (1998–present)

ASA   American Surfing Association

ASP   Association of Surfing Professionals (1983–2014)

ATP   Association of Tennis Professionals

CT   Championship Tour (under WSL, 2014–present)

ESA   Eastern Surfing Association

HWS   History of Women's Surfing; www.historyofwomensurfing.com

IOC   International Olympic Committee

IPS   International Professional Surfers (1976–1982; precursor to the ASP and WSL)

ISA   International Surfing Association (1976–present; formerly the ISF)

ISF   International Surfing Federation (1964–1972; precursor to the ISA)

IWS   International Women's Surfing (2000–present)

NSSA   National Scholastic Surfing Association (1978–present)

QS   Qualifying Series (under WSL, 2014–present; formerly the WQS under the ASP)

USSF   United States Surfing Federation

WCT   World Championship Tour (under ASP)

WISA   Women's International Surfing Association (1975–1993)

WQS   World Qualifying Series (under ASP)

WSL   World Surf League (prior to 2014, the Association of Surfing Professionals)

WT   World Tour (under WSL; formerly the WCT under the ASP)

Acknowledgments

The critical surfing studies field is currently undergoing a scholarly renaissance of sorts and, at the time of publication, contributions to the field continue to emerge from diverse academic disciplines and wave-riding communities across the globe. In this moment of tremendous growth and expansion of core academic research related to surfing, we owe a debt of gratitude to the many surfers with whom we have discussed this volume and the social, political, and cultural state of surfing around the world. We have encountered countless fellow surfers concerned with how surfing culture, sport, and industry can be more socially meaningful and politically influential, as well as less environmentally damaging. We are grateful to everyone who has shared an insight or a laugh that contributes to critical conversations within the surfing world, and to those who demand that surfing retain social, political, and environmental value.

We have the contributors to thank for the project's success, and we wish to thank the authors for their patience, cooperation, and enthusiasm throughout the process of coordinating this collection. As we have stated from the project's outset, we hope that this collaborative effort has been a joyous experience! It has certainly been rewarding for us, and every exchange—in person, via email, and over the phone—has been a pleasure and a privilege.

Several contributors merit an expression of our gratitude. Krista Comer met with us on several occasions from project genesis through completion, providing us with valuable insights along the way. Glen Thompson, Robin Canniford, and Doug Booth contributed ideas and support for the project from its very inception, and Clifton Evers provided excellent advice at the planning stages of the volume. Pat Moser was kind enough to show us around his Northern California stomping grounds and connect us with several veteran authors. Conversations with Cori Schumacher and Dina Gilio-Whitaker contributed to our sense of the field's reach beyond academia and its intersections with their work.

Special thanks are also due to lisahunter, Rebecca Olive, and Belinda Wheaton for organizing and hosting the University of Waikato's February 2016 Surfing Social Hui in Raglan, New Zealand. Several contributors were present among the distinguished panelists, and many used this forum to explore and challenge themes found in this volume. Additionally, it provided occasion for members of the international research community to meet one another and share ideas, laughs, and waves in a true surfing mecca.

Others who are not represented in the table of contents have contributed much to this project in correspondence and conversation, including Matt Warshaw, Pat Snee, Rebecca Olive, Tetsuhiko Endo, Rafael Fortes, Rory Parker, Derek Rielly, Elliot Pill, Cleber Dias, Yago Colás, Juan Poblete, Hector Fernández L'Hoeste, and J'aime Morrison. Thanks to each of you!

At Berkeley, Dexter would like to thank Emilie Bergmann, Estelle Tarica, Natalia Brizuela, Michael Iarocci, Ignacio Navarrete, Lisa Trever, and Todd Olson. Each has shaped this project more than they might suspect! Alex extends his gratitude to Billy Acree and Ignacio Sánchez Prado at Washington University in St. Louis for taking surfing seriously and believing in this, and other, works of surf scholarship. Additional thanks are due to Alex's colleagues at Dartmouth College for their support and encouragement, in particular the members of the Society of Fellows and Reena Goldthree.

Many thanks are due to Courtney Berger at Duke University Press for her commitment to seeing this project through to print. We would also like to express our deepest thanks to Sandra Korn for her contributions from Durham, as well as those of Lisa Bintrim, Christopher Robinson, Heather Hensley, and Rosanne Hallowell. It has been an honor to work with the Duke University Press family, and we are grateful to have had such a wonderful editorial team from day one. On behalf of all involved with the project, we would like to extend our thanks to the anonymous readers assigned to the manuscript. Your contributions to the volume are much appreciated!

This volume was possible only with the advocacy, support, and encouragement of our graduate mentors. We would like to extend our utmost gratitude to Ivonne del Valle and Billy Acree, unfailing mentors, readers, teachers, and friends during our nascent scholarly careers. In spite of their distance from the surfing world, their enthusiasm, rigor, political conviction, and intellectual curiosity are each present in this volume.

The infinite support and endearment of Claudia and Elvita Zavalza and Meghan Kyle are essential not only to this project but to every word we've ever written. Thank you.

Introduction

DEXTER ZAVALZA HOUGH-SNEE AND
ALEXANDER SOTELO EASTMAN

Surfing is fun! Anyone who has dedicated a lifetime—or even five minutes—to playing in the ocean is quick to acknowledge that, at its most visceral level, riding a wave is a unique thrill. As the push of a wave takes over, the human body cheats gravity ever so briefly, rendering the rider weightless, the body's fitness challenged to harness raw aquatic energy and convert brute natural force into the sensation of gliding across time and space toward no particular destination but the wave's culmination, lapping onto the shore, smashing into the rocks, or folding back into the ocean's currents. To ride a wave is to steal a fleeting glimpse into what it might be like to live as a human intermediary between land, sea, and heavens, to live without resolve and yet embrace some intangible, inexpressibly beautiful purpose. And so, surfing engenders a romantic attraction and emotional entanglement with nature, beauty, performance, the body, and uninhibited play, further heightened by the surf's apparent distance from earthly concerns.

While many an athlete is a fanatic, few are romantics and even fewer, mystics. But surfers are romantics, their calling mystical, the appeal of riding waves capable of miraculously rousing the young, old, infirm, and overworked in the twilight to convene at the beach or set out overnight in search of distant surf, new experiences, and companionship found only in shared pursuits. As a good day's fishing does not necessarily involve catching fish, a good day surfing is about much more than riding waves. It is the interplay of elements involved that provides relief, however momentary, from the mundane, the predictable, the sedentary, and the purposeless. Nature dictates swell, wind, and tide, each proctoring tests of devotion, patience, knowledge, and skill, aptitudes acquired only with endless hours on the water and relationships forged with individual roads, beaches, footpaths, rocks, sandbars, and skylines. And, after the thrill of the first ride, it is these relationships that form the common bond among the hopelessly addicted, who congregate time and time again to revel in the nuances of conditions braved, waves caught, and boards ridden.

This volume is, at its core, a collection of scholarly essays about surfing and all of its mystical, performative, and communitarian trappings that together make surfing an enchantingly powerful form of good clean fun. And given the intense appreciation for bobbing in the ocean that those who enjoy riding waves share, it is unsurprising that the marriage of this pastime to critical inquiry is not new. After all, wave-riding spans millennia, including the ancient navigational wave-riding of north-central Peru atop Mochica *tup* (reed kayaks; *caballitos de totora* in Spanish), the aquatic cultures of West Africa, and the variants of stand-up and prone surfing that characterized pre-occupation Hawai'i and the precolonial Pacific. Surfing's phenomenological appeal has long proved capable of leading all kinds of people to the water's edge, and the way in which the joys of wave-riding have moved across time and space is infinitely more complex than the simple pleasures of playing in the surf zone. Fundamentally shaped by indigenous, colonial, industrial, and neoliberal histories, surfing—as religion, cultural practice, ludic pursuit, countercultural iconography, competitive sport, multinational industry, and consumer culture—is a profoundly complex global practice, rife with contradictions. And four centuries of writing about surfing has emerged from and reflected on these contradictions, impacting diverse peoples, connecting distant geographies, and linking their constituent cultural, social, economic, and political practices.

At its core, this volume is also an intervention, reflecting on surfing's *longue durée* to further illuminate surfing's relationship to those practices and the ways that unadulterated wave-riding, fun at its core, can become entwined with the nuances of social life. The essays included here approach surfing from wide-ranging geographic perspectives, as scholars, activists, public intellectuals, and surfers seek to demystify wave-riding cultures' entanglements with social and political life. Many essays posit realities dissonant with mythic rhetorics of an idyllic or monolithic surfing past. Others engage archives and active partici-pant research to identify surfing in unexpected times and places, challenging colonial and patriarchal appropriations and destabilizing hegemonic narratives of surfing as exclusive to white bourgeois beach culture. Yet others imagine and advocate for alternative futures realized through surfing, suggesting the pos-sibility of affecting social change in the microcosm of the surfing world before carrying it outward. But even in light of often-activist intentions, this volume is still, at its core, a collection of scholarly essays about surfing.

And scholarly appropriation of culture is, itself, a form of colonization. Rec-ognizing this maxim cannot reverse such an appropriation. And reification of surfing, scholarly or otherwise, risks rendering wave-riding something inordi-nately special, independent of the social, political, and economic worlds that have shaped it. With that in mind, this volume emerges in a moment of much thinking about how to render surfing—as culture, iconography, competitive sport, industry, and area of scholarly inquiry—a more egalitarian social space. In opposition to shallowly conceived, surf-centric neoliberal organizations in the private and nonprofit sectors, the last decade has seen the rise of countless activist initiatives pushing to recast surfing—past and present—in restorative feminist, queer, ethnically and racially inclusive, and decolonial modes.[1] And while one might rightfully note that there is a certain irony in attempting to decolonize or "queer" a pastime whose modern cultural legacy is generally (if inaccurately) associated with bourgeois whiteness and coastal affluence, there is much practical value in moving surfing culture and sport—the spoils of two and a half centuries of cultural colonization—toward a recognition and correc-tion of their violent pasts.

These corrections are not easily realized, especially given the entanglement of development initiatives with for-profit entities and superficial denomina-tions of surfing as social good. Under such claims, surfing and its industries are lauded, often uncritically, as capable of correcting profound structural in-equalities produced by enduring global North–South disparities inherent to surfing's very popularization across the world. However, by occupying a schol-arly position divorced from the profit-driven surfing industry, this collection seeks to take one more step—if, admittedly, largely theoretical—toward such a correction. In its collective interventions, this volume contributes to rethinking and redeploying surfing outside its long-standing colonial and patriarchal origins and beyond recent neoliberal manifestations.

In recent decades, the emergence of humanities and social sciences scholarship related to surfing has stemmed from the undeniable contradictions of surfing's historical development and its accompanying narratives, those "changing images" that have long enthralled surfing's commentators.[2] Wave-riding was originally a ritual practice and a mechanism of political and social organization in pre-occupation Hawai'i.[3] Upon European arrival to the islands in the eighteenth century, the act of wave-riding was actively opposed by European authorities who, after initial wonder, sought to moderate the "indecency" and "idleness" that missionaries perceived in an indigenous Hawaiian beach culture that revolved around hierarchized modes of surfing.[4] On the eve of the nineteenth-century annexation of the Hawaiian Islands, white settlers, investors, and developers would appropriate the sacred practice as a leisure activity to attract mainland tourism to the islands.[5] Yet surfing was first practiced on the mainland in 1885, not by returning tourists, but by Native Hawaiian royalty studying in Northern California.[6] Introduced across North America and Australia as a recreational novelty during the 1910s by Native Hawaiian Duke Kahanamoku and part-Hawaiian George Freeth, surfing quickly reached elite circles in coastal environs worldwide, taking hold in Peru, Brazil, and South Africa, among other coastal nations, in the 1930s.[7] In these same decades, surfing would be touted alongside sea bathing to attract homebuyers to the California coast and promote aquatic leisure elsewhere in the world.[8] During surfing's first decades as a modern practice, wave-riding appeared more a tool of promotional fun than a sporting culture or stand-alone industry.

Surfing continued during World War II, with a new contingent of American servicemen picking up the practice in the Pacific, although international travel to Hawai'i, still surfing's epicenter, diminished. Upon the war's conclusion, materials developed via military technologies, such as fiberglass and composite foam, became surfboard construction materials. After incipient failures at organizing surfing competitions, surfing's previous promotional value for coastal tourism and development yielded the consolidation of surf-riding exhibitions into formal competitive affairs, laying the groundwork for the organization of competitive surfing and the onset of global surf travel in the 1950s.[9] Consumer airlines simultaneously opened new modes of overseas transportation that enabled nascent surf travel. By the mid-1950s, international competitions became annual events with standardized judging criteria, beginning with the Makaha International Surfing Championships (1954–1971) and the Peru International Surfing Championships (1956–1974).[10] As competitions grew and the World Surfing Championships (1964–1972) were established, governing bodies quickly emerged to further regulate judging criteria and administer prizes. Surf-specific media arose to cover these events and promote a wide array of new surfing consumer goods and fashions, beginning with California's *Surfer* magazine, founded 1960. With ABC's *Wide World of Sports* covering the Makaha contest for American audiences between 1962 and 1965, surf-specific media exploded. Australia's first publication, *Surfing World*, appeared in 1962, followed by *New Zealand Surf Magazine* in 1965 and California-birthed *International Surfing* in 1962 (abbreviated to *Surfing* in 1974). By the 1970s, the appearance of numerous other global publications—South Africa's *South African Surfer* (1965–1968), *Down the Line* (1976–1977), and *ZigZag* (1976), the Florida quarterly *Wave Rider* (1975–1982), Peru's *Tabla Hawaiiana* (1971) and *Tabla* (1983–1984), and the Brazilian *Brasil Surf* (1975–1978), *Quebra-Mar* (1978), and *Surf Sul* (1979), among others—marked the rise of endemic surf media that would inaugurate dozens of global publications in the 1980s. Anchored by the International Surfing Federation (ISF; 1964–1972) and its successor, the International Olympic Committee (IOC)–recognized International Surfing Association (ISA; 1976–present), competitive surfing became professional surfing with the formation of the International Professional Surfers (IPS; 1976–1982) group, the precursor to the Association of Surfing Professionals (ASP; 1983–2014) and the World Surf League (WSL; 2014–present). The cooperation of surfing media with competitive surfing infrastructure, the rise of surf industry, and continued coastal development in surfing places led to a vast network of twentieth-century institutions centered around promoting and profiting from surfing.

As this network emerged, the contradictions inherent in surfing's cultural makeup intensified. During California's postwar economic boom, surfing in North America came to be associated with Anglo-American leisure and countercultural resistance to the labor demands of capitalism in Southern California, this in spite of the sport's decidedly elite following, especially in the Global South.[11] As postwar technological advances enabled the material evolution of the equipment used to ride waves—surfboards, board shorts, wetsuits, and essential accessories—the cottage industries manufacturing the requisite wares for surfing exploded into a massive commodity-driven global supply chain. The industrialization of surf goods production further rendered surfing a Western—and, eventually, neoliberal—practice.[12] All the while, as commoditized surf culture and its goods and personalities continued circulating in the diverse imaginaries and landscapes of the ever-globalizing world of the last half century, the sport has maintained constant contact with the frontiers of local and global politics, gender and race relations, and emergent economic practices and ideologies.[13]

Through renewable marketing iconographies, surfing continues to hold connotations of an indigenous ritual practice and a heathen temptation. It enables Westerners both to purportedly "go native" and to recolonize the postcolonial world with blissful ignorance, surfboards under arm. Idle time in the waves implies a surfer's resistance to participation in capitalism, yet the sport's most recognizable brands are publicly traded, multinational entities, and corporate-sponsored professional surfers gross millions of dollars annually. In spite of their self-cultivated identity as feral travelers and countercultural icons, Western surfers are often associated with affluence—or, as one surf journalist put it, "surfing is now perceived as a pastime nestled between golf and yoga, as opposed to a vice favored by coastal juvenile delinquents."[14] Surfing is simultaneously an impetus for tourism, a local economic stimulus, and a source of great socioeconomic disparity in terms of wave-riding destinations. Surfing practice implies phenomenological liberation, while unidirectional tourism from the Global North to the Global South and overseas manufacturing highlight structural and material barriers to any sort of surf-inspired socioeconomic egalitarianism. Women feature prominently in surfing iconography and constitute a major surfing population worldwide. Yet all too frequently, female surfers are relegated to the realm of eroticized beach spectators or emissaries of exotic seduction.

Surfing is rife with contradictions that beg further scholarly inquiry. It is these tensions that this volume seeks to confront.

Critical Surfing Studies: Envisioning Surfing's Radical Potential

Critical surfing studies are, simply enough, the aggregate of scholarly production in which the history, culture, and practice of surfing, its practitioners, and its cumulative media and industry institutions are central to inquiry and analysis. As the below review indicates, surfing scholarship is decades old. However, until recently, many surfing scholars have worked in relative isolation without direct dialogue across disciplinary boundaries or national academic traditions. This volume marks the conversion of a set of once-isolated specialists into a consolidated international community of scholars of surfing culture, history, and politics, coming together to envision the radical potential of surfing studies to dialogue with contemporary issues in the surfing community, to review prevailing academic debates in the humanities and social sciences, and to develop activist networks. This is not the first academic collaboration with surfing as its subject, and it does not purport to mark some new field that is only now emergent. Rather, the present volume constitutes a rigorous, collaborative gesture, uniting scholarly voices from diverse academic disciplines, institutional profiles, and national university systems.

Surfing's historical dissemination globally and its sundry manifestations and discourses have impacted the development of the field in a way that is not the case for many national or regional sporting traditions. The field is unique in that many scholars employ hybrid methodologies marking the intersection of their home disciplines and broader means of leveraging historical archives and giving voice to contemporary surfing practitioners. In doing so, historicizing the surfing world and interrogating its massive popular archive are imperative. So, too, is the need to incorporate fieldwork and active participation research in order to accurately position the voices of surfing's practitioners, from celebrated figures to common beachgoers, commercial enterprises to community activists. Each contributor takes a unique approach informed by his or her disciplinary training and distinct relationships with the surfing world in an attempt to posit critique, allude to programmatic outcomes for the direction of surfing studies, and couple scholarship with the broader surfing world.

While surfing—as indigenous tradition, recreational activity, professional sport, culture, industry, and social act—is the unifying theme, this volume is more concerned with analyzing and theorizing the flow of ideas, bodies, and commodities between beach communities than it is with wave-riding in its strictest sense. The collection features self-reflective, deeply historicized interventions that collectively push to define the limits of surfing's relationship to academia, activism, and development, as well as industry, media, and governance, uniquely plotting the coordinates of contemporary surfing scholarship. Many of the essays strive to transcend critique and allude to programmatic outcomes for surfing, scholarship, and activism to attempt to overcome the modern surfing world's colonizing, commercial, patriarchal, and neoliberal impulses, wherever they may be identified, from the classroom or holiday villa to the factory or the beach.

Within the rapidly rising field of surfing-related studies, the volume has three primary objectives. First, it further consolidates surfing's scholarly legitimacy as a means of analyzing social, cultural, and economic relations. Surfing is not a mere object for theoretical dissection. Instead, it is a practice suggestive of the need for systematic engagement and critique cognizant of the theoretical debates central to cultural studies (including, but not limited to, the theoretical coordinates of gender and women's studies, ethnic studies, postcolonial studies, and indigenous studies). In dialoguing with the paradoxes and plight of multinational surf industry, international tourism, political activism, and environmentalism, surfing's constitutive global flows of people and capital are the protagonists of these essays, which aim to speak not only to scholarly researchers, but also to the surfing community at large.

Second, this volume forges core disciplinary connections with the humanities and social sciences by providing a small sampling of current global research on surfing taking place across a variety of traditional academic disciplines. Whereas surfing has gained some traction in business, hospitality, and international development schools in the United Kingdom and the United States, much research on surfing exists in a disciplinary and theoretical vacuum. This volume seeks to position surfing scholarship within core humanities and social science disciplines, demonstrating the interdisciplinarity of surfing studies and the theoretical rigor of scholarship taking place outside of revenue-driven inquiry. As such, the volume ultimately questions the appropriation of surfing studies within corporate university models and resists surfing's academic institutionalization in profit-driven fields.

Last, the volume responds to recent trends in competitive surfing, manufacturing, media, tourism, nonprofit sectors, and higher education that champion surfing as an unquestionable, categorical social good. Competitive surfing has gone mass market in its broadcast tactics, crafting an accompanying poetics of philanthropic benevolence. In summer 2016, the IOC added surfing to the 2020 Tokyo Olympics, lauding it for its youth appeal and potential for cross-cultural understanding. In less than a decade, surf-specific nongovernmental organizations (NGOs) with myriad missions and charters have become pervasive in the coastal developing world. In higher education, numerous study-abroad programs have deployed surfing as a pastime resonant with student populations for diverse purposes, including revenue. And while our volume does not share the objectives of these programs—in fact, it contests them—it is a clear supplement to the rising institutionalization of surfing beyond its traditional manufacturing and media boundaries. Through collective reflections on surfing in local and global contexts, this book provides a scholarly anthology to reorient surfing studies as a rigorous, deeply politicized, cultural studies subfield relevant across disciplines.

Like the current surf studies field, this collection is a product of the genesis and maturation of an identifiable critical surfing literature. We turn now to its history, tracing popular surf writing's relationship to the university to plot the present field.

WRITING ABOUT SURFING

While scholarly work on surfing was limited until recent decades, there has never been a shortage of writing about surfing. On the contrary, beginning with the colonial chronicles and missionary accounts accompanying European colonization of the Pacific and spanning practically every literary and nonfiction genre since, there is such an abundance of literature on the practice that it would be impossible to proffer a comprehensive bibliography of surfing publications.[15] Instead, we would like to signal a few trends, pivotal moments, and issues in the development of writing about surfing while paying special attention to the intellectual and critical undercurrents within popular media that gave rise to critical surf studies.

It is difficult to overstate the centrality of popular surf media—including magazines, films, and documentaries—to the history and historiography of surfing. The initial wave of magazines from the 1960s was primarily a regional affair that centralized the visually captivating aspects of surfing. The first issue of what would become the longest-standing surf magazine to date, *The Surfer* (now simply *Surfer*), contained just two articles, one entitled "Surfing for Beginners," and sold 5,000 copies.[16] These early magazines did not approach surfing through a critical lens but aimed to entertain and inform the public through explanations and depictions of what constituted surfing and its related lifestyle. Light-heartedness and carefree tones aside, by offering definitions of surfing—visually or verbally—surf publications and writers limited the possibilities of expression and diversity for surfers and their culture. Magazine directors came to be seen as the authorities of a rapidly spreading activity popular with the coastal, white, middle-upper class.

Surf media's attempt to control the direction and representation of surfing became more explicit and heavy-handed as the riding of waves—and, in particular, the representation of it—proved to be a lucrative commodity. Were surfers countercultural rebels, beach bums, athletes, or everyday citizens? Was surfing a recreational activity, hobby, or sport? Surfing was unquestionably fun, but did it encourage a wholesome lifestyle or usher in idleness and vice? On the whole, editors and directors of surf magazines and films from the 1960s denounced the rebellious manifestations of surfing and set out to promote a "scrubbed up" and decidedly "whitewashed" version of it.[17] These conservative and even repressive publications are far from what we conceptualize as critical surf studies today. Riddled with silences, omissions, and distortions, they embody a foundational moment and stand as an unavoidable source base in their purposeful recording of modern surfing history. If attempts to control the image and representation of surfing are clearly expressed in the pages of surf magazines, the goal in doing so was less apparent. Much clearer is the trajectory that surfing and surf writing would take in the following decades.

Historically, writing for major surfing publications has been an exclusive affair limited to small circles in specific geographic areas (Southern California and Australia's east coast, for example). Outsiders to these circuits, and particularly women, are noticeably absent from the ranks of mainstream surf media, whose content has long been attached to sponsor agendas. These circuits allude to perhaps the most defining feature of surf writing: proximity to the subject matter. In 1983, world champion (1966 and 1970) Nat Young took on the ambitious endeavor of writing a history of surfing.[18] Following suit, today's most prolific popular surf historians, Matt Warshaw and Drew Kampion, cut their teeth as writers and editors at major surf magazines.[19] Kampion is a prime example of this insider positionality in the surf industry, where writers wore multiple hats as practitioners, competitors, business owners, advertising agents, popular historians, or all of the above. An editor of *Surfer* from 1968 to 1972 and *Surfing* from 1973 to 1982, Kampion then headed the advertising department for apparel brand O'Neill before penning several foundational popular histories.[20] Likewise, former *Surfer* writer and editor (1984–1990) Warshaw's intensively researched print publications have culminated in his curatorship of the History of Surfing (http://Historyofsurfing.net) and the Encyclopedia of Surfing (http://Encyclopediaofsurfing.com/) websites; the latter was sponsored by *Surfer* magazine between 2011 and 2016. Platforms somewhere between "a museum, an archive, and even a theater," alternately described as "a conservation project . . . a digital place where the sport can be presented, stored, celebrated, archived, and accessed," the innovative projects' ties to the legacy publication *Surfer* further highlight the embeddedness of even the most rigorous and self-aware surf writing in long-standing media and industry circles.[21] The surf industry's "revolving door" between publications, advertisers, and competitive governance has hampered investigative journalism and created what critics have called an "incestuous relationship" in which select insiders dominate the pulpit and rebut dissent.[22]

One is hard-pressed to find more exaggerated claims than those of the popular histories celebrating the anniversaries of surf magazines. Take, for example, Warshaw's foreword to *The Perfect Day: 40 Years of Surfer Magazine*, in which he gushed that *Surfer*'s moniker, the "bible of the sport," did not fully recognize the magazine's merit and scope, arguing that it was "surfing's greatest yearbook and archive, forum and marketplace, gallery and parade ground."[23] Hyperbole aside, Warshaw correctly observed the vast import of magazines for the dissemination and maintenance of surf culture and history, a complex phenomenon that he understands well as surfing's most prominent popular historian. Warshaw then went on to recognize a lack of critical distance as a defining feature of surf publications before shrugging his shoulders and proceeding: "Because I am a former *Surfer* editor, my appraisal of the magazine's literary worth could be biased to the point of worthlessness. Or forget the editorship, I'm a 31-year subscriber. So of course I'm biased."[24] These issues not only plague popular surf history, but also confound scholars engaged in critical surf studies who rely on a limited source base and are often immersed in surf culture themselves. Still, countless academics have referenced *The Perfect Day*'s selection of iconic articles, given that university libraries have not prioritized the acquisition of surf magazines. While scholars from all disciplines must account for bias and subjectivity as they consult primary source material, questions of accessibility, reliability, and distinctions between primary and secondary sources are particularly acute in surfing scholarship.

This is not to say that writers from within the surf industry have not been critical of the subject, nor that popular histories written by entrenched surf personalities are without critical or scholarly merit. Steve Barilotti penned perhaps the first surf magazine article that significantly broke the insularity of surf media. In "Lost Horizons: Surfer Colonialism in the 21st Century," Barilotti indicted modern surf travel as a form of colonialism, effectively challenging a centuries-long mainstay of the surfing imaginary.[25] Though ambiguous and problematic in its concluding gestures, "Lost Horizons" set a new tone for surf writing in the twenty-first century which has witnessed an outpouring of reflective and critical publications acutely aware of surfing's inextricability from broader social, cultural, and political issues.

The heightened critical approach, in which a much more diverse cast of writers and thinkers has voiced hitherto marginalized or silenced perspectives, exists mostly outside of mainstream surf media outlets. Indeed, many of the writers who have denounced surf media's incestuous relationship with corporations turned to independent outlets after growing disgruntled with the lack of journalistic integrity in mainstream media.[26] Digital media has played an essential role in the democratization and critical turn of surf writing. Through blogs, online journals, and open-access documentaries, politically minded writers have forged communities across myriad borders and succeeded in adding much needed nuance to popular historical narratives focused on California, Hawai'i, and Australia and male surf culture therein.[27] Although surf cultures throughout the Global South have produced autonomous writings for decades, they have only recently, and in piecemeal fashion, been given the critical attention they deserve.[28]

Cultural studies scholar Clifton Evers, writer Stuart Nettle, and anthropologist Alex Leonard broke new ground in the history of critical surf writing in 2008 when they founded *Kurungabaa: A Journal of Literature, History, and Ideas from the Sea*, a surf-specific, biannual academic journal and literary magazine. Featuring an editorial board of international academics, graduate students, and countercultural surf personalities, *Kurungabaa* combined digital and print formats to connect readers and writers across geographic borders. Yet its most innovative contribution was to forge a democratic space for diverse contributors, including university researchers, veteran surf writers, artists, and everyday aficionados, to discuss surf culture and human–ocean interaction in a critical manner, be it in feature articles, editorials, or online comments. *Kurungabaa* adamantly resisted commercialization in order to retain scholarly credibility and, notably for an academic journal, did not require a university-affiliated subscription. Although the project was shuttered in 2014, *Kurungabaa* demonstrated the potential for critical collaborations that challenged divisions between popular and academic surf studies.[29]

Kurungabaa's debut coincided with numerous alternative initiatives that together constituted an explosion of counter-hegemonic texts, films, and publications. For instance, in 2010 a former *Surfer* staffer launched a contributor-built online platform for ideas outside of surf culture's journalistic mainstream. *The Inertia* garnered a fervent following by repeatedly questioning whether the surfing world had ever counted an "honest" investigative journalist among its ranks.[30] By 2016 the site purported a monthly readership of 1.5 million and boasted some 2,000 contributors. However, accompanying such popularity came a commercial overhaul and a softening of any potential political or critical editorial angle. In contraposition to *Kurungabaa*, the decidedly mainstream *Inertia* raises an oft-asked question in the surfing world: is it possible to be countercultural when a critical mass is reached?

If there is a critical approach that can offer insight as to how to sustain a radical politics, it is likely found in what lisahunter identifies in this volume as a "queer wave in new media and social media." Across the globe, women have been among the most systematically exploited, silenced, and ignored surfing demographic. Consequently, they constitute a public, far from singular or homogenous, that has diligently forged outlets with a more critical and rigorous approach to surf writing than traditional, male-dominated surf magazines. In subverting the limitations of Orientalist and heteronormative discourses, many female writers have taken to blogs and created their own outlets for circulating surf writing.[31] A burgeoning surfeminism "critiques the industry's sexploitation of elite stars and images of women across global surf media, and offers itself as counter-discourse."[32] As further elaborated in part III of this volume, Feminist Critical Geography, surfeminism encompasses more than media platforms; it constitutes an evolving theoretical approach and activist practice that hinges on collaboration across numerous borders, thus presenting a promising future for critical surf studies.

Such media have blurred the lines between popular and academic writing and precipitated the arrival of the first wave of university press books about surf studies. With *The World in the Curl: An Unconventional History of Surfing* (2013), Peter Westwick and Peter Neushul succeeded in veritably erasing the boundaries between popular history and critical scholarship of surfing. The first popular surfing history by career academics, their text retains the rigor, research relevance, and teaching value characteristic of scholarly monographs, although conceived of as a trade publication. Often in dialogue with or in contraposition to popular surf histories, *The World in the Curl* also reflects how popular work has generated lively debates around specific narratives of surfing's dissemination and appropriation, a practice that has intensified with scholarly histories of the sport.[33]

THE RISE OF CRITICAL SURFING STUDIES

The advent of critical surf studies has accompanied the natural evolution of rigorous and increasingly politicized nonacademic prose and scholarly forays into popular surf writing, as well as university presses' embrace of surf culture.[34] And as people passionate about surfing built scholarly careers, it was only a matter of time until critical writing about surfing emerged, accompanied by courses in sociology, literary studies, sports history, and anthropology with surf culture at their center. Surfers will, after all, always be surfers.

But critical surfing inquiry has also had an organic genesis with nonsurfer scholars in a variety of academic disciplines, perhaps because of the intersection of surfing's histories and iconographies with many of the fundamental critical categories of humanistic and social scientific inquiry. Not coincidentally, surfing's arrival to the academy (and relative acceptance therein) accompanied the broadening of the cultural studies field to privilege countercultural practices and marginal identities at the onset of the twenty-first century.

Niche scholarly articles and monographs first register as academic novelties beginning in the 1950s and 1960s with a series of notes and articles by anthropologist Ben Finney in Hawai'i.[35] In the 1970s, sociologists John Keith Irwin and Kent Pearson published the first serious scholarship on surfing in California and

Australia, respectively.[36] Adopting methodologies still relevant today, both sociologists couple analysis of popular surfing books and magazines with ethnographic research. Tanis Thorne published two academic notes historicizing surfing culture in 1976. In 1983, semiotician and media scholar John Fiske contributed another early work, followed by a 1986 article by historian Edwin Jaggard and Pierce Julius Flynn's discussion of surfing as a semiotic system in 1987. In spite of these early contributions, scholarly work on surfing began to gain traction only in the mid-1990s. When articles by Douglas Booth (1991, 1994, 1995, 1996), Jaggard (1997, 1999), Dean Scheibel (1995), Leanne Stedman (1997), and Jeff Lewis (1998) appeared, they too had to depend on an archive of popular material, merging it with contemporary theory and methodologies in their respective fields.[37]

If not a coordinated effort and rarely informed by coherent transnational or cross-disciplinary dialogue, the period of 1995–2010 saw several important— some indeed seminal—short-form contributions to the field from sociology, communications, history, geography, ethnic studies, film studies, and cultural studies more broadly, each allusive to the potential and future of the field. The significance of those essays, authored by Booth (1995, 1996, 1999, 2000, 2001, 2004, 2005, 2006, 2008), Mark Stranger (1999), Robert Rutsky (1999), Margaret Henderson (2001), Keith Beattie (2001), Eric Ishiwata (2002), Joan Ormrod (2003, 2005, 2008, 2009), Kevin Fisher (2005), Clifton Evers (2004, 2006, 2008, 2009), Kevin Dawson (2006, 2009, 2013), Robin Canniford (2007, 2009), Leslie Heywood (2008), Heywood and Mark Montgomery (2008, 2012), Gary Osmond (2008, 2010, 2011a, 2011b, 2016), Osmond and Murray Phillips (2004, 2015), Osmond, Phillips, and Mark O'Neill (2006), Gordon Waitt (2008), Waitt and Andrew Warren (2008), Belinda Wheaton (2007, 2008), and David Wood (2009, 2012), cannot be understated in plotting the field's vast critical matrix.[38]

And while hundreds of articles, book chapters, and volumes on so-called action sports more broadly have emerged over the last decade, monographs remain scarce relative to the abundance of popular surf books and scholarly studies of mainstream sport. Commenting on the limited bibliography of long-form surf scholarship available when preparing her 2010 monograph *Surfer Girls in the New World Order*, Krista Comer noted that "as a topic of critical inquiry, . . . surfing has barely registered."[39] If true of scholarly books when Comer was writing, this has quickly changed only a few years later, especially given forthcoming works.[40] Marking the first surfing studies book in American literary and cultural studies, Comer's work built upon a decade of field work focusing on the experiences of women and girls in the surf zone to argue that female surfers "have brought critical perspective not just to norms of femininity but to understandings of the material places (oceans, beaches) in which counterfemininities are enacted."[41] Embedding her analysis in feminist politics, globalization theory, and critical theory, and driven by activist convictions, Comer's work was quickly accompanied by several monographs that now anchor the surf studies field across the disciplinary spectrum.

Once an isolated case of surf scholarship in the social sciences (and one of the few texts available when Comer was writing), geographer Nick Ford and sociologist David Brown's *Surfing and Social Theory* informed and anticipated subsequent contributions in both fields.[42] Without a doubt, Kristin Lawler's study of the iconographies and rhetorics of the surfer in twentieth-century capitalism, *The American Surfer: Radical Culture and Capitalism*, constitutes the most important contribution to surfing studies from US sociology. In the same year, Australian sociologist Mark Stranger's *Surfing Life: Surface, Substructure, and the Commodification of the Sublime* deployed rigorous ethnographic research to examine surfing as an example of postmodern culture, rife with tensions between commodification and authenticity in surfing experience.[43] Both Lawler's and Stranger's monographs emerged as geographers Andrew Warren and Chris Gibson were engaged in the fieldwork that yielded *Surfing Places, Surfboard Makers* (2014).[44] In their study of surfboard manufacturing practices in Hawai'i, California, and Australia, Warren and Gibson focused on cultural and human geography in the rising tensions between handicraft and mechanization, local and global markets, and personalization versus standardization, all long-standing issues in surfboard construction.

The above studies of surfing have, by necessity, often cited journalism, popular histories, and reference texts in order to compensate for the lack of long-form scholarly source material available to authors. Indeed, popular historiography's dominance as the prevailing mode of surf writing has provided a reliable corpus for scholars to draw from in lieu of scholarly works. Surf culture is rife with contentious debates, and trade surf historiography first pushed these debates toward the type of work that critical surf studies seek to accomplish in revising earlier thinking about the sport embedded in and, at times, sponsored by, media, industry, and surf culture.

And with the argumentative turn in trade surf history taking place somewhere between the work of Finney, Kampion, John Clark, and Warshaw, historical scholarship has also yielded texts that now anchor the field. Isaiah Helekunihi Walker's *Waves of Resistance: Surfing and History in Twentieth-Century Hawai'i* (2011) examines surfing's cultural and political importance in Hawai'i, arguing that Hawaiian surfers have resisted colonial intrusions from the surf zone, using surfing to develop and articulate coordinated assertions of local indigenous identity and powerful decolonizing critiques.[45] Walker's work is informed by—and contributes to—postcolonial, ethnic, indigenous, and Pacific Studies literatures, which endow his work with a strong political character of particular interest to scholars.

Following Walker's *Waves of Resistance* was Scott Laderman's *Empire in Waves: A Political History of Surfing* (2014), a singular contribution given his background as a historian of foreign policy specializing in Southeast Asia. Laderman's monograph argues that in spite of surfing's rhetoric and iconography of pleasure and leisure, surfing has always necessarily operated within and alongside domestic politics, foreign policy, and political conflict. Surfing, says Laderman, is inseparable from broader political contexts and their local consequences, regardless of the sport's recurrent association with hedonistic ideals. Westwick and Neushul's offering also merits mention here, as it demonstrates precisely the manner in which historiography connects popular and critical histories: as studies across the disciplines have deployed popular histories as a result of the paucity of scholarship, scholarly histories now seek to challenge the wagers of prevailing popular narratives. Westwick and Neushul join Walker and Laderman in revising popular historiography through academic research methods and arguments of not-so-subtle differentiation from their trade history peers and predecessors.

Also published in 2014 was ethnomusicologist Timothy Cooley's *Surfing about Music*. Somewhat of a disciplinary outlier, Cooley's work plotted the diverse modes and means by which music has accompanied surf culture from ancient Hawai'i to the present. Seeing musicality "as an integral part of group imagination and invention," Cooley explores how surfers and their allies and admirers have come to associate the cultural practices of riding waves and making music as intimately connected human practices.[46] While he sees making music and surfing as homologies (they are fundamentally the same phenomenon, he says, as experiencing the surf and experiencing music engender affective responses), Cooley also contends that musical sharing enables surfers engaged in a predominantly solitary practice to form and nurture community. Unique in its disciplinary scope within surf scholarship, Cooley's rigorous and rich work rounds out the corpus of monographs at the center of current critical surf studies.

During and since the elaboration of these monographs, many book chapters have also appeared.[47] Accompanying them was a significant surge in journal publications, as well as a broadening of journals willing to publish about surfing.[48] Interdisciplinary and field-specific collections on sport, regional themes, and special topics have also yielded significant contributions on surfing, each further relating surfing to critical concepts relevant to specific local and national contexts.[49] With this brief outline of the critical surfing studies field, we turn now to the contents of the present volume.

Volume Outline

The volume is organized into four parts, grouping chapters into categories that have long intersected with surfing's histories and iconographies: coloniality, race and ethnicity, feminisms, and capitalism. As there is much critical overlap between these categories, many chapters transcend the conceptual boundaries of where they are situated, dialoging across the book's contents.

The chapters in the first part, Coloniality and Decolonization, contribute to thinking and working toward the decolonization of surf culture in historical, pedagogical, and theoretical modes. In the opening chapter, Patrick Moser takes up the accounts of Hiram Bingham to resituate the nineteenth-century missionary's rhetoric of surfing's demise. Identifying Bingham's influence on annexationists and, later, modern surf historiography, Moser cogently highlights the destructive stakes of indigenous erasure perpetuated by Bingham's canonization in Western histories of Hawai'i. Moving forward into the twentieth century, Scott Laderman questions surfing's reputation for rebelliousness by interrogating surf travel narratives generated between the 1960s and 1980s. Taking up accounts of the notorious Miki Dora and surfers traversing Latin America, the Caribbean, and much of the developing world, Laderman adroitly shows how surfers' tastes for the exotic and the isolated, masked under the guise of rebellion, manifest a range of dangerous tendencies, from the self-indulgent and hedonistic to the imperial and anti-Semitic. Within the matrix of ongoing debates about Hawaiian autonomy, Isaiah Helekunihi Walker explores how Native Hawaiian professional and competitive surfers understand and broadcast their identity within the context of global sport and Hawaiian political identity. Skillfully building upon active-participant collaborations and media surrounding key Hawaiian competitive surfing successes, he contends that the Hawaiian concept of *kuleana*, roughly translated as responsibility to community and environment, endows surfing with meaning and inspires Native Hawaiian surfers on the world stage.

In chapter 4, Dexter Zavalza Hough-Snee and Alexander Sotelo Eastman demonstrate how surfing institutions—industry, competitive governance, tourism, and media (among others)—shape participation in surfing, arguing that the evolution of a modern surfing state places ever-stricter limits on surfer creativity.[50] Exploring the career of Mexican-American professional surfer Bobby Martinez and the local reorganization of the Oaxaca surf community of Salina Cruz to suggest how individuals and communities creatively resist the superstructures of professional surfing governance and Global North–South surf tourism, they seek to envision radical creative futures outside of the broader surfing state. Tara Ruttenberg and Pete Brosius also seek to encourage alternative futures by suggesting the possibility of decolonizing the realm of sustainable surf tourism. Writing as coordinators of the University of Georgia's summer program, "Surfing & Sustainability: Political Ecology in Costa Rica," Ruttenberg and Brosius propose that the very foundations of sustainable surfing tourism need rethinking. Recognizing that "income-oriented 'status quo' sustainability" programs perpetuate conventional forms of exploitation, they encourage alternate forms of tourism governance and alternatives to development as a means of decolonizing the surf tourism industry.

Kevin Dawson forcefully opens part II, Race, Ethnicity, and Identity, by interrogating a broad archive of colonial observations of surfing and aquatic culture generated between the 1590s and the 1790s in Atlantic Africa and Oceania. Dawson suggests that Europeans who colonized oceanic landscapes, lacking any identifiable aquatic traditions of their own, had to become native, simultaneously allowing indigenous water cultures and practices to prevail in spaces with traditional meanings. Glen Thompson explores the development of the South African surfing lifestyle during the 1960s, historicizing how local surf culture was raced, gendered, and shaped by transnational surfing trends. Identifying the "whitewashing" of surfing in South Africa as an attempt to institutionalize global surf culture's mythic trope of a tanned whiteness, Thompson analyzes and problematizes how apartheid and lifestyle consumption imported the "California dream" to render surfing a white pastime. In the wake of these discussions of surfing in Africa, Belinda Wheaton collaborates with African American surfers in Southern California to explore the experiences of black surfers around Los Angeles. Debunking the notion of a "white" Californian surfing culture, Wheaton's timely exploration of black surfing participation in California paints a portrait of individuals who actively move surfing beyond its historically racialized connotations and promote "an expanded image of self and black culture." In chapter 9, Colleen McGloin challenges the notion that surfing was "introduced" to Australia, resituating the ocean as a "country"—a cultural and spiritual place of origin—and site of history in aboriginal geographies. With such understandings of the ocean, McGloin argues, indigenous surfing in Australia becomes an act of cultural restoration as well as a form of epistemic disobedience. Moving from Australian to Hawaiian indigeneity, Dina Gilio-Whitaker examines how concepts of blood quantum prevalent in US Native American relations contributed to the canonization of Duke Kahanamoku as surfing's modern figurehead. She then turns to George Freeth's marginalization in surf history to understand how surfing's notions of cultural authenticity have been equated to racial purity, perpetuating *fin de siècle* racial categories into the present.

The third part, Feminist Critical Geography, begins with an intervention by Krista Comer, who invokes surfeminism, critical regionalism, and public scholarship to narrate an origin story of how current feminist efforts in surfing have evolved and taken on a character of their own in the present wave of feminism. Writing in the wake of recent activist and public humanities work with the Institute of Women Surfers, Comer insightfully reports on initiatives indicative of how "surfeminist, place-based knowledges" might push such collaborations beyond gender equity and into the realm of decolonizing surfing more broadly. Lisahunter playfully weaves together a series of corporeal metaphors to question whether surfing's collective body is metaphorically "screwed" and if it might ever be desexed. She begins by proposing that surfing is indicative of what she terms "patriocolonialism"—patriarchal and colonial practices that further capitalist modes, Western knowledge systems, and heteronormativity—experienced as an illusory semblance of gender equality and feminist victory in the surf. She then asks a fundamental question as to whether surfing could be anything but sexed, responding in the affirmative "by offering several queer lines of flight with pedagogies of possibility." Writer, activist, and world-champion surfer Cori Schumacher provocatively concludes the section by suggesting that instead of limiting themselves to a "stealth feminism" that merely resists heteronormative sexualization and objectification of women, surfers should embrace a surfeminism that challenges the very nature/culture and subject/object divides common to Western understandings of surfing. She figuratively invokes the mermaid as a symbol of women's communion with the ocean, and posits its likeness as an activist icon to rally around in working toward such a surfing future.

The final part, focused on the commodification of surfing, begins with Kristin Lawler's fascinating exploration of the image of the "surf bum," through which surfing was historically deployed in contraposition to work. Lawler resurrects the surf bum from John Rawls's idea of the "Malibu Surfer Problem" in the 1970s, updating the image to what conservative US news media have coined the "Food Stamp Surfer." She then explores how this image, deployed by the political right to instill divisiveness, can become a symbol of liberation, contributing to "a culture of freedom that inspires workers to resist work" by slowing down, enjoying life, and embracing the omnipresence of the avatars of leisure in their midst. Moving from avatars to industry, Douglas Booth takes a historical materialist approach to trace the evolution of surfing's 1950s cottage industries into the emergence of today's global surfing industry. Booth begins by examining the crises that the industry has recently faced before proceeding to historicize three types of labor—industrial, free-surfing, and competitive labor—and concludes by highlighting the demographic and social trends that have divided surfing culture. Andrew Warren and Chris Gibson draw upon active participant research in pairing labor geography and cultural economy theory to examine the labor experiences of workers in the surfboard industry during major transitions toward mechanization and industry globalization. They commandingly argue that, despite working within a culture of precariousness, these workers contest the conditions of employment, their agency shifting over time and space, corresponding to the ebbs and flows of the industry.

Engaging earlier discussions in the volume, Robin Canniford skillfully tracks the construction of surfing as a pure nature experience for marketing purposes. Capitalizing on surfers' understanding of the idealized surfing experience as "a magical encounter with pure nature," he argues that surf marketing connects nature back to markets by creating a linkage through the image of the primitive, a construction of nature that enables a distinction of surfing-as-pure-nature from modern cultures. Illustrating the pervasiveness of such linkages wherever mass marketing promotes surfing, Clifton Evers takes up the global surfing industry's hyperbolic claims to the profitability of China as surfing's next frontier. Coupling active participant research with a nuanced portrait of surfing's current status in China, Evers strongly concludes the volume by highlighting how Chinese surfing culture finds itself at the intersections of the global and the local. Examining the environmental, economic, cultural, and political conditions of surfing in China, Evers contemplates the antagonistic relationship between the global surfing culture industry and local realities that may not render China the lucrative surf destination that it was once forecast to be.

As critical literatures on surfing continue to expand, the collective contents of this volume serve to mark where the field stands today. In highlighting specific disciplinary and political questions that surfing brings to the fore around the globe, each author employs unique archives and references that provide a starting point for further reading and inquiry. It is our hope that this project contributes to the field's growth by anchoring critical studies to core disciplinary research and identifying areas for further exploration of surfing through teaching, scholarship, activism, political participation, and, of course, riding waves.

NOTES

1. Women's initiatives are most numerous in this respect, embodying what Krista Comer has identified as "a global contemporary social movement with feminist, environmental, pacifist, and antipoverty commitments" (Comer, *Surfer Girls*, 18). These initiatives include, among others, the History of Women's Surfing (http://www.historyofwomensurfing.com/), curated by Sheri Crummer, Cori Schumacher, and Carla Rowland-Zamora; Crummer and Schumacher's Inspire Initiative (http://www.theinspireinitiative.org/); surfeminism, directed by Nicole Grodesky (http://www.surfeminism.com/); Farhana Huq's Brown Girl Surf group (http://www.browngirlsurf.com/); and the Institute for Women Surfers (http://www.instituteforwomensurfers.org/), organized by Comer. The Black Surfers Collective (http://www.blacksurferscollective.org/) originated in Southern California in 2012. Thomas Castets founded GaySurfers.net in 2010, an online LGBTQIA surfing community "promoting diversity and inclusion in the lineup" that boasts chapters worldwide (http://www.gaysurfers.net/). Sofia Mulanovich's Sofia Proyecto (http://www.sofiaproyecto.com/en/) brings together top Peruvian junior surfers from varied socioeconomic and ethnic backgrounds in an attempt to propel local youth from across the social spectrum into elite competition. Anchored by Apish Tshetsha and Bongani Ndlovu, Waves for Change (http://www.waves-for-change.org/) was founded by Tim Conibear in 2011 to provide therapeutic benefits to urban youth in South Africa, simultaneously diversifying Cape Town lineups. Surfing New Zealand's Auahi Kore Aotearoa Maori Titles and Surfing Australia's Australian Indigenous Surfing Titles provide competitive outlets for Maori and aboriginal surfers, respectively, and celebrate indigenous aquatic traditions.

2. Moser, *Pacific Passages*, 1.

3. See Walker, *Waves of Resistance*.

4. See Westwick and Neushul, *The World in the Curl*.

5. See Laderman, *Empire in Waves*, 8–40.

6. See Walker, *Waves of Resistance*, 37.

7. On Kahanamoku and Freeth, see Gilio-Whitaker, this volume; Walker, this volume; and Moser, this volume. See also Walker, *Waves of Resistance*; Laderman, *Empire in Waves*, 3, 25–36; Westwick and Neushul, *World in the Curl*, 44–69.

Surfing was exported from Hawai'i when travelers returned home during the political prelude to World War II. Peruvian Carlos Dogny, for example, returned to Lima from O'ahu during the war's onset, taking surfing with him. On Dogny, see Wood, "On the Crest of a Wave," 228, and Zavalza Hough-Snee, "You Have the Right to Surf," 203–204.

8. See Laderman, *Empire in Waves*, 34; Westwick and Neushul, *World in the Curl*, 65–66.

9. See Warshaw, *Encyclopedia* (2005), 132.

10. See Warshaw, "Makaha International Surfing Championships," and "Peru International Surfing Championships," http://encyclopediaofsurfing.com/.

11. See Lawler, *The American Surfer*. On surfing's white-collar foundations, see Westwick and Neushul, *World in the Curl*; Wood, "On the Crest of a Wave"; and Warshaw, *History of Surfing*.

12. See Warren and Gibson, *Surfing Places, Surfboard Makers*.

13. See Comer, *Surfer Girls in the New World Order*.

14. Lewis Samuels, "Secret History," *Surfline.com*, July 27, 2015. Professional surfers of recent generations have embraced golf and tennis as hobbies, actively documenting their forays into these sports and pushing competitive surfing back toward the spectrum of club sports where it existed in the first half of the twentieth century. According to the 2011 Surfrider Foundation study, *A Socioeconomic and Recreational Profile of Surfers in the United States* (http://surfridercdn.surfrider.org/images/uploads/publications/surfrider_report _v13(1).pdf), the typical US surfer is university educated and earns $75,000 per year.

15. For anthologies of surf writing from the eighteenth to the twenty-first centuries, see Moser, *Pacific Passages*, and Warshaw, *Zero Break*.

There have been attempts to compile comprehensive bibliographies of surfing literature, although each has been outdated with the corpus's ongoing growth. Representative of such attempts is DeLaVega, *200 Years of Surfing Literature: An Annotated Bibliography*. We limit our discussion here to works in English, although there are numerous national and local histories of surfing from around the globe, most prominently from early surfing nations such as Peru, Brazil, South Africa, France, New Zealand, and Australia. Hundreds of popular works offer histories of specific locales in Latin America, Australasia, and Europe. In the interest of brevity, the present discussion of surfing literature has no pretensions to comprehensiveness and admits focus on writings from the United States, Hawai'i, New Zealand, Australia, and the United Kingdom.

16. Matt Warshaw, "Articles of Faith. 35 Years of Surf Magazines: An Insider's View," *The Surfer's Journal* 5.1 (1996): 89.

17. Patrick Moser, "The Custodian, Interview with Steve Pezman," *Gingko Tree Review* (2013); Warshaw, "Articles of Faith." The documentary *White Wash* (Trespass Productions, 2011) addresses the racial segregation of beaches in the United States and the erasure of African Americans from the history of surfing. In 2016, the *Journal of Ethnic History* (35.2) published a special issue dedicated to analysis of the groundbreaking film. Glen Thompson has been a leading voice in untangling the racialized history of surfing in South Africa. See, for example, "*Otelo Burning* and Zulu Surfing Histories" and his chapter in this volume. Kevin Dawson has shed light on the rich and little-known histories of water sports in early modern Africa and Oceania; in addition to his work in this volume, see "Enslaved Swimmers and Divers in the Atlantic World" and his monograph *Enslaved Water People in the Atlantic World*.

18. See Young and McGregor, *The History of Surfing*. Young authored six additional titles.

19. See Warshaw, *Surf Riders* (1997), *Maverick's* (2000), *Zero Break* (2004), *The Encyclopedia of Surfing* (2003), *Surf Movie Tonite!* (2005), *Photo/Stoner* (2006), and *The History of Surfing* (2010). See Encyclopediaofsurfing.com for the encyclopedia's digital evolution as reference text and multimedia archive, and Historyofsurfing.net for the digitized, updated

version of the *History of Surfing*, complete with links to archival material and primary sources. Warshaw has also generously helped many scholars to find and access rare materials and sources in spite of his distance from academia. Kampion has authored a host of surfing travel guides, biographies, and popular histories. See *Stoked!* (2003), *The Way of the Surfer* (2003), *Waves* (2005), *Dora Lives* (2005, with Stecyk), and *Greg Noll* (2007).

20. For more on the "revolving door" in the surf industry, see Westwick and Neushul, *World in the Curl*, 290.

21. Matt Warshaw in Mark Lukach, "The Glory of the Digital Encyclopedia of Surfing," *TheAtlantic.com* (September 30, 2013) (https://www.theatlantic.com/technology/archive/2013/09/the-glory-of-the-digital-encyclopedia-of-surfing/280120/).

22. Numerous scholars have pointed out the incestuous business model of surf media, advertisers, and brands. See, for example, Westwick and Neushul, *World in the Curl*, 290, and Thompson, "Disturbed Waters."

23. Warshaw, "Foreword," 4.

24. Warshaw "Foreword," 5.

25. Steve Barilotti, "Lost Horizons: Surfer Colonialism in the 21st Century," *The Surfer's Journal* 3.11 (2002): 88–97.

26. For example, Lewis Samuels, a former contributor to prominent surf forecasting website *Surfline*, was fired after he published an incendiary post on his *PostSurf* blog in which he criticized the CEO of a major surf company. Samuels stated that his intention in creating *PostSurf* in 2009 was "to change the landscape of the surf media" and to contemplate alternative histories for surfing (Nick Carroll, "The New Sarcasm," *Kurungabaa.net* [September 7, 2010]).

27. Accompanying this turn to online content, *Surfer* is transitioning its print publications from monthly to quarterly beginning in 2017.

28. A comprehensive study of the history of surf publications that takes into account regional particularities remains to be written. Critical surf studies would benefit from more comparative studies, such as Joan Ormrod's "Surf Rhetoric in American and British Surfing Magazines Between 1965 and 1976." Brazilian scholar Rafael Fortes has published several articles on the history and evolution of Brazilian surf media. See, for example, "Making Surf Media in Brazil."

29. See Clifton Evers, "Kurungabaa says Goodbye," *Kurungabaa.net* (January 28, 2014).

30. See Zach Weisberg, "Sensationalistic, Scummy Journalism," *The Inertia* (November 14, 2010), and "Surf Media: Living the Dream?," *The Inertia* (December 6, 2010). For a similar critique of surf journalism's lack of ethical standards, see Morgan Williamson, "Surf Journalism in the Age of Kardashian," *Stabmag.com* (August 2015). Tetsuhiko Endo, a journalist and fiction writer trained in postcolonial studies, authored some of the most compelling intellectual prose about surfing to emerge in recent years, primarily during his tenure as editor of *The Inertia*.

31. Among representative critics is Rebecca Olive, a trained sociologist and lecturer whose blog *Making Friends with the Neighbours* (http://makingfriendswiththeneighbours.blogspot.com/) has focused on women's issues in surfing for over a decade, often overlapping with her scholarly work and contributions to niche media. Cori Schumacher has written for nonsurfing periodicals and women's surfing publications since 2011, simultaneously

maintaining an active blog. Dina Gilio-Whitaker, a research associate at the Center for World Indigenous Studies, has also dedicated much ink to scholarly topics relating surfing to indigeneity in popular print, also publishing on her blog *RumiNative* (https://dinagwhitaker.wordpress.com/). In 2014, Australian women's media collective The Mermaid Society (http://themermaidsociety.com.au/) was founded to independently cover women's surfing.

32. See Comer and Schumacher, this volume.

33. Academic presses have also published noteworthy trade histories of surfing and related reference texts, most notably the University of Hawaiʻi Press, which released John Clark's history, *Hawaiian Surfing: Traditions from the Past* (2011), and Tony Butt's *Surf Science: An Introduction to Waves for Surfing* (2004). Columbia University Press recently released Pete Maguire and Mike Ritter's *Thai Stick: Surfers Scammers, and the Untold Story of the Marijuana Trade* (2015), a trade history of the cannabis industry that details surfing's relationship to pot at great length. The University of Nebraska Press is responsible for Jeremy Evans's *The Battle for Paradise: Surfing, Tuna, and One Town's Quest to Save a Wave*, a narrative of the conflicts surrounding Costa Rican surf destination Pavones. MIT Press published Richard Kenvin and Christine Knoke's *Surf Craft: Design and the Culture of Board Riding*, an accompaniment to the 2014 exhibition of the same name at San Diego's Mingei International Museum, marking a consideration of surfcraft in an art historical mode. That same year, the University Press of Florida issued Paul Aho's *Surfing Florida: A Photographic History*, which accompanied several exhibitions statewide.

34. As writings of journalists and popular historians have garnered scholarly attention, career academics have also contributed to popular literature on surfing. Ben Finney, Professor of Anthropology at the University of Hawaiʻi since 1973, a longtime research associate at Honolulu's Bishop Museum, and an authority on the Pacific world, co-authored (with James Houston) the seminal *Surfing, the Sport of Hawaiian Kings*, one of the earliest trade press surfing histories. The tome was republished as *Surfing: A History of the Ancient Hawaiian Sport*. Patrick Moser's anthology of surf writings, *Pacific Passages*, compiles sources spanning from indigenous and colonial Polynesia to the twenty-first century. Since publication, Moser's volume has anchored teaching of surf-related curricula and provided valuable primary source matter for researchers, including rare and unpublished archival materials. Moser has also coauthored two books with South African world champion surfer Shaun Tomson: see Tomson, *Surfer's Code* and *The Code*. Douglas Booth has also contributed to surfing nonfiction, elaborating a comprehensive reference text that complements more than two decades of scholarly writing on surfing. For his trade text, see Booth, *Surfing: The Ultimate Guide*. His *Australian Beach Cultures* discusses surfing at great length in exploring the role of the coast in Australian culture. Clifton Evers aimed to open the minds of young surfers to promote social justice and critical thought with his popular text *Notes for a Young Surfer*.

35. See Finney, "Surfboarding in Oceania," "Surfing in Ancient Hawaii," "The Development and Diffusion of Modern Hawaiian Surfing," and "Surfboarding in West Africa."

36. Published in 1973 and 1978, respectively, Irwin's and Pearson's works are among the earliest scholarship of surfing. See Irwin, "Surfing: The Natural History of an Urban Scene"; Pearson, *Surfing Subcultures*; and Pearson, "Conflict, Stereotypes, and Masculinity

in Australian and New Zealand Surfing." (An ironic anecdote concerning one of these authors is reflective of midcentury surf culture: Irwin, the first mainland American scholar to publish on surfing, served a five-year prison term for armed robbery, earning college credit while incarcerated. He took sociology degrees at UCLA [BA] and Berkeley [PhD] upon his release and taught at San Francisco State University for twenty-seven years.)

37. See Booth, "War off the Water," "Ambiguities in Pleasure and Discipline," and "Surfing Films and Videos"; Jaggard, "Chameleons in the Surf" and "Australian Surf Life-Saving"; Scheibel, "Making Waves"; Stedman, "From Gidget to Gonad Man"; and Lewis, "Between the Lines."

38. Previous scholarly literature reviews have understated the importance and magnitude of these authors and their works, perhaps owing to editorial limitations.

39. Comer, *Surfer Girls*, 9.

40. Kevin Dawson's *Enslaved Water People in the Atlantic World* accompanies this volume to print. Patrick Moser is currently elaborating a history of surfing from 1788 to 1944, and Californian performance studies scholar J'aime Morrison (California State University, Northridge) is also preparing a monograph examining surfing's relationship to dance.

41. Comer, *Surfer Girls*, 18.

42. Ford and Brown, *Surfing and Social Theory*.

43. Stranger, *Surfing Life*. See also Stranger, "Surface and Substructure" and "The Aesthetics of Risk."

44. Warren and Gibson, *Surfing Places, Surfboard Makers*.

45. Walker, *Waves of Resistance*.

46. Cooley, *Surfing about Music*, 16.

47. Comer, Lawler, Stranger, Walker, Laderman, and Dawson each published articles or chapters while preparing their books.

48. A comprehensive list of journals that have published articles on surfing exceeds the scope of this introduction. We refer our reader to the bibliography for a large sample of these journals.

49. For a small sampling of chapters about surfing in edited collections focused on broader themes, see Ormrod, "Endless Summer" (2008); Thompson, "Certain Political Considerations"; Laderman, "Reds, Revolutionaries, and Racists"; Roy and Caudwell, "Women and Surfing Spaces"; Heywood and Montgomery, "Ambassadors of the Last Wilderness" and "Economies of Surf"; and Zavalza Hough-Snee, "You Have the Right to Surf." As for edited collections, see Ormrod and Wheaton, *On the Edge*, as well as individual works coordinated by lisahunter, Wheaton, and Holly Thorpe, among others.

50. For origins of the modern sporting state concept, see Colás's "Getting Free" and *Ball Don't Lie*.

Part I / Coloniality and Decolonization

PATRICK MOSER

Hiram Bingham stepped ashore on the island of Hawai'i on Tuesday, April 4, 1820. By his own account he was eager to track down King Kamehameha II and ask for permission to settle in the Islands to spread the Gospel. There were twenty-two people in his company: seven married couples, five children, and three Native Hawaiians who had arrived by various routes at the Foreign Mission School in Cornwall, Connecticut, and been trained as missionaries. After spending 163 days at sea—a grueling voyage around the tip of South America filled with seasickness, morning sickness (four of the women were pregnant), tight quarters, and stifling heat—Bingham had no idea if the King would even allow the New Englanders to stay.[1]

Bingham certainly had things on his mind that morning other than surfing, but the sport was present from the first moments of his arrival. As he boated in from the *Thaddeus*, he remarked that "a great number of the natives—men, women and children, from the highest to the lowest rank, including the king and his mother, were amusing themselves in the water," some of them "float-ing on surf-boards."[2] This is no surprise. He'd come ashore at Kamakahonu on the north end of Kailua Bay, on the west side of the island. This had been the residence of King Kamehameha I, an expert surfer who lived out the last years of his life at this spot.[3] His twenty-two-year-old son, Kamehameha II—also known as Liholiho—may have been one of the surfers that morning. "Amuse-ment" is a word often used to describe surfing during this time period (as when Bingham later presented "sporting on the surf" as "the favorite amusement of all classes").[4] It is possible, then, that Liholiho—and perhaps his mother, the sacred queen Keōpūolani—were catching waves as Bingham prepared to lay at their doorstep an ideology that, in its eagerness to show positive gains for Christian donors back home, falsely trumpeted the decline of surfing in the Hawaiian Islands. Bingham's inflated public rhetoric proliferated a warped view of surf history, influencing later writers and surf historians who accepted his words as historically accurate rather than as religious propaganda. The re-sult has been a narrative, still repeated in academic and popular histories, that surfing nearly died out in nineteenth-century Hawai'i. A careful reconsidera-tion of our primary source for surfing's supposed early demise—Hiram Bing-ham's writings—calls into question Bingham's reliability and starts the process of recuperating Native Hawaiians' practice of their national pastime. Surfing did not nearly "die out" in nineteenth-century Hawai'i, as so often has been reported. Riding waves continued to be a part of Hawaiian daily life during the missionary era and well after Bingham's departure in 1840.[5]

Bingham was in a hurry that first day. He waited until Liholiho came in from the ocean, then presented his offer to the young king: eternal life and edu-cation for his people in exchange for sponsoring the missionaries—providing them with homes, churches, and eventually schools.

The king listened, but was noncommittal. The next day, to boost their cause, the missionaries brought ashore gifts: elegant bibles and a spy glass. The following day they invited the king and his retinue back to the *Thaddeus* to dine. After dinner, the missionaries sang hymns on the quarterdeck at the king's request, accompanied by a bass viol played by one of the young Hawaiians, George Kaumuali'i, who'd studied at the Foreign Mission School.

On April 7, the missionaries went back ashore for more lobbying, then again on the 8th. They decided to ask the king to split their company: some to remain with him at Kailua on the Big Island, the rest to settle on O'ahu in Honolulu, an up-and-coming port town. Prescient leader Liholiho responded: "White men all prefer Oahu. I think the Americans would like to have that Island."[6]

But the king still did not give them a definitive answer. Instead, he offered them temporary shelter in a thatched hut at Kailua. Captain Andrew Blanchard of the *Thaddeus*, impatient to get on with his fur-gathering expedition to the North American coast, urged the missionaries to accept. Bingham took a look at the hut—he described it as a barn-like structure—and hesitated: the whole company under one roof, a dirt floor, no ceiling or walls or windows or furniture, and miles away from a fresh water source? He needed something firmer from the king. He stalled, and told Liholiho that it was taboo for them to unload on the Sabbath (April 9); then he stayed aboard and planned a full-court press for the next day.

On Monday, April 10, from morning until late afternoon—"hearts burning with the desire to be advantageously and *speedily* settled down in our work"(my emphasis)—the whole company lobbied the king and local chiefs for permission to stay. This urgency on Bingham's part, manifest in his writing through the repeated use of words like "speedily" and "eagerly," was not merely a quirk of character or a clash of two cultures with fundamentally different concepts of time.[7] Rather, it was a sign of religious anxiety: the missionaries believed they had a duty to save Hawaiians before the Second Coming of Christ, an event predicted among Congregationalists (the denomination of the two ordained ministers in the group, Hiram Bingham and Asa Thurston) to occur in 1866. So there was urgency to their project, and no amount of effort was too great to begin saving "heathens" around the world.[8] Beyond their personal religious convictions, however, it turns out that Bingham and the other missionaries consistently used a rhetoric of urgency as a basic strategy to alarm their readers back home in order to incite donations and fund their mission. On a side note, we can remark that narratives of urgency parallel much of surf history, as when fiction writer Jack London famously exclaimed, early in the twentieth century, that surfing "was at its dying gasp" when Alexander Hume Ford arrived in Waikīkī and took the sport under his wing with the founding of the Outrigger Canoe Club. More recent urgency arrives in mailboxes around the globe on a monthly basis as the surf media hypes travel alerts for the latest perfect wave.[9]

Back to the Big Island: King Liholiho continued to put Bingham off. He wanted to wait until his *hānai* mother and co-ruler, Ka'ahumanu, returned from a fishing trip before he gave an answer to the missionary. After the death of Kamehameha I the year before, Liholiho accepted a radical change to the taboos that had governed Hawaiian society for centuries: the old gods and shrines were abandoned—some of them burned—leaving a vacuum that Bingham saw as providential for his mission to create a kingdom of Jehovah in the middle of the Pacific. He did not know that Liholiho's mothers—his biological mother Keōpūolani, and his father's favorite wife Ka'ahumanu, who had raised Liholiho in her household—were the primary movers behind this change. Both women would eventually be critical to the mission's success. Ka'ahumanu especially became the linchpin for Bingham's rise to power and his ability to suppress native traditions like surfing for a number of years. For her part, Ka'ahumanu was able to use the new religion to solidify and extend her rule in Hawai'i until her death in 1832.[10]

But all that was yet to come. On April 10, 1820, Ka'ahumanu unexpectedly arrived back from her fishing trip and, together with the king, sat ready to give an audience to the newcomers.

But only after calling for an impromptu hula. "While the eyes and ears of this great multitude were engrossed with this idle, time-killing employment," Bingham wrote—he estimated 2,000 natives were gathered at the event—"we longed to interest their souls with the news of the great salvation."[11]

Finally, at sunset, after "a time that seemed indeed long to us," Bingham got the chance to present his case to the rulers. He went over it all again—why they'd come, what they hoped to achieve, the benefits to the Hawaiians, their plans to establish two missions on Hawai'i and O'ahu—and answered the sovereigns' questions. He hoped they would give his request careful thought "and *early* grant us a favorable answer" (my emphasis).[12]

The king's advisor, John Young, later told Bingham that, if the Hawaiians followed their normal practice, he'd be lucky if they gave him an answer within six months.

Bingham wasn't willing to wait six months. The next day he came back with a new proposal: allow the missionaries to stay for one year. It was a compromise for Bingham—the time was much too short for his grandiose plans—but he desperately needed a foothold. The souls of 130,000 Hawaiians and the success of the American Board's inaugural mission to the Pacific rested on his shoulders.

Liholiho granted his request. Bingham and most of his party eventually ended up in a thatched hut in Honolulu. One of the reasons the missionaries noticed surfing in the coming days was because their residence sat on the path to Waikīkī, the traditional surfing grounds of Hawaiian royalty, and the king and his court would parade by Bingham's front door when they wanted to get some waves. When it happened on Sunday, Bingham sometimes followed the king and preached to him down at the beach.[13]

The American Board of Commissioners for Foreign Missions

Bingham's charge once he got settled in Honolulu was to save Hawaiian souls by converting them to Christianity. Everything in his life was directed toward that purpose. Surfing itself was a fairly low priority for him. The polygamy and incest of Hawaiian chiefs (Liholiho had five wives; his favorite, Kamāmalu, was his half-sister), the prostitution of Hawaiian women who swam out to incoming ships, the gambling and rum drinking, the hula dancing, which Bingham connected to worship of pagan gods—all ranked above surfing on Bingham's to-don't list.

But surfing played an interesting role for the missionaries. To understand its unusual appeal, it is necessary to turn toward Boston a moment and consider the organization that sent the missionaries to Hawai'i in the first place: the American Board of Commissioners for Foreign Missions. A brief look into the early history of the mission to Hawai'i, and the goals of the Congregational Church in general, will provide critical context for understanding how the missionaries used surfing to further their financial and religious goals, and why their actions necessarily cast doubt on the veracity of Bingham's statements about the state of surfing.

The mission to the Sandwich Islands (as they were dubbed by Captain James Cook in 1778) was the first independent venture by the American Board, an organization founded by Congregationalists in Boston in 1810 during the Second Great Awakening, an era of religious revival in the United States. The Board sent several groups of missionaries into Asia and the Middle East during its first decade, but these were in areas under the control of Britain and the London Missionary Society. The mission to the Sandwich Islands, writes John A. Andrew III in *Rebuilding the Christian Commonwealth*, captured "the attention of New Englanders almost at once. . . . Never before in the history of American foreign missions had so much attention been directed toward a single object."[14] The success of the mission—and advertising its success— quickly became the driving force of the American Board. Success abroad, the Board hoped, would dispel growing factionalism among Protestant denominations at home (Methodists, Baptists, even differing sects among the Congregationalists) and pave the way for a new Christian commonwealth around the world. The Sandwich Islands, situated in the middle of trade routes in the

Pacific Ocean, would be the ideal launching pad for their global evangelism. For Americans, the Board tied its mission to Manifest Destiny by arguing that a principal goal was also the Christianization of the West Coast (mainly Native Americans).[15] Like their Pilgrim ancestors, the Board sought a new City on the Hill in the Sandwich Islands: a Kingdom of Jehovah in the heart of the Pacific. At home there was growing competition for parishioners among the various Protestant denominations (not to mention the Catholics); moreover, as Americans steadily emigrated north and west out of New England following the Revolutionary War, the Methodists and Baptists held an advantage because their ministers were itinerant.

But the Congregationalists could be the first ones to the Sandwich Islands.

So the missionaries, like the romantic philosophers of the previous century who projected Eden onto Tahiti and Tahitians, arrived with their own utopian ideals. Instead of glorifying leisure and low-hanging breadfruit, however, the missionaries valued toil and tilling the land: this was their vision of recreating heaven on Earth—or, to be more specific, an idealized New England in the Sandwich Islands. Failure of this first mission would call into question the Board's credibility and its entire foreign mission project. Such were the pressures behind Bingham's relentless push in those first days to secure royal permission for his group to stay.[16]

But it took more than tenacity and strong convictions to "save" the world. The price tag to outfit and send the first group of missionaries to the Sandwich Islands was more than ten thousand dollars. How could they fill the coffers? How would they sustain public interest in a mission that would take time to arrive, set up, and produce hard results in the form of native converts? This was where "exotic heathen" customs like surfing came in. The Board had its own publication, the *Missionary Herald*, which turned into "a useful propaganda organ" for their fundraising activities.[17] After the big news that the missionaries would be permitted to stay *and* that the Hawaiians had officially abandoned their traditional system of religious beliefs, the *Missionary Herald* and other New England publications begin to focus on news from the Sandwich Islands. "Each issue of the *Missionary Herald* reproduced long segments of the missionaries' journal," Andrew writes. "These proved good propaganda and stimulated the flow of donations."[18] The following is an excerpt from one of those published journals—Bingham's first description of surfing—which appeared in the *Missionary Herald* in August of 1822. After describing surfboards and how Hawaiians paddled them out through the waves, Bingham wrote: "Then choosing one of the highest surges, adjusting his board as it approaches him, directing his head towards the shore, he rides on the fore front of the surge, with great velocity, as his board darts along swifter than a weaver's shuttle, while the whitening surf foams and roars around his head, till it dies on the beach, and leaves him to return or retire at pleasure. . . . Sometimes the irregularity or violence of the water tears their board from under them, and dashes it on the rocks; or threatening to carry them into danger, obliges them to abandon it, and save themselves by diving and swimming."[19]

The excitement and novelty of riding waves, along with many other native customs, was used by the Board essentially as a marketing device for the missions: to grab readers' attention and shock them into donating money so that the missionaries could continue the work of eradicating such dangerous customs. Bingham had chosen his subject wisely: at least four newspapers in Vermont and Connecticut picked up his description of the sport over the next two months, one article giving the sport its first headline: "The Surf-Board of the Sandwich Islands." Such articles had already begun to increase interest and donations to the mission, so much in fact that by December of 1821, the Board began preparations to send a second company of missionaries to the Sandwich Islands. Eventually they would finance twelve groups and 153 missionaries over the next thirty years.[20]

PALAPALA

After the second company of missionaries arrived in April of 1823 (fourteen adults, one baby, and four more Hawaiians), modest stations were established on Hawai'i, O'ahu, Kaua'i, and Maui.[21] The first company of missionaries had brought their own printing press and printer—Elisha Loomis—and had begun churning out spelling sheets and religious pamphlets in the Hawaiian language, which the missionaries had codified for easy learning (up to that point the Hawaiians had no written language). Reading and writing—known as *palapala*—was the key to conversion. It was the most successful meeting ground between missionary and native because the Hawaiians loved to learn and the missionaries loved to teach. The Congregationalists had planned this strategy from the beginning of the mission. Reverend Herman Daggett, the principal of the Foreign Mission School back in New England, had advised that the founding of schools was the way "to befriend the natives and gain their confidence before attacking their religious system." He continued: "This will probably be grateful to the Natives . . . & may serve as a cover to the ultimate object, which if too soon presented to their view, might excite prejudice & resentment."[22]

The strategy worked very well. The missionaries organized exams that played into the Hawaiians' love of public display, competition, and storytelling. They adapted their curriculum to native strengths in music and oral history by having Hawaiians memorize long biblical passages and "cantillate" them in unison.[23] When the king's mother, Keōpūolani, decided to relocate to Lahaina on Maui in 1823, she brought with her two missionary families and a Tahitian tutor named Tau'ā, who instructed her in reading and writing. Keōpūolani's death later that year became a watershed moment for the mission. She was baptized on her deathbed—the first Hawaiian to undergo this rite by the missionaries—and so became the first converted Christian in the Islands.[24]

This was a newsworthy event for supporters back home. The publication of *Memoir of Keopuolani, Late Queen of the Sandwich Islands* in 1825 became a means to announce concrete progress of the mission in the Sandwich Islands and put in a plug for more donations: "Let the friends and supporters of missions to the heathen, into whose hands this short narrative may fall," wrote William Richards, the missionary who penned the narrative and accompanied the Queen to Lahaina, "call to mind that their offerings furnished a part of that light, which shone around her path to the grave, and dispelled the darkness which otherwise would have hung over it."[25]

The appendix, which offered general remarks about the Sandwich Islands for New England readers, was more blunt about funding: "The evidence that Almighty God looks kindly upon the enterprise, is overwhelming. Who is on the Lord's side? Let him not hesitate to lend his decided and generous aid. Every thing is to be hoped from prompt and vigorous action; and much to be feared from vacillating and feeble efforts."[26] We can see Bingham's touch here: the hyperbolic prose, the need for urgency. Given Bingham's deeper knowledge of the Islands (Richards did not arrive until 1823), it is probable that he authored the appendix. Authorship aside, we can say, generally speaking, that in addition to any religious urgency driving Bingham due to the Second Coming of Christ, his rhetoric reflects an urgency that was manufactured for the sake of propaganda, one that "became a familiar theme among supporters of foreign missions."[27] In terms of surf history, Bingham's hyperbole about the decline and disappearance of surfing has long been taken at face value rather than as part of a larger promotional campaign by the Congregational church to secure funding and extend its influence. Understanding the context of Bingham's words—that they were meant to demonstrate religious progress in order to win donations from New England congregations—helps us reevaluate the state of surfing in nineteenth-century Hawai'i as reported by Bingham (and subsequently repeated by surf historians). He amplified his limited success at suppressing activities like surfing while glossing over (or ignoring altogether) the status quo or outright failures to eradicate the sport in the long term. The very existence of the mission depended upon good news. For the missionaries, that meant a decline in surfing and other native traditions. Whether these traditions were actually declining or not is another question. It need not be a matter of outright lies on the part of the missionaries, simply a choice of what to report, what not to report, and how to give the daily uphill battle of conversion in this remote Pacific archipelago the best spin possible for the people back home.

It is worth noting that the marketing arm of the American Board had already had great success publicizing the death of another Hawaiian: Henry Obookiah ('Ōpūkahaʻia), a young native educated by the Board's Foreign Mission School in Connecticut. The four Hawaiians who had shipped out with the first group of missionaries had in fact been recruited by 'Ōpūkahaʻia, who was the School's first student and became the "symbol of the essential goodness and intelligence of heathens everywhere."[28] The American Board intended that 'Ōpūkahaʻia would return to Hawaiʻi to convert other natives, but he died of typhus fever in 1818. His death was a galvanizing moment for the entire mission. Several of the missionaries who ended up going to Hawaiʻi did so because of the influence of *Memoirs of Henry Obookiah*, a slim volume published in 1818 which eventually sold 50,000 copies in twelve editions (a huge best seller of the day). Lyman Beecher's funeral sermon, appended to the *Memoirs*, predicted the positive impact that 'Ōpūkahaʻia's death would have on the Foreign Mission School, the mission to Hawaiʻi, and fundraising efforts in general: "His death will give notoriety to this institution—will awaken a tender sympathy for Owhyhee, and give it an interest in the prayers and charities of thousands who otherwise had not heard of this establishment, or been interested in its prosperity."[29] Seven years later the *Memoir of Keopuolani* "was published primarily to indicate missionary benevolence and progress to the American people."[30]

The confluence of education and hyperbole for the sake of mission propaganda appears throughout Bingham's own memoir, *A Residence of Twenty-One Years in the Sandwich Islands*, and has led to a distorted perspective on the history of surfing. In his section for the year 1824 entitled "School Exercises Substituted for Heathen Sports," Bingham follows the missionary practice of using inflated rhetoric to highlight success while glossing over (or simply omitting) any failures.[31] After describing the success of his public exams and how Western education "spread rapidly over the whole group" of Islands, "extending more or less . . . to a third of the whole population," Bingham added: "In the meantime, the heathen sports of the nation nearly disappeared."[32] This summary dismissal of "heathen sports" represents the kind of missionary statements that laid the foundation for the myth of surfing's demise in the nineteenth century.

Bingham saying so does not make it so. Not for him, and not for later writers influenced by his rhetoric who looked favorably on the mission enterprise to "civilize" Hawaiians by eradicating their native culture.[33] We know from other sources that surfing endured in Native Hawaiian communities.[34] But Bingham was riding his own wave of success during the mid-1820s, and there were few Westerners around to contradict his brash assertions.[35]

KA'AHUMANU

The *kuhina nui* or co-ruler with Liholiho, Ka'ahumanu, was the force behind Bingham's rise in influence. After Liholiho and his wife Kamāmalu suddenly died from measles in 1824 while visiting England, Ka'ahumanu became the de facto ruler of the Islands (Kamehameha III was a young boy at the time). It was Ka'ahumanu who, under the persistent efforts of Bingham and the other missionaries, decreed in December of 1824 that there was to be no work or play on the Sabbath. Her decision was partly guided by the need to convince the missionaries that she was worthy of baptism, which they denied her at first. "We dared not authorize such a step," Bingham wrote, "till we had more decisive evidence that she had been born from above by the power of the Spirit of God."[36] Part of the "decisive evidence" Ka'ahumanu could give the missionaries concerning her Christian faith was banning amusements like surfing, at least on Sundays.

This was a significant step for Ka'ahumanu, whom Hawaiian historian John Papa 'Ī'ī described as one of the top surfers in the Islands, a woman who expertly wove her way through rock outcroppings with her husband, Kamehameha I, as the two raced ahead of big waves into shore. "This was a difficult feat and one not often seen," 'Ī'ī wrote, "but for Kaahumanu and the king it was easy."[37] Ka'ahumanu had learned to surf as a young girl to escape her isolation at Kohala on the island of Hawai'i where Kamehameha I kept her confined until she was old enough to marry.[38] Surfing remained a favorite activity for Ka'ahumanu in the first years of the missionaries (she was in her mid-forties by then). Early in her relationship with Bingham—in July of 1821, a couple of days before Bingham wrote his first description of surfing that appeared in the *Missionary Herald*—Ka'ahumanu visited the missionary leader in his home in Honolulu. He was due to depart that day for Kaua'i and rendezvous with the island's ruler, Kaumuali'i, before they both disembarked for Tahiti to meet with British missionaries and learn from their success. Bingham had already asked Ka'ahumanu her thoughts about the trip, and she told him she approved. She'd come down to ask him to bring her several items back from Tahiti, including "a royal surf-board" from the Tahitian king Pōmare.[39] It was a sign of her high esteem for surfing and her strong desire to connect with her Tahitian counterpart. Unfortunately the trip was scuttled, so we do not have the rich irony of Hiram Bingham hauling an enormous *olo* back from Tahiti and facilitating the queen regent's depravity. Ka'ahumanu never got her Tahitian surfboard, but she did eventually get Western religion.

She was finally allowed to convert in December of 1825. From one of Hawai'i's top surfers to the woman who banned surfing on Sundays, Ka'ahumanu maintained her loyalty to Christian practices until her death in 1832.

By the early 1830s—the zenith of missionary influence—Bingham and the others had recruited some 50,000 Hawaiians to attend 1,100 schools throughout the island chain; this represented about 40 percent of the population and included the highest chiefs in the kingdom.[40] One of Bingham's entries for this period shows how drastically the schools had changed the lives and culture of Hawaiians who had adopted the new faith: a group of students were building a seminary at Lahainaluna on Maui using the traditional methods that, a decade before, would have been the same ones used to build canoes and surfboards. Bingham wrote: "The walls and roof of the school-house being erected by their own hands, the pupils, in the summer of 1832, went to the mountains for plank and timber for writing-tables.... They must cut down trees, and hew them away to the thickness of the plank needed; then bring them on their shoulders, or drag them on the ground, by hand, for miles. This was the common method of procuring plank and boards, by natives, throughout the islands before the pit-saw and the saw-mill, moved by water power, were introduced."[41] We could not have a clearer picture of how much the missionaries affected surfing and other native customs among devout Hawaiians during Ka'ahumanu's reign: instead of crafting surfboards, the new *kāhuna* at the seminary were building writing tables to study language, history, math, and Western religion. Two years earlier Bingham had declared enthusiastically that "the slate, the pen, and the needle, have, in many instances, been substituted for the surf-board, the bottle, and the *hula*."[42]

Bingham had high praise for the students at Lahainaluna—"What class of pupils in America, without funds or patrons, would have shown more zeal . . . while pursuing their studies?"—but his personal influence had already reached its peak. The death of Ka'ahumanu that same summer and the ascension of Kamehameha III began a return to native traditions—including surfing, which the king practiced regularly at Lahaina—that would continue until the end of his reign in 1854. By that point the mission had been decommissioned. Surfing resurfaced in Native Hawaiian communities that had formerly embraced Christianity. For those communities that had not embraced Christianity, surfing quietly endured: not a relic of former customs but a tradition that continued to be a vital part of daily life.

Surfing stuck with Bingham as well. Back in New England, penning his memoir in the 1840s, he felt the need to justify himself several times for the missionaries' negative impact on the sport. Here is his most well-known attempt:

> The adoption of our costume greatly diminishes their practice of swimming and sporting in the surf, for it is less convenient to wear it in the water than the native girdle, and less decorous and safe to lay it entirely off on every occasion they find for a plunge or swim or surf-board race. Less time, moreover, is found for amusement by those who earn or make cloth-garments for themselves like the more civilized nations.
>
> The decline or discontinuance of the use of the surf-board, as civilization advances, may be accounted for by the increase of modesty, industry or religion, without supposing, as some have affected to believe, that missionaries caused oppressive enactments against it.[43]

Bingham tried to deny any political influence over the Hawaiians, which would have been against missionary policy, but for him and the others out in the field, a Christian commonwealth meant Christian laws, and they ultimately decided to subvert Board policy and "legislate morality."[44] Sometimes this was done indirectly, as when the missionaries used their apprentice, Native Hawaiian Thomas Hopu, to communicate to Ka'ahumanu (via her servants) that those "who do not observe the Sabbath of the Lord, will go '*i ke ahi a roa*,' (to the endless burning)."[45] On the particular day in question, in early February of 1822, Ka'ahumanu had declined Bingham's invitation to attend church in Honolulu and gone down to Waikīkī for a Sunday surf session. She was entertaining the visiting king of Kaua'i, Kaumuali'i, whom she would marry (along with one of his sons) to solidify political power over Kaua'i.[46]

Another denial by Bingham appears in his section for 1824, "School Exercises Substituted for Heathen Sports": "It was not a matter of wonder that any agreeable substitute, moral, literary, or religious, which should be generally adopted by the people in the place of gambling, or any influence that should speedily put an end to the practice of that vice, while our proposed substitute was openly and diligently, but kindly, urged upon the mass, should be supposed, whether correctly or not, to have nearly abolished the sports of all classes of the people throughout the Sandwich Islands. The experiment was interesting."[47]

Bingham's phrasing here is dense and difficult to read. The long first sentence is convoluted, as if he were trying to dodge behind multiple layers of words, a verbal buffer of sorts to protect himself against the accusations of others.[48] His rhetoric of urgency is present here as well ("or any influence that should *speedily* put an end to the practice of that vice" [my emphasis]), but one wonders if his multiple denials about trying to abolish surfing and other sports do not go beyond the zealous public rhetoric of the missionary enterprise to a deeper and more personal urgency that threatened the foundation of his spiritual convictions.

We know the missionaries disapproved of surfing for many reasons—its connection to idleness and gambling, for example—but perhaps the sport affected them most strongly through its sheer physicality. Hawaiian women surfed naked, and Hawaiian men nearly so (typically in a *malo* wrapped around their hips), and sexual activity abounded in and around the surf zone.[49] Sheldon Dibble, who arrived in 1831 with the fourth group of missionaries, provided a typical (and the most often cited) response to the carnal associations that surrounded what he called "sensual sports": "But the greatest evil of all resulted from the constant intermingling, without any restraint, of persons of both sexes and of all ages, at all times of the day and at all hours of the night."[50]

Part of surfing's enduring appeal is the strongly physical nature of the act itself—riding waves—which produced what the missionaries were nervous about: powerful emotions like joy, pleasure, and desire.[51] Surfing accounts by Native Hawaiians in the nineteenth century are filled with such words as *puni* (pleasure), *makemake* (desire), *walea* (enjoyment), and *ʻoliʻoli* (joyful).[52] For the missionaries, such feelings were the temptations of the physical world that must be fought with self-control and self-denial. All human nature was corrupt, they had been taught and believed, and activities like surfing or the hula, with their communal power, their overt sexuality, their bodily performance, were threats to spiritual purity.[53] These customs and others were probably constant reminders to the missionaries of human weakness—including their own—which constantly pulled them toward the temporal life and away from God.[54]

So surfing for the missionaries, I will argue, beyond an activity that pulled Hawaiians away from Sunday mass and encouraged them to vice, had a strong visceral element that was at odds with their Protestant understanding of religion: they could not reconcile the corporal pleasure of riding waves with the spiritual pursuit of redemption. In her study of the first group of female missionaries in Hawaiʻi, Mary Zwiep comments on their ornate rhetoric as a defense mechanism: "Sexual passion, like the raw pain of grief or the heathen customs surrounding them, was dangerous and needed controlling. More than simply expressing or decorating experience, their language also creates it. Their need for control—whether linguistic, theological, or cultural—is evident in this overly elaborate, even obsessive, prose."[55] Returning to Bingham's rhetoric of urgency: beyond the Second Coming of Christ, beyond even the propaganda of fundraising, we can posit an ever-present need for his own emotional control when faced with the raw physicality and sexuality that were an inherent part of activities like surfing.[56]

Surfing survived the missionaries because it was ultimately a source of great pleasure for the Hawaiians. And conversion worked both ways. By 1843 we have the likes of Reverend Henry T. Cheever, not a missionary but a man of the cloth nonetheless, who published *Life in the Sandwich Islands*, which included an enthusiastic description of surfing from his visit to Lahaina, Maui: "For my part, I should like nothing better, if I could do it, than to get balanced on a board just before a great rushing wave, and so be hurried in half or quarter of a mile landward with the speed of a race-horse, all the time enveloped in foam and spray, but without letting the roller break and tumble over my head."[57] Surfing made its own converts among a later generation of visitors to the Islands, those perhaps less concerned with either their personal salvation or the need to show congregations back home that their donations and prayers for a new Christian commonwealth had not been offered in vain. Included among them were Chester S. Lyman, a teacher at the Royal School for Young Chiefs in Honolulu and later at Yale University, who in the summer of 1846 "had the pleasure of taking a surf ride towards the beach in the native style" at Waikīkī. And Mark Twain, who describes his tumbling experience riding waves at Honaunau, Hawaiʻi, in July of 1866.[58]

But missionary propaganda had already made its impact on the history of surfing. Travelers amplified Bingham's words throughout the nineteenth and twentieth centuries—a gospel, as it were, that (for them) either accurately described the state of surfing or fell into line with a reality they wanted to believe in and construct. Annexationist G. W. Bates, for example, would turn Bingham's religious rhetoric to political advantage and insist that surfing, by the early 1850s, was "rapidly passing out of existence."[59] Today, in an era of billion-dollar surf apparel companies that cater to millions of wave riders around the globe, we can smile at such naive statements. But the propaganda that surfing nearly died out, still repeated today in histories of the sport, masks darker implications.[60] Beyond reminding those of us who write history to study closely the context of the writers and sources we rely upon so heavily, the idea that Hawaiians abandoned a cultural activity that they developed more highly than any other people on earth—not just in practice but in song and story—does a grave injustice to them and to their long history of cultivating, celebrating, and passing down this unique human activity.

NOTES

1. The best resource for Bingham's account is his *A Residence of Twenty-One Years in the Sandwich Islands*, originally published in 1847. The record of the mission's first contact with Hawaiians can be found on pages 85–91. This information is supplemented by journal excerpts published in the *Panoplist, and Missionary Herald* (later simply the *Missionary Herald*) in 1820 and 1821. Online access can be found through Yale University: http://guides.library.yale.edu/content.php?pid=319014&sid=4999149. A fourth Hawaiian, George Kaumuali'i (son of the king of Kaua'i), also sailed with the missionaries but was not considered part of the mission. See the *Missionary Herald*, 1820 (16, 12), 570. Information centering on the missionary wives' experiences (four of the women being pregnant) is from Zwiep, *Pilgrim Path*, 73.

2. Bingham, *Residence*, 85–86.

3. "They were at Kamakahonu, where a spring, Kī'ope, mixes with sea water, a favorite gathering place for swimmers and surfers." Mookini, "Keōpuōlani," 4.

4. Bingham, *Residence*, 136. Bingham's original description from the *Missionary Herald* for 1821: "As we drew near the shore, we saw him [Liholiho] bathing in the surf, in company with others" (17, 4), 116. "Bathing" was also a verb used to describe various forms of surfing in the nineteenth century. This volume of the *Missionary Herald* presents the first accounts from the missionaries themselves about their arrival in Hawai'i (111–121).

5. The starting point for early surf history has traditionally been Ben Finney and James D. Houston's *Surfing: The Sport of Hawaiian Kings* (1966), revised in 1996 as *Surfing: A History of the Ancient Hawaiian Sport*. The authors argue convincingly that many causes led to a decline in surfing in nineteenth century Hawai'i (disease and depopulation among them), yet their acceptance of missionary rhetoric resulted in an uncritical reception and repetition in various forms of such statements as "With these activities [gambling and sexuality] forbidden, interest in surfing quickly died. The Hawaiians apparently found little value in the sport when it lacked these attractions" (*Ancient Sport*, 56). Beyond Bingham, key primary sources in surf history include missionary William Ellis's *Narrative of a Tour Through Hawaii* (1826); Samuel Mānaiakalani Kamakau's *Ruling Chiefs of Hawaii* (1961); and Blake's *Hawaiian Surfriders 1935* (2006). Contemporary popular and academic histories that repeat Finney's and Houston's claims include Kampion, *Stoked! A History of Surf Culture* (2003), and Westwick and Neushul, *The World in the Curl* (2013); histories that challenge the myth of surfing's demise include Warshaw, *The History of Surfing* (2010); Clark, *Hawaiian Surfing* (2011); Walker, *Waves of Resistance* (2011); and Laderman, *Empire in Waves* (2014). See also note 34.

6. Bingham, *Residence*, 89.

7. Bingham, *Residence*, 90.

8. Andrew, *Rebuilding the Christian Commonwealth*, 79. Andrew also mentions how guilt factored into the missionary mindset: "Theological principles and biblical command

also instilled a sense of guilt. Why had foreign missions been so long delayed? This guilt drove the men toward completion of their missions and energized those at home to support their efforts" (152).

9. For a reading of London's and Ford's influence on surf history, see Patrick Moser, "Revival," *Kurangabaa* 3, no. 1 (2010): 46–49, https://kurungabaa.wordpress.com/2011/02/25/revival-by-patrick-moser/.

10. For Ka'ahumanu's use of the missionaries, see Barrère and Sahlins, "Tahitians in the Early History of Hawaiian Christianity," 22–25.

11. *Missionary Herald* 17, no. 4 (1821): 120.

12. Bingham, *Residence*, 90.

13. For Bingham preaching at Waikīkī, see *The Missionary Herald* 19, no. 4 (1823): 100, and Bingham, *Residence*, 182.

14. Andrew, *Rebuilding*, 97.

15. Andrew, *Rebuilding*, 103.

16. In terms of missionary idealism, Wagner-Wright notes in *The Structure of the Missionary Call to the Sandwich Islands*: "All were under the spell of their theology and the romantic image of missionary life" (113). Bingham exerted himself so much that he was unable to hear Liholiho's final response to his request. He stayed on board the *Thaddeus*, exhausted "by the long continued negotiation"; Asa Thurston and Thomas Holman went in his place (*Missionary Herald* 17, no. 4 [1821]: 120).

17. Andrew, *Rebuilding*, 122. A detailed account of expenses for the trip can be found in the *Missionary Herald* 17, no. 1 (1821): 3.

18. Andrew, *Rebuilding*, 126.

19. *Missionary Herald* 18, no. 8 (1822): 242.

20. *Missionary Herald* 17, no. 12 (1821): 396. Bingham's description appeared in *Spooner's Vermont Journal* (vol. XL, no. 2036, p. 1) on August 12, 1822; the *Connecticut Journal* (vol. LV, p. 2) on August 6, 1822; the *Times, and Weekly Advisor* (vol. VI, no. 297, p. 4)—"The Surf-Board of the Sandwich Islands"—on Sept. 3, 1822; and *North Star* (vol. XVI, no. 34, p. 1) on Sept. 5, 1822.

21. Zwiep, *Pilgrim Path*, 198–199. Their number included Betsey Stockton, an African American who eventually ran a school on Maui for the commoners or *maka'āinana*.

22. Andrew, *Rebuilding*, 104–105.

23. Bingham, *Residence*, 214.

24. Silverman notes in *Kaahumanu, Molder of Changer* that the high chief Kalanimoku "accepted the opportunity to be baptized as a Christian aboard the French ship *l'Uranie*" in 1819 (66). This would have been conversion to Catholicism. Kalanimoku is later converted to Protestantism with Ka'ahumanu and other high chiefs on December 5, 1825 (Bingham, *Residence*, 277).

25. Richards, *Memoir*, 44–45. Accessed through Google Books.

26. Richards, *Memoir*, 53.

27. Andrew, *Rebuilding*, 77. I am indebted to Andrew for the connection between missionary rhetoric and the American Board's fundraising efforts. Anna Johnston mentions a similar pattern for the London Missionary Society: "Most published missionary texts are the end result of a well-oiled and efficient production machine run by the missionary

societies and their supportive evangelical publishers. They are thus, fundamentally and frankly, propagandistic in nature. As a result, published missionary texts tend to conform to an identifiable set of generic regulations. Unsurprisingly, there is always an emphasis on the positive achievements of missionary work, for example, whilst the limited successes or spectacular failures are rarely mentioned" ("Antipodean Heathens," 70).

28. Andrew, *Rebuilding*, 101.

29. Dwight, *Memoirs of Henry Obookiah*, 125. Accessed through Google Books.

30. Andrew, *Rebuilding*, 168.

31. Andrew, *Rebuilding*, 92.

32. Bingham, *Residence*, 215.

33. A prominent example is Nathaniel B. Emerson's "Causes of Decline of Ancient Hawaiian Sports" in *The Friend* 50, no. 8 (1892): 57–60. Finney and others cite this source to demonstrate the near demise of surfing. Emerson was the son of missionary John S. Emerson, who arrived in 1832. For a reading of Emerson as used by Finney and Houston, see Moser, "The Endurance of Surfing in 19th-Century Hawai'i." See also Laderman's reading of Emerson (8–10).

34. For the endurance of surfing in the nineteenth century see Moser, *Pacific Passages*, 53, 108; Clark, *Hawaiian Surfing*, 33 et passim; Moser, "Reports of Surfing's Demise," 195–204; Walker, *Waves of Resistance*, 26–31; Laderman, *Empire in Waves*, 8–17; and Moser, "The Endurance of Surfing in 19th-Century Hawai'i" (411–432).

35. Bingham's statement about heathen sports disappearing was most likely written in the 1840s after his return to the United States, as he composed his memoir (published in 1847). But he made similar statements in the late 1820s (see note 42).

36. Bingham, *Residence*, 214.

37. 'Ī'ī, *Fragments of Hawaiian History*, 51, 133–137.

38. Silverman, *Kaahumanu*, 7.

39. Bingham, *Residence*, 135. This would have been Pōmare II.

40. Daws, *Shoal of Time*, 90.

41. Bingham, *Residence*, 425.

42. Stewart, *A Visit to the South Seas*, 259–260. Bingham's words appear in a joint missionary letter appended to Stewart's account for November 22, 1829.

43. Bingham, *Residence*, 137.

44. Andrew, *Rebuilding*, 160.

45. *Missionary Herald* for 1823 (19, 4), 100. See also Bingham, *Residence*, 158.

46. Daws, *Shoal of Time*, 67.

47. Bingham, *Residence*, 215.

48. Naval surgeon W. S. W. Ruschenberger wrote in 1836 (*Narrative of a Voyage Round the World*, 373–375): "Can the missionaries be fairly charged with suppressing these games? I believe they deny having done so. But they write and publicly express against the laws of God, and by a succession of reasoning, which may be readily traced, impress upon the minds of the chiefs and others, the idea that all who practice them, secure to themselves the displeasure of offended heaven."

49. For Hawaiian women surfing naked and the sexuality of surfing in Hawaiian legends, see Moser, *Pacific Passages*, 17–18, 80.

50. Dibble, *A History of the Sandwich Islands*, 102; "sensual sports," 53. Dibble's description of "playing on the surf-board" is on page 99.

51. An excellent discussion of the spiritual life versus the temporal one can be found in Zwiep, *Pilgrim Path*, 122–123: "Sybil [Bingham] felt the tension between such spiritual truths and the attraction of life in all its physicality."

52. In his *Tales and Traditions of the People of Old*, nineteenth-century Native historian Samuel M. Kamakau describes the surfing exploits of Kelea-nui-noho-ana-ʻapi-ʻapi (45–49): "Surfing was her greatest pleasure" (*"O ka heenalu hoi kana puni"*); "When Kelea heard the word 'surfing,' desire rose in her, for surfing had been her favorite pastime" (*"A lohe keia i ka hua heenalu, makemake loa iho la keia, no ka mea, o kana puni no hoi ia o ka heenalu"*); "the kamaʻaina said [about Waikīkī]: 'This is a place of enjoyment'" (*"O kahi walea o keia wahi"*); "Joyful at the thought of surfing" (*"Olioli keia i ka heenalu"*). The Hawaiian derives from the original story published in *Ka Nupepa Kuokoa* on August 19, 1865, p. 1, cols. 5–6, and p. 2, col. 1 (accessed through papakilodatabase.com). Similar accounts and vocabulary by Native Hawaiians in the nineteenth century can be found in Clark, *Hawaiian Surfing*, 394–395.

53. "[T]he natural disposition of our race is to indulge the sordid, sinful passions" (Bingham, *Residence*, 23).

54. Note Mercy Whitney's comment on the death of the princess Nāhiʻenaʻena: "O may it lead us all to look well to our ways, lest we also fall & deny the faith we now possess" (Zwiep, *Pilgrim Path*, 281).

55. Zwiep, *Pilgrim Path*, 146.

56. Another example of Bingham's ornate, periodic prose—with a description of natives "riding more rapidly and proudly on their surf-boards, on the front of foaming surges, as they hasten to the sandy shore"—can be found in *Residence*, 217–218.

57. Cheever, *Life in the Sandwich Islands*, 66–68.

58. For Lyman and Twain, see Moser, *Pacific Passages*, 106–107, 117.

59. Bates, *Sandwich Islands Notes*, 288–289.

60. The website for the Outrigger Canoe Club, for example, notes: "When the Outrigger Canoe Club was founded, the ancient Hawaiian water sports of surfing and outrigger canoeing were on the verge of extinction." https://www.outriggercanoeclub.com/web /pages/history.

2 / A World Apart: Pleasure, Rebellion, and the Politics of Surf Tourism

SCOTT LADERMAN

Just who was Señor Bormanito? A handful of surfers, at most, might today recognize the name. This is not surprising, as it appeared in the pages of the sport's flagship publication only once—and that was in the early 1970s. But what that long-ago reference suggests about one of the more celebrated figures in modern surfing history is something that should interest us all.

In 1971, Miki Dora published a dispatch from South America for *Surfer* magazine about his alleged encounter with the enigmatic figure.[1] The details he provided were telling. According to Dora, "Senor Bormanito" was a German "gentleman now residing in Paraguay" with a fondness for South African wines, Nordic folklore, and Richard Wagner. The young American, it quickly became obvious, could barely contain his enthusiasm. Dora raved about the unfettered access he enjoyed to the German's private plane (complete with a sommelier) and private yacht, as well as the lodging volunteered by Bormanito at his opulently adorned estate. That estate—and here Dora was clearly speaking to his sixties-era audience—contained "experimental greenhouse laboratories" in which, in "one of the [world's] major horticultural breakthroughs," a "most imaginative grafting process" was fusing "the cocaine leaf of the upper high-lands of Ecuador with the unique Kamodo [sic] Island monitor poppy." The "great vintage crop" that resulted, Dora proclaimed, was awaiting export to the "jet set" crowds of Europe, Asia, and North America. As "a shy man," however, the mysterious German "experienced acute paranoia at the sight of my cam-era," Dora noted next to a blurry photograph he claimed to have snapped of him. Nevertheless, Bormanito was a "man of great taste and *dégénère supérieur*," which Dora undoubtedly intended as a compliment. "Our host's talents never cease to amaze me," the American surfer gushed.[2]

Reading's Dora's missive today is an exercise in frustration. The prose is overwrought and self-absorbed, and the piece is at times incomprehensible. But what makes the screed not just bizarre but downright repugnant is Señor Bormanito himself. Only the most astute readers might have picked up on the clues. A Wagner-loving German with a penchant for apartheid-grown wines? Señor Bormanito was quite clearly meant to be Martin Bormann, who at the time was one of the most wanted Nazi fugitives said to be residing in South America. Bormann was in fact dead; a DNA test in 1998 confirmed that he died in Berlin in 1945.[3] But in 1971, when Dora penned the piece for *Surfer*, his fate was still uncertain. Indeed, a representative of the militant Jewish Defense League sent a copy of the *Surfer* article to the US Embassy in Buenos Aires and asked the magazine "to contact Mr. Dora" so that his organization could "ques-tion him about this matter." The blurry photo of "Senor Bormanito," Rabbi David Komonor wrote, "bears a certain resemblance to Martin Borman [sic], second in command of the Third Reich, perhaps the most hated and wanted man on the face of the earth by the Jewish people."[4] So why would Dora con-coct a glowing portrait of one of the principal architects of the Nazi terror?

Surfers fancy themselves a rebellious bunch, and there are few "rebels" more celebrated than Miki Dora. To Ben Marcus he was "an outsider and a noncon-formist and a rebel without a cause."[5] Dora's "eloquent railing (often in print) against the forces of greed and growth," Drew Kampion wrote of the same man who collected a handsome sum for his product endorsements and Hollywood appearances, "became the sport's conscience."[6] *Surfer* magazine's Justin Hous-man said in 2015 that Dora's "outlaw mystique still sets the bar for rebellion decades after the peak of his power."[7] The sentiment is consistent with the subtitle of one of his biographies: Dora was nothing less than a "rebel surfer," proclaimed David Rensin in 2008.[8] But none of these tributes could surpass the fawning obituary that appeared in the *Times* of London following Dora's death from pancreatic cancer in 2002. Dora—"a Kerouac in shorts, the soulmate of Jack Nicholson in *One Flew Over the Cuckoo's Nest*: a subversive, restless wildman"—was "so much a rebel that he rebelled, in the end, against surfing" itself.[9] Such unidimensional paeans notwithstanding, there was another side to this oft-touted legend. As Peter Westwick and Peter Neushul reminded us in 2013, Miki Dora was a notorious bigot with a soft spot for fascism.[10]

Indisputably possessing a rare talent for wave-riding, Dora embraced a "rebellion" predicated on violent aggression, white supremacy, criminal activity, and personal betrayal. He was the best known of the so-called surf Nazis who adopted the emblems (the swastika and the Iron Cross) of the genocidal Third Reich. But for Dora it was not just about Jews. In 1965, he staffed an anti–civil rights desk at a UCLA protest. He railed against Mexicans and "niggers." And, in 1982, he professed his love for "American Nazis."[11] Sought by the law for various transgressions, Dora fled the United States in the 1970s, spending much of his exile in apartheid South Africa, where, writing from "deepest darkest Africa" in 1986, he intoned that black South Africans are "not like the blacks in the US who just kick your ass and take your wallet. These MF's are flesh-eaters. Give these guys the rights and you'll get white-man jerky for export." When apartheid finally ended, Dora bemoaned the change. "The good times are over," he told his friend Steven Taussig. "I'm trying to make a move to South America somewhere before the Blacks take everything. It was great while it lasted."[12]

Dora's contemporaries too often gave him a pass. It says something about modern surf culture that his praise-filled 1971 dispatch from three of the worst human rights violating states in the Americas—Brazil, Paraguay, and Argentina—engendered nary a peep. It also says something about modern surf culture that Dora's glowing portrait of Martin Bormann has, in the forty-something years since its publication, been almost entirely forgotten.[13] The fact that Dora never actually met Bormann is immaterial. What is telling is that he, just like countless neo-Nazis, saw fit to write so affectionately about this paragon of the Third Reich. Some might dismiss this as evidence of Dora's mischievousness. But this is a form of rebellion from which surfers surely ought to recoil. There is nothing admirable in glorifying *genocidaires*.

Such spurious rebellion is hardly unique to Miki Dora, of course. The annals of surf history are filled with self-congratulatory accounts of surfers staking a claim to the countercultural vanguard. Generally speaking, however, theirs is too often a counterculture bereft of serious political meaning. "From the start," wrote famed surf explorer Kevin Naughton in a retrospective piece in 1990, "traveling surfers picked up where the fifties' Beat Generation left off." If the Beats were "a wandering group of writers and poets who went against the grain of society bent on producing thousands of ants in pinstripe suits," Naughton suggested, "add a surfboard" and "what emerges is the prototypical traveling surfer."[14]

While there is perhaps a kernel of truth in Naughton's analogy, for the most part it is difficult to take his claim seriously. Equating the hedonistic journeys of self-absorbed surfers with the politically driven work of artists railing against modern industrial capitalism simply strains credulity. Indeed, surfers were often wont to celebrate their conscious disregard of precisely those things on which the Beats focused their attention. As journalist and bestselling author Leonard Lueras noted in the 1980s, "[p]olitically, surfing has managed to remain relatively pure and blind to the world's greatest social problems."[15] To associate surfing's purity with its detachment from an inevitably politicized world, as Lueras did, was, and is, significant, suggesting the risk posed by social realities to the supposed transcendence of the wave-riding experience. For wandering surfers taking to the globe, this had meaningful implications. A surfing paradise, a young Australian wrote in 1966, became a place "completely devoid of crowds, society, and [the] pressure of modern civilization, politics, and world affairs."[16] So, we might ask, what exactly made surf tourism so rebellious?

TO BE SURE, Miki Dora's travelogue from South America was not representative of the genre. Most surfers did not fantasize about cavorting with Nazi fugitives. But Dora's account is significant for making explicit what most pieces buried: There could be a politics to surf travel. Kevin Naughton erred, however, in characterizing this politics as countercultural, by which he meant rebellious. Hedonism is hardly rebellion. Yet the surfers from around the world who undertook journeys of exploration in the 1960s and 1970s did so as political actors unable to escape the larger realities of that era. The years following World War II were of course marked by global struggles for decolonization and independence. Imperial powers that had taken for granted their claims over most of Africa and Asia and portions of Latin America and the Pacific faced insurrections by the exploited masses that had toiled under colonial domination. Many of these struggles became subsumed by the Cold War and its vernacular, from "communism" and "freedom" to "totalitarianism" and "democracy." To oppose the spoils accruing to colonial masters was to be "communist," even if those doing the opposing were not themselves members of a communist party. This was because revolutionary nationalism, like nonalignment, was perhaps an even greater sin than communism in the eyes of Washington, as it suggested a Cold War alternative outside the American and Soviet axes. It thus had to be opposed.

This was the case in Chile, for instance, where Henry Kissinger, Richard Nixon's national security advisor, warned of the insidious "model effect" that Salvador Allende's 1970 democratic election could present to independent-minded peoples beyond the Southern Cone. "The example of a successful elected Marxist government in Chile would surely have an impact on—and even precedent value for—other parts of the world, especially in Italy," Kissinger warned the president. "The imitative spread of similar phenomena elsewhere," he continued, "would in turn significantly affect the world balance and our own position in it."[17] In an effort to destroy Allende's vision for the country, Nixon ordered his national security team to "make the [Chilean] economy scream."[18] And in 1973, with Allende still in power, the United States backed a military coup that overthrew the elected government, ushering in nearly seventeen years of dictatorship under Augusto Pinochet.

The story of Chile is in fact instructive for surf history. Surfers today know the country as a land of outstanding waves and a regular stop on the professional world circuit, a sort of "cold-water Indonesia" with some of the world's longest point breaks. But for most of the 1970s and 1980s, Chile was probably best known internationally for its vicious military regime. This might have come as a surprise to thousands of young, clueless surfers—at least if the treatment afforded by *Surfer* magazine is any indication. When the magazine presented its Chilean debut in 1982, running a six-page spread that touched not only on the country's waves but also its geography, economy, and people, the article included not a single reference to the Pinochet dictatorship. Instead, readers learned, the people in "all of Chile" are "warm and entertaining" and manage to "enjoy themselves in whatever they do." Politically astute surfers might have wondered whether these "warm" Chileans included those populating the state's repressive apparatus, and whether the oppressors found enjoyment in the torture, execution, or "disappearance" of tens of thousands of political opponents during that period. But if one was not already aware of Chile's political realities, as was presumably the case with many readers of the magazine, one was not going to discover them in the pages of *Surfer*. The closest the magazine came to acknowledging the country's political repression was a vague, possibly suggestive reference to a concert attended by the article's author. "The second day I was in Chile," Erik Aeder wrote, "I went to a 'Police' concert and watched people jump as they sang 'When the world is running down, you make the best of what's still around.' "[19]

If Aeder failed to situate Chile within the extant political universe—that is, within empirical reality—he instead offered an idyllic vision of a country marked by bucolic splendor to which surfers might just wish to immigrate. The countryside was dotted with "snow-capped volcanoes, azure lakes, forests, and country towns." The coast featured "long beaches . . . dissected [sic] by rocky headlands where birds gathered and capped the rocks white with guano." Those beaches "literally crawl" with purple sand crabs, penguins, sea urchins, eels, and scallops that were "some of the best" the author had ever eaten, while the "fertile valley" in which the capital city of Santiago sat sported grapes used to "produce excellent, inexpensive red wines that are known throughout South America." Both the capital and the resort area of Viña del Mar were "modern cosmopolitan cities." And the surf? "With almost four thousand kilometers of coastline, Chile has [wave] potential beyond belief." Indeed, "with so much unexplored coastline, Chile is another frontier for surfing that has yet to be realized," the magazine pronounced. This led to what many human rights activists might have considered startlingly counterintuitive advice. At a time when Chile had spawned an exodus of political refugees fleeing Pinochet's repression, *Surfer* took a different tack: "If isolation surrounded by natural beauty is what you seek[,] this could be the place" for you.[20]

Such counsel does not seem unusual when one considers the extent to which wandering surfers overlooked repression elsewhere. Brazil, which today is a competitive surfing powerhouse, underwent a comparable treatment in the 1960s following the US-backed overthrow of João Goulart, the left-wing president who was deposed by the military in 1964.[21] Like Chile, Brazil was addressed as if it were a world apart: there was not even a hint of its political repression in the surf media's coverage. Instead, the country appeared to be one big party. "A few years ago," *Surfer* reported in 1968, "Brazil was strictly the land of carnival, samba, bossa nova, soccer, coffee, jungles, and sun. But today, way down among Brazilians," it continued, "something new has been added—surfing."[22] Did it matter that *Surfer* was an American magazine written for American surfers who were traveling in American client states? Perhaps. The case of El Salvador, which sponsored the surf exploration of Monty Smith in a tourism-boosting effort in 1969, suggests that US foreign policy was treated quite differently across the Pacific, with the Australian periodical *Tracks*, for example, running a scathing piece on US support for the right-wing Salvadoran junta.[23] The United States was "propping up the corrupt government," Rob Debelle wrote in 1981, and "history has shown the peasants that they have to die fighting rather than take any more oppression."[24]

Even when the American surf media explicitly addressed the repression of US client states, its treatment could seem remarkably superficial. Bernie Baker, who would later pen a somewhat shallow piece on his "return to El Salvador," wrote in 1970 about the "perils" of surfing in Central America and the West Indies.[25] (In an indication of the stature afforded it, the 1970 account, which was said by Chris Mauro and Steve Hawk to have "usher[ed] in the golden age of surf travel," was reproduced nearly forty years later in *The Best of* Surfer *Magazine*.[26]) Trinidad, Baker said, was a "beautiful place" even though it had "some of the poorest people" he had ever seen. "Revolution and politics were in the air," he wrote without explanation, and he was quite blunt about wishing to not stick around. Baker left when "riots broke out"—over what is left unstated—"bringing a US Navy convoy to [the island's] shores to evacuate the Americans." Baker then made his way to Panama, where he stayed with a family in the Canal Zone. "Panama is controlled by a military junta," he noted, "and that fact will be on your mind day and night." But what follows is a nod only to what this means for a visiting American. "Their police system is efficient, and they make up their own rules. If they don't like your hair, bell-bottom pants, or sandals, they'll let you know with a swift clop on the head and an undetermined length of time in one of their prisons."[27]

The same problem afflicts Baker's coverage of Nicaragua, which in 1970 was suffering under decades of a US-backed dictatorship. His twinned assumptions that it would take foreigners to seed revolution but that the rebellious potential of Nicaragua was an inner-familial matter—a very bourgeois notion, and one belied by the rise of the Sandinista movement that overthrew the Somoza regime in 1979—are startling. "I was learning that the feeling among the people was that any wandering youth with long hair was one of those 'student radicals' pictured in last week's international edition of *Time* or *Life*. In general, a rock-throwing, cop-hating revolutionary. And these people have enough on their hands trying to keep their own youth in order without 'student radicals' planting seeds of revolution in their children's minds. But don't worry, most of the kids I met were in the midst of leading their own quiet revolt against the binding Spanish traditions and beliefs of their parents."[28] If Baker was dismissive of the actual revolutionary ferment in Nicaragua, he witnessed the violence such rebellion invited as he left Nicaragua for points north.

El Salvador, where Baker scored great surf, was also at the time ruled by a US-backed authoritarian regime. This is never acknowledged, however, though Baker does write cryptically about what he periodically witnessed late in the evenings in La Libertad. There, "under the secrecy of night, arms and ammunition were unloaded off foreign vessels anchored in deep water, and whisked away under armed convoy."[29] What nation provided these weapons and for what purpose was a mystery—or at least not worth mentioning. But it is difficult not to read this as an oblique reference to the funneling by the United States of millions of dollars of military aid into the country, an arrangement that invited so much repression of Salvadoran civil society that, by February 1980, Archbishop Oscar Romero famously implored the Jimmy Carter administration to cut it off.[30] (Romero was assassinated just weeks later. According to the United Nations Commission on the Truth for El Salvador, the assassination was ordered by the US-backed death-squad leader Roberto D'Aubuisson.[31]) Baker did get a "good look at war" when crossing the heavily militarized Honduran–Salvadoran border and seeing a bridge attacked by the Honduran armed forces, but the account is used not to illuminate the political repression of the region but to demonstrate the intrepid nature of Central American travel. None of this violence, in fact, precluded Baker from calling El Salvador a "paradise."[32]

In a section of his piece on how to "rout[e] around revolts," Baker offered what he must have considered sage counsel for his compatriots at home. "The safest and easiest way of traveling through is to pick up an air mail edition of the *Miami Herald*, found in every major city down there, and find out who's revolting at the moment," he began glibly. "Then pick your route and make a run for your destination." True, to some readers this might have "sounded a little too heavy for your nerves and peaceful, flowing way of life." But if "you're wondering what uncrowded waves look like, and long for a little adventure," his advice was simple: "take off." What Baker's report suggested more than anything was that war and revolution exist, and surfers may be forced to confront them during their global sojourns, but why people revolt, and the West's role in aiding the repression that often gave rise to such strife, were of little importance. This blithe dismissal was intimated by *Surfer*'s applause for its correspondent's ability to "sidestep revolutions" and "r[i]de a bus through the middle of a war" just to report on surf conditions in the West Indies and Central America.[33]

Baker's relative ease of travel was of course facilitated by his status as a white-skinned tourist from the First World. While he sought to distinguish himself from better-heeled travelers—the resorts in Barbados cater mostly to wealthy tourists, he wrote, and "that doesn't help you or me"—he nevertheless enjoyed far more privilege than did most of the local people.[34] It is not clear whether he recognized this. Some later surfers certainly would not, such as Timmy Turner, who surmised during an Indonesian camping trip in the early twenty-first century that the local fishermen looked at him "not with your typical Indo look" but "with respect and . . . like this guy's living harder than us."[35] Of course, Turner's deprivation, which he filmed and sold commercially, was temporary and a matter of choice. Not so for the Indonesians he encountered.

Other Western men during surf tourism's "golden age" proudly adopted the pleasures that accompanied life amongst the neocolonial class. An example would be the handful of surfers who "discovered" and publicized the world-class waves of Tamarin Bay in the 1960s. Mauritius had been a sugar-producing, slavery-dependent French colony in the eighteenth century until its capture by the British in 1810. While the British abolished slavery in 1835, colonial planters came to rely on a large pool of indentured laborers imported from India. This created a mixed society in which those of Indian and African descent predominated, while small numbers of wealthier Europeans and Chinese maintained a stable presence. Mauritius remained a British colony until 1968.

When Joel de Rosnay, a Frenchman from Biarritz whose family owned a sugar plantation on the island, wrote about his experiences surfing there in 1963, he seemed to harbor nary a critical thought about this "surfing paradise."[36] Little appeared to change in the years that followed. By 1965 a surf club was beginning to form within the colonial ranks, and in 1966 *Surfer* provided a report ("Mauritius: Surfing Paradise") by an Australian who, the magazine wrote, "always dreamed of finding the almost deserted tropical island where the only sounds at night are bull frogs and the boom of surf breaking on a reef." The author in question, Ian Harewood, who traveled to Mauritius for six weeks as an escape from the crowded Durban lineups of apartheid South Africa that he toured with *Surfer* correspondent Ron Perrott, was said by the magazine to be the type of surfer who regretted his birth falling well after the Congregationalist missionaries ventured to Hawai'i and Fletcher Christian to Tahiti in the early nineteenth century. How he would have loved to accompany them! But Mauritius proved the next best thing.[37]

Harewood spent his time on the island at the "weekend beach bungalo [*sic*]" of local surfer Bernard Koenig, dining on French cuisine—tournedos chasseur, steak au poivre, cervelle de boeuf au beurre noir, et cetera—and imbibing French cognac and wine. The bungalow "looked as if it had been created by a Hollywood movie set designer for an exotic island picture," Harewood boasted. It featured a sun deck and a cocktail bar, and it was conveniently situated over the water at Tamarin Bay, site of the island's premier surf break. It was "six of the quickest and easiest weeks of my life," he crowed. And no wonder: he occupied a colonial dreamscape. The "mess of dishes and pans" from the sophisticated menu he enjoyed, for instance, would "miraculously vanish [by the next day]—cleared away by one of our servants."[38]

Readers learn nothing about these servants, and certainly nothing critical is said about the master–servant arrangement, but the local people did provide a colorful backdrop that lends to the experience's romance. When Harewood and his traveling companion first arrive on Mauritius, for example, they are dashed through Port Louis in "a vintage English-built Morris VIII" taxicab. They zoom down "narrow streets with leaning buildings on each side, heavy shutters hinged back and everywhere strange shops: hardware, a grocery shop next to a man with a sidewalk display of coffins. . . . There were street peddlers selling watches, deformed, pitiful beggars, Chinese shops, Indian shops, French shops, small dingy bars, dark and forboding [sic] in contrast to the bright sun. There were pavement stores where Indians cooked on open braziers, scavenging dogs, oxen pulling heavy timber carts and everywhere people shouting in French, selling things, cars tooting." Elsewhere there were "lean-tos of timber, corrugated iron, and reeds," as well as "long-haired, scruffy urchins" who "played in the roads, many without pants on." "This was Mauritius," he says at one point, "and it was fantastic."[39]

Harewood does, of course, acknowledge the island's poverty, but, in his strange telling, the fault appears to lie with the poor themselves, whose "apathy"—or is it their penchant for "procreation"?—is at the heart of the problem. "There is a lot of the easy going, slow colonial atmosphere on Mauritius[,] and there's a great contrast between the well-to-do minority and the mass of undernourished poor," he writes. "There is unemployment and squalor[,] and apathy among the lower class is almost a religion. The economy, which relies almost entirely on sugar cane, is in a poor state and procreation is probably Mauritius's number one industry. There is talk of independence for this Indian Ocean island and that could make things worse—at least in the opinion of many of the local colonials. In short, Mauritius has many economic problems with no real solution in sight and consequently many of the younger people—certainly the most useful—leave the island for more productive climes." But potential visitors need not have worried. "These few drawbacks shouldn't bother any visiting surfer as the people on the island are tremendously friendly," Harewood assured his First World audience. And none of these real-world distractions would temper his view that Mauritius was a "dream island, a paradise of surf and solitude in the middle of the Indian Ocean."[40] It seemed almost a shame that he had to return to Durban, where he would continue to enjoy the privilege but without the solitude.

To their credit, some surfers did acknowledge and criticize the injustices or inequities they witnessed while traveling in what was then called the Third World. Such was the case with Craig Peterson in Western Sahara, the one-time

Spanish colony occupied by Morocco and Mauritania following the Spanish withdrawal from the territory in 1975—a withdrawal during which, former US senator George McGovern said, the Gerald Ford administration brokered "a backdoor deal that effectively sold out the fundamental right of the people of [Western Sahara] to determine their own destiny."[41] Peterson's account of his travels through North Africa highlighted both the menace and the incompetence of the occupation forces. "The band of guerrillas formed from the independence of what was once Spain's claim in Africa, Spanish Sahara, are backed by Algeria and strike under the name 'Polisario,'" he wrote. "They are defenders against invasion and occupation on the part of Morocco and Mauritania, and frequently make raids on both countries to stress their seriousness."[42]

A similarly critical perspective appeared in Craig Lockwood's dispatch for *Surfing Action Around the World* in 1969 on the Peru International Surfing Championships. Lockwood expended considerable ink on the otherwise forgotten travails of Gerardo Alberto Bejarano Ybarra, a young man called Negro Soto by the local surf community. Ybarra, wrote Lockwood, was one of the best surfers in Peru. A dark-skinned nineteen-year-old, he progressed to the last semifinal heat in that year's contest. This was remarkable, Lockwood explained, because in Peru surfing was "a rich man's sport"—"only the rich surf"—and Ybarra had the singular misfortune among the Peruvian contestants of being born into poverty. When Ybarra competed, in fact, he could not even use his own board, for he did not have one. "Each of his heats was surfed on a board he had borrowed for the first time," Lockwood wrote. "Once he traded boards during a heat."[43]

Ybarra's story reveals something about the elitism of Peruvian surfing and the privilege that more generally accompanied the sport. Surfing may have originated as a cross-societal pastime in the Pacific Islands, but by the 1960s it was, at least outside Hawai'i, largely confined to the better-off First World classes who had the time and resources to take to the waves. In Peru the class distinctions were quite pronounced. Most of Peruvian surf culture centered on the high-end, members-only Club Waikiki in Lima. There, Peruvian elites could dine on a multicourse meal, play a game of squash, or shake a leg on the club's marble dance floor, all while waiting for the staff to wax and carry their boards to the water.[44]

This was not the world enjoyed by Gerardo Ybarra. "I used to hang out at the beach watching the others surfing," he said.

> They were all rich and could afford surfboards. I asked to borrow a board to try it out, and they laughed at me and told me that I had to wax

everybody's board and get the boards when they washed in. I had to act like a servant, but the first time I went out on a board I stood up and rode it all the way in. That was the first time and I earned their respect. That was three years age [*sic*] on a balsa log. You see, here in Peru, those who have the money ride the waves. I'm the only one without money who surfs. It's a waste of time to come down alone without a board. Even when I borrow one it is only for a few hours at the most. Sometimes, though, I've had a little luck and had a board for a whole day.

Ybarra's poverty—the sole structural condition that kept him from owning a board of his own—was "the one thing... keeping him from getting any better," Lockwood believed. And the contest was no help. There was a new board being given out as a prize, but it went to the thirteen-year-old winner of an "unimportant interclub contest," Lockwood wrote. Meanwhile, Ybarra was "out trying to hustle up a board to ride for a few minutes." Lockwood felt dispirited. He pointed to the vast distance that separated the Peru of touristic imaginings with the realities faced by people such as Ybarra. " 'Peru,' say all the travel brochures, 'is a land of contrasts,' " he noted. But "not all the contrasts are quaint, or picturesque. Some shake the gringo's sense of fair play and decency, and leave a taste as bitter as the endless alkaline dust that blows across the mesa of Punta Rocas." In the context of late-sixties surf culture, this was about as damning a statement as one could make.[45]

BUT THE ACCOUNTS by Peterson and Lockwood proved the exception rather than the rule. Not a single travelogue in *Surfer* (or, across the Pacific, in *Tracks*) of the dreamscape discovered by surfers in Indonesia in the 1970s mentioned the invasion and genocidal occupation of East Timor by the US-backed Suharto regime, for example.[46] And to surfers, the world looked similarly uncomplicated in the Middle East. When a feature on Israel appeared in the American surf press in 1987, there were vague references to the region's "troubles" or "political struggles" and "the wars that Israel was involved in," but the Jewish State's illegal occupation of the Palestinian territories, including East Jerusalem, was overlooked amidst the author's exhortation to visit the Israeli-occupied Old City. The ubiquitous "people in uniform," moreover, might at first seem scary with their "M16s or Uzis," Abraham Paskowitz wrote to his readers-cum-potential tourists, but "the presence of the military tends, instead, to give a feeling of real security."[47] One wonders whether the local Arabs would have agreed. What emerges from the surf tourism of the 1960s through 1980s, in other words, is a culture convinced of its rebelliousness yet largely eliding the revolutionary ferment and injustices of the era.

Surfers may have savored their perceived coolness while envisioning themselves modern-day iconoclasts, but, with few exceptions, their countless journeys during the "golden age" of surf travel reveal a misguidedly smug culture occupying a world apart. It is not difficult to be a "rebel" when one defines rebellion as simply choosing to surf. Yet that seems an extraordinarily facile conceptualization. Was it really the case that, amidst the twentieth century's campaigns for peace, national liberation, and class revolution, wave-riding could seriously be equated with these extraordinary struggles? Surfers apparently thought so. But surf tourists were not in fact rebels: they were hedonists and gluttons. Surfers did not take to the road in an effort to change the world. They did so because discovering and riding waves is fun. Surf tourism, in other words, was about pleasure. Nothing more, nothing less.

NOTES

1. Drew Kampion wrote that the story was originally written by Allan Carter, but Dora, according to Carter, "went back in and doctored it all up with his weird surreal shit" (Stecyk and Kampion, *Dora Lives*, 88).

2. Mickey (née Miki) Dora, "To Whom It May Underestimate." The man in the photo, according to Allan Carter, was "actually some guy with his son on the Baltic" (Stecyk and Kampion, *Dora Lives*, 88). Dora's account suggested that Bormanito was involved in the drug trade (Dora, "To Whom It May Underestimate," 59).

3. Imre Karacs, "DNA Test Closes Book on Mystery of Martin Bormann," *Independent* [London], May 4, 1998, www.independent.co.uk/news/dna-test-closes-book-on-mystery -of-martin-bormann-1161449.html.

4. Komonor, "M. S. D.," 11.

5. Marcus, *Surfing USA!*, 69.

6. Kampion, *Stoked!*, 74. On Dora's commercial involvement, see Warshaw, *The Encyclopedia of Surfing*, 161.

7. Housman, "Rebel Whisper," 36.

8. Rensin, *All for a Few Perfect Waves: The Audacious Life and Legend of Rebel Surfer Miki Dora*.

9. "Mickey Dora," *Times* [London], January 12, 2002.

10. Westwick and Neushul, *The World in the Curl*, 169.

11. Rensin, *All for a Few Perfect Waves*, 117, 175–176, 275. I am indebted to Westwick and Neushul (*The World in the Curl*) for identifying some of the most significant details contained in Rensin's *All for a Few Perfect Waves*.

12. Warshaw, *The Encyclopedia of Surfing*, 161; Warshaw, *The History of Surfing*, 120; and Rensin, *All for a Few Perfect Waves*, 317, 359. In fairness, Dora seemed to be a misanthrope in general. His solution to crowds in the lineup, given the failure, he said in a 1965

interview, to implement birth-control policies twenty years earlier, was to "send them to Saigon" ("Mickey Chapin Dora," 30). Dora's flippancy annoyed a Californian serving in Southeast Asia. "There are a large number of surfers over here at the present time who left their homes and beaches behind to fight for their country," he wrote to *Surfer*. "What is Mr. Dora doing for his country?" (Lamont, "Viet Nam on Dora," 12).

13. In his *All for a Few Perfect Waves*, for example, David Rensin mentioned Dora's "classic magazine travelogue" but failed to acknowledge its praise for the Nazi (Rensin, *All for a Few Perfect Waves*, 199). Rensin did include Allan Carter's story about Carter and Dora declining an invitation to a dinner party for Paraguayan dictator Alfredo Stroessner that they worried might turn into a reunion for "a Wermacht [*sic*] SS unit" at which he and Dora, who "didn't look Aryan," could potentially face physical harm (Rensin, *All for a Few Perfect Waves*, 199).

14. Naughton, "A Feel for the Road," 56.

15. Lueras, *Surfing*, 197.

16. Harewood, "Mauritius," 49.

17. "Memorandum from the President's Assistant for National Security Affairs (Kissinger) to President Nixon," November 5, 1970, in McElveen and Siekmeier, *Foreign Relations*, 440–441.

18. Notes of Richard Helms, September 15, 1970, in McElveen and Siekmeier, *Foreign Relations*, 254.

19. Aeder, "Southern Cone Expedition," 44–45.

20. Aeder, "Southern Cone Expedition," 42–45.

21. Even the *New York Times* has noted Brazil's surfing ascendancy; see Juliana Barbassa, "What Explains Brazil's Surfing Boom?" *New York Times*, March 29, 2015.

22. "Rio: City of Love . . . and Surf," 50. For an American exchange student's account of Brazilian surfing, see Pete Johnson, "Esta Na Onda."

23. On the Salvadoran government's sponsorship of Smith, see Naughton, "A Feel for the Road," 56. On the marked difference in coverage of El Salvador in *Surfer* and *Tracks*, see Laderman, "Reds, Revolutionaries, and Racists," 416–419.

24. Rob Debelle, "El Salvador," 15.

25. Baker, "Return to El Salvador," 88–89, 122.

26. Mauro and Hawk, *The Best of* Surfer *Magazine*, 31.

27. Baker, "Perils of the Tropics," 73.

28. Baker, "Perils of the Tropics," 75.

29. Baker, "Perils of the Tropics," 77.

30. US Embassy in San Salvador to the Secretary of State, "Text of Archbishop's Letter to President Carter," February 19, 1980, http://www2.gwu.edu/~nsarchiv/NSAEBB /NSAEBB339/doc04.pdf.

31. Commission on the Truth for El Salvador, "From Madness to Hope," 354–357.

32. Baker, "Perils of the Tropics," 75, 77.

33. Baker, "Perils of the Tropics," 66, 77.

34. Baker, "Perils of the Tropics," 70–71.

35. Turner, *Second Thoughts*.

36. De Rosnay, "Discovery: Mauritius," 49, 51.

37. Bernard Koenig, "SI Notes," 9; Harewood, "Mauritius," 42.

38. Harewood, "Mauritius," 44, 46.

39. Harewood, "Mauritius," 44.

40. Harewood, "Mauritius," 48–49.

41. McGovern, "Foreword," xiii.

42. Peterson, "Sojourn into the Western Sahara," 75–76.

43. Lockwood, "Peru," 25–26.

44. For more on Club Waikiki and Peruvian surf culture, see Laderman, *Empire in Waves*, 46–47. On the cultural impact of surfing in Peru, see Zavalza Hough-Snee, "You Have the Right to Surf," and Wood, "On the Crest of a Wave" and "Representing Peru." I am grateful to Dexter Zavalza Hough-Snee for bringing Wood's articles to my attention.

45. Lockwood, "Peru," 25–26.

46. Laderman, *Empire in Waves*, 61–90.

47. Paskowitz, "Israel: Surfing in the Land of King David," 122–124, 126. Paskowitz is the son of Dorian Paskowitz, who introduced surfing to Israel in 1956 and later co-founded Surfing for Peace; see Laderman, *Empire in Waves*, 160–162.

3 / *Kai Ea*: Rising Waves of National and Ethnic Hawaiian Identities

ISAIAH HELEKUNIHI WALKER

Native Hawaiian activists are working to reestablish an autonomous Hawaiian government today. Although Hawaiians have differing views of political sovereignty, there are essentially two prevailing agendas. The first is to achieve federal recognition as a Native people under the US government in order to establish a path toward self-determination and Hawaiian governance, and possibly enter into a government-to-government relationship with the United States, similar to American Indians.[1] The other approach seeks international recognition of Hawai'i's unrelinquished sovereignty and the deoccupation of Hawai'i by the United States military.[2] While Hawaiian activists are seeking recognition and autonomy today, Hawaiian surfers have already earned political independence in the waves and are universally recognized as an independent nation distinct from the United States.

In competitive and social settings, Hawaiian surfers, teams, and organizations are identified as Hawaiian rather than American. For example, in November 2015, the World Surf League Women's Championship Tour narrowed to a title race between two top competitors. The rivalry between Hawaiian surfer Carissa Moore and American Courtney Conlogue culminated in the final event of the competition year held in clean, double-overhead waves at Honolua Bay, Maui. After a day of flawless right-handed barrels, the Hawaiian prevailed over the number 2–seeded American, winning the contest in dominant fashion. In fact, the Hawaiians prevailed over almost everyone at Honolua, with three Hawaiians arriving to the semifinals before Moore cemented her third professional world title. Jubilantly hoisting the Hawaiian national flag overhead while being carried to the winners' stage, Moore clearly expressed a sentiment held in common among all surfers: she was a *Hawaiian* world champion.

Hawaiian surfers represent Hawai'i, not the United States, in virtually every contest and on every competitive level in the surfing world. While competitive surfing leagues such as the World Surf League (WSL), the International Surfing Association (ISA), and the National Scholastic Surfing Association (NSSA) define Hawai'i as an independent region, Hawaiian surfers nonetheless view this as a national distinction. If nationalism is a social construct imagined by members of that particular community, as Benedict Anderson contends, then Hawaiian surfing nationhood is also authentic.[3] As if transported into an alternate dimension where nineteenth-century Hawaiian society leaped onto a different historical timeline years ago, Hawai'i surfers represent the *lāhui* (people and nation of Hawai'i) on a world stage. This allows Hawaiian surfers to develop unique and empowering identities, in contrast to other Hawaiians who have struggled to value themselves and their culture in the face of longstanding cultural, political, and economic struggle evolving from a 150-year history of colonization. "I love being identified as a Hawaiian surfer rather than an American surfer," Carissa Moore confesses, "Hawai'i is a part of America but I consider us separate." She continues, "We really are strong, independent thinkers and passionate, loving human beings. . . . We are special. There is no place like Hawai'i and I am happy the surfing tour recognizes that."[4]

However, Native Hawaiian professional surfers carry additional *kuleana* (responsibility) in comparison to other surfers—including other non-ethnically Hawaiian surfers from Hawai'i. Since Native Hawaiians often link *he'e nalu* (surfing) to their *mo'okū'auhau* (genealogy) from their *kupuna* (ancestors and elders), their identities are imbued with additional significance and *kuleana*. For most Hawaiian surfers, this *kuleana* means preserving he'e nalu as a Native practice and maintaining Hawaiian reign in the surf. It can also mean inspiring youth, toppling negative stereotypes, and even winning surfing competitions. Ultimately, it is about representing the lāhui (people/nation of Hawai'i) with he'e nalu. Although some have erroneously suggested that Hawaiian surfing slipped into near-extinction at the turn of the twentieth century, surfing has perpetually been an avenue for sustaining and disseminating a thriving Hawaiian culture.[5] Thus, maintaining Hawaiian prominence in the surf is central to a proxy battle for preserving Hawaiian nationalism, political autonomy, and cultural existence. Since the surf occupies this alternate realm of independence for Hawaiians, a position lost on land to colonialism, preserving that space is an essential *kuleana* for Hawaiian surfers. This helps explain why to Kanaka Maoli (native Hawaiians), surfing is still, very much so, Hawaiian.[6]

In this chapter, I will recount the expressions and experiences of particular surfers (and surf teams) to explore the cultural and national identities of Kanaka Maoli surfers in the context of larger discussions of Hawaiian sovereignty. This includes (1) Hawaiian professional surfers Carissa Moore, Ezekiel Lau, Keanu Asing, Makuakai Rothman, and Ulu-boy Napeahi; (2) the all-Hawaiian, two-time NSSA High School National Champions, the Kamehameha Schools Surf Team; and (3) Hawai'i's 2012 and 2014 multiethnic ISA World Junior Team and their Gold Medal victories for the "nation of Hawai'i."

Strides for Hawaiian Political Autonomy

Over the last two decades, activists and legislators have written and revised several bills (like the Akaka Bill) supporting US federal recognition for Native Hawaiians, whereby the United States would officially recognize indigenous Hawaiians as Native peoples.[7] With this recognition, they hope to preserve Native entitlements and start a process whereby Hawaiians can form a Native government similar to other tribal governments in the United States through elected Hawaiian delegates and constitutional conventions. Federal recognition is supported by many influential Hawaiians and non-Hawaiians, including Hawai'i State elected officials, the Office of Hawaiian Affairs, and even President Barack Obama, although many Hawaiians oppose it. Although federal recognition bills have yet to pass, organizations like Na'i Aupuni have already begun a process whereby delegates are mapping out a contemporary Native Hawaiian government.[8]

In contrast to such movements favoring US federal recognition of Native Hawaiians, the deoccupation agenda inspired by political scientist Keanu Sai draws from World Court arbitration and the support of the international community to begin a process of deoccupation.[9] Drawing from nineteenth-century treaties signed between the Hawaiian Kingdom and various world powers, Sai contends that the US annexation of Hawai'i was null and void because (1) the Hawaiian kingdom was internationally recognized as an independent and neutral state in the late 1800s, and (2) the US domestic joint resolution bill (Newlands Act) used to claim control over Hawai'i in 1898 (during the Spanish American War) was not a legal treaty of annexation.[10] The absence of an actual treaty between the United States and the Hawaiian Kingdom, Sai contends, means that Hawaiian sovereignty never ceased and the Kingdom was technically occupied as a temporary wartime possession.[11] In his PhD dissertation, Sai outlines a process whereby the Hawaiian kingdom government is deoccupied by the US military.[12] This deoccupation model has gained considerable momentum over the last decade. And while both movements continue to advance toward greater political autonomy for Native Hawaiians, surfing continues to afford Hawaiians a unique autonomous position both locally and internationally.

Historical Surfing Independence

Why does the surfing world recognize Hawai'i, the fiftieth state in the Union, as an independent entity from the United States? Randy Rarick, the former director and founder of both the Triple Crown and International Professional Surfers (the association that preceded the WSL and ASP), provides historical context: "Traditionally, prior to statehood ('59), Hawaii was considered a separate entity in the old Makaha Championship [1954–1971] and Peru International [1956–1974]—and even the US Championships in Huntington Beach [1964–1972]. For purposes of distinguishing those surfers who were from the US mainland (both east and west coast), they were designated USA and those from the islands were obviously designated Hawaii. . . . tradition has carried over even into the pro ranks and is accepted practice worldwide."[13] Though informative, this explanation does not consider the social factors that led to the creation and maintenance of this tradition. As I theorize in *Waves of Resistance* and elsewhere, the surf zone remained an autonomous Hawaiian realm throughout the nineteenth and twentieth centuries because Hawaiian surfers adamantly preserved it as a native social space.[14] While colonial hierarchies were absent in this borderland (or boarder-land) and resistant native identities thrived, the *po'ina nalu* (Hawaiian surf zone) was a place that colonial powers were less able to conquer.[15] As Hawaiian surfers maintained control over the po'ina nalu in the early twentieth century, shortly after annexation to the United States, they were recognized as governing chiefs in the surf. This was most notably the case in Waikīkī at the turn of the century, where famous surfers like Duke Kahanamoku, Prince Jonah Kuhio, and others contended against a segregated "whites only" Outrigger surf club in the early 1900s.[16] Made up of the same elites who imprisoned Hawai'i's Queen Liliuokalani a few years earlier, these Outrigger elites were thwarted by strong, resistant Hawaiian surfers. Likewise, in decades to follow, Hawaiians asserted themselves often, preserving a distinct Hawaiian space. Hence the surf zone, and the surfers who reigned therein, remained distinctly Hawaiian to the outside world.[17]

Since surfing, or he'e nalu, was a Hawaiian practice that survived an era of cultural decline lasting throughout much of the twentieth century, Hawaiians have been very protective of wave-riding. While Kanaka Maoli are aware and proud that the origins of surfing are inextricably Hawaiian, Kanaka Maoli surfers of various generations have had to repeatedly preserve their autonomy in the contemporary waves. Examples include Eddie Aikau and Ben Aipa, who fought for Hawaiian seats in the predominantly *haole* (white, foreigner) professional surfing competitions of the 1960s (most notably the Duke Invitational of 1965); the Save Our Surf organization, which, since the 1960s, slowed development and demanded access to Hawaiian waves for Kanaka Maoli and local people; and the 1976-formed Hui 'O He'e Nalu club that organized to preserve he'e nalu for Hawaiian families against the encroachment of corporate and competitive surf industries on the North Shore.[18] While resistance in the po'ina nalu sometimes translates into Hawaiian control over surfing lineups, various community groups have also worked to preserve Hawaiian access to surfing spots and competitions, and have led service projects to care for or preserve the sea and the land (*E mālama i ke kai* and *E mālama i ka 'aina*); notable among them are Duane Desoto's Na Kamakai and Keith Nehls Skibbs's Basic Image Inc.[19] And like the conservation of historically Hawaiian spaces and cultural traditions, preserving Hawaiian voices in historical surfing narratives and contemporary surfing culture has also been a recurring battle.

Despite clear evidence that proves otherwise, many surf historians have undermined early twentieth-century Hawaiian surfers as less influential and nearly extinct.[20] Perhaps initiated with Alexander Hume Ford's writings or Ben Finney's popular 1966 book *Surfing*, the notion that he'e nalu went extinct until resurrected by Ford has contaminated surf history narratives for decades.[21] In *Waves of Resistance* I tackle this myth by reiterating the continued contributions of Hawaiian surfers throughout this period of colonization.[22] While scholars are more conscientious of this fact today, many still reinforce the misconception (intentionally or not) that once surfing was transplanted onto the mainland United States, Hawaiian surfing became inconsequential, and in some cases invisible.[23] While searching for the origins of modern surfing, Scott Laderman recognized in *Empire and Waves* that Native Hawaiians revived surfing at the turn of the twentieth century. However, he then concluded that since Ford promoted the sport in an American capitalistic manner, he was the founder of modern surfing and its industry. Although Laderman is critical of Ford's racist and imperialist character, he nonetheless overlooks the contribution of Native Hawaiians in surfing's modern history—including the establishment of one of surfing's first businesses, the lucrative, Hawaiian-run Waikīkī Beachboy concessions.[24]

Marketing and tourism entities have also worked to claim Hawaiian surfing for their benefit. For example, while Hawaiians have looked to Duke Kahanamoku as a native icon, the tourism industry has also used him as a marketing tool. For example, although they initially excluded Hawaiians from their whites-only club and supported the annexation of the Hawaiian Kingdom at turn of the twentieth century, the Outrigger has more recently claimed contested ownership to Duke Kahanamoku's name for branding purposes—for Duke's restaurant chain, in particular.[25] Many Hawaiians resent such entities for appropriating Duke's iconic Hawaiian persona to benefit corporate agendas in Waikīkī and elsewhere. More recently, the Hawaiian surf club, the Hui 'O He'e Nalu, has made a move to reclaim Duke, so to speak, for Native Hawaiian surfers today. In 2015 and 2016, Da Hui Backdoor Shootout, an event and organization run by Native Hawaiians to benefit the local and Hawaiian community, dedicated their professional Pipeline event to the memory of Duke Kahanamoku. As competitors voiced their gratitude for Kahanamoku and commentators emphasized Duke's historical contribution to the Hawaiian surfing community over live Internet feed, Duke's memory was recontextualized. While the tourist industry insists that Duke is exclusive to and synonymous with Waikīkī tourism, Da Hui Backdoor Shootout reminded viewers that Duke has relevance to Hawaiians on the North Shore and beyond. Recently crowned WSL Big Wave World Tour Champion Makuakai Rothman conveyed at the Shootout, "Duke Kahanamoku is my inspiration. . . . He's my hero, one of the greatest Hawaiians to ever live. . . . Thank you very much to Duke for paving the way."[26] Bruce Irons explained, "When I think of Duke, I think . . . it's about time we brought his name back into surfing . . . here at the Shootout."[27] Professional surfer Mason Ho recalled, "He is definitely one of my heroes."[28] Freeing the memory of Duke from the confines of Waikīkī at Da Hui's Backdoor Shootout enabled Hawaiian surfers to publicly reclaim Duke.[29]

Being Hawaiian is most commonly defined as an ethnic or racial classification based on biological and genealogical connections to Native Hawaiian kupuna (ancestors) and ʻaina (land). Although not all Native Hawaiians agree with the practice, non–Native Hawaiʻi surfers are also identified as Hawaiian in surfing competitions and surf media. However, most Hawaiʻi locals clearly understand that Hawaiian means Kanaka Maoli (Native people), as opposed to just any-one living in the state, like a Californian. Calling non-Native surfers Hawaiian remains highly problematic in contemporary Hawaiʻi. Perhaps most Hawai-ians are reluctant to expand "Hawaiian" to include non-natives because they do not yet enjoy the security of political autonomy on land. In *Hawaiian Blood: Colonialism and the Politics of Sovereignty and Identity*, J. Kehaulani Kauanui defines "Hawaiian" as a racial category, but theorizes that Hawaiian obsession with blood quantum is the product of US imperialism. "Many Hawaiians and non-Hawaiians" she argues, "have become invested in blood quantum as proof of indigeneity and rely on the fractionalizing measurements of one's ʻblood amount' as a marker for cultural orientation and identity, even though the racial categories this logic depends on are the product of relatively recent colo-nial taxonomies."[30] Moving beyond blood quantum, under Keanu Sai's deoc-cupation model, non–Native Hawaiian citizens who lived under the Hawaiian kingdom government (of the past and the possible future) would be consid-ered Hawaiian nationals. Perhaps Hawaiian surfers will eventually expand their definitions of "Hawaiian" to include non-Hawaiians, thereby emphasizing national citizenship as Sai does. However, these expanded definitions, even for Sai, are contingent upon a restoration of Native Hawaiian political autonomy on land, and any shifting of definitions of Hawaiian identity assumes the pos-sibility of a sovereign Hawaiʻi as nation (independent) or nation within nation (under the United States).

Within these larger debates, highly accomplished Hawaiian professional surfer Ezekiel Lau considers Hawaiian identity inextricably linked to heritage and ancestry. Speaking about non–Native Hawaiian surfers labeled as Hawai-ians, Lau explained, "I think it's cool that we recognize Hawaiʻi surfers as rep-resenting Hawaiʻi, but it's kind of weird to me when non–Native Hawaiians are called Hawaiians. Not that I don't like it, it's just weird to me."[31] He further explained that although he has many non-native surfing friends in Hawaiʻi, being Hawaiian still means being a native. For example, he continued, "I really looked up to Andy Irons as a great surfer from Hawaiʻi. However if you would ask me who was the last [men's] Hawaiian world champion, I would say, Sunny

Garcia. . . . It's hard, because you don't want to disrespect, but . . . I want to make it known, for sure, that there is a difference with having that bloodline."[32] With this observation, Lau highlights a fundamental distinction long observed in the islands: being Hawaiian versus being *from* Hawai'i.

As a Native Hawaiian on the elite WSL men's Championship Tour (CT), Keanu Asing articulates that qualifying for the CT constituted his proudest moment as a Native Hawaiian surfer. He states, "Being a real Hawaiian is something I couldn't be more proud of. There are only a few of us that are Native Hawaiians in the surfing world . . . that is something we can treasure."[33] He continued, "Surfing to me is the essence of Hawai'i . . . Hawaiians are the true inventors of surfing and were the ones who introduced it to the world."[34] As with Lau and Moore, Asing aligns his ethnic identity with being Hawaiian *and* a surfer. Such identification not only bolsters his sense of self, but also qualifies his identity through a distinctive cultural heritage and history: he'e nalu, or surfing. This is a common sentiment among Hawaiian surfers.

Hailing from *Moku o Keawe* (Big Island), young Hawaiian professional surfer Jimmy Ulualoha "Ulu-boy" Napeahi expresses a similar sentiment about what it means to be Hawaiian. "Surfing is my connection to who I truly am as a Kanaka Maoli. It is a part of my life. It is in my blood." He continues, "I believe that it is greatly important for the Native people of Hawai'i to be recognized as their own out there in the water. However," he clarifies, "there are a lot of foreigners that claim Hawai'i as their home, marking themselves as Hawaiian surfers. A lot of people don't know what it is to be a Hawaiian, and many don't carry themselves as our ancestors would. Nonetheless, I am so happy that surfing is the one thing that we have that no one can take away."[35] Napeahi also recognizes that Hawaiian autonomy, while yet to be fully realized on land and in politics, is still alive in the waves today: "We cannot today claim the land as ours, although I still believe that Hawaiians still rightfully have claim to the land. But, Hawaiians definitely have their right to the ocean today. In the ocean, especially on the North Shore, every one recognizes that the Hawaiians have claim still. The ocean will forever be a place where Hawaiians will be a minority, but people still respect us."[36]

The rising disparity between Native Hawaiians and a burgeoning group of wealthy transplants and land speculators is rapidly increasing. Such disparity increases social and cultural divisions along class lines, even in the surf. As escalating real estate prices and short-term leases targeting vacationing tourists continue to push Hawaiians off their land (or into homelessness), limited access to beaches along expensive and exclusive coastlines threatens Hawaiian presence in the surf. "Where's all the local people?" asks Eddie Rothman, "They are nowhere on the North Shore . . . there are only, maybe, one, two, or three local families, because rich people keep coming and buying."[37] During our interview, Lau lamented that there seems to be fewer Hawaiian surfers in the professional ranks today, and reasoned that economic privilege and opportunity has much to do with it.[38]

Growing up in a small apartment in a Kamehameha Schools Kapālama dormitory where his family lives as dorm advisors, Lau noticed that Hawaiian surfers have fewer opportunities because they are "just trying to survive and fit in to society, to do well in school and sports."[39] Lau explained that he was raised in an athletic family, where sport was seen as a ticket to college or other successes in life. While his father excelled in football, and his sisters in soccer, Lau was required to play a variety of sports in his youth (like soccer, baseball, and basketball) well into high school. Once his career path in surfing seemed secure, he could focus exclusively on that sport. Although his parents did as much as possible to support his surfing, he was still at a disadvantage. For example, while he attended eight hours of school daily, most of Lau's fellow sponsored surfing competitors did not attend school at all, but instead spent most of their time surfing while undergoing home-schooling programs of questionable rigor. While his peers had the luxury of traveling during the school year and surfing every day, Lau struggled to scrounge rides to the beach after a long day of school. Having less time and opportunity to venture to the North Shore on weekdays, Lau was often relegated to surf the less-impressive nearby breaks of Oʻahu's south shore. Money was also an issue—"it's an expensive sport," he confessed—and many of his non-Hawaiian peers had ample financial support from their families to pay for travel, competition fees, equipment, and so forth. Fortunately, Lau reported, "my sponsors eventually provided me with that support."[40]

Native Hawaiian Identities

After an accomplished junior career (4 NSSA national championships) and a strong showing on the WSL Qualifying Series, Lau qualified for the WSL's elite 2017 Men's Championship Tour and is anxious to represent Hawaiʻi on the CT. For Lau, being Native Hawaiian is essential to his identity as a professional surfer. He says that being Hawaiian "means everything to me, I am wearing that out there on my sleeve."[41] Because he touts traditional and contemporary Hawaiian tattoos on his arms and torso, this statement is actually quite literal. Among those tattoos is an iconic sketch of Duke Kahanamoku and another of the helmeted warrior Kamehameha. Kamehameha—who was a powerful

Hawaiian surfer—conquered all the Hawaiian islands in the early nineteenth century and established the Kingdom of Hawai'i. Kahanamoku is an early twentieth-century surfing icon and a great source of inspiration for Lau, who states that "Duke is the reason I surf today, everything he has done, he has given the path for me today."[42] Lau takes great pride in his ancient surfing forefathers, but also in the fact that his own grandfather was a regular surfer at Kewalos, Lau's home break. Lau expounded, "It's in my blood, my roots. It is what I was born to do."[43] Lau links his ethnic identity to his genealogical ancestry, and is motivated in his professional career by such identifications. Of all the surfers interviewed for this project, Lau most conspicuously draws from his Native Hawaiian heritage as a motivation for his surfing success. While native surfers like Lau strive to represent their culture through their competitive accolades, it is important to clarify that competitive results do not sustain or destroy Hawaiian autonomy in the waves. Instead, competitive leagues and organizations merely reflect a historical and social reality: that Hawaiians have maintained the surf zone as a sovereign Hawaiian space. However, as seen with Lau, competitive Hawaiian surfers increase native pride through competitive success.

I kū mau mau
I kū wa
I kū mau mau
I kū huluhulu
I kū lanawao
I kū wa
I kū lanawao
I kū wa
I kū wa huki
I kū wa ko
I kū wa a mau
A mau ka eulu
E huki e
Kūlia

Stand up together!
Stand and shout!
Stand together!
Haul with all your might!
Under the mighty trees!
Stand at intervals!
Stand up among the tall forest!

Stand at intervals!
Stand at intervals and pull!
Stand at intervals and haul!
Stand in place and haul!
Haul branches and all!
Haul now!

Encouraged by the chanting, Kamehameha Surf Team member Chasen Kim explained, "People were staring and didn't know how to react. At that point I was really proud to be Hawaiian."[44] One reporter noted the swinging momentum in the final heats after the ʻoli was performed. "[After chanting] a chant designed to inspire ancient Hawaiians when hauling heavy koa trees [to build canoes], Imaikalani DeVault started ripping into the rights. The 16-year old, regular foot snagged the biggest set waves of the final and came from behind to decisively beat San Clemente High School's Kei Kobayashi 15.06 to 10.5."[45] Winner of the women's division, Cayla Moore expressed, "It feels awesome knowing that surfing came from Hawaiʻi and we are bringing the [NSSA National High School Team Championship title] back to Hawaiʻi, making everyone at home proud because a Hawaiian surf team has never won the title before."[46]

Paradoxically, the Kamehameha High School Surf Team won the US National title as Hawaiian nationals. While other schools may have displayed their particular high school banners and flags at the competition, the Hawaiians were the only ones waving national colors. This is a fortunate contradiction. Although the NSSA recognizes Hawaiʻi as its own region, the NSSA still invited Kamehameha to participate against the American teams in their annual national championships. This arrangement is ideal for Hawaiian surfers, as they are granted a kind of dual citizenship in the NSSA events. The Kamehameha Schools' NSSA national victory provided a stage for a historical reenactment where a proxy battle bequeathed a metaphoric counterconquest where Hawaiians prevailed over America.[47] Perhaps that is why emotions ran so high for these Hawaiian surfers at the nationals in California. While other schools probably saw it as just another surfing competition, the Hawaiians were jubilant—but respectful—in their victory precisely because of the internalization of Hawaiian identity in local and international contexts and an understanding of the political significance of representing Hawaiʻi not as state, but as lāhui (a people, a nation).

The Kamehameha Surf Team returned pride to the Hawaiian community with this championship title. Upon the team's return home, they appeared on every major Hawaiʻi television station, where surfers expressed their pride in being Hawaiian. Team member Uapili Lucy uttered, "It felt amazing. The uni-fication we have separates us from everyone. We have all our flags, we just wave it up, we are proud to be Hawaiian."[48] Although you would expect the conversation to be centered on the technical side of their surfing or the narrative of their victory, almost all the youth instead expressed their pleasure in representing their Hawaiian culture as surfers. Charlie Akao reiterated, "I think that we should all be really proud because we are all Hawaiians and Hawaiians created this sport. So it's even more of an accomplishment, showing that we can bring it back home."[49] He continued, taking up Lau's thoughts on education and competitive surfing: "We go to school every day, some kids are home-schooled so they surf all day, but we don't do that."[50] Strengthening and consolidating this Hawaiian cultural pride, the Kamehameha team returned and defended their title in 2015. Through their success in the NSSA, these Hawaiian students simultaneously expressed a strong sense of national and ethnic pride in being Hawaiian, an opportunity unique to native youth surfers today.

Like her younger sister on the Kamehameha team, three-time WSL women's champion Carissa Moore has linked her success in competitive surfing with her identity as a Native Hawaiian. She says, "One of the proudest moments I have felt for being a Native Hawaiian surfer was when I won my first world title in France and I got to raise the Hawaiian flag above my head." Moore explains that this sentiment is fundamentally about shared Hawaiian identity and collective pride felt by Hawaiian surfers, even when competing against one another overseas: "My fellow Hawaiians Megan Godinez, Geodee Clark, Melanie Bartels, Coco Ho and Kelia Moniz were there as well and had brought me a flag all the way from home. It meant so much to share that excitement with them."[51]

Moore's identity is not contingent upon her success in competition, but grounded in her roots as a Hawaiian and the common connection of Hawaiian ancestry that she shares with her fellow competitors from the Islands. As with every surfer interviewed for this chapter, Carissa sees herself as an ambassador for her culture and kupuna (ancestors): "Surfing originated with my Native Hawaiian ancestors and I feel blessed to be able to carry on this tradition." She continues, "I think my relationship with surfing is different because I am a Native Hawaiian. I surf because I love it. I don't do it for the money, for the fame or accolades. That stuff is great, but I do it because it fills up my soul and that is why my ancestors did it. I feel most at home and at peace with myself in the ocean. I don't think, I just let it flow from my na'au [gut, heart] I feel especially connected to the ocean when I am at home in Hawai'i. Surfing at Honolua Bay the past two years was a comfort, knowing in my heart that the ocean would provide for me."[52]

Like the elder Moore, Ulu-boy Napeahi's Hawaiian cultural identity is also intertwined with his love for surfing. "Hawaiians introduced surfing to this world, and I feel that it has given many great opportunities. Being a minority, I am proud of who I am. Surfing allows me to express my *aloha* by sharing my spirit with everyone that I meet. That is how I carry on my culture and the goodness that has been instilled in me."[53] Born and raised in the rural Big Island villages of Keaukaha and Kalapana, each comprising a high concentration of Native Hawaiians, Ulu-boy had a more traditional Hawaiian upbringing than most of his Hawaiian surfing peers. Attending Ka'umeke Kaeo, a Hawaiian language immersion school in his youth, Napeahi learned Hawaiian language, culture, and history in a unique Hawaiian enclave. Furthermore, while in Kalapana, he survived off the land and off the grid, living with his family in a humble home, on beautiful 'aina (land) without the amenities of municipal or county water or electricity.[54] His expressions reflect a Hawaiian perspective imbued with these experiences: "Every single time I walk down the beach, no matter where I am, I look up to the mountains, and I look at the water that touches my feet. Emotionally, spiritually, and physically I am connected. My spirit, my presence . . . through surfing, I am able to share my spirit of *aloha* worldwide. That makes me proud!"[55]

Makuakai Rothman likewise draws cultural and spiritual strength from being in the ocean as a Hawaiian. "The ocean is my place of worship, it's my church . . . Hawai'i is the birthplace of surfing . . . my ancestors created this sport."[56] Growing up on the North Shore, Makua has found success in charging big waves from a young age, and his prowess in large surf helped him win the WSL's inaugural Big Wave World Tour. Like Carissa, Rothman attributes his competitive successes to cultural roots and a pride in representing the nation of Hawai'i. In comparison to other surfers interviewed for this chapter, Rothman most clearly articulates a connection between his identity and Hawaiian nationalism. He states, "A lot of my drive comes from my culture, from being proud of who I am and where I am from. I am proud to be Hawaiian. . . . You know, what really fuels my fire is to be a champion for a nation. . . . When I win, I win for Hawai'i. When I surf, I surf for Hawai'i."[57]

Although each professional surfer interviewed for this chapter found pride and motivation from their Hawaiian heritage, such identification adds weighted *kuleana* (responsibility) for these athletes.[58] In addition to surfing for one's family, self, and sponsors, Hawaiian surfers often symbolically carry the Hawaiian culture and *lāhui* (people/nation) on their shoulders as cultural representatives. This is precisely the phenomenon that Eddie Aikau committed his life to in 1978 when he joined the crew of the traditional double-hulled

Hawaiian voyaging canoe *Hōkūleʻa*. Constructed in the midst of a Hawaiian cultural revival movement, the creation of a traditional Polynesian vessel to traverse the Pacific inspired Hawaiians like Eddie Aikau. *Hōkūleʻa* embodied and symbolized the survival of a Hawaiian culture in peril and the emergence of a still-nascent cultural renaissance. An artifact that spurred restoration through the preservation of ancient Polynesian navigating technologies and techniques, *Hōkūleʻa* was envisioned as the vehicle for carrying the Hawaiian renaissance into the future, and Eddie saw himself as a steersman for that voyage. When *Hōkūleʻa* capsized miles offshore in rough seas during its 1978 voyage from Hawaiʻi to Tahiti, Aikau further embraced this weighted *kuleana*, risking and eventually giving his life to save his vulnerable crew by paddling his surfboard to find help.[59] Although his *kuleana* cost him his life, Eddie's spirit soars with *Hōkūleʻa* and in Hawaiian waves today as his sacrifice fueled the progression and continuation of Hawaiian cultural revitalization movements and traditional voyaging, in particular. As ambassadors of heʻe nalu, most Hawaiian professional surfers carry a similar kind of stewardship, which is to uplift the lāhui through surfing. However, each surfer interviewed for this chapter uniquely defines and balances their own sense of *kuleana*.

Carissa Moore defines her *kuleana* as a responsibility to inspire and uplift the next generation of Native Hawaiians to excel in life by overcoming negative stigmas and stereotypes. Through her example and influence, Moore hopes to uplift a suppressed and often misunderstood people who are inextricably tied to the sport of surfing and the cultural politics of Hawaiian colonization. "The Native Hawaiians have been suppressed for so long I think many have given up on their dreams to venture out and make a name for themselves. For me getting to travel the world and represent our small island in the Pacific makes me so proud. What makes me feel even prouder inside is the thought of possibly giving a breath of fresh air to our dying culture and a little bit of hope to our people."[60] However, *kuleana*, to her, also means to educate and correct misconceived and negative perceptions of Hawaiians: "They were a forward-thinking culture, traveling outside of the islands to explore new waters. Their way of life was so efficient that they found time to relax and enjoy recreational activities such as surfing. If the Native Hawaiians weren't suppressed, I believe they could thrive in the world today more so than they are now. We are just as capable as anyone else and can do anything we set our hearts and minds to. We are good enough. . . . I want to break that negative stereotype that Native Hawaiians are lazy and uneducated and represent what we really are."[61]

Since surfing is a Hawaiian sport, some believe that Kanaka Maoli should be among the top surfers in the professional ranks in order to keep heʻe nalu relevant on a global competitive stage. Native Hawaiian presence in contemporary competition does reflect the continuity of heʻe nalu, and by extension Hawaiian culture, as an intact and relevant practice, connecting the practice from ancient times until today. Although competitive success (or failure) does not alter the reality of this historical continuity, it is a powerful tool for marketing this notion. Thus, for Lau, Asing, and others, representing Hawaiʻi in competitive surfing is a part of their *kuleana*. Perhaps because of his physical appearance (Lau has a notable Polynesian build and appearance), his family's socioeconomic status, his educational training at the Kamehameha Schools, or his family's athletic background, Lau outwardly shoulders this particular *kuleana*. Through his frank declaration that, "as Hawaiians, we are supposed to be the best at surfing," Lau's expectation on himself to win, as a Hawaiian, is palpable.[62] Currently, Lau's main focus is to excel on the WSL men's CT where he can showcase his Hawaiian power surfing on the elite level. While Asing was the only Native Hawaiian surfer of the thirty-four surfers on the men's CT in 2015 and 2016, he defines his *kuleana* as representing the lāhui on the main stage. Asing admits that this *kuleana* adds pressure, but also motivation. Such *kuleana*, he explains, "absolutely gives me motivation to push and push myself to be better. When I come home and I'm at the beach and people are telling me they're proud and cheering for me that makes me feel . . . like I want to do it for Hawaiʻi."[63] In addition to representing Hawaiʻi and Hawaiians at home, Asing also feels responsible for representing his culture honorably abroad, stating that "I feel it is my job . . . to spread that Aloha Ambassador spirit to the world stage of surfing today."[64] Although the weight of this *kuleana* (to succeed in competition) can generate extra pressure, most surfers interviewed for this chapter revel in the challenge.

Speaking of this additional pressure, Ezekiel Lau explained, "Sometimes it does play on your mind. But I like it. I like that pressure."[65] Since he feels that Hawaiians should be the "best at surfing," Lau confesses that losing causes the most stress for him.[66] Although he does not admit it, the pressure to succeed by way of representing a cultural birthright is wearing. But Lau explains that he hates losing because it is often difficult to remain humble and gracious in defeat. Since he does not want to shame his culture or family, or give surfing media an excuse to highlight another Hawaiian warrior as an angry savage, he restrains his frustrations in public view. He expresses that the surfing media uses a double standard when representing Hawaiian and non-Hawaiian surfers in competition. For example, he explains that when haole surfers lose and throw a fit after a heat, people think it's funny, as seen with Kolohe Andino, and other WSL professionals, who are regularly observed punching their surfboards and flipping off judges after a heat.[67] But when Hawaiians get upset over a bad heat or controversial score, the media emphatically depicts Hawaiians as angry and volatile, a phenomenon that is especially visible in representations of 2000 World Champion Sunny Garcia.[68] Perhaps it is because the surfing media often compares Lau to Garcia that Lau makes a conscious effort to curtail his emotions in public view. Although different from W. E. B. Du Bois's notion of double consciousness, and Fanon's dual consciousness, in this regard Hawaiian surfers still find themselves juggling dual objectives within their surfing identities.[69] They simultaneously surf for themselves and their reimagined nation. However, in Lau's case here, the notion of double consciousness is applicable as media gazing "only lets him see himself through the revelation of the other world."[70] Lau consciously sees himself through the eyes of onlookers in this scenario and uses this mechanism to cultivate a positive image of his Hawaiian identity, long misrepresented in surfing media.[71]

Hawaiian Nationalism at the ISA World Junior Championships

In 2012 and 2014, the Verizon-sponsored Team Hawai'i won multiple gold medals at the ISA World Junior Championships in Panama and Ecuador, including the overall national team division medal. Winning gold over a host of national teams (including the United States) while wearing the same red and yellow colors of the ancient Hawaiian *ali'i* (chiefs, nobility), Team Hawai'i was clearly representing a distinct nation. Although their surfing was remarkable, the award ceremony held after the competition was particularly memorable. As the 2014 ISA World Junior Team Hawai'i stood on the podium to receive their gold medals, they waited for their national anthem to play. Although, theoretically, one could argue that Hawai'i does not have a national anthem anymore, the Hawaiian Kingdom's national anthem came over the loudspeaker, *Hawai'i Pono'ī*, written by Hawai'i's "Merry Monarch" King David Kalākaua. Composed in 1876, *Hawai'i Pono'ī* is a *mele* (song) of pride and respect for the Hawaiian kingdom. It is also an ode to the *mo'ī* (king), ali'i, and lāhui. It is very nationalistic, and very Hawaiian. The ISA surprisingly knew this song, and played it for the Hawaiian gold medalists.

> Hawai'i pono'ī,
> Nānā i kou mo'ī,
> Ka lani ali'i
> ke ali'i

Chorus:
Makua lani ē
Kamehameha ē
Na kāua e pale
Me ka ihe
Hawai'i pono'ī,
Nānā i nā ali'i
Na pua muli kou
Nā pōki'i
Hawai'i pono'ī,
E ka Lāhui e,
'O kau hana nui,
E u'i e

Hawai'i's own,
look to your king,
the royal ruler,
the chief.
(Chorus)
Royal father of the nation,
Kamehameha,
We shall defend
with spears.
Daughters and sons of Hawai'i,
look to your chiefs,
the children after you,
the young.
Those true to Hawai'i,
O Nation, the Hawaiian people,
your great duty

A contributing member of that winning team, Napeahi, recalls that moment on the podium when they played *Hawai'i Pono'ī* with great pride. "I remember that day, specifically. Out of the whole team, I was the one person that it really hit hard. I was in tears. I had chicken skin. That was one of those moments I was so proud, I took it all in."[72] For Napeahi, the significance of that victory and awards ceremony meant more than simply winning an event. He reveled in the larger picture, a Hawaiian picture, where the nation of Hawai'i won a gold medal, in its own sport, over the United States, Australia, and other world powers. Napeahi continued, "When I hear the Hawaiian words, I can tell you what they are saying. *Hawai'i Pono'ī* is a powerful song. The words are very straightforward. It is Hawai'i's song. It was a proud moment."[73]

Although Napeahi viewed this noble moment as powerfully Hawaiian, not everyone on the team saw the surfing victory as an accomplishment of the same magnitude. He explained, "Everyone was happy, but looking into their [my teammates'] eyes, I think they were just proud to win the contest, they didn't look at the big picture." In fact, he continued, "There were some kids that didn't know the song, it was weird."[74] Unlike the Kamehameha Surf Team, the Hawai'i ISA Junior Team was comprised of both Native and non–Native Hawaiian surfers. In his comments, Napeahi notes that the transplanted Hawai'i surfers (non–local born and non-native surfers) on the team did not grasp the larger picture of Hawaiian nationalism. Perhaps because of this difference, Napeahi did not always feel integral to the Hawai'i team.[75] Napeahi's critique of some of his teammates' inability to grasp the significance of Hawaiian ethnic and national pride highlights another important contrast between Native and non–Native Hawai'i surfers. While Native surfers carry a distinct and nuanced identity that is interwoven with cultural and nationalistic undertones, non-native surfers from Hawai'i do not identify with surfing in the same way; nor do they carry the additionally weighted *kuleana* of representing kupuna (ancestors) or uplifting the lāhui (Hawaiian people). Although some non–Native Hawai'i surfers do sympathize with and support these agendas, it is ultimately optional. All the surfers interviewed for this chapter, although they were gracious and respectful in saying it, recognized the difference between Native and non-native surfer identities and *kuleana*. For Kanaka Maoli surfers, the recognition of Hawaiian autonomy in the surf has historic significance, shapes and empowers their identities in the present, and comes with a weighted *kuleana* to the *lāhui*.

Conclusion

While generations of Hawaiian legislators, activists, and scholars have sought recognition of Hawaiian autonomy on land, the surfing world has always recognized the independence of Hawaiians. Although the politics of autonomy are complex, surfers have bolstered Hawaiian national pride on a global scale for decades. Such autonomy has also encouraged strong Native identities in the waves, even among top ranked amateur surfing teams (NSSA and ISA) and Hawaiian professional surfers competing in today's WSL. For these surfers, Hawaiian national identities are empowering and essential. As Keanu Asing explains, "We deserve to be our own country in the surfing world. Like . . . the great Hawaiian Duke has done for this sport, we deserve to have the chance to carry the Hawaiian legacy in the sport of surfing."[76] While these surfers embrace a strong pride in Hawaiian ancestry, culture, and nationalism, they define their *kuleana* to the *lāhui* in various ways, including being a positive influence on Hawaiian youth, overturning negative stereotypes, and exceling in surfing competitions. Such *kuleana*, or responsibility, to Hawaiian culture and community, although motivating, is admittedly emotionally taxing for athletes who are already under great competitive pressure. Despite such weight, Hawaiian surfers inspire other Kanaka Maoli by waving Hawai'i's national flag, singing the kingdom's national anthem, and representing the nation of Hawai'i on a global scale. Such representation provides symbolic redemption from the colonial occupation of Hawai'i and stirs feelings of pride, nationhood, and autonomy in a nation and culture developed long before colonization. *Mahalo nui no ko 'oukou hana maika'i. Imua!*

NOTES

1. For further analysis see Kauanui, "Precarious Positions: Native Hawaiian and US Federal Recognition"; Sai, "A Slippery Path towards Hawaiian Indigeneity"; and the Na'i Aupuni website, http://Naiaupuni.org.

2. See Sai, "The American Occupation of the Hawaiian Kingdom."

3. Anderson, *Imagined Communities.*

4. Carissa Moore, email interview with author, February 3, 2016.

5. Many have suggested that surfing itself plunged into extinction at the turn of the twentieth century; see Finney and Houston, *Surfing: The Sport of Hawaiian Kings;* and Kampion, *Stoked! A History of Surf Culture.* See also Peralta, *Riding Giants.*

6. While the surfing world refers to all Hawai'i surfers as Hawaiian, Hawaiian typically means Kanaka Maoli, or Native Hawaiian. In this chapter I will use the term Hawai'i surfers when referring to non–Native Hawaiians and I will contextualize and analyze the differences between these identifications.

7. Such congressional legislation was initially referred to as the Akaka Bill after Senator Daniel Akaka, who first proposed Senate Bill 2899 and House Bill 4904 to the 106th US Congress in 2000. Proposed legislation has evolved over time, especially under processes of congressional amendment.

8. See the Na'i Aupuni website, http://Naiaupuni.org.

9. Sai, "The American Occupation."

10. Sai, "The American Occupation." See also Sai, *Ua Mau Ke Ea, Sovereignty Endures.*

11. Sai, "The American Occupation."

12. Sai, "The American Occupation."

13. Randy Rarick, quoted on the *Surfline.com* "Who Knows?" blog.

14. Walker, *Waves of Resistance;* Walker, "Hui Nalu, Beachboys, and the Surfing Boarderlands of Hawai'i"; and Walker, "North Shore Reign."

15. For a more comprehensive explanation of borderland theory see Anzaldúa, *Borderlands/La Frontera;* Brooks, *Captives and Cousins;* LaDow, *The Medicine Line;* Johnson, *Roaring Camp.* On "boarderlands," see Walker, "Hui Nalu, Beachboys, and the Surfing Boarder-lands of Hawai'i."

16. Walker, *Waves of Resistance.* See also Walker, "Hui Nalu, Beachboys, and the Surfing Boarder-lands of Hawai'i."

17. Walker, *Waves of Resistance.* See also George, *Hawaiian: The Legend of Eddie Aikau.*

18. See Walker, *Waves of Resistance,* for details on these examples.

19. See the Nā Kama Kai website, http://nakamakai.org, and the Basic Image, Inc., website, http://www.pakalove.org/.

20. See Peralta, *Riding Giants.*

21. See Finney and Houston, *Surfing: The Sport of Hawaiian Kings;* and Kampion, *Stoked!;* see also Peralta, *Riding Giants.*

22. Walker, *Waves of Resistance,* 26–30.

23. Clark, *Hawaiian Surfing;* Moser, "The Endurance of Surfing in 19th Century Hawai'i."

24. Laderman, *Empire in Waves.* See also Walker, "Review: *Empire in Waves.*"

25. Patti Paniccia, "Who Owns the Duke," *Honolulu Magazine,* November 1, 2006.

26. Makuakai Rothman, January 2015, "Da Hui Backdoor Shoot Out 2015-Final Day," 6:30–7:07, https://youtu.be/R1L36YYklXg.

27. Bruce Irons, January 2015, "Da Hui Backdoor Shoot Out 2015-Final Day," 0:05–0:40, https://youtu.be/R1L36YYklXg.

28. Mason Ho, January 2015, "Da Hui Backdoor Shoot Out 2015-Final Day," 4:50–4:55, https://youtu.be/R1L36YYklXg.

29. See Backdoor Shootout contest opening, interviews: "Live—Dahui Back Door Shoot Out—Day 1," 0:30–1:30, 3:00–4:20, https://www.youtube.com/watch?v=GgHUBfhetVg.

30. Kauanui, *Hawaiian Blood,* 5–6.

31. Ezekiel Lau, email interview with author, January 31, 2016.

32. Lau, email interview.

33. Keanu Asing, email interview with author, February 14, 2016.

34. Asing, email interview.

35. Jimmy Ulualoha "Uluboy" Napeahi, email interview with author, February 1, 2016.

36. Napeahi, email interview, February 1, 2016.

37. Eddie Rothman, in "Being: Makua Rothman," *Being,* Vol. 1 (film), http://xgames.espn.com/xgames/video/12664395/being-makua-rothman.

38. Lau, interview.

39. Lau, interview.

40. Lau, interview.

41. Lau, interview.

42. Lau, interview.

43. Lau, interview.

44. Daniel Ikaika Ito, "The Kamehameha Surf Team Wins the NSSA National High School Championship," *Freesurf Magazine,* n.d., http://freesurfmagazine.com/the-kamehameha-surf-team-wins-the-nssa-national-high-school-championship/.

45. Ito, "Kamehameha Surf Team."

46. Ito, "Kamehameha Surf Team."

47. For a discussion on staging, performing, and reenacting history, see Dening, *Mr. Bligh's Bad Language*.

48. Uapili Lucy, in "Kamehameha Surf Team Wins NSSA Title," KHON2, June 23, 2014, http://khon2.com/2014/06/23/kamehameha-surf-team-wins-nssa-title/.

49. Charlie Akao, in "Kamehameha Surf Team Wins NSSA Title."

50. Charlie Akao, in "Kamehameha Surf Team Wins NSSA Title."

51. Moore, email interview.

52. Moore, email interview.

53. Napeahi, email interview.

54. See "Waves4Water: Hawaii," December 13, 2014, http://www.worldsurfleague.com/. See also Etienne Aurelius, dir., "Ulualoha," 2016, https://vimeo.com/174619296.

55. Napeahi, email interview.

56. Rothman, "Being: Makua Rothman."

57. Rothman, "Being: Makua Rothman."

58. Keanu Asing also finds strength as a professional surfer in his native identity and his Hawaiian roots. "I'm carrying that Hawaiian flag with me and not only doing it for myself but for Hawai'i too. I love where I'm from and love the people." He finds pride in "being a part of the latest few born, blooded Hawaiians carrying that flag on the world stage and giving the Hawaiians a true Kanaka Maoli to cheer for and be proud of." Asing, email interview.

59. See Coleman, *Eddie Would Go*; Peralta and Taublieb, *Hawaiian*.

60. Moore, email interview.

61. Moore, email interview.

62. Lau, interview.

63. Asing, email interview.

64. Asing, email interview.

65. Lau, interview.

66. Lau, interview.

67. See Danny Nieves, "5 Competitions Freak-outs: Broken Boards, Punches, Head-butts," *TheInertia.com*, November 4, 2014; and Dashel Pierson, "Kolohe Andino Flips Off the Judges as He Loses to Mick Fanning," *TheInertia.com*, September 11, 2015. In the latter article the author explains that unlike his dark-skinned Mexican counterpart, Bobby Martinez, Andino was composed and controlled despite his flagrancy in the water.

68. Lau, interview. See also Pete Thomas, "Garcia's Aloha Tour: Volatile Hawaiian Says He Is Done with Professional Surfing After this Season," *LA Times*, September 13, 2015.

69. See Du Bois, "Of Our Spiritual Strivings."

70. Du Bois, "Of Our Spiritual Strivings."

71. See chapter 4 and chapter 7 of *Waves of Resistance* where I analyze misrepresentations of Hawaiian surfers in the media, including films like Gosch's *Bustin' Down the Door*.

72. Napeahi, email inteview.

73. Napeahi, email inteview.

74. Napeahi, email inteview.

75. For example, Napeahi explained that while others were selected after a single tryout, Napeahi had to fly to Oʻahu on six different occasions for multiple tryouts before eventually earning his spot on the team (email interview).

76. Asing, email interview.

4 / Consolidation, Creativity, and (de)Colonization in the State of Modern Surfing

DEXTER ZAVALZA HOUGH-SNEE AND
ALEXANDER SOTELO EASTMAN

"Surfing is a creative outlet, the ocean is an escape," proclaims surf filmmaker Kai Neville. "The pursuits of surfing . . . are creative by their very nature," writes a blogger and start-up founder. A feature on hallowed surf photographer Thomas Campbell explores how he "captures the surf world's creative spirit."[1] Creativity has long been a trope of surfing culture and its practitioners, an ideal that marketing powers have exploited since Alexander Hume Ford lauded entrepreneurial creativity as a means to advance colonial Hawai'i.[2] Such celebrations of creativity often fail to take into account that surfing, as journalist Tetsuhiko Endo reminds us, "has been, in varying degrees, the pet project of corporate entities from its very re-inception in the 20th century, when Hume Ford saw that it could be used . . . to market Hawaiin [*sic*] Holidays."[3] In spite of a deeply commercial character, modern surf culture's adherents continue to espouse the practice's inherently creative foundations.[4] Such iterations of surfing's creative makeup, of course, have their origins in colonial observations of Native Hawaiians' ludic interactions with the surf zone, novel to eighteenth-century European sensibilities.[5] These origins were then revitalized by 1960s and 1970s "hippy and soul surfing rhetoric" which "expounded a form of 'fraternal' individualism that extolled creativity and self-expression" above all else, against commercial ideologies evolved from colonial enterprise.[6] And as countless individuals and institutions profit from surfing through "high consumption, materialism, and competition," the rhetoric of surfing's innate creativity remains.[7]

This volume's contributions are united by their unique engagements with those nebulous entities commonly referred to as the "surf industry," "surfing media," "surfing industrial complex," and "surfing culture industry," loose institutional networks that simultaneously pander to surfing's fabled creativity and rigidly define boundaries of surfing activity. Many allude to the nexus of these institutions and surfing's myth of creativity, as well as the means by which riding waves and related practices (production, consumption, and circulation of media, commodities, and travel) construct subjectivity. These two oppositional coordinates of surfing's institutionalization—renewable assertions of surfing's creativity and the visceral pressures that such institutions excise on individuals—beg the question: to what extent can individual surfers really express technical (wave-riding), cultural, and social creativity within surfing institutions? Can modern surfers, deeply influenced by a century of surf marketing and the resulting social pressures of local beach culture to look, act, and surf in certain ways, really be creative? Although surfing is often opposed to work, can surfers ever escape the confines of capitalism, embodied by the surfboard as commodity, to express radical creativity? Simply, can one surf beyond capitalism?

Yago Colás's recent theorization of the "modern basketball state" provides a point of entry to consider how a similarly conceived, metaphoric "state of modern surfing" demarcates the limits to creativity expressed by those interacting with surfing from any angle of engagement.[8] At the heart of this comparison is the conviction that there are "certain fundamental parallels in function between" institutions seeking to control and profit from surfing "and modern nation-states as they emerged, developed, and expanded in Europe and the Americas," as both limit individual agency and demand allegiances to enjoy the privileges of citizenship.[9] Like Colás, we also acknowledge that individuals— surfers—within the collective retain agency and seek to creatively negotiate the state of modern surfing. It is this agency that we celebrate, as we challenge the designation of all surf-related activity as creative in order to push the limits of surf-related activity further into potentially radical futures beyond, or even outside of, the surfing state and its institutions.

Defining the State of Modern Surfing

Colás's metaphoric modern sporting state refers to "public entities and private capitalist interests cooperating to maximize the profits they can extract from labor, stabilize the system by which they do so, and foster the impression that this arrangement is . . . desirable, . . . natural and . . . inevitable."[10] Anchored by professional sporting governance, the modern sporting state is embodied by the cluster of agents responsible for growing and promoting the sport while simultaneously defining the limits of player creativity and agency and restricting her or his ability to profit from the sport's growth.[11] In justifying these limitations, the sporting state then produces legitimizing narratives—myths—that vindicate the central role of its constitutive groups as essential to that sport's very existence.[12] Rendering athletes as passive objects, the sporting state places itself at the center of a sport's historical development, declaring its own responsibility for the sport's existence. While focused on basketball, Colás admits the possibility of "other parallel, or intersecting similar . . . universes" in organized, professional sport, a possibility that we extend to surfing cultures here.

In referring to the "state of modern surfing" (SMS), we regard surfing "as a semi-autonomous modern world of its own" under which the right to surf—"citizenship (i.e., the right to play)"—is governed by pressures exerted by those seeking to institutionalize and profit from modern surfing.[13] These pressures define what surfing is, what surfing "should" look like, and who can surf in different contexts. SMS organizations include amateur and professional competitive surfing governance; commodity manufacturing and marketing; specialty media, including independent photographers, filmmakers, and bloggers who compete with longstanding mainstream counterparts; travel, tourism, and hospitality infrastructure; wave pool enterprises; nonprofit, philanthropic, and charitable organizations; as well as scholarly engagements with surf culture, history, and the aforementioned entities. A comprehensive list of SMS institutions and actors is elusive, rendering it more befitting to conceive of the SMS as the collective pressures placed on surfers that limit participation in surfing to SMS institutions and the ideologies that they support, instead of a group of specific historical institutions.[14]

We employ the term *modern surfing* to refer to the practice of riding waves on any form of surfcraft after Western appropriation and exploitation of surfing. The very notion of modern surfing—where the surfboard is commodity, the surfer is athlete, and citizenship is contingent on the ability to accrue resources (catch and ride waves) according to prescriptive technique—admits surfing's indigenous, preindustrial past. As such, unlike basketball, which emerges in and expresses a "characteristically modern mix of feelings" around modernity, iconographies and affective expressions of modern surfing harken back to idyllic visions of surfing's premodern origins, prominent in media, marketing, and popular associations of surfing's freedom with the primitive. Such primitivism then necessitates claims to creativity—and celebrates it—for modern surfing's progress and growth ad infinitum.[15]

Our exploration of the SMS attempts to conceptualize the broadest potential definition of the global surfing collective in order to demonstrate how limits are placed on individual creativity and profitability within this global collective, which is hypothetically unified by surfing subjectivity over all else.[16] This is meant to challenge the way in which surfing has long been perceived—and marketed—as a manifestation of independent agency, countercultural politics, aesthetic creativity, and ludic freedom in wave-riding practices and expressions of surfing culture.[17] Surfers continue to celebrate surfing as the manifestation of endless creativity outside the confines of mainstream culture, in terms of both technical innovation (maneuvers, equipment, etc.) and entrepreneurs' never-ending quest to engineer "new" (and decidedly neoliberal) ways to profit from surfing.[18] Ironically, this insistence on abundant creativity potentially renders surfing a totalizing and globalizing phenomenon in which creative expression and the very concept of creativity are reduced to the logic of capital in the water and on land.

From one-time surf holiday novices to diehard recreational surfers to professional athletes, individual creativity in riding waves and profitability from that creativity is largely predetermined, artificially constructed, and potentially absent from much surfing experience. The same can be said of the creation of surf artifacts (boards, fashions, media, performances, etc.). Those individual actors enabling citizenship (the right to surf) through the construction of necessary commodities (board, fins, etc.), often revered for their innovation, also function within strict limits of productive possibility. Including the spectrum of self-employed, cottage industry shapers and unskilled production workers employed by multinational corporations in overseas industrial parks, the surfboard maker (and the surfboard), like the surfer, operates in a confined field, crafting equipment endorsed and authorized by the SMS. Surfing's creativity in wave-riding practice and the crafting of artifacts is, we suggest, a construction that accompanies the fundamental myths of self-legitimization that Colás's sporting state identifies.[19] While this myth is not unique to wave-riding, it is amplified in surfing and other lifestyle sports because the follower/participant exists in greater proximity to the state apparatus. Surfers are primarily practitioners, not mere spectators, and thus direct consumers of surfing institutions' wares and ideas of what surfing is; embracing SMS technologies and attitudes, they are participants in beach spectacle, as much as they are consumers of it. And it is upon this participation—purportedly democratic, yet crafted in the strictures of the SMS—that claims to surfing's creative makeup are built.

The objective in signaling the trappings of a mythologized creativity in the SMS is not to condemn the efforts of surfers and entrepreneurs, but to open a space to imagine alternate, potentially radical surfing futures beyond the foundation of another brand, company, nongovernmental organization, or nonprofit. Recognizing the limitations imposed by the SMS might be considered a theoretical precursor to "queering surfing," "desexing surfing" (see lisahunter, this volume), or truly decolonizing any single aspect of surf-related practice (travel, business operations, philanthropic initiatives, etc.) across global North–South power differentials. The remainder of this chapter focuses on two examples from Latin/o America to examine some of the ways in which the SMS excises control and how this power grid has been contested and challenged. We focus on Latin/o America because of its centrality within the surfing imaginary: for at least half a century, traveling surfers have idealized Latin American coasts as a frontier to be explored, conquered, and commoditized. Before considering one community in the Global South's creative attempt to decolonize surf tourism, we turn to the story of professional surfer Bobby Martinez, whose fiery rhetoric and mere presence unsettled the idea of a singular surfing image.

Bobby Martinez and the Professional Surfer in the SMS

Long Beach, New York—September 7, 2011. Against a media backdrop emblazoned with Association of Surfing Professionals (ASP) imprints and Quiksilver brand logos, twenty-nine-year-old professional surfer Bobby Martinez bobs his head, ducking and weaving as he fields the first question of his post-heat interview from ASP media representative Todd Kline. A tremendous grin overcomes the 2006 ASP Rookie of the Year as he shelves the acquiescent media persona donned by many professional competitors. And he has every reason to grin: Martinez has just narrowly defeated Australian Bede Durbidge at the first-ever World Championship Tour (WCT) contest in New York City, and his advancement from round two fares well not only for his campaign to requalify for 2012, but also for his chance to claim the winner's $250,000 share of "the richest prize purse in surfing history," a cool $1,000,000.[20]

Kline sputters, "Bobby, you haven't competed since Brazil [the third tour stop in 2011], you've missed two events [Jeffreys Bay, South Africa, and Teahupo'o, Tahiti]. What brings you to New York?" Martinez's response reveals what his smirk had concealed: "First of all, I'd like to say—an' the ASP are going to fine me—'cuz I don't want to be a part of this dumb, fucking-wannabe tennis tour. All these pro surfers want to be tennis players. They want to do a halfway cutoff . . . Come on now. Bullshit. That's why I ain't goin' to these stupid contests no more. This is my last one, because FTW, my sponsor, is here and I just tell it like it is. This is my last one, and I don't like tennis. I don't like the tour . . . Who gives a fuck? You know what I mean?"[21] As Martinez drops his second and third expletives, Kline betrays an incredulous grin, simultaneously expressing shock and delight at the strikingly candid, if incendiary, broadcast. Kline asks Martinez his opinion of New York, to which the surfer responds, "I love this city. [But] I'll tell you right now, if my sponsor wasn't here, I wouldn't be here for this dumb contest. [The] ASP? . . . surfing's going down the drain thanks to these people."[22] And with this interview criticizing the ASP requalification system, Martinez effectively ended his competitive career: within hours the adroit goofy-footer was dismissed from the event and subjected to a one-year suspension from ASP competition.[23]

The sixty-eight-month WCT career of the Santa Barbara, California, native is ripe for exploring the means by which the SMS limits individual creativity in professional surfing, seeking "to exercise its power to exclude from participation players who, for one reason or another, its agents have determined to be a threat to its integrity and stability."[24] Martinez's de facto retirement speech highlights two prominent elements of the SMS's ability to regulate its professional denizens. First, it demonstrates the regulation of professional surfers' discourse by punishing athletes who speak out against pro surfing outlets.[25] Martinez's unauthorized narrative of ASP history garnered immediate competitive and financial sanctions. Beyond his New York interview, earlier criticism of the ASP and its principal sponsors via social media—reflective of Martinez's frustrations with the institutional limits placed upon professional surfers occupying a privileged position in the SMS—contributed to his loss of lucrative sponsorships in 2008 and 2010.[26] Second, and more importantly, the rules used to discipline Bobby indicate how the ASP and sponsor partners frame and re-position themselves as surfing itself, constructing wave-riding as exclusive to organized competitive surfing, marginalizing other unauthorized and thus stigmatized forms of wave-riding.

Limits to Professional Surfers in the SMS

After garnering seven National Scholastic Surfing Association (NSSA) titles and being embraced by sponsors for his smooth technique and effortless style, the adolescent Martinez was expected to quickly ascend the WCT ranks.[27] As a junior competitor, Bobby was the perfect citizen of the SMS: his surf-ing was attuned to the rhythms of judging criteria, his style reminiscent of champion goofy-footers Mark Occhilupo and Tom Carroll, and he naturally surfed to the highest levels of competitive governance, aspiring to advance his career within the framework of competition and industry sponsorship. That is, he limited his athletic performance—as any performer in a subjec-tively judged sport does—to focus on techniques endorsed and promoted by judging criteria designed to yield fun-to-watch surfing that could grow view-ership and sponsorship revenues.[28] By surfing to the criteria, the professional surfer must conform to the hierarchization of a regulated, sanctioned set of narrowly defined "innovative and progressive manouevres."[29] Rewarded for prescribed techniques, competitors surf to the criteria at the expense of inno-vation, instead reinforcing a hierarchy of technique asserting the "best" way to surf. And, paradoxically, as more technically difficult maneuvers are born of free-surfing attempts to best previous techniques, the more limited surfing's competitive repertoires become, seeking repetition of newly canonized tech-niques instead of innovation.

For Martinez, like most skilled surfers, his attempts to profit from surfing were limited to riding for and in the name of a corporate entity as a paid athlete, using only the prescribed equipment: the archetypical three-finned, high-rocker shortboards pervasive since the 1980s, best suited to the acrobatic maneuvers and explosive turns salient to judges and marketing directors. Under palpable sponsor pressure, Martinez took five long years on the World Qualify-ing Series (WQS) to qualify for the WCT. But he displayed dominance during his first WCT season, garnering 2006 Rookie of the Year honors, winning con-tests at Mundaka (Basque Country) and Teahupo'o, and concluding the season fifth in the overall rankings. Finishing in the top ten during his first four years on tour, Martinez's results showed the makings of a WCT stalwart destined for a fruitful career.[30]

Yet by his sixth WCT season in 2011, Martinez was skipping contests, uninterested in surfing for the judges—whose scores he often disputed—in poor waves.[31] After ducking the Jeffreys Bay competition without contacting ASP officials, he also skipped the Tahiti event, where he was a favorite after winning in 2006 and 2009. And this is where Martinez began to collide with the limits of the ASP and the SMS more broadly. In 2011, Martinez, (then soon-to-be) eleven-time world champion Kelly Slater, and marquee talent Dane Reynolds each scratched WCT events to (1) surf in better conditions elsewhere that afforded opportunities to practice wave-riding skills outside of the judging criteria and (2) advance their careers through non-ASP coverage of their travels. Having denied the ASP of viewership by nullifying their prominent fan appeal, the three would collectively incite league officials to ratify and implement financial sanctions for athletes failing to attend WCT events. New rules, sustained through the ASP's rebranding as the WSL, stipulated that a seeded surfer could be fined up to $50,000—no small sum when even partial participation in the qualifying (WQS) tier costs upwards of $50,000—and mandated potentially career-killing suspensions from the WCT ranks.[32]

Meant to ensure that the sport's most popular names were on hand to attract viewership for official events financed, broadcast, and owned by the four largest surf companies, such policies indicate the means by which the pro surfer's creativity—to surf when, where, how, and with whom he or she wants—is engineered by SMS institutions.[33] Further consolidating ASP control, surfers were also restricted from competing outside the ASP and obligated to participate in top-tier qualifiers.[34] To surf professionally, then, meant to surf in the ASP. The freedom of competitive surfers such as Martinez to travel and surf at will outside of SMS structures became regulated through competitive bylaws that further limited surfers' profitability inside and outside the ASP, banishing them to the margins for dissidence. This was precisely what Martinez had resisted for years when he skipped contests and publicly criticized the ASP for funneling profits to the handful of ASP-authorized sponsors who owned event rights: "These surf companies don't want the sport to grow . . . they are holding everyone in a tight niche and got everyone by a rope and no one can grow."[35] If the ASP was to grow, it was on its own terms.

Martinez's contest absences coincided with diatribes across social media critical of the restructuring of the WCT to include a midyear cutoff that opened up the elite tour for new qualifiers at the midway point in the season, a concept adapted from the Association of Tennis Professionals (ATP) tour that would allow rising WQS talent to replace lower-tier WCT competitors at midseason.[36] Earlier in 2011 at the Bells Beach contest, Martinez had a public outburst against judges for what he perceived to be the overscoring of his heat competitor, also filmed and immediately posted online.[37] Bobby's discontent with the ASP was all too clear, and his season's results, marred by contest withdrawals, were meager in comparison to past years. Arriving at the fifth contest in New York, Martinez was barely in position for requalification, especially given the ASP's experimental midyear cutoff. But as his new sponsor (FTW) had been recently licensed to a Long Island surf entrepreneur, Bobby surfed in New York. And he surfed well, until he was disqualified from the contest. While Martinez's expletive-laden critique would not be admissible within most professional circles (sporting or otherwise), media and public responses collectively served to reiterate the ASP's decision and the surfing state's collective retraction of the surfer's privileged status.

Damage to Surfing's Image

In disciplining Martinez, the ASP threw the veritable rulebook at the twenty-nine-year-old surfer. Punishment was doled out in accordance with ASP rulebook Article 151, which "outlines that all Surfers shall not at any time damage the image of the sport of Surfing."[38] Citing Martinez's comments in full, the ASP Rules and Discipline Committee then deployed Article 147 to immediately suspend Martinez from the World Tour and prohibit him from finishing the event.[39] Furthermore, his suspension would be upheld indefinitely until a report could be submitted on behalf of the commission.

Prior to 2011, an expectation developed that competitors would uphold a certain code of conduct, especially in formal competition and related media. The "rebel" behavior previously championed by surf brands and surf culture more generally had rapidly declined in the competitive realm, as the SMS collectively shifted dominant definitions of surfing from a countercultural pastime, hobby, or culture toward a competitive sport and professional industry. In 2008, notorious bad boy Chris Ward, who anchored incendiary marketing by edgy surfboard and apparel manufacturer . . . Lost Industries in the late 1990s, ushered in such change with his own apologies to the ASP and his sponsors "for the negative publicity . . . generated to [*sic*] the sport and to the tour" after allegedly punching three women outside a bar.[40] After the Ward incident, then-ASP Rules and Disciplinary Committee Chair Robert Gerard responded that "there has been a trend in surfing that has brought attention to athlete issues and one of my missions is to insure [*sic*] that pro surfing does not get the image of a 'bad boy' sport."[41] In this overt campaign to eradicate the "bad boy" image once part and parcel of surfing as counterculture, the ASP asserted, quite overtly, its role as a gatekeeper organization necessary for the sport's very existence. Whereas competitive surfing has a long history of transgressive behavior and personalities unwilling or unable to fit into a professional mold, the ASP's revised code of conduct restrained surfer behavior as a protective measure not of the ASP, but of surfing itself.

And therein lies the supposition behind ASP Article 141: the ASP *is* surfing, and damage to "the image of the sport of Surfing"—surfing with a capital S—constitutes damage to the ASP and vice versa. While still implicit during Bobby's interview, this rule would be stated overtly in subsequent rulebooks: "Individuals bound by this Policy shall not engage in any conduct which could cause damage to the image of the sport of surfing... defined as any act, regardless of time or place, which casts the sport of surfing or WSL in a negative light."[42] Reflective of the way that competitive governance defines itself and its brand of surfing as the privileged—and only—surfing culture, the language of the rulebook cited in disqualifying Martinez coopts the very definition of surfing: to ride waves outside of competitive infrastructure becomes something other than surfing, making surfing synonymous with acrobatic performance maneuvers calibrated to a judging scale. Frolicking in the shore break on a plank, bodysurfing, even riding in a straight line: these are no longer surfing, and imaginaries of other surfcraft, from the Peruvian *caballito de totora* to more contemporary recreational forms, are excluded from surfing's very definition.

The Limits of Discourse: Critique as Competition

On paper, Martinez's competitive profile, contest winnings, and list of sponsors resembled the typical resume of a top-tier professional surfer. Yet there was more to Martinez's relationship with the ASP and industry brands than his contest results revealed. A third-generation Mexican American and "a rare Latino surfing superstar from a working-class background," Bobby was an anomaly in the largely white, generally affluent professional surfing world who "for years had the gangster hat hung on him by the makers of the surf world's often limited worldview."[43] Reporters were enraptured with the rise of this surfer of color from a "nontraditional" surfing community, penning countless features proclaiming him "a *cholo*, or a gangster, or coming from the hood," the product of a violent barrio upbringing.[44] His major apparel sponsor, Reef (2005–2008), pushed the Mexico angle, designing Martinez's signature apparel around Mexican flag iconographies and Day of the Dead skull and skeleton motifs. Reef even titled his 2008 feature film *Mixed Tape*—without Martinez's support—in homage to his "mixed" heritage. Within the SMS, Martinez was assigned the uncomfortable role of ambassador of Mexican culture and liaison to mainstream Anglo surf culture, restricted from forging a public persona as a professional surfer on any grounds beyond ethnic and racial heritage. In his own words, Bobby was "being fucking portrayed as an idiot," racialized, nationalized, and tokenized for marketing purposes, seen not as a talented surfer, but as a talented brown surfer. And although other competitors shared his frustrations with the WCT and butted heads with their handlers, Martinez was quickly singled out as a surfer of color "who would not bow when he disagreed with his bosses."[45]

In a 2009 feature for Australian *Stab* magazine, veteran writer Derek Rielly and Sydney-based artist Ben Brown would caricature Bobby as trapped between inner-city Mexican-American culture and white coastal California. Titled "Bobby Martinez is Baby G[angster]," the cartoon opens with the heavily tattooed Martinez in front of a sunburst reminiscent of representations of the Virgin of Guadalupe. He turns to face the viewer, planted between a group of Latino "gang bangers" and a trifecta of blonde surfer dudes, each claiming Bobby as their own. Martinez's speech bubble proclaims, "It was always hard for me to fit in. I got shit for being a gay surfer dude on one side, but I was always in awe of the gang bangers."[46] Martinez was rightfully offended by the spread, which was published without his input. But Rielly, an ardent media advocate for Bobby since his ASP exit, alludes rather accurately, if provocatively, to Martinez's uncomfortable positioning between the institutions of the SMS (industry, ASP, media) and his local community, generally outside of the SMS.[47]

In occupying the liminal space between his community and normative surf culture at the beginning of his career, sponsors, judges, competitors, and spectators could not deny Bobby's raw talent, his citizenship based on his ability to perform the acrobatic techniques most celebrated in competition. Still, as an outsider brought into the SMS for marketing purposes, he was regularly discredited by marketing executives as uncooperative in spite of widespread accounts of his tremendous work ethic and humility.[48] Prior to the New York incident, refusals to publicly cheer for his sponsors' other team riders and play brand ambassador at events favoring other surfers—whom he saw as competitors, not fellow company representatives—led to industry perceptions of Martinez as what Sara Ahmed has termed a "killjoy," his ethnic background earning him the tag of "melancholic migrant" in a sport prominently marketed as the ludic manifestation of happiness.[49] Martinez's competitive seriousness and attempts to control his public persona caused marketing executives, media, and some fans to deem him an angry person of color, and worse yet, an ingrate, for not conforming to marketing pressures to cultivate the exuberant hyperpositivity expounded by many professional surfers.[50]

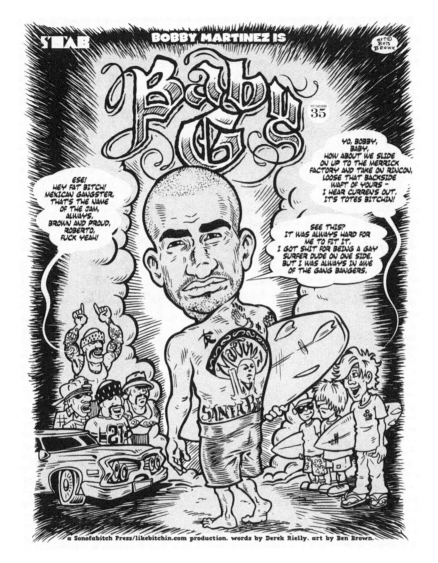

FIG. 4.1 Ben Brown's cartoon of Martinez in *Stab* magazine, 2009.

Martinez's reputation came to a head when he lost his principal sponsor O'Neill in 2010, his third such separation after departing Reef in 2008 and Oakley in 2005. Within the SMS, Martinez's criticism of professional surfing's apex organization tested and found the limits to profitability, these limits enacted by critical speech and individual agency (to forge a professional career as one pleases). As a result, surfing's foremost governing body and its corporate partners ostracized Bobby, leading him to claim that "the surf world has given up on me. . . . It's a small world and there is this image that all the big bosses of every surf company have of me. I'll remain sponsor-less from a major surf company the rest of my life."[51] As Martinez recognizes, under "the slow but steady consolidation" of an apex organization, those aspiring to surf "for a living must abide by the laws—in each domain—of the . . . state or be exiled to a kind of uncharted wasteland of . . . economically and culturally marginal minor leagues, sideshow traveling teams, or some combination of these."[52] Martinez was relegated to just such a competitive "uncharted wasteland" through his suspension and inevitable fall from WCT qualification. Yet unlike professional team sports, a pro surfer's primary income is contingent on product endorsement and brand sponsorship. As Martinez notes above, he was also exiled from endemic sponsorship for not surfing by the rules.

Although his talents remained intact, and he found support in several streetwear start-ups and Monster energy drink, Martinez's WCT finale saw him placed at the margins of the SMS, a positioning that forced him to once again confront his origins outside of the normative surf culture endorsed by the SMS. Racially driven commentary abounded following the New York interview. A *Stab* magazine commenter chirped, "never worked a day in their life . . . comes from a minority, where victim culture and blaming everyone else for there [*sic*] problems is standard."[53] Deeper, darker, epithet-laden critiques emerged. Bobby had taken on what industry stalwart Jonathan Paskowitz has called "this big, nepotistic group of industry individuals that all hang out together and work together," precisely the promoters and profiteers behind the SMS institutional network.[54] As outsider to Southern California surf industry and a person of color, Bobby was doubly deprived of his creativity—to express himself against the norms of "stoke" and "froth" and surf when and where he pleased—and profitability within the SMS, relegated to sponsors (FTW and Monster) on the fringe of the SMS institutional network.

Bobby Martinez originated in a community underrepresented, even marginalized, in surfing institutions.[55] However, his sheer talent engendered such aesthetic epiphanies that he was granted exceptional status in the highest tiers of the SMS.[56] The fact that he deployed his talents in formal shortboard competition, the surfing discipline that grants the greatest cultural capital and financial reward, furthered his position in the SMS, placing him in a position to negotiate the institutions promoting and profiting from surfing with greater independence than recreational wave riders or surfers divested from the industry. Of course, his arrival at that position was the result of corporate sponsorship, and his targeted branding toward a niche audience (Latin/o surfers) became a civic responsibility for retaining his status in the SMS. Even with such privileged citizenship in the SMS, Martinez was limited to embodying a typified ethnic caricature, which suggests that the surfing world has its own "unresolved racial tensions in the history of the sport" charted across surfing's appropriation.[57]

Martinez's career transitioned from the competition circuit to free surfing as a representative of several financially precarious small surf ventures and a large youth brand (Monster Energy). As a free surfer, Martinez refocused his energies to produce promotional surf clips from California and abroad, traveling to global surf destinations in the service of marketing surfing through "exploratory" modes. As Martinez transitioned away from the institutional framework of professional competition, his career shifted to one of the foundational components of the SMS. International surf travel, primarily from the Global North to the South, has long been a pillar of the surf imaginary. And while a full account of the evolution and impact of these travel circuits requires greater discussion than this chapter permits, this closing section glosses three pivotal moments in the development of international surf tourism before considering a recent innovative response from the community of Salina Cruz, Oaxaca, Mexico.

In 1907 Jack London set sail around the South Pacific and popularized what has become the bread and butter of surf journalism: the travelogue. Surf-specific magazines would not flourish until decades later, so London published about his fascination with dark-skinned men "conquering . . . bull-mouthed monsters" in the *Woman's Home Companion*. The majority of London's readers did not have the opportunity to hop on a boat and follow his ship's wake around the world, but settled for the vicarious thrill provided by reading about his adventures in the burgeoning industry of widely distributed commercial magazines. Consequently, "Riding the South Sea Surf" helped to insert surfing and international exploration and discovery into the mainstream fold.[58] Notably, London lodged in the Royal Hawaiian Hotel, where he hobnobbed with patrons such as tourism bureau member Alexander Hume Ford, the orphaned son of a wealthy South Carolina plantation and a tireless promoter of surfing and Hawaiian beach culture since settling in the Islands in 1907.[59]

After a half century of rapid technological advances that brought international exploration to the masses, Bruce Brown released the now-iconic documentary *The Endless Summer* (1966), in which two Southern Californian surfers traipsed around the Global South in order to escape crowded beaches at home, the consequence of linking surf culture and exploration to freedom and nonconformity. Perhaps more than any other surf production to date, *The Endless Summer* presented the Global South as a land of endless possibilities and potential. The blatant colonialism of the film was overlooked by viewers, as was the reality of its impossibly perfect waves, most notably those of Cape St. Francis, which upon further exploration proved to be notoriously fickle. In spite of the superficiality of the documentary that glorified the virtue of exploration and glossed over the viewpoints of the local populations it portrayed—or perhaps precisely because of the film's overt orientalism—international surf travel boomed in the following decades, as surfers from the Global North set out in search of their own discoveries and creative freedom.[60]

Near the turn of the twentieth century, when surfing had been commercialized and mainstreamed to the point of losing its marketability as alternative-cool, Rip Curl designed a new marketing campaign in an attempt to capitalize on the foundational linkage of modern surfing and international exploration. "The Search" began in 1992 as an ad campaign that depicted world-class waves with nobody in sight, welcoming consumers of the images to insert themselves in the idyllic scenes and, as the slogan suggested, search the globe for unknown surfing locales. In 2006 the company set a new precedent for the marketability of search-and-discovery narratives when it hosted a WCT event under the "floating license." The "Rip Curl Pro Search" advertised the summertime event to be held "somewhere in Mexico" and promised that it would "ad[d] a spice to the tour."[61] Fueled by marketing professional and media outlets, rumor and speculation buzzed as to the exact location in Mexico, which was not officially unveiled until 2010.

Several notable points regarding surf travel and exploration are worth unpacking. First, "The Search," with its print and digital advertisements and promotional videos of "exotic" locations, is the stripped-down core of a century of surf travel writing laid bare. That is, as opposed to previous travelogues such as "Riding the South Sea Surf" and *The Endless Summer*, which encouraged surfers to trot the globe while only explicitly selling the creative fantasy of travel,

"The Search" directly linked the consumption of surf travelogues and photography to the marketing of exploration and travel. The ads sold prepackaged "creativity credentials" to be earned through global exploration, ideally while donning Rip Curl's travel gear. That the surf travelogue genre culminated in pure advertisement, wherein the line between content and advertisement has been erased, reveals the extent to which the SMS hinges on myriad (capitalist) interests. More specific to the WCT event, it is remarkable that a multinational corporation maintained a public ruse for over four years, repeatedly printing a fictional name, "La Jolla," in place of the actual community—Barra de la Cruz—where local residents' lives were increasingly affected by the influx of international surfers following the WCT event. Although Rip Curl marketed Barra de la Cruz as an international surf tourism destination, by concealing the town's name it attempted to channel the allure and profit of the main attraction—the wave—toward the company itself.

Owing in part to its proximity to one of the modern epicenters of the surf and film industries (Southern California), Mexico has long held a special place in the cosmography of surf travel. Yet ease of travel for those from the North is only part of the appeal. Like many other locations in the Global South, Mexico has been portrayed as a dangerous, mythic, and adventured-filled frontier for the feral surfer. As one surf journalist wrote in 1965, "There have always been many myths of huge green waves, undiscovered spots, perfect breaks abounding in Mexico. But like the El Dorado sought by the ancient Spanish Conquistadores, the treasure is always over the next hill, beyond the distant jungle." Much like the contemporary discourse on surf exploration, the author romanticizes the notion of an endless search where only the most dedicated persevere. He does not hesitate in likening himself to an imperial enterprise whose mission is wealth and conquest: "I had to find out and so I was on the trail tracking the myth to its source."[62]

In the decade since the WCT event, Barra de la Cruz has been transformed from a social democratic collective based on fishing and agriculture to a divided, neoliberal town centered around the surf tourism industry. In the midst of the 2006 WCT event, Pablo Narvaez, a community leader of the 800-resident Chontal indigenous village, stated, "Go ahead, name it [the town]. What's in a name? We have control. We will always have control."[63] Perhaps unfamiliar with the nuances of surf travel and the ensuing surfer colonization that follows exploration and exploitation by actors in the SMS, Narvaez underestimated how many surfers would "track the myth to its source" once the name and location of the wave-rich village were revealed. Like many rural beach towns in the Global South, Barra de la Cruz has struggled to curtail the myriad issues—environmental, social, and political—involved with the rapid growth of tourism. For instance, the $30,000 that Rip Curl paid the town to host the event—a mere fraction of the (often seven-figure) going rate in locations in the Global North—was insufficient to fund the health clinic that villagers had hoped to construct. Further demonstrating the ASP's limited investment in the community, the winner of the contest won $30,000, and the top eight finishers earned $106,000 in total prize money.[64] Rip Curl's global marketing director bluntly stated that the company did not pay more in Barra "because we did not have to. We had another relationship with the village."[65]

The rapid and uneven transformation of Barra de la Cruz since 2006 was surely fresh in the minds of residents in neighboring Salina Cruz when *Surfing* magazine published the provocatively titled feature "The Life and Times of Salina Cruz: A Pointbreak Sensation." The anonymous essay personified Salina Cruz as a promiscuous woman who responded to the interviewer's question with double entendre and sexual innuendo.[66] While the surf world was disturbingly silent regarding the overt misogyny of the article, the publication that named, promoted, and visualized the wave-rich region renewed debates about the politics of exposure and the "outing" of secret spots.

Fearing a flood of unbridled foreign investment and development, a group of resident surfers and lifeguards formed the Unión de Surfistas y Salvavidas de Salina Cruz, Asociación Civil (USSSC; Union of Surfers and Lifeguards of Salina Cruz, Civil Association) to protect the local economy and coastline and to control the influx of foreigners: "The result of this article helped us realize that we ought to work together so that our beaches will not be exploited by people outside of our community."[67] The association disseminated a public letter to the surfing community in which it explained its intentions and policies, including the obligatory hiring of a local guide and a fee for photography so as to invigorate Oaxaca's economy, referenced as one of the three poorest in Mexico. In an interview with the popular surf website Surfline, founding USSSC member Cesar Ramírez elaborated on why the revelatory article infuriated many natives of Salina Cruz: "It wasn't even a story. I don't know what it was. But it showed Salina Cruz as something that is easy to access for anyone [a promiscuous woman]. And they didn't show the real point of view of the local people. They made it a fictional story—that's the part that pissed everyone off."[68] Surfline's interview generated hundreds of reader comments, some of which empathized with the USSSC's wariness regarding the "paradise-discovered" myth cycle in the SMS: "We deal with this same surf media BS in the Caribbean. The surf media comes, they get their 'story,' they leave and then we are stuck with crowds and disrespectful surfers." What this commenter and

Ramírez denounced were the fictions of beaches without communities, of empty waves waiting to be "found" and the ensuing commodification of the resources (waves) and lives of peoples in the Global South.

It is too early to say whether the local community in Salina Cruz will successfully mediate the development and intensification of surf tourism. However, the transmission of locals' perspectives and the problematization of surf discovery tales is a step in the direction toward decolonizing surf tourism and narratives. Unsurprisingly, many readers were quick to criticize the USSSC as a "killjoy" that threatened to dismantle the purported purity, happiness, and creative freedom of surfing and related travel. Take the following comment as example, which succinctly embodies the tensions within surf tourism as practice and discourse that we have attempted to develop here: "The beauty of surfing is that the ocean is free and a way to express athleticism in a one of a kind dance with nature free of politics and all the other trappings of society such as greed and materialism where the ultimate bonus is possibly finding a spiritul [sic] connection and inner peace . . . I see none of the GOOD things about surfing as it relates to The Salina Cruz Surf Council [sic] and their controlling quest . . . It's a complete abomination and rape of surfing freedom."[69]

Other readers similarly attacked the USSSC for aiming to privatize a public space, and lumped the association into a stereotypical portrayal of Mexico as a land of corruption and extortion, with one commenter comparing the association to a drug cartel, expressing doubt that the profits would actually support community projects. The title, "Extreme Localism . . . or Just Plain Extortion," revealed one surf magazine's refusal to interpret the USSSC as a creative and emancipatory response to exploitation.[70] The backlash against a grassroots civil organization aiming to protect local autonomy and to disrupt the hegemonic model of North–South surf tourism was, perhaps, to be expected. As Ahmed theorizes, "killjoys," or those who expose the often troublesome paths to sustaining happiness, "disturb[ing] the very fantasy that happiness can be found in certain places," are charged as unhappy deviants whose own supposed unhappiness frequently eclipses the structural or systemic issues that provoked unhappiness in the first place.[71]

The USSSC's attempt to control the development and representation of Salina Cruz seemed to mark an affront to the hegemony of the surf media. In the words of the organization, "We want Salina Cruz to be a surf destination free from foreign control and the economic revenue derived from tourism to be for the sole benefit of the local population and the visitors' stay to be pleasant, safe, comfortable, worry-free, and fun!"[72] The surf tourism model the USSSC adopted, however, has meshed with the overarching narrative and structure that the SMS promotes. After a few years of indecision regarding how to approach Salina Cruz, surf media and companies now openly promote travel to the region. A popular surf-news website included Salina Cruz in its promotional travel section, "#GoThere." Although written by the editor, the byline, "This installment of #GoThere is powered by WaterWays Surf Adventures," rendered unclear the "owner" of the article's message: "A lot of people get to Puerto Escondido and stop there, because of both its waves and reputation. But south . . . to surfers is like west to pilgrims. There is always that call to head just a little farther down; that pull to see what's around that next bend. And guess what's around it? Salina Cruz."[73] As the media entities constitutive of the SMS promoted Salina Cruz as the new frontier to be conquered, the organization of the region's surf camps quickly became part and parcel of the globalizing state of modern surfing, the creativity of their decolonial response to media and tourism exploitation eroded by the masses.

The Salina Cruz case demonstrates the bounds of creativity when working within the structures of international surf tourism. The tension between local tourism operators and the fear of losing appeal as an adventure destination is palpable in the way that the now-numerous Salina Cruz surf camps all insist on being the "first" and "original" local tour operator.[74] One commenter to a promotional article about Salina Cruz, apparently offended that a surf magazine would deter readers from "real" exploration and discovery by funneling them into charted territory, wrote, "I think anybody that stays at a surf camp—is more of a surf tourist—than real surfer. Don't believe it when they say surf camps are the only option—maybe [the] surfing mag really is getting kick-backs."[75] This comment registers unmediated travel's centrality to the surfing imaginary, and reveals a certain naiveté about how destinations are put on the map and, in chiding visitors who pay for the camps, a disregard for the fates of the communities to which they travel. That surf magazines receive "kickbacks" (ad revenue) from tourism operators, and that local companies require publicity to stay afloat, is unquestionable. Even more certain, however, is the continuation of the "discovery and conquest" cycle that will convert rural coastal towns like Salina Cruz into international tourist destinations.

How much autonomy and governance local peoples have on the future form and practice of surf travel will depend on the ethics and actions of people like "tony," a surfer who responded to the USSSC's regulation of surf-related business practices: "who has 2 grand to spend on mexico, thats an indo trip at that point. if I'm going to mexico i want to spend as little as possible."[76] The desire to economize is understandable, but it behooves all of those implicated in the SMS to reckon with the uneven costs of seemingly unmediated and unbridled surf exploration. As Krista Comer observed about another developing surf destination in Mexico, "the surf industry nods toward indigenous local rights or sovereignty issues without actually having to give up much."[77] Minimizing the pay gap between events held "somewhere in Mexico" and Southern California, in addition to letting go of the paternalistic narrative that surf tourism invariably helps communities in the Global South by introducing them to the joys of wave-riding and dollars, seems like a fine place to start.

The State of Modern Surfing as Starting Point

The actions of Bobby Martinez and the members of the USSSC register attempts to humanize, decenter, and reconceptualize the SMS. Martinez and the USSSC shared a mission to embrace diversity in surfing by forging a more democratic and transparent public forum under which individual surfer-citizens could readily exercise their creativity and mobility within surfing superstructures. The shortcomings of their projects attest to the nimbleness of the SMS and its ability to marginalize dissenters and profit from those who define its boundaries. When Martinez tested the ASP's authority and refused to acknowledge the ASP as surfing, the ASP retaliated with sanctions and censorship. The battle over surfing's image(s) ultimately afforded professional surfing greater visibility as the controversy fueled viewers' desire for a "countercultural moment" while Martinez's surfing career shifted to the less profitable margins of the SMS. When surf media reduced Salina Cruz to a fictionalized, faceless town awaiting discovery and exploitation, local surfers mobilized and disrupted long-standing surf tourism practices by organizing, demanding recognition, and setting their own rules and rates. The USSSC gained leverage in its ability to self-represent and profit from its natural resources, though challenges—including competition among guides—have since slowed Salina Cruz from achieving its emancipatory goals of community and environmental improvement. Similar to the way Martinez's protests stoked the fire of surfing's mythical rebelliousness, Salina Cruz's denunciation of surf travel's orientalist narratives spurred new fantasies about traveling beyond the beaten path. Yet both were resurrected—as sponsored athlete and commercial tourism operators—from within the confines of the SMS. The takeaway is not to idealize Martinez's protests or to replicate the USSSC's regulatory model around the Global South, but to reconsider the factors and institutions that shape our views of creativity, progress, and surfing's productive potential in and out of the waves. By deconstructing the myth of surfing's inherent creativity—showing how surfing's radical potential is muted by its folding back into capital—we allude to a space in which another sustainably sourced business, another philanthropic effort, or another inclusivity initiative acknowledges its own limits, ideological allegiances, and contradictions, and seeks to operate in the name not of redemption, but of truly radical creativity.

NOTES

1. Primoz Zorko, "Surfing Is a Creative Outlet: Meet Kai Neville," *El Dorado Journal* 15 (2015), http://eldoradoexperience.org; Shawn Zappo, "Interview with Chris Miller," July 29, 2015, http://surfandabide.com/chris-miller-skateboarding-surfing-yoga-and-the -creative-life/; Jonathan Feldman, "Thomas Campbell Captures the Surf World's Creative Spirit," February 25, 2013, http://www.papermag.com/thomas-campbell-captures-the-surf -worlds-creative-spirit-1426829619.html.

2. Ford's *Mid-Pacific Magazine* regularly lauded entrepreneurial creativity and derided trade unions for hindering creativity. See Kanda's "Japan at the Great Conference," which claims "what we want is no longer the acquisitive genius . . . but the creative genius, which has an elevating and enriching effect on humanity in general," going on "to advocate . . . the spiritual and creative conquest of the world" (434). Against unions as stymying creativity, see Chen, "Chinese Guild," where Chen states that a worker "must either blindly follow the guild regulations, or suffer a common boycott for exercising his creative intelligence" (533).

3. Endo, "Crimes Committed in the Spirit of Play," 85.

4. Excessive iterations of surfing's creative legacy have yielded satirical interventions lampooning self-proclaimed creativity. See Phil Watson, "Opinion: You Are Riding a Pure Wave of Creativity," April 13, 2015, http://beachgrit.com/2015/04/opinion-you-are-riding -a-pure-wave-of-creativity/.

5. See Dawson, "Surfing Beyond Racial and Colonial Imperatives," this volume; and Dawson, *Enslaved Water People in the Atlantic World*. For colonial expressions of European wonder at surfing, see Moser, *Pacific Passages*, 55–125.

6. Surf 4.4 (1974): 28 in Ormrod, "Surf Rhetoric," 93.

7. Surf 4.4 (1974): 28 in Ormrod, "Surf Rhetoric," 93.

8. See Colás, "Getting Free" and *Ball Don't Lie*.

9. Colás, *Ball Don't Lie*, 37. Here, "institutions" refers to the aforementioned surfing industry, surf media, and surfing industrial complex and their corporate, nonprofit, and governmental agents.

10. Colás, *Ball Don't Lie*, 37.

11. Colás, "Getting Free," 278–279, and *Ball Don't Lie*, 37–38.

12. Colás, *Ball Don't Lie*, 9–14, 27–28, 38.

13. Colás, "Getting Free," 268, 280; and Colás, July 15, 2015, email to author. It is worth noting that we invert Colás's syntax ("state of modern surfing" instead of "modern surfing state") in recognizing that precolonial Polynesian forms of surfing—unlike basketball, an invention of nineteenth-century recreational promotion that lacked indigenous forms—are largely excluded from official state narratives, except as avatars of premodern national origins. Isaiah Walker has repeatedly demonstrated how Native Hawaiian surf-

ers have challenged marginalization in the state of modern surfing by forming their own institutions and forging a uniquely Hawaiian participation in competition and industry. See Walker, *Waves of Resistance*.

14. It might be alternately understood "less as a thing (or a network of things) and more as a set of functions" consisting of "potentially antagonistic or . . . unrelated entities collaborating to control and exploit the creative labor of . . . players as well as [to generate] . . . mythic narratives legitimating that control and exploitation." Colás, July 15, 2015, email. In lieu of deeply historicizing surfing institutions' competition and collusion for control over the surfing population here, we refer the reader to Walker, *Waves of Resistance*; Laderman, *Empire in Waves*; Westwick and Neushul, *World in the Curl*; Sheri Crummer, Cori Schumacher, and Carla Rowland-Zamora's History of Women's Surfing website, http://historyofwomensurfing.com/; and Warshaw, *History of Surfing*, among others.

15. For example, Canniford, "Branded Primitives," this volume.

16. See Heywood, "Third Wave Feminism," 64; Thorpe, *Transnational Mobilities in Action Sport Cultures*.

17. See Lawler, *The American Surfer*.

18. This is seen in the overwhelming abundance of NGOs, "sustainable" businesses, media outlets, and higher education initiatives employing surfing as a fundamental part of their business model in the twenty-first century.

19. Colás, *Ball Don't Lie*, 9–14.

20. In 2011, all other ASP WCT contests had total prize purses of $425,000–$500,000.

21. Todd Kline, "Bobby Martinez Interview Quiksilver Pro New York 2011," uploaded on September 7, 2011, https://www.youtube.com/watch?v=MC4WQmc-O4k.

22. Kline, Bobby Martinez interview.

23. Jon Coen, "Bobby Martinez Retires from Competition," August 19, 2011, http://www.espn.com/action/surfing/story/_/id/6874940/bobby-martinez-retire-asp-world-tour. Martinez had announced plans to retire at the season's end because of differences with the ASP.

24. Colás, "Getting Free," 279.

25. Attempts to forge a professional career outside of industry limits—for example, as a freesurfer/model using social media to create an individual "brand"—are quickly co-opted by the SMS. Such media engagements can be seen as requisite civic duties—responsibilities—for professional denizens in the SMS.

26. On Martinez's use of social media to criticize the ASP, see Tibby Rothman, "Bobby Martinez's Rebel Cry," January 5, 2012, http://www.laweekly.com/news/bobby-martinezs-rebel-cry-2173522. On his sponsorship loss, see Coen, "Bobby Martinez Retires."

27. Martinez won titles in 1994 (Explorer Menehune), 1995 (Open Boys, Explorer Boys, Explorer Menehune), 1997 (Explorer Boys), and 1998 (Open Juniors, Explorer Juniors), a feat bettered only by current women's Championship Tour competitor Carissa Moore (eleven titles, 2004–2007). See *Mixed Tape*, 2007, directed by Pete Santa Maria.

28. For more on competitive surfing judging criteria, see WSL Rulebook, 67; Warshaw, *Encyclopedia* (2005), 132–33 and 357–58. In Sam George's words, "Competition surfing has a built-in limitation" (quoted in Warshaw, *Encyclopedia*, 133).

29. WSL Rulebook, 66.

30. Martinez placed fifth (2006), tenth (2007), ninth (2008), and eighth (2009).

31. For Martinez's comments against judging decisions, see Emma Schiller, "Bobby Martinez Accuses Judges of Giving Unfair Scores," April 21, 2011, http://www.foxsports.com.au /surfing/american-surfer-bobby-martinez-accuses-judges-of-giving-unfairly-high-scores -to-australian-taj-burrow-at-bells-beach/story-e6frf6bl-1226042929497. On judging inconsistencies favoring more marketable athletes, see Andy Davis, "Judge Dread," October 25, 2011, http://www.mahala.co.za/?s=judge+dread.

32. Jake Howard, "The Price of Qualifying," May 13, 2015, http://stabmag.com/news /the-price-of-qualifying/; and ASP Rulebook 2014, 59. Articles 147.18–19 stipulate that failure to attend an event with notice but without medical excusal is punishable by a fine of $12,500 on the first offense and $25,000 on the second; the third offense carries an automatic suspension for three CT events and concurrent top tier qualifiers. Financial penalties double if the surfer fails "to attend the WCT Events entered without warning."

33. See Davis, "Judge Dread." For more on the economics of event sponsorship, see Stu Nettle, "The ASP: It's On, But Who's Watching?," Parts I–III, May 8, 2014, through January 14, 2015 (Part I accessed at http://www.swellnet.com/news/surfpolitik/2014/05/08 /asp-its-whos-watching).

34. ASP Rulebook 2014, Article 22 (16–17), Article 13.03 (10).

35. "Bobby on Pro Surfing and Sponsors," uploaded on May 23, 2009, https://www .youtube.com/watch?v=qQdAyNixEqw.

36. The ASP dropped the mid-season cutoff after the 2011 season.

37. "Bobby Martinez Unloading on Judges—Rip Curl Pro Bells Beach," April 21, 2011, https://www.youtube.com/watch?v=RRiL9aAK1rc.

38. "ASP's Official Disciplinary Letter to Bobby Martinez," September 7, 2011, http:// www.surfline.com/surf-news/asp-statement/asps-official-disciplinary-letter-to-bobby -martinez_59308. Preserved almost verbatim, the rule cited here is Articles 141 and 171, respectively, in the ASP 2014 and WSL 2015 rulebooks.

39. "ASP's Official Disciplinary Letter to Bobby Martinez."

40. Shawn Price, "Ward Faces Long Road Back," *Orange County Register,* February 12, 2008, http://www.ocregister.com/articles/ward-92158-asp-case.html. In 2015 and 2016, further domestic abuse incidents led to Ward's incarceration and prompted longtime sponsor . . . Lost to drop the Californian.

41. Price, "Ward Faces Long Road Back."

42. WSL Rulebook 2015, Article 171 (70).

43. Rothman, "Bobby Martinez's Rebel Cry"; Brad Melekian, "Almost Not Famous," *Surfer* 48, no. 7 (July 2007), http://www.surfermag.com/.

44. Melekian, "Almost Not Famous." For an example of such sensationalism, see Scott Frampton, "Santa Bruta Don't Surf," *ESPN Magazine* (2006). For Martinez's thoughts on misconceptions about his life and neighborhood, see Melekian, "Almost Not Famous," and Derek Rielly, "Bobby's Closing Statement," March 21, 2013, http://stabmag.com/style /bobbys-closing-statement/.

45. Rielly, "Bobby's Closing Statement"; Rothman, "Bobby Martinez's Rebel Cry."

46. Derek Rielly and Ben Brown, "Bobby Is Baby G," 2009, http://stabmag.com/style /bobby-martinez-in/.

47. Martinez would later publicly comment on the social challenges of being a surfer in a largely Latino community. See Rielly, "Bobby's Closing Statement."

48. Rothman, "Bobby Martinez's Rebel Cry." Frequently mentioned in reference to pro surfers, humility has long been valued by the modern professional surfing infrastructure. The quality takes on an uncomfortable semantic coexistence encompassing residual expectations of colonial servitude (perhaps originating in Anglo colonization of Hawai'i), the indigenous Hawaiian value of *ha'aha'a* (humility, pride in self-growth, valuing importance of all in the family), and corporate observations of hierarchy and expectations of compliance.

49. Ahmed, *The Promise of Happiness*, 50–87, 121–159.

50. See Chris Mauro, "Dear Bobby," GrindTV, September 7, 2011, http://www.grindtv .com/surf/dear-bobby/#m1qZXVsHkFWWW4Pi.97. For a contrast to Martinez, see the Gudauskas brothers, who are marketed as ambassadors of hyperpositivity through primary sponsor Vans, their "Stoke-O-Rama" contest, and Positive Vibe Warriors NGO. See http:// positivevibewarriors.com and http://www.vans.com/article_detail/positive-vibe-warriors .html.

51. Coen, "Bobby Martinez Retires."

52. Colás, "Getting Free," 279.

53. Rothman, "Bobby Martinez's Rebel Cry."

54. Rothman, "Bobby Martinez's Rebel Cry."

55. Few US Latino professional surfers precede Martinez; among them is Chuy Reyna. On marginalization of people of color and access to beaches in global contexts, see Glen Thompson, Kevin Dawson, and Belinda Wheaton, this volume.

56. Hans Ulrich Gumbrecht defines "epiphanies," quite common to surfing spectatorship, as "an unexpected . . . appearance of a body in space, suddenly taking on a beautiful form that just as quickly and irreversibly dissolves . . . the source of the joy we feel when we watch an athletic event, and . . . the height of our aesthetic response" (Gumbrecht, *In Praise of Athletic Beauty*, 54).

57. Colás, *Ball Don't Lie*, 28. On surfing's historical development, see Walker, *Waves of Resistance*; Laderman, *Empire in Waves*; and Moser, "Endurance of Surfing."

58. Jack London, "Riding the South Sea Surf," *Women's Home Companion* (October 1907). London's writings allegedly inspired South African Tony Bowman to build a surfboard and surf around Cape Town circa 1922. See "Surfboards Made in Muizenberg in 1920s," Surfing Heritage South Africa, http://surfingheritage.co.za/site/1922_tony _bowman.

59. Moser, *Pacific Passages*, 6; and Westwick and Neushul, *The World in the Curl*, 36. For more on London and Ford, see also Dina Gilio-Whitaker, this volume; and Walker, *Waves of Resistance*.

60. For in-depth analysis of *The Endless Summer*, its colonial gesture, and place within surf history, see, for example, Comer, *Surfer Girls*, 23, 53–65; Lawler, *The American Surfer*, 142–146; Laderman, *Empire in Waves*, 48–51; and Ormrod, "*Endless Summer*: Consuming Waves and Surfing the Frontier."

61. A company history of "The Search" is available on Rip Curl's website, http:// thesearch.ripcurl.com/en/.

62. Cleary, "Through Arid Desert and Steaming Jungle."

63. Quoted in Kimball, "The Spot." For more on the struggles in Barra de la Cruz and the community's response to growing tourism, see Serge Dedina, "Mexico's Election: Citizens Seek to Succeed Despite Government," *San Diego Union Tribune*, June 23, 2012; and Serge Dedina, "The Coastal Wonders of Oaxaca," March 14, 2012, https://sergededina.com/2012/03/14/the-coastal-wonders-of-oaxaca/.

64. Transworld Surf, "Andy Irons Wins Rip Curl Search WCT in Mexico—Moves to #2 in WCT Ratings," June 23, 2006, http://www.grindtv.com/surf/andy-irons-wins-rip-curl-search-wct-in-mexico-moves-to-2-in-wct-ratings/.

65. Kimball, "The Spot," 115.

66. "The Life and Times of Salina Cruz: A Pointbreak Sensation," *Surfing Magazine* (November 2011): 62–73.

67. "A Message from the United Surfers and Lifeguards of Salina Cruz," April 18, 2012, http://www.surfline.com/surf-news/press-release/a-message-from-the-united-surfers-and-lifeguards-of-salina-cruz-on-current-state-of-surfing_69347/.

68. Mike Cianciulli, "Southern Oaxaca: Update," April 19, 2012, http://www.surfline.com/surf-news/southern-oaxaca-update_69344/.

69. Mike Cianciulli, "Southern Oaxaca: Update."

70. Sean Radich, "Extreme Localism . . . or Just Plain Extortion," *Surfing Life*, April 19, 2012, http://www.surfinglife.com.au/news/sl-news/9882-extreme-localism—or-just-plain-extortion.

71. Ahmed, *The Promise of Happiness*, 66–68.

72. "Message from the United Surfers." See also Parkin, "Points of Common Desire"; and "Your Next Trip: A Salina Cruz Long Weekend," *Surfing Magazine* (July 24, 2014).

73. Alexander Haro, "#GoThere: Salina Cruz," *The Inertia* (March 13, 2014).

74. Salina Cruz Surf Tours, run by Cesar Ramírez, declares that it is "The Original Local Surf Company" (http://salinacruzsurftours.com/). Las Palmeras Surf Camp similarly claims that it "is the first locally owned and operated Surf Camp in Salina Cruz" (http://surflaspalmeras.com/). Punta Chivo Surf Camp takes an even more aggressive stance: "We were the 'Original surf camp' in Salina Cruz, Mexico and the only camp run by local experts . . . The other surf camps uses [*sic*] non surfers for surf guides and you will be sharing your tour with more of [*sic*] 8 surfers" (http://www.puntachivosurfcamp.com/).

75. "Freerider" comment in "Your Next Trip."

76. "Your Next Trip."

77. Comer, *Surfer Girls*, 208.

5 / Decolonizing Sustainable Surf Tourism

TARA RUTTENBERG AND PETER BROSIUS

The global expansion of surfing has been described as a colonizing process of Western socioeconomic and cultural domination. As a leading factor in the growth and spread of surfing to areas previously off the global tourism map, the mobility of surf tourists from the Global North has transformed coastal communities in myriad ways. The effects of this development include displacement, social exclusion, cultural hybridization, and environmental degradation. Surf scholars have used the word *neocolonial* to identify the tendency for wealth to accumulate among foreign business owners in surf destinations to the detriment of local communities. In response, conscientious surfers have developed action-oriented approaches in attempts to remedy these challenges by designing projects and models to support the sustainable development and conservation of surf tourism destinations. By making it more sustainable, these projects envision surf tourism as a meaningful driver for the positive socioeconomic development of local communities while safeguarding against negative environmental impacts.

While prescient in recognizing the neocolonial nature of surf tourism, and well intentioned in designing frameworks for a more sustainable brand of surf tourism, we argue that many of the solutions proposed by proponents of sustainable surf tourism are in need of fundamental rethinking. By aligning itself with income-oriented, status quo sustainability, the emerging field of sustainable surf tourism runs the risk of becoming sustainability greenwashing while reproducing conventional forms of exploitation. We offer a critical examination of the field's current approach to sustainability as a basis for reconsidering the "surf-tourism-for-sustainable-development" model. Our aim is to encourage experiments in endogenous forms of assets-based surf tourism governance aligned with diverse community economies and alternatives to development as a decolonizing approach to sustainable surf tourism.

Surf Tourism as Neocolonialism

The characterization of surfing tourism as a colonizing activity is not new.[1] A number of surf scholars have identified the ways in which the global expansion of surfing, much like the history of colonialism, has prompted the cultural homogenization of surf tourism spaces in the Global South through imported modes of development catering to the demands of hypermobile, predominantly white, male, middle-class surfers from the Global North.[2] As surf tourism locales grow from surf secret to surf city, foreigners reap the economic benefits of tourism through unregulated investment, favorable terms for land ownership, weak environmental standards, and lax labor laws characteristic of tourism in the Global South.[3] Local people, by contrast, receive few economic benefits from surf tourism, and are often relegated to the social margins as low-salaried workers in foreign-owned tourism businesses, when they are not otherwise displaced from their homes owing to upward pressure on land prices resulting from the influx of foreign capital.[4]

In its power to similarly transform the natural, social, and cultural landscapes of coastal communities the world over, surf tourism invariably produces a "relation of structural domination" and a subsequent "suppression of the heterogeneity" of sociocultural landscapes characteristic of colonialism.[5] Structurally speaking, Uluwatu is Tamarindo is Puerto Escondido is Lagundri

Bay, places dominated and homogenized by and for foreign surfers, where local people are seen as obstacles to riding waves (localism), are valued as means of production (labor), or at the very best, are treated as cultures to be consumed when the surf has gone flat.[6]

Given this sort of development in surf tourism destinations, Butler's analysis of the seemingly predictable destiny of open-access, boom-and-bust tourism provides further impetus for concern among conscientious surfers who refuse to see their favorite spot turn into the next Uluwatu.[7] According to Butler's Tourism Area Life Cycle Model, tourism development follows a continuum of linear phases: (1) exploration, (2) involvement, (3) development, (4) consolidation, and (5) stagnation, at which point a tourism destination will either find ways to rejuvenate and maintain its appeal, or self-destruct because of oversaturation by mass tourism and the appeal of new attractions elsewhere. This inevitable tourism trajectory is particularly troublesome given the explosive growth in the number of surfers worldwide, estimated at 20 to 35 million and growing as fast as 15 percent per year.[8] With waves perceived as finite resources among a growing surf population, surfers seek to escape the crowds they help grow at their home breaks. And as the surf media and industry continue to construct a travel-to-surf narrative of tropical surf nirvana to satisfy an insatiable endless summer dream, the demand for surf tourism amenities is set to increase exponentially, along with all the pathologies that accompany them: environmental degradation, the depletion of coastal aquafers, sex trafficking, and mafioso-style organized crime, among others.[9]

Vital to considerations of Butler's model, however, is an acknowledgment that the trajectory of such tourism development is not as natural or inevitable as it may seem. Rather, it functions within a governance structure and associated ideology built on a constructed system of beliefs, values, practices, and regulatory frameworks all constitutive of neoliberalism, defined here as a capitalist political-economic system and ideology founded on economic liberalization, privatization of public enterprise or commonly shared resources, and deregulation of investment, finance, and ownership.[10] In our discussion of surf tourism as a process of colonization we bear in mind the power of neoliberal governmentality to pervade the ways we see, behave, and interact in surf tourism spaces, which both informs and dictates the present realities and future constructs of surf tourism destinations around the world.[11] In other words, surf tourism and its associated development are inextricably conflated with neoliberalism, itself a construct only decades in the making, and its hegemony in defining values, beliefs, practices, and forms of governance.[12]

In response to the numerous social and environmental challenges associated with surf tourism we see a florescence of efforts in the emerging field of sustainable surf tourism (SST) in which surfing academics have joined forces with surfer philanthropists and environmentalists, the majority of whom hail from the Global North and work on and in surf tourism destinations in the Global South. Less than a decade old, SST has come to include a number of projects and models proposing solutions to issues of both conservation and development in surf tourism spaces, drawn together under the umbrella of sustainability. The SST framework encompasses, but is not limited to, sustainability certification standards and best practices for resorts and surf tourism providers; surf voluntourism for development; surf philanthropy through monetary assistance and environmentalist campaigns in surf tourism destinations; surfonomics as a policy-oriented mechanism for valuing and preserving surf breaks; educational surf travel; academic publications, research, and conferences; and surf tourism management plans.

While these initiatives operate in unique ways, their approach to sustainability unites them in proposing similar solutions to the problems of surf tourism. As such, the field of SST represents both a discursive ideology and an action-oriented movement based on a shared recognition that host communities should reap the socioeconomic benefits of surf tourism, and that efforts should be made to minimize the environmental impacts of related development. Together, the emerging forms of SST seek to harness the potential of surf tourism as a benevolent source of environmental conservation and socioeconomic development, the realization of which, it follows, would contribute to greater sustainability in surf tourism spaces.[13]

Operating within a discursive framework of sustainability, the field of SST aligns itself with the discourse of sustainable development, a concept defined by the 1987 Brundtland report, *Our Common Future*, as "development that meets the needs of the present without compromising the ability of future generations to meet their own needs."[14] As an attempt to improve upon decades of failed pursuits in international development, with an eye toward addressing the challenges of climate change, the Brundtland report served as a manifesto for neoliberal attempts to reconcile development and conservation goals to satisfy the needs of human life within the natural limits of the biosphere, paving the road for the Earth Summit in 1992 and the adoption of international agreements such as Agenda 21 and the Rio Declaration. Transitioning into the twenty-first century, and driving the international policy agenda in the post–Millennium Development Goals era, sustainable development is proposed as the overarching means for alleviating poverty, supporting human dignity, and curbing environmental degradation. Maintaining continuity with the foundational tenets of its development predecessor, micro-level sustainable development policies are income oriented and geared toward Western modes of modernization.[15] These policies include investment in health, education, and infrastructure; an emphasis on job creation and local entrepreneurship to encourage savings and consumption; and conservation strategies like payments for ecosystem services and the promotion of eco- and nature-based tourism. At the macro-level, the philosophy behind the global sustainable development agenda is unquestionably neoliberal. Social objectives rely on an economic-growth-for-development model, and environmental goals align with a neoliberal environmentality in conservation initiatives where nature is valued as resource and commoditized as a supposed means toward sustainability.[16]

Our analysis of contemporary SST initiatives reveals that leveraging surf tourism for sustainable development is the overarching objective connecting the spectrum of projects and models within the field of SST. This assertion is consistent with recent publications by Borne and Ponting, which explicitly offer sustainable development as a conceptual foundation for sustainability trends in the surfing world.[17] Although the field of sustainable development has been the subject of critical scrutiny by numerous practitioners and scholars from a broad range of disciplines, this critique has yet to be extended to the field of sustainable surf tourism. We offer the following critique of SST as a step in that direction.

Surf Tourism for Sustainable Development

As Mach discusses, leading scholars in the field of SST present a five-part framework for sustainable surf tourism:

1 A move away from Western business models whereby locals are "empowered" and encouraged to participate as owners in their local surf tourism industries

2 Formal, long-term coordinated planning in the form of surf tourism management frameworks based on a recognition of the limits to growth through taxation of visiting surfers, reef fees, quotas on the number of surfers granted entry, and exclusivity rights for so-called sustainable resorts at certain breaks

3 Systematic attempts to foster cross-cultural understanding geared toward informing locals of their natural wave resources vis-à-vis surf

tourism and educating them on sustainability to support shifts in local practices and means of livelihood toward more sustainable income-generating pursuits like surf tourism

4 Encouraging locals to learn to surf as sport, along with the promotion of local competitions to further the development of surfing while promoting social change and community well-being

5 Contribution to poverty alleviation among the host community through income-oriented approaches to local employment, ownership, entrepreneurship and social welfare.[18]

Currently, many initiatives that operate under the umbrella of SST align their principles with these five sustainability objectives, while offering a few additional goals similar to those promoted by sustainable development. For example, surf voluntourism nonprofits leverage the dollars and energy of philanthropically minded surfer-volunteers to invest in local community development projects in income-poor surf destinations. Such projects include building schools to teach indigenous youth; installing health clinics to provide immunizations and pharmaceuticals for disease prevention and treatment; establishing computer labs and internet in rural areas; teaching local youth to become surf instructors and surf photographers; supplying micro-credit loans for local entrepreneurs; and offering mentoring and capacity-building programs geared toward income generation for poverty alleviation as a development strategy.[19]

Best-practices frameworks and sustainability certification schemes for surf tourism operators are also gaining popularity.[20] Notable in this regard is the STOKE Certification for surf resorts and surf-related businesses. Aligned with the standards set in 2012 by the Global Sustainable Tourism Council (GSTC) of international experts "working together for the universal adoption of sustainable tourism practices," the STOKE framework is based on a checklist of 142 sustainability metrics that, in exchange for consulting and evaluation services, is intended to be applied as a one-size-fits-all sustainability benchmark in surf tourism areas around the world. Proposed as the tourism industry's response to the challenges of the UN Millennium Development Goals—in particular, poverty alleviation and environmental sustainability—the GSTC model deploys experts to train business personnel and to build capacity through education on a predefined notion of sustainability. Certification criteria emphasize "social and infrastructure community development . . . , education, health, and sanitation," and encourage companies to support local entrepreneurship.[21] STOKE's certification criteria adapted the GSTC standards to the surf tourism context through a three-year process of "working closely with surf resort owners, community leaders, nonprofits and government officials in surfing destinations" to quantify "the highest standards of sustainable surf tourism practice" and to measure the "efficacy of sustainability management systems, surf resource conservation, quality and safety of surf experience delivery, as well as social, economic, cultural heritage, and environmental impacts" as a "comprehensive multisectoral approach" to assess the sustainability of surf tourism operators.[22] Tailoring their sustainability efforts to meet STOKE's standards, businesses like Turtle Bay Resort in Oʻahu, Hawaiʻi; Wavepark Surf Resort in Mentawai Islands, Indonesia; and Tavarua Island Resort in Fiji have been awarded the STOKE certification based on varying degrees of compliance. Such resorts cater to high-end surf tourists who can afford to "surf easy knowing that their trip is part of the solution to global and local challenges to sustainability and not part of the problem."[23]

Mach highlights the foundational challenges of applying a singularly defined, universal approach to sustainability in surf tourism given the varying understandings of a concept like sustainability among people representing diverse sectors and interest groups in surf tourism destinations.[24] The malleability of sustainability as a conceptual category is further complicated by considerations of diverse world views, livelihoods, and cosmologies. Such acknowledgment of difference renders problematic a singular definition of sustainability and the creation of universally applied sustainability certification standards that do not consider local determinants and grassroots conceptualizations of sustainability. The surf resource sustainability index (SRSI) created by Martin and Assenov and O'Brien and Eddie's work on benchmarking global best practices represent additional examples of externally designed, locally applied approaches in need of similar reevaluation.[25] Though well intentioned, sustainability indices and certification frameworks created by experts, professionals, and scientists—such as those offered by the SRSI, GSTC, and STOKE certified models—ignore situated local knowledges while imposing external views, logics, and practices on social and natural landscapes in surf tourism spaces. Here, as in Fletcher's analysis of tourism that sustains global capitalism, the questions of "what is being sustained and for whom?" merit greater attention.[26]

Educational surf travel represents another approach to SST. A growing number of universities and for-profit service providers offer study-abroad courses for high school and college students to study surfing and surf tourism's impacts on coastal communities. One such service provider, Groundswell Educational Travel, premised its programs on making surf tourism's impact a "positive one" through "cross-cultural understanding and sustainability."[27] Groundswell's successor, Sea State, offers a range of educational surf travel options with the explicit mission to enhance students' "compassion, global citizenship, environmental stewardship, and marketability for our globalized world."[28] The course we teach through the University of Georgia, Surfing and Sustainability: Political Ecology in Costa Rica, takes a different approach, interrogating issues at the intersections of sustainability, conservation, and development in surf tourism destinations through a critical political ecology framework that employs an ethnographic lens. While offering different approaches to issues of sustainability in surf tourism, educational surf travel programs situate themselves within the framework of SST by contributing to the production and sharing of knowledge regarding the ways surf tourism affects coastal communities. Whether these programs contribute to surf tourism having a positive impact on those communities remains to be seen.[29]

Finally, the nascent field of surfonomics has been promoted in sustainable surf tourism circles for its utility in determining the monetary value of surf breaks as an advocacy mechanism to influence government policies toward preserving famous waves like Uluwatu, Mundaka, and Mavericks, as well as cultural heritage surfing spots like San Miguel in Baja Mexico, Huanchacho in Peru, and Pichilemu in Chile.[30] Surfonomics seeks to "determine the economic value of a wave and surfing to local communities to help leaders make better choices to protect their coastal resources and waves" as an alternative to infrastructure and industry that would destroy them.[31] Surfonomics has contributed in significant ways to the Save the Waves' World Surfing Reserves (WSR) program, which designated itself as the "global model for preserving wave breaks and their surrounding areas by recognizing and protecting the key environmental, cultural, economic and community attributes of surfing areas."[32] So far, WSR includes nine "outstanding" surf spots currently in varying stages of the designation process: Punta de Lobos, Chile; Bahia Todos Santos, Baja Mexico; Huanchaco, Peru; Santa Cruz and Malibu, California; Ericeira, Portugal; Manly Beach and Gold Coast, Australia; and Guarda do Embaú, Brazil.

The incentive framework of surfonomics in which the WSR program is situated operates within the same rationale of sustainable development's popular approach to payment for ecosystem services (PES), whereby conservation is arguably motivated by valuing nature in monetary terms as in situ resources, such that the income benefits of preserving natural resources outweigh the costs of their destruction. Fletcher describes this approach as "harnessing in situ resources as the basis of income generation sufficient to cover the opportunity costs of alternative (i.e., extractive) land use and thereby incentivize stakeholders to 'freely' elect preservation."[33] This approach has been fundamental to the promotion of nature-based tourism and ecotourism as livelihood incentives versus cattle farming, logging, or other forms of forest conversion. Fletcher outlines how the shortcomings of PES are representative of neoliberal conservation and characteristic of the "paradoxical situation in which progressive biodiversity conservation closely conjoined with ecotourism has expanded in concert with environmental degradation."[34] Demonstrating how and why this "neoliberal conservation strategy has rarely actually worked effectively in practice," Fletcher's conclusions support earlier studies on neoliberal conservation and development models, determining that "win–win scenarios, where both natural resources are conserved and human well-being is improved in specific places over time, have been difficult, if not impossible, to realize."[35]

Similarly, as the case for surfonomics demonstrates, the contradiction inherent in the PES approach is such that the same incentive structure for the economic valuation of conserving surf breaks also relies on the steady income generated by the influx of surf tourism associated with those breaks as the economic incentive for governments and communities to conserve wave resources rather than destroy them. In this way, both conservation and development become vital to the neoliberal tourism-for-development governance model, despite the deleterious environmental consequences of tourism development associated with conserving natural resources—in this case, preserving surf breaks. Thus, while preventing the destruction of reefs and local environments from non-surf-related infrastructure or industry, "saving" surf breaks through a policy tool such as surfonomics similarly condemns their social and natural landscapes to deeper degradation and exploitation through neoliberal forms of surf tourism development and the commodification of nature as resources to be exploited sustainably.

Herein lies the cyclical conundrum of neoliberal approaches to tourism for sustainable development, whereby conservation requires tourism development, just as development spawns the need for conservation.[36] It is within this framework of tourism for sustainable development, itself part and parcel of the larger economic growth for development model vital to the global capitalist economy, that the field of sustainable surf tourism has situated itself quite (un)comfortably to date.[37]

In examining the sustainability approach of the SST field, we see that its singular rhetoric and universalizing perspective unravel as its material and sociological foundations represent yet another means of colonizing surfing spaces, local landscapes, and ideologies, just as the neoliberal sustainable development paradigm has colonized billions of minds, bodies, and natures under the seductive guise of doing good in the world.

The field of post-development challenges us to envision and to create new approaches to development by rejecting the neocolonial paradigm of development as we know it and replacing it with alternatives that acknowledge a rich multiplicity of ways of knowing, seeing, doing, and being in the world.[38] Stemming from a deep disillusionment with the post–World War II development project, critiqued by the left and exposed for its failures of environmental degradation, social inequality, and extreme poverty, post-development discourse is founded on a critique of Western development inspired by Foucauldian poststructuralism.[39] This critique is both compounded and complemented by neo-Marxist perspectives on the neoliberal economic-growth-for-development paradigm wherein traditional development schemes are perceived as reliant on insertion into the global economy through the promotion of export-led growth and income-oriented approaches to poverty alleviation.[40] Given the discursive and practical insertion of SST into neoliberal modes of development and sustainable development, the post-development perspective offers a useful critique for deconstructing and reimagining the field of sustainable surf tourism.

Post-development theory underlines the interplay between power and politics as a process of establishing a singular hegemonic vision which maintains that economic development and social well-being are achievable only through capitalist production and modernization. At the same time, it perpetuates a monoculturalizing meta-narrative of a Western-modern materialist world view.[41] This logic has far-reaching implications, creating a univisional sense of social norms and beliefs governing right and wrong ways of being and doing, thus contributing to a culturally homogenized set of accepted realities in all spheres of life: education, agriculture, health care, political systems, production, and culture itself, where the dominant practices developed in the North have been exported through historic processes of colonization and present-day neocolonialism. These processes begin to explain the internalization of the social values of both modernity and neoliberalism in the field of sustainable surf tourism, as well as the subsequent distortion of traditional social relationships and deterioration of respect for local ontologies and cultural diversity inherent in its approach to both sustainability and surf tourism for sustainable development. Sachs writes:

> It is not the failure of development which has to be feared, but its success. What would a completely developed world look like? We don't know,

but most certainly it would be both boring and fraught with danger. For development cannot be separated from the idea that all peoples of the planet are moving along one singular track towards some state of maturity, exemplified by the nations "running in front." In this view, the Tuaregs, Zapotecos or Rajasthanis are not seen as living diverse and noncomparable ways of human existence, but as somehow lacking in terms of what has been achieved by advanced countries. Consequently, catching up was declared to be their historical task. From the start, development's hidden agenda was nothing else than the Westernization of the world.[42]

This dominant meta-narrative of the Western world view operates at the levels of culture, knowledge, and practice, and is founded on both a modern cultural habitus and the hegemony of scientific, linear-rational logic characteristic of Enlightenment thought, whereby anything "other" is both noncredible and nonexistent.[43] The challenge for post-development, then, is to transcend this "unequal discourse" and its oppressive monocultural logics by divesting them of their power and hegemony through imagining alternatives to development and creating a counter-hegemonic premise by which to recognize diversity in knowledge, culture, and economic interaction.[44] Gibson-Graham refers to this process as the "deconstructive project of post-development thinking," which focuses on "unhinging notions of development from the European experience of industrial growth and capitalist expansion; decentering conceptions of economy and de-essentialising economic logics as the motor of history; loosening the discursive grip of unilinear trajectories on narratives of change; and undermining the hierarchical valuations of cultures, practices and economic sites."[45]

This approach is relevant for the field of SST, whose singular narrative on sustainability perpetuates neoliberal and colonizing strategies in conservation and development, and thus requires significant re-evaluation. Maiava writes of the constructive shift from intentional to immanent development, with practitioners moving to support what people are already doing to enhance social well-being, recognizing people and communities as agents of their own development instead of imposing a top-down interventionist model with predetermined objectives.[46] This approach requires a fundamental shift in world view as the means to reject preconceived notions of development and sustainability.[47] From there, post-development practice seeks to recognize indigenous and endogenous efforts to improve well-being, and to support and strengthen existing efforts as the means to promote localized, pluralistic grassroots movements and development initiatives outside the confines of a materialist world view and its associated sociocultural dictates.[48] Understood in this way, we see post-development as a decolonizing mode of thinking, as well as an emerging experiment in practicing development alternatives that support the local and the endogenous while rejecting the universalization, control, and limitation of possibilities characteristic of development as we know it.[49] If taken seriously by the field of SST, this approach to working with communities toward locally defined sustainabilities based on what people are already doing may open space for the types of innovative thinking and exchange necessary for re-imagining interactions in surf tourism scenarios.

The post-development framework is conceptually situated within the debate on sustainable development, providing a well-articulated critique of efforts that seek to address interrelated environmental and socioeconomic challenges without acknowledging the underlying need for systemic/structural change at the very core of modernity's local and global crises. As such, post-development promotes a transformationist approach to sustainable development, in sharp contrast to arguments for both (1) market-based solutions characteristic of the status quo economic growth-for-development paradigm and (2) reformist strategies championing technical fixes that promote "sustainable, equitable capitalism" through renewable energy, technology, and policy reform within existing social and economic structures.[50]

The post-development approach challenges the fundamental myth upon which status quo and reform approaches to sustainable development both rely: that environmental destruction and social injustice can be remedied without a transformation in the economic systems and structures of power that cause and perpetuate them. This myth ignores the key Marxian insight that persistent poverty and social inequality are requisite conditions for the sustainability of capitalism, and what James O'Connor calls the second contradiction of capitalism, whereby the economic system inherently aggravates ecological crisis and impairs its own conditions of reproduction by depleting the natural resources on which it depends for its very survival.[51] In a world of finite resources, and thus finite growth, the second contradiction is impossible to reconcile beyond the very short term, as transformationist critiques of mainstream sustainable development have recognized, when status quo and reform approaches ignore, obscure, and deny such realities.[52]

Dismissing as a "disenchanted cosmos" the entire sustainable development paradigm, the post-structuralist perspective offers a complementary critique, articulating the ways in which sustainable development co-opts social movements and conquers indigenous peoples and their knowledge. In similar fashion, sustainable development brings about the death of nature through the capitalization and commodification of the conditions of production in the service of economic growth, using the environmental problematic as the impossibly futile, yet all-the-while attractive attempt to reconcile nature and capital without disrupting the market system—that is, believing in an impossibly sustainable growth as a means of conveniently circumventing the second contradiction of capitalism as its short-term solution to crisis.[53] Founded on the dominant rational logic of Western thought and modern science as previously described, sustainable development thus becomes another tool of sociocultural and ecological exploitation that divests people and non-human nature of their intrinsic value and active agency to then relegate them to passive roles as resources to be economized, means of production through which to capitalize, and "reservoirs of value" to be commoditized and consumed.[54]

Similarly, the governance framework for sustainable development gives little value to the conservation of nature for nature's sake, but rather seeks to conserve the system of capitalized nature through processes of control and conquest: the aspects of nature worth conserving (read: valuable as resources or commodities) are categorized under the term "environment," and the people responsible for their conservation and sustainable exploitation are given the honorable roles of environmental stewards, custodians, and managers. Status quo sustainable development thrives in both discourse and practice, an all-encompassing catch-phrase industry for saving the planet from destruction and its people from poverty and misery by converting nature and humans into means of production to both propel economic growth and conserve a commodified Earth. In the process, the unsustainable consumption patterns and dominant power interests of the Global North continue while income-poor populations are consigned to a new round of "gluttonous vision" in which modernization via Western standards of knowledge, livelihoods, wealth accumulation, and lifestyle is touted as a template for living a decent life, despite the obvious natural limits to the growth model on which this vision relies.[55] This type of status quo sustainability is the colonizing mantra of sustainable development, and we see it manifest as materially and discursively indistinguishable from the ways in which SST is being promoted and implemented in the world today.

In adopting the monoculturalizing meta-narrative of the modern materialist paradigm in discourse and practice, and adapting its interventions to the status quo framework of sustainable development in the service of the neoliberal economic growth-for-development paradigm, SST inherits and imposes the same neocolonial attitude and practices it seeks to transcend. In alignment with Audre Lorde's famous words, "the master's tools will never dismantle the master's house," the call to decolonize SST, then, requires that we create and acknowledge alternative practices of sustainability in surf tourism spaces outside the frameworks of status quo sustainable development and its persistently pervasive neoliberal governmentality.

And while the power of neoliberal governance operates through deeply entrenched dynamics of coercion, consent, and resistance to the economic growth-for-development paradigm, alternative constructs in surf tourism management may represent a fundamental shift in those power relationships. That is, in presenting a different approach to surf tourism, local communities—perhaps in concert with critically engaged SST practitioners—can assert power by withdrawing their consent to the cyclically exploitative structures and ideologies of neoliberalism, with an eye toward the creation of non-neoliberal and post-capitalist forms of interaction in surf tourism spaces.

Decolonizing Sustainable Surf Tourism: Experiments in Diverse Community Economies and Alternatives to Development

The principal objective of this chapter has been to challenge the discursive and practical foundations of the emerging field of sustainable surf tourism through a decolonizing lens on surf tourism-for-sustainable development, offering the post-development critique as a vital impetus toward re-imagining conceptualizations of sustainability and alternatives to development in surf tourism scenarios. In concordance with a transformationist approach to sustainable development, we have argued that solutions to the problems of neoliberal surf tourism governance require fresh alternatives beyond the confines of the colonizing status quo sustainability that is currently proposed and implemented within the field of SST. Acknowledging that we cannot solve contemporary challenges from within the same mindset that created them, we consider non-neoliberal, decolonizing, and post-capitalist approaches as vital to transcending both neoliberal structures of governance and governmentality responsible for perpetuating persistent modes of domination, exploitation, and oppression in (sustainable) surf tourism encounters. At the intersection of culture, nature, conservation, and development, surf tourism destinations offer unique milieus for reinventing tourism as a means of critically acknowledging diversity and moving toward truly sustainable futures in surf tourism and beyond.

To those ends, we propose flexible, context-specific approaches to recognizing difference as a means of exploring experiments in localized sustainabilities and surf tourism governance. This approach aligns with (1) a non-essentializing hybridity lens on cross-cultural interaction in surf tourism spaces, (2) an assets-based diverse economies approach to endogenous community development, and (3) a call for profound self-reflexivity among SST practitioners in deliberations on sustainability in surf tourism.[56]

The cultural lens of hybridity offers a nuanced means by which to experience and interact with host communities in surf tourism destinations, moving beyond a primitivizing narrative of a romanticized "other" or an essentializing of cultures into unrealistic, homogenized categories of traditional or modern.[57] Escobar describes hybridity as a synthesis whereby new cultural identities emerge in the space where "traditions have not yet left and modernity has not yet settled in."[58] In their treatment of hybridity, MacGinty and Sanghera acknowledge the complexity of "composite forms of practice, norms and thinking that emerge from the interaction of different groups, worldviews and activities," as well as the ways in which the agency of local actors subverts external interventions and constructs "alternative visions" of lived experience.[59] These perspectives open space for deeper engagement with the myriad ways in which coastal communities may respond to the presence of surf tourism.

In tourism encounters in general, and in surf tourism spaces in particular, the hybridity lens provides a means of acknowledging heterogeneity and context-specific cultural dynamics in ways that allow ample opportunity to see people and places as they are in relation to their interactions with different types and stages of tourism.[60] This approach could serve the purposes of decolonizing sustainable surf tourism by recognizing locally determined modes of engagement and allowing practitioners to support existing initiatives rather than imposing external, universalist, and therefore colonizing models out of touch with local realities.

Important to this discussion is the recognition that hybrid cultures in tourism spaces are mutually constituted and mutually constituting, and involve complex processes of subjection in cross-cultural interaction that are steeped in dynamic interplays of power and agency.[61] These processes require that SST practitioners recognize relationships of power in knowledge exchange and community engagement in tourism spaces, and adapt their interventions accordingly.[62] In other words, cross-cultural encounters do not occur in power-neutral environments, but rather carry with them the histories and processes of coercive and consensual cultural imperialism that dictate power dynamics between dominant and nondominant cultures.[63] Through decolonizing methods, including post-structuralist participatory action research, critical ethnographies, and assets-based approaches to mapping diverse community economies, strategies for surf tourism governance might reflect truly local (albeit hybrid) ideologies, world views, and cultural practices.[64] These types of decolonizing methodologies would support a discursive and practical shift from simply reproducing dominant constructs on what is considered desirable, right, good, or sustainable that result from our collective social conditioning into modernity and local subjection to the dominant Western world view.[65] Unpacking what is meant by local or participatory engagement in surf tourism space is a vital first step in any such process.[66] For example, to what extent does the surf tourism management framework in Salina Cruz, Mexico, represent a "for local, by local" approach to mitigating the social and environmental consequences of surf tourism, when considered within a decolonizing perspective on local internalizations of Western values in reproducing structural and ideological patterns of a neoliberal governmentality in local surf tourism management?[67]

Given the overwhelming dominance of Western structures and ideologies, such questions point to the persistence of "reluctant subjects."[68] These subjects represent a significant challenge for decolonizing SST, particularly where coastal communities in surf tourism destinations have internalized the values of the hegemonic "monocultural logics of scientific knowledge, linear time, hierarchical classification, global scale and capitalist productivity" in relation to Western modes of development and modernization.[69] These values may prevent them from wanting to see and be other than what the dominant social narrative tells them they ought to be. Cameron and Gibson's framework for post-structuralist participatory action research supports decolonizing processes for community engagement, promoting the development of fresh subjectivities as a useful platform for the field of SST. Working with local teams across social sectors in surf tourism destinations, this approach would include the following:

1 Documenting and acknowledging existing community representations, subjectivities, and feelings related to the current state of affairs in surf tourism and sustainability

2 Contextualizing and deconstructing the current situation vis-à-vis dominant Western constructs, while simultaneously creating space for new representations to emerge by tapping into existing skills, capacities, and assets of community members that may have been marginalized or denied by existing perceptions and self-understandings within status quo social structures

3 Community inquiry and assets-mapping to strengthen new community representations with the potential to enable new subjectivities among social actors

4 Workshops and brainstorming sessions, as opportunities to offer a forum for communities to create and implement strategies for action

on sustainability in surf tourism governance, aligned with any new representations of community and subjectivities of self that may have emerged in the previous stages of the process.[70]

The post-structuralist nature of this kind of project recognizes the interplays of power and agency in ways that would allow for transformative processes of community interaction toward shared goals in locally determined approaches to sustainability and surf tourism governance.

As a complementary contribution to decolonizing methods in surf tourism scenarios, Cameron and Gibson-Graham provide a useful, context-specific design for engaging with communities toward endogenous development alternatives.[71] Their approach emphasizes the utility of a diverse economy perspective as a basis for interacting with communities whereby SST practitioners can better understand the many interrelated processes of economic interaction in which capitalist forms of production and exchange are only a piece of the puzzle, thus opening the way for a re-evaluation of non-capitalist socioeconomic relationships. As Gibson-Graham demonstrates, building on similar work done by Ledesma, the diverse economy approach shows how the "thin veneer of capitalist economic activity" we have been programmed to recognize as the sole arbiter of economic interaction is indeed "underlain by a thick mesh of traditional practices of gifting, sharing, borrowing, volunteering, and reciprocated individual and collective work."[72] These rich and diverse economic practices are those "that have been rendered non-existent, 'non-credible alternatives to what exists' by the monoculture of capitalocentric thinking."[73] Furthermore, "they are the substance and process of what we have termed the 'community economy'—those economic practices that sustain lives and maintain well-being directly (without resort to the circuitous mechanisms of capitalist industrialization and income trickle-down), that distribute surplus to the material and cultural maintenance of community and that actively make and share a commons."[74]

The commons as described here goes beyond the "sustainable governance of common pool resources" approach to sustainable tourism by de-linking the conceptualization of the commons from a market- or property-oriented understanding of community resources to be equitably distributed and therefore equitably or sustainably exploited.[75] Instead, the diverse economy approach expands the concept of the commons away from a capitalized resource-centric model of governance toward a nuanced view on how community assets align with community well-being in post-capitalist, often non-exploitive modes of individual and collective livelihood. Stemming from that premise, and serving as an action research methodology for engaging with community economies in surf tourism spaces, the Diverse Economy Assessment builds on other assets-based approaches as a process of mapping existing economic interaction at the community level such that interventions can support the strengthening of non-capitalist modes of exchange and well-being toward locally self-determined, socially and environmentally sustainable futures.[76]

This approach offers a powerful way to shift the surf tourism-for-sustainable development narrative away from the "monotonously stylized representation of lack" characteristic of "monocultural logic"–imbued participatory community appraisal methods that tend to produce the locality as "inferior, residual, non-productive and ignorant" as their starting place for "needs-based" development interventions.[77] In contrast, the community economy approach begins with assets-mapping rather than needs-mapping, to elicit greater understanding of community members' actions and experiences with collective development, focusing on residents' capacities and "networks of flow" contributing to "resilience, identity and well-being."[78] From there, SST practitioners can offer support in bringing awareness to these assets and drawing on them to help communities strengthen and expand their diverse community economies as a foundation for strategies of sustainability and surf tourism governance. Applying this approach to the practice of surf voluntourism and surf tourism governance, for example, could have profound effects on the types of projects implemented in coastal communities, generating shifts in identities, roles, and power dynamics among local people and philanthropically minded surfers in surf tourism scenarios. The diverse economy approach thus has the potential to revolutionize the ways in which the field of SST practices and approaches surf tourism, in its ability to both unsettle a neoliberal governmentality and transform structures previously mired in Western-modern capitalocentric ideologies and institutions.

An assets map might follow the format outlined by Kretzmann and Mc-Knight and adapted by Gibson-Graham identifying three categories: business and physical infrastructure; local associations and institutions; and people and practices.[79] Following the assets-mapping process, the Diverse Economy Assessment is the follow-up step to provide a clear understanding of all of the economic relationships that exist in a community, arranged into three sets of relations: (1) "transactions of goods, services and finances," divided then into market transactions, alternative market, and nonmarket sub-categories; (2) "the performance and modes of remuneration of labour," divided into wage labor, alternative paid labor, and unpaid labor; and (3) "the production, appropriation and distribution of surplus within different kinds of enterprise," divided into capitalist, alternative capitalist, and non-capitalist enterprise.[80] Re-inserting capitalist economic activity within and among non-capitalist modes of interaction de-centers its discursive superiority and allows for the visualization of non-capitalist economy as a basis for seeing and strengthening diverse means of fostering community well-being.

These forms of community-based trends in assets-mapping and the diverse economy may prove worthwhile in re-envisioning the role for SST practitioners from one of intervention to one of support and engagement, thus strengthening post-development theory's utility in the field as a driver for socioeconomic alternatives toward sustainable, non-neoliberal futures in surf tourism scenarios. In this way, SST can support the opening of space for endogenous development experiences and social realities outside the confines of modernity's dominant monoculture, re-valuing cultural diversity in sustainability and recognizing the agency of subaltern or otherwise-marginalized communities in determining their own development paths outside the hegemonic tourism-for-development paradigm.[81] By adopting an ethics of solidarity toward a decolonizing role, SST practitioners can re-imagine their interventions as a means to "disrupt the daily performance of power relations" rather than continuing to "reproduce the world as seen by those who rule it."[82] In this way, decolonizing SST research and practice seeks to transgress colonial patterns by highlighting alternative development paradigms and self-determined representations of cultures and communities in surf tourism spaces, not to be confused with "giving voice" to the subaltern, which is neither our place nor desire.[83] Re-imagining the role for the SST researcher/practitioner, then, imbues it with a performative aspect of situated activity founded on a praxis-based ethic for constructing counter-narratives, acknowledging our interrelated subjectivities within the understanding that research and practice are never objective, but always political in their processes of construction, production and outcomes.[84]

This decolonizing role for SST practitioners requires a simultaneous openness to self-reflexivity in thought and praxis, an acknowledgment of the ways in which our values and actions stem from world views, discourses, and associated practices that may exist in opposition to, and often perpetuate, the challenges we hope our interventions might somehow remedy. This reflective willingness to see ourselves critically in relation to our beliefs and knowledge systems and to adjust our actions accordingly breeds a deep humility in honoring that experiences of right and wrong and sustainable and unsustainable are subjective, values-laden, context-specific, and cultural—in effect, unseating the centrism of our own certainties and positioning them instead as possibilities among a plethora of possible others. Viewing ourselves in this manner, as embedded within our own life ideologies and structures, themselves in constant relationship with the world's multiplicity of ways of seeing, being, knowing, and doing, we enter into a space for decolonizing our own minds as a foundation for action and interaction in acknowledgment of difference. And it is precisely this willingness to see ourselves as other, to "be and become anew," that allows us to experiment with solutions and sustainabilities in surf tourism spaces that we may have never considered before, as "thought turned toward difference readies itself for encounters with random, alternative arrangements and events emerging through the dynamic, interactive encounters of materiality."[85]

The dream of supporting ecologically sustainable lives of dignity and well-being, complemented by the drive to decolonize the systems, contexts, ideologies, and frameworks in which (sustainable) surf tourism operates, finds its ultimate integrity and deepest utility in our own willingness to turn the mirror toward ourselves as the basis for transforming our role as practitioners from one of power-over to one of power-with. The initial call to action for decolonizing sustainable surf tourism, then, requires that we as critics, academics, and practitioners "acknowledge and place on the table for discussion what we can see of our own foundations, that we negotiate in awareness of our histories, and that we be assured of our partial ignorance of the multitude of understandings of the many historical and current relations that constitute those occasions when we consider the lives of those whom we suffer the conceit of believing we are fit to serve."[86]

NOTES

1. See volume introduction.

2. Dolnicar and Fluker, "Who's Riding the Wave?"; Tom, "Surfer Exploration."

3. O'Brien and Ponting, "Sustainable Surf Tourism"; Tara Ruttenberg, "Stealing Pura Vida: Surf Tourism on Trial in Costa Rica," *The Inertia* (March 20, 2014), http://www.theinertia.com/surf/stealing-pura-vida-surf-tourism-on-trial-in-costa-rica/.

4. Buckley, "Surf Tourism . . . I," "Surf Tourism . . . II," and *Adventure Tourism*; Ponting, McDonald, and Wearing, "De-constructing Wonderland"; Ponting, "Projecting Paradise"; O'Brien and Ponting, "Sustainable Surf Tourism"; Mach, "From the Endless Summer"; LaTourrette, "Land Grab"; Walker, "El Confessor"; Ruttenberg, "Stealing Pura Vida" and "What's Sustainable about Sustainable Surf Tourism," *The Inertia* (August 11, 2014).

5. Mohanty, "Under Western Eyes," 61.

6. Barilotti, "Lost Horizons"; Canniford and Karababa, "Partly Primitive."

7. Butler, "The Concept of a Tourist Area."

8. Lazarow, "The Value of Coastal Recreational Resources"; O'Brien and Eddie, "Benchmarking Global Best Practice"; Buckley, "Surf Tourism . . . I"; Mach, "From the Endless Summer."

9. Comer, *Surfer Girls*; Ford and Brown, *Surfing and Social Theory*; Kavanagh, *Manufacturing Stoke*; Ormrod, *"Endless Summer"*; Canniford and Shankar, "Purifying Practices"; Canniford and Karababa, "Partly Primitive"; Ponting, "Projecting Paradise"; Ponting and McDonald, "Performance, Agency, and Change"; Ponting and O'Brien, "Liberalizing Nirvana"; Mach, "From the Endless Summer"; Tom, "Surfer Exploration"; Barilotti, "Lost Horizons"; Buckley, "Surf Tourism . . . I"; Hugues Dit Ciles, "Sustainability of Surfing Tourism."

10. Harvey, *Neoliberalism*; Foucault, *The Birth of Biopolitics*; Ruuska, "Ideological Transformation"; Ruttenberg, "Economic and Social Policy."

11. Here we refer to Foucault's framing of "neoliberal governmentality" as a hegemonic discourse and "art of governance" determining ideology, associated structures, and socialized patterns of behavior aligned with the tenets of neoliberalism, the overwhelming power-through-hegemony of which allows it to be perceived as normal and therefore all but unseen (*The Birth of Biopolitics*).

12. Fletcher, "Neoliberal Environmentality" and "Using the Master's Tools?"; Harvey, *Neoliberalism*.

13. This perspective builds on Martin and Assenov's review on trends in the field of SST, which highlights that most SST researchers suggest direct policy approaches geared toward the sustainable management of surf resources ("The Genesis")

14. Borne and Ponting, *Sustainable Stoke*; UNWCED, *Our Common Future*.

15. Ruttenberg, "Wellbeing Economics."

16. Harvey, *Neoliberalism*; Escobar, "Construction Nature"; Ruttenberg, "Wellbeing Economics"; Fletcher, "Neoliberal Environmentality" and "Using the Master's Tools?"

17. Borne and Ponting, *Sustainable Stoke*.

18. The example of the Surfing Association of Papua New Guinea (SAPNG) is provided as a flagship model for sustainable surf tourism, satisfying the sustainability criteria described here, and seen as a successful surf tourism management approach to the sustainable governance of "common pool resources." See Mach, "From the Endless Summer"; Ponting and O'Brien, "Liberalizing Nirvana."

19. Examples include WAVES for Development in Lobitos, Peru; Give and Surf in Bocas del Toro, Panama; Project Wave of Optimism in Gigante, Nicaragua; and Kwepunha Retreat in Robertsport, Liberia. Similarly, the foundation SurfAID raises funds to provide monetary assistance to support projects in health, "positive change," and development in the coastal communities of select islands in Indonesia (surfaidinternational.org).

20. O'Brien and Eddie, "Benchmarking Global."

21. Global Sustainable Tourism Council, "Global Sustainable Tourism Criteria," 2012, http://www.gstcouncil.org/en/gstc-criteria-hotels-tour-operators-destinations/criteria-for-hotels-tour-operators-industry.html.

22. See STOKE Certified website, http://www.stokecertified.com/.

23. STOKE newsletter, June 11, 2015.

24. Mach, "From the Endless Summer."

25. Martin and Assenov, "Developing a Surf Resource"; O'Brien and Eddie, "Benchmarking Global."

26. Fletcher, "Sustaining Tourism"; Mowforth and Munt, *Tourism and Sustainability*.

27. See Groundswell Education Travel on the World Minded website: http://worldminded .com/groundswell-education-travel/.

28. Sea State website, http://theseastate.com/.

29. As an avenue for future research, critical studies might interrogate whether educational surf travel programs contribute to nuanced perspectives and decolonizing practices in SST, or simply create a fresh batch of concerned "global citizens" perpetuating a neocolonial vision on sustainability in surf tourism and development.

30. See, for example, Gregory Thomas, "Surfonomics Quantifies the Worth of Waves," *The Washington Post*, August 24, 2012; Lazarow, "Coastal Recreational Resources," "Using Observed Market Expenditure," and *The Value of Coastal Recreation*.

31. See Save the Waves Coalition website, http://www.savethewaves.org/.

32. Save the Waves Coalition website, http://www.savethewaves.org/.

33. Fletcher, "Between the Cattle," 80.

34. Fletcher, "Between the Cattle," 70.

35. Fletcher, "Between the Cattle," 80; McShane et al., "Hard Choices," 970.

36. Fletcher, "Between the Cattle."

37. Fletcher, "Sustaining Tourism."

38. The conceptual treatment of the field of post-development offered here draws on the seminal work of Arturo Escobar, Wolfgang Sachs, Ivan Illich, Gustavo Esteva, Constantino, Nandy, Kothari, Rist, Lind, Matthews, Nusted, Rapley, Ziai, J. K. Gibson-Graham, Rob Fletcher, Ahorro, COMPAS, and Maiava, among others.

39. Sachs, "Preface"; Ahorro, *The Waves;* Gibson-Graham, "Surplus Possibilities."

40. Harvey, *Neoliberalism.*

41. Sachs, "Preface"; Escobar, *Encountering Development.*

42. Sachs, "Preface," xvii.

43. Fletcher, *Romancing the Wild*; Said, *Orientalism*; Santos, "The WSF"; Gibson-Graham, "Surplus Possibilities."

44. Escobar, *Encountering Development*; Santos, "The WSF"; Gibson-Graham, "Surplus Possibilities."

45. Gibson-Graham, "Surplus Possibilities," 411.

46. Maiava, "When Is Development Not Development?"

47. Gibson-Graham, "Surplus Possibilities"; Maiava, "When Is Development Not Development?"

48. COMPAS 2007; Maiava, "When Is Development Not Development?"; Ahorro, *The Waves.*

49. Maiava, "When Is Development Not Development?"

50. Hopwood et al., "Sustainable Development." See also Christie and Warburton, *From Here to Sustainability.*

51. O'Connor, "Capitalism, Nature" and "Uneven and Combined"; Escobar, "Construction Nature"; Fletcher, "Using the Master's Tools?"

52. Hopwood et al., "Sustainable Development."

53. Daly, "Sustainable Growth"; Grossman and Krueger, "Economic Growth"; O'Connor, "Capitalism, Nature"; Visvanathan, "Mrs. Bruntland"; Escobar, "Construction Nature"; Fletcher, "Using the Master's Tools?"

54. Escobar, "Construction Nature."

55. Escobar, "Construction Nature."

56. Escobar, *Encountering Development*; MacGinty and Sanghera, "Hybridity in Peacebuilding"; Guerrón-Montero, "Tourism and Afro-Antillean"; Cameron and Gibson, "Participatory Action Research"; Van Veldhuizen and COMPAS, *Learning Endogenous Development*.

57. Canniford and Shankar, "Purifying Practices"; Canniford and Karababa, "Partly Primitive."

58. Escobar, *Encountering Development*.

59. MacGinty and Sanghera, "Hybridity in Peacebuilding," 3.

60. Guerrón-Montero, "Tourism and Afro-Antillean."

61. Woodward, Dixon, and Jones, "Poststructuralism"; Gibson-Graham, *A Postcapitalist Politics*.

62. Buckley and Ollenburg, "Tacit Knowledge Transfer."

63. Said, *Culture and Imperialism*; Lindner, *A Dignity Economy*.

64. Cameron and Gibson, "Participatory Action Research"; Canniford, "Moving Shadows"; Gibson-Graham, "Surplus Possibilities"; Cameron, "Collaborating with Communities."

65. Smith, *Decolonizing Methodologies*.

66. Esteva, "Development."

67. Mike Cianciulli, "Southern Oaxaca: Update," April 19, 2012, http://www.surfline.com/surf-news/southern-oaxaca-update_69344/; "Salina Cruz Surfers & Lifeguarding Association—Discuss," April 22, 2012, http://www.boardroomshow.com/salina-cruz-surfers-lifeguarding-association-discuss/. See Zavalza Hough-Snee and Sotelo Eastman in this volume.

68. Gibson-Graham, *A Postcapitalist Politics*.

69. Gibson-Graham, "Surplus Possibilities," referencing Santos, "The WSF."

70. Cameron and Gibson, "Participatory Action Research."

71. Cameron, "Collaborating with Communities"; Gibson-Graham, "Surplus Possibilities."

72. Gibson-Graham, "Surplus Possibilities," 16; Ledesma, *Landless Workers*.

73. Santos, "The WSF," 238.

74. Gibson-Graham, "Surplus Possibilities," 16.

75. Ostrom, *Governing the Commons*; Agrawal, "Sustainable Governance" and "Common Property Institutions"; Briassoulis, "Sustainable Tourism"; Healy, "The Common Pool"; Holden, "Achieving a Sustainable Relationship"; Ponting and O'Brien, "Liberalizing Nirvana"; Mach, "From the Endless Summer."

76. Kretzmann and McKnight, *Building Communities*.

77. Gibson-Graham, "Surplus Possibilities," 10–11. See also Esteva, "Development."

78. Gibson-Graham, "Surplus Possibilities," 12.

79. Kretzmann and McKnight, *Building Communities*; Gibson-Graham, "Surplus Possibilities," 11.

80. Gibson-Graham, "Surplus Possibilities," 12.

81. Van Veldhuizen and COMPAS, *Learning Endogenous Development*; Santos, "The WSF."

82. Pensky, *Ends of Solidarity*; Woodward, Dixon, and Jones, "Poststructuralism"; Escobar, *Encountering Development*.

83. Spivak, "Can the Subaltern Speak?"

84. Denzin, Lincoln, and Smith, *Handbook*; Said, *Orientalism* and *Culture and Imperialism*; Foucault, *Truth and Power*; Wallace, "Grassroots Community-Based Peacebuilding."

85. Gibson-Graham, *A Postcapitalist Politics*; Woodward, Dixon, and Jones, "Poststructuralism," 402.

86. Tamas, "Misrecognitions and Missed Opportunities."

Part II / Race, Ethnicity, and Identity

6 / Surfing beyond Racial and Colonial Imperatives in Early Modern Atlantic Africa and Oceania

KEVIN DAWSON

Our story begins off the Island of Hawai'i in Kealakekua Bay. Here, on January 22, 1779, surgeon's mate David Samwell wrote an early account of surfing that captured Western apprehensions of water and other people's—water people's—affinity for gliding through liquid infinities, penning, "these People find one of their Chief amusements in that which to us presented nothing but Horror & Destruction, and we saw with astonishment young boys and Girls about 9 or ten years of age playing amid such tempestuous Waves that the hardiest of our seamen would have trembled to face." The sailors "looked upon this as no other than certain death." Conveying Western land-oriented beliefs that water was an unnatural element, Samwell revealed how whites misconstrued Hawaiian aquatic valuations, categorizing surfing as mere "amusement" and swimming a life-threatening pursuit. The playground of Hawaiian youth remained a place of "Horror & Destruction" for white men who just spent three years at sea.[1]

Societies carve diverging cultural identities from their interactions with and historicization of the same ocean, as Samwell illustrates. Westerners are terracentric, treating waterways as cultureless ahistorical voids. For more than a millennium there has been a concerted effort to suppress the sea. Science explains that human existence began after our common ancestor slithered ashore. Historical narratives begin ashore, sometimes using transoceanic voyages to frame accounts of explorers, pilgrims, priests, conquistadors, colonists, and slaves. Scripture tell us humanity began in the Garden of Eden.[2] The ocean symbolized the unfinished chaos predating civilization, a metaphor for God's vengeance. It was the "realm of Satan," an "abode of monsters stirred up by diabolical powers," while stories of the Great Flood and drowning of pharaoh's army depicted water as an "instrument of punishment." Swimming was equated with eternal damnation, with sinners compared to "a shipwrecked swimmer" who "is tumbled about in the depth of the sea, so the ungodly, being shipwrecked from salvation, are tumbled about in the abyss of Gehenna," or "hell."[3]

Scholars encapsulate societies into binary reductive spheres, assuming individuals were landspeople or mariners, farmers or fishermen—not both. Most conclude that cultural creation was land-bound. Many early modern Africans and Oceanians were fishing farmers and farming fishermen. Weaving terrestrial and maritime experiences into amphibious lives, they equally incorporated water and land into their lives in ways that scholars have largely overlooked.[4]

Situating water at the confluence of its analysis, this chapter considers how Atlantic Africans and Oceanians from the seventeenth into the early twentieth century treated waterscapes as social, cultural, spiritual, and political spaces despite the onslaughts of Christianity and colonialism. Africans and Oceanians merged water and land into unified culturescapes, forging discrete yet similar communities of practice and meaning.[5] Immersionary cultures required people to become strong swimmers. Many Oceanians and Africans employed aquatics as passages to honor, masculinity, and femininity. Water was a natural place for culture, pleasure, and spirituality.

Conversely, white people formed negative connotations of aquatics, deploying them to support claims of racial and cultural superiority and colonial designs. Even as Western powers colonized tropical landmasses, and blue water navies projected imperial might across oceans, perceptions of aquatics and seminude bodies precluded the annexation of "coastscapes" (the area bounded by surf and seashores' inland reaches) before World War I. Coastscapes could not be colonized without adopting dark-complexioned water people's traditions and affirmative perceptions of seminudity.[6] Cultural differences obviously existed within and between Atlantic Africa and Oceania. Still, similarities, especially when compared to Western valuations, allow us to deliberate the cultural process from the vantage point of surfboards rather than from shore or tall-sided Western ships.

Travelogues, ship records, newspaper accounts, and Oceanian oral traditions document surf cultures. Unfortunately, no known African-authored sources exist. Although white authors richly related practices, racism tainted their interpretations, portraying activities they admired as uncivilized. Authors averred that Africans and Oceanians underused their bodies and land. Hence, quixotic surfing accounts insidiously promoted the sexual pleasures and profits that could be extracted from colonized dark-complexioned bodies and tropical places while decrying perceived indecencies.

Water covers some 70 percent of Earth. Most people live near water. Atlantic history seems ideally suited for considering aquatic cultures as it examines trans-Atlantic connections to dispute traditional national and imperial methods of historical organizing.[7] Even as most scholarship focuses on waterside communities, we marginalize the Atlantic, pushing it to our parched intellectual peripheries.[8]

Oceanian paradigms can enhance Atlanticists' analysis of waterscapes. Stressing that previous studies misconstrued the Pacific by assuming Oceanians were sea-locked peoples stranded on islands, Oceanian scholars borrowed concepts of cultural geography from scholar-activists writing in the wake of African independence who forged broad integrative frameworks to correct the historiographic fragmentation that shattered Atlantic Africa into "a historical jigsaw puzzle." Epeli Hau'ofa charted Oceania, rejecting the "belittling" tendency of "continental" scholars who shrank this expanse by focusing on dry spaces and how Europeans carved it into Polynesia, Micronesia, and Melanesia. Water did not confine Oceanians, nor was it a liquid void; it was a broader existence in which islands and seas formed a seamless culturescape, a "sea of islands." "Oceania" signifies the region's vastness and human connections to the sea. While this sea of islands "would suffer a colonial tsunami," it did, as Nicholas Thomas stressed, "remain an Islanders' world."[9]

Social and Cultural Meanings of Aquatics

Water people accommodated themselves to marine environments, weaving spiritual and secular beliefs, economies, social structures, political institutions—their very way of life—around relationships with water. Immersionary cultures valued swimming as a life skill capable of extending fortunes, saving lives, and obtaining honor. Parents inculcated this ability into children at a young age, transforming dangerous waters into safe play spaces.

Atlantic Africans were taught how to swim after learning to walk, between ten and fourteen months of age, or after weaned at approximately two to three years of age. After "children begin to walk," they "go to the water in order to learn how to swim," wrote Pieter de Marees. William Bosman commented, "the Mother gives the Infant suck for two or three Years," then go "to the Sea-side to learn to swim."[10]

Oceanians learned when equally young. "Most" Tahitians "learn to swim as soon as walk." They "lose all dread of it [water] before they are old enough to know the danger to which" Europeans "should consider them exposed." Hawaiians were "taken into the sea by their mothers the second or third day after birth, and many . . . can swim as soon as they can walk." Most became proficient surfers by the age of "seven or eight."[11]

Africans and Oceanians developed the crawl, concluding that its alternate overarm stroke and fast scissor-kicks, which make it the strongest and swiftest style, was the proper method. Virtually every traveler was amazed by African fluencies. Dutchman Pieter de Marees described Gold Coast Africans' crawl during the 1590s, writing, "They can swim very fast, generally easily outdoing people of our nation in swimming and diving."[12] Oceanians were equally impressive. At Honolulu "men and boys" leaped and dove from ships' yards, swimming "under their bottoms" to "reappear on the other side."[13]

Westerners were enthralled, as they nearly abandoned swimming during the Medieval period. Those who swam used variants of the breaststroke akin to the dog paddle. They regarded the breaststroke as the "sophisticated" white method of swimming, deeming the crawl "savage," as it generated considerable splashing.[14]

Aquatic youth transformed coastscapes into playgrounds. At Elmina (Ghana), Jean Barbot watched "several hundred . . . boys and girls sporting together before the beach, and in many places among the rolling and breaking waves, learning to swim."[15] Oceanians equally enjoyed these spaces. As King David Kalākaua explained, coastscapes were the nucleus of Hawaiian culture, where the gods went to "taste of mortal enjoyments." Oʻahu, or "the gathering place," has long been the heart of the surfing world. Oceania's "Garden of Eden" lay in the waters of Waikīkī, a surf mecca affording mile-long waves, while its North Shore was the "spawner of big steep waves." Beaches were places for remembering. Duke Kahanamoku (1890–1968) captured the milieu, remembering how surfers gathered "at a *hau* tree on Waikiki Beach and discuss[ed] boards, waves, the delights of surfing, and the latest thing in experiments. It was a poor man's club, but it was made up of dedicated surfers."[16]

In some ways, surf zones were liminal culturescapes between insinuating shoreside missionaries and colonists and the open ocean, where shipmasters wielded absolute authority. As historian Isaiah Helekunihi Walker explained, Kānaka Maolis (Native Hawaiians) conceptualized this space, calling it *ka po'ina nalu*. Children learned to surf small waves close to shore. Experts paddled several hundred yards out to larger surf thundering on outer reefs. Jack London observed that Waikīkī's shallows were "the kindergarten where the little Kanaka boys were at play," the "deep water [was] where the big smokers came rolling in." Mark Twain similarly noted that Waikīkī's playground, located "three or four hundred yards out to sea," was where Hawaiians "of both sexes and all ages" pursued "the national pastime surf-bathing."[17]

Play is a liberating pursuit, allowing humans to escape time and place while bonding. Children favor play spaces affording adventure, creativity, and at least illusions of danger. Coastscapes provided Oceanians and Africans with these criteria. Girls and boys pretended to be sharks or crocodiles pursuing playmates. Leaping over and ducking under crashing surf, they learned the physics of breakers.[18]

Play allowed youth to absorb societal values, develop social and conversational abilities, and craft individual and group cohesion. People visited waterscapes almost daily to rejuvenate body and soul while enjoying the community spirit of surfing. Camaraderie was cultivated in Tahitian surf zones, with "fifty to a hundred persons, of all ages sporting like porpoises in the surf . . . cheering and animating each other." The communal thrill of Hawaiian surfing was "heightened by the shouts and laughter" as people shared waves, perpetuating childhood joys into adulthood.[19]

Scholars generally believe the first account of surfing was written in Hawai'i in 1778. They are only 140 years too late, and some ten thousand miles off the mark. The first account was written during the 1640s in what is now Ghana. (Oceanian oral traditions are older still.) Surfing was independently invented throughout Atlantic Africa and Oceania. African surfing developed in Senegal, the Ivory Coast, Liberia, Ghana, Cameroon, and West-Central Africa. Like Oceania, Africa possesses thousands of miles of warm, surf-filled waters and populations of seagoing fishermen and canoemen who knew the surf patterns. Traditionally one surfed in a prone, kneeling, sitting, or standing position, and in one-person canoes.[20]

Surfing takes years to master, and thus gauges societal understandings of waterscapes, aquatics, hydrography (the marine geography, including the effects of tides, winds, and currents), and hydrodynamics (physics concerned with the motion of fluids and forces acting on solid bodies immersed in and in motion relative to fluids). It was only developed by societies with deep aquatic roots and powerful swimmers, as London learned. "The man who wants to learn surf-riding must be a strong swimmer, and he must be used to going under the water," as far more time is spent paddling than surfing, and one must match a wave's speed to catch it. Surfing is more than an individual accomplishment; it is the expression of generational wisdom.[21]

Several factors restrict our understanding of surfing. Europeans traversed Oceania for centuries before documenting surfing. Few whites attempted to surf prior to the twentieth century, when London romanticized the Hawaiian surfer as a masculine, muscular, "black" and later "brown Mercury," whose "heels are winged, and in them the swiftness of the sea."[22] Surfing scholarship focuses on post–World War II circumstances, overlooking how subtleties in surfboard designs and surfing techniques reflected early modern hydrographic and hydrodynamic understandings. Surfing, especially in Hawai'i, was more developed than previously assumed.[23]

Few early modern descriptions of African surfing were transcribed. Michael Hemmersam provided the first known African account. Believing he was watching Gold Coast children learn to swim, he wrote, "[Parents] tie their children to boards and throw them into the water." Swimming was not taught in this manner, as such lessons would have resulted in many drowned children. Atlantic Africans learned to swim as toddlers, and surely with more positive reinforcement.[24]

Later accounts are unambiguous. In 1834, while at Accra, James Alexander wrote: "From the beach, meanwhile, might be seen boys swimming into the sea, with light boards under their stomachs. They waited for a surf; and came rolling like a cloud on top of it. But I was told that sharks occasionally dart in behind the rocks and 'yam' them."[25] In 1861, Thomas Hutchinson observed surfing in southern Cameroon. Fishermen rode surfboard-size canoes "six feet in length, fourteen to sixteen inches in width, and from four to six inches in depth" and "made of light wood." Describing how work turned to play, Hutchinson penned:

> I observed that from the more serious and industrial occupation of fishing they would turn to racing on the tops of the surging billows which broke on the sea shore; at one spot more particularly, which, owing to the presence of an extensive reef, seemed to be the very place for a continuous swell of several hundred yards in length. Four or six of them go out steadily, dodging the rollers as they come on, and mounting atop of

them with the nimbleness and security of ducks. Reaching the outermost roller, they turn the canoes stems shoreward with a single stroke of the paddle, and mounted on the top of the wave, they are borne towards the shore, steering with the paddle alone. . . . They come, carried along with all its impetuous rapidity. . . .

It sometimes happens that a prowling shark, tempted to pursue the fish which the fisherman is hauling on the line, comes within sight of the larger bait of the negro leg and chops it off without remorse. . . . But this did not diminish the number of canoes riding waves, nor render one of the canoe occupants less energetic or daring than before.[26]

African surfboards seemingly resembled Hawaiian *alaia*. Alaia are round-nosed, square-tailed surfboards about one to three inches thick, eighteen inches wide, and three to seven feet long. *The Endless Summer* (1966) illustrates Ghanaians' use of alaia-like boards. Filmmaker Bruce Brown followed two Americans on a global surf trip. Jones assumed they introduced surfing to Africa, proclaiming it the "start of bellyboard surfing in Ghana." This was not the start of surfing, but rather a display of old traditions. Indeed, several kids had round-nosed body boards, while their surfing fluencies indicate that they were not neophytes.[27]

Westerners perceived surfing as people's attempt to conquer nature. Jack London described waves as "bull-mouthed monsters," and surfing was, for him, to "wrestle with the sea." Herman Melville equated surfing to a battle in which "billow battalions" of waves "burst like bombs," and intrepid surfers risked being "run over by the steed they ride."[28]

Water people knew better: they knew surfing as a synchronized, sublime, liquid "dance." Hawaiian Gerry Lopez captured surfing's sensory ecstasies, saying, "[I]t's probably as close as humans can get to being able to fly like a bird . . . it's a sense of freedom. . . . It is much more than physical and mental; there must be some spiritual stimulation that we may not be aware of." London eventually learned it was not "surf-fighting," but the art of "non-resistance," requiring surfers to "never be rigid. Relax." Flow with "waters that are now tearing at you."[29]

Aquatics have long been a way for men and women to attain honor and convert themselves into heroes, as illustrated in art, literature, and oral traditions.[30] Scholars argue that concepts of honor largely motivated African behavior, as societies devised cultures valuing heroic honor that stressed prowess, brawn, courage, and bravery. John Iliffe proposed a minimalist definition of honor, "stripped of cultural specificity and designed for cross-cultural comparison," characterizing honor as "a right to respect." Notions of honor varied, yet in most societies masculine honor pivoted on bravery, courage, strength, expertise, and prestige.[31] Scholars contend similar concepts of manhood were imposed upon males across cultural boundaries, allowing for cross-cultural understandings.[32]

Hawai'i provides opportunities for considering how honor and masculinity were braided into surfing, or *he'e nalu*. Hawaiian surfing was situated at the vortex of the social, cultural, religious, and political life. "This art," explained John Papa 'Ī'ī, "was held in high esteem" and there were "rules to be observed." Surfing became a metaphor for brawn, expertise, sex, and courage. Strength was, as Ty P. Kāwika Tengan explained, "gendered as *masculine* and coupled with authenticity, by men and women," who surfed to display control. Surfboard makers followed sacred rituals, while surfboards were icons infused with spiritual meaning and "held in high estimation." Urban areas were often situated near prime breaks.[33] The *ali'i*, or hereditary chiefly aristocracy, were the most dedicated, staking reputations on wave-riding expertise, which were extolled in *mele*, or chants. While ashore, ali'i did not carry their own surfboards, and when waves were exceptional, they surfed "from sunrise to sunset, taking [their] meals of poi during the day without ever coming ashore." Commoners and lower nobles could be executed for dishonoring chieftesses or chiefs by catching waves they rode, allowing their boards to strike one of higher status, or riding *olo*, a design reserved for *ali'i*.[34]

Surfing remained a communal pursuit, "practiced equally by king, chief and commoner," allowing *wāhines* (Hawaiian and Māori for women), men, and children of every social status to enhance their prestige. Women surfed as "dexterously as the men," and histories and legends indicate that "empowered women" routinely "defeated" male surfers. Kelea, a Māui princess, illustrates how women harnessed concepts of masculine bravery to exercise control over their lives and gain honor. She was "the most graceful and daring surf-swimmer." When the waves were big, "Kelea, laughing at the fears of her brother, would plunge into the sea with her *onini*, or surf-board, and so *audaciously* ride the waves that those who watched and applauded her were half-inclined to believe that she was the friend of some water-god, and could not be drowned." At O'ahu she beat "all the chiefs at surf-riding."[35]

Oceanians and Africans used surfing to enhance their prestige in other ways. Paddling into shark-filled waters demonstrated honor and masculinity, while allowing youth to claim manhood. Males probably did not abstain from surfing when sharks were present lest they be ridiculed as effeminate or boys. Surfers' status was elevated when they battled sharks. Africans also engaged in ritualized blood sport when fighting sharks, crocodiles, and hippopotamuses, as did Oceanians when battling sharks.[36]

Likewise, the "larger the waves, in their opinion the better the sport," providing optimal opportunities for glory as community members surfed together in conditions that could impose injury or death. Villages were abandoned as residents surfed or gathered on the beach to watch experts. As Kahéle and Charles Stoddard walked down Méha Valley, Oʻahu, they passed through a semi-deserted village. Kahéle knowingly "kept an eye on the reef," informing Stoddard of the good surf. He gracefully demonstrated "prowess" upon a borrowed surfboard. Patient surfers waited for "a heavy wave" as illustrated when, according to Hawaiian oral history, Hauailiki selected waves to impress Laieikawai, his would-be love.[37]

Surfing was also a "courting tool" that, coupled with males' and females' wet, muscular bodies, captured the attention of would-be suitors. If Hawaiian men and women rode the same wave, "custom allowed certain intimacies when they returned ashore."[38] Surfing simultaneously enabled wāhines to exercise control over their selection of sexual partners and spouses. The aforementioned Maui princess Kelea used surfing, which sculpted her "shapely limbs and shoulders," to escape an unhappy marriage and obtain the desired husband, Kalamakua.[39]

Surfing allowed a person to test him- or herself. It was a performance ritual evoking praise and criticism from surfers and shoreside observers. Spectacular wipeouts while pushing boundaries were applauded. Smaller spills and "the temporary loss of" surfboards evoked "the laughter of the rest of the swimmers as well as the spectators on shore."[40] Within frameworks where male and female strength were gendered, cowardice was ridiculed. Not surfing large waves or when sharks were present and frequent falling illustrated an emasculating lack of control.[41]

Hawaiians' *alaias* and *papa hé nárus* (wave sliding-boards) harnessed the sea's energy. Stained "black, and preserved with great care," papa hé nárus were "five or six feet long, and rather more than a foot wide," and the bottom was slightly concave. This concave feature demonstrated an understanding of hydrodynamics; it allowed the surfboard's rails to cup the wave's face, permitting surfers to ride parallel across breakers rather than slide sideways to the bottom, so "those who are expert" stayed in the curl to get barreled. Alaias equally enabled "skilled surfers" to glide across a steep wave "as it begins to curl over," engulfing themselves in tubes of liquid light. "The greatest difficulty, and therein the chief merit of the performance, consists in keeping upon the steepest part of the rolling sea, which brings the swimmer so near its foam, that he is sometimes lying in almost a perpendicular position." As large barrels collapsed, they ejected a gush of air and spray, called "spit," blowing surfers out of their open mouths. Those who emerged earned considerable respect, as Melville documented. "At last all is lost in scud and vapor, as the overgrown billow bursts like a bomb. Adroitly emerging, the swimmers thread their way out." Experts also struck stylistic poses, changing "position on the board, sometimes sitting and sometimes standing erect in the midst of the foam," to articulate elegance, virtuosity, poise, and control. Lopez reflected traditional valuations, explaining the serenity of accomplished tube riders "standing calmly in the center of a terrifying explosion of ocean," where "the man and water join energies to become a single force of non-commercial almost religious union."[42]

Africans and Oceanians were also versed in riding waves in surf-canoes and outrigger canoes, respectively. Since Atlantic Africa possesses few natural harbors, and "Uncle Sam's boats are not built" for passing through surf, white voyagers hired surf-canoemen to convey them between ship and shore, with surf-canoeing becoming an exotic thrill for nonswimming whites. Horatio Bridge's exaggerated account of Cape Coast, Ghana, captured the excitement of surfing waves he inflated to "fifty feet in height," saying: "There is a peculiar enjoyment in being raised, by an irresistible power beneath you, ... upon the high rollers, and then dropped into the hollow of the waves, as if to visit the bottom of the ocean, at whatever depth it might be." Some surf-canoes were modified to enhance passengers' pleasures by attaching a "seat" to "the bow."[43]

Contested Bodies and Spaces

Scholars explain that post-annexation (1898) Hawaiians planted the "roots of global surf culture" before considering how surfboards became imperial implements. Scott Laderman provocatively explained how America, Australia, South Africa, Britain, and France used surf tourism to fabricate "empire[s] in waves" throughout the world. Isaiah Helekunihi Walker documented how Hawaiians challenged these incursions. Both illustrate that twentieth-century coastscapes were embattled political spaces. Prior to about 1910, white people were conspicuously absent from and unprepared to colonize surf zones. The lack of drugs to treat malaria precluded African colonization before the 1870s. Likewise, aquatic inability and insufficient sunscreens prevented the appropriation of coastscapes and dark-complexioned wet bodies.[44] Coastscapes did not favor pale skin, as the "insidious, deceitful sun" diminished the thrill of surfing, rendering "sunburned," blistered, "skin-peeling" bodies incapacitated for days.[45] Surfing compelled attitudinal shifts in what white bodies should look like. The development of commercial sunscreens in the 1920s and acceptability of tanning during the 1930s allowed whites to don "blackface," or, more precisely, dark-complexioned bodies.[46]

Surfing helped sculpt Oceanian and African bodies into portraits of masculinity and femininity as societies in both regions honored strength and agility. Dark, wet, glistening, semi-nude, muscular bodies enunciated skill, strength, and endurance. Africans did not stigmatize nudity, believing their bodies were beautiful gifts from their creator that should be proudly exhibited. Shaka, ruler of the Zulu, expressed as much, saying, "the first forefathers of the Europeans had bestowed on [them] many gifts," yet withheld "the greatest of all gifts, such as a good black skin, for this does not necessitate the wearing of clothes to hide the white skin, which was not pleasant to the eye."[47] Oceanians held similar beliefs that cut across traditional Western valuations, and early twentieth-century Hawaiian surfers proudly flexed during stylistic poses so photographers could capture their masculinity.[48]

The unclothed bodies of Oceanian surfers became spectacles of exploitation as tourism, sex tourism, and colonialism conspired to extend Western influence. Shortly after annexation, Jack London employed surfing and Hawaiian bodies to promote tourism. In racist prose, he described Hawaiian great George Freeth (1883–1919) as "carelessly poised, a young god bronzed with sunburn" and unrealistically promised white men "what that Kanaka can do, you can do yourself." Simultaneously, he allowed white women to lust "vicariously over the strength and speed of a bronzed man."[49]

Descriptions equally alerted white men to Oceanians' acceptance of same-sex relationships, inviting them to "Chum with a Savage." Travelogues provided armchair travelers with the sights, sounds, smells, tastes, textures, and real and imagined sexual pleasures of the tropics. In 1873, Charles Stoddard extolled male Hawaiian surfers as "agile, narrow-hipped youth, with tremendous biceps and proud, impudent heads set on broad shoulders, like young gods." Stoddard obscured his homoerotic miscegenation, illegal and taboo in America, behind a satirical veil while casting "friendships" with Oceanian males as civilizing missions. He described his sexual partner, Kahéle, whose "biceps" were sculpted by surfing, as "the most promising specimen of the reorganized barbarians."[50] Kahéle eventually rejected attempts to "civilize" his body, yet descriptions of athletic male and female surfers remained a siren call, beckoning white men and women to tropical coastscapes where annexation did not adhere to grand narratives written from above.

Ashore, white men subjugated black and brown bodies, while prohibiting dark-complexioned males from touching white women lest they impassion "alien cultural longings." On the American mainland, an "accidental [black] touch might be transformed in white minds into sexual violence." Yet surf zones allowed Hawaiian men to enjoy white women's bodies. Seminude Hawaiian men, often called "black" and subjected to continental Jim Crow racism, embraced white women, whose form-fitting swimsuits were illegal on the mainland. Paddling out, a woman lay on the front of a surfboard while an instructor lay between her spread legs, his arms extending over her thighs, his face a few inches above her buttocks. While tandem surfing, men held women's hips or torsos and cupped them in their arms. Sharing the pleasures of the surf, Hawaiians enjoyed "intimacies" with these women ashore. Many married white women; others were biracial—both illustrating how Hawaiians ignored colonial imperatives. Understandings of American standards undoubtedly accentuated taboo desires.[51]

Late nineteenth-century and early twentieth-century whites applauded water people's expertise while racializing them to conform to white racial/social hierarchies. Many believed Oceanian and African aquatics displayed "all the eager action and muscular power of savages" who formed "*a link in creation, connecting man to the brute*," while missionaries decried surfing as "pagan sport." Missionary William Ellis spent six years in Oceania before arriving at Hawai'i in 1822, where he rejoiced that Christianity stripped the Sabbath of its traditional sounds. "No athletic sports were seen on the beach; no noise of playful children, shouting as they gambol'd in the surf. . . . It could not but be viewed as the dawn of a bright sabbatic day for the dark shores of Hawaii."[52]

Hawaiian surfing was routinely depicted as savage pageantry, permitting whites to gaze upon the "sport of kings"—albeit uncivilized kings—while justifying Hawaiian annexation.[53] In a 1913 newspaper article, Jim Nasium lauded Duke Kahanamoku's swimming prowess while racializing Hawaiians. Claiming the "South Sea islander" ashore was an "indolent, shiftless being," in the "shark-infested waters of his native islands he apparently realizes for the first time what his hands and feet are hitched onto his body for, and he is all action and exhibits a skill that is little less than marvelous." Hawaiians were "brown skinned hydro-men," distinct from the urbane white man who "kept his feet incased in patent leather shoes." Aquatic prowess sprang from innate tropical abilities. Even as Kahanamoku became a national hero, winning gold and silver at the 1912 Olympics and being proclaimed "the greatest swimmer the world of sport has ever seen," white people believed his dominance arose from instinct, as "bodily contact with the waves" permitted him to break records in a "leisurely manner" unattainable by "civilized" whites.[54]

Water became a stage for watching uncivilized sports akin to the late nineteenth-century and early twentieth-century ethnological shows.[55] Ethnic, racial, and regional distinctions were ignored as Africans, Oceanians, Aboriginal Australians, and Filipinos were subsumed into a new murky race of "frizzy-haired . . . tropical savages," indifferently known as "Pacific negroes," "Kanakas," or just "niggers." Ultimately, their land and labor were stolen.[56]

Despite Christian and colonial incursions, the equilibrium of the sea prevailed. Coastscapes remained indigenous culturescapes. Spaces too dangerous for white men were places of play, learning, and memory for Africans and Oceanians. Inexperience precluded whites from challenging perceived racial inferiors. They were outlanders who never entered African waters to surf or fight crocodiles, sharks, or hippopotamuses, and marginalized themselves on Oceanian shores for over one hundred years before attempting to surf. In 1769 Joseph Banks marveled at "ten or twelve" Tahitian boys riding surf "impossible for any European boat to have lived in it; and if the best swimmer in Europe had, by any accident, been exposed to its fury, I am confident that he would not have been able to preserve himself." In 1872, Mark Twain conceded: "None but the natives ever master the art of surf-bathing."[57]

It is perhaps superbly ironic that modern white people eventually learned to swim like Africans and Oceanians. In 1898, the stroke that water people used for centuries was appropriated and renamed. Richmond Calvin was credited for inventing the "Australian crawl," which he learned from Alick Wickham, a Solomon Islander.[58] Surfing became Hawaiians' gift to the world when George Freeth, Duke Kahanamoku, Kahanamoku's brothers, and other Hawaiians inspired white people to strip down to bikinis and board shorts to indulge in water peoples' long-celebrated beach cultures. By the 1920s, whites viewed themselves as coastscapes' rightful heirs while indigenous bodies facilitated exotic pleasures. Using "ceremonies of possession," like segregation, "beach apartheid," and a "tyranny of blondness," they forged "empires in waves," pilfering Hawaiian, North American, Australian, and South African coastscapes before embarking on "surfaris" to "discover" tropical waves "occupied by ocean expert."[59]

It can be argued that even as Hawai'i's dry spaces were annexed, Hawaiians prevented the physical and intellectual colonization of their *ka po'ina nalu*. During the early twentieth century, Alexander Hume Ford and Jack London sought to marginalize Hawaiians while using surfing to promote tourism. A South Carolinian transplant to O'ahu and product of the Jim Crow South, Ford "embraced the racist suppositions of the post–Civil War era." After Freeth and other Hawaiians taught Ford and London to surf, they founded the segregated Outrigger Canoe Club (1908), proclaiming it "an organization for the haole (white person)." Hawaiians countered, forming the multiracial Hui Nalu (Club of Waves), which expressed their affirmative concepts of multi-racialism, "maintained control of their social standing in the waves, and helped preserve the ocean as a Hawaiian domain."[60] During the late twentieth century Oʻahu's Hui ʻO Heʻe Nalu (Wave Sliding Club) resisted professional surfing's attempts to "marginalize them from their aquatic cultural sanctuary." Using surfing and fighting abilities, they reasserted their "masculinity against prevailing stereotypes that belittled Native Hawaiian men."[61]

Africans, like Hawaiians, controlled surf zones, even as the Atlantic slave trade, colonialism, and missionaries redefined terrestrial realities. Surf zones terrified whites, as illustrated when Warren Henry approached Sierra Leone during the 1920s. Pleading in his best "pidgin' English" for surf-canoemen to take care, he exclaimed: "I know savvy swim." Lamenting the dearth of calm waters for Englishmen to cool off in, Henry said: "We could frolic on the fringe of the surf, but not being born that way, could never go so far as to swim in it." Knowing whites were poor swimmers, surf-canoemen demanded respect even from those seeking to purchase human bodies. Whether intentionally or accidentally, canoes manned by the best watermen could overset in the surf, and offended canoemen could swim away from, rather than toward, drowning Europeans. In 1693, slave ship captain Thomas Phillips advised Europeans to shelve racial suppositions, saying, "We venture drowning every time we go ashore and come off again, the canoos [sic] frequently over-setting, but the canoo-men are such excellent divers and swimmers, that they preserve the lives of those they have any kindness for, but such as they have any displeasure to they will let shift for themselves" and will "impute all to accident." Imprudent voyagers could pay with their lives. During the 1890s, "a bad" Englishman employed on the Colony of the Gold Coast "ill-used his men." Paddling him "through the surf to go aboard the ship that was to take him home, there was the usual catastrophe, which no one thought much of." When his body was found the truth was revealed, as it had "three iron shark hooks, with lots of line attached, wherewith the men had . . . played him like a fish, until the surf beat the life out of him."[62]

Quinine and machine guns facilitated African colonization, while Oceanians could not defeat gunboat diplomacy. Still, water people found power in waves and their aquatic acumen long after land masses were colonized. Exploiting Mother Nature to achieve violent responses to white affronts, they side-stepped culpability while drowning Western social/racial hierarchies of power to command white respect.[63]

History is typically studied through the Western lens: scholars bind themselves to myopic farmers-or-fishermen paradigms, even as Western aquatic valuations remain irrelevant to cultural understandings of amphibious spaces Westerners sought to physically and intellectually colonize. Early "race ethnographies" were, as Anoop Anayak explained, "produced through and against a cultural standard of white normalcy." James Sidbury and Jorge Cañizares-Esguerra observed that historians continue to make the "historical experiences of Europeans" the "normative standard against which judgments about Atlantic people and their histories are made." Such biases reduced Oceanian and Atlantic histories to parched disciplines, ignoring indigenous aquatic understandings. Refusing to take the plunge, most scholars conclude that maritime history only existed aboard the tall-sided ships from which they view the past.[64]

Colonizers projected Western social/racial hierarchies of power across the globe. Yet, as historian James Sweet, cautioned, "European domination was never a forgone conclusion." Even as they sought to control open oceans and dry spaces, they could not colonize African and Oceanian surf zones prior to World War I.[65]

The examination of surfing shatters the chains binding scholars to intellectual shores, adding hundreds of thousands of miles of liminal space to our analysis. Discrete, yet similar, cultures of meaning and practice existed throughout Atlantic Africa and Oceania. Surf zones were social, cultural, and political spaces and land was the periphery. Beaches were where Oceanians waited for distant storms to deliver surf, and where indigenous people reflected upon surfing feats. Land was where whites watched Oceanian and African aquatics.

White men enjoyed considerable success projecting hierarchies of power across landscapes and onto ships. Yet they could not drown aquatic cultures beneath the bow of waves of colonialism and Christianity. Silently defying Western notions of civilization, wet African and Oceanian bodies did not behave as elite white men wanted them to. Upon surfboards, seminude Oceanian men and white women defined race according to their valuations, disregarding insinuating Western constructs of race and gender.

Likewise, as the twentieth century progressed, white bodies increasingly refused to conform to Western imperatives. Beachgoers accepted their bodies as gifts from the creator that should be displayed, tanning and ornamenting them with tattoos, piercings, and scarifications. Many donned "tribal" face paint in the form of neon pink, yellow, or blue Zinka sunblock. Whites slid into the drink to swim and surf. Some wrestled alligators; others rode great white sharks. True,

Western powers colonized tropical waterscapes. But, lacking their own aquatic traditions, whites "went native" to enjoy themselves, permitting African and Oceanian immersionary cultures to prevail in waters retaining traditional meanings and practices.

NOTES

1. Beaglehole, ed., *Journals, III*, 1164–1165; Moser, *Pacific Passages*, 1.

2. Gillis, *Human Shore*, esp. 7; Dening, "Deep Time, Deep Spaces"; King James Bible, Genesis 1–2; Leed, *Mind of the Traveler*, esp. 19; Corbin, *Lure of the Sea*, 1–18; and Connery, "There Was No More Sea."

3. Corbin, *Lure of the Sea*, 1–18, esp. 2, 7; Cañizares-Esguerra, *Puritan Conquistadors*, 35–55, 123–125, esp. 123; Bruce, *Commentary on the Gospel*, 79–81, 85, 227, 462–463; Orme, *Early British Swimming*, esp. 24–25; Camporesi, *Fear of Hell*, esp. 15–17, 21–22, 38, 57, 82, 140; Dawson, "Enslaved Swimmers."

4. For examples of scholarship stressing the need to reconsider maritime history, see Mack, *The Sea*, esp. 21–23; Bentley, Bridenthal, and Wigen, *Seascapes*; Gillis, *Islands of the Mind*; Klein and Mackenthun, *Sea Changes*; Steinberg, *Social Construction*; Games, "Atlantic History"; Vickers and Walsh, *Young Men*; Bolster, "Putting the Ocean"; Norling, *Captain Ahab*; Linebaugh and Rediker, *Many-Headed Hydra*; Dawson, "Enslaved Swimmers;" Dawson, "Swimming, Surfing."

5. Atlantic Africa extends from Senegal to Angola. To consider how societies were culturally connected through migration and internal, trans-Saharan, and trans-Atlantic commerce, see Thornton, *Warfare in Atlantic Africa*, esp. 12–16; and Falola and Childs, *Changing Worlds*. Waterscape is defined as freshwater and saltwater cultural spaces that actively participated in personal and group identities.

6. Dawson, "Enslaved Ship Pilots," esp. 74, 89; Lindberg and Todd, *Brown-, Green- and Blue-Water Fleets*.

7. The following exemplify Atlantic history's broad contours: Bailyn and Denault, eds., *Soundings*; Games, "Atlantic History"; Cañizares-Esguerra, Childs, and Sidbury, *Black Urban Atlantic*.

8. Bolster, *Mortal Sea*, 13; Bolster, "Putting the Ocean."

9. Hauʻofa, "Our Sea of Islands," 31–32, 39; Barry, *Senegambia*, xvi; Thomas, *Islanders*, 20; Te Punga Somerville, *Once Were Pacific*; Igler, *Great Ocean*; Okihiro, *Island World*; Matsuda, "Pacific"; Dening, "Deep Time."

10. De Marees, *Description*, 26; Hair, Jones, and Law, *Barbot on Guinea, II*, 501n16, 532, 640; Bosman, *New and Accurate Description*, 121–122; Jones, *German Sources*, 109; Smith, *New Voyage to Guinea*, 210.

11. Maxton, *After the Bounty*, 215; Ellis, *Polynesian Researches*, I, 303–304; Ellis, *Narrative of a Tour*, 373; Hill, *Travels*, 197; Korn, *Victorian Visitors*, 70; Bingham, *Residence*, 136–137; Broeze, *Merchant's Perspective*, 24; Silvers, *Land of the O-O*, 112.

12. De Marees, *Description*, 26, 32, esp. 186–187; Dawson, "Swimming and Surfing."

13. Jarvis, *Scenes and Scenery*, 279–282; Greene, *Talofa, Samoa*, 39–40; Ellis, *Polynesian Researches*, 304.

14. Dawson, "Enslaved Swimmers," 1329–1334; Dawson, "Surfing and Swimming," 83–84.

15. Hair, Jones, and Law, *Barbot on Guinea, II*, 532; Jones, *German Sources*, 219; Smith, *New Voyage to Guinea*, 210.

16. Kalakaua, *Legends and Myths*, 483; Kahanamoku and Brennan, *World of Surfing*, 31, 59; Moser, *Pacific Passages*, 135.

17. Walker, *Waves of Resistance*, 2; London, *Cruise of the Snark*, 86, and 82–87; Twain, *Roughing It*, 526.

18. Packard, *Our Endangered Children*, 64–66; Reinier, *From Virtue to Character*, 60–61.

19. Ellis, *Polynesian Researches, I*, 299, 304–305; Ellis, *Narrative of a Tour*, 372, 374. For play, see King, *Stolen Childhood*, 107–115; Huizinga, *Homo Ludens*, 1–27; Packard, *Endangered Children*, 65; Mintz, *Huck's Raft*, 18–19, 104–105, 107–108; Mergen, *Play and Playthings*, 3, 22.

20. Jones, *German Sources*, 109; Finney, "Surf Boarding in West Africa"; C. Béart, "Jeux et Jouets de L'Oust African: VII. Le Surf-Riding," *Mémoires de L'Institut Français D'Afrique Noire* 1, no. 42 (1955): 329–331; Finney, "Surf Boarding in Oceania"; Jean Fouch, "Surf-Riding sur la Cote d'Afrique," *Notes Africaines: Bulletin D'Information et de Correspondence de l'Institut Francais d'Afrique Noir*, 42 (April 1942): 50–53.

21. London, *Cruise of the Snark*, 88.

22. Jack London, "Riding the South Sea Surf," *Women's Home Companion* (October 1907), 9; London, *Cruise of the Snark*, 76, and 75–90; Moser, *Pacific Passages*, 4–5.

23. Wheaton, *Cultural Politics*, 19.

24. Jones, *German Sources*, 98, 109; Hair, Jones, and Law, *Barbot on Guinea, II*, 532.

25. Alexander, *Narrative of a Voyage*, I, 192.

26. Quoted in Dawson, "Swimming and Surfing," 100–101.

27. Béart, "Surf-Riding," 329–331; Fouch, "Surf-Riding," 50–53; Brown, *The Endless Summer*; Jones, *German Sources*, 103, 109; Hair, Jones, and Law, *Barbot on Guinea, II*, 532; Alexander, *Narrative of a Voyage*, 192; Rattray, *Ashanti*, 60–65. For alaias, see Finney and Houston, *Surfing: A History*, 43, 52; 'Ī'ī, *Fragments of Hawaiian History*, 135.

28. London, *Cruise of the Snark*, 82, 83–90, esp. 82, 75, 88; Melville, *Mardi and a Voyage*, 238–239.

29. Lopez, "Aftermath Winter 1976"; Glenn Sakamoto, "Gerry Lopez," *Liquid Salt*, November 30, 2009, http://www.liquidsaltmag.com/volume1#/gerry-lopez/; London, *Cruise of the Snark*, 82–90, esp. 75, 82, 88.

30. Moser, *Pacific Passages*, 17–47; Westervelt, *Legends of Old Honolulu*; Kalakaua, *Legends*; "Eora First People Exhibit," Australian National Maritime Museum; "Pacific Cultures Exhibit" and "Indigenous Australia Exhibit," Australian Museum.

31. Iliffe, *Honour in African History*, esp. 1–8, 1–118; Desch Obi, *Fighting for Honor*; Stewart, *Honor*.

32. Gilmore, *Manhood in the Making*, esp. 9–29; Sigrid, "The Wrestling Tradition"; Iliffe, *Honour*; Tengan, "(En)gendering Colonialism"; Tengan, *Native Men Remade*; Burstyn, *Rites of Men*; Law, Campbell, and Dolan, *Masculinities in Aotearoa*.

33. 'Ī'ī, *Fragments of Hawaiian History*, 133–137; Tengan, *Native Men Remade*, 3–13, esp. 13; Melville, *Mardi and a Voyage*, 239; Stoddard, *Summer Cruising*, 232; Walker, "Terrorism or Native Protest?"; Okihiro, *Island World*, 49–60, esp. 50.

34. 'Ī'ī, *Fragments of Hawaiian History*, 133–137; Ellis, *Hawaii*, 103, 375; Kahanamoku, *Surfing*, 25–26; Maxton, *Bounty*, 214; Ellis, *Polynesian Researches, I*, 304–305; Stewart, *Residence in the Sandwich Islands*, 256; Walker, *Waves of Resistance*, 22; Bingham, *Residence*, 135, 217–218.

35. Malo, *Hawaiian Antiquities*, 204; Hill, *Sandwich and Society Islands*, 200; Kalakaua, *Legends and Myths*, 231 [author emphasis on "audacious"], 245; Brassey, *Voyage in the "Sunbeam,"* 276–277; Walker, *Waves of Resistance*, 25; Ellis, *Polynesian Researches, I*, 304; Stoddard, *Cruising*, 233.

36. Hill, *Sandwich and Society Islands*, 203; Korn, *Victorian Visitors*, 96; Kalakaua, *Legends*, 231, 245; Twain, *Roughing It*, 552; "Hawaiian Surf Riding," *Hawaiian Annual* (1896), 106–107; Walker, *Waves of Resistance*, 25. For blood sport, see Dawson, "Swimming and Surfing," 101, 104–107; Dawson, "Enslaved Swimmers," 1342–1344.

37. Ellis, *Hawaii*, 373–374; Stewart, *Residence*, 256; Haleole, *Laieikawai*, 448–450, 624n48; Stoddard, *Cruising*, 232–234; 'Ī'ī, *Fragments of Hawaiian History*, 133–136; Kamakau, *Ruling Chiefs*, 53, 106; Bingham, *Residence*, 136; Anonymous, "Surf Riding," 109; Blake, *Hawaiian Surfriders*, 22–29, 38, 46.

38. Jim Nendel, "Surfing in Early Twentieth-Century Hawai'i," 2434; Finney and Houston, *Surfing: A History*, 38–40; Haleole, *Laieikawai*, 444–450; Fornander, *Fornander Collection, IV*, 116–118; Blake, *Surfriders*, 27.

39. Kalakaua, *Legends*, 229–246; Anonymous, "Surf Riding"; Finney and Houston, *Surfing: A History*, 38.

40. Hill, *Sandwich and Society Islands*, 200; London, *Cruise of the Snark*, 85; Blake, *Surfriders*, 24; Hague, "Our Equatorial Islands," 665.

41. Tengan, *Native Men*, 3, 9, 13; Kalakaua, *Legends*, 213; London, *Cruise of the Snark*, 85.

42. Ellis, *Hawaii*, 373; Hill, *Sandwich and Society Islands*, 199–200; Melville, *Mardi and a Voyage*, 239; Lopez, "Aftermath Winter 1976," 102; Kalakaua, *Legends*, 231; 'Ī'ī, *Fragments of Hawaiian History*, 133–136; Stewart, *Residence in the Sandwich Islands*, 255–256.

43. Thomas, *Adventures and Observations*, 212; Bridge, *Journal of an African Cruiser*, 137; Leonard, *Records of a Voyage*, 258; *The Endless Summer* (film).

44. Laderman, *Empire in Waves*, esp. 3–5; Walker, *Waves of Resistance*; Conner, *A People's History*, 95–96.

45. London, *Cruise of the Snark*, 9; Shaath, *Sunscreens*, 3–17, 71–81; Driscoll, "Artificial Protection," 459–462. Commercial sunscreens became available in 1928 and were significantly improved during World War II.

46. Fynn, *Diary*, 81–82; Emerson, "Causes of Decline of Ancient Hawaiian Sports," 57.

47. Fynn, *Diary*, 81–82; Emerson, "Causes of Decline of Ancient Hawaiian Sports," 57.

48. Kalakaua, *Legends*, 229–246; Malo, *Antiquities*, 204, 220; Tengan, *Native Men*, esp. 51, 145–147, 155; Blake, *Hawaiian Surfriders*, 22–28; DeLaVega, *Surfing in Hawai'i*.

49. London, "South Sea," 9–10; London, *Cruise of the Snark*, 76, 78, 87; Okihiro, *Island World*, 56; Laderman, *Empire in Waves*, 17–20, 33–34; Walker, *Waves of Resistance*, 31–32; Musick, *Hawaii*, esp. 72–74, 226–227.

50. Stoddard, *Cruising*, 29–75, 233–234, 239; Edwards, *Exotic Journeys*, 33–47; Aldrich, *Colonialism and Homosexuality*, 130–135; Poole, "Cannibal Cruising," 71–85; Austen, "Stoddard's Little Tricks," 73–82.

51. Stoler, *Carnal Knowledge*, 155–157; Hodes, *White Women, Black Men*, 203; Smith, *How Race Is Made*, esp. 24–25, 58–59, 83–86; Gross, *What Blood Won't Tell*, 178–210. For images of tandem surfing, see DeLaVega, *Surfing in Hawai'i*, 54, 62–88, 119, 122–123, 126; Blake, *Surfriders*.

52. Stewart, *Residence in the Sandwich Islands*, 88; Bates, *Sandwich Island Notes*, 87; Ellis, *Hawaii*, 417; Finney and Houston, *Surfing: A History*, 51–57; Dawson, "Enslaved Swimmers," 1331–1333, 1341–1344; Laderman, *Empire in Waves*, 1–40. For colonialism, see Laderman, *Empire in Waves*; Silva, *Aloha Betrayed*, 15–44; Trask, *From a Native Daughter*; Okihiro, *Island World*, 59, 43–97. For racial hierarchies, see Dawson, "Enslaved Ship Pilots," 93n16.

53. Laderman, *Empire in Waves*, 8–40; Eperjesi, *Imperialist Imaginary*, 105–129; Hague, "Our Equatorial Islands," 665–667; Musick, *Hawaii*, cover, 72–74. Alexander Hume Ford penned a two-part article attributed to Duke Kahanamoku to promote tourism by, among other things, claiming Hawaiians were simplistic people and white men were the natural heirs of Hawaiian waves as they easily learned to out-surf Hawaiians. Paoa, "Riding the Surfboard."

54. Jim Nasium, "Kanaka Swimmer Has No Equals in the Water: This Hawaiian Is a Human Fish," *Salt Lake City Tribune*, February 2, 1913, 34. Also see London, *Cruise of the Snark*, 75–78; Nodaway, *Rollo in Hawaii*, esp. 31–33.

55. Linfors, *Africans on Stage*; Crais, *Pamela Scully*; Holmes, *The Hottentot Venus*; Poignant, *Professional Savages*; Qureshi, *Peoples on Parade*; Trachtenberg, *Shades of Hiawatha*; Brownell, *1904 Anthropology Days*.

56. Douglas and Ballard, *Foreign Bodies*, esp. 104, 157–201; Silvers, *Land of the O-O*, 112; Bradley, *Imperial Cruise*; Firmin, *Equality of the Human Races*, 155; Horne, *White Pacific*, esp. 46, 133, 129–145.

57. Hawkesworth, ed., *An Account of the Voyages Undertaken*, I, 135; Twain, *Roughing It*, 526; Walker, *Waves of Resistance*, esp. 11.

58. "Evolution of the Australian Crawl," Australian Screen website, http://aso.gov.au/titles/documentaries/australian-crawl/clip1/; Colwin, *Breakthrough Swimming*, 14–16.

59. Seed, *Ceremonies of Possession*; Thompson, "Otelo Burning," esp. 325–326; Laderman, *Empire in Waves*, esp. 3, 5; Walker, *Waves of Resistance*, 14–16, 26–39; Okihiro, *Island World*, 43–71; McGloin, "Aboriginal Surfing," 93–100. Also see Karhl, *The Land Was Ours*; Corbin, *Lure of the Sea*; Gillis, *Human Shore*, esp. 143, 128–157; Wheaton, *Lifestyle Sports*, 121–137.

60. Laderman, *Empire in Waves*, 17–33, esp. 20, 25–26; Eperjesi, *Imperialist Imaginary*, 114–116; London, *Cruise of the Snark*, 78; Walker, *Waves of Resistance*, 57–82, esp. 57; Gross, *What Blood Won't Tell*, 178–210.

61. Walker, "Terrorism or Native Protest?," esp. 576, 577; Walker, *Waves of Resistance*, 127–172; Tengan, *Native Men Remade*.

62. Henry, *Confessions of a Tenderfoot*, 109; quoted in Dawson, "Swimming and Surfing," 87; Kingsley, *Travels in West Africa*, 513–515. Also see Thomas, *Adventures*, 212.

63. Canoemen also employed work disruptions to gain concessions, while Hawaiians used violence to prevent professional surfing from annexing their ka po'ina nalu. Priestly,

"An Early Strike in Ghana," 25; Gutkind, "Trade and Labor," 30–42; Walker, *Waves of Resistance*; Dawson, *Enslaved Water People*.

64. Nayak, "After Race," 413; Sidbury and Cañizares-Esguerra, "Mapping Ethnogenesis," 208; McGloin, "Aboriginal Surfing," 93–100.

65. Sweet, *Domingos Álvares*, esp. 6; Dawson, "Ship Pilots," 71–100.

GLEN THOMPSON

This society has appropriated dimensions of consciousness and nature that formerly were relatively unspoiled. It has formed historical alternatives in its own image and flattened out contradictions, which it can thus tolerate . . . the subjective and objective space for the realm of freedom has also been conquered. —HERBERT MARCUSE, "Foreword," *Negations: Essays in Critical Theory*

This chapter seeks to push under the whitewash of South African surfing's history.[1] It looks to historical explanations of why surfing in contemporary South Africa is perceived to be a white, male sporting lifestyle despite the evident histories of black and women's surfing.[2] As a counterpoint to that present, this chapter revisits the 1960s as the founding moment of modern South African surfing history. It explores how a tanned whiteness and exemplar masculinity, as configured by beach apartheid and an imported "California dreaming," were essential to the making of the South African surfing lifestyle during the years of grand apartheid—a lifestyle that was seen in early 1965 by the newly published *South African Surfer* magazine "to give favorable publicity to another feature of the South African way of life, as well as establishing South Africa as a leading surfing nation."[3]

A decade later this surfing mythology had become normative. "Surfing is an ideal South Africa sport," Cornel Barnett observed in 1974. "It raises those involved in it above the mundane levels normally prescribed by our social environment."[4] This echoed Anthony Morris's views of surfing in 1966: "It is an escape from the drabness of everyday life" and "the freedom attained beyond the breakers is perhaps unequalled in any other sphere."[5] Despite these imaginings, apartheid shaped the everyday lives of white surfers whether they acknowledged it or not.[6] However, what is missing from political accounts of South African surfing history was how "assertions of racial identity are inextricable from the subject of masculinity."[7] Thus, gender needs to be included in historical analyses on surfing, race, and culture in the making of white surfing in South Africa, an approach I have undertaken in this chapter—first by setting out how beach apartheid and lifestyle consumption framed local surfing identities, and second by considering how transnational currents from California birthed South African surfing. Implicit in these processes was the reiteration of a male-dominated gender order. The period under review is 1959 to 1968, when the emergence of the local longboard surfing era overlapped with the genesis of beach apartheid and the importation of Californian surf culture.[8]

Surfing, Beach Apartheid, and Lifestyle Consumption

The sixties were the so-called golden years of South Africa surfing.[9] These were the years that saw the emergence of a distinct surfing lifestyle associated with a South African outdoors lifestyle. Surfing's popularity was the preserve of a small coastal population of surfers, although the surfing cultural industry and the organization of competitive surfing nationally made for a larger sporting presence than would have been expected based on the number of surfers. In 1964, journalist Anthony Morris estimated that there were "about 350 riders in Durban and the South Coast," and by the end of 1965, wrote Morris, there were "about 20" women surfers in Durban.[10] In 1966, the national surfing association president, John Whitmore, reported 800 surfers around Cape Town's peninsula.[11] South African surfers, therefore, made up a tiny part of the reported 200,000 surfers worldwide—and an even smaller percentage of the total white coastal population in South Africa.[12]

In contrast to the austerity of the immediate post–World War II era, access to the South African beach was enhanced by the greater affordability of automobiles in the 1960s. This was a result of increased white prosperity and consumerism during the sixties economic boom.[13] Along with racially exclusive group areas legislation, "car culture in the apartheid years greatly facilitated the development of the suburbs and helped whites to insulate themselves from a common urban life."[14] Apartheid laws privileged white society's consumption of outdoor leisure spaces, including the beach, and curtailed black South Africans' use of these public amenities from the early 1950s. A cursory reading of the history of petty apartheid as regulating beach leisure supports the argument that "regimes of race have co-produced regimes of consumption" in South Africa.[15] Thus, enforcing apartheid on the beaches demarcated pleasure within a politics of difference. "Racial hierarchies ratified and legitimized the social and economic inequalities that were in turn held up as evidence of a hierarchy of racial differences. From this perspective, then, whiteness was an entitlement to privilege and relative affluence; blackness became an official judgment about being unworthy of certain modes and orders of consumption."[16] The consumption of pleasure and "freedom" at the beach therefore came to be a white cultural practice and a sign of white power and privilege—especially when socially constructed as part of the architecture of grand apartheid laws and policies phased in at most urban beaches from 1966.[17]

The mechanisms for beach apartheid were complex, and the apartheid state under the National Party government expanded it through several iterations of racial legislation.[18] Petty apartheid in the Reservation of Separate Amenities Act of 1953 was used to structure and limit race relations by creating separate social and sporting spaces for blacks and whites. The Reservation of Separate Amenities Amendment Act of 1960 expanded group areas to include the coastal sea and seashore within its definition of "land," thus extending racial segregation into the surf zone. While its effect was not part of the sixties, the Sea Shore Amendment Act of 1972 tightened the enforcement of beach apartheid at the municipal level. This web of apartheid legislation provided the structural conditions limiting social contact between "races" at the beach.[19]

Beach apartheid reinforced white anxieties about "mixed bathing" and racial "pollution": as Robert Archer and Antoine Bouillon explained, "at the heart of white social life swimming is subject more than any other leisure activity to a pitiless, indeed pathological segregation . . . far from separating swimmers of different races (or sexes) water dissolves the physical barriers between them."[20] "Whites only" signs thus regulated both direct and indirect social contact in the littoral zone. Another sign of entrenched whiteness at the beach was the advent of shark nets. Installed in Durban in the early 1950s and on the north and south coasts of KwaZulu-Natal in the early 1960s, shark nets created protected swimming beaches for coastal residents and upcountry holiday-makers. The fact that shark nets were found exclusively at white-designated beaches, which were usually resourced with lifesavers, went far to further *laager* (that is, enclose) white oceanic pleasure.[21]

In this context of racial exclusion, white surfers benefited from safe, pristine beaches and "remained at all times unconcerned in their racially cosseted world."[22] Herein, the tanned whiteness of the surfing lifestyle displaced white English and Afrikaans ethnicities, and to some degree class. This process did not effect a "complete disintegration" of white identities, but rather their re-imagination due to socioeconomic and cultural processes in the 1960s.[23] Drawing on critical race theory in forming his concept of "tanned whiteness," David Goldberg cites both the material and discursive entanglements of local and transnational identities and culture formations.[24] With beach apartheid, tanned whiteness was implicit in the "California dream," with its free-and-easy fun ethos at the beach, an associated affinity with the surfer image, and a genuflection to surfing's roots in Hawai'i.[25] By "the late twentieth century, in fact, the California surfer, male or female alike, had become an icon of the California lifestyle, celebrated in song, film, advertising, and other media."[26] What was elided from that myth was how California's beaches were historically racially segregated spaces that excluded African Americans, and how coastal private property development in California effectively continued racial exclusion in the guise of maintaining middle-class values.[27] The transnational mobility of these Californian images that traveled to Cape Town and Durban was part of the Americanization of South African society and economy during the Cold War years.[28] In place of local white ethnicities shaped by language, culture, and history there was a re-imagination of the surfing self through the consumption of (southern) Californian surfing culture. Yet this consumption imbibed a politics too, as "in its hedonistic values and cultural orientations [Californian] surf culture was *adaptive* rather than rebellious. Rather than confronting or resisting the dominant cultural order, the 1960s surf phenomenon" played a part in "pioneer[ing] and populariz[ing] new, expressive and indulgent lifestyles integral to white, middle-class America's move away from an ethos of inhibition and restraint into a world of pleasure and personal gratification."[29]

These sociocultural and economic processes occurred as South Africa left the British Commonwealth to become a republic in 1961. The "Californication" of surfing thus not only reoriented the South African beach away from the British imperial past and an imagined Brighton seashore in the Cape and Natal, it also distanced itself from the cultural nationalism of the mid-twentieth-century Afrikaner beach resort project as envisaged for vacationing railway workers in Hartenbos in the southern Cape.[30] The South Africa surfing subculture was therefore a reshaped Anglo-world identification of sun, sand, and surf for youthful whites—a process itself part of the bourgeoisation of white society in which identity was uncoupled from ethnicity through lifestyle consumption. This was part of the emergence of new white subjectivities in the middle classes determined more by individualism and consumer choice, irrespective of language and culture, open to create new social and subcultural lifestyle formations.[31]

These processes of self-fashioning began to break with the submission to political and patriarchal authority encouraged by the official discourse of the conservative apartheid state. As part of the process of globalization in South African society, lifestyle consumption can be seen as drawing on "liberal," or more "open," ideals and values that pushed against apartheid's political regulation of social life and the moral authoritarianism of the apartheid state. However, identities shaped by lifestyles were not necessarily politically progressive. Rather, they were socially and morally permissive—as such, from the mid-1960s, South African authorities saw youth anti-social trends (as evidenced by sexuality, rock music, alternative religions, drugs, and surfing) as drawing inspiration from Western "liberal" influences from outside of the country.[32] Surfing's Californication was part of this process—an American recolonization of post-1945 settler culture through youthful lifestyle consumption. Herein, the consumption of pleasure and fashioning of surfing identities should rather be seen as impetuses for maintaining, and not challenging, the status quo in South Africa, despite the countercultural image of the surfer that emerged in the late 1960s. Material possessions such as cars and surfboards took on values that defined social and racial status as well as an outdoor manliness. Advertising in surfing and other lifestyle sport magazines in the mid-1960s reveals the values as well as the semiotic linkages between whiteness, consumption, and the gender order. In short, surfing became a mode of conforming to apartheid society as surfers benefited socially and economically from the cultural capital of whiteness. The Californication of the beach thus reinforced apartheid's sociocultural bubble. This was evident in South African surfing icon Shaun Tomson's recollection about his adolescent surfing life in Durban: "Still, world events and the beginnings of our ostracism of our government from the Western world were not part of our daily reality as gremmies. Barely teenagers, we were interested mainly in the beach and the surf and in emulating the Southern California style that was filtering south, mainly through surf magazines and surf movies.... Overall, though, the surf explosion of the sixties never penetrated our country's mainstream culture as it did in the USA, never moved off the sand into a national fad.... So to the lives of us kids on the beach there was a cosseted innocence."[33] Unlike California, sixties South Africa remained socially and morally conservative, and "far from taking up the flame of the counter-culture, South Africa got stuck in a McCarthy-like era."[34]

Tomson's account also points to other contextual factors. From 1960, decol-onialization in Africa threatened white political and economic privilege. During the making of apartheid, South Africa acted in the geopolitical interests of the West as a Cold War beachhead against Communist support for national lib-eration movements, including the African National Congress (ANC) in exile. Internal political dissent in South Africa was repressed by the apartheid state with increasing violence through the decade. The ANC and the Pan African Congress (PAC) were banned. In response to the pervasiveness of racial seg-regation in society, an international antiapartheid movement supported by the United Nations and Commonwealth countries lobbied for political, eco-nomic, and cultural sanctions against South Africa as well as the boycott of racialized sport. Yet in the sixties, South African surfing remained outside of international political scrutiny except for one episode. In 1966, the racially seg-regated nature of South Africa's beaches reached an international surfer pub-lic when a photograph by Australian Ron Perrott of a young black man and three white surfers at Durban's Dairy Beach was published in *Surfer* magazine. Perrott's photograph came to symbolize surfing and politics in South Africa as *The Endless Summer* screened nationwide in the United States.[35] However, the image's anti-apartheid commentary was undermined by the accompany-ing text of the "Surf Suid Afrika" article. While it did address the segregated beach, it was more touristic surf journalism than social commentary; its intent was to describe the Durban beachfront as a place of freedom, desire, and plea-sure. Thus it did more to perpetuate surfing's tanned whiteness (nonetheless diminishing South Africa as a surfing nation by noting that "the general surfing standard is well below Australia's") and the exotic appeal of Zulu cultural tour-ism at the beach.[36] Ironically, it was an appropriation of Zuluness that was used by the *South African Surfer* magazine (1965–1968) to turn attention to white surfing. In a genuflection to the Californian *Surfer* magazine and borrowing from cartoonist Rick Griffin's "Murphy," the cover of the first issue of the local surfing magazine was illustrated with a white male "stokie" surfing a wave at a Durban beach. This 1965 cover of *South African Surfer* was a figurative prelude to Perrott's 1966 photograph, but with a political effect that reinforced surf-ing's settler whiteness: watching the surfer from the white sand was "Takkies," a caricature of an African male in Zulu traditional dress.[37] The Zulu Other was thus deployed to make sense of this new Anglo-world sporting culture where whites rode, or rather "civilized," waves.

There was a significant social distance between Perrott's photograph and the beach in the local popular white imagination. This politics of play was reiterated in advertisements promoting beach culture. In this cultural imaginary, which mirrored the South African gender order, strong links were made between male dominance and supportive femininities, especially among the middle classes.[38] Surfing culture as represented in the *South African Surfer* magazine was replete with portrayals of active men on waves and women in bikinis on the beach that imitated an aspirational California beach lifestyle—this was before the Gunston cigarette advertisements came to be ubiquitously associated with surfing on the back page of surfing magazines from the 1970s. Herein, masculinities and whiteness were an important citation of the surfer identify in South Africa. For example, Surfer's Corner at Muizenberg Beach was the epicenter of Cape Town surfing by the mid-1960s, and had been zoned for "whites only" in 1966.[39] It was on these white sands that David Butler, recently out of high school and a printer by trade, had taken up surfing with friends. His sense of manliness was linked to surfing prowess. "There was no feeling like it anywhere in the world; angling on the swell. . . . As we got better, we gradually moved up the line, so to speak, and progressed to Muizenberg Corner. Once you had surfed the Corner, in the mind and language of a surfer, you had officially arrived, big time. You were now in the big boys' league; you were now a full-blown surfer." He continued, noting the distinguishing characteristics of the youthful, white, male, heterosexual surfer which seemingly balanced male fantasy, a fun ethic, and the responsibilities of a newly found adulthood: "God, what a feeling to be a surfer—you were so many miles higher than mere rugby or cricket players. Chicks swooned when they saw you. . . . Tanned, blond hair, healthy—you represented everything good about being alive, even if you had to pay rent."[40] Butler's account of his social capital linked to tanned whiteness, masculinity, and surfing prowess was framed within the consumption of the surfing lifestyle in South Africa's sixties. It thus becomes necessary to understand how these identifications, caught in wider currents of utopianism and individualism, were reproduced by means of an imported Californian surfing imaginary.

The Californication of South African Surfing

Nascent homegrown trends existed as precursors to the Californication of South African surfing.[41] By the 1950s, according to sixties surf media entrepreneur Harry Bold, "we were worlds away from the source and hub of surfing."[42] This was to change in early 1959, when twenty-six-year-old goateed Californian Dick

Metz arrived in South Africa. Metz was to become a key actor in establishing linkages between certain South African surfers in Cape Town and Durban and the "Dana Point mafia," the surfing fraternity at the hub of the Californian surf industry and surf media.[43] The result was that South African surfing leapfrogged into the modern surfing era within a few years.[44] In exploring the Californication of local surfing, this section looks to four key moments in this transnational history: Metz's visits to Cape Town and Durban as a turning point in South African surfing history, the allure of *The Endless Summer* frontier narrative of surfing in South Africa, how authenticity in surfboard manufacturing was reliant on nods to the Californian surf industry, and how Californian Phil Edwards's surfing style was vital to the construction of an exemplar surfing masculinity in South Africa.[45]

Inspired by reading men's adventure magazines, Metz's global travels began in the South Pacific; he then moved on to Asia before landing in East Africa. From there he hitchhiked south to the border of present-day Zambia and Zimbabwe. Arriving in Victoria Falls at night, Metz "made a decision that changed a lot of lives."[46] He chose to go on to the driver's destination of Cape Town, South Africa. This unplanned trip resulted in a meeting at a Sea Point beach (not Glen Beach in Camps Bay, as the story is usually told) with John Whitmore, who came to be known as the "father" of South African surfing.[47] For Metz, Cape Town mirrored California's Laguna Beach, where he grew up surfing, in its climate, geography, and its easygoing beach lifestyle. During his stay in Cape Town, Metz shared some of his surfboard-shaping knowledge with Whitmore. Six months later, Metz traveled up the east coast of South Africa to Durban.[48] Here he met a group of beachboys and lifesavers at Durban's South Beach where the "strange American" asked to hire a surfboard.[49] Surfer and city lifeguard Harry Bold offered his Finn Anderson–designed hollow wooden board. As Baron Stander recalled:

> Dick then dropped to his knees next to the board, and started waxing from the tail end, eventually moving forward and started waxing over the fancy paint-job. We never ever put wax that far forward, especially over painted designs. . . . A perplexed Harry asked: "Why are you doing that?" "In California we walk to the nose and stand there, and it is good if you can put your toes right over the nose," said our man from the States. One of the boys asked: "Why the hell would you want to do that. The nose will plough in, and you will just fall off." Anyway, D[ick] M[etz] takes the board to the water, paddles out at Kontiki [South Beach], takes off on a nice little well shaped right, turns, walks right up to the nose and puts five toes over the front.[50]

Not only did Metz reframe wave-riding styles for the Durban surfers, he also introduced Californian sartorial style in the surf trunks he wore. Stander noted, these were "the biggest pair of board shorts we had ever seen. They were sort of knee length and had bands, similar to the long shorts that were worn by [black] apartment cleaner staff in those days."[51] The Durban surfers, on the other hand, wore lifeguard uniforms rolled down to their waist or sported short tight-fitting trunks. Yet it was Metz's account of his travels that opened up the surfing world outside South Africa for the local surfers. As Bold recollected, Metz regaled them with "stories of Baja Mexico, Malibu, Makaha, Laguna ... and of an up and coming young surfer by the name of Phil Edwards. . . . It was that encounter where it was decided," Bold continued, "we have to go and take a look at California and Hawaii."[52]

Bold started on a world surf tour in 1960 and traveled to California. Through Metz and others, Bold was introduced to magazine publisher and filmmaker John Severson, filmmaker Walt Philips, and surf entrepreneur Hobie Alter. Bold also met Bob Olsen from Pacific Beach, who shaped under the Ole Surfboards label. Bold purchased an Olsen's polyurethane surfboard, and transported the "American-type board" in an empty cabin on his return trip by freighter to South Africa in 1961.[53] Metz sent a letter to John Whitmore, alerting him to Bold's docking in Cape Town en route to Durban. This was to be Whitmore and Bold's first meeting. Whitmore took measurements of the Ole surfboard, which he then used to remodel his surfboards.[54] A further significance to their meeting was that it created the first cultural and commercial surfing linkages between Durban and Cape Town. Whitmore, who was also a Volkswagen automobile salesman, traveled to Durban in late 1961 and sold a few of his Ole-inspired surfboards to Durban surfers. A photograph taken on Durban's South Beach attests to the evolution in local surfboard design, waterman masculinity, and differences in surf trunk sartorial style (fig. 7.1). Whitmore's trip was evidence of his interest in commercializing surfboard manufacturing. By the mid-1960s, his business in Cape Town was thriving.[55] In Durban, Bold too entered the surfboard-making business and joined Max Wetteland and Baron Stander in setting up Safari Surfboards in late 1963.[56] These surfers pioneered the South Africa surf industry, but were by no means the only surfers to do so in the local market.

Through their Californian links, Bold and Whitmore became South African cultural brokers. They were distributors of *Surfer* magazine, wrote South African content and took photographs for the magazine, and promoted Californian-made surf films. Films such as *Surf Mania* (1961), *Waterlogged* (1963), and *The Performers* (1965) were screened in South African surfing centers.[57] These films featured surf rock music soundtracks that further popularized

FIG. 7.1 Sixties surfer boys, South Beach, Durban, 1961. Bold, third from the left, Whitmore to his right. Photograph from Harry Bold Collection, SHSA.

Californian surfing culture. Yet even outside of the subculture, the sounds of surfing were circulating widely in white South African popular culture at the time. Songs like The Mamas and Papas' 1965 "California Dreamin,'" along with the lyrical rhythms of South Africa's own fronting of a Californian band, The Fantastic Baggies, offered a sonic imaginary of a romanticized, youthful, carefree, outdoors lifestyle. The Beach Boys' song "California Girls" reached number one on the Springbok Radio chart in 1965.[58] However, more so than surf rock music, it was the moving image that brought surf culture to life in halls and cinemas along the South African coastline. And it was from the movie reel, more so than through the efforts of organized surfing in the mid-1960s, that South Africa was inducted as a surfing nation into the American-Australian surfing order.[59] A corner of the South African surfing wilderness was "discovered" in the cinematic climax of Bruce Brown's travelogue surf movie, *The Endless Summer.* The film, initially released in 1964 to surfing audiences in the United States, traveled globally after its movie theater release in 1966. *The Endless Summer,* brought into the country by John Whitmore under a local distribution license from Brown, played to packed audiences in Cape Town and Durban, and inspired many young women and men to take up surfing.[60]

The Endless Summer's focal point was the sequence that Brown filmed when he, along with Californian surfers Robert August and Mike Hynson, visited Cape St. Francis, in the Eastern Cape, in November 1963. This surf spot had been chosen for filming on the suggestion of Whitmore, their South African host, who had been introduced to Brown through Metz. It was the discovery of what came to be called "Bruce's Beauties" that made South Africa an international surfing destination.[61] The cultural imperialism of the film also semantically removed from the records the local name for the surf spot, "Sea Vista," the name for a nearby holiday resort. The renaming as "Bruce's Beauties" followed the rhetoric of American frontier conquest as an act of cultural consumption—especially when Brown described the American travelers as finding a perfect, pristine wave over the sand dunes.[62] Hynson, in his surf memoirs, and appealing to a Southern Californian postwar nostalgia, called the wave "little Malibu."[63] The filmic myth surrounding this wave inspired local and international surfers to seek out this "perfect" wave. It should be noted that the film captured an idyllic and dehistoricized view of South Africa. It depicted a pleasurable sameness for the white American tourist gaze to explore—adding African wildlife to the familiar sight of white beaches. Politics, however, was absent; *The Endless Summer* made no direct mention of South Africa's apartheid.[64] Rather, the film reveled in displaying how the Californian surfers' littoral manliness seduced the "natives," that is, female beachgoers at Cape Town's Long Beach.

The cultural effect of the film resonated with the American hosts of the 1966 World Surfing Titles held in San Diego, California. In the official contest program, it was proposed that the 1970 world championships be held at "Bruce's Beauties." This remained no more than a Californian dream, as the 1970 contest was held in Australia owing to political pressure against apartheid sport. Nevertheless, in an amicable rebuttal to the idea in 1967, Harry Bold, as editor of *South African Surfer* magazine, noted, "Don't expect to come over the sand dunes and find [the waves] tubing as Bruce did."[65] "Bruce's Beauties" was in fact a fickle surf spot, its geography requiring the alignment of specific swell, wind, and tidal conditions before it was surfable. However, Bold offers a further interpretation of this surf spot, one located as surf colonialism within the emerging tensions between nostalgia and progress, individualism and organization, in the sport of surfing. "It is a legendary spot which will continue to be exaggerated by those who in their own minds, like to dream of a far off endless tube, constantly hissing spray out of the vortex. Maybe such a dream helps to relieve the tensions of the competitive world in which the dreamer exists. We all like to think that there is an ultimate, unspoilt, perfect wave somewhere, just waiting to be conquered. Cape St. Francis comes close to this dream."[66]

The local surf industry was another means of strengthening cultural, material, and financial linkages to California. Despite the small size of the South African surfing population in the 1960s, surfers provided enough of a market for the consumption of surfwear and surfboards. Surfboard manufacturing became the material base for the Americanization of surfing in South Africa, located specifically in the importation of polyurethane foam blanks. While it was the surfboard that made the act of stand-up surfing manageable, it was innovation in the use of polyurethane materials for surfboard construction in California during the late 1950s that made modern surfing possible and popular.[67] Whitmore and Bold, who had been introduced to Gordon Clark through Metz, began importing Clark Foam blanks in the early 1960s.[68] By the mid-1960s, Walker Foam, another Californian product, was imported by other South African surfboard makers. Claims that foam blanks were California-made soon became a signifier of quality and authenticity in the local industry. This could be seen in the advertising of South African surfboard manufacturers, adding fuel to a growing rivalry between Cape Town and Durban. Besides a clear identification with the local surfboard shapers, who themselves were surfing icons, such as Max Wetteland in Durban and John Whitmore in Cape Town, advertisements run by surfboard makers publicized the Californian supply of their materials or surfboard design knowledge. In the April 1965 issue of *South African Surfer,* Durban-based Surf Centre advertised its Wetteland Custom Built Surf Boards, and claimed that Max Wetteland had "returned from California with a greater knowledge of surfboard manufacture" and that "Walker foam as used in California" went into the construction of Wetteland Surfboards. On the other hand, Whitmore Surfboards in Cape Town promoted the use of Clark Foam in the July 1966 issue of the same magazine. Both advertisements illustrated the replication of the Californian dream in local surfer aspirations for subcultural authenticity through the consumption of surfboards. Moving beyond which foam was used, the Whitmore Surfboards advertisement added two further layers of legitimacy to their surfboard business: "We specially import a cloth from California to wrap around it, double. . . . We even use Redwood and balsa so that you Mr. Surfer can have in your surfboard exactly what a surfer in California can get."[69]

Yet as South African surfers gained cultural capital in their own right in national contests in the late 1960s, advertisements by Safari Surfboards, Whitmore Surfboards, and Wetteland Surfboards emphasized less the Californian linkages and more a sense of South Africa as a surfing nation. Three factors pointed to the loosening of transnational cultural identifications. First, most surfboard manufacturers used top local surfers to promote their surfboards—with membership of a branded surf team designating elite status. Second, while many surfboard makers designed decals using their names, some explicitly drew on the cultural iconography of ethnicity and nation to promote distinction in their surfboard advertising. Durban-based Safari Surfboards appropriated symbols of Zulu tradition (the cowhide shield, knobkerrie, and assegai) in its company logo. In Cape Town, Whitmore Surfboards drew on John Whitmore's Afrikaner heritage and surf pioneer status. In a September 1967 Whitmore Surfboards advertisement in *South African Surfer,* the already iconic imagery of a surfer carrying a surfboard and the sun on the horizon, inspired by the film poster for *The Endless Summer,* was combined with an Afrikaner cultural nationalism nostalgically referencing the Great Trek as symbolized by an ox wagon (fig. 7.2).[70] In this visual bricolage, settler (anti)colonial whiteness was conjoined with a sense of surfing's freedom and pleasure, a reinterpretation of Afrikaner nationalist historiography as opening up of the "empty" South African coastal frontier to surf exploration. Furthering Afrikaner cultural identification in the Whitmore Surfboards advertisement was the spelling of South Africa in the Afrikaans language as *Suid-Afrika,* and "pioneers" referencing the founding fathers of Afrikaner republicanism. However, this foregrounding of a mythic Afrikaner nationalist past as an assertion of South Africanness was a rare instance in the archive of whiteness explicitly configured as central to the making of surfing's utopianism.

Cultural politics aside, the practical implication of the use of American-sourced foam materials for surfboard manufacturers was that surfboards could be made much lighter than in earlier years. Andrew Ogilvie, a Safari Surf Centre surfboard shaper in the mid-1960s, indicated that the average weight of a standard 9 foot 6 inch (3m) board dropped by more than half from forty-five pounds. This had practical implications for increasing surfing's popularity: it enabled teenager "stokies" to carry a surfboard more easily down to the surf.[71] In April 1965, the newly launched *South African Surfer* magazine noted, "during the past few years South Africa surfers have 'caught up' to their counterparts in Australia and America in the art of riding a surfboard."[72] In November 1967, on a return trip to South Africa, Metz's comment on the growth of surfing in South Africa was reported on in the *Daily News* newspaper. "He could not believe the transformation which had taken place over the last eight years in Cape Town and Durban," and, more specifically for Durban, Metz said, "Man, this is 'outasight,' sort of like Waikiki [Hawai'i] on 4th July."[73] This is not to say surfing was as popular as cricket, rugby, or tennis. Yet surfing's broader cultural visibility in 1960s South Africa, as it was in California, was greater than the number of its practitioners.

FIG. 7.2 Whiteness and the surfing dream, 1967. Advertisement in *South African Surfer* 4, no. 1 (September 1967): 11. Photograph from Harry Bold Collection, SHSA.

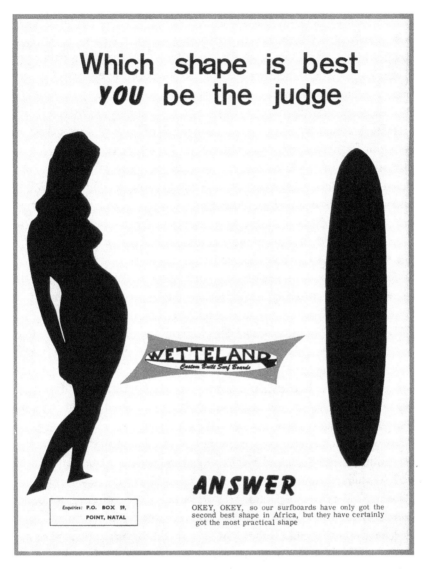

FIG. 7.3 Surfboards and male desire, 1967. Wetteland Surfboards advertisement, *South African Surfer* 3, no. 2 (April 1967): 2. Photograph from Harry Bold Collection, SHSA.

Two further sociocultural consequences of surfboard innovation in South Africa can be observed as a reflection of the male-dominated gender order of the day. The first concerns how South African surf industry advertising maintained the male gaze. Women were regularly cast as objects of male desire within surfing's promotional culture to create an allure for the consumption of products by associating sensuality (and sex) with surfing. Examples of this, specifically referencing American consumer culture in the *South African Surfer* magazine, were phallocentric advertisements for Pepsi-Cola beverages and Lexington cigarettes.[74] Surfing as a male domain was also exhibited as a play on body/board "shape" in a 1967 Wetteland Surfboards advertisement (fig. 7.3). This citation discursively functioned to gender the surfboard as a feminine object and subordinated women as secondary to male surfer *jouissance* (despite the advertisement's protestation to the contrary). A 1965 article in the *South African Surfer* scripted a similar gendered fantasy, in this case that of an adolescent male surfer's heteronormativity: "The surfboard (second hand, R40), is the most cherished possession. Even the girlfriend takes second place." The author continued, chauvinistically stipulating the place of his girlfriend in his surfing life as "she must grin and bear surf talk . . . sit on the sands and watch the rides and the wipe-outs, or better still train her camera on the conquering hero."[75] Even the surf zone was a space for strengthening male bonding and power. In 1966, female surfer Cecile Charlesworth observed of the backline, "Board riding bristles with male terminology, techniques, and a rather healthy sounding barroom chatter."[76]

The gender order was also seen in the construction of an exemplar surfing masculinity institutionalized in the regional and national surfing associations and drawing stylistic imitation from the functional surfing of Californian Phil Edwards.[77] The initial impetus for the organization of South African amateur competitive surfing was prompted by initiatives from the International Surfing Federation (ISF) to hold world titles. As a result, the first Springbok surfing team was selected at the inaugural national champions in Durban in July 1966. The team participated in the World Titles held in San Diego, California, later that same year. Herein, national prestige and surfing prowess shared the same goal: how to codify the judging of competitive surfing style to determine a Springbok surfer as exemplary.

It should be noted that local organized surfing conformed to the whites-only membership requirements of the apartheid state's sporting structures. For example, the membership of several Durban surf clubs that were affiliated to the Natal Surfriders' Association (NSA) were for "Male and Female South African citizens of the White Group."[78] At the leadership level, most clubs and association committees were comprised of men, except where they were assisted in administrative duties by women. Furthermore, female surfers themselves were marginalized within the sport. Despite the rhetoric of including women in the competitive domain—it was the ISF's requirement for a national team to include two women surfers that was the driving force behind local surf administrators promoting women's surfing—the official judging criteria, as agreed on for the first national surfing championships in South Africa held in Durban in July 1966, focused on longboard surfing styles that displayed athleticism and a muscular manhood.[79]

Yet the importance of determining normative standards in the sport of surfing ensured that the judging system was a contested site in competitive surfing culture during the mid-1960s. Dave Lee, chairman of the NSA and a head judge, observed that one of the most significant issues in the association was how to codify a judging system and ensure objectivity when scoring surfing contests.[80] The aesthetic criteria for judging the world surfing contests from the mid to late 1960s informed the South African Surfriders' Association (SASA) idea of good surfing: determining "functional" surfing—smooth and stylish surfing, alternating between displays of controlled power turns and spontaneity on a wave—as "muscular, heroic and technically competent."[81] This style of surfing became hegemonic primarily owing to the influence of the Californian surfboard shaper and surfer Phil Edwards.[82] It was made popular in South Africa in three ways: influential top local surfer and shaper Max Wetteland adopted Edwards's style as his own after his participation in the world championships in Australia (1964) and Peru (1965); the circulation of international and local surfing magazine imagery of Edwards, and other surfers, provided representations of exemplary surfing style; and the screening of surf films produced in California—such as Bruce Brown's *Waterlogged* (1963)—transported Edwards's functional style of surfing to local audiences.

This is not to say that functional surfing was the only approach to riding waves or the construction of surfing masculinities. There was a range of embodied surfing styles, from hotdogging (tricks) to graceful (flow) to aggressive (power) and functional (control, with elements of the others). Nevertheless, with SASA's push to regulate the sport and to gain national and international acceptance, "functional" surfing was to be cited as good surfing. Thus, it was with the aligned interests of the surf media and organized surfing that the functional surfer was manufactured as *the* "good surfer" by the time of the 1966 national championships. Anthony Morris used his weekly newspaper column to educate the Durban community about surfing standards. In July 1964, Morris cited functional surfing as follows: "The 'functional' man adapts his riding to the mood of the sea. His is characterized by his smooth riding, by his blending with the wave. He never does anything unnecessary. . . . But no matter how the waves are breaking, the 'functional' always strives to stay in the 'hottest' section of the wave. And he does this with smooth, functional manoeuvres."[83]

Morris further described the masculine functional surfing style as epitomizing a utilitarian economy of motion, where "the truly functional surfer is the one who can 'trim' his board properly. And to do this he must move his board fast and control it. This involves quick thinking and perfect timing with the changing movements of the wave."[84] In the "Hints to Competitors" in the official program for the 1996 national championships, a surfer was seen having "a good chance of being a surfing champion" when integrating three criteria into his performance: "the smooth stylish surfer with plenty of graceful, fluid, maneuvers has the edge in any contest . . . [with] a proper blend of '*riding the board*' and '*riding the wave*' as well as a thorough *knowledge of the rules* of his event" [my emphasis].[85] In both Morris's and the NSA's contest program, an exemplar white male surfer made visible the supposed invisibility of masculinity in surfing and its ideological mirroring of the gender order beyond the beach. The discursive construction of an idealized surfing man in the competitive surfing area thus embodied the masculine as normative. If the 1966 Natal and South African Surfriding Championships was the surf administration's template from which all other national contests were to be run, it could be argued that this contest provided the founding moment of how making waves made men.

There is a further implication of this sixties exemplar surfing masculinity as part of the gender order. It leaned toward becoming a hegemonic masculinity, although it did not "stand out as a sharply defined pattern separate from all others" available in the sporting lives of white South African men. Rather, competitive surfing offered a sociocultural space for men where "a degree of overlap or blurring between hegemonic and complicit masculinities [wa]s extremely likely if hegemony [wa]s [to be] effective" within the surfing lifestyle.[86] In this way, and owing to the marginalized status of surfing as a sport, exemplar surfing masculinity should be seen as complicit in the privileged social world of white South Africa. Nevertheless, the chauvinism of South African white men in this period produced "brittle masculinities" that were constructed within "the uneven distribution of power [that] gave them privileges but also made them defensive about challenges (by women, blacks, and/ or other men) to that privilege."[87] While the gender and racial orders limited the challenges from women and blacks to male surfers, in surfing's sixties these challenges came from other men with longer hair (a marker of youth and nonconformity), drug use (a precursor to the influence of the counterculture), and demonstrations of "good" surfing outside of the contest arena (indicative of competing surfing masculinities).[88] Constructions of masculinity in this way were therefore as much a part of maintaining surfing's tanned whiteness as they were in perpetuating the male domination of the Californian surfing imaginary.

Conclusion

In focusing on the making of South African surfing in the sixties, this chapter has sought to historicize and politicize surfing's tanned whiteness. In a context of increasing international and internal political opposition to apartheid, and in a bubble of white male privilege at the South African beach, a self-fashioned insular white surfing identity and lifestyle had emerged by the late 1960s. With the internalization of those cultural practices and discourses associated with the Californian dream, a South African surfing lifestyle began to de-emphasize the global and accentuate the specificities of the local. In this way, the tanned whiteness of South African surfing was shaped by the racial exclusionary policy of beach apartheid and a Californian cultural imperialism. Together, these local and transnational currents maintained white privilege and power at the South African beach in the 1960s (and beyond). Yet solely looking to race and cultural politics was insufficient in accounting for surfing's tanned whiteness. Also evident in its making was how white men shaped sixties surfing. Not only were men actors in establishing links to California, the birthing of the local surfing cultural industry, and the formation of organized surfing, they also further maintained the gender order as male-dominated. This was undertaken in the surfing cultural industry through the male gaze and in the codification of judging criteria in organized surfing based on male bodies in the waves. The resultant gendered effects were the social and discursive subordination of women at the beach and in the waves, as well as the construction of an exemplar surfing masculinity. In short, considerations of race, gender, and culture make for surfing's tanned whiteness in the sixties along with its utopian inclinations and politics of withdrawal.

The specter against which this chapter writes is how South Africa's surfing sixties persists in the present by flattening contradictions and marginalizing alternative historical narratives: both whiteness and male domination remain largely uncontested despite changes in the post-apartheid wavescape. The project of pushing under the whitewash, the unsettling of surfing's past, opens up a radical critique of racial power and the patriarchal dividend within South African surfing culture.

NOTES

1. "Whitewash" references the film *White Wash,* directed by Ted Woods.

2. See Thompson, "Surfing, Gender and Politics."

3. Bold, "Editorial" (1965), 3.

4. Barnett, *Hitting the Lip,* 30.

5. Anthony Morris, "Sport of Pagan Kings Now Rules Thousands," *The Natal Mercury,* July 4, 1966.

6. Laderman, *Empire in Waves,* 97–105 and 130.

7. Newell, "Postcolonial Masculinities," 244.

8. The effects of the countercultural turn to "soul" and shorter boards, evident from 1968, are outside the scope of this chapter.

9. Hift, *Legends of Jeffreys Bay,* 15.

10. Anthony Morris, "Hurtle Ashore in a Flurry of Foam," *The Natal Mercury,* June 25, 1964, and Anthony Morris, "Now the Girls Discover that Stoked Feeling," *The Natal Mercury,* December 3, 1965.

11. Whitmore, "Surfing Around the Cape," 5.

12. Morris, "Hurtle Ashore." The total white population was estimated in 1965 at 3,395,000 (5.25% of the total South African population); see Horrell, *A Survey of Race Relations,* 110.

13. Grundlingh, " 'Are We Afrikaners Getting Too Rich?,' " 144–51.

14. Beinart, *Twentieth-Century South Africa,* 174.

15. Posel, "Races to Consume," 172.

16. Posel, "Races to Consume," 168.

17. Apartheid was more an unfolding policy than a monolithic stratagem, despite the consolidation of white power during grand or "high" apartheid (1960 to late 1960s).

18. Preceding apartheid laws, Durban's beaches were already racially segregated in the early 1900s.

19. By the early 1980s, much of the South African coastline had been set aside for whites; see Durrheim and Dixon, "The Role of Place and Metaphor," 436.

20. Archer and Bouillon, *The South African Game,* 105.

21. Van Oordt, "A Historical Overview of the Origins of Anti-Shark Measures in Natal," 58–61.

22. Heard, *Cape of Storms,* 2.

23. See Grundlingh, " 'Are We Afrikaners Getting Too Rich?,' " 158.

24. David Theo Goldberg uses the term "tanned whiteness" to describe how culture, including adventure sport, is raced (*The Threat of Race,* 365). Laderman, in *Empire in Waves,* notes that the Americanization of surfing "soon resembled an endless sea of bronzed skin" (40).

25. See Lawler, *The American Surfer,* 155.

26. Starr, *California: A History,* 300.

27. See Jefferson, "African American Leisure Space."

28. See Campbell, "Americanization of South Africa."

29. Osgerby, *Playboys in Paradise,* 108.

30. Hughes, "Struggling for a Day in the Sun," and Grundlingh, "Holidays at Hartenbos."

31. Hyslop, "Why Did Apartheid's Supporters Capitulate?," 37–39.

32. Hyslop, "'Days of Miracle and Wonder?,'" 495.

33. Tomson, *Bustin' Down the Door,* 16–17.

34. Morrell, "The Times of Change," 16.

35. See Laderman, *Empire in Waves,* 97.

36. Perrott, "'Crocodiles,' Zulus, and Surf Suid Afrika," 59.

37. The racist "Takkies" cartoon featured in most *South African Surfer* issues.

38. Mager, *Beer, Sociability, and Masculinity,* 47–52.

39. The Cape Town City Council delayed beach apartheid implementation until December 1968 owing to a liberal political agenda that frustrated the state's conservative Afrikaner nationalist agenda; see "Apartheid in Action on Beaches," *The Star,* December 28, 1968.

40. Butler, *The Adventures of a Reluctant Printer,* 6–7.

41. "Surfboard riding" on short belly boards was already popular in 1910. There is evidence for stand-up surfing in the interwar years. The surfing centers of Durban, East London, and Cape Town were birthed largely in isolation, except for loose linkages between organized swimming and lifesaving.

42. Harry Bold, "Surfing Recollections (South Africa)," Manuscript, n.d.: 3, Harry Bold Collection, Surfing Heritage South Africa (SHSA).

43. See my interview with Dick Metz, Surfing Heritage and Cultural Centre (SHCC), San Clemente, California, February 20, 2012, digital audio recording.

44. Some Australian surfers also influenced South African surfing; however, until 1968 this was largely part of the same Californian impetus.

45. While I draw on Krista Comer's use of "Californication," I do not use it as a marker for neoliberalism; see her *Surfer Girls,* 219–20.

46. Surfing Heritage and Cultural Centre, *Travel Adventuress with Dick Metz.*

47. See Deon Bing interview with Dick Metz and John Whitmore, Elands Bay, December 1999, video tape, Deon Bing Collection.

48. Harry Bold, "Dick Metz," Scrapbook, n.d., Harry Bold Collection, SHSA.

49. See my interview with Harry Bold, Tauranga, New Zealand, February 17, 2016, digital audio recording.

50. Baron Stander, "1959 Toes on Nose in Durban," 2001, South Africa File 3, SHCC.

51. Stander, "1959 Toes on Nose in Durban."

52. Harry Bold, "Dick Metz," Scrapbook, n.d., Harry Bold Collection, SHSA.

53. "Novel Surfboard in His Luggage," *The Natal Mercury,* May 16, 1961.

54. Interview with Harry Bold.

55. Masterson, "Well Connected," 82.

56. Interview with Harry Bold.

57. Australian surf films were also screened locally, for example, Bob Evans's *High on a Cool Wave* (1966).

58. Tertius Louw, "Springbok Hit Parade: 1965–1971: No 1 Hit Records: SA Pressings," South African Rock Encyclopedia website, November 2004, http://www.rock.co.za/files/springbok_hits_1965.html.

59. The sixties surfing pantheon also included Peru. The ISF validated Hawaiian exceptionalism in seeing Hawai'i as a separate surfing nation from the US mainland.

60. See my interview with Bernie Shelly and Therese Russell, Cape Town, September 16, 2010, digital audio recording.

61. Wilson, "Cape St. Francis," 17.

62. See Ormrod, "*Endless Summer* (1964)," 49–50.

63. Hynson and Jost, *Mike Hynson*, 34.

64. There was an obscure reference to racial segregation in *The Endless Summer*. Brown narrated, "[S]harks and porpoises have yet to integrate in South Africa."

65. Bold, "Bruces Beauties," 23.

66. Bold, "Bruces Beauties," 23.

67. Warren and Gibson, *Surfing Places, Surfboard Makers*, 85–87.

68. Letter from Gordon Clark to Harry Bold, October 10, 1963, Harry Bold Collection, SHSA.

69. See Whitmore Surfboards advertisement in *South African Surfer* 2, no. 2 (July 1966): 24.

70. The political mythology of the Great Trek (1829–1835) provided a symbol for Afrikaner unity and British anti-imperialism, and was also used by apartheid architects to justify racial segregation and the separate development of African homelands.

71. See my interview with Andrew Ogilvie, Durban, May 27, 2011, digital audio recording.

72. Editorial to Evan, "Body Surfing," 7.

73. Stokey [Harry Bold], "Surfing," *Daily News*, November 23, 1967.

74. See *South African Surfer* 2, no. 3 (July 1966), 10 and 22, for the respective advertisements.

75. Rorvick, "A Certain Kind of Madness," 27.

76. Charlesworth, "Girls Overboard," 33.

77. For a more detailed discussion, see Thompson, "Judging Surf Culture."

78. For these surf club constitutions, see Natal Surfriders' Association (NSA) Files, Dave Lee Collection, South African Surfing History Archive (SASHA); this is my personal archive.

79. See "Outline of the Contest Judging System," *1966 Natal and South African Surfriding Championships Souvenir Program*, 6. NSA Files, Dave Lee Collection, SASHA.

80. Author's telephone conversation with Dave Lee, March 11, 1997.

81. Ford and Brown, *Surfing and Social Theory*, 87.

82. Warshaw, *History of Surfing*, 185–187.

83. Anthony Morris, "Expressing Yourself in Surfing," *The Natal Mercury*, July 15, 1964.

84. Anthony Morris, "Trimming Is the Secret," *The Natal Mercury*, August 13, 1964.

85. "Hints to Competitors," *1966 Natal and South African Surfriding Championships Souvenir Program*, 13.

86. Drawing on Connell and Messerschimdt, "Hegemonic Masculinity," 839.

87. Morrell, "The Times of Change," 18.

88. For hair, see Paarman, *Lunatic Surfer or Destiny?*, 15; for drugs, see Bold, "Editorial" (1967), 3; for a questioning of surfing style, see Bold, "S.A. Titles 1966," 9.

BELINDA WHEATON

Surfing's White Tribe

Surfing has a long history as a Polynesian cultural form that, through colonization, was appropriated by white North Americans and Australians in the
mid-twentieth century. As part of this well-documented process of appropriation, the activity was redefined and reorganized, drawing "nostalgically on an
imagined cultural authenticity from Hawai'i's pre-colonial surfing past."[1] Since
the 1950s, the quintessential image of the surfing body has been "phenotypically
White," specifically, a young, white, male subject, slim, toned, tanned—but not
dark skinned—with a mop of sun-bleached hair.[2] Fueled by the Hollywood
beach movies, and the surf music craze epitomized by the Beach Boys, in the
United States the white, blonde surfer became so iconic he—and increasingly

she—became the face of California.[3] As Isaiah Walker details in *Waves of Resistance*, this colonial appropriation has not been without resistance in Hawai'i. Yet this particular image of surfing has subsequently been perpetuated more globally in both the surfing niche media and through wider mass media surfing discourses. Thus, although surfing's imagery as a white, male, youthful, privileged activity and space is a relatively recent and contextually specific social construction, globally it has been and remains the hegemonic one.[4]

My focus in this chapter is on the experiences of surfers who do not fit this hegemonic ideal—specifically, those racialized as nonwhite. Surfing participants often claim—indeed believe—that surfing culture is inclusive of all, and that race and gender do not matter. However, despite a desire for an inclusive and cosmopolitan citizenship, as I illustrate, surf culture and the surfing media continue to perpetuate what Chivers-Yochim terms an "imagined community" of whiteness.[5] This chapter draws on a research project that explored the formative and contemporary experiences of minority ethnic surfers, predominantly African Americans, who lived and surfed around Los Angeles, California. I explore how these black surfers negotiate space and identity in the surfing culture, and their experiences of belonging and exclusion.[6]

First, I situate the case study within a broader understanding of sport, whiteness, and exclusion, highlighting research that reveals surfing in the United States and beyond as a gendered and racialized space. I also consider the central and problematic roles that surfing media and industry play in developing our sporting imagination. I then turn to the contradictory experiences of belonging of the black surfers in my case study, identifying some of the difficulties and barriers experienced by these surfers carving a space in a white-dominated cultural practice. While some aspects of their experiences and identities were shared with white and other ethnic-minority surfers, what was most revealing was the range of difficulties or constraints that many of these surfers had faced and which they saw as barriers to other African Americans becoming surfers.

Surfing, Whiteness, and Inclusion

Given the close association between whiteness, surfing and Western imperialism, the paucity of research on surfing and ethnicity is surprising.[7] The voices of minority ethnic and indigenous surfers are often absent from surfing culture, media, and research. This is an absence, however, that has started to gain academic and media attention. Of particular significance is Walker's detailed history of the changing role and meaning of surfing in Hawaiian cultural identity. He details how throughout the twentieth century indigenous Hawaiians successfully resisted and challenged colonial hierarchies and categories through surfing spaces.[8] Although the empirical focus in this chapter is California, I highlight some of these more international sources to illustrate that these are issues that affect many dominant surfing nations, including Australia, New Zealand, South Africa, and countries in South America.[9]

Kyle Kusz's work has been foundational in highlighting that, in the United States, "extreme sports" including surfing have become important contemporary sites of whiteness, celebrated as the "symbol of a new American zeitgeist," promoting and reviving traditional and specifically white American values, including "individualism, self-reliance, risk taking, and progress."[10] These sports are represented as cultural spaces that are overwhelmingly white, yet "rarely ever imagined as a racially excusive space."[11] That is, whiteness acts as an invisible and unmarked norm to most whites. As Krista Comer highlights, racial and national-based tensions exist between the dominant blonde "California surfer girl" image and other discourses and experiences of surfing in the United States, such as the "Muslim surfer girl."[12]

Glen Thompson's historically rooted research on surfing masculinity in South Africa reveals the history of black Zulu experiences of the South African beach and surfing, and changing representations of surfing as a white sport pre- and post-apartheid.[13] Thompson illustrates that although surfing as a sporting lifestyle is undergoing transformation, and has been opened up to all ethnicities, there is a persistence of "racialised cultural relations."[14] This is vividly illustrated in Thompson's work on the documentary *Otelo Burning*, a film that provides the context for a broader discussion of the history of black male surfers in KwaZulu-Natal, and the range of ways in which the "Zulu surfer" has assumed meanings.[15] While surfing waves is presented as "more individualistically redemptive (and hedonistic) than socially transformative for these participants, surfing is presented nonetheless as a metaphor for changing subjectivities."[16]

In the Australian context, the racialized geographies of the contemporary Australian surf beach are evident in the punitive treatment of "outsiders" documented in discussions of localism. The power of contemporary discourses to exclude bodies racialized as nonwhite from surf spaces has been graphically illustrated in the so-called race riots at Cronulla Beach in December 2005.[17] A number of commentators have begun to unpack the whiteness of the "quintessentially Australian surf space," recognizing that surfing's whiteness is rooted in, and associated with, the white settler Australian identity.[18] Colleen McGloin most systematically explores the genealogy of the relationship between surfing, the nation, and white masculinity in Australian culture. As she writes, "in white conceptions of nation, the Australian male surfer represents the national corpus... the individual body of the male surfer, often represented within mainstream surfing texts as white, blond, tanned, fit, competitive, and heterosexual. The ocean is his performative place of becoming."[19] Importantly, McGloin also explores contemporary indigenous surfing culture, highlighting that indigenous surfing has gained increasing momentum in communities across Australia. Drawing on research with Aboriginal surfers and elders, she argues that there is "a distinction in philosophy and practice, in conceptions of the beach and the ocean."[20] Aboriginal ways of understanding and relating to the ocean are, she suggests, different from dominant white representations of surfing and beach life. The perspectives of Aboriginal participants and contributors provide a counterdiscourse, contesting dominant projections of nation and of surfing as a form of cultural expression.

Mihi Nemani also reveals indigenous experience of the ocean. Her research focuses on understanding intersecting experiences of gender and ethnicity in New Zealand body-boarding culture. Drawing on her own experiences of being a Samoan-Maori elite brown body boarder and on interviews with male and female Maori, Pacific Island, and New Zealand European body boarders, Nemani's research provides a fascinating perspective on how indigenous participants negotiate space in a place that is predominantly white.[21] She argues that a unique form of cultural capital exists among Maori and Pacific Island participants in which respect, courtesy, and fairness were given more value than demonstrations of physical capital.

Surfing's Global Village? The Industry and Media Rhetoric

The media play a central role in developing our sporting imagination, and surf media are no exception. Surfing has long been seen, and represented itself, as a leisure practice that embraces a style of life that offers a different and better way of living than the mainstream.[22] Yet despite various claims to ethical, environmental, and humanitarian credentials, the surf industry and media are often exploitative, operating in unethical ways and manipulating various non-Western communities and their resources, such as reefs.[23] The surf media also continue to play a role in racializing surfing, reproducing constructions of surfing as a white male space, adopting stereotypical discourses about black athleticism and erasing the black surfer subjectivity.

In this context, the colonial imaginary informing the surf safari genre of discovery films like *The Endless Summer* (1966) has received most widespread commentary and critique.[24] Although this genre continues to infuse contemporary mainstream Hollywood surf films and niche media, travelogue discourse is usually based on white, heterosexual, privileged young men from the Global North searching out perfect waves in exotic distant lands, often around the Global South. Racial stereotypes underpin this narrative, emphasizing cultural and racial differences, suggesting that postcolonial countries and subjects are more primitive than the civilized West. For example, where images of black subjects are used, they tend to be as the native Other, depicted in traditional clothing or performing primitive tasks like fishing or hunting for food. Occasionally, local surfers are portrayed, but predominantly the white surfer befriends and tames the primitive native black Other, with whom he shares an affinity for nature and the ocean, the basis of the soul surfing ethos and transcendent experience.[25] As Lewis argues in his reading of *The Endless Summer*, the "romantic project" of the surfer seeks to "parenthesize issues of indigenous poverty, global exploitation and apartheid through good-humoured engagement with locals as curios."[26] While the "pilgrim surfer" is not oblivious to the different material conditions of the local communities where he travels, such difference cannot "detract from the importance of [his] journey for spiritual enlightenment."[27] The film aestheticizes less powerful cultures into First World texts, creating a form of Orientalism and exploitation wherein the naturalness of surfers' subject position as white, male, and Western is reinforced.[28]

For the participants in my research, US surf media were seen to play a central role in sustaining the myth that surfing was a white activity, denying or erasing the potential for their black surfer subjectivity. Some of the black surfers interviewed said that the postcolonial mentality in films and media travelogues was one of the aspects of surfing culture that most angered them: "Because what you're saying is, you're going into these third world countries, [and] we are still uncivilized. You came, you're going to teach us how to surf! ... It amazes me to think that we are so ... and I'm going to say [that we are the worst offenders in the] United States because I don't see it [this attitude] so much in other places, as we [US citizens] feel like we have to find everything. Our white culture has to discover everything. You don't need to discover us [people of color]; we've already been here."[29]

The surf film genre, however, encompasses a broad range of styles and formats.[30] One of the more progressive recent developments is the emergence of art house films and surfing documentaries. These often focus on challenging dominant discourses about surfing space and identity, and appear to have gained traction with audiences at international surfing film festivals, where there is a "growing appetite for 'indigenous' surfing stories."[31] Poignant examples include *Wave of Change* (2002), which explores Balinese surfers, and *Surfing the Healing Wave* (1999), an Australian indigenous surfing film that foregrounds personal histories, and asserts Aboriginal conceptions of nation and country through the cultural practice of surfing and conceptualizations of the ocean.[32] As noted earlier, *Otelo Burning*, a Zulu-language film with English subtitles, presents young black men searching for freedom through surfing in late apartheid South Africa. It premiered at the Durban International Film Festival (July 2011) and has subsequently gained significant academic attention.[33] Particularly relevant to the present chapter is *Whitewash* (2011), which explores "the complexity of race in America through the struggle and triumph of the history of black surfers."[34] The film, which emerged during my research project to critical and scholarly acclaim, resonates with many of the themes discussed herein.[35] These independent filmmakers challenge dominant histories and myths about surfing culture and history, including representations of race, gender, and sexuality, disrupting the idea that there is a singular, monolithic surfing culture or history.

Surfing Culture, Inclusion, and Exclusion

Researchers have established that in the United States, black and minority ethnic (BME) peoples underutilize nature-based outdoor recreation spaces and resources, including beaches.[36] Their research has identified a range of sociocultural, economic, and practical barriers for these communities' ability to access general recreational spaces. Through the course of my discussion, I outline how many of these barriers have also hindered BME participation in surfing. Initially, the surfing lifestyle can be expensive, with high-performance surfboards and wetsuits costing several hundred dollars. In addition to the financial outlay, there are also practical barriers, such as transport of person and board to the beach. Garcia and Baltodano's study exemplifies that "people of color and economically disadvantaged communities disproportionately lack efficient access to the beach."[37] They cite city bus stops up to "half a mile from a public path to the beach" that create "a significant burden," particularly for those with young children or recreational gear.[38] The most exclusive surf beaches, such as Malibu (in the most affluent, predominantly white communities), were those that were least accessible by public transport.[39] Yet while such economic and logistical barriers to participation in lifestyle sports are consistently acknowledged, often absent in understandings of beach underutilization by BME groups are considerations of "the historical and cultural patterns of oppression" that become systematically embedded in "society's norms and daily practices."[40]

To understand the contemporary experiences of black surfers in the United States requires a historical and spatial perspective, considering the impact of formal and de facto segregation on the African American community, and how the spatialization of race has had—and continues to have—a profound impact on the use of beaches by black communities. That is, the contemporary California beach suburbs, like many other seaside spaces, are constructed through "imaginary notions of whiteness."[41] Reinforcing historic patterns of segregation, postcolonial anxiety has fueled white flight from inner city urban areas to the seaside suburbs, spaces that operate as places of white retreat and safety. As research across contexts, including white suburbia and the countryside, has shown, "ethnic minorities are made to feel out of place" in these nonurban spaces.[42]

Literature investigating how racialized "social relations are spatially expressed" proves particularly useful for exploring how these issues affect beaches and surfing spaces.[43] This turn to spatiality has been influential in revealing how sporting spaces are gendered, sexualized, and racialized, as well as how "power geometries" of "white space [are] produced and exercised on the bodies of Others."[44] Nirmal Puwar's book *Space Invaders* is a seminal text in illustrating that "some bodies are deemed as having the right to belong, while others are marked as trespassers, who are, in accordance with how both spaces and bodies are imagined (politically, historically and conceptually), circumscribed as being 'out of place.' Not being the somatic norm, they are space invaders."[45]

In the remainder of this chapter I seek to understand the ways in which black surfing bodies reside in and take up space, and if BME bodies are made to feel out of place, rendered as Other to this surfing collectivity. I highlight some of the historical, cultural, ideological, and economic factors that underpin and sustain the difficulties experienced by a group of African American male and female surfers in California. While some factors are clearly specific to these individuals and the Californian context, other factors are also applicable to other geographic spaces and other groups of minority surfers.

Developing the Surfing Habitus

In his account of how leisure preferences are acquired and reproduced, which he terms *habitus*, Bourdieu suggests that a range of cultural factors, including an individual's upbringing (i.e., education, family influence, community, peers), values, and disposition, are central in acquiring both the taste for, and experience of, leisure activities.[46] For Bourdieu, taste is not just the result of individualistic choices, but rather is socially patterned, and a key means by which the social distribution of symbolic resources is organized. Bourdieu's work helps us consider the ways in which participation and accessibility in surfing is related not only to material factors—their cost (economic capital)—but also to the cultural and physical capital required, or rather, the particular and distinctive cultural knowledges that participation demands, and the ways these knowledges are embodied, in gestures, manners, and being in space.[47]

While Bourdieu was primarily concerned with the reproduction of social class, his theories have increasingly been used to explore the gendered and racialized aspects of (body) habitus, and how they are reproduced historically and spatially.[48] Cultural capital in sporting activities like surfing includes the range of cultural, social, and historical knowledges and resources a person possesses, and can take various forms from the embodied to the institutionalized. These knowledges are passed on from generation to generation, but can also be learned through various life experiences. The surfing habitus is also "corporeally informed by social position and expectations."[49] It is a marker of distinction, and a signifier of identity based on maintaining similarities and differences between selves and others. Habitus, gender, and race operate in becoming an insider in a cultural field like surfing: "people are differentiated as to the extent to which they are included, and the extent to which they are insiders in accordance with how well their habitus is adjusted to the demands of the field."[50]

Thus, habitus can help explore the degree to which BME individuals share or are invited to participate in the dominant cultural habitus, and ways in which they are excluded.[51]

Water Enlightened and Whiteboy Wannabes: Childhood Experiences and Family Life

Following Bourdieu's theory, family influences and values are central to acquiring the habitus for visiting the beach and the ocean. Many of the surfers I interviewed were exposed to the beach and the water through their families. Yet they were in the minority, recognizing that black families tended not to go to the beach: "I wouldn't call it a white thing, but we don't do it so regularly. Black families that are quite 'water enlightened' do. But they're still a minority. You know, the majority of people that live in the inner city don't use the facilities of the beach. They don't feel for whatever reason either comfortable because they're brought into it [from outside], or because there's not enough black people down there to allow them to feel comfortable."[52]

Despite being from water-based families and strong swimmers, none of the black surfers I interviewed had grown up with surfers in their families or family-based friendship groups. The attitudes of their parents ranged from support through ambivalence to hostility. Josh, who became a competitive surfer, had complete support from his family. His mother saw surfing as something positive, and so drove him to the beach and to surf contests: "My mom was very proud that her son could surf so well and was happy that I found something that I was so passionate about."[53] However, among some families surfing had retained its 1950s-rooted public image, still associated with juvenile delinquency and drug use.[54] That is, surfers were characterized as youth who "shied away from order and structure" and who were "wasteful and selfish."[55]

School-based friendships and associations led to some interviewees' first surfing experiences. Conversely, as Michael recounted, his son grew up enjoying beach life with his family and surfing with classmates, but as a teenager he rejected surfing in favor of activities popular with his black peers, such as basketball. Josh also highlighted that school was an environment where people took issue with him surfing and not playing basketball: "They figured since I surf I was trying to be white which was totally NOT why I surfed."[56] Irrespective of experiences or opportunities, the perception of surfing being a white sport remained an issue for many black families and communities. Jennifer recounts, "I think it's a difficult thing when I talk to young black people and I try to encourage them to come out and try the sport. They look at me and just go 'that's a white sport.'"[57] This experience was widespread among interviewees. Stevie recounted how driving around his neighborhood with a surfboard on the roof of his car provoked comments like, "Oh you're trying to be a white boy." Michael reflexively narrated the personal difficulties he experienced "being black, and being a surfer" in the (black) middle-class neighborhood where he lived: "I kind of found myself when I was young in limbo, in no man's lands. You know, I knew I couldn't really fit in with the traditional white surf community down there, so to speak. I didn't really fit in here in the black community because people would call me an Uncle Tom, they'd call me an Oreo, they'd call me a white boy, 'oh you're a white boy wannabe.'"[58] As Erickson et al.'s research exploring African Americans' use of nonurban leisure spaces in the United States illustrates, because "recreating in natural areas" is not considered a "black thing" to do, those who choose to take part risk "being associated with 'white culture' by other African Americans, and are perceived as rejecting African American culture."[59]

Such cultural values are not fixed, however, but shift over time. Younger participants recognized that attitudes to youth and BME participation in surfing culture have changed, suggesting that parental and community disapproval was less widespread than for previous generations. Nonetheless, these accounts clearly illustrate how ideas about racial difference, "racialized structures," and "ways of seeing the world" were reproduced in school and family life and through sporting participation.[60] Stereotypes about race were reproduced in and through both white and black communities.

Cultural Stereotypes: "Blacks Can't Swim"

In 1990, at an event in Los Angeles to celebrate Nelson Mandela's release, African-American comedian Nell Carter "joked with the seventy thousand spectators, most of whom were black, that swimming was 'un-black'; if blacks knew how to swim, he said, there would be no African Americans because their enslaved ancestors would have all swam back to Africa."[61] While this common stereotype about black bodies is rooted in racial ideologies—that is, historically constructed differences, not biological facts—it is nonetheless a stereotype that is widely perpetuated by the media, and by black and white Americans. In the documentary *Whitewash*, African American youth at an inner-city basketball court are shown laughing at the notion of them swimming.

Statistics also drive these erroneous beliefs, illustrating, for example, that more minorities in the United States drown than whites.[62] A study by *USA Swimming* suggested that 70 percent of the African American children surveyed had no or low swimming ability, in contrast to 42 percent of white children.[63] Swimming is clearly a powerful signifier in differentiating the black body from the white body, and these myths have ongoing relevance for developing a surfing habitus.[64] Interview participant Jennifer suggested that a lack of swimming proficiency is "one of the main reasons why blacks don't surf."[65] She recounted training to work for the Coast Guard and being amazed that many black recruits couldn't swim. Numerous economic and cultural factors contribute to contemporary African American children being less likely to swim confidently, many of which were alluded to in interviews.[66]

Many of the surfers, however, were cognizant of the fallacy of these discursive constructions of blacks as nonswimmers: "black surfers and black watermen know that there is a heritage, an African heritage of watermen, and waterwomen, and that goes all the way back . . . but culture is powerful."[67] Jennifer suggested that "other minorities," particularly Hispanics, frequented the beach much more than the African American community, arguing that visiting the beach was a part of their diasporic community's identity, and did not seem to have the same connotations as a place of fear.[68] The effect of this, she suggested, was to help break down stereotypes about the beach and surfing as white spaces: "And they've got much stronger tradition with the water and using the beach for picnics and for families' events and for parties, because they did it in their homeland. And they felt comfortable doing it and they don't seem to have some of the same stigmas that we have, that belief that if we go down there we're not going to be able to have fun because white people are going to keep us from it. And they go and do it, and it changes the dynamic."[69] Jennifer's observation is supported by research exploring the use of beaches and urban parks in the United States.[70] Both studies suggested that Hispanics used these recreation sites primarily for social gatherings such as family picnics, illustrating that people from different ethnic groups construct "different meanings for natural space based on their own values, cultures, histories, and traditions."[71]

Perceptions about surfing's exclusivity as a white sport remain widespread. These surfers discussed how they had been affected, at least initially, by stereotypical views about what blacks did and didn't do, but once they had their first taste of surfing, those stereotypes—including self-imposed ones—were quickly broken. As Alicia contended, as a kid she spent a lot of time with her family at the beach, but never asked her mother if she could try surfing because she assumed "surfing was for rich people, that could afford to buy that stuff."[72] Thus, as outlined in Wolch and Zhang's analysis of the use of beach space in California, "race and class matter."[73]

White Racism in Beach Spaces

Racism was part of everyday life for most of my interviewees, particularly when growing up, and surfing spaces were not immune, as many graphically recounted:

> I didn't like to go there [the beach] because I felt very uncomfortable. People ignored you, they didn't talk to you, they stared at you, they threw things at you, they slit your tires, they wrote with wax on your car, they keyed your car and scratched names, you know . . . [names] like "niggers go home" and things like that, with regularity. So it was really an uncomfortable situation. . . . But you know we experienced racism everywhere, so you know I live in the inner city of Los Angeles, it's a black community in which all my life I've experienced some sorts of racism, and at the beach, I've experienced quite a lot.

Interviewees recognized that racial harassment today is much less prevalent than it was in the 1960s, but observed that racism nonetheless continues to exist, often taking more subtle forms. As Carrington highlights, racialized bodies "can become subject to a panoptic form of white governmentality" that seeks to oversee, control, and regulate the behavior of black people and is underpinned by the constant threat of racial harassment and violence.[74]

Drawing on Bonilla-Silva's influential work on the concept of "colorblind racism," Burdsey argues that there has been a shift to more subtle forms of racism, such as racial microaggressions, defined as "brief, everyday exchanges" evident in "gestures, looks, or tones."[75] While surfers I interviewed who had been the recipients of physical abuse were in the minority, most had experienced or witnessed verbal racism in some form, or a particular look or stare. The stare or gaze operates to make minority ethnic individuals feel unwelcome or out of place, and is significant in their surveillance.[76] As Michael recounted: "When you're the only black person sitting out there you know it. And the general vibe in the water sometimes became tense. The staring and the twisted facial expressions sometimes gave way to a slur or negative comment."[77] Alicia suggested that "I have never been aggressively or negatively approached," but that "you are looked at—people stare at you." Alicia believed the stares were benevolent: "It's just odd, not something that is common, they don't know how to place me and I understand that and accept it."[78] As Carrington discusses, being black in a white space can provoke intrigue and fascination as well as surveillance. However, he also argues that while this "new fact of blackness" appears to be more tolerant, it is nonetheless a "moment of post/colonial racism, a double bind. Of intrigue and interest and objectification and racialized inscription all at once."[79] Furthermore, the effectiveness of these microaggressions is their often "subtle and unconscious character," and their "accumulation over a period of time."[80] Jennifer admitted she often felt fearful, and at times fear stopped her surfing altogether: "There were no black people surfing at [surf break]. I would drive up to [place] to sit and watch because I was too afraid to join in."[81]

The Surfing Brotherhood, Race, and Belonging: Contradictory Discourses

Michael argued that surfers themselves were more enlightened than most beach users. He saw the values of surf culture as inclusive and not exclusive, commenting, "Generally the reaction was great because surfers, I think, are enlightened people." Michael was not alone in holding the belief, as well as desire, that the surfing brotherhood was inclusive of all backgrounds. Stevie outlined how surfing in the 1960s had "a sense of communalism" and an openness to difference. Despite being the only black surfer, he was soon "one of the group": "So, you could go to beaches and say, 'can I use your surfboard?' 'Sure use my surfboard, go and play around in the water.' They don't do that at all now, but that was very common."[82]

Josh, an elite, lifelong surfer in his thirties who had competed regularly, said he had not experienced *any* racism when surfing, nor had he really even thought about race, suggesting that, if anything, black surfers were generally seen as "cool." "I've never experienced racism while surfing. Sure, I've had clashes with people in the water but it had nothing to do with my skin color. . . . Tell you the truth I don't think about skin [color] while I'm in the water. I have my focus on getting another wave and thinking about what I'm going to do on it. Maybe if I'm in the water with other black surfers I notice color but I tell myself that it's nice to see that they discovered surfing."[83] Crissy, who had successfully become an elite female surfer in the United States, claimed she was "welcomed with open arms" by the elite surfing fraternity, but experienced "real issues" with her own (black) community.[84]

Nonetheless, many of these narratives were contradictory: their accounts gave numerous examples of ways they were marked as different (looks, stares, etc.), and described exclusion or racism instigated by surfers. Yet they didn't want to see surfers as the problem. Their belief in the inclusivity of the surfing brotherhood made it hard for black participants to hold white surfers accountable. As Puwar highlights, in many spheres "the systematic fantasy of imagined inclusiveness makes it difficult to see racism" and to confront the fact that racism exists.[85] As illustrated in many sporting contexts, this color-blind ideology is so entrenched in many Western sports that "minority ethnic participants can also enforce its interpretive framework."[86] For example, research has shown that individuals adopt various strategies seeking to "simultaneously downplay or deny incidents of racism while trying to exonerate those accused of engaging in such acts."[87]

Despite having experienced racist incidents with white surfers, Michael blamed those (nonsurfers) who lived in middle-class white beach communities: "The people that dwell there, they are not necessarily exposed to a variety of things, one of which is black surfers. And they feel entitled to the ocean already, believing that it's theirs and they could fence it."[88] Yet in conversation, he also recognized that he didn't *want* surfers to be the problem. Having worked hard to become a surfer, and having started to see himself as a surfer, he needed, at least discursively, to disavow surf culture as being excluding or racist. In subsequent conversations I discussed this contradiction with him, and he conceded that the racism he experienced at the beach came from both surfers and nonsurfers, although the latter was more prevalent: "Yes I do find it difficult to talk badly about anyone or anything that I identify myself with . . . I think you're right about me not wanting to see surfers in that light."[89]

Alicia suggested that white surfers held a range of views, from "respect just for being a surfer, and being good at what I do" to "exotified [*sic*] just because you have a different skin color." Yet she believed that once she had developed a level of involvement and commitment to be considered a real surfer, she gained insider status and respect: "If you get to the level in which you can truly say you *are a surfer*, that level of commitment to the ocean, then you see like-minded people who are doing the same. But if you get past that threshold, other surfers who are at the same place, some sort of positive energy and connection that's really not about color or gender or anything, it is just about acknowledging that we are people who love the ocean; and how lucky we are to be able to get to that point. And I just feel very lucky, like being in on a secret, a nirvana with no connection to people, just water."[90]

As Puwar discusses, in the process of becoming an insider, individuals racialized as nonwhite develop what Bourdieu calls a "feel for the game."[91] This is an "embodied form of knowledge and skills that operate beneath the level of conscious discourse" that arises from achieving a level of "synchrony between their habitus, its social trajectory and the institutional space"—or here, as Alicia outlines, in the cultural field of surfing.[92] As Alicia argues, there is an "unspoken understanding" about being a real surfer. Moreover, implicit in the feel for the game is a "denial of the body," a narrative that "prides itself on being based on neutral standards that apply across the board to everybody."[93] Thus, by describing surfing as a spiritual activity, about connecting to water/nature and not bodies, Alicia was able to negate the importance of the visible embodiment of gender and race. As she put it, "a community was open to me by my commitment to surfing."[94]

This belief that commitment to the surfing *activity* superseded other factors was widespread. The association between the "complicity of habitus and field and social capital" that these surfers had achieved through their commitment to surfing has "immense implications for the opportunities that are made available."[95] Certainly, in some spaces and contexts, these surfers were able to feel at home, to become, as Puwar terms it, "familiar strangers" who have in Bourdieu's terminology gained "ontological complicity."[96] The beach was described as a different and liminal space; as Michael put it, kind of like a "foreign country" outside of social control: "Surfing is an exclusive thing, it takes part in the time of day when other people are asleep or doing something else, and we could go and just be, and enjoy and do that. . . . from six in the morning to . . . eleven in the morning ... when we were surfing we were ... brothers. ... And so we all got to just go and be, and hang, and it didn't matter."[97]

Conclusion

In this chapter I have highlighted a range of the cultural, structural, spatial, and ideological difficulties of being a minority ethnic surfer in a white culture and space. The experiences outlined here need to be understood as contextually specific to the place and time and are certainly not generalizable to all minority ethnic surfers or surfing spaces. Yet it is a starting point in deconstructing and challenging our often-uncritical acceptance of surfing culture, media, and space as an important contemporary site where privileged white masculinity is both constructed and reproduced.

The surfers in this research were not a homogenous group; their surfing identities were shaped by a multitude of experiences that differed in relation to factors including (but not limited to) gender, social class, life stage, and residence. Therefore, it was not surprising that while some surfers had been able to transcend difficulties and had become lifelong surfers, for others, the varying forms of exclusion and white racism they experienced continued to have an impact on their surfing experiences.

Following Puwar, I have described these surfers as space invaders who, as Michael reflexively illustrated, did not fit in with the "traditional white surf community" or "in the black community" but were "in limbo, in no-man's lands."[98] Most experienced some exclusion from the black communities, ranging from hostility to being called a variety of abusive names such as "white boy wannabes," "Uncle Toms" and "Oreo cookies." Yet in some spaces and contexts they were able to feel at home.[99] These black surfers found various ways to negotiate their insider identity and difference in these surfing spaces, and their surfing experience provided a space of relative freedom. As Alicia put it, "Through surfing I came to realize Bob Marley's lyrics 'Heaven is here on Earth,'" while for Josh, "My love of surfing outweighed the negative feelings I had when I was told I was trying to be white."[100] While recognizing that the idea of insider and outsider is fluid and complex, racialized minorities do "become in significant ways, insiders."[101] Nonetheless, blackness is still conditional, and measured in relation to a narrowly prescribed set of roles and an imagined community from which the black surfer is still at least partially excluded.

For some, this marginality had been channeled into wanting to confront, challenge, and change the opportunities and experiences for black surfers, and the culture and representation of surfing. Individuals have been active as filmmakers and writers, contesting mass media depictions of surfing and providing opportunities to get more people on the beach and into the water. As Michael suggested, their unique experiences gave them "something that's special . . . we carry a little greater gratitude." In rejecting stereotypes and thinking and living differently from most white surfers, Michael suggests that black surfers embody, and can promote, "an expanded image of self and black culture."[102]

NOTES

1. Thompson, "*Otelo Burning*," 325.

2. Kusz, *Revolt of the White Athlete*, 136.

3. Booth, *Australian Beach Cultures;* Stenger, "Mapping the Beach"; Comer, *Surfer Girls*.

4. Wheaton, *Cultural Politics of Lifestyle Sport*.

5. Chivers-Yochim, *Skate Life*.

6. I use the term *black* in this chapter to refer to self-defined African American surfers. While some factors are clearly specific to these individuals as members of an ethnic minority in the cultural context of California, other factors explored here are applicable to both other geographic spaces and other groups of minority surfers.

7. Laderman, *Empire in Waves*.

8. Walker, *Waves of Resistance*.

9. Usher and Kerstetter, "Surfistas Locales."

10. Kusz, "Extreme America," 209.

11. Kusz, "Extreme America," 207.

12. Comer, *Surfer Girls*, 228.

13. See Thompson, "Judging Surf Culture" and "Reimagining Surf City."

14. Thompson, "Reimagining Surf City."

15. Samuelson and Thompson, "Introduction," and Thompson, "*Otelo Burning*."

16. Samuelson and Thompson, "Introduction," 305.

17. Barclay and West, "Racism or Patriotism?," and Evers, "The Cronulla Race Riots."

18. Waitt, " 'Killing Waves,' " 78; McGloin, *Surfing Nation(s), Surfing Country(s)*.

19. McGloin, "Aboriginal Surfing," 94.

20. McGloin "Aboriginal Surfing," 93.

21. Nemani, "Getting Deep" and "Being a Brown Bodyboarder."

22. See Comer, *Surfer Girls*; Wheaton, "Identity, Politics, and the Beach."

23. On claims of positive impacts, see Thorpe and Rinehart, "Alternative Sport and Affect"; Wheaton, "Identity, Politics, and the Beach." On manipulation of reefs in surfing destinations, see Ponting and O'Brien, "Liberalizing Nirvana."

24. See Beattie, "Sick, Filthy, and Delirious"; Lewis, "Between the Lines"; and Ormrod, "*Endless Summer* (1964)."

25. See Booth, *Australian Beach Cultures*, and Stranger, "Aesthetics of Risk."

26. Lewis, "In Search of the Postmodern Surfer," 70.

27. Lewis, "In Search of the Postmodern Surfer," 71.

28. Lewis, "In Search of the Postmodern Surfer," 71.

29. "Jennifer," interview.

30. On the diversity of surf film genres, see Beattie, "Sick, Filthy, and Delirious"; Booth, "Surfing Films and Videos"; and Ormrod, "Representing 'Authentic' Surfer Identities."

31. Samuelson and Thompson, "Introduction," 305.

32. On the latter film, see McGloin, "Surfing Nation(s), Surfing Country(s)."

33. See Samuelson and Thompson, "Introduction," which introduces the special number of the *Journal of African Cultural Studies* coordinated by the duo.

34. Woods, *White Wash*.

35. In 2016, the *Journal of American Ethnic History* (35, no. 2) published a special issue dedicated to *White Wash*.

36. Garcia and Baltodano, "Free the Beach"; Wolch and Zhang, "Beach Recreation."

37. Garcia and Baltodano, "Free the Beach," 201.

38. Garcia and Baltodano, "Free the Beach," 201.

39. Garcia and Baltodano, "Free the Beach," 201.

40. Erickson, Johnson, and Kivel, "Rocky Mountain National Park," 531.

41. Nayak, "Race, Affect, and Emotion," 2375.

42. Nayak, "Race, Affect, and Emotion," 2372.

43. Neal, "Rural Landscapes," 443.

44. Doreen Massey in Puwar, *Space Invaders*, 7; Carrington, "Leeds and the Topography of Race," 201.

45. Puwar, *Space Invaders*, 8.

46. Bourdieu, *Distinction*.

47. Bourdieu calls all forms of power "capital," and discusses different forms, such as cultural, symbolic, economic, and physical capital, thus recognizing that wealth is not just economic (or political) but also symbolic (Wheaton, "Habitus"). These different types of wealth, which are inherited or accumulated, and tend to be unevenly distributed, constitute part of a person's habitus. Through the formation of their habitus, people acquire cultural capital, a "range of cultural competencies" that "makes particular activities more or less accessible for them" (Haywood et al., *Understanding Leisure*, 240).

48. Puwar outlines how Bourdieu's ideas, particularly "a feel for the game," helps explain how minorities become insiders in institutions dominated by whiteness. See Atencio, Beal, and Wilson, "The Distinction of Risk"; Erickson et al., "Rocky Mountain National Park"; Thorpe, "Bourdieu, Feminism and Female Physical Culture" and "Bourdieu, Gender Reflexivity, and Physical Culture."

49. Evers, "The Cronulla Race Riots."

50. Puwar, *Space Invaders*, 125.

51. Burdsey, "One of the Lads," 764.

52. "Jennifer," interview.

53. "Josh," interview.

54. On associations of surfing with drug culture, see Booth, *Australian Beach Cultures*; Lawler, *The American Surfer*, 126–140; and Ormrod, "Issues of Gender," 2.

55. Booth, *Australian Beach Cultures*, 95.

56. "Josh," interview

57. "Jennifer," interview.

58. "Michael," interview. Such derogatory terms are discussed in Nayak, *Race, Place, and Globalization*, and Carrington, "Double Consciousness."

59. Erickson et al., "Rocky Mountain National Park," 540.

60. Carrington, *Race, Sport, and Politics*, 175.

61. Dawson, "Enslaved Swimmers and Divers," 1354.

62. Dawson, "Enslaved Swimmers and Divers," 1354. Of course, *where* people swim may be a key factor attributing to this statistic, with whites being more likely to have access to safer swimming pool environments.

63. Finlo Rohrer, "Why Don't Black Americans Swim?," *BBC News*, September 3, 2010, http://www.bbc.com/news/world-us-canada-11172054. In one study, respondents were asked if they could swim across a 25-yard pool.

64. It is also the focus of an insightful editorial by Tetsuhiko Endo, "Debunking the Stereotype that Blacks Don't Swim," *The Inertia*, February 20, 2012, http://www.theinertia.com/surf/debunking-the-stereotype-that-blacks-dont-surf-or-swim/.

65. She described the documentary *White Wash*, which "shows an interview with African American youth at a basketball court in New York, laughing at the notion of them swimming."

66. Of course such experiences are not universal but context dependent. As explored in Wheaton, *The Cultural Politics of Lifestyle Sport*, street children in Durban, South Africa, grow up in proximity to the sea and learn to swim and surf in the ocean.

67. "Alicia," interview.

68. "Jennifer," interview. This fear of water, and natural places more generally, is widely commented upon. See Wheaton, *Cultural Politics of Lifestyle Sport*.

69. Wheaton, *Cultural Politics of Lifestyle Sport*.

70. Wolch and Zhang, "Beach Recreation," and Garcia and Baltodano, "Free the Beach," 197.

71. Garcia and Baltodano, "Free the Beach," 197.

72. "Alicia," interview.

73. Wolch and Zhang, "Beach Recreation," 437.

74. Carrington, "Fear of a Black Athlete," 107.

75. Bonilla-Silva, *Racism Without Racists*; Burdsey, "That Joke Isn't Funny Anymore," 268.

76. See Puwar, *Space Invaders*.

77. "Michael," interview.

78. "Alicia," interview.

79. Carrington, "Leeds and the Topography of Race," 176.

80. Burdsey, "That Joke Isn't Funny Anymore," 268.

81. "Jennifer," interview.

82. "Stevie," interview.

83. "Josh," interview.

84. "Crissy," interview.

85. Puwar, *Space Invaders*, 137

86. Burdsey, "That Joke Isn't Funny Anymore," 275.

87. Burdsey, "That Joke Isn't Funny Anymore," 268.

88. "Michael," interview.

89. "Michael," interview.

90. "Alicia," interview.

91. Puwar, *Space Invaders;* Bourdieu, *Homo Academicus,* 56.

92. Puwar, *Space Invaders,* 127.

93. Puwar, *Space Invaders,* 132.

94. "Alicia," interview.

95. Puwar, *Space Invaders,* 129.

96. Puwar, *Space Invaders,* 129.

97. "Michael," interview.

98. "Michael," interview.

99. Puwar, *Space Invaders,* 129.

100. "Alicia," interview; "Josh," interview.

101. Puwar, *Space Invaders,* 119.

102. "Michael," interview.

9 / Indigenous Surfing: Pedagogy, Pleasure, and Decolonial Practice

COLLEEN McGLOIN

Although the legend of Duke Kahanamoku is often revered as the beginning of Australian surfing, the notion that surfing as an activity, a form of play, or indeed a cultural practice that was "introduced" into Australia is questionable. Indigenous people in Australia have for millennia used the ocean as both a food source and a playground. The ocean is an indicator of "country" depending on a group or clan's location. It is also a site of history.[1] Aunty Rita Timberey, a local elder from the southeast coast of New South Wales, says of the ocean, "For my people, it was a life source. . . . It's all about a different worldview. The beach owns us. It gives us life. . . . For white Australians it's different. The beaches right along the south coast are sacred to us, our middens are there. Some are now in the ocean because of the last ice age when the waters rose and covered them over. The beach is our history. We played there as well, like other kids."[2]

There is a paucity of work dealing with indigenous surfing in Australia, or reference to the surfing practices of indigenous people either pre- or postcolonization. However, it is reasonable to assume that prior to colonization, an aspect of the beach "play" referred to by Aunty Rita was riding waves, whatever form that took, and that surfing, for indigenous coastal dwellers, comprised a form of pleasure, and indeed, cultural expression that identified "country" for surfers as both a geographical and cultural site. In its contemporary state, indigenous surfing in Australia constitutes a pedagogical practice as well as a form of pleasure; surfing is both a reclamation of cultural pride and an affirmation of precolonial sovereignty.

Indigenous surfing as a modern-day activity can be understood according to its many formations and practices. Australian indigenous surfing enjoys collective interactions with other, global indigenous surfers through a shared history of colonization, although it remains distinctive owing to the particularity of the Australian colonial experience. Indigenous surfing is, for some, an individual pursuit; not all surfers belong to groups or engage in competitive surfing. For others, the competitiveness of the marketplace is an attraction. Similar to white mainstream surfing, therefore, Australian indigenous surfing is not neatly definable, but at this historical juncture it is distinctive in that indigenous surfers share the historical legacy of colonialism and the persistence of colonial discourses that continue to define indigenous people in Australia according to colonial relations of power. For the purpose of this discussion, I use the term "indigenous surfing" in its broadest sense: as an activity undertaken by indigenous (Aboriginal and Torres Strait Islander) surfers, for whom the brutal legacy of colonialism and its plethora of contemporary manifestations remains a daily reality.[3]

In this chapter I engage with the ways in which indigenous surfing as a pedagogical force disrupts dominant discourses of national identity. Deploying work in critical pedagogy that identifies the relationship between cultural practices and the broader, political domain of corporate neoliberalism as a site for teaching, learning, and knowledge production and consumption, I examine the ways in which indigenous surfing constitutes a form of critical pedagogy that recenters indigenous knowledges, *epistemes*, histories, and spatiotemporalities.[4] When examined through this lens, indigenous surfing encompasses a politically motivated cultural impetus that reinvigorates Australian indigenous cultures by providing the basis for unlearning and relearning, for dissociation and retrieval. Indigenous surfing can be understood as the repossession of culture, of landscape and seascape, a practice of resistance to the enduringness of colonialism. This is not to suggest it constitutes a heroic act of agency that sits comfortably with white fantasies of a defiant Other. Rather, the seizing back of surfing as an expression of precolonial practice can be understood as a revival of surfing according to *epistemically* relevant knowledges: a decolonizing pedagogical force that foregrounds oppositional ways of knowing and being as a deliberate reversal of power, or, following Walter Mignolo, as a form of "epistemic disobedience," an act of "decolonial thinking" as "an unveiling of the epistemic silences of Western epistemology" that is grounded in the body politics of knowledge.[5]

This chapter takes the following trajectory. First, I discuss briefly the emergence of contemporary white mainstream surfing movements' association with the development of white, masculinist Australian identity. Second, through evidence and examples, I theorize indigenous surfing's localized reclamation of surfing as a pleasurable and pedagogical practice enjoyed by indigenous children and teenagers.

In a previous work, *Surfing Nation(s) Surfing Country(s)*, I explored the discursive terrain of surfing in Australia, identifying a popular cultural movement that dictated particular forms of white masculinity. These modes of masculinity have been historically mobilized to support dominant discourses of national identity in Australia. Although expressions of masculinity changed over time, these transformations always need to sit well with the shifting constructions of "Australian-ness." In other words, following Homi Bhabha's discussion about how nations can become blurred or camouflaged, newer forms of representation and cultural practice bolster a renewed attempt to reconfigure the appearance of national unity.[6] What was once disavowed is now validated in the interests of nation.

White mainstream surfing culture contributed to this renewal. In the mid- to late twentieth century, representations began to incorporate changes in culture, gender, sexuality, race, and class as these reflected shifts in the national cultural perception of surfing. Competitive surfing, taking hold in the 1970s and 1980s in Australia, provided the impetus for surfing's remaking as a market-driven enterprise. Surfing's cultural meanings were *re*-presented, *re*-packaged, and *re*-badged—"branded" with the help of large surfing corporations such as Rip Curl and Billabong—but also ideologically sanctioned in collaboration with other nationalist discourses. Surfing was given a new set of meanings, new images, and associated paraphernalia to accompany new marketing strategies.

A refocusing of Australian national identity away from the enduring colonial bush iconography of the nineteenth and early twentieth centuries toward the seascape as surfing culture became marketable paved the way for white Aussie surfers to become integral to revitalized visions of nationhood. There was a notable shift in much media representation of surfing, for example, from stereotypical notions of "laid-back" hedonistic people where the stereotypical "laziness" of surfers prevailed to a more corporate view of surfing that fits with national re-imaginings of a market-driven economy. National interests now endorsed competitive surfing as a commercial, market-driven industry that conformed to both national and transnational neoliberal economies. Over time, this refashioned connection between surfing and nation articulated a symbolic narrative of progress that worked hard to contain its contradictions and slippages and to represent itself as coherent. This narrative was accompanied by the rise of women's surfing, which, although stylistically and perhaps in some ways philosophically different from mainstream male surfing, has nonetheless also been incorporated into a mainstream, market-oriented political economy.

Indigenous surfing as a practice taught to indigenous children and teenagers destabilizes the dominant surfing movement's claims to white masculinities, and to a national identity grounded in a white male ethos artfully removed from a violent history of colonial dispossession. Indigenous surfing, or the surfing practices of indigenous surfers, constitutes a disruption precisely because indigenous peoples' daily realities are experienced through the lens of colonial rule and the ongoing legacy of that history.

For many young indigenous surfers, as I will illustrate, surfing is encoded with social and cultural meanings. Surfing as a pedagogical tool is often presented to young indigenous surfers in accordance with different knowledges, histories, experiences, and cultural values. This does not imply that indigenous surfing as a movement is removed from the market-driven forces that corporatized mainstream surfing in the 1980s. Nor am I suggesting that indigenous surfing is somehow beyond the domain of the individualism encoded in neoliberal ideology. I note, though, that particularly since the 1990s, many sports teachers and indigenous surfers have been active in teaching surfing to young indigenous females and males, not necessarily with a competitive impulse, but as fun, an esteem-building activity that promoted the reclamation of cultural pride and pleasure in the act of surfing as a fun and pleasurable activity. This was a time in Australia's history when indigenous politics was firmly on the political agenda through much-publicized land rights issues and discussions about reconciliation. It was a brief time when possibilities for social and political change were both envisaged and, to some degree, realized.

Although many young indigenous surfers entered the competitive surfing domain, my research at the time demonstrated that indigenous surfers often spoke of surfing using quite different frames of reference than those used by their white counterparts. Many indigenous surfers approached surfing with different foci; for example, emphasis was placed on surfing's capacity to teach, to impart pedagogical tools for the preservation, maintenance, and proliferation of indigenous culture and indigenous knowledge. The pleasure of surfing over the pleasure of winning is also noted: "Some fellas, they talk about ripping the waves to pieces. I reckon the wave tells you what to do, just catch the wave and ride the wave, flow with what the wave's doing and if you get a good score for it, well that's good. If you don't you had a good time riding the wave."[7]

Surfing schools for indigenous youth are places where cultural values are imparted alongside individual prowess. Indigenous surfing is a way of connecting the individual surfer to her or his community, to issues of health and well-being, and, on a global scale, to wider indigenous surfing communities. So although indigenous surfers did, and still do, compete on the international surfing circuit, another way of conceiving surfing is being taught to indigenous youth through surf schools that herald surfing as a kind of decolonizing cultural practice. Surfing is reclaimed as a longstanding cultural activity that preceded and has endured the imposition of colonialism, not as a static form, but as a continually evolving practice of cultural affirmation and resistance to colonization.

Australian Colonial History: The Legacy of Dis-ease

Since Australia was colonized by the British in 1788, the indigenous population has been subjected to all forms of violence imaginable. This has manifested directly as a result of frontier warfare and racism, and indirectly as a result of social regulation through government policies and their attendant practices of child removal, enforced relocation, prescribed miscegenation, overrepresentation in the legal system, deaths in custody, the outlawing of languages, and the imposition of Christianity; the list is endless. The legacy of colonization in Australia mirrors that of many colonized cultures, but needs to be seen according to the specific and ongoing discursive formations that have structured, and continue to structure, the nation's self-identity. Australia's identity as a nation was formed according to the doctrine of *terra nullius* (land belonging to no one), a doctrine in place since a proclamation issued by the colonial government in 1835 and overturned as recently as 1992 following the efforts of Torres Strait Island activist Eddie Koiki Mabo and the famous Mabo ruling.[8] Australian nationhood was also reinforced racially according to the principles of the White Australia Policy, officially introduced in 1901 and officially revoked as recently as the late 1970s.

Knowledge of Australia's colonial history reveals that although resistance to colonialism has been ongoing since 1788, and manifested through a multitude of political and social activities, it is only in recent decades that indigenous cultural revival has been discursively acknowledged in mainstream white Australian culture. It is still the case, however, that indigenous people continue to suffer alarming rates of disease, disability, infant mortality, deaths in custody, and social disadvantage. These disparities are well documented, and will provide the reader with staggering information about the ongoing effects of colonialism.[9] In the face of relentless and systemic violence, punitive and cruel policies, and ongoing disadvantage, indigenous people in this country have fought back, resisted, and subverted, individually and collectively, through actions that have been documented in works on Australian colonization from an anticolonial standpoint.[10] In small groups, pockets of resistance, and larger, organized political groups, resistance has been core practice since invasion. Most texts detailing indigenous resistance are published by nonindigenous scholars who have come to see colonialism in this country as an enduring enterprise that systemically subjugates indigenous knowledges and practices according to a binary position within Western knowledge production and consumption. So although we—nonindigenes—acknowledge and pay tribute to the extraordinary resilience of Australian Aboriginal people as the oldest and longest-surviving indigenous culture in the world, and to their relentless efforts to resist colonial violence, we are latecomers to this salutation, in fact, sluggish respondents to the acknowledgment of the extent of historical violence, and discomforted by our own complicity in the enduringness of its dehumanizing force. Although institutions of "higher learning" have in recent decades given a nod to indigenous studies, we still struggle with the prospect of competing *epistemes*. Despite our often well-intended commitment to indigenous issues, we still do not sit well as "critical allies."[11] Shifting uncomfortably in our skin and often harried by our dis-ease, we are at times immobilized by guilt, shame, and the astonishing fact that indigenous people continue to survive the onslaught of colonial violence. What is also disturbing is that we have no suitable language yet that will allow us to be easy with this knowledge as it relates to the way we see ourselves as *humane* beings, democratic citizens, or national subjects. The forms of colonial violence are arguably more subtle, more clever and manipulative than they once were during the official "protection" and "assimilation" policies that regulated the lives of indigenous people in Australia throughout much of the nineteenth and twentieth centuries. The current sway of neoliberalism has effectively incorporated into its domain a human rights agenda that we latch onto at times to provide comfort and assure ourselves we are alert to the inhumanity of colonialism, that we "heed" the call. And when that fails, we assuage ourselves by invoking the notion that we shouldn't indulge in self-flagellation, that this further immobilizes our potential for understanding and for forming ethical and supportive alliances. Self-flagellation is often a recipe for retreat, and can be understood as what Lewis Gordon describes as "disciplinary decadence," an avoidance of critical thought or acknowledgment of reality. Drawing from Fanon, Gordon refers to disciplinary coercion as "self-devouring methods" where "getting it right" is a methodology rather than a conscious attempt to engage with the real, lived realities of our own implication in suffering.[12] Nonindigenous responses to colonialism invariably do—and will continue to, no doubt—invoke this form of "decadence," where, for example, in relation to surfing culture, it is still the case that indigenous surfing is rarely represented in surfing texts as a pursuit that represents a vastly different epistemology. Rather, indigenous surfers' prowess is incorporated into a white mainstream marketized ethos that retains the paternalism of colonial discourses. Davis and Shpuniarsky mark the ways that indigenous/nonindigenous relations play out in the social domain, "When Indigenous and non-Indigenous people come together in alliances and coalitions, paternalism may be mobilized, subtly or overtly. There are often breeches of Indigenous social codes of which non-Indigenous people are simply not aware. . . . Despite the good intentions of allies, colonial relations can be reproduced."[13]

The project for new ways of understanding is thus ongoing. We are still searching for a language to come to terms with, or to articulate meaningfully, the ways in which we are implicated as social subjects, citizens, advocators of democracy and human liberty, in the continuity of paternalistic colonial domination. We find it difficult to locate an ethical standpoint that does not position us as compliant, or indeed, a position that allows us to situate the persistence of colonial violence (and our complicity in that) within the much broader discursive domain of global politics. In our self-obsession and struggle to "get it right," what many of us fail to recognize is the cultural heritage of precolonial indigenous life, where knowledge and cultural practices were inextricable from law, kinship relations, and social regulation, and linked to both harmonious relationships and conflict, tribal wars and peaceful coexistence.

Into the mix of survival techniques founded on tens of thousands of years of acquired knowledge, indigenous cultures, of course, included play, recreation, and relaxation in their social relations. To reiterate, it is inconceivable to imagine that surfing—the artful, skillful, and playful gliding across the ocean—was not an activity practiced by indigenous people whose countries were located on the Australian coastline. I note the connectivity between knowledge and recreation as captured by Dina Gilio-Whitaker: "Most indigenous wisdom teaches [that] everything is connected, someway, somehow, including surfing and indigeneity. In Hawaiian culture the connection between these two things is well known, since for something like 2,000 years wave riding was a central element of the culture. The same is true in Peru and other places."[14]

What Gilio-Whitaker points to is a way of being that proposes connectivity between indigenous knowledges and cultural practices that was severed when languages, cultural practices, and rituals were outlawed. Indigenous surfing in its contemporary Australian context thus foments a discontinuity, where surfing represents a *re*-presentation or *re*-identification that is accompanied by the pleasure of surfing, undoubtedly, but is also implicated by resistance to the enduringness of colonial policy and practice. Ossie Stuart's discussion of the way in which football has been taken up in colonial Africa echoes this point: "The game was wrested from European control and used by the African population to assert their new urban identity. The game became an expression of defiance towards the state and of independence from their colonial oppressors."[15]

Stuart points to the way football was "wrested," seized, or reclaimed. Again, it would be naive to assume that pre-colonial African cultures did not kick objects as forms of recreation or as an organized form of play, as it would also be naive to assume indigenous people did not engage in oceanic forms of recreation such as surfing. I will return to a more comprehensive discussion of indigenous surfing that supports Stuart's point, albeit from a different colonial context. First, I want to consider neoliberalism as the current political orthodoxy that organizes all social and cultural practices within what we might call "mainstream" surfing culture, with all its shades and nuances.

Neoliberalism and Public Pedagogy: Surfing the Market

Henry Giroux argues that neoliberalism cannot simply be understood as an economic theory. Rather, he suggests, it is a discourse that pervades all aspects of the public arena, imposing a form of pedagogy whereby knowledge is produced, circulated, and consumed in the public domain, primarily according to corporate interests.[16] Corporate interests reflect the power relations inherent in dominant discourses where particular knowledge is validated, sanctioned, and authorized institutionally, and other knowledge deemed invalid or irrelevant to the interests of the nation. Neoliberal economies have a vested interest in mainstream surfing and the kind of knowledge that accrues around its practice. Whether this refers to the spiritual, competitive, or pleasure-seeking aspects of surfing practice, or the geographical, cultural, or tourism foci that accompany surfing, it is the case that mainstream surfing constitutes a form of pedagogy that "teaches" not simply about surfing, but about race, gender, heteronormativity, and the dominant precepts of what constitutes nation. Surfing in its mainstream form is about particular ideas of nation, gender relations, sexuality, religious belief, environmental concerns, corporatism, and all that can be absorbed into the ideological framework of market economies, whether constitutive of a mainstream or subcultural impulse. This is not to say that mainstream surfers are unaware of this. Nor is it to imply that somehow no agency can be effected to sidestep, appropriate, or subvert market forces if so desired. What it does tell us, though, is that mainstream surfing has been stridently assimilated into corporate market ideology, perhaps because of its already competitive impulse grounded in competitive white masculinities, but also, I would argue, because of surfing's connection to nationalist discourses. To reiterate, as bush iconography and its associated ethos were less representative of an increasingly urbanized body politic, from around the 1960s onward surfing was integrated into the national psyche as a prominent marker of national identity through mainstream media, literature, and the political domain; at the outset of surfing's incorporation into nation, Australians were to be seen as a beach-loving culture, relaxed, outdoorsy sun-worshippers.

It is not a difficult task to commoditize any sport or cultural practice whose focus is primarily competitive in nature. Surfing was, and remains, integral to the construction of Australia as a modern nation-state and its imperative as a thriving capitalist economy on the global stage. Global Industry Analysts, Inc., estimates that the world surfing market will reach an astounding US$13.2 billion by the year 2017.[17] Australian surfing contributes significantly to surfing's global economic success. In fact, SurfingAustralia's annual report for 2013 boasts that "surfing remains one of the most marketable sports in Australia."[18] I have discussed in detail elsewhere mainstream surfing's various manifestations of "soul surfing," environmentalism, spirituality, and connection to nature as a countercultural ethos that reignited the national imagination and, to some degree, attempted to sidestep the onslaught of capitalism.[19] It is the case, though, that Australian mainstream surfing depended on its development elsewhere for its branding as a "homegrown" practice. The "elsewhere" was invariably in the landscape of other indigenous cultures, such as those of Bali, Samoa, Tonga, and Hawai'i. Professional surfer Stephen Cooney confirms this practice, speaking of the Balinese surfing destination Uluwatu as a "real life experience . . . it was pristine, there was a coral reef, there was [sic] fish, there were sea cows. The locals continued to tell us you shouldn't be out there[,] 'don't go out there, you shouldn't be in the water[,]' because they felt that Uluwatu had some sort of mystical power, well I think they thought it was an evil place so when we actually started paddling out, they couldn't quite work out what we were doing."[20]

This representation of Balinese people fits well with many stereotypical depictions of "natives" which I won't reproduce here. However, it is hard to countenance that a culture subjected to colonialism would have been in any way puzzled by Australian surfers ignoring warnings; they are probably accustomed to disrespectful responses to their belief system. The disregard of culture implicit in the above statement heralds a form of cultural arrogance that was not unusual—in fact, it was characteristic of Australian surfers' escapades to many Pacific Island nations during mainstream surfing's commodification into the global marketplace. As noted by another pro surfer, Mark Richards, Australian surfers built camps in Samoa and Tonga. Overseas travel, he claimed, is "the essence of surfing."[21] Competitive surfing was often practiced and nurtured elsewhere, and was a kind of backlash to the "soul surfing" movement of the 1970s. Competitive surfing relied on aggression, on winning, on "stealing" waves, being ruthless; to borrow a description of Australian surfing icon Nat Young, "He wanted to . . . rip the wave to pieces, like shred it to bits. . . ."[22]

The competitive impulse of surfing was complemented and reflected by the global shifts in economic and political power during this era where corporate forms of capitalism commoditized all cultural pursuits in many Western nations. To borrow from Giroux, "Neoliberal ideology re-scripted citizenship as: an energized plunge into consumerism," where market forces celebrated all expressions of individualism through a competitive free market.[23] Thus began the era of large surfing corporations, where nationalism could be performed through the act of surfing as well as its associated brands, logos, texts, and other paraphernalia. Surfers were, and still are, in Australia and globally, identified and sponsored through large corporations. As Clifton Evers notes in his critique of corporate surfing, "Pro surfers are enlisted in the army of the service industry," and "The professional surfing tour and corporations attached to it preach creativity and freedom in the slogans but it's possible to argue that they actually bury them, destroy them, make them only connote *sales*."[24] It is not unusual to hear critiques of corporatized surfing, especially from surfers who lament that surfing should be ideologically removed from corporate interests.

Corporate interests reflect individualism, individual competition, and free markets, and are entrenched in neoliberalism, an ideology whose core principles of market dominance infiltrate every facet of everyday life in what is identified as the Global North. It is difficult, therefore, to remove or delink the practice of surfing from the ideology that gave rise to its prominence as a national symbol.

Also, following Giroux, neoliberalism constitutes a mode of public pedagogy whereby all spheres of social and cultural activity are sought out, assessed for their "value," for incorporation into the market, and for their potential use in proliferating neoliberal values.[25] This is not to say that mainstream surfers are a homogenized group incapable of resistance to market-driven economies. There are always interventions into dominant discourses; as Zygmunt Bauman reminds us, "Culture is a permanent revolution of sorts."[26] New formations in Australian surfing culture are continually emerging and include Christian surfers, gay surfers, and disabled surfers.[27] New surfing formations, however, do not necessarily constitute oppositional ideologies. Although denoting difference, they may complement existing mainstream ethos or, conversely, refute it by reproducing an even more fundamentalist value system. Whatever the case, mainstream and so-called subcultural surfing cultural formations produce narratives, ideas, practices, and sets of imagery and iconography that constitute a pedagogical force for surfers and potential surfers: to reiterate, surfing is to teach, to interpellate, and to produce subjectivities. In the case of indigenous surfing, interpellation is always inflected by the knowledge of colonialism, the theft of land, and the differential power relations that construct subjectivities according to the dominance of imposed systems of knowledge.

Cultural Reclamation

Australian indigenous knowledges are grounded in pedagogical practices that predate colonialism and comprise tens of thousands of years of survival. One of those practices was surfing. Indigenous people have always surfed, a point raised by John Ogden, a surfer, cinematographer, and former photojournalist of the Australian surf magazine *Tracks*.[28] Ogden states, in reference to the Aboriginal people of Sydney's northern beaches, "These were very good water people, with excellent surf skills. It was their livelihood. Theirs was a canoe culture and they were known to take these craft out in large surf. . . . Their traditional way of life broke down within a couple of years of the arrival of the First Fleet, mainly due to smallpox."[29]

During much of the colonial era, Aboriginal people were not seen at beaches, either because of forced relocation onto missions or as an effect of the racist ideology that relegated all indigenous people to "fringe dwellings" out of sight of the white public domain. During the past twenty to thirty years, though, coinciding with the rise of surfing culture as a "respectable" and more marketable sport, indigenous surfing has become popular. Many Australian indigenous surfers are well-known high achievers and well known in mainstream surfing (e.g., Otis Carey, Russell Molony, Soli Bailey, Robbie Page) and in indigenous surfing titles. Much of the popularity of indigenous surfing has been nurtured through indigenous surfing competitions, and from the inception of many localized surf schools around the coastlines of Australia. The 1999 film *Surfing the Healing Wave* depicts an indigenous surfing competition on the north coast of New South Wales. This film is one of a kind, and I have used it in my teaching to encourage students to explore the expression of cultural pride that is at the forefront of this surfing competition. The film's blurb states, "This film is a lively and uplifting look at the positive steps taken by an Indigenous community as it strives to achieve cultural continuity for future generations."

Indigenous surfing as an explicit form of cultural expression—*as culture* — can be understood as a form of epistemic disobedience, following Walter Mignolo, who tells us that "the task of decolonial thinking and the enactment of the decolonial option in the 21st century starts from the epistemic de-linking: from acts of epistemic disobedience."[30] I understand this to mean acts that are transgressive through opposition, through a systematic insistence on other cultural codes, other ways of practicing culture, other epistemes directly at odds with Western thought and action, acts that comprise modes of defiance in order to destabilize existing colonial relations of power, not simply by a reversal, but by a concrete act of dismantling the logic on which those power relations rest—that is, the (il)logicality of colonial thought.

George Sefa Dei argues that "it is imperative to recognize that there has been incessant pressure for Indigenous bodies to Indigenize Western ideologies and practices, sometimes for survival in local contexts and other times to fit into the Western-centred globalization project order."[31] *Surfing the Healing Wave* provides an example of the indigenizing of Western practices. The film depicts an indigenous surfing competition at Fingal Bay on the north coast of New South Wales, where indigenous surfers from Australia and worldwide congregate to celebrate the surfing abilities of indigenous youth. It is a film about competitive surfing that is interspersed with snippets of narrated colonial history and, echoing Mignolo, "fit[s] into the Western globalization project order" to some degree through its use of globally recognizable surfing paraphernalia.[32] These visual cues of global marketing are peripheral, though. The film centralizes a view of indigenous cultural life at the local, national, and global level, and de-emphasizes a neoliberal market orientation of indigenous surfing. This is achieved through oral and visual vignettes of a past steeped in the loss of land and kinship networks, and a present exhilarated by the connection between and among indigenous peoples from across the globe who come to compete, but also to meet, to be part of the ceremonial gathering of local, national, and global indigenous surfers and their families. The film illustrates a local indigenous surfing school where surfing is taught as a confidence builder without an emphasis on "success" or winning, and with deference to the power of the ocean as a teacher. As the winner of the surf competition in the film explains, "I reckon the ocean decides the winner on the day.... The ocean don't care what colour you are or how good you can surf."[33] The surfing school at Fingal Bay was initially sponsored by Billabong, but now attracts no corporate sponsorship and is funded by the local community as a cultural event that, according to a local elder, initiator of the first indigenous surfing competition in the area, reminds him of "the old days, the gathering of people, Corroborree, meeting of all tribes throughout our great nation...."[34]

The film speaks of indigenous surfing through culture and history; surfing narratives are combined with colonial histories of dispossession and juxtaposed with representations of the role of surfing in reclaiming cultural pride and identity. As Mignolo reminds us, "a politics of identity is different from identity politics—the former is open to whoever wants to join, while the latter tends to be bounded by the definition of a given identity."[35] The politics of identity for Australian indigenous people is about an enforced and regulated colonial identity, one formulated through policy and administration that has rendered fraught issues of Aboriginal identity in Australia, and that continues to do so.[36] As a cultural identity both ascribed and destroyed by colonialism, indigeneity in Australia in contemporary times is expressed in surfing primarily as a site of cultural reclamation and restoration, a reminder of an erased subjectivity grounded in a precolonial history: "Yeah, surfing helps me get back to who I am. Even if I'm by myself it connects me back."[37] This response suggests surfing offers an opportunity for retrieval where a sense of cultural identity grounded in memory is temporarily reactivated and where the seeds of decolonial thought and action might be mobilized. *Surfing the Healing Wave* provides a starting point, a text that exemplifies the potential for cultural reclamation and affirmation. Coinciding with the release of this film, and perhaps as a response to it, many local indigenous surfing schools were introduced nationwide. I focus here on the locale of the south coast of New South Wales, where such schools are still in operation and offer indigenous youth a program of health, well-being, fun, and cultural knowledge.

Surfing as Pedagogy: The Locale

Indigenous knowledge (sometimes referred to in academia as IK) refers to both pre- and postcolonization ways of knowing and being. In the context of teaching surfing to youngsters, indigenous knowledge constitutes an understanding of connections to kinship relations through the ocean and the practice of surfing whereby indigenous youngsters are made aware of the importance of resilience and their place within communities. During the 1990s, surf schools for children and teenagers became popular sites for Aboriginal people and Torres Strait Islanders in the south coast regions of New South Wales. Jodie Edwards was instrumental in starting a local surf school named Healthy Cultures, held at various beaches south of Sydney. At this school, surfing was used as a vehicle to teach kids about healthy living, and in the process, to try and shift the connection between white mainstream surfing and unhealthy practices. Participants in the school were given a two-hour surfing lesson and a healthy lunch, followed by discussions and guest speakers. Jodie described the school to me as follows: "The surf school was initiated to give our kids an awareness of culture alongside an interest in pleasure and play. We taught the kids about the importance of maintaining health, of being aware of the potential dangers of drugs, alcohol, and the risks of HIV in conjunction with a program that introduced them to the joys of surfing. The program, therefore, was never just about surfing per se. It was intended to be about how surfing could connect the kids with community in ways that would enrich their knowledge of their Aboriginality through surfing, through fun activities."[38]

Another local Aboriginal initiative, the Koori Youth Network, ran a surfing and diving program in Wollongong on the New South Wales south coast for several months.[39] This program introduced local indigenous youth to surfing through a program similar to Healthy Cultures, where aspiring young surfers were taught culture. The locale of this network has a particular history of colonial dislocation identified by miscegenation and enforced relocation; many fair-skinned Aboriginal youth have difficulty identifying and being identified as Aboriginal, or "proving" their Aboriginal heritage, owing to the destruction of records, but also the local suspicion of lighter skin based on embedded colonial assumptions about skin color and Aboriginality. The Koori Youth Network addressed these identity problems by teaching local Aboriginal surfers about culture and local history, and by instilling a sense of cultural pride through surfing and other activities.

At the national level, the Australian government's "Closing the Gap" program produced a paper entitled "Supporting Healthy Communities through Sports and Recreation Programs," a joint initiative whereby the positive effects of sport and recreation were inextricably connected to culture: "Within Indigenous communities, a strong component of sport and recreation is the link with traditional culture."[40]

Indigenous surfing as it is taught to indigenous children and young adults is a teaching tool that combines play, fun, and learning according to indigenous cultural values. The indigenous surfing schools disrupt colonial discourses by foregrounding indigenous ways of knowing and being. This pedagogical mode of teaching and learning operates at the site Martin Nakata refers to as the "cultural interface," a real and symbolic site of tension, struggle, and productivity. Nakata refers to the interface as "points of intersecting trajectories. It is a multi-layered and multi-dimensional space of dynamic relations constituted by the intersections of time, place, distance, different systems of thought, competing and contesting discourses within and between different knowledge traditions, and different systems of social economic and political organisation . . . a space that abounds with contradictions, ambiguities, conflict and contestation of meanings that emerge from these various shifting intersections."[41]

Nakata's concept refers specifically to the ways in which Torres Strait Islander people negotiate the daily exigencies of colonial rule. It can be adapted, though, as a means to understanding the processes, struggles, and possibilities that inform all Australian indigenous peoples' negotiations and realities in all daily pursuits; as Nakata explains, it is a "space of possibilities as well as constraints, which can have negative or positive consequences for different people at different times."[42] Indigenous people who teach surfing are aware of the possibilities and constraints Nakata speaks of, and while teaching young indigenous people to surf and have fun, do so with an awareness of colonial power and a form of active resistance that seeks to reinstate indigenous cultural values as an integral aspect of fun, health, and cultural well-being.

Concluding Thoughts

Indigenous surfing in Australia transforms indigenous peoples' social relations from a colonially imposed discursive regularity to a mode of resistance whereby the affirmation of indigenous knowledge and cultural practices is reinstated. While indigenous surfing is a restoration of culture or cultural pride, indigenous surfing can also be understood as a form of "epistemic disobedience" whereby the promotion of indigenous epistemology is enacted through a practice that predates colonial invasion: riding waves. Reinstating cultural identity as non-national and specific to precolonial notions of "country" or "nation," indigenous surfing validates indigenous peoples' knowledge of the seascape as a pedagogical device taught to youth by experienced indigenous surfers, teachers, and elders. Operating at the "cultural interface," indigenous surfing reclaims the seascape and the precolonized knowledge that continues to assure the survival of Australian indigenous people. In the context of decoloniality, indigenous surfing represents a vital aspect of indigenous peoples' cultural and political survival that depends on collective memories through a pedagogy of resistance and affirmation.

NOTES

1. McGloin, "Aboriginal Surfing," 93. *Country*, in the indigenous context, refers to a cultural and spiritual place of origin. It can refer to land or sea. Country incorporates cultural values and practices, stories and histories. The term *country* does not carry the meanings associated with a nation-state. It is, however, a political entity that ascribes identity and stewardship, and dictates the law and the obligations of indigenous custodians. Country encompasses the geographical location of spiritual belief and communal kinship networks.

2. Aunty Rita, quoted in McGloin, *Surfing Nation(s) Surfing Country(s)*, 171.

3. There are two officially recognized and distinct indigenous groups in Australia, Aboriginal people and Torres Strait Islander people. However, it is important to note that the homogenizing of these cultures is a colonial enterprise that does not recognize the diversity within and among each group.

4. There were over 250 different language groups prior to European colonization; thus, pluralizing knowledge invokes that vast range of knowledge systems that were encoded in all aspects of survival, in all "nations" and "countries" from desert to outback to coast, throughout the continent.

5. Mignolo, "Epistemic Disobedience," 4.

6. Bhabha, *Nation and Narration*, 86.

7. From *Surfing the Healing Wave*, quoted in McGloin, *Surfing Nation(s) Surfing Country(s)*.

8. See Langton, "Native Title, Poverty and Economic Development."

9. See "Overview of Aboriginal and Torres Strait Islander Health Status 2015," Australian Indigenous HealthInfoNet website, http://healthinfonet.ecu.edu.au/health-facts/overviews/introduction#, for detailed information on current Australian indigenous health status.

10. See, for example, the work of Henry Reynolds and Richard Broome.

11. "Critical allies" is a concept that refers to nonindigenous activists and supporters and advocates of indigenous rights who see themselves as working with indigenous people as allies, comrades, and learners as well as teachers, rather than as spokespeople for indigenous people and rights. The notion of critical alliance, a somewhat nebulous term, requires continual scrutiny in order not to be perceived as a folksy descriptor for support of indigenous peoples and rights. Rather, the term *critical allies* denotes an active role, where participation or activism takes the form of a genuine alliance alongside recognition of white privilege and the ongoing effects of colonial power relations *and* the conscious efforts to undermine those relations. See McGloin, "Listening to Hear," and Aveling, "Critical Whiteness Studies."

12. Gordon, "Shifting the Geography of Reason," 98.

13. Davis and Shpuniarsky, "The Spirit of Relationships," 337.

14. Dina Gilio-Whitaker, "Surfing and the Politics of Sovereignty and Identity," November 17, 2014, Center for World Indigenous Studies, cwis.org/FWE/2014/11/17/surfing-and-the-politics-of-sovereignty-and-identity/

15. Stuart, "The Lions Stir," 28.

16. Giroux, *The Terror of Neoliberalism*, 105–110.

17. Phil Gee, "Surfing—A Growing Industry," Surfcareers.com, March 4, 2014, http://surfcareers.com/blog/surfing-a-growing-industry/.

18. https://d3oeiojhgxjdue.cloudfront.net/uploads/ckeditor/attachment_file/data/276/uploads_2F1435204805063-54zzne6bmr4wjyvi-133cb642f101a604160efb1333196a42_2Fannual_report-2013.pdf.

19. McGloin, *Surfing Nation(s) Surfing Country(s)*.

20. Steve Cooney, quoted in "Gone Surfin'," ABC Radio National, *Hindsight* (Australia), April 6, 2003.

21. Mark Richards, quoted in "Gone Surfin.'"

22. Mark Richards, quoted in "Gone Surfin.'"

23. Giroux, *The Terror of Neoliberalism*, xvii.

24. Clifton Evers, "The Society of the Spectacle: The Association of Surfing Professionals and Corporations," Swellnet.com, November 25, 2013.

25. Giroux, *The Terror of Neoliberalism*.

26. Zygmunt Baumann, quoted in Giroux, *The Terror of Neoliberalism*, 111.

27. See the Christian Surfers Australia website, http://www.christiansurfers.org.au/#home; Gaysurfers.net; and The Disabled Surfers Association of Australia, Inc., website, http://disabledsurfers.org/.

28. Ogden, *Saltwater People of the Broken Bays*.

29. Steve Meacham, "Writer Challenges Myths of Aborigines and Saltwater Culture," *The Sydney Morning Herald*, November 26, 2011.

30. Mignolo, "Epistemic Disobedience," 15.

31. Sefa Dei, "Revisiting the Question of the Indigenous," 27.

32. Mignolo, "Epistemic Disobedience," 15.

33. McGloin, *Surfing Nations(s), Surfing Country(s)*, 140.

34. Samantha Morris, "Indigenous Surfing Title Makes a Comeback," Blank Gold Coast, July 30, 2015, http://blankgc.com.au/indigenous-surfing-title-makes-a-comeback/.

35. Mignolo, "Epistemic Disobedience," 14.

36. Carlson, *Politics of Identity*.

37. Aboriginal surfer, quoted in McGloin, *Surfing Nations(s), Surfing Country(s)*, 172.

38. Jodie Edwards, research participant in author's PhD thesis, 2004.

39. The Koori Youth Network was introduced by local Aboriginal academic and activist Bronwyn Carlson in 2003. The word "Koori" is often used to refer to the Aboriginal people of southeast Australia, i.e., New South Wales and parts of Victoria.

40. Vicki-Ann Ware and Veronica Meredith, "Closing the Gap Clearinghouse: Supporting Healthy Communities through Sports and Recreation Programs," December 2013,

Australian Institute of Family Studies, Australian Institute of Health and Welfare, http://www.aihw.gov.au/uploadedFiles/ClosingTheGap/Content/Publications/2013/ctgc-rs26.pdf.

41. Nakata, *Disciplining the Savages*, 199.

42. Nakata, *Disciplining the Savages*, 200.

10 / Appropriating Surfing and the Politics of Indigenous Authenticity

DINA GILIO-WHITAKER

In 1992, mayor of Huntington Beach Tom Mays wrote a bill petitioning the California legislature to recognize his city as California's official Surf City, sparking a contentious debate about whether the real Surf City was Huntington Beach or Santa Cruz. Santa Cruz argued its case on the grounds of the city's historic significance to surfing, beginning with three Hawaiian princes who first surfed there in 1885.[1] Huntington Beach contended that it was the "real" Surf City because it was the home of the big-money West Coast Surfing Championship and United States Surfing Championship, more commonly known as the US Open. Then-assemblyman Sam Farr from Santa Cruz, in the committee power seat and with the ability to have the last word, killed the bill. Popular surf historian Matt Warshaw notes that the television news show *Current Affair* aired a segment in which Hillary Clinton, stumping for her soon-to-be-president husband in Santa Cruz, claimed, "This is the real Surf City where only real surfers surf."[2] He also notes that the real reason Farr gave for killing the bill was "because we all know the surfers in Huntington Beach are barneys. And not even soul-barneys at that."[3] In surf lingo the term *barney* is another word for kook, meaning someone who surfs badly or calls himself a surfer regardless of his ability or level of dedication to the sport, just for the cultural cachet. A *soul surfer*, on the other hand, is the epitome of a true, authentic surfer, someone who surfs for the love it, not for commercial benefit or for an image of cool. As Warshaw notes, "The soul surfer is often thought of as the 'pure' surfer."[4]

A legal battle for the right to claim the Surf City moniker eventually resulted in Huntington Beach winning the title in an out-of-court settlement in 2008.[5] At the root of both perspectives were contradictory and competing claims to authenticity—and thus surfing's perceived purity—which has been a recurring theme in surfing's historical narratives, going back to American surf culture's roots in fin de siècle Hawai'i. The battle over the Surf City name reflects a larger fixation on purity and authenticity that has deep and longstanding roots in American culture, and surf culture's obsession with authenticity is inextricably bound up with the United States' racial histories more broadly. Even surf culture, despite popular surf historians' implicit and explicit claims to surf culture's racial tolerance, is rooted in a profoundly racialized (and racist) episode of American history.[6] In a settler colonial framework, indigenous authenticity is enmeshed with state projects to dispossess indigenous peoples of their lands through denying their political existence as indigenous peoples. This chapter explores the relationship between the American obsession with indigenous authenticity and the American appropriation of surfing to illuminate how *haole* surf culture has unendingly reproduced these racialized social structures in its own cultural productions for over a century.

In 1885, when the three Hawaiian princes first surfed at the San Lorenzo river mouth, the United States was deeply embroiled in its expansionist adventures on the North American continent and in Hawai'i. Forty years earlier, Manifest Destiny had first become articulated as the guiding principle for the growth of the country, underpinned as it was by the twin pillars of Euro-American ethnocentrism and the evangelical imperative of Christian fundamentalists to save the Indian soul. The "white man's burden" was based on social Darwinist ideologies of the racial inferiority of nonwhite peoples, a concept whose social currency had, by the 1880s, become shored up by evolving scientific racism.[7] Modern scholarship reveals the willingness of both religious fundamentalists and secular intellectuals and scientists to embrace the misconception that Indians (and all nonwhite peoples) were racially inferior.[8] This ideology of indigenous racial inferiority was the foundation, for example, of the nearly half-century tenure of the 1887 Dawes Act, with its three-pronged strategy to forcibly assimilate Indians into American society by stripping them of their collective traditional cultures. The privatization of tribal lands through individual allotments broke up communal landholdings, while a compulsory boarding school system aimed to "kill the Indian and save the man."[9] With the granting of citizenship in 1921, Indian assimilation was thought to be complete.

The history of American racism toward Indians is directly connected to the Euro-American fixation on racial purity and, by extension, authenticity, as Americans struggled to develop a uniquely white national identity.[10] Philip Deloria, for example, argues that American policy vacillated between extermination and assimilation, because Indians—however reviled they may have been—were necessary to validate a sense of authentic "Americanness"; this was coded in the "noble savage" trope.[11] Similarly, Huhndorf explains that Americans' growing fascination with "going native" in the nineteenth and twentieth century was partly reflective of an ambivalence about modernity and a need to distance white America from a violent past irreconcilable with the principles of democracy.[12] Meanwhile, the politics of Indian identity became bound up with physical, cultural, and political elimination through land dispossession and Americanization during the Dawes years. Simultaneously, the concept of blood quantum—the measure of Indian authenticity in a calculus where culture is equivalent to blood purity—became increasingly central to defining who was and was not Indian.[13] Intermarriage with nonnative populations decreased blood quantum, making individual allotments easier to sell, almost invariably, to settlers.[14] Conforming to an image based on a frozen past, Indians came to be thought of as a vanishing race, while those who endured as mixed-race moderns, often disconnected from their lands, were perceived as inauthentic and thus erased from the American social landscape as indigenous peoples.[15]

Laura Basson's study on indigenous race mixing in the fin de siècle era exposes a moment in American history where mixed-blood natives challenged the presumptions and common-sense understandings about American subjectivity.[16] Where property ownership was a necessary precondition for full belonging in the national body, whiteness itself was constructed as property.[17] Likewise, the logic associated with individual physical whiteness was extended to the populations of America's overseas colonial possessions, where race became essential to discussions of local governance. In congressional hearings on Hawai'i's annexation, debates raged regarding Hawai'i's fitness for self-determination as an inferior, racially mixed place. On Indian reservations, American power was consolidated and self-government denied to tribal nations on the basis of their racially determined inability to self-govern, a status that would not be revisited until the passage of the 1975 Indian Self-Determination and Education Act.

While Basson's study focuses on conceptions of nation and statehood, it does this by revealing the ways that social discourses on race and race-mixing—indigenous race-mixing in particular—influenced court decisions on allotment cases, congressional hearings on Hawaiian annexation, and other indigenous land claims. These cases exposed not only the underlying commitments to white supremacy maintained by the hierarchical, monoracial categories that structured the US sociopolitical order, but also the centrality of race to national identity, and how those of mixed race collapsed those categories. Mixed-race bodies denaturalized the assumptions of national identity and belonging based on blood/racial/ethnic purity and whiteness. The result, Basson argues, was an increased shoring up of those racial boundaries.[18] The logic of authenticity based on racial and cultural purity that dominated turn-of-the-century Indian policy was the basis for Native Hawaiian land dispossession and identity politics well into the new century, evidenced by the Hawaiian Homes Commission Act (HHCA) of 1921.[19] By the turn of the century, the deeply cemented American obsession with cultural authenticity in both white America and Native America would be deployed in the telling of surf history from its beginnings in pre-American Hawai'i.

The Decline of Surfing in Hawai'i

The significance of surfing in Hawaiian culture is impossible to overstate. However, for over a century, popular surf histories have narrated an indigenous sport that became nearly, if not completely, extinct as a result of the deadly combination of Christianization and depopulation due to foreign diseases, only to be resurrected by a handful of well-intentioned haole businessmen. But emerging scholarship challenging this assumption casts new light on such histories of settler revitalization of surfing. Indeed, debunking the myth of surfing's extinction is one of the most important objectives of revising surf history today.[20] Isaiah Walker emphatically states that "although fewer people surfed in the late 1800s than in centuries prior and after, he'e nalu was neither extinct, nor even nearly extinct, as often purported."[21] Likewise, Clark maintains that "during the late 1800s the popularity of surfing among Hawaiians declined considerably. . . . They continued to surf, which is evident from many sources, including the *kanikau* in the Hawaiian-language newspapers, but in fewer numbers."[22] Walker and Clark's research shows that while surfing was being enjoyed by fewer people in the late 1800s, there were still enough people engaging in wave-riding (in all its forms) for it to be considered a vital activity, despite outsider claims of extinction. A survey of the Hawaiian-language literature cited by Clark indicates that there were still significant pockets of vitality well into the 1880s, if not the 1890s, and characterized surfing as a sport that "changed into an activity practiced by individuals rather than a nation."[23]

The narrative of surfing's extinction cannot be seen outside of this colonial history, and the differences between the English and Hawaiian language accounts raise important questions. That surfing experienced a decline is indisputable, but how we describe the decline—that is, decline versus extinction—is crucial to understanding the way the conventional historical narrative of surfing unfolds from this point. Characterizing the sport as "dead" or "extinct" sets up a dialectic rendering an implied need for rescuing, and this is precisely what has been perpetuated throughout decades of popular surf culture literature. And in this narrative, who rescues surfing from its neglect by Native Hawaiians, thus preventing its inevitable final demise? None other than a group of elite white male settlers, many of whom were responsible for the political overthrow of the independent nation of Hawai'i.

Surfing's Salvation, the Great White Hope, and the Question of Race

In canonical surf literature, perhaps the most overlooked aspect of this era of surf history—generally referred to as surfing's "renaissance"—is how the racial dimensions inherent in the relationships between haole and Kanaka Maoli have been narrated. Until recently, race has been largely dismissed or portrayed as inconsequential in surf history, often analyzed outside the broader context of American relationships with indigenous populations.[24] Within this fold, a figure who has also been underanalyzed is George Freeth. He was instrumental in surfing's renaissance and, as a mixed-blood Native Hawaiian, Freeth stood at the intersection of several historic processes, exposing the social tension inherent in his racial liminality, especially as he was—and still is—seen outside the Hawaiian community by popular non-Native surf writers. Freeth's role in surf history is emblematic of how the racial dynamics during surfing's renaissance has been downplayed for over a century. In order to thoroughly revisit George Freeth's significance for conceptualizing race in Hawaiian surfing history, however, we first need to examine the events leading to Freeth's relative lack of notoriety in surf literature.

In the conventional telling of it, surfing's extinction would be reversed thanks to the efforts of globetrotting adventurer Alexander Hume Ford, with the help of fellow traveler Jack London. This is due, undoubtedly, to the happy coincidence that both were professional writers with the "power of the pen" to influence how the story of surfing's resurrection would occur. Born in postbellum South Carolina in 1868, Ford had made a name for himself as a freelance journalist, and arrived in Honolulu in 1907, bringing with him a love for surfing instilled by photos he'd seen as a boy.[25] Not long after his arrival, Ford met Hawaiian surfer George Freeth, who taught him how to surf standing up in one session after months of unsuccessful attempts with other instructors.[26] Ford was so impressed by Freeth that he wrote, "A young hapahaole (half white, half native) took pity on me. He was the champion surfer of the Islands. . . . I learned in half an hour the secret I had sought for weeks."[27] On May 29, 1907, Ford met Jack London and his wife Charmian who'd sailed in on their boat *The Snark*, an adventure London would write about in his 1911 book *The Cruise of the Snark*. Ford had spotted the Londons drinking in the foyer of the Royal Hawaiian Hotel. Jack London, arguably the most famous writer in America at the time, acknowledged that he knew of Ford's own work, and the two became immediate friends.[28] It didn't take long for Ford to begin hatching a strategy for how he and London could approach the broader objective of exposing the outside world to life in Hawai'i. A few days later, Ford introduced London to Freeth, whom both had seen surfing at Waikīkī. Equally impressed by the young George, London would later write about him: "Shaking the water from my eyes as I emerged from one wave and peered ahead to see what the next one looked like, I saw him tearing in on the back of it, standing upright on his board, carelessly poised, a young god with sunburn. We went through the wave on the back of which he rode. Ford called to him. He turned an airspring from his wave, rescued his board from its maw, paddled over to us and joined Ford in showing me things."[29]

Now newly infected with the surf bug, Ford and London would proceed unrestrained in their enthusiasm to share the sport with the rest of the world: London, because he was a natural storyteller, and Ford because he was a natural promoter. London recounted his surfing adventures (as well as his encounter with Freeth) and the thrill of wave-riding in an article that would be reprinted in *Women's Home Companion* and England's *Pall Mall Magazine*, and later become a chapter in *The Cruise of the Snark*. He also published other articles about surfing. Ford's new mission was to highlight surfing as a way to promote tourism in the Islands. He founded the *Mid-Pacific Magazine* for just that purpose in 1911 (the inaugural issue featured an image of a surfer on its cover), and he wrote prolifically on surfing. In 1908, just a year after his purported arrival in the islands, he was appointed secretary of the Transportation Committee by the territorial governor, where his role was to advance the Pacific territory's interests. From Ford's perspective, this meant intensifying America's colonial efforts by opening Hawai'i up to greater white settlement. In 1911 he also created the Hands-Around-the-Pacific Club (in 1917 renamed the Pan-Pacific Union), and was a founding board member of the Pan-Pacific Congress in 1911, both formed for the express purpose of promoting tourism.[30] Ford's influence on tourism in Hawai'i by promoting surfing is legendary and well documented, earning him the reputation of almost single-handedly resuscitating the "nearly-dead" sport that Hawaiians themselves had shamefully allowed to die. Jack London minced no words about it when he wrote, "Not only did the Hawaiian born not talk about it [surfing], but they forgot about it. Just as the sport was at its dying gasp, along came one Alexander Ford from the mainland. And he talked. Surfboarding was the sport of sports. There was nothing like it anywhere else in the world. They ought to be ashamed for letting it languish. It was one of the Islands' assets, a drawing card for travelers that would fill their hotels and bring them many permanent residents, etc."[31]

For London, Ford was clearly surfing's great white hope. Yet for all the ways surf culture has remembered him as the savior of the Hawaiian sport for promoting surfing in the tourist market, Ford is perhaps best known in his role as a founder of the Outrigger Surf Club in 1908. The club was established, as Ford wrote, "to give an added and permanent attraction to Hawai'i and make Waikiki always the Home of the Surfer," and to ensure coastal access to people of "limited means."[32] The club soon became the domain of some of Hawai'i's most wealthy and powerful haole aristocrats, including proannexationists and some of the prime architects of the overthrow of the Hawaiian Kingdom. Among its membership, the club counted Lorrin A. Thurston, J. P. Cooke, and Sanford B. Dole, and as Ford boasted, "Judges of the Supreme Court in Hawai'i with their wives and daughters, ex-governors and their families, and the greater portion of the prominent business men."[33] Surf literature is replete with accounts of the Outrigger's discrimination against Hawaiians, and according to the conventional narrative, a group of Kanaka Maolis formed their own club in response, which they called Hui Nalu ("club of the waves"). Walker writes that "William A. 'Knute' Cottrell explained that he, along with Duke Kahanamoku, Kenneth Winter, Edward Kaleleihealani 'Dudie' Miller, and other Hawaiians created the Hui Nalu after being 'disgusted' by offensive remarks made by Outrigger members."[34] Walker also points out, however, that Hui Nalu was not created as a knee-jerk response to Outrigger. Created in 1905, three years before Ford's club, it existed as a loose affiliation of Hawaiians prior to garnering official sanctioning in 1911.[35] Surfing, he contends, was already experiencing a resurgence among Hawaiians prior to the growing tourist industry fueled by Ford, and increased among Kanaka Maolis as an expression of autonomy and political resistance to the colonial regime.[36]

Here is where academic and popular surf historians part company on the issue of race, and popular, media-based writers undermine the role race had in the shifting landscape of political power in Hawai'i and its impacts on historical surf narratives. If race is mentioned at all, it is given only a passing glance, as Drew Kampion does by saying only that the two groups (Hui Nalu and Outrigger) "often went head-to-head in competition."[37] Warshaw acknowledges Ford's thinly veiled white supremacism when the latter wrote that "The white man and boy are doing much in Hawaii to develop the art of surf-riding. Games and feats never dreamed of by the native are being tried," and boasted that "white boys and girls" were "most expert" in the water.[38] Warshaw also notes that "race [and class] was still an issue in the sport," but praises Ford and London for naming surfing the "Sport of Kings," where the assumption was that everyone knew they meant *Hawaiian* kings.[39] "Gestures mattered, and this was a nice one," Warshaw says, seeming to imply that even if London and Ford had appropriated the Hawaiians' sport and claimed it for haoles, the Hawaiians must have at least been grateful for the rhetorical nod in their direction.[40] He devotes one paragraph to the overthrow of the Hawaiian monarchy, but only to highlight the Hawaiians' loss of culture. In other words, racial difference is downplayed and disconnected from asymmetrical power relations and then-recent American depredations against the Hawaiian Kingdom government.

Westwick and Neushul come only a little closer to connecting the racism prevalent in Hawaiian surf history to larger political processes. The racial tension, they write, "is sometimes, but wrongly, viewed through the competition between two clubs, the Outrigger and Hui Nalu, representing, respectively, haoles and natives."[41] They argue that a strict definition of Hui Nalu as a purely Native Hawaiian organization blurs the fact that it was composed of native and nonnative members, and make the dubious claim that two of the three founders were haole.[42] They also note that George Freeth was a charter member, but refer to him as "ethnically only one-quarter Hawaiian."[43] For them, this begs the question of who was Native Hawaiian—"Was it just someone born there? Or was it determined by ethnicity, and if so, what degree of Hawaiian ancestry qualified?"—before proceeding to discuss the creole nature of the population.[44] Thus, instead of connecting haole racism to broader political relationships rooted in imperialism and colonialism, such analysis of racial tension among Hawai'i's early surf clubs is viewed as a local conflict limited to defining who is and who isn't native based on a fetishized, "common-sense" understanding of blood quantum as the sole arbiter of cultural authenticity.[45]

Isaiah Walker has essentially been the first to deeply interrogate the problem of racism in this era of surf history and, as he shows, the racist assumptions that undergird the American colonization of Hawai'i are still very much alive in Hawaiian and American surf culture today.[46] Scott Laderman's work also exposes racism in great detail, although he adopts a different approach by focusing on Ford and uncovering his underlying motivations. Laderman directly connects Ford's ideological positioning to his Southern, postbellum upbringing and a deeply ingrained sense of white superiority, what Kristin Lawler calls "an abstract 'white man's burden'-style racism," a trait she also attributes to London.[47] Laderman sees Ford's work as a product of the belief that by virtue of an inherent, benevolent superiority, whites had "global obligations," in the case of Hawai'i, to bring "Asiatics better things and better government."[48]

Ford's views were far from unusual. America's expansionist agenda was explicitly animated by this earlier version of benevolent superiority, underwritten by the racial hierarchies that were systematically embedded in all levels of society, especially at the governmental level. From the top down, the principles of racial inferiority that drove America's Indian policy on the continent flowed seamlessly into the ideology of conquest in the Hawaiian Islands and beyond.[49] As Basson writes, "Hawaii's designation as a mixed-race territory by both proponents and opponents of Hawaiian annexation expressed the challenges it posed to conventional definitions of the US nation and state as homogenous entities in which white, European Americans were demographically, as well as politically and economically, dominant."[50]

The logic of (and need for) cultural authenticity was not lost on Ford with his aspirations to build a Hawaiian tourist industry. Nothing, after all, said "Hawai'i" more than the image of a smiling, brown-skinned native balanced gracefully on a rolling Waikiki wave (except, perhaps, the image of a scantily clad, grass-skirted, brown-skinned *wahine* performing the hula). In 1905, Ford wrote an article titled "Give the Tourists More Variety," in which he claimed that tourists needed "an insight into the wild life of the Polynesians. . . . Native color is what the pleasure seeker likes to have imbued in his entertainment."[51] And, as Westwick and Neushul write: "What better introduction to wild Hawaiian life than the sport of surfing? Surfing also presented a benign image to counter the popular misperception . . . that Hawaiians were violent and warlike, even persisting in cannibalism. Surfing images instead portrayed Hawaiians as peaceful and fun-loving."[52] In other words, surfing images of this era performed the work of presenting an image of Native Hawaiians as "authentic" and "natural" natives.[53]

The "Americanization of surfing" through tourism promotion was no less than the process of appropriating surfing as a haole sport where, as Michael Willard writes, haoles were surfing's "saviors."[54] In order to effectively promote surfing as an authentically Hawaiian cultural phenomenon, however, the nascent tourist industry needed an ambassador: a recognizable icon that embodied everything haole tourists expected from their prospective Hawaiian experience. The commercialization of Hawaiian tourism by selling it through the images of surfing in this era marks surfing's transformation from a strictly Hawaiian cultural practice to its emergence as an industry, embedded in tourism, and is the origin of its commodification.[55] But because surfing was "uniquely Hawaiian," it needed to maintain an image of Hawaiian cultural authenticity for years to come. Whoever surfing's ambassador was, they had to be an appropriately Hawaiian body, one who unambiguously portrayed all that was purely Hawaiian, who could surf and play the part well. Two particular people were at the forefront: George Freeth and Duke Kahanamoku. But as time has shown, only one would earn the title of the "Father of Modern Surfing," as perpetuated by the modern, haole-controlled surfing industrial complex.

George and Duke

Far more is known about Duke Kahanamoku than is known about George Freeth. Duke lived to be seventy-seven years old before passing away in 1968; Freeth, on the other hand, died at the age of thirty-five in 1919. George Douglas Freeth, Jr., was born on November 9, 1883, to Elizabeth Kaili, who was half Hawaiian and half English. Freeth's father, George Freeth, Sr., was an Irish sea captain.[56] George's maternal grandfather was the English-born William Lowthian Green, an amateur geologist-turned-businessman and politician. Having arrived in Hawai'i in 1850, Green quickly rose to prominence in Honolulu through a variety of business ventures, and by 1874 he'd been appointed to the King's Privy Council under King Kalākaua and, later that year, was appointed Minister of Foreign Affairs, an office that he held for many years. He also served in a number of other positions under the king, but he was most notable for his role as a countersigner of the Reciprocity Treaty of 1875. He remained in his post as Minister of Foreign Affairs through the American-imposed Bayonet Constitution of 1887, a precursor to the overthrow that eroded the power of the Hawaiian monarchy while granting power to haole interests. Green later appointed Lorrin A. Thurston, one of the masterminds of the overthrow, to the newly formed cabinet.[57]

George Freeth, Jr., grew up swimming in the waters of his birthplace at Waikīkī and became an accomplished swimmer and high diver with the prestigious Healani swim team, where he met the younger Duke Kahanamoku, who became one of his students. By the time he met London and Ford and taught them how to surf, Freeth was already widely known for his swimming and surfing prowess, and had rightly earned Ford's praise as "the champion surfer of the islands."[58] Based on George's own account, apparently no one in Waikīkī was surfing in the standing position, and he would become the first to do so in his era. In the only known written account by Freeth, a 1917 article from the *Los Angeles Evening Herald*, he recounts his experience learning to surf. He notes that everybody the world over knew of the Hawaiian Natives' skill in surf-riding: "Every boy knew from the tales handed down from his father that the Hawaiians had at one time, ridden the waves but then not a one of them could stand. I listened to the tales told by the boys of how their ancestors could stand on a board speeding over the water at a terrific speed. I hardly believed it at first."[59]

He then describes how he first attempted to ride a surfboard in 1902 after several trips to the United States and how he learned about water feats after "bathing" at Atlantic City. He found a large board and shaped it to suit his weight, began by riding on his hands and knees, and, in time, became able to ride an entire wave "standing at full height." At first the native boys laughed at him, he said, but then "they all hailed me as the reviver of the lost art" and they all took to riding standing up.[60] In 1907, not long after his foray with London and Ford, he left Hawai'i and went to Southern California, surfboard in tow, and became the first to expose southern Californians to the joys of surfing, just as the three Hawaiian princes had in Santa Cruz twenty-four years earlier. It didn't take long for real estate magnate Henry Huntington to "discover" Freeth, and within six months the Hawaiian was working for Huntington and tobacco tycoon Abbot Kinney, helping to promote the newly built saltwater plunges that constituted part of their burgeoning real estate developments in Redondo Beach and Venice Beach. Dubbed the "Hawaiian Wonder," Freeth gave surfing exhibitions at both beaches, showcasing his aquatic talent to the growing crowds of beachgoers. The nascent beach culture of settler-dominated Southern California, now seeded with the "new sport" of surfing and Freeth's superior water skills, became the laboratory for the evolving art and science of ocean safety and awareness. Virtually single-handedly, Freeth pioneered lifesaving, and trained male and females alike to become expert watermen and waterwomen, as well as practitioners of medical first aid. After innovating lifeboat surf rescue in the Venice Volunteer Lifesaving Corps, in 1908 Freeth was awarded the Congressional Gold Medal, the highest civilian honor, for a daring December rescue of eleven Japanese fishermen from the frigid Pacific. He was also commended by the United States Lifesaving Corps for rescuing more than 250 people during his lifeguard career in Southern California.[61] For the rest of his short life, Freeth lived in Southern California, dedicated to the advancement of water safety. He died in 1919 at the age of thirty-five as a result of the 1918 Spanish flu epidemic that killed over twenty million people worldwide.[62]

Duke Kahanamoku greatly admired Freeth, and they remained friends until the end of George's life.[63] A note preceding Freeth's *Los Angeles Evening Herald* article claims that "Duke Kahanamoku who broke the world's record in the 100-meters race both at Stockholm and in Germany under the American colors, is one of Freeth's swimming companions who owes his success to the Redondo star."[64] Attributing Duke's successes to Freeth is a tremendous gesture, as Kahanamoku's accomplishments are things of sporting legend: from 1912 until 1932 he participated in four Olympics, garnering numerous medals and establishing record-breaking times. He was a founding member of the Hui Nalu Surf Club, and later became a lifelong member of the Outrigger Canoe Club; he went on to act in a few Hollywood films, and his name lives on in a chain of restaurants that he helped to found in Hawai'i and California. By 1925 (just six years after Freeth's death), Warshaw claims, Duke was the world's best-known surfer.[65]

For decades, surf writers and popular historians have widely recognized Duke Kahanamoku as the "father of modern surfing." Only recently, however, have writers begun to question why Duke retained this title when Freeth was known to be his predecessor and elder waterman, the first to revive stand-up surfing at Waikīkī, and a surf teacher to London and Ford. Laderman notes that of the two, Freeth remains the least known, which for him is surprising since it was Freeth, "a mixed blood Hawaiian," who was considered the most skilled surfer of the time, and "who firmly planted the seeds of what would become California's renowned surf culture."[66] Because Ford's views suggested haole appropriation of surfing, Westwick and Neushul wonder why Kahanamoku had risen to such prominence, neglecting Freeth's role in the revival. They conclude, "One might say that Freeth was neglected precisely because he was more Caucasian than Hawaiian, and that Duke became known as the father of modern surfing because he was a full-fledged 'native.'"[67] Or, stated another way, since surfing had clearly been appropriated as a white man's sport, Freeth could not have been dubbed the modern sport's patriarch since his racial profile (read: blood quantum) more closely resembled Caucasian than Hawaiian. In a logic where racial purity equals cultural authenticity, he was simply not native enough. Freeth's identity as a mixed-blood Hawaiian presented too many ambiguities to comfortably retain white surf culture's lofty title of the Father of Modern Surfing, a designation that demands that authenticity accompany racial purity, the determination of culture based on blood quantum.

So little is known about George Freeth and his family that we cannot know how he would have negotiated his liminality as a *hapa haole* within Hawai'i as a settler colonial space or how he perceived himself.[68] George left the islands at the age of twenty-four, never to return; he passed away in San Diego and was never married or had any children. Smith reports that George's grandniece May Borthwick described George's family as "dysfunctional," attributable, Smith guesses, to the family's hapa haole status in a "highly race conscious society," adding that "though most Americans today are multi-ethnic if not multi-racial, such was far from the case in George's time—even in Hawaii."[69] Yet such claims that the family's mixed-race status was unusual for turn-of-the-century Hawai'i are patently wrong. Quite the contrary: census records show that the "part-Hawaiian population" experienced an astronomical growth rate at the turn of the century, having grown from 2,487 in 1872 to over 16,000 in 1919, quadrupling in a span of less than fifty years.[70] And that is to say nothing of the other racially mixed non-Hawaiian people in the islands. Social scientists had long been fascinated by the race-mixing of the population after the influx of Asian migrant workers in the early nineteenth century (as well as haole settlers), and considered it a "racial laboratory," or racial "melting pot."[71] Smith does seem to be making a larger point, however: that as hapa haoles, the family was likely subject to intense racism. As Hawaiians (or even "part Hawaiians"), the white supremacy inherent in the colonial environment of Hawai'i would not have escaped them. As mixed-race, hapa haole Hawaiians, they would have been subject to another, qualitatively different type of racism, however, one that constructed their Hawaiianness as inauthentic, in the same way the authenticity of mixed-blood North American Indians would have been dismissed in light of prevailing assimilationist social ideologies and political policies.

Duke Kahanamoku, on the other hand, was unambiguously "pure" Hawaiian. He was the eldest son in a family of six boys and three girls, and the family on both the maternal and paternal sides descended from lower ranking *ali'i* known as *kaukau ali'i*.[72] As a very dark-skinned native, he was no stranger to racism, and was at times mistaken as a "negro" (and treated accordingly) on the mainland and overseas, though his authenticity as a Hawaiian was never questioned. Reinforcing the persistent (hegemonic) racialized understandings of Hawaiianness, however, James Nendel refers to him as "a vivid reminder of the old dying breed of pureblooded Hawaiians."[73] Indeed—but as Willard observes, representations of Duke would come to convey different meanings about Native Hawaiians at different stages of his career. Echoing Jane Desmond's contention that Hawaiians came to be marked as "ideal natives" in an epistemological framework that she calls "physical foundationalism," where bodies function as material signs for categories of gendered, racial, and cultural difference, Willard reasons that Duke represented the brown native body that white civilization was destined to replace, simultaneously recovering white "manliness" and racial superiority.[74] After his Olympic wins in 1912, which accompanied Olympic laurels by several Native American athletes (Jim Thorpe among them), an African American runner, and other Hawaiian swimmers, Duke came to symbolize a racially unified American nation.[75] Later media representations came to emphasize "not his primitivism or any racial ambiguity that stemmed from his Hawaiianness but instead his assimilability."[76]

Being an original member of Hui Nalu and the Waikiki Beachboys, Duke's legendary swimming and surfing abilities contributed to the cultural clout needed for his image as the ultimate symbol of everything Hawaiian in the promotional machinery of Hawai'i's early tourism industrial complex—engineered in large part by Alexander Hume Ford—and later the American surfing industrial complex, which constructed Duke's image as the father of modern surfing.[77] As Nendel argues, Duke came to symbolize both the old and new Hawai'i, pre- and post-overthrow, and the potency of his representation of Native Hawaiian continuity and pride cannot be underestimated.[78] Although George Freeth did more initially to reinvigorate surfing (at least in Waikīkī) and sowed surf culture throughout Southern California, it was Duke's longevity and highly racialized image of Hawaiian cultural authenticity that earned him the title Father of Modern Surfing. The denomination, however, raises certain concerns. It exposes and substantiates the underlying assumptions constitutive of the discursive production of surfing as a dead sport—a dead sport that was saved thanks to the benevolent superiority of haole patriarchs. And no matter who would be granted the lofty title of surfing's primordial patriarch, that problem would remain. Surfing's worldwide spread has carried with it the story of Hawai'i and her people. But only a truncated, carefully whitewashed version of this story survives, one that by and large has been divorced from the conditions of imperialism that circumscribed its renewal and obscured it as a form of cultural appropriation, and thus as a tool of settler colonialism.

Assessing the hows and whys of Duke Kahanamoku's ascendancy over George Freeth as the patriarch of modern surf culture should not be taken as an argument that Freeth (or anyone else for that matter) better deserved the title. The rhetorical title as perpetuated in haole-constructed surf narratives only exists in the context of a logic that constructs Hawaiian surfing as having been dead and resurrected. Given the evidence that the sport was nowhere near extinct, the title itself is absurd. While they honor Duke for his accomplishments as a waterman, Hawaiians themselves don't consider Duke—or anyone else—as surfing's patriarch.[79] The comparison between Duke and George only serves to demonstrate how popular haole historical surfing narratives have reproduced the racialized social structures that existed in fin de siècle colonial Hawai'i and the United States.

Conclusion

Viewing the master narratives inherent in the conventional origin stories of modern surf culture through the racialized lens of settler colonialism brings into sharp relief the relationship between appropriation and authenticity. In this equation, the cultural appropriation of the Hawaiian sport of surfing and the politics that surround it are grounded in a logic where cultural authenticity equals racial purity. Surf culture's fixation on authenticity arises out of the same American racial anxiety that mobilized whites to "go native" at various points in US history, and it is but one particular form of such appropriation. In the highly racialized environment of fin de siècle colonial Hawai'i, discourses and images of Hawaiian authenticity, coupled with stories of the haole rescue of surfing, lay the groundwork for perpetual appropriation vis-à-vis ever-unfolding textual and visual representations of surf culture. In the context of settler colonialism, appropriation is always about the continual remaking of indigenous space into settler space, at both material and discursive levels of culture and politics. American surf culture is thus reflective of and complicit in larger, ongoing colonial projects to dispossess indigenous peoples—in this case, Kanaka Maoli—of their ancestral places and culture.

NOTES

1. David Kawananakoa, Edward Keliiahonui, and Jonah Kuhio Kalaniana'ole, the adopted sons of King David Kalākaua and his wife, Queen Consort Esther Julia Kapi'olani, are the first known people to surf on the continental United States when they were students at St. Matthew's Military Academy in San Mateo. See Walker, *Waves of Resistance*.

2. Warshaw, *Encyclopedia* (2003), 575.

3. Warshaw, *Encyclopedia*, 575.

4. Warshaw, *Encyclopedia*, 552. The concept of "soul surfing" has its roots in the 1960s, as surfing aligned itself with the counterculture and in opposition to corporate-driven pro-

fessional surfing. While the surfing industry delivered yet another seismic wave of change to surf culture in the mid-1970s—one that has since characterized the sport through the twentieth and twenty-first centuries—at the root of each era of surf culture were the concepts of purity and authenticity, expressed in different terms commensurate with varying time periods.

5. "Surf City USA Legal Battle Is Over," January 23, 2008, Surfertoday.com, http://www.surfertoday.com/surfing/408-surf-city-usa-legal-battle-is-over.

6. For instance, under the heading "racism and surfing," Matt Warshaw makes the bold claim that "while sexism has long been a surf culture hallmark, the sport for the most part has been free of racism" (*Encyclopedia*, 491). Although he cites several examples of blatantly racist events in surf history (most of them outside the American context) and suggests that surfing's nineteenth-century "collapse" was the result of "imperialist-based racism" (491), Warshaw's view reflects a common brand of surf history-telling that lacks deeper social-scientific analysis.

7. Horsman, "Scientific Racism," and Daniel, "Either Black or White."

8. See especially Horsman, "Scientific Racism," Berkhofer, *White Man's Indian*, and Omi and Winant, *Racial Formation in the United States*.

9. The phrase is attributed to Richard Pratt, the founder of the Carlisle Indian Industrial School (1879–1918) and the compulsory education system that would subsequently serve as a model of forced cultural assimilation for other minority groups.

10. Deloria, *Playing Indian*; Garroutte, *Real Indians*; Barker, *Native Acts*; Huhndorf, *Going Native*.

11. Deloria, *Playing Indian*, 3–5.

12. Huhndorf, *Going Native* (see especially chapter 1).

13. Wolfe, "Settler Colonialism"; Barker, *Native Acts*; Peck, "What Is a Real Indian?"; O'Brien, *Firsting and Lasting*.

14. Under the Dawes Act (a.k.a. the General Allotment Act), allotments were subject to a twenty-five-year holding period for Indians with higher blood quantum. Allotments could not be sold during that period, based on the idea that Indians with higher blood quantum were not as competent to manage their affairs as were mixed-blood Indians. Those with a lower blood quantum were not subject to the waiting period. This created a devastating proposition, however, in which the more mixed Indians became, the more easily they could be separated from their lands. The possibility of selling their land offered a way out of intractable poverty, on the one hand, but it led to a massive loss of native land, on the other. This largely explains what is referred to today as the "checkerboarding" of the reservations.

15. O'Brien, *Firsting and Lasting*.

16. Basson, *White Enough to Be American?*

17. Harris, "Whiteness as Property"; Lipsitz, "The Possessive Investment of Whiteness."

18. Basson, *White Enough to Be American*, 184.

19. Kauanui, *Hawaiian Blood*. The HHCA imposed a blood quantum of 50 percent in order for Hawaiians to qualify for Hawaiian homestead land.

20. Walker, *Waves of Resistance*, and Clark, *Hawaiian Surfing*, have, so far, gone furthest toward debunking the myth of surfing's extinction.

21. Walker, *Waves of Resistance*, 30.

22. Clark, *Hawaiian Surfing*, 32–33. *Kanikau* refers to a type of chant that honors the memory of a deceased person by recounting various aspects of his life, which could name particular places, deeds, or beloved activities, like surfing.

23. Clark, *Hawaiian Surfing*, 32–33.

24. Warshaw, *Encyclopedia*, 495.

25. Most accounts have Ford arriving in 1907, although Laderman and Walker cite various accounts dating Ford's arrival to 1905 or 1906.

26. Joel Smith, "Reinventing the Sport, Part III: George Freeth," *Surfers Journal* 12, no. 3 (2003): 90–95. So invisible is Freeth in the historical narrative that this is one of the few accounts in mainstream surf literature that names Freeth as having taught Ford how to surf, despite Ford's written mentions of Freeth. See Verge, "George Freeth," for the most detailed historical account.

27. Verge, "George Freeth," 85.

28. Verge, "George Freeth," 85. In the online article "Alexander Hume Ford (1868–1945)," accessed at http://files.legendarysurfers.com/blog/ahford.doc.pdf, Malcolm Gault-Williams notes a correction: because the Royal Hawaiian wasn't built until 1927, the hotel was most likely the Moana Hotel.

29. London, "Riding the South Sea Surf," 10.

30. Laderman, *Empire in Waves*.

31. London, *Our Hawai'i*, 8.

32. Laderman, *Empire in Waves*, 23.

33. Walker, *Waves of Resistance*, 61. Dean Saranillo notes Thurston's fears of the threat of Asian immigration by pointing out his involvement with developing tourism as early as 1890. "After facing defeat at the voting polls in 1890, Lorrin A. Thurston became heavily involved in promoting tourism as a means to attract a 'desirable population' to replace Kanaka 'Ōiwi. In 1911, the Hawai'i Territorial Legislature would act on this same sentiment when it passed a bill urging Congress to pay the fares of White farmers to Hawai'i to provide a militia to protect US interests" (Saranillo, "Why Asian Settler Colonialism Matters," 286). This helps explain Thurston's foundational role in the founding of the notoriously white-dominted Outrigger Club.

34. Walker, *Waves of Resistance*, 62.

35. Walker, *Waves of Resistance*, 62. Clark also notes that in 1897 a group of Hawaiians formed what was probably the first canoe-surfing concession on Waikīkī Beach. Called *Hui Pākākā Nalu*, the group further evidences surfing's vitality in the late 1800s if one considers canoe surfing as a legitimate form of wave riding more generally categorized as surfing. See Clark, *Hawaiian Surfing*, 69.

36. Walker, *Waves of Resistance*, 57.

37. Kampion, *Stoked*, 38.

38. Warshaw, *History of Surfing*, 44–45.

39. Warshaw, *History of Surfing*, 44–45.

40. Warshaw, *History of Surfing*, 44–45.

41. Westwick and Neushul, *World in the Curl*, 53.

42. Westwick and Neushul, *World in the Curl*, 54. Westwick and Neushul cite Tom Blake and Hal Prieste as founding the club with Freeth.

43. Westwick and Neushul, *World in the Curl*, 54.

44. Westwick and Neushul, *World in the Curl*, 54.

45. Westwick and Neushul's comment is a revealing demonstration of how deeply entrenched the logic of blood quantum remains as a determinant of cultural authenticity.

46. Walker, *Waves of Resistance*.

47. Laderman, *Empire in Waves*; Lawler, *American Surfer*, 35.

48. Laderman, *Empire in Waves*, 33.

49. Go, *American Empire and the Politics of Meaning*; Kauanui, *Hawaiian Blood*; Basson, *White Enough*.

50. Basson, *White Enough*, 106. The topic of Hawai'i's fitness for statehood was taken up only a few years after its annexation in 1898. In 1907 a congressional delegation came to Hawai'i on a more than two-months-long fact-finding mission to consider the possibility of Hawaiian statehood. It would be half a century before Hawai'i was admitted as a state.

51. Quoted in Westwick and Neushul, *World in the Curl*, 37.

52. Westwick and Neushul, *World in the Curl*, 37.

53. Desmond, *Staging Tourism*, 57. Referring to the representational power of hula dancers at the turn of the century, Desmond writes, "The Hawaiian native comes to represent an ideal type in the Euro-American imaginary—oscillating between the noble and the romantic savage." The "ideal native" trope is easily applicable to images of native surfers and is commonly deployed throughout surf historiography, as Westwick and Neushul's second chapter alludes to.

54. Laderman, *Empire in Waves*, 3, 8–40; Willard, "Duke Kahanamoku's Body," 19.

55. Laderman makes this point most succinctly, stating that "visual representations of Hawai'i—images that spoke to the exotic splendor unique to the island chain—could go some distance in selling the Hawaiian dream. And nothing spoke more fully to what was uniquely Hawaiian than the sport of surfing" (*Empire in Waves*, 29).

56. In spite of providing the most extensive research on Freeth to date, Verge writes that Freeth Sr. "was English born and bred" ("George Freeth," 4), while Warshaw claims that he was "an Irish sea captain" (*Encyclopedia*, 214), and Freeth Jr. writes that his father was "native of Cork, Ireland" (Moser, *Pacific Passages*, 154). It is important to note that many Irish surfers claim Freeth Jr. as their own; see, for example, the film *Waveriders*.

57. For more on Green's relationship to the Hawaiian League and Bayonet Constitution, see Osorio, *Dismembering Lahui*; on the Hawaiian League, see Walker, *Waves of Resistance*, 51–52.

58. Quoted in Verge, "George Freeth," 85.

59. Moser, *Pacific Passages*, 153–154. Contradicting this claim, Walker wrote that Princess Ka'iulani surfed regularly at Waikīkī from 1895 to 1899 on a traditional *olo* board, typically ridden upright and reserved for royalty. See Walker, *Waves of Resistance*, 58–59.

60. Moser, *Pacific Passages*, 153–154.

61. Moser, *Pacific Passages*, 153.

62. Verge, "George Freeth."

63. Duke referred to Freeth as "the world's greatest diver" immediately after the 1912 Olympics where Duke won gold in the 100-meter freestyle. See Smith, "Reinventing the Sport."

64. Moser, *Pacific Passages*, 153.

65. Warshaw, *Encyclopedia*, 309.

66. Laderman, *Empire in Waves*, 33.

67. Westwick and Neushul, *World in the Curl*, 52.

68. In the little existing information about his life, Freeth seems conflicted about his identity. Curiously, in the 1917 article he wrote for the *Evening Herald*, he refers to the "natives" and "their" ancestors, speaking as though from an outsider's perspective. Yet in the last paragraph he says, "Today many of the life guards on our western coast are proficient riders and can do feats that make the spectator hold his breath. But 10 years ago there was no surf board riding in America. It is an art that belongs to the natives of the Hawaiian Islands" (in Moser, *Pacific Passages*, 154). He doesn't explicitly connect himself to the "natives," but at the same time he implicitly rejects the claims that Ford and others made about surfing being a white man's sport and (re)claims it as the rightful domain of Native Hawaiians. While he does not necessarily include himself in that category, he nonetheless defends the authenticity of the sport as Hawaiian, and expresses an underlying sense of pride.

69. Smith, "Reinventing the Sport," 93.

70. Kauanui, *Hawaiian Blood*, 126.

71. Manganaro, *Assimilating Hawaii*, 7; Ledward, "On Being Hawaiian Enough," 118.

72. Nendel, "Duke Kahanamoku," 7.

73. Nendel, "Duke Kahanamoku," ix.

74. Desmond, *Staging Tourism*, xiv; Willard, *Duke Kahanamoku's Body*, 21.

75. Willard, *Duke Kahanamoku's Body*, 23.

76. Willard, *Duke Kahanamoku's Body*, 25. Willard notes that racial discourses of primitiveness and national belonging have existed sided by side in sport and even "reinforced each other."

77. Much written about in popular and scholarly surfing literatures, the famed Beachboys were young Hawaiian men who for decades (well into the mid-twentieth century) worked Waikīkī Beach, hiring themselves out as surfing instructors and companions to wealthy white tourists (mostly women). See Timmons, *Waikiki Beachboy*; Westwick and Neushul, *World in the Curl*, 56–70; Warshaw, *History of Surfing*, 52–59.

78. Nendel, *Duke Kahanamoku*, iv.

79. Isaiah Walker, email correspondence, February 17, 2016.

Part III / Feminist Critical Geography

11 / Surfeminism, Critical Regionalism, Public Scholarship

KRISTA COMER

I want to challenge you to see [surfer girls of Bangladesh] as more than cool girls in a salwar kameez getting up on a surfboard and surfing ... —FARHANA HUQ

It's not all about me (Cori), but a growing "we" that wants the best for our future. —CORI SCHUMACHER

I wanted something a little more edgy, something a little more of the reality of who we are at Ocean Beach. —DAYLA SOUL

On September 12, 2013, bearing a protest petition with some 22,000 signatures, Cori Schumacher met with Roxy executives at corporate headquarters in Huntington Beach, California. I joined her in feminist solidarity, and as part of the public humanities work I have been doing with activist surfers since 2011. An explosion of public outrage following Roxy's release of a video promoting the 2013 Roxy Biarritz Pro had forced the meeting, with Roxy senior executives Danielle Beck, then Vice President of Marketing, and Cathey Curtis, then Senior Vice President of Marketing. The video showed a faceless and mainly undressed surfer getting ready to go out surfing: tousled hair in bed, vamping in the shower, cleavage shot on the beach, butt shot as she paddled out. No shots of her surfing. The hashtag on Twitter #WhoAmIJustGuess asked viewers to weigh in on the identity of the surfer, which presumably invited them to become familiar with or "know" her body, since surfing was not featured. Response on social media was instant and furious. "You would never see a men's surf brand do this!" declared one woman, "Roxy, I fear this will hurt for a while."[1] A nerve among surfing publics had been struck, clarifying how little people wished for Roxy's brand, widely held to be the "face" of global women's surfing, to resemble a Victoria's Secret lingerie ad. Outraged by the video herself, and seasoned in the art of negotiating industry forces as a three-time world champion longboarder and former Roxy rider who left the brand behind, Cori Schumacher began a petition drive demanding Roxy "Stop All Sex, No Surf" ads.[2] She challenged Roxy to represent women in ways that all "women and girls can admire."[3] The petition blew up into a major campaign, fueled by Change.org, which would bring us both, eventually, to the executive conference table.

When one does business (including activist work) at the headquarters, it is impossible not to engage the glamor of the Roxy/Quiksilver project: its state-of-the-art architectural self-presentation, floor-to-ceiling rolling surf/skate/snow videos, polished cement floors, slatted-wood design elements, vertical high-modern white spaces, glass walls running end to end to cordon off public lobby space from "the inside." Cori Schumacher and I each crossed over behind those glass walls, as it were, to take a seat at the behind-closed-doors table. This gorgeous Orange County facility covers some fourteen thousand square feet, three separate buildings; Roxy is but one. The compound is among the ground zeros or epicenters of a multifaceted global empire. Brands like Roxy/Quiksilver of course are image brokers, visual culture machines, as well as employers of innumerable people at all levels of formal and less formal global economies. I mention these few facility details (by no means all that could be noted) to say that Roxy/Quiksilver is in the business of selling, among other things, itself, and the way it does business. In an era over the last few years of shattered surf economies and devastated profits (Quiksilver filed for Chapter 11 bankruptcy in 2015), to attack the brand, to demystify its "beauties," as the Stop Roxy Ads campaign did, is to get the empire's attention, at least for a bit.[4]

Roxy/Quiksilver headquarters is a productive site from which to open this chapter, since it frames key critical issues I pursue pertaining to subcultural publics and activist publics, as well as to the dynamic emerging field of surf studies. How will the disparate but overlapping knowledge arenas engage the political economies of surfing? Why are these crucial questions for feminism and surfeminism? One argument of this chapter is that feminist epistemologies and methodologies offer surf studies ways to think through its location as a cross-disciplinary knowledge project tied intimately both to social theory and disciplinary knowledges and also, crucially, to the expertise of subcultural publics. The question of how the field or individual researchers will work with lay experts is a big one, whether a particular scholar's work is explicitly activist or not. Feminist research presence in universities today, of course, grew in part out of global civil rights movements and has from the outset grappled with navigating social and academic boundaries to further critical knowledge and social justice projects. Feminist work and its long histories of creating alternative models of knowledge production can help surf studies think through problems of democratic relations between and theoretical framings of the work of researchers with community knowledge creators.

I focus my arguments through a discussion of the history and emergence of the Institute for Women Surfers (IWS), and an examination of what the IWS can teach researchers about the public humanities and the possibilities of scholar/activist collaboration. The IWS is an ongoing instance in which a particular very strong and effective subcultural base in the world of surfing, mainly from California, has come together for feminist activist purposes with scholar allies, some of whom are surfers. Projects that have come about through the IWS, or that have developed alongside or intersected the IWS, serve as examples for related topical discussions, including, toward this chapter's end, reflections on what political theorist Kathi Weeks calls postwork imaginations. The three conceptual terms in my title—surfeminism, critical regionalism, public scholarship—invoke theoretical, political, and methodological priorities for the work, and they need elaboration. By way of doing so, I briefly tell a kind of origin story for how the work and the IWS itself came to be. In this story, we see interests that organically cross and inform each other in feminist representations of women, matters of place or what I call "related local" geographies, and from-the-ground-up expertise.[5] We see also a driving political and activist vision owing broadly to commitments between US-based and transnational queer, women of color, and indigenous feminisms. The definitions and meanings of feminism, not surprisingly, are components of our work.

I try, in the chapter's first and middle parts, to set up and then fine-tune key concepts as a way to track what became important new, and unforeseen, topics of interest and of theory for the surfers and scholars contributing to this current work—namely, livelihood as an emergent concern, as well as storytelling (representation). I report on specific initiatives that show how surfeminist place-based knowledges (critical regionalisms) can focus our work in broad decolonial directions. I also note the unavoidable limits of collaborative dynamics, the growing pains, and the lessons under way and bound to continue. From the projects as sources of social theory, I then offer some thoughts going forward for the field imaginary of surf studies—including what I call theoretical humility. I use the language of "report" to indicate that the research is ongoing; I am still coming to terms with the archive that activists and other scholars and I have created, and it seems almost premature to write about it. Additionally, the IWS is understood to belong to those who participate, not to me personally, so one important question beyond the publication of this chapter is: to whom does IWS knowledge belong?[6] Ultimately, it seemed important to contribute to this collection. The rapid growth of surf studies as a young field, and the occasion of this collection to promote conversation among scholars from all over the world, marked this as an important moment for bold feminist presence. As I see it, the impulse of the collection to locate a critical surf studies in the self-aware and critical relation of scholars to profit-driven surf industry forces dovetails with the ideals of IWS as a collaborative project accountable to vernacular and community publics and their extensive surf microeconomies. This mindfulness of the complexities and politics of subcultural authority also establishes values by which scholars and other participating publics might evaluate any of our efforts so that research design and execution is responsive to grassroots change agents.

Situating Surfeminism: Plotting the Field

The Roxy example through which we began, alongside an already burgeoning surfing scholarship, establish as foundational field investments the importance of the racialization and gendering of nationalist and global imaginaries as well as worldwide subcultural economies. Interweaving with, but distinct from, the problem of racialized gender and difference are questions of indigeneity, sovereignty, and country claims and, often accompanying them, projects in cultural heritage and revitalization. Scholarship working from the contact zones of the present day shows us how much there is yet to learn about contests between indigenous and settler colonial interests over "local" status, visions of environmental justice, and histories of surfing and its precolonial and contemporary meanings beyond those of the Polynesian Triangle.[7]

To be sure, surf studies has a strong showing of work along the path of women, gender, and sexuality analyses, in both qualitative and quantitative research arenas. But there is a distinction to be made between analyses that "add women (gender or sexuality) and stir," so to speak, as opposed to analytics that frame gender through some engagement with or either deliberate or unaware distance from feminist theory. Here I take up scholarship working with feminist epistemologies explicitly. Initially, feminist surf work came through history and media studies, and operated via what we might think of as an informed skepticism and critique, as in Douglas Booth's incisive term "surf fraternities" to cast feminist doubt on industry's claims of 1990s girl friendliness, or in exposures by Margaret Henderson of intense sexism in several national subcultural media contexts, or by Leslie Heywood and myself of the prominence of gender and girls in producing postfeminist neoliberal subjectivity.[8] Drawing from the social sciences, in *Surfing and Social Theory* Nick Ford and David Brown elevated that discussion by conceptualizing surfing as experience and knowledge through gender as a central analytic, framing understandings of embodiment, ontology, and global gender orders in direct conversation with, among other things, feminist subcultural studies. My own work, coming out of feminist American studies, blended social science and humanities methodologies, employing feminist history, analyses of representation, political economy, and critical ethnography.

Recently, a threshold has been crossed related to the volume of new feminist work available. Clusters of texts speak to one another across global geographies and disciplinary difference. Journals like *Sport in Society* showcase a lot of work that approaches surfing through gender and feminist frames, and major presses like Routledge sponsor lists with titles in fields such as sports and leisure studies. The sociology of sport, along with human movement studies, has produced very active areas of feminist inquiry. Much of it has come from a productive group of scholars whose paths crossed at the University of Waikato, Aotearoa (New Zealand). Among these scholars is Belinda Wheaton, who shows that lifestyle sports, including surfing, should be distinguished from traditional organized sports, with far-reaching implications for comprehending late modernity, the politics of the everyday, and problems of difference.[9] Who are these different Others (including ourselves as women athletes), and what research methodologies will be helpful to understand them/us? Holly Thorpe takes on the proliferation of sport for development and peace (SDP) organizations and their complex politics in relation to Muslim women who participate in board sports in Afghanistan.[10] Interested in feminist research methodologies, Rebecca Olive theorizes the interactivity of social media (e.g., blogging, Instagram), and links recreational surfing in Australia to gendered embodiment, risk, and pleasure.[11] In the masculine surf spaces of the United Kingdom, Georgina Roy considers lesbian networks, bodies, affectivity, and desire, as well as the complexities in the relationships of researchers to "informants" who become surfing friends.[12] Patriocolonial visual economies across the worlds of surfing media serve as points of critique for lisahunter, who points us toward the possibilities of female physical capital, including her own, and feminist critical pedagogies.[13] Among other things, running through all the above work is a strong feminist methodological insistence on positionality and self-reflexivity—an acknowledgment of the partiality of knowledge, and the inescapable implication, in that knowledge, of the located "I," the knowledge producer.

The expanding archive in surfing masculinity developing alongside, but separate from, the above indicates again how prominent gender study is for the emerging field. How the archive relates to feminist thought, or does not relate, is an interesting question for both surf scholarship and for masculinity studies more broadly. Increasingly, feminists are asking of this kind of work: does it see itself as having something to do with feminist studies? One cannot simply assume a link. Clifton Evers's important memoir, *Notes for a Young Surfer*, does what we might consider public humanities work by telling a tale, very self-consciously, of the formation of a masculine surf subject (himself, the narrator).[14] What is feminist about it, beyond its self-reflexivity, is the care with which Evers details how surf settler heteromasculinity spreads over and claims place—that is, that certain configurations of gender/sexuality produce a power that is historically suited to spreading until something stops it. Andrew Warren and Chris Gibson are interested in the production of cottage industry surfboards through the interweaving of masculine cultures of place, craft, and an aggressive heteronormativity. An alternative masculinity importantly but implicitly underwrites their analysis, as it does for much work on masculinity. Whatever relation it has or wants with feminist thought or politics is not articulated.[15]

Approaching masculinity as an indigenous world-building project, Colleen McGloin shows genealogical relations between surfing, the Australian nation, and white masculinity, in order to counterpose notions of Aboriginal country, ocean epistemologies, and relations of indigenous surfing to anticolonial lifeways.[16] Indigenous cultural revitalization of Hawai'i is a shared principle for Isaiah Walker as well, whose work offers an epistemological accounting of surf life and history centered through Hawaiian language sources, oral histories, and the *po'ina nalu*, a gendered social space devoted, in contexts of repeated invasion, to the renewal of native masculinities.[17] Again, what relation these masculinity studies have to feminist genealogies or to indigenous or native feminisms (perhaps issues of feminist sovereignty or gender justice pertain?) is not, however, yet a topic.

What seems accepted in general thus far in scholarship is that modern surfing usually cannot be understood apart from histories of coloniality and modernity. Histories of surfing and its travels implicate it fundamentally in the politics of empire.[18] Even so, surfing imaginaries and communities, and individual surfers, are hardly unified in political outlook or self-understanding. If most scholars agree that the social site and practice of surfing is often one of profound political contradiction, scholars also find that surfing as representation can fuel anticapitalist mass cultural fantasy.[19] It offers radical sources of embodiment and pleasure; fosters environmental literacy; produces place-based knowledge conducive to indigenous and other subjugated knowledge; and provides platforms for social/political transformation. Participatory activist research initiatives as well as literatures on critical pedagogy offer needed instruction in how to undertake forms of knowledge generation tied into ideals of social justice.[20] Many scholars, prominently including those in SDP, perceive that surfing and surf tourism, as international development strategies, raise questions about relative geographies of international power and the need to define models and economic philosophies driving surfing as a Western export product. Some theorists of SDPs, Simon Darnell and Lyndsay Hayhurst well known among them, urge decolonial methods and theoretical frameworks, which also encompass sustainability and social well-being.[21] Hayhurst urges a feminist decolonial effort, as does Tara Ruttenberg in her clear-thinking work for this volume. Certainly in the present, when activist projects or business ventures bring surfing to new places or emergent markets in the name of freedom or stoke, as happens all the time, coloniality/modernity and its gender/racial orders will travel alongside.

To return to the point about feminist studies in the field and what they offer surf scholarship: Clearly, a strong, foundational impulse toward women, gender, and sexuality analysis is present. At the same time, it is key to notice that the practice of "including women" or "addressing masculinity" or "activating sexuality" in particular texts or surf histories, or across large-scale analyses of states or international political economy, is not the same kind of analysis as is one in which conceptual genealogies, or disciplinary departure points, crucially theorize and historicize whatever specific instance of women/gender/sexuality is at hand. This holds strongly also for analyses that prioritize racial formation or indigenous revitalization. Women of color feminists, indigenous feminists, feminist philosophers of the coloniality of power—all have insisted that visions of social life for decolonial futures must filter through feminist lenses.[22] "Gender" should not signal a category of analysis reduced to women or to masculinity and separate from renderings of surfing's "big picture," such as its socioeconomic life, ontological appeal, global pop cultural presence, history of travel, vision of environmental justice, imposition of colonial structures, current Western export as "empowerment" philosophy, or indigenous revitalization. All of the above "big ticket" intellectual topics are fundamentally constituted via gendered difference, its colonial/race politics, and so on. Indeed, Roxy's production of ideal white femininity is a statement as much about masculinity, sexuality, settler geographies, and surf political economy and its preferred definitions of freedom and development as it is about "women's surfing."

Foundations: Toward a Feminist Public Humanities

In 2010, I published *Surfer Girls in the New World Order*, about local/global subcultures of girls' surfing, globalization and surf political economy, and surfing's established intergenerational feminist communities. There was no indication at the time *Surfer Girls* went to press that something like the field of surf studies would come to be. The book combined multisited ethnographic study with theories of globalization and cultural/historical analysis to make an argument about transfers of feminist knowledge (through what I call "girl localism") happening across women's and girls' surf subcultures in California, Mexico, and the Transpacific. When I got to the end of the book and speculations about Muslim girls' surfing and the markets of Indonesia, I thought I was done with surfing as a research pursuit—until, to my surprise, I began to get emails from surfers who had read the book and were posting comments on blogs and Amazon.com. They were sharing the book with friends in different parts of the surfing world, because, they said, it put a "big picture" on the gendered globalist dimensions of surfing, and explained for them, in spite of it being branded as girl-friendly, the subculture's persistent, even escalating, sexisms, and the use of girls to cover, or "girl-wash," Western imperial land grabs in surfing's new emergent markets. Readers remarked upon the difficulty of the "more academic" parts of the book (its theorization) even while the challenges did not stop them from completing or understanding the book or using its ideas to grapple with their own subcultural situations.

Not all of these were simply "thanks for the book" emails. Two respondents in particular—the activist and social entrepreneur Farhana Huq and the already-noted world champion surfer and activist Cori Schumacher, both from California—wrote to me to make feminist connections. Both of them, independently, were mapping projects that complemented the political architecture I had theorized in the book. Huq was launching the entrepreneurial social change and media platform BrownGirlSurf.com, dedicated to diversifying the lineup and subcultural media, and putting women of color surfing at the center of networks of alternative belonging; Schumacher was finalizing The Inspire Initiative, to generate activism, develop subcultural political literacies, and train new leaders. Both are 501c(3) nonprofit organizations. With a bit of happy shock, I perceived the theoretical work of the book was in direct conversation with activist projects. My claims were circling back to me, and being expanded, at that time not yet by critics or colleagues, but by ambitious nonacademic feminist readers. Would I be a partner in this moment of theory as new forms of practice?

Theorizing what I am doing by saying "yes" to these and other queries that followed from them has been an ongoing process of new learning. What is research? What is research good for? How can activists and scholars collaborate? In "Activisms and Epistemologies," the historian and theorist Laura Briggs urges scholars to see themselves as bringing critical and conceptual tools to activist projects at the same time, she notes, that activist intellectual offerings are often underappreciated by university researchers. Obviously, however, where scholars get their ideas is important. Briggs suggests crafting a "politics of solidarity" that would refuse any simple activist/scholar divide. Briggs's politics of solidarity overlaps philosophically with the concept of "engaged research." The eminent Latin American anthropologist Charles Hale defines engaged research as a practice in which "people who are the subjects of research play a central role, not as 'informants' or 'data sources,' but as knowledgeable participants in the entire research process."[23] Research ethics are understood not just at the level of personal relations between researcher and "informant." Hale distinguishes between "activist research" and "cultural critique," arguing that the former builds alliances for political goals between activist scholars and the organizations with whom they work. If the outcomes of research founded on alliance and not on critique are "troubled" or "imperfect" or "full of contradictions," Hale holds the research to be nonetheless valuably informed by the "complexities of political contention."[24] The idea is to forward a model of analysis and group work that lets the inevitable loose ends show as productive lessons.

The feminist sociologist Nancy Naples and ethnographers Craven and Davis (among many others) observe that the dilemmas of public scholarship bear strong similarities to those of feminist research: they bring into relief tensions between theory and practice, expert and informant, and strongly critique positivist science and the neutrality or objectivity of the observing knowledge producer.[25] Indeed, the literature in feminist studies on the specific dilemma of "speaking for" others runs very deep, especially in feminisms derived from postcolonial, indigenous, and women of color contexts.[26] Feminist thought is constituted by precisely these challenges, offering methodological and epistemological models that should be called upon as theoretical and practical resources far more often than they are in research projects collaborating with social change actors that are devoted to public address.

With ideals of engaged scholarship in mind, I began to think of and talk about this work publicly as performing a feminist "public humanities."[27] As do public humanities projects generally, I took as one goal the translation of humanities research findings or theoretical concepts into everyday language that most of us can understand. The idea is to bring people together for engaged public discussion on topics of social significance to everyone—like democracy, security, technology, well-being, sustainability, sovereignty, cultural heritage. A specifically feminist public humanities engages the ways in which "big topics" (democracy, the realm of the public, environment, security and the state, globalization, etc.) are deeply rooted in and serve to further or intervene upon gendered ideologies. These topics require feminist analysis.

Public humanities as a feminist undertaking seemed (in my developing thinking) to be potentially responsive, moreover, to the understandable desire of activists to see or create better images, more accurate representations of social life than often is found in the pages of major magazines and global media. It could offer a more sophisticated sense of the slipperiness of representation, its investments and instability, those audiences implied or unconsidered, and the fact that representations elude authorial intention. All these matters seemed important because issues of representation had surfaced as among the most important activist concerns. On reflection, what had drawn activists to make the leap from reading my book to contacting its author with collaborative intentions is the fact that they felt represented by what was written. They had been hailed as subjects of political theory.

That is, what was happening with the Roxy campaign, as well as the hope that drove Brown Girl Surf, had to do with the social implications of representational politics. Industry's notorious exploitation of images of women for profit, and its narrow and racist productions of "blonde babe" female types, were nothing new, though they had consequences both for women paddling out and for their making a living through surf economies. What was new, perhaps, was a moment ripe for change. Showing how high the stakes of protesting these realities really are, Schumacher (during the Stop Roxy ad campaign) faced homophobic death threats on social media.[28]

Through the Brown Girl Surf social media platform and blog, Farhana Huq hoped to represent the local breaks of the San Francisco Bay Area of California in ways that would enable and empower a more diverse lineup. Indeed, she hoped, through her work, to produce the very women of color South Asian community she longed for. Huq also was drawn to do transnational activist outreach to the few girl surfers in Bangladesh, where Huq had family and personal history, as well as in south India. For these projects, film seemed the obvious medium, because in her mind, how else would one represent them, and herself, in the same frame, and do it between "there" and "here"? In partnership with Cara Jones of Storytellers for Good, a social change organization working in the medium of video, Huq created two short activist films about girls' and women's surfing in India and Pakistan. The complex process of editing the films and presenting them to Bay Area audiences fed self-consciously into the goal of putting issues of representation and decolonial storytelling on activist tables.

The Institute for Women Surfers: Practices of Surfeminism

The IWS is a grassroots educational initiative in the public humanities that brings together activist women surfers and their allies to create spaces of peer teaching, learning, and mutual aid. As a public political intention and cluster of relationships, the IWS has been growing since 2011. The Institute conducts in-person trainings, publicizes issues and events via social media, and hosts a website (InstituteForWomenSurfers.org) where educators and activists can find out about participants' projects in filmmaking, art, photography, hip-hop, nonprofits, business, blogging, healing justice, and scholarship. Collaboration of activists and educators is the organizing principle of Institute knowledge creation. To date, two IWS trainings have been held; a third institute is planned for fall 2018, to be held in San Francisco.

The initial idea for the IWS came out of discussions I had with family members who are senior collective bargainers for the California Nurses Association (CNA), which has since become the National Nurses Association (NNA), the only major US trade union to commit official union platforms to feminist issues like reproductive justice. The NNA offers extensive political education for its members in global health, food security, and movement building. Taking a page from their playbook while simultaneously immersed in conversations with surfers about next steps in political action, I imagined a social space devoted to political education of activist women surfers.

If trade unionist political education models inspired an organizational model for the Institute, the full-blown IWS grew and matured only once Schumacher and I began to work on it together. The pilot Institute meeting, held in July 2014, in Oceanside, California, at the North County LGBTQ Resource Center, brought together an international group of women surfers and activists for three days of discussion, mutual learning, participant presentations, and communal surfing. We focused on "big picture issues" for surfing subcultures as well as on building coalitions for activisms of the future. Schumacher worked tirelessly on the organizational logistics, and she and I designed a curriculum that intertwined five topical workshop sessions with invited participants' various projects—films, blogs, nonprofit programs, surf hip-hop, and

FIG. 11.1 Selected participants of Institute of Women Surfers (IWS). *Left to right, back row*: Lynn Bryant, Elizabeth Pepin Silva, Camille Ramini, Sarah Soul, Alison Rose Jefferson, Krista Comer, Margaret Cariño-Condon, Dina Gilio-Whitaker, Tara Ruttenberg, Margaret Seelie. *Left to right, middle row*: Nicole Grodesky, Beth O'Rourke. *Left to right, front row*: Mira Manickam-Shirley, Christina Baldwin, Mercy Cormier, Lauren Callahan. *Foreground*: Dayla Soul.

FIG. 11.2 IWS/Wahine Banner, with Project Wahine Director Dionne Ybarra.

FIG. 11.3 IWS Grassroots Political Education poster.

FIG. 11.4 IWS logo, Collaboration Across Generations.

oral history. The topics were chosen for their relative political urgency. Each workshop had as homework an essay reading or film. Workshops, along with precirculated essay summaries, highlighted equality vs. liberation feminisms, place-knowledge, feminisms over Global North/South geographies, and the complexities of storytelling and of "doing" history. Issues of women's well-being and livelihood featured additionally as movement-building priorities. At times, Muslim women's surfing garnered special focus, given that Brown Girl Surf had just produced the two film shorts noted earlier about Bangladeshi and Indian surf girls. The explicit Institute goal, overall, was to develop new political vocabularies. This curriculum can be found, archived, on the IWS website.[29]

"Surfeminism" as a term emerged out of the group gestalt. It seemed to float atop or "pop" from conversations to name a loose desire or hope or political direction—that is, "surfeminist!" with an exhilarated laugh, a surprise that the term made sudden sense, was not oxymoronic. Not systematically pursued or defined or fought over, the term was perhaps, initially, an affective recognition or exhortation. What surfeminism means or does, what worlds it names or values, its relation to other feminisms, is under construction. In an extended blog exploration immediately following the Institute's 2014 meeting, Schumacher theorized, "This becoming-Surfeminism" is a "visceral" body knowledge emerging from "dialogue" about "shared experience."[30] Surfeminism, for Schumacher, takes third-wave feminist commitments, identified through "intersectionality," and puts them in service of the life of the body that surf women live individually, and live as groups. Generally, I would say, "surfeminism" is hopeful, suggestive, productive of the new; it marks becomings, transformation. The term instances a new moment of political energy, spontaneous consciousness and sociality, and feminist demand, in the sense that political theorist Kathi Weeks describes "demand" as formulation of a political statement.[31] Surfeminism critiques industry's sexploitation of elite stars and images of women across global surf media, and offers itself as counterdiscourse.

Eighteen months later at the 2015 IWS meeting, participants worked to develop further the understanding of surfeminism—including immediately posting #surfeminism to social media sites to see what conversations would come of it. Again, an international group of participants gathered for three days of interactive learning and surfing, this time in Ventura, California, at the Brooks Institute Film and Photography School. Enabled by a change from invitation-only to public application, the Institute's 2015 participant list grew to nearly twenty-five. The 2015 themes, "Storytelling, Sustainability, Building a Movement," gave focus to a weekend of dynamic discussions, workshop presentations, participant skill-sharings, and collaborative organic intellectual and creative work. Co-facilitated by the rapper and youth culture worker Mira Manickam of Brown Girl Surf Oakland, who led an inspired series of "Bring Yourself" exercises culminating in the creation of a group coral reef mural, the weekend featured as additional workshop leaders Michelle Habell-Pallán of the University of Washington's "Women Who Rock Public Humanities Project" and Dina Gilio-Whitaker of the World Center for Indigenous Studies.[32] Doctoral candidate Tara Ruttenberg from University for Peace, Costa Rica, led a discussion on decolonial sustainability. Carly Thomsen, a feminist studies queer theorist experienced in engaged research pedagogy, attended the 2015 meeting as an ally to help craft conversations about our own activist/scholar politics of solidarity. Clearly, IWS 2015 manifested deeper scholar/activist relations. The original 2014 curriculum served as a model that Thomsen and I took in new directions: all were asked to think about the meanings of collaboration, of "co-vivencia" (Habell-Pallán's term for feminist co-living in community), and political alliance. A highlight everyone reported was the extensive grassroots participant "Skill-Shares" featured throughout the weekend: film projects in process, surfeminist hip-hop, surfeminist art, tips and tricks for social media campaigns, as well as transnational projects in photography, surfboard recycling and international board sharing, mental health justice, and youth education. Again, the curriculum and select Skill-Share videos are archived on the IWS website.[33]

In the nearly three years since the inaugural Institute meeting, postings on our closed IWS Facebook group have noted new optimism about the possibility of feminist subcultural intervention. Individuals have written about boosts of encouragement taken from both the IWS real-time events and the ongoing online community following them. Some people report major transformations in gendered aspects of personal affairs or in moving feminist activist projects forward. New formal and informal partnerships have been formed; women have reached out to one another to skill-build or to problem-solve, as well as to collaborate officially via fiscal sponsorship or merged strategic partnerships, in ways that did not happen before the Institute existed. The photographer and filmmaker Elizabeth Pepin-Silva has begun new film projects on the surf giants Linda Benson and Joyce Hoffman, and finished *La Maestra* (2015), with Paul Ferraris, a thirty-minute surf documentary about Mayra Aguilar, a Mexican teacher and inspirational figure in her home community of Baja.[34] Nicole Grodesky, with the enthusiastic support and counsel of IWS allies, has launched the website Surfeminism.com, which features interviews, new stories, and analysis, and publicizes surfeminism as a movement that is still building. The provocative *It Ain't Pretty*, directed by Dayla Soul, opened the San Francisco documentary film festival in June 2016, to a standing-room-only audience of

Soul's home-turf and surfeminist-minded filmgoers. The IWS was enthusiastically represented. Taking the surf world by storm and winning awards as it goes, the film has propelled Soul, along with big wave surfers like Bianca Valenti, into the political limelight. The film's interest in sexism and surfing (the subtitle is "The Women's Big Wave Movement") has played an important publicizing role in the battle of female big wave surfers for access to the legendary Mavericks contest.[35]

Inevitably, conflict has arisen—about political differences, personal differences, and the need to set limits about how much can be given by participants to one another and on what terms. What is political solidarity, what is friendship, and what is labor that should not be given for free? Some people post a lot on the closed Facebook group, some not so much. It has been a particular challenge for me to incorporate this new social media aspect of a project into existing workloads, though I am learning. Perhaps the biggest challenges the Institute has faced grow from the legacies and contexts that the surf industry has created, over a half-century, for the representation of women. The initial campaign against Roxy that opens this chapter showed Roxy—the "leader" in women's surfing and the corporate face of global women's amateur and professional competitive surfing—as incapable of understanding there were politics to its representations, or as unable to be accountable to a protesting base. Where, then, will activist surfers find accountability? Alternative cultural movements and activist alliances in collaboration with scholarly partners raise hopes about being able to offer a better chance at accountability and creating the new worlds people long for.

Yet one of the steepest learning curves is to understand the degree to which even a feminist public humanities effort is subject to subcultural strain related to representation. Since the surf industry is foundationally structured around trafficking in women's images, and depends upon exploiting women surfers and their celebrity stars for maximum market share, it is imperative that representations of surfing feminism be as accurate, balanced, and real-time as possible. But this is easier said than done. Why? Beyond the ambiguities of representational practices, many difficulties boil down to different timelines and expectations of activist versus scholarly representational practices. Institute participants and I have had many conversations about how imperfectly the two meet up. Activists must see themselves in and be credited in the work as it develops in real time to continue to trust in collaborative intentions, at the same time that academic and publishing protocols present serious challenges to the whole idea of real-time representation (i.e., temporal lags for revision, fact-checking, citation, peer review, revisions, delays for academics' day job duties). Public scholarship thus requires that scholars get better, quickly, at translating into public forums the relational nature, and perhaps "intermediate findings," of collaborative labors so that, as it is ongoing, the collaboration-in-process sees the public light of day. Information appearing on websites or traveling in social media offers many stages along the way for giving credit where it is due and for the renewal of group purpose.

There is also the related issue of immediacies surrounding social media and activism. Cori Schumacher has often remarked that surfers are among the most online of global subculturalists, checking weather patterns, planning where to surf, and communicating topical events as well as tracking or protesting surf news. The looseness of social media platforms, the preference for sound-bite expertise, the "instantaneous" and "Wild West" environment where sometimes anything goes and recognition of sources is lax—these features of social media as a virtual space of thought and of activist mobilization are distant to scholarly communal life (in-person lectures, conferences, theory reading groups, teaching). Nonetheless, hashtag activism research is changing how scholars understand social media politics. It typically is precisely because of the possibility of broader democratic dialogue that scholars doing public work will want to retrain themselves, as quickly as they can, to navigate across competing intellectual temporalities so they can move capably between complex concepts and sound bites. Some scholars already are very good at this navigation: Rebecca Olive, for instance.

I have taken time to narrate above the development of the IWS as a collaborative project in order to theorize surfeminism as an evolving public intellectual enterprise constituted also by practices of recognition and reciprocity, and through them, research ethics. One of the big issues going forward for critical surf studies, when working with nonacademic experts, is to distinguish scholars' behavior from that of macro- or micro-industry. As this new field grows, scholars may be in more of an "industry" role in terms of public authority or recognized expertise than most of us imagine now. And it will not always be a bad thing; sometimes we may be able to "credential" projects that otherwise would have been dismissed. Still, I see how my fate as a thinker or writer or public figure is now tied to subcultural economies and historical legacies in ways I did not imagine.

Surfeminism and Critical Regionalism

If the Roxy campaign might be read as a protest of the ways industry travels the world's financial/media circuits not just via generic "babes" but also via the competitive tour world map, other feminist campaigns go forward with less fanfare or public awareness to make a case about the importance of place. These campaigns are no less significant examples of feminist work digging in and making a difference. The ones I report on here in the final section of this chapter show their feminist work through what I call "critical regional" emphases. Critical regionalism is a developing body of thought associated with critical architectural genealogies (Frampton, most prominently); theories of critical transnationalism or literary regionalism/border study, such as that of Jameson, Campbell, Comer, or Limón; and postcolonial and some Latin Americanist thought—for example, Spivak and Moreiras, respectively.[36] One of the key conceptual terms of my *Surfer Girls* work was "related locals"—meant to theorize subcultural social/political imaginations as well as modes of translocal embodiment and travel, which I noted as an instance of feminist critical regionalism. Here I extend and develop that theoretical work toward critical regionalism as a geopolitical concept with decolonial and democratic abilities. I tease out what critical regionalism is as a set of informing theoretical precepts for surf studies through its on-the-ground enactment in two feminist projects in particular.

The first is Farhana Huq's BrownGirlSurf.com: from its inception, Huq perceived connections between San Francisco's Ocean Beach scene and the emerging female surf worlds in southern Bangladesh and southern India. The connections had to do with her sense of who was missing—that is, women of color, especially South Asians—in dominant surf media representations. Huq was learning about surf scenes cropping up in new places, and as somebody with a history of activism and family, language, and cultural heritage in Bangladesh and Pakistan, the "grabby" sensational media stories—about the Muslim surfer girls on the Gaza strip in Palestine, for instance—piqued her sense of solidarity.[37] Raised as a Muslim in New Jersey, and an accomplished competitive athlete, Huq felt a personal connection to these stories. She encountered them, that is, from a sense of situated place knowledge produced between Pakistan, Bangladesh, New Jersey, and now the Bay Area, where she had founded but recently left a nonprofit, and was living her life as a single woman, thinking about new work, and spending a lot of time surfing Ocean Beach. Place knowledge, that is, entangled itself in questions of relative livelihood options between the starkest poverties of Bangladesh, the relative privilege of southern Indian economies, and Huq's own privilege relative to both sites, but her real need nonetheless to make a living.

What is unique about the activist work of Huq and Brown Girl Surf is its mapping of Ocean Beach as a site of transformative feminist politics between women surfers in San Francisco, Cox's Bazaar, Bangladesh, and southern India. This geography of linked "related locals" is what I am calling the project's feminist critical regionalism. The political programs under way through it have been several. One is ongoing collaboration with the Indian surfer Ishita Malaviya, founder of the Shaka Surf Club, who has become a familiar figure of emerging South Asian women's surfing in global surf media including Roxy. Another program supports the Bangladesh Surfer Girls Project, founded by Hazera Khanam, essentially an informal feminist SDP project aimed at providing educational opportunities, work opportunities, or health care to extremely poor girls, often orphans. Both efforts developed from film projects that were the official initial purpose of Huq's travel to Bangladesh.

The two short films, *Surfing Possibility: The First Surfer Girl of India* and *Surfing Possibility: The Surfer Girls of Bangladesh*, proved incredibly dynamic as public humanities and activist ventures. They are free online, and one of them (about Ishita Malaviya, "The First Surfer Girl of India") has "gone viral."[38] The story of making the films, revising them to edit out elements that "didn't feel right" to Huq (we came to call them "orientalisms"), and then the public presentation of the revised films, as well as our public comments about the process of revision, deserves attention. Made with crowdsourced funds from a Kickstarter campaign, the idea was to use grass-roots media to create public forums for raising transnational awareness about women's issues. We gave the first screening/presentation of the films, along with their "complicated backstory," at Patagonia in San Francisco on the International Day of the Girl in October 2013. This event framed for its audience a story about surfing in parts of the world where surfing is relatively new (southern India and Bangladesh). The actual shooting of the films turned out, however, to be a more complex undertaking than initially anticipated. Complications had to do with international relations (visa refusals for Muslims traveling on US passports to India), histories of development (expectations Bangladeshi collaborators had of Huq), and Christian surf development in Bangladesh (the global evangelical organization Surfing the Nations was an early sponsor of the Bangladeshi surf club). What was so creative and interesting was the perspective brought by Huq to the interface of these issues with race and poverty, mothers and daughters, sports for women, and the concept of "possibility." What did "possibility" mean? Did the West have a monopoly on stories of female freedom?

The questions *Surfing Possibility: The Surfer Girls of Bangladesh* raises in particular, and the "backstory" Huq told online and in social media about the complications of making it, are part of a larger and rare conversation about Muslim women's surfing and Indian women's surfing. When Huq challenges film audiences (as I note in this chapter's opening epigraph) to see more than "cool girls in a salwar kameez" learning to surf, we reach the most pointed question relevant to surf cinema about women in emergent markets: how do "we" understand a good life for women? How are we in Western surf audiences seeing these films? What visions of feminism or women's liberation typically inform the work of activists?

Such questions will help us think through, in future surf activist projects, the special claim for Muslim women's victimhood that has long informed colonial imaginations and gained traction in post-9/11 "war on terror" political rhetoric. As we discussed at the 2014 Institute gathering, the now-classic work of feminist political theory by Lila Abu-Lughod asks: "Do Muslim Women Really Need Saving?"[39] Her project calls attention to the ways that the US war on Afghanistan repeatedly utilized women's liberation goals as an ideological justification for imperial intervention. Institute discussions examined the work of empire performed in the name of Western feminism, teaching us that, in order to create more fruitful collaborations, we must recognize the need for more sophisticated political educations so that we can intervene effectively in postfeminist foreign policy—and always, the need for positionality.

Of course, other recent films featuring Muslim women's surfing as a topic are well known by those involved in surf activism. Viewers familiar with the high-visibility documentary projects *Into the Sea* (directed by Marion Poizeau), about the efforts of Irish big wave surfer Easkey Britton to introduce surfing to Iranian women, and *Beyond the Surface* (directed by Crystal Thornburg-Homcy and Dave Homcy), about Western women surfing south India with Ishita Malaviya, may well wish for a comparative analysis of these projects here.[40] While I do not provide that, I will say that Huq's project allows surf scholars to grapple with why a feminist critical regionalism may help theorize power in what is sure to be an extremely global knowledge project. The places from which any of us speak or locate analyses or theory cannot but inform whatever politics we bring or projects we conceive. The focus of Huq's films on issues of related-place locations, which is not a typical given in feminist theory, makes more textured and politically accountable the transnational activisms that are commonplace in surfeminism. Feminist critical regionalism critiques ideals of "flow," and global circulations, by calling attention to the uneven politics of mobility, of who moves when, why, and how.[41] Huq implicates herself in the histories and cultural and language practices of Bangladesh when she imagines, from northern California, a project of Muslim outreach. She does not begin her storytelling through impulses of "adventure" or "pioneering," since she and "we" the audience of the films enter a world that is not foreign, not "Other" or otherworldly. She loops "them" through "us" in "our" Western world home places.

These framing devices—the fact we are not put into place via a border zone of the civilized and primitive—is what I find remarkable about the Brown Girl

Surf shorts. They break the mold of exotica in what audiences expect from surf cinema—which means a new story can open. All the tropes of classic surf narrative are present: travel, joy, love of ocean, living life through the body. But the kinds of complicating elements introduced by a story that pivots around sequences of male domination over women and girls in Bangladesh makes for a tale that, in spite of its authentic smiles and visual high production values, is jarring. "Wait a minute," we are saying. People who know surf narratives well must pause.

And wait another minute: it is not "there," without also being "here," because there *is* here, "we" are not separate from "them." Returning now full circle to the feminist challenges of life in the West, since the critical mapping of Bangladesh links it to issues of hierarchy in one of the most feminist-friendly places on earth—the Bay Area, and Ocean Beach—we have a new kind of decolonizing political impulse. It does not depict the West as "the best" in terms of its gender order. This is a very important act against imperial forms of feminism, or a politics of empire deploying "feminism" for its own ends, and it is important because we began with the fact of subcultural structural violence "at home," with male domination and subcultural struggles over issues of branding, profits, and livelihood.

Surfeminism for the Future: Postwork Imaginaries, Autoethnography, Public Scholarship

Let me move toward a conclusion by focusing on issues of livelihood and work under late capitalism through the concept of "postwork imaginations" forwarded by the feminist materialist Kathi Weeks. I have spent much time in this chapter with problems of representation, telling, among other stories, a Roxy story, my own story, a story of the IWS, as well as a story about Huq and Brown Girl Surf, who are telling stories through film about Bangladeshi surfer girls. It is fair to say that storytelling demanded more from the project and its participants than anyone anticipated. In a sense, so too have issues of female livelihood demanded more from us, or something other, anyway, than the initial terms on which people came together. The work of collaboration (including for me) has gotten more personal. It is now definitely as much about "us" as about "them"—whomever was the object of organizers' initial activities.

What has created this shift is the accidental, but nonetheless full-blown, intrusion of discussions of work into our activist vision. What should work be or do? In this set of questions, we pursue the proposals of Kathi Weeks that work become a renewed subject of political theory. One of the most exciting concerns emerging as clearly important but always, in a sense, hanging back, making itself hard to see on its own terms, has had to do with this matter of livelihood, the rationale of its production, and surfers' long-standing philosophy of skepticism about organizing life around work, about having one's life rhythms and primary locations (where one lives or the life and place one inhabits) be utterly disciplined or determined by capitalist work logics. Surfers have long been unpersuadable that work, in itself, articulates an ethical life or governing social vision. In this conviction, surfers are perfect subjects for the kind of critique Weeks brings to the devotions of capitalist social orders to work as a moral good.

What is becoming clearer as the activists' projects go forward is that challenged livelihood is a shared (however unevenly) situation of surfing female life. Most of the surf activists with time for unpaid activist work and also time to surf are not regularly employed in the full-time labor force, have been recently on unemployment insurance, or are employed in full-time ventures, like small businesses or nonprofits, that barely break even. Some surfers work in jobs that allow them to prioritize activism and surfing. Many earn wages from participation in surf microeconomies (teaching surf lessons, for instance). None of the surfers involved here is supported by a partner. Serious activists who also surf seriously are not typically working full time at highly demanding jobs, since surfing and activism *are* their serious activities. The above situation is true notwithstanding wide variety in activists' class and educational backgrounds. So there is a fair amount of scrambling among US-based activists to meet basic expenses of life such as housing, food, transportation, and health care. That is, there is a lot of scrambling to meet basic needs.

Even so, debates about what constitutes "need" itself strongly directed our discussions, and the telos of surfing lives is unmistakably *not* public accomplishment or upward mobility per se, but "passion," as in living in accord with one's passions in life. A distance from the moral discourse attending Protestant work ethics, in tandem with what we might think of as subcultural legacies of antiwork philosophies, provide ideological counterweights to normative values that insist upon the organization of a life around work, its networks and social relations, its provision (or withholding) of status, and of course its benefits of income and securities (e.g., health insurance, retirement savings). Postwork imaginations, that is, lives directed by "passion," are on regular display in the world of surfing. "Passion" alerts us to issues of both desire and need broadly defined, including needs for creativity, joy, community, living in the female body powerfully, and living in conscious relation to the natural world. If the meeting of some needs is insecure in this world of challenged female surfers' livelihoods, other needs of activists—for living a passionate life—are not themselves *made* insecure by the world of work, its temporalities, its bodily or affective demands. This is an important point, because for some of us, like me, "security" efforts have created *in*securities like being away from the water, and chronic overwork with its own health hazards. Discussions of work, "security" and its hidden complexities, and precarity have raised issues of public health and well-being as IWS priorities. Female surfing is a wonderful site for staging a global conversation across borders about feminist public health and what contributes to it, as well as one related to the influence of gender on issues of life quality and flourishing.

The Wahine Project is a site for just this kind of discussion about work, passion, and politics. Founded by Dionne Ybarra, The Wahine Project is very friendly with, but functioning autonomously from, Brown Girl Surf.[42] It is a business-model nonprofit organization geared to girls from economically challenged neighborhoods of the Salinas Valley and Monterey County. It offers both surf camps during the summer, where girls learn to surf, as well as a nine-month feminist curriculum during the school year. Girls learn to swim and surf, to connect with other girls, to identify and withstand social pressures to mistreat other girls or themselves, and to engage in local project-based eco-learning. Ybarra sees the most important lesson not as surfing, but as girls' friendship. As of September 2014, IWS began collaborating with Project Wahine Teen; the curriculum for the teen program includes reading select feminist short essays and discussing films, with me as a video chat presence occasionally on Sunday afternoons. Project Wahine also fosters transregional political solidarity with other challenged girl surfers. For a time it collaborated, through Facebook and video chats as well as real-time surfboard exchanges, with the Gaza Surf Girls and they continue to be linked to surfers in Punta Mita, Mexico, as well as the Philippines.

The Wahine Project sees its mission as one of intergenerational nurture, and toward that end, some months ago, I drove down to Monterey from the Bay Area, where I stay with one or another of my sisters, to visit Project Wahine's surf camps for girls.

It is a Wednesday, and in the summer of 2015, Ybarra devoted Wednesdays to the theme of Waterwomen. I park and walk onto the sand at Municipal Wharf #2. Perfect blue-sky day, no wind, little lapping waves, and fifty or so girls under umbrellas and Project Wahine tents. They had been doing a "try-athalon" earlier, a run–swim–paddle event; the boards are still on the beach, and the tide is rising under the pier where a bit earlier big starfish were clearly visible underwater. I learn I am the "Waterwoman Wednesday" featured speaker.

I do not think I can overstate how much I love, as a woman with four younger sisters, to see all these wet-haired girls sitting together on beach towels, feeding each other pieces of oranges. Some of them, including Ybarra, are painted up in blue sunscreen. This weekly surf camp part of Wahine Project is a critical revenue stream that keeps the nine-month curriculum going, with all its many scholarship offerings for those who cannot pay. The youngest of the large group today is five and the oldest is seventeen, about to go to college. The latter's name is Sam, and she was one of the girls doing Wahine Teen—I remember her from our video sessions. Ybarra prompts me to tell the girls something about my life as a waterwoman, and eventually to take questions. I tell them I am a professor now, I used to live by the water and it organized my life, but my work on surfing helps bring me back again, and makes me happy. I am not sure what else I say, something about loving seeing all the girls, something about Project Wahine, and about the importance of understanding the place you come from so you can understand who you are. I have labored into a borrowed wetsuit so Ybarra and I can paddle out and look at the starfish when we're done, and I am looking forward to that.

Ybarra joins me in front of the girls and surprises me by talking about what I do, the importance of what I have done for women's surfing—it did not occur to me to think this way or raise it even indirectly as a part of my Waterwoman Wednesday talk. Then she gets to the heart of what she wants to say to them, the core curriculum. She talks about "male domination" in the water, its influence in the ads one sees in surf magazines, and its effects on women and girls on land. We need one another to be strong, she says, and to know our own value. We also need to be able to stand up for ourselves, and to back each other in doing that. Meanwhile, the sun shines, the girls are giggling but attentive, they are together and focused. They take this all in stride. Now it is Q & A time. One of the girls asks how long I have been surfing, and I say I do not really surf, I have always been more of swimmer, and if I lived all the time by the water, maybe things would be different. The group takes in this information, and one of the girls then raises her hand; she forgets what she wants to say, so we wait until she remembers. She says, "Well, I think you're what we mean by a Project Wahine Waterwoman." Everybody is taken by this observation, especially me. It is probably one of the kinder observations anyone has made recently. Given how high-performance the surfers are that I typically run with, and how competitive, if the truth be told, I feel usually either insufficient or subjected to efforts to improve me: a better bodysurfer, boogie boarder, a longer-distance swimmer. But thinking about this now, none of these comparisons really matters, because the fact is that I am returning to a life of the body in place, one I have known, and know how to know again, and the path toward it today involves these women and girls, and our postwork talents.

I include this final moment of autoethnography so as to show, for real, that there are stakes in this kind of public scholarship project that are different, and I take them seriously. What I have admired about Project Wahine from its beginning is the ontological work it does with girls to "place" them in the place they already might be from but cannot claim and do not know. Ybarra is one such girl grown into womanhood herself, daughter of Mexican American migrant farmworkers, raised in East Salinas, mother of four sons, a woman who taught herself to swim in her thirties, then taught herself to surf, and figured, with her training as a teacher, she would teach others. If Roxy exists to create future markets of girl surfers or consumers by offering lessons in coming of age, Project Wahine is also creating a future for girls and women, but obviously, this is counter-education, accomplished not through consumption of sexist images or competition as the only means of self-esteem and social recognition, but through in-person intergenerational nurture and transfers of feminist knowledge. The geographic scale here is translocal. Like Farhana Huq, Ybarra loops her activist project in Monterey back through her own communal roots and history in East Salinas. Though it supports international projects, Project Wahine sets its political sights on *this* place and not some other place, and feminist ontologies and place knowledges *here*. There is no narrative of adventuring or "discovery"; the claims are more humble. This is not, however, a vision of a simple-minded or parochial "local." It is a microview of a preferred social order where the totalizing effects of competitive capitalism and the traffic in women's images are critiqued and discarded in favor of feminist ontologies of place, and postwork notions of social purpose and community.

A few final thoughts are in order about these projects as sources of feminist social theory for surf studies. To the degree they exhibit humility, a regard for place and its accountabilities, they take us in the direction of decolonial politics. Humility is not naiveté; it is a statement about the limits of "our" knowledge or authority to proclaim Authority. Decolonial theory urges us to avoid totalizing visions, including of liberation, since they so routinely revert to Eurocentric epistemologies and re-center the world again through the primacy of Europe.

If there is any cautionary tale told here, it is one that urges surf studies not to travel the world of an emerging field and, through theoretical finesse, claim and name it. Theory provides needed big explanations and linkages, yes, but the grace of the concept of feminist critical regionalism is that it speaks its geographies and observes boundaries, places where "we" may not be invited. It is important to reiterate that all of the projects here matter, whether critical of representational politics (the Roxy campaign or Huq's films) or interested in critical pedagogies (like the IWS or Project Wahine). Whatever projects in surfing are forthcoming from the ground up will depend greatly on how we honor the production of knowledge from below.

NOTES

Epigraphs: Huq, "Backstory to *Surfing Possibility*: Stories of India's and Bangladesh's First Surfer Girls," *Brown Girl Surf*, http://www.browngirlsurf.com/surfing-possibility .html, accessed September 26, 2014. The webpage is no longer available. *Surfing Possibility: India's First Surfer Girl* is available at https://vimeo.com/77648509 (accessed March 8, 2017); *The Surfer Girls of Bangladesh* is available at https://www.youtube.com/watch?v =VhrpS1Tcnkc (accessed March 8, 2017).

Schumacher, "quick someone shoot that . . . feminist dyke," *Cori Schumacher: State of Flux*, July 16, 2013, http://www.corischumacher.com/2013/07/16/quick-someone-shoot -that-feminist-dyke/.

Soul, "Not Your Stereotypical 'Surfer Girls,'" Sound Cloud: KALW San Francisco Radio, February 25, 2014, https://soundcloud.com/kalw/not-your-stereotypical-surfer.

1. Martha De Lacey, "'I am utterly disgusted': Fans Slam Surf-wear Brand Roxy's Online Video Starring Faceless Female Surfer's BOTTOM . . . and NO surfing," *Daily Mail*, July 9, 2013, http://www.dailymail.co.uk/femail/article-2358917/Utterly-disgusting-sexist-Roxy -Facebook-fans-outraged-new-online-video-female-surfers-surfing.html#ixzz4b70CherM.

2. Schumacher held the 2000, 2001, and 2010 Women's World Longboard Champion world titles. For political reasons, she boycotted the Association of Surfing Professionals (ASP) 2011 Longboard Competition to be held in Hainan Island, China. For details, see Zach Weisberg, "For Female Surfers, Challenges Out of the Water," *The New York Times*, March 26, 2011.

3. See Schumacher's web page, http://www.corischumacher.com/.

4. International financial media have reported crushing losses in recent years for major industry retailers Billabong, Quiksilver, and Rip Curl. See, for instance, Russell Jackson, "Billabong's Downfall May Signal the Death of the Entire Surfwear Industry," *Business Insider*, November 7, 2013, http://www.businessinsider.com/billabong-demise-surfwear-2013 -11. Suggesting silence is better than confirming the spiral downward, the Surf Industry Manufacturers Association (SIMA) has offered no industry data since 2013. At the 2014 Institute meeting, Cori Schumacher offered analysis of the increasing sexism in advertising as a desperate response to losses. On Quiksilver's recent emergence as Oaktree Capital Management (a private company) after restructuring its debt, see Tim Corrigan, "Quiksilver Wins Court Approval to Exit Bankruptcy," *Wall Street Journal*, January 28, 2016, https://www.wsj.com/articles/quiksilver-wins-court-approval-to-exit-bankruptcy -1454012044.

5. I develop the concept "related locals" in *Surfer Girls in the New World Order* to theorize how world subcultures of surfing imagine being in place—specific surf spots are understood culturally against a larger backdrop of global surf breaks well known in subcultural life. The concept is important as a way of thinking about the body in place and the materiality of places and activisms in contexts of contemporary traveling cultures and world geographies of surfing (22–25).

6. In what ways the IWS archive contributes to work in progress by any of its participants is an active question. My current book in progress, *The Feminist States of Critical Regionalism*, explores literary and activist strategies of feminist storytelling that contend with the broad political climate and confusions of postfeminism. Political imaginations associated with surfeminism offer important insights into topics of interest in this chapter: work, well-being, the materiality of bodies, intergenerationality, and the possibilities for democracy of critical regional alliances.

7. On environmental justice, see Gilio-Whitaker, "Panhe at the Crossroads." For histories of precolonial surfing, see Zavalza Hough-Snee, "You Have the Right to Surf"; Wood, "Representing Peru"; Dawson, "Enslaved Swimmers and Divers."

8. Booth, "From Bikinis to Boardshorts"; Henderson, "A Shifting Line Up"; Heywood, "Producing Girls and the Neoliberal Body"; Comer, "Wanting to Be Lisa."

9. Wheaton, *Cultural Politics of Lifestyle Sports*.

10. Thorpe, "Action Sports for Youth Development."

11. Olive, "Making Friends with the Neighbours."

12. Roy, ' "Taking Emotions Seriously." '

13. lisahunter, "Becoming Visible."

14. Evers, *Notes for a Young Surfer*.

15. Warren and Gibson, *Surfing Places, Surfboard Makers*.

16. McGloin, *Surfing Nation(s), Surfing Country(s)*.

17. Walker, *Waves of Resistance*.

18. Laderman, *Empires in Waves;* Comer, *Surfer Girls*.

19. Lawler, *American Surfer*.

20. lisahunter, emerald, and Gregory, *Participatory Activist Research*.

21. Darnell and Hayhurst, "Sport for Decolonization"; Ruttenberg, "Wellbeing Economics and Buen Vivir."

22. Smith and Kauanui, "Native Feminisms"; Smith, *Decolonizing Methodologies;* Hall, "Managing Our Own."

23. Hale, *Emerging Contradictions*, 4.

24. Hale, *Emerging Contradictions*, 4.

25. Craven and Davis, *Feminist Activist Ethnography*; Naples, *Feminism and Method*.

26. Spivak, "Can the Subaltern Speak?" (1988) is the classic formulation, but a literature in the problems of feminist witnessing also pertains. For a cogent rendering of the ethics of this problem as related to ethnographic practice, see Angel-Ajani, "Expert Witness."

27. Moments in which scholars define "public humanities" for non-specialist audiences are interesting to perform. An early example from my own experience is "On Philosophies of Storytelling" for a public event at Patagonia commemorating the International Day of the Girl, in San Francisco. It is archived on the Brown Girl Surf website, which currently is under reconstruction.

28. Schumacher, "quick someone shoot."

29. For 2014 curriculum, see the Summer Institute 2014 page on the ISW website, http://www.instituteforwomensurfers.org/summer-institute-2014/.

30. See Cori Schumacher, "Thoughts on a Surfeminism," *Cori Schumacher: State of Flux*, July 23, 2014, http://www.corischumacher.com/?s=thoughts+on.

31. Weeks, *The Problem with Work*, 116–117.

32. For more information about Habell-Pallán's work, see http://womenwhorockcommu nity.org; for more on the work of Gilio-Whitaker, see http://dinawhitaker.wordpress.com.

33. See the Institute 2015 page on the ISW website for meeting details, http://www .instituteforwomensurfers.org/summer-institute-2015/, accessed March 7, 2016.

34. For a gloss on Pepin-Silva's impressive work, see the Institute Participant webpages at IWS, http://www.instituteforwomensurfers.org/participant-test-2/, accessed March 7, 2017.

35. The film is available on Amazon and iTunes. For information, see https://itunes .apple.com/us/movie/it-aint-pretty/id1191057209.

36. For more discussion of the critical regional thought informing this work, see Comer, "Thinking Otherwise."

37. For an early example of Western press representation of this story, see Sarah Topol, "Gaza's Surfer Girls," *The Atlantic*, October 21, 2010.

38. Upworthy reported over four million views as of December 2016. See https://www .facebook.com/Upworthy/videos/1076627229044801/.

39. Abu-Lughod, "Do Muslim Women Really Need Saving?"

40. *Into the Sea*, available at http://surfmovies.org/free-surf-movies/938-into-the-sea .html; *Beyond the Surface*, available at https://www.beyondthesurfacefilm.com/.

41. Comer, "Thinking Otherwise."

42. See the Wahine Project website, http://www.thewahineproject.org/, for details of these exchanges and the mission statement. For reporting on the Gaza Surf Girls, see Harriet Sherwood, "Gaza's Girl Surfer Battles Pollution and Prejudice," *The Guardian*, August 29, 2011.

LISAHUNTER

I ka au ana a hiki I kulana heenalu, au waiho ia mai iloko ko ke kamaaina, a lana wale aku la no keia I waho, me ke kali hoi no ke ku ana mai o ka nalu. Ia ia no hoi e lana ana, ku mai la ka nalu mua, aole keia I pae, a pela no hoi I ka lua a me ke kolu o ka nalu, aka, I ka opuu ana mai o ka ha o ka nalu, o koi a nei hoomo iho la no ia a pae. I ka hoomo ana no, ua oi kau no ke Akamai, a me ka hiehie hanohano luaole. Ia wa, ua uwa kapihe a haalele wale, uwa hou no a haalele wale, uwa hou haalele wale. O na alii a pau a me ka poe makaikai no ke Akamai o Kelea. Ka Nupepa Koukoa.

When [Kelea] reached the place where the surf broke, she left that place to the kamaiāina and paddled on out to wait for a wave to rise. As she floated on her board there, the first wave rose up but she did not take it, nor did she take the second or third wave, but when the fourth wave swelled up, she caught it and rode it to the shore. As she caught the wave, she showed herself unsurpassed in skill and grace. The chiefs and people who were watching burst out in cheering—the cheering rising and falling, rising and falling. —SAMUEL MANAIAKALANI KAMAKU, "Kelea-nui-noho-'ana-'api'api," August 19, 1865

This opening passage from a newspaper over 150 years ago identifies the surfer, Kelea, and her surfing prowess.[1] It is used by John Clark to identify how "position changes and different stances in a traditional surfer's personal style may have also been marks of athleticism and aesthetics."[2] The image of females surfing is also captured in Figure 12.1, an engraving from 1874. Today athleticism and aesthetics are still significant qualities of surfing, but during the last one hundred years or so the female surfer, and possibilities for the subject position "female surfer," have been stolen, ignored, marginalized, or wiped out. *Wāhines* (Native Hawaiian females) were repositioned as nonsurfers; *haole* females (white

"Kahéle and I watched the surf-swimmers for some time, charmed with the spectacle."—(*See p.* 234.)

FIG. 12.1   Early sketch c. 1779 of female and male surfers. Courtesy Bishop Museum.

settler females) were positioned as subservient to males and largely dismissed as "lesser" than men in and out of the surf; female participation was not deemed worthy of recording through historical artifacts; and the female was positioned as a passive object of the heterosexual male gaze—in "her place" on the beach. Clearly sex, gender, and sexuality count in and around the surf, and while these are not the only identity markers that intersect in an individual, they are the focus of this chapter.

Is Surfing Screwed?

Despite the workings of race, economics, globalization, capitalization, colonialization, and competition, sex (the category and act, along with gender and sexuality) is arguably the most pervasive influence in constituting the field of surfing and the habitus of surfers. I mount an argument that sex has defined surfing, and that its current form continues to rape participatory subject positions. In tracing its presence in the localized precolonial Hawaiian form to its contemporary globalized diaspora, I then focus on ethnographic evidence from Australasia. Here, a hegemonic androcentric, patriarchal, (hetero)normative doxa that I term *patriocolonialism* facilitates an illusion of equitable participation for males and females, and therefore feminist victory, while symbolic violence reproduces a spectre of patriarchy, albeit in new or hidden forms.[3] Courting the structural (field) systems that enable and constrain the doxa and the resourceful appropriation of the body (habitus), I draw on multiple field texts to unpack the constructedness of sex/gender/sexuality (herein referred to as SGS) and their boundary work in surfing, to "deconstruct the cultural teachings of heteronormative orthodoxy."[4] Practices of sex, heteronormativity, dichotomized hegemonic gender, queer absence, hyperfemininity, surf porn, carnalities, and biological masking are explored in contemporary Australasian settings to ask whether surfing is "screwed" and whether it could be anything other than sexed. I finish by offering several queer lines of flight with pedagogies of possibility to provoke discussions about the future of the habitus/field of surfers/surfing.[5] I use hybrid theory to go beyond just penetrating the field and practices of surfing, seeking to engage with the sensual pleasures of desexing surfing.

Background: Historical and Conceptual Frameworks

The socially constructed and heteronormative gender binary of woman (feminine) and man (masculine) is intricately enmeshed with the simplistic biologized sex binary of female and male. As such, to speak of gender one must also consider sex (biology and the act of) and sexuality. Many modern forms of (Western) physical pursuits reflect these relationships:

> From the mid-nineteenth century, when modern sport in the West took an organized form, right up until the present day, it has been a distinctly gendered activity... because sport has been dominated by men, the focus on gender is very often equated with the story of "women in sport" and their struggles over many years for equality with men.[6]

Surfing waves, in various forms, was a common cultural practice of indigenous Polynesian peoples prior to colonialization. In precolonial times up until the 1800s, in what is now geopolitically known as Hawaiʻi, *heʻe nalu*, or wave sliding, was considered a widespread pastime of Hawaiians regardless of sex, age, or social class.[7] The pastime became appropriated and redeveloped in the twentieth century by Western patriarchal colonial violence, both materially and symbolically.[8] As I have argued elsewhere, the patriocolonial ontology that framed the development of a modern form of surfing acts as a doxa, "an orthodoxy, a right, correct, dominant vision which has more often than not been imposed through struggles against competing visions."[9]

I also argue that surfing's doxa takes for granted normalized and naturalized notions of SGS, intersecting with other markers such as race, and assumes these categories to be normative markers of a surfer's disposition, or surfer habitus. Such normative markers are used to recognize, make intelligible, and position a surfer within the field. In a dialectical manner, it is the individuals' and groups' social practices that establish and reinforce potentially fluid social structures (field), and these same social structures, in turn, influence the nature of the individuals' or groups' habitus. Practice, therefore, is "the product of a habitus that is itself the product of the embodiment of the immanent regularities and tendencies of the world."[10] The practices associated with SGS in surfing—for example, heteronormativity/homophobia—are produced by the SGS (heteronormative/homophobic) bodies who participate—the (assumed straight) surfer habitus and (assumed straight) field each constituting the other and marginalizing or absenting other forms of sexuality. *Practice* is both the result and the process by which field and habitus are evoked.

It is within the surfing field, through individual and group practices that legitimize capital, that the field is made stable by those invested in it, rewarded by it, and positioned more powerfully in it to the point where they are "fish in water," unable to see the logics of practice that they embody.

Including a discussion of surfing's diaspora, I focus on ethnographic evidence from the geopolitical space of Australasia. Here, a hegemonic androcentric, patriarchal, (hetero)normative doxa facilitates an *illusio* of equitable SGS participation and feminist victory, while symbolic violence reproduces patriarchy, sometimes in new or hidden forms.[11] Courting the structural (field) systems that enable and constrain the doxa and the resourceful appropriation of the body (habitus), I draw on multiple field texts and previous surf- and gender-order literature to unpack the constructedness of SGS and their boundary maintenance in surfing, to "deconstruct the cultural teachings of heteronormative orthodoxy."[12] Practices of sex, sexualization, surf porn, heteronormativity, dichotomized hegemonic gender, hyperfemininity, queer absence, and carnalities are practices to be explored in the contemporary setting to ask whether surfing could be anything other than sexed.

But what of each point of the triad: sex, gender, sexuality?

In this section I consider each element of the SGS triad—sex, gender, and sexuality—separately, and relating to levels of sport and, specifically, in surfing. This exploration identifies some of the complex interactions of practices that reinforce simplistic and normative SGS relationships and a cishet binary normative doxa for, through, and as surfing.[13] While complex, these practices are separated as points of an SGS triad only for the purposes of discussion, and I acknowledge that some of the power of doxa is in the complexity and fluidity in the definition and relationship between the three. Nevertheless, I will explore some of the practices that embody a patriocolonial orthodoxy as the ontology that sits deep below the surface of surfing, including sexualization, heteronormativity, dichotomized hegemonic gender order, hyperfemininity, surf porn, and queer absence. After this section, I briefly discuss how the field is being penetrated queerly, and whether new moves, such as queering surfing or exploring surfing's carnality, might be employed to dismantle entrenched identities and practice, birthing new possibilities for expression, connection, and experience.

Sex: A Normalized Biological Binary and an Act

SEX IN SPORT

Sport, particularly in its dominant forms and as a valued marker of Australia, has been described as "an ideological institution with enormous symbolic significance that contributes to and perpetuates cultural hegemony."[14] Sport, and more specifically, competitive sport, has historically been perceived in Australia as a male domain, controlled by men, and a context where hegemonic masculinity, the idealized and normalized dominant masculine image, is constituted and promoted.[15] Competitive sport explicitly values and rewards dispositions of competitiveness, self-confidence, aggression, dominance, risk taking, independence, and emotional control; these are characteristics of the successful athlete, but also of normative masculinity.[16] While this relationship has been the focus of considerable critique for some time, it remains a relationship strongly embedded in stereotypes and in sports media representations, and the doxa of sport in Australia.[17]

SEX IN SURFING: ERASURE AND REPLACEMENT

The failure to systematically record the history of female involvement in surfing reflects the absenting of histories of female involvement in sport and Western society more generally. So while sex contributed to aspects of being and doing in pre-patriocolonialized Hawai'i, where early forms of surfing were part of the very structure of society, and female involvement was recorded in oral legends and sketches, the sex, gender, and sexuality categories may have been markedly different from the patriocolonial society that colonized native Hawai'i in the 1900s. Precolonization, *wāhine* (females) and *kāne* (males) both surfed with great skill and power, as evidenced in this chapter's opening passages and image.[18] Native oral legends position females not as passive but as active and present. Even early colonial traveler records included sketches and stories of wāhine surfing, although more to document the "quaint native" than to celebrate female power, I suspect. The sensual nature of surfing and the role surfing took in forming relationships, "flirting," and as a precursor to the act of sex are also documented in Clark's compilation of mid- to late 1800s traditional surfing lore:

> O ka nalu e heenalu ai o ke kaikamahine a Hoolae, o Keanini; He nalu no ia maloko o ke kaikuono o Kapueokahi; a he nalue poha wale I waho, a ua maa ua kaikamahine nei a Hoolae I ka heenalu. A o Kiha-a-Piilani, he keiki heenalu no Waikiki, a ua kaena oia I kona mau nalu e holo ai I ka lala; O ka nalu o Kalehuawehe a o ka naly o Maihiwa. Elua a eha la heenalu o Kiha-a-Piilani me Koleaamoku I lilo ma ka heenalu ana, a me na hooppoipo ana no ka ike mai I keia kanaka maikai. (Ke Au Okoa, December 8, 1870, p.1)
>
> [Kamakau also told this story in Ka Nupepa Koukao, November 18, 1865, p.1]
>
> The surf on which Ho'olae's daughter [Kolea-moku] surfed was called Ke'anini. It was inside the bay of Kapueokahi, a surf that broke easily. Ho'olae's daughter was accustomed to surf-riding. Kiha-a-Pi'ilani was used to surfing at Waikiki, and he often boasted of those [waves] with a long sweep, the surf of Ka-lehau-wehe and the surf of Mai-hiwa. Two to four days Kiha-a-Pi'ilani and Kolea-moku spent in surf-riding. Noticing his handsome appearance, Kolea-moku made love to him.[19]

Clark preempts this passage by saying that "for traditional Hawaiian surfers, there was something magical about men and women surfing together. The ocean is alive, constantly in motion, soothing and sensual when it's calm, and exciting and challenging when the surf is up and surfers are enjoying the pure pleasure, the adrenaline rush, of riding a moving wave. When men and women shared this experience in the same place, on the same wave, or even on the same board, it was stimulating for everyone and sometimes led to romantic interludes."[20]

However, the active participation and equitable positioning of females was erased or destroyed as part of the patriocolonial violence in Hawai'i during the eighteenth and nineteenth centuries. The positioning of and by one's sex became reshaped by the hegemonic culture of white Euro-American binaries in sex and race: positioning wāhine as "hula girls" and servants to the whites; females (Hawaiian and haole) as subservient to males; and male Hawaiians subservient to white hegemony. There is little evidence of wāhine surfing in the early 1900s, but Euro-American tourists and haole were entertained and guided by kāne known as beachboys: these were the Hawaiians who kept a tradition of surfing going, and renewed it as the "modern" form of surfing.[21] This modern form developed in several ways: as appropriated by haole in Hawai'i; through diaspora communities initially in California, Australia, and Europe via surfing demonstrations; and then, in the mid-twentieth century, through the idea of "surfaris," travel trips to unpopulated waves around the world. This modern form of surfing carries little female history, owing in part to history being viewed and recorded by patriocolonial males who had the monopoly on roles and resources to create that "surfing history." But as surfing history's origins and politics are being challenged, and new evidence from the past excavated and voiced, there is growing evidence of a female resistance to passive positioning all along in the form of surfing participation, albeit erased or treated tokenistically in surfing's imaginary.[22]

Today, sex in the form of a male–female biological binary is strongly evident in surfing epiphenomena. At the annual Quiksilver-sponsored World Surf League (WSL) World Tour surfing competition held on Australia's Gold Coast since 2002, two divisions exist: the Quiksilver Pro for males and the Roxy Pro for females. In 2015, seventeen females, rated as the world's best from the previous year, competed for a total prize purse of $262,500 (the winner getting $60,000).[23] At the same site but during different times of the day—with more optimal wave conditions—thirty-four males competed for US$525,000 (the winner receiving $100,000). This disparity has not gone unnoticed.[24]

Among those who promote the sexualization of female surfing and the heterosexual gaze of female surfer bodies are the mainstream media, commentaries and articles in surf magazines and websites, and embodiments by well-known "babe"[25] models and professional surfers seeking to exploit the gaze of their bodies, for example, Alana Blanchard, Elli-Jean Coffey, and Anastasia Ashley.[26]

This phenomenon does not go unchecked, however. Females and other supporters are (still) asking whether surfing is hypersexualized with a "sex sells" attitude, and how this might be alienating and marginalizing females from

FIG. 12.2 Male surfer "dropping in" on a female surfer.
FIG. 12.2 Male surfer "dropping in" on a female surfer.

surfing or wanting to participate in surfing. Such a debate has haunted surfing for a long time, as illustrated by surfer biographies and narratives from previous generations.[27]

The ongoing work of researchers like Mary Jo Kane and Janet Fink has unpacked some of the complexity in the sexualization of females in sport.[28] They and others, like Mike Messner, have shown how the sports media commercial complex, or what Dexter Zavalza Hough-Snee and Alex Sotelo Eastman refer to in this volume as "the state of modern surfing," heavily influences how female sport and female athletes are framed and therefore represented in society.[29] While they argue that athlete marketability depends on gender and racial stereotypes and upholding dominant ideologies of the preservation of hegemonic masculinity, male power, and male privilege, we cannot ignore that this is also about sex and sexuality, about "gender" that is normatively aligned with biologized sex and the heteronormativity of reproductive opposite sex acts. Discourses of sex provide the grounds for gender division. Females are still portrayed for their sex, as a sex, and for sexualization, rather than for their surfing. As a result, some female surfers can gain something from the situation: economic capital in the form of wealth (sponsorship and modeling) that can translate to some forms of success in surfing, whether it is the economic opportunity to participate in the WSL world tour, and therefore compete or be paid to "freesurf" as part of promotional trips; the social capital of being noticed and sought after by sex-based commercialization; and/or the symbolic capital from the territory of the dominant heterosexual male gaze, where female bodies act as commodified and sexualized objects of desire. The challenge female surfers face is to negotiate a dual identity of heterosexual specificity in the form of "performing femininity" and a "soft essentialism" that is athletic *and* heterosexually feminine.[30]

"Sex appeal" and "flaunt it if you've got it" justifications of sexualizing one's body for individual gain or for "getting more coverage for the sport" is an ongoing trope in sport more widely, and surfing in particular.[31] Self-sexualization requires one to "buy in" to the easily accessible story of female availability and value through sex via idealized bodies—idealized through both their "look" and the apparent aspiration to hegemonic heterosexuality for dominant male pleasure. "Female athletes' decision to pose in sexually provocative ways commoditizes their bodies for the 'male gaze,' and as a result, they become complicit in reinforcing the exploitation of women's sports overall."[32] These deep-seated cultural associations, also prevalent in the surfing field, explain why some athletes embrace self-sexualization and seek portrayal as traditionally feminine rather than as physically big and powerful, qualities reserved for the "opposite" sex—a hierarchical binary that keeps heteronormativity in prime place. Kane and colleagues also noted that the nude/seminude and "soft porn" portrayals that nearly always present the female athlete as passive, with little attention to athletic musculature, are in sites (magazines, websites, television channels) designed for normative heterosexual male gaze, not for female sport appreciation. In their study, female fans reacted negatively to hypersexualized images, seeing the "sexy babe" image as simply a marketing tool aimed at cishet males and counterproductive to the promotion of female athleticism.[33]

In the state of modern surfing, the athletic female surfer possibility of premodern surfing times is replaced with that of the babe in order to uphold patriarchal domination and, as part of that doxa, heteronormativity. While that is also under challenge, again, there is much to suggest that elite female surfers have yet to break from the babe idealization.[34] In her research investigating the lifestyle marketing practices of the three major surfing companies and the sponsorship experiences of fifteen elite female surfers, Ros Franklin found that "the attributes of female surfers recommended for sponsorship selection were surfing ability, an appropriate look or image, engaging personality and the ability to communicate effectively in public," the "look" being pivotal.[35] In contrast, male surfers are not sexed as a primary means for sponsorship. While "image" and "personality" are also important for males to achieve sponsorship, image is associated with surfing strength, power, and speed rather than sex appeal.

Erasure of the competent and athletic female surfer has also been produced through what Robert Rinehart offers as "surf porn."[36] This refers to practices where surfers, waves, locales, "beach babes," and the like are configured as objects of the scopophilic gaze, wherein a commodified culture exists that supports a subject–object stance, surf media exploits its subjects without reflexivity or taking a critical stance, and surfing is a popular culture artifact whose fundamental purpose is to make money. The doxa of a modern surfing state is continually reinforced through the mechanism of surf porn embedded in nostalgia for patriocolonial "golden eras" captured in iconic surfing films such as *The Endless Summer* (1964), in which females are "in their place" as sexual objects, and waves are for consumption by adventurous or alternative males.[37]

The Gold Coast, springboarding from the sensual nature of the beach, embodies surf porn: the giants of the surfing industry, located on the Gold Coast, sell products that are a commodification of the surfing lifestyle, such as fashion and beach or lifestyle products that are not actually purchased for participating in surfing.[38] The WSL-sponsored competition is hosted by a surfing industry that promotes and reinforces the "sex sells" and "babe factor" discourse, one's sex and one's performance of sex acts strongly determining how one is politically positioned in the field. Even the female world champion, Stephanie Gilmore, saw economic opportunity in tapping into such discourses to attract a sexual gaze rather than exploit her competent, athletic, strong, fast, and powerful body.[39]

Sex, sex stereotypes, the act of sex, and surf porn have been central to erasing females as competent and athletic surfers, and constructing the passive "babe" in surfing doxa and the contemporary ontology of the field. Yet as discussed in the final section of this chapter, other practices trouble the boundaries of sex and patriocolonial surf porn, or exist beyond them, providing the sensual pleasures of surfing while also challenging normative identities and subject positions. Before discussing these queer practices, there are two other points to this sex triangle to be discussed—that is, gender and sexuality.

Gender

GENDER IN SPORT

Lindsey Meân and Jeffrey Kassing argue that "gender remains the primary categorization of women athletes, re/producing female athletes as women who play sport rather than as athletes first and foremost."[40] There is much evidence that modern sport generally, but also specifically in Australia, has been heavily rooted in heteronormative binary cisgender relations: hegemonic masculinity equated with a sporting habitus showing, in particular, speed and strength. Not only do sports and leisure activities divide populations along gender lines, but they also dictate what movements constitute being hegemonically masculine and hyperfeminine. In Australia, males gain capital in demonstrating their masculinity through hegemonic sport forms mostly seen as one form of football code or another, and, alternately, in cricket. Like females in other countries during the last century, females in Australia had to carefully negotiate an athletic identity alongside that of patriarchal femininity. It was not uncommon to see females competing in full makeup, passing as feminine for fear of being ostracized by derogatory labels such as "butch" or "dyke" or claims that they were not being sufficiently female.[41] In Australia's colonial development, it strongly identified as a sporting nation, and now has a global presence in sport. Yet females were, and still are, denied access to sport's resources; selling sex becomes a more available route, negotiating the tension between athleticism and feminine beauty by absenting the athletic, and replacing or supplementing it with the babe.

GENDER IN SURFING

Similarly, in surfing, gender expectations and relations have been maintained by denying a more inclusive history of female participation, together with an insistence on females embodying the particular femininity that satisfies male desire. As already discussed, noticing and valuing feminine characteristics of a particular form, legitimated as beauty and captured as a reference to the "beach babe," are prevalent in early surfing magazines and still, to a large extent, in contemporary magazines (and surf media and entertainment more broadly) targeting male youth. Colleen McGloin makes the point that "misogyny in surfing texts is commonplace and has a specific textual function. . . . It can recuperate surfing masculinities inflected by the patriarchal feminine."[42]

Up until recently, females were expected to demonstrate a femininity that provided a passive beachside spectator for their male surfing partners. As gendered and sexualized "Others," they were, and in some situations still are, present to recognize the position of the hegemonic male, and in return were/are valued as a naturalized and naturalizing object of male desire. The "page 3 girl" in the popular Australian surf magazine *Tracks* epitomizes the tokenistic inclusion of females in modern surfing's broader history. The bikini shot or near-nude photo of an assumedly heteronormative female model has often been the only portrayal of females in *Tracks* magazine.[43] The absence of female surfers in the public face of surfing (magazines and more recently film) until very recently, the "model" or "babe" presence of females in surfing magazines, and the to-kenistic representation of female surfers in history books and museums made it clear that the female role was to be passive and only intelligible through hegemonic masculinity.

Building on the valuing and legitimation of females through appearance, en-trepreneurial surf industry drivers such as Quiksilver/Roxy, Billabong, and Rip Curl found new markets in clothing lines for femininity.[44] As others and I have discussed elsewhere, clothing lines such as Roxy were born out of the commodi-fication of surfing along gender lines, enabling a reinscription of femininity through passive street clothing as well as through the burgeoning and now intel-ligible position of female surfer.[45] In the 1990s, board shorts for females finally became available beyond niche and boutique local producers.[46] This, while re-flecting and constructing a possibility of female as surfer rather than spectator or decorative beach piece, has also conversely reinforced a hegemonic male–female and masculine–feminine binary through color, patterns, volume, and styles.[47] This same binary is evident in other surfwear, and recently in wetsuits.[48] Inter-estingly, and speaking directly to the point of this chapter, while enjoying a brief popularity amongst female professional surfers, in warm-water climes board shorts often give way to bikinis. Exposure of the flesh for sexual gaze overrides the protection from sun, wax, and board afforded by board shorts.[49] Within the broader surf industry, aesthetic taste has become a gendered category as major brands recognized the marketability of surf-specific products to female surfing demographics. The increased visible media of female surfing, the production of films for female audiences, and higher volumes of female relegation to the less-valued longboarding "soul style" in marketing all work to capture a market while the same time reinscribing what it means to be female.

As in modern surfing more generally, gender positioning in Australia is heavily linked to sponsorship. This has meant that surfing females have to dem-onstrate hyperfemininity if they are to gain sponsorship.[50] Competitive and professional surfers talk about the need to appear "feminine" in order to be sponsored, and the surveillance of female appearance not just by media and the industry but also by other surfers and spectators. Swimwear chosen for displays of femininity rather than functionality can be strategically employed to catch a good wave in competitive, hierarchical lineups. The visual stimulation of fe-male montes, buttocks, and breasts revealed through bikinis, the smaller the better, earns waves. Some female surfers have even admitted that they nurture their hyperfemininity and lack of body cover to gain value in the lineup and "score more waves," relegating ability to second place, often because one has to score a wave to prove one's ability. Alana Blanchard, a professional surfer, draws capital from the "sex sells" ethos by appearing in sites such as *Stab* and Network A, where her minimalist bikinis, part of the Rip Curl range, are predicted to appeal to the site's audience. With the title "Alana Blanchard Designed Her Own Tiny Bikinis for *Sports Illustrated*'s Swimsuit Issue," the site's author notes, "In case you have been living under a rock, Alana Blanchard, the star of Network A's Surfer Girl, appeared in the 2013 *Sports Illustrated* Swimsuit Issue. But who reads magazines anymore? So being the nice folks that they are, *SI* put together this behind the scenes video of Blanchard's photo shoot in Las Vegas. Blanchard actually designed the bikinis that she wore in the Swimsuit Issue and made sure that they were tiny, just the way she likes them. We like them that way, too."[51] In reality, the "we" who "like them that way" are interested in the objectified body exposed by the lack of bikini.

Although not herself a world champion, Blanchard has appeared in a recent Air New Zealand airline safety video alongside men's WSL world champion Brazilian Gabriel Medina, three-time WSL world champion Australian Mick Fanning, and American big wave legend Laird Hamilton.[52] The press release explicitly names Blanchard's *Sports Illustrated* fame, highlighting that for male surfers, performance is high capital, whereas for female surfers, appearance mobilizes capital.[53] So while Blanchard's (and others') moves to capitalize on their perceived "sexiness" can be framed as taking control of her sexuality by presenting as sexy *and* athletic, it is perhaps more insidiously a pimped Trojan horse for the reinscription of previous (hetero)sexualized SGS binary relations in surfing doxa.[54]

Surfing Sexuality/ies

SEXUALITY IN SPORT

Passing as heterosexual and a technique that Tiffany Myrdahl refers to as "covering"—"temporally and spatially determined muting of certain enactments of identity"—were and are ways that lesbians and gays reported to negotiate their participation in sport spaces.[55] Players' and spectators' use of derogatory slurs to categorize their competitors as "gay," "lesbian," "dyke," or "fag" have been and continue to be used to disrupt participation and legitimate hegemonic masculinity and femininity throughout the sporting world. Numerous recent examples include Sacramento Kings guard Rajan Rondo yelling in a game, "You're a f***ing faggot, Billy" to NBA referee Bill Kennedy.[56]

Jayne Caudwell unpacks the action of soccer players and fans using gay sexuality as the pedagogic device of en-masse derision toward particular players or opposition teams. She describes the Mexican National football (soccer) team's followers' use of the term *puto*—a derogatory Spanish term for a homosexual male—against the opposition at the 2014 World Cup.[57] Males showing what are deemed to be "feminine" characteristics in the form of appearance (beautiful, fine), gesture (grace, poise), or choice of sport (ice skating, netball) are often seen as emasculated and less male. Eric Anderson notes that "a significant use of Western sport in the 20th century has been to reproduce what Connell describes as hegemonic masculinity by turning young boys away from qualities associated with femininity or homosexuality."[58] The feminine and female are devalued. As athleticism is tightly bound to hegemonic masculinity, suspicions toward one's sexuality are invited if a female is athletic or a male athlete shows female-identified dispositions. Some female athletes overcompensate, hyperfeminizing in order to be read as heterosexual, that is, passing as cisgendered, the hegemonically desired position for a female.

SEXUALITY IN SURFING

Modern surfing cultures have been groomed by narrow, limited, and limiting modern patriocolonial Western possibilities.[59] "Grooming" is the process by which an offender—in this case, modern patriocolonial surfing culture—draws an unsuspecting person or identity category into a sexual relationship and maintains it in some form of secrecy. While the secret of sexism, misogyny, and heteronormativity is "out," as a doxa, it remains absented, almost as a secret. This is despite the counterculture of the 1950s and 1960s, where, as Krista Comer argues, subculture served "as an everyday locus for struggles over the expectation that male coming-of-age meant lives organized around breadwinning for a nuclear family," the presence of "surfer girls" enabling subcultural revisions of male gender roles, and expanded gender norms related to femininity enabling countermasculinities.[60] This may have been a counterculture in some respects, but, I would argue, very much a conservative and SGS doxa-conserving culture in relation to a broader patriocolonial society and sport within it.

While binarized gender performances were perhaps loosened and expanded in the 1960s, surfing's counterculture did little to challenge binaries within heteronormative sexuality or in relation to a new binary with homosexuality. Arguably, despite more homosexual visibility, it is nevertheless still not a well-accepted or safe identity throughout Australia or in surfing. Queer is absent from the epiphenomena of surfing—or it has been until this decade, in which we now see early signs of a queer wave in new media and social media, and in groundbreaking films, including less queer or specialized sites, albeit "straightened" a little.[61]

In 2013, heteronormativity and homophobia in surfing were rendered publicly visible by the release of the film *Out in the Lineup*. Not only were heteronormativity and homophobia the topic of the film, but its reception arguably speaks to a deeply held homophobia in the surfing community. One member of a well-known surfing community in the Gold Coast was very disappointed at the low attendance at the screening, as "normally surfing films are sold out." Although some prominent surfers, such as female longboard world champion Cori Schumacher and professional world tour female surfer Keala Kennelly, have made public their queer identities, literally putting their bodies on the line, many still remain fearful of exposing their sexuality because of concerns about potential sponsorship loss, retaliation by their fan base, and slurs and physical assault in and out of the water. While professional surfers such as Matt Branson and Craig Butler have revealed they are gay, as the film makes clear, no professional male surfer has "come out" while competing.

Cori Schumacher embodies the social activist surfer. She is outspoken and very well versed in post-structural feminism, and has been vocal on issues of sexism, sexualization, and homophobia in surfing. Cori is a three-time WSL world champion in the Women's Longboarding category, and therefore has some capital to negotiate social networks both within and outside of the surfing field. After the release of a now-infamous hypersexualized and sexually objectified video to advertise an upcoming international surfing competition, people were strongly polarized, and many blogs were inundated with opinions.[62] The video showed "sexy" pictures of an "unknown" surfing female champion, never once shown surfing. One industry representative, the then–Quiksilver Surf Program manager, reportedly later dismissed for his actions, commented on his Facebook site that "some butchy lesbos were representing surfing [in the past]—not rigged out sexy women who are in touch with their sexuality and know exactly how they are represented and marketed."[63] Cori Schumacher responded: "That three generations of female surfers have had to navigate the limitations of lesbian-baiting ought to bring us pause when considering the unapologetically sexualized image of female surfing we are currently receiving from Roxy and elsewhere in the surf industry. Reclaiming the narrative of women's surfing from that which is controlled by the surf industry, one that is constantly on the defence about sexuality, is the first step in truly advancing women's surfing." As a world champion surfer, Cori's critique of the industry and media—powerful players in setting the heteronormative professional surfing field—is telling. Ultimately, by having to endure the sexualized image as an insider competitor, she actively rejected her competitor position and withdrew from competition.

Much of the media associated with surfing has been engineered and produced by heterosexual men (and perhaps homosexual men passing as heterosexual) and for heterosexual men; their collective homosocial gaze rendered it important to maintain the prominence of white Western male heterosexual surfing over all other forms. Homophobia has been central in the creation of acceptable masculinities, and arguably femininities, with decreasing homophobia in sport making variable SGS possible.[64] This "virtuous circle of decreasing homophobia" makes way for a more inclusive form of SGS that "intentionally avoids theorizing patriarchy in order to avoid the structural trap of hegemonic masculinity, which asserts causation between the hegemonic masculine stratifications of men and patriarchy, while simultaneously postulating that hegemonic masculinity will always exist."[65] As discussed in the next section, some of these more inclusive forms dismantle, interrupt, and disrupt old patriocolonial forms or stimulate new queer futures.

Penetrating the Old Field or Stimulating a New? Queering Futures?

To shift away from the limitations to participation based on SGS, we can notice practices that queer or interrupt, dismantle or disrupt, the fixedness of categories rooted in SGS. Steven Martin and Ilian Assenov emphasize the need to understand "multiplicities of difference" rather than multiplicities of the same, what Olkowski might refer to as "an ontology of static hierarchies and objectified structures."[66] To penetrate the relatively stable surfing field, we can destabilize, explode, and blur current SGS categories so that they are no longer intelligible as identity categories, or if intelligible, hold no more power than other identities, all the while actively promoting multiplicities of difference in subject positions. Disrupting practices include an increased presence of females in the surf and the growing awareness of the (micro)violences toward females in surfing (albeit contradictory and patchy); gay surfers "coming out"; the opportunities afforded by surf schools, surfing at school, and surfing as school; public pedagogies of sport, industry sponsorship, and media; possibilities of new media; and new directions in surfing research that make space for the Other in inclusive ways. While each of these warrants considerable investigation, owing to space constraints they are explored more thoroughly in forthcoming publications.

Conclusion

As compound and separate SGS mechanisms of practice affect field/boundary maintenance and therefore habitus recognition or exclusion, the enfleshed practices of sexual gaze, sexualization, dichotomized hegemonic gender order, sexism, heteronormativity, surf porn, hyperfemininity, hegemonic masculinity, homonormativity, and queer absence have defined the surfing field of today. Yet boundary maintenance, membership, capital legitimation, and field definition have always been negotiable, to greater or lesser extent. The patriocolonial practices prevalent in the late twentieth century, captured in Figure 12.2, have prevailed to date, but seem to be in decline as new waves of members explore new lines of flight for position changes and different stances about who a surfer is, and what surfing can be. This is evidenced by this book. While there is much to be learned and appreciated from the last one hundred years or so of patriocolonial self-pleasuring in the form of who had access to waves, to documenting those who had access to waves, and celebrating such homosociality in magazines, films, and museums, there is also much to be dismantled, disrupted, interrupted, reclaimed, and opened up so that Others may catch the wave and ride it to shore. Like the early surfer Kelea captured at the beginning of this chapter, waiting for the fourth wave—desexing and resexing surfing—may create new spectacles and pleasures. As the power of multiple celebrations of difference in surfing continues to become intelligible and expand, those embodying difference also need to consider protecting themselves from the reproductive power of already established doxa. Perhaps surfing in its modern form *is* screwed with SGS metaphors and practices that reflect the patriocolonial carrier; entitlement, aggression, domination, localism, and narcissism akin to cultural rape and pillage have reduced the surfing field's potential. But also, perhaps these practices are beginning to experience impotence in the longer unfolding timeline of surfing, as those who have been marginalized, erased, or violated embody the field, and even those with dominant habitus adopt remorseful and more inclusive practices.[67] As aspects of the modern surf complex go limp (e.g., the decline of clothing companies, smaller board manufacturers, and misogynist and racist magazines) and past practices are dismantled, disrupted, penetrated from a different direction, and interrupted by new possibilities, I believe there is hope. Although it is unlikely we will erase SGS as a set of powerful categories in the very near future (though I propose this as a worthy undertaking), work is under way to destabilize dominant SGS constellations, opening up who can be a surfer and who can surf.

NOTES

Many thanks to elke emerald, who offered support, critique, and advice on drafts of this chapter. Also to Dexter and Alex for their patience and collaboration to bring this book project to fruition.

1. Samuel Manaiakalani Kamaku, "Kelea-nui-noho-'ana-'api'api," in Moser, *Pacific Passages*, 22; and Clark, *Hawaiian Surfing*, 48.

2. Clark, *Hawaiian Surfing*, 48.

3. I use the term *patriocolonial* to emphasize the ontology of patriarchal and colonizing practices. It is also intended to include taken-for-granted assumptions from capitalism, Western knowledge systems, and heteronormativity, and therefore hegemonic masculinity and hyperfemininity as the assumed SGS (sex/gender/sexuality) binary.

4. Caudwell, "Sporting Gender," 2.

5. See lisahunter, "Visualising Herstory: Pedagogies of Participation," paper presented at the Third International Visual Methods Conference, Wellington, New Zealand, September 4, 2013.

6. Hargreaves and Anderson, *Handbook of Sport*, 3.

7. Malo, *Mo'olelo Hawaii*.

8. The modern history of surfing over the last hundred years has been framed by the patriocolonial males who were positioned to write that history. More recently, Native Hawaiian historians have written a history from a Native Hawaiian perspective. One such scholar is Isaiah Helekunihi Walker (*Waves of Resistance*), who develops the argument that native Hawaiians kept surfing alive during the time the patricolonial "history" tells of it nearly dying out. Walker also repositions Native Hawaiian men as pivotal to the development of surfing and its diaspora.

9. lisahunter, "Stop"; lisahunter, "Positioning Participation"; Bourdieu, *Practical Reason*, 56.

10. Bourdieu and Wacquant, *Invitation to Reflexive Sociology*, 138.

11. Illusio, "an investment in the game," is the level of personal investment one has in the practices and valued capital of a field. See Bourdieu and Wacquant, *Invitation to Reflexive Sociology*, 98; see also lisahunter, "Exploitation and (Unqueering)."

12. See Booth, *Australian Beach Cultures* and "From Bikinis to Boardshorts"; Evers, "The Point"; Franklin, "Making Waves"; Henderson, "A Shifting Line Up"; lisahunter, "What Did I Do-See-Learn"; Olive, McCuaig, and Phillips, "Women's Recreational Surfing"; Ford and Brown, *Surfing and Social Theory*; Caudwell, "Sporting Gender," 2.

13. *Cishet* (also, *cisgender*) is a queering term that refers to a heterosexual identity where the normative sex binary identification of male or female aligns with the normative gendery binary identification of feminine and masculine, that is, a hegemonically masculine male and a hyperfeminine female. A range of queer identities, fluid identities, and non-identities trouble the normative cisgender, such as gender-nonconforming, queer, questioning, and trans*.

14. Hall, "Knowledge and Gender," 38.

15. Phillips, "An Illusory Image"; Connell, *Gender and Power*.

16. Fiebert and Meyer, "Gender Stereotypes."

17. See Messner, *Power at Play*. See also Bryson, "Sport and Maintenance"; Lenskyj, "'Inside Sport'"; Mikosza, *Inching Forward*; Phillips, "An Illusory Image"; Stoddard,

"Invisible Games"; Wensing and Bruce, "Bending the Rules"; Bruce, "Reflections on Communication."

18. See Clark, *Hawaiian Surfing*.

19. Kamakau, *Ruling Chiefs*, in Clark, *Hawaiian Surfing*, 25.

20. Clark, *Hawaiian Surfing*, 45.

21. See Walker, *Waves of Resistance*, 57–82.

22. Comer, *Surfer Girls*.

23. Roxy is a brand operated under parent company Quiksilver. The company primarily manufactures swimwear and fashion goods associated with surfing lifestyle commodification for hyperfeminine heteronormative markets rather than functional surfwear. Roxy often promotes its clothing using models and sexualized female images rather than surfers in action images (see Schumacher, Comer, this volume). Roxy is the primary sponsor of several significant surfing competitions.

24. See Lucy Ardern and Emma Greenwood, "Despite an Increase in Winnings, the Gender Gap Has Not Been Bridged in the Surfing Prize Pool," *Gold Coast Bulletin*, March 3, 2014, http://www.goldcoastbulletin.com.au/news/gold-coast/despite-an-increase -in-winnings-the-gender-gap-has-not-been-bridged-in-the-surfing-prize-pool/story -fnj94idh-1226843213573; Franklin, "Making Waves."

25. "Babe" refers to an idealized femininity of a sun-bronzed hourglass figure of beauty with long blonde hair, often portrayed in advertisements and media (Heywood and Dworkin, *Built to Win*) or captured by one blogger as the "Damsel" as opposed to its binary the "Dyke" (Schumacher, "Women in the Sub-Culture of Surfing").

26. See, for example, the *Sunrise* interview with Coffey and Elliot Struck, "Ellie Jean Coffey Says Gurl Surfers Are sxc," Stabmag.com, http://stabmag.com/news/ellie-jean -coffey-says-gurl-surfers-are-sxc/; and surfer Rachel Brathen's response, "Apparently My Butt Is the Issue," *Curl Magazine*, January 29, 2015, *Curl Women's Surf Mag*, http://www .curl.co.nz/. See also "Hot Surfer Anastasia Ashley Visits Controversial Photographer Terry Richardson," *Network A*, May 8, 2015, http://www.networka.com/surfer-anastasia -ashley-visits-terry-richardson-studio; "Alana Blanchard Becomes a Better Person in the Water," *Network A*, August 23, 2013, http://www.networka.com/stories/6264/alana -blanchard-becomes-a-better-person-in-the-water.

27. See unpublished interviews of surfers by lisahunter, 2010; Gordon and Beachley, *Layne Beachley*; Kohner, *Gidget*; CoriSchumacher.com; Stell, *Pam Burridge*.

28. For example, see Fink, "Homophobia and Marketing"; Fink, Cunningham, and Kensicki, "Using Athletes"; Kane, "The Better Sportwomen Get"; Kane and Lenskyj, "Media Treatment of Female Athletes"; Kane, LaVoi, and Fink, "Exploring Elite Female Athletes;" Kane and Maxwell, "Expanding the Boundaries."

29. Messner, *Power at Play*, and Messner and Montez de Oca, "The Male Consumer as Loser."

30. Kauer and Krane, "Scary Dykes and Feminine Queens"; Messner, "Gender Ideologies, Youth Sports, and the Production of Soft Essentialism."

31. For a list of examples, see Kane, LaVoi, and Fink, "Exploring Elite Female Athletes."

32. Kane, LaVoi, and Fink, "Exploring Elite Female Athletes," 275.

33. See Antil, Burton, and Robinson, "Exploring the Challenges Facing Female Athletes as Endorsers"; Kane and Maxwell, "Expanding the Boundaries."

34. See lisahunter, "Positioning Participation."

35. See Franklin, "Making Waves."

36. Rinehart, "Surf Film, Then & Now."

37. See Booth, "Surfing Films and Videos"; Comer, *Surfer Girls;* Ormrod, *"Endless Summer"* (2008); Rinehart, "Surf Film, Then & Now."

38. See Stranger, *Surfing Life*; Lawler, *The American Surfer.*

39. For example, see the interview with *Elle* magazine on how to be a beach babe: Christiana Molina, "Beauty Chat: Surfing Champ Stephanie Gilmore on How to Be a Beach Babe All Year Round," *Elle*, September 16, 2013, http://www.elle.com/beauty/news/a15246 /stephanie-gilmore-interview/. See also the passive nude pose for *ESPN Magazine*, "Stephanie Gilmore Poses Nude for ESPN Magazine," *IndoSurfLife*, October 6, 2011, http:// indosurflife.com/2011/10/stephanie-gilmore-poses-nude-for-espn-magazine/.

40. Meân and Kassing, " 'I Would Just Like,' " 127.

41. Kauer and Krane, " 'Scary Dykes and Feminine Queens.' "

42. McGloin, "Reviving Eva," 112.

43. See Henderson, "A Shifting Line Up," and Booth, "(Re)reading The Surfers' Bible," for further debates about female positioning in the magazine

44. Comer, *Surfer Girls,* 178.

45. lisahunter, "Becoming Visible" and "Positioning Participation"; Comer, *Surfer Girls*; Lawler, *The American Surfer.*

46. Comer, *Surfer Girls,* 80–83.

47. lisahunter and emerald, "(A)dressing the Long (Boardies)."

48. lisahunter, "The Long and Short of (Performance) Surfing: Tightening Patriarchal Threads," *Sport in Society* (under review); lisahunter and emerald, "(A)dressing the Long (Boardies)."

49. This too is again being challenged by grassroots surf clothing brands such as Salt Gypsy with their surf suits and the encouragement of surfing for females in places such as Iran. See, for example, Marion Poizou's film *Into the Sea*, https://www.reelhouse.org/x -tremevideo/into-the-sea.

50. Franklin, "Making Waves."

51. "Alana Blanchard Designed Her Own Tiny Bikinis for *Sports Illustrated*'s Swimsuit Issue," December 4, 2013, http://www.networka.com/stories/6729/surf-behind-the -scenes-of-alana-blanchard-in-si-swimsuit-issue, and "Alana Blanchard Surf Girl Season 2," *Network A*, February 11, 2013, https://www.youtube.com/watch?v=433XRqZhJls&feature =youtu.be.

52. See https://www.youtube.com/watch?v=ADqb6ovsasE, accessed March 13, 2016.

53. lisahunter, "Sex(ed/y/uality) Positions in Surfing."

54. lisahunter, "A Stranger Surfing Life," "Exploitation and (Unqueering)," and "Stop."

55. Myrdahl, "Lesbian Visibility."

56. "Basketball: NBA Player Denies Being Homophobic after Using Gay Slur," *New Zealand Herald*, December 15, 2015, http://m.nzherald.co.nz/sport/news/article.cfm?c _id=4&objectid=11561413.

57. Caudwell, *Sport, Sexualities.*

58. Anderson, "Assessing the Sociology of Sport," 364.

59. Bronwyn Adcock, "Is It Hard to Surf with Boobs?," *Griffith Review* 40 (2012): n.p.; Thorpe, "Boarders, Babes and Bad-Asses"; lisahunter, "A Stranger Surfing Life"; Waitt, "'Killing Waves'"; Waitt and Warren, "'Talking Shit over a Brew.'"

60. Comer, *Surfer Girls*, 37.

61. Evers, "Queer Waves"; Cori Schumacher, "ROXY Pro Trailer: One Year Later," September 24, 2014, http://www.corischumacher.com/2014/09/24/roxy-pro-trailer-one-year -later/; Gaysurfer.net; Thomas Castets, "Coming Out: To Be a Gay Surfer," *The Inertia*, http://www.theinertia.com/business-media/coming-out-to-be-a-gay-surfer/.

62. "Roxy Pro Biarritz 2013 Official Teaser—#WhoAmIJustGuess," June 26, 2013, https://www.youtube.com/watch?v=GCji6TiJjbE.

63. Quoted in Alexandra Pieffer, "Staffer Compares Roxy Ad to 'Butchy Lesbos' Past," *9News.com*, July 13, 2013, http://www.9news.com.au/national/2013/07/13/14/15/staffer -compares-roxy-ad-to-lesbian-surfer-past.

64. Anderson, "Assessing the Sociology of Sport," 365.

65. McCormack, *The Declining Significance*, 63; Anderson, "Assessing the Sociology of Sport," 366.

66. Martin and Assenov, "Measuring the Conservation Aptitude"; Olkowski, *Gilles Deleuze*, 14.

67. At the recent international academic Surfing Social Hui, a well-known surfer and producer of surf media explained his realization that acting as an entitled rather than social surfer in the lineup meant he negatively impacted others. He has changed his behavior in the waves and in what he writes, more often, to be more inclusive. Like others in this position, he has the positional power to educate others like himself. See "Surfing Social Conference," Raglan, Aotearoa New Zealand, February 10–12, 2016, http://www.waikato .ac.nz/wmier/news-events/surfing-social.

13 / "My Mother Is a Fish": From Stealth Feminism to Surfeminism

CORI SCHUMACHER

"My mother is a fish." —VARDAMAN, IN WILLIAM FAULKNER, *As I Lay Dying*

I have always surfed. My mother surfed until she was eight months pregnant with me, switching to a mat when she could no longer knee-paddle the long-board she had transitioned to after her belly became too large to paddle a short-board prone.

The progression of splashing about in the shallows at the beach to modeling both my parents' masterful surfing was a simple transition, one that did not seem at all odd to me, despite being a five-year-old girl surfing during arguably the most male-dominated, misogynistic era of surfing in the United States and Australia: the early 1980s.

Frieda Zamba had not yet won the first of her four world titles, Wendy Botha was a decade away from posing in Australian *Playboy,* and Lisa Andersen was just thirteen years old when I rode my first wave.[1] My father, mother, and sister were the entirety of my world, and in that world, women surfed.

The life I led as a child was cordoned off by family, surfing, private school, books, and surf contests. Both my mother and father competed when I was young, though my mother often achieved higher levels of competitive success than my father, who eventually shifted his sights away from competition.

I listened to my parents occasionally discuss the politics of surf competitions—the problems associated with subjective judging, overly aggressive competitors, sore winners, sore losers—but what emerged specifically around women's competitions was a very clear sense that lesbians were "ruining the image of women's surfing," and that they were one of the main reasons that women's surfing was being held back at the highest levels of competition.

There was a palpable tension at contests between heterosexual and homosexual women. This tension did occasionally explode in verbal and physical altercations. Mostly, the tension bubbled just below the surface on the beach, and the women would unleash their aggression during their contest heats, promptly reapplying their smiles as the air horn signaled the end of the heat. I learned all of this before I discovered that women's surfing was undervalued, ignored, and often openly ridiculed in the male-dominated surf media, surf industry, and professional surfing circuit.

This chapter is informed by my thirty-plus years of competitive experience in surfing, as well as archival material ranging from journalism to digital media. It examines how the identity of the prototypical "surfer girl" was sculpted through a dogmatic policing of female desire and agency. This was executed initially through bifurcating female surfers as a group through a widespread anti-gay sentiment that functioned in part to malign and devalue lesbian-identified and feminist female surfers. This gave rise to the hypersexualized, fun-loving, non-threatening "surfer girl" trope espoused by the current decade's generation of female surfers, an image and representation that serves a narrow, heteronormative, neoliberal, Global North surfing narrative promoted by surf companies, surf media, and competitive organizations.

Despite this, or perhaps because of it, for female surfers "the very place of identification, caught in the tension of demand and desire, [has become] a place of splitting" that ruptures the master narrative of surfing and provides a starting point from which to critically engage emerging identity formations, narratives, and activisms in women's surfing.[2] However, engaging this rupture critically entails a shift from current ideations of women's surfing as a "stealth feminism" toward the deployment of a surfeminism that consciously engages its own complicity in neoliberal economic values, while understanding emerging female surfing identities as not only potential feminist subversions of the heteronormative scopophilia of surf culture, but also sites of resistance to the nature/culture, subject/object divide.[3] One such ontological experiment—and metaphoric representation of such resistances for women surfers—is the mermaid, upon whose body we might read "a double narrative, two living stories: one that describes how the monster came to be and another, its testimony, detailing what cultural use the monster serves."[4]

The Power of the Closet: Overt Homophobia in the 1980s and 1990s, and Its Impact on Combatting Sexism

Most accounts of the "surfer girl" trope and women's surf history begin with Gidget and skim the eras from the mid-1970s to the early 1990s, focusing next on the year 1993 with the eruption of the female surf market through Lisa Andersen and Roxy.[5] Yet it was precisely from the mid-1970s through the 1980s that the treatment of female surfers by competitive surfing organizations, the surf media, and burgeoning surf brands led to a feminist revolt, the formation of the Women's International Surfing Association (WISA), that would serve as inspiration for future unions of professional female surfers.[6] This organization, a collaborative effort between lesbian and nonlesbian female surfers, opened the doors for late-1970s female surfers and future generations of professional female surfers to compete alongside their male professional counterparts.[7] The WISA folded in 1993 due to a lack of sponsorship dollars as well as a change in amateur competitive organizations that siphoned away many competitors.[8]

Sponsorship resources available to women during this time were minimal: women were not given equal opportunity to ride the best waves in competitions, they were rarely, if ever, visible in surf media, and the prize money for women was substantially less than for their male counterparts. These disparities continued to persist in the 1980s and 1990s, but instead of tackling the issues through collaborative effort, the women's competitive surfing population began to turn on itself, lesbian-identified surfers to one side and heterosexual female surfers to the other.[9] Surf media provided a platform for this infighting and overtly encouraged it. Surf culture influencers, like brands and the surf media, symbolically excluded women in the 1980s, and in the mid- to late 1990s they began to make visible only those voices and images of female professional surfers considered "feminine" and "straight."[10]

Jodie Cooper, a lesbian surfer who competed professionally throughout the 1980s and 1990s, retiring after a back injury in 2002, says of her competitive career, "There was never a time when I thought surfing was tolerant enough to accept my sexuality. Certain individuals were fantastic, didn't care at all, but in general, no way in the world—surfing was the most bigoted, closeted sport. It was terrible."[11]

In 1982, a letter addressed to WISA by Dr. Gary F. Filosa, founder of the American Surfing Association (ASA) and longtime advocate for surfing as an Olympic sport, who had developed connections with the American Athletic Union (AAU) and the International Olympic Committee, exposes the tensions and misunderstandings around homosexuality in surfing during this time.[12] Filosa openly admits the intentional exclusion of gay surfers from his organization, as well as an open and growing "contempt" for gay surfers in "international sports circles, internatipal [sic] journalism circles, et cetera."

Much of what was going on in the 1980s revolved around the increased orientation of the surf industry and surf media around competition, which had embraced a more radical, aggressive style of surfing with the introduction of the shortboard in the late 1970s.[13] What began as a gender-deviant surf environment transformed into a stodgy gender-conformist environment by the 1980s.[14] An inflated, paranoid homophobia, amplified by surf media and surf industry marketing, was used to regulate women and enforce gender norms in the lineup, in sponsorship relationships, and within competitive settings.

Leanne Stedman has argued that the symbolic community generated by and through the surf media illustrates the transition from gender nonconformity to strict gender conformity through her analysis of the longest published surf magazine in Australia, *Tracks,* where feminists and lesbians were conflated, images of women in G-strings were run "to get up feminists' noses," and it was even explicitly stated that "*Tracks* hates all poofters and thinks they should be put inside a giant piston and squashed."[15] Stedman's examples illustrate the prevailing attitude toward homosexuality and women in Australia and the United States (excluding Hawai'i).

In the 1980s, new "swimsuit editions" of American magazines added to pressures to conform to strict gender norms. *Surfing* magazine published its "swimsuit preview" in 1983. Female surfers of the 1980s and early 1990s questioned the use (and salaries) of nonsurfing models used by swimwear companies that very well could have been sponsoring female surfers who hungered for sponsorship support. It was argued that these swimsuit companies who were ostensibly advertising, at least in part, to women who surfed, would surely benefit from sponsoring female surfers.

When the world's largest female surf brand, Roxy, first launched in 1990, it chose to use surfers as models specifically because this was an ongoing

Gary Fairmont R. Filosa, II

24 May 1982

Dear ████████,

The president of the GAY SURFING LEAGUE has just written me a
letter castigating me for a private letter I had written you
and Mrs. ████████████, which he says puts down gays, and which
he indicates is being widely distributed by ███████████████. I
regret that ████ would give a private letter to a person of
such low moral fibre as ███████████████, but my experience in
surfing continues to convince me that the lowlife types like
████ most probably stole it when ████ wasn't looking. We
do not permit gays in USIC nor shall we, whatever the pressure.
The recent incident in San Diego county of an NSSA officer
veing arrested on the beach during a competition because he
was wanted for molesting boys in 4 states proves my decision
is correct.

In any regard, this is minor. I write because as you know we
now have a monthly half-hour surf series on cable nationwide
(48 affiliate stations), and are adding new stations weekly,
and shoot these competitions the last two days of every month
at Trestles with the cooperation of the USMC and the Department
of Parks of the State of California, and we would be delighted
to give our surfing friends in WISA some coverage whenever you
deem it appropriate. We reach with one segment more people
than all surf magazines combined together have reahced since
they started publishing 22 years ago, so you see the magazines
have lost any punch they use to have with our surfers. This
was why I was determine to have this show, why we improve it
continually, and expand its telecast enthusiastically.

You have moved, so I must send your mail to this box, pleaze
send your new address. Now that we are with WEST NALLY as a
client, as is world tennis, world soccer, world swimming, and
world gymnastics, lights are going on in many places, and it
has been made clear to everyone if they continue their collusive
effort to harm ICAS, its affiliates, or its officers, which is
illegal, they will be called to task and will have to pay for
their illegalities. I suppose I should have sued years ago
but who can take such garbage from such garbagemen seriously.
Anyone who believes ██████████████ is a leader in surfing has
a very low opinion of our sport. He is only a leader among
a group who think they own this sport, but have laready lost
it for the contempt for this group grows daily ininternational
sports circles, internatipnal journalism circles, et cetera.

In any rgeard, our best to you as wlaus, our best to WISA,
and come and see us on the beach, we will do a WISA show.

213-246-7603 / Box 1315 / Beverly Hills 90213

P.O. Box 2622 • Newport Beach, California 92663
714-760-7073

FIG. 13.1 A 1982 letter addressed to the Women's International Surfing Association
(WISA) by Dr. Gary F. Filosa of the American Surfing Association.

conversation within female surfing circles. They were lauded for this choice, but it soon became apparent that Roxy surf models would represent an exclusively "feminine" (an industry code word for "heterosexy") ideal.[16] During Roxy's casting call for the 2003 MTV show *Surf Girls,* for example, one featured interview highlighted that the potential cast member was "not a lesbian . . . and [didn't] have multiple personality [disorder]."[17] The Roxy feminine ideal of slim, smiling, fun-loving, and "not a lesbian" reshaped women's surfing by exploiting the homophobic divide in women's surfing, slamming the closet door shut on lesbian-identified female surfers and supporting a damaging double standard.[18]

This double standard demands women surf more like men to gain respect and equal prize money, and to enjoy access in the lineup, yet disparages and excludes those deemed "too manly." Being labeled or rumored to be a lesbian was, and continues to be, a "death sentence" for professional female surfing athletes. This (mis-)labeling problematically extends to those women who speak out against sexism in surfing.[19]

Building on the Roxy Feminine Ideal: Normalizing Inequality and Hypersexuality

Along with the fear of being labeled a lesbian, one of the greatest challenges to systemic change in surfing for women is the persistent masquerade of surfing being a simple meritocracy (an argument that has been used to justify lower pay for women and serves to erase challenges faced by surfers of color), and a numbers game in which the allocation of fewer sponsorship resources and less event prize money is justified because female surfers constitute a lower percentage of the total surfing population.[20]

Yet these numbers don't add up. In an analysis of the gender participation distribution and prize allotments on the World Surf League's (WSL's) Qualifying Series (QS), the global competition circuit that surfers must compete in to qualify for the elite Championship Tour (CT), 19 percent of the total QS participants were female in 2014, yet only 10 percent of the total QS prize money was allocated to the women's qualifying tour in 2015.

Given such disparity in competition earnings, corporate sponsorship is essential for female competitors, as the women's QS requires a minimum of approximately $40,000 (for travel including boards and baggage fees, lodging, food, ground transportation, WSL membership, and contest entry fees) to reach the necessary events scattered around the world that enable a surfer to earn enough points to qualify for the CT.[21] In most cases, surfers need to travel to lower-rated events in order to make up for lost points, which adds to this amount substantially. Philippa Anderson, an Australian surfer from Newcastle, started a crowdfunding venture to fund her QS campaign after losing her major sponsor. Her goal was to raise $50,000 by August 28, 2015, for travel to four events in California, El Salvador, France, and Spain.[22] It is nearly impossible to achieve the necessary points to enter the elite CT realm without a sponsorship, but there are far fewer sponsorship opportunities for women at this level, and, not surprisingly, female QS surfers frequently self-sexualize in order to attract endorsements by companies who see surfers with crossover advertising (model) appeal.[23]

One notable exception to this trend is Silvana Lima, a talented Brazilian of short stature, dark skin, and strongly Portuguese-accented English, who holds that "beaches are not catwalks and athletes are not fashion models."[24] Lima crowdfunded her QS run (after tearing her ACL in 2012 during a CT competition and being dropped immediately by major sponsor Billabong) in order to make it back onto the 2015 CT.

That year, in her first event back on the CT, Lima posted the year's first perfect scoring ride, delivering "the most dominant performance of the Roxy Pro to date."[25] Lima's story, as well as other dominant athletic performances sans sponsorship, strongly challenges the idea that surfing is a simple meritocracy.

Other top female surfers, many of whom have dropped off the tour because they have not been able to maintain solid competition results, have adapted to the inequality and gender bias of professional surfing by self-sexualizing and self-objectifying by crossing over into swimsuit modeling and related marketing.[26] This is illustrated by a 2010 interview with (then) nineteen-year-old Laura Enever, who discusses a soft porn–style photo shoot with *Stab* magazine's editor, Derek Rielly. Rielly asks: "Were you specifically warned about the Stab shoot? That we were devils? (laughter detonates)," to which Enever responds, "I was! I was! I heard from Alana (Blancahrd) [*sic*] and Bruna (Schmitz) who you did the photo shoot with last year. They told me how they were freaked out about how you, like, tried to get them naked. I'd been warned a few times, but it's fine, because you guys are a men's magazine and it's an amazing magazine. At the shoot, I was told my first couple of photos weren't sexy enough and that *I had to take some clothes off*, but it ended up being really cool [emphasis added]."[27] In this interview, the process of shifting a female surfer toward self-sexualization is exposed. Enever later explains that there are "great surfers [who] don't get sponsors" because they are not deemed sexy enough to be marketable.

In an environment where women compete, not only for the QS points to qualify for the CT, but also for the financial resources to do so, an additional layer of competing for "the most sexy" is added. This process is facilitated by predatory media. Sexualizing female surfers, defining women's empowerment through commodification and a language of self-objectification, along with an uncritical application of "sex sells" marketing rhetoric in nearly every visible conversation about and with female surfers in surf media, builds upon the Roxy feminine ideal that intervened in women's surfing in the 1990s, naturalizing a hypersexualized surfer girl and accompanying gender script that has exploded across the modern surfing sphere.

WSL Webcasts and the Competitive, Noncompetitive Professional Female Surfer

The current version of the surfer girl gender script that emerged in surf media just after the recent generational shift on the women's CT (circa 2009) includes an attitude that is fun-loving and deferential. The attitudinal aspect of the surfer girl script, when used in tandem with self-sexualization, diminishes her appearance of being a threat to men. The professional surfing world tour (now the WSL's CT), in particular, has served to disseminate the message that this new generation of elite female surfers is a happy-go-lucky, nonthreatening, playful, and, only incidentally, extremely talented, crew of girls.[28] Both male and female commentators on the live webcasts of professional events frequently note how humble, fun-loving, noncompetitive, and ever-smiling female pro surfers are when compared to their stoic, competitive, and serious male counterparts.

For example, during the WSL Rip Curl Pro webcast, held at the historic Bell's Beach in Victoria, Australia, in April 2015, both male and female WSL commentators actively bolstered the prescribed attitudinal gender script with countless comments, like those of host Chelsea Cannell, who remarked to competitor Alessa Quizon, "We love to see that smile!" and "She's so positive!" Other comments during the event focused on the competitors' relationships with one other: "They're all happy, friends. There are no real rivalries." Terms used to describe women's surfing technique ranged from "smooth little hack" and "cheeky carve" to "one of the prettiest techniques on tour" and "amazing grace and style." By contrast, on the men's side, comments ranged from "He's angry. I love it!" to descriptions of "solid," and "powerful" surfing, chatter about "the working man's wave," and copious references to "manhandling" waves and executing "man-hacks," and "man-turns."

The WSL media attention afforded Courtney Conlogue, a powerful and focused Californian who, like Silvana Lima, distances herself from sexualized representations, was especially curious during the event. One commenter's pre-occupation with Conlogue's "intense" look during one of her heats led to an uncomfortable interview with Conlogue, who felt the need to explain why she wasn't smiling (which, she stated, was in order to focus on winning). Later, after Conlogue lost in the semifinals to Australian Stephanie "Happy" Gilmore (so nicknamed, viewers were told, because Gilmore is always smiling), Cannell and her camera crew sought out Conlogue on the beach. While Conlogue signed autographs, Cannell talked at length about how Conlogue was finally smiling, "doing her job" by connecting with the beach audience, and stating how happy this exchange was for fans. WSL broadcasts are routinely gendered along these lines.

The function of the surfer girl gender script, and the regulation of those who deviate from it, is to neutralize challenges to the dominant masculine hegemony embedded in surf media, brand marketing, advertising, and endorsements, while perpetuating a monolithic myth of a fun-loving, perpetually happy, and nonaggressive women's surfing.[29] The overall result of these efforts to date is the use of the "feminine" side of surfing as the narrative carrier of surfing's cultural ideals, whereas the "masculine" communicates and contains the authoritative expression of surfing's performance, the "sportization" of surfing.[30] The two paradigms work in concert, supporting the mission of surf industry globalization.

An example of the "feminine" side of surfing being used as a narrative carrier of surfing's cultural ideals occurred in 2011 when the ASP Swatch Girls Pro Women's World Longboard Championships were chosen as the inaugural ASP event run in China.[31] Women's professional longboarding has a reputation for being full of friendly camaraderie and being the least aggressive of all ocean board sports. Women's longboarding, in other words, is the most "feminine" of the board sports.

The event spokesperson, Kassia Meador, who was featured on the billboards, trailers, and advertisements, and in the post-event broadcasts, is also well known as a free surfer.[32] This event, then, sponsored by Swatch and populated by surfing's "ambassadors of goodwill"—female longboarders flown in by the Chinese government from around the world—was meant to showcase the cultural ideals of surfing as a gospel of fun, fashion, art, freedom, and friends through the graceful, nonaggressive elegance of women's longboarding.[33] This was the surf industry's official introduction to China's growing middle class, a new market opportunity that surf industry leaders identified back in 2003, stating that they were "excited to begin to capitalize on [women's surfing]" through their "lifestyle message."[34] The fact that the foremost point of surf industry's global outreach continues to be a "feminine," noncompetitive competitive representation belies the surf industry's awareness of the power of using the female surfing body to communicate problematic notions like "fun is freedom."[35]

Competitive vs. Soul vs. Free Surfers and Stealth Feminism

In order to understand the investment that surf industry, surf media, and competitive organizations have in the female surfer as an iconographic figure carrying surfing's cultural narrative forward, we first need to step back to the 1960s, when the distinction between soul surfers and competitive surfers originated, making way for the professional free surfer of the early 2000s.

The splitting of surfing along the lines of soul surfer and competitive surfer emerged in the late 1960s. The distinction is somewhat self-evident: competitive surfers are endorsed by clothing and surfboard brands to represent surf companies and use their products in formal competition (often as a part of a team of brand-sponsored competitive surfers), whereas soul surfers refuse to surf in competitions, and because of this, rarely garner the attention or financial support of sponsors. This is a source of pride for the soul surfer, whose identity is, at least hypothetically, defined by her or his desire to keep surfing free of any and all financial interests.

To the soul surfer, it was the competitive surfer, contests, and those who financially backed them, that ultimately ruined surfing, and it was from the tensions between the soul surfer and the competitive surfer that the free surfer sprung.[36] The free surfer is typically a surfer who has tasted competition and gained the attention of sponsors, but instead of pursuing competition, opts to travel and compile photographs and film for formal and informal marketing campaigns. The sponsored free surfer is generally male, and serves a similar purpose to the surfer girl in today's surf culture, though his iconography and messaging is inwardly focused in an attempt to connect surf industry and surf media to the "authentic" core of surfing.[37] It is no coincidence that the free surfer and the Roxy feminine ideal both solidified by the early 2000s, right at the time that surf brands were strategizing an expansion of their market to nontraditional surfing markets through surfing's "lifestyle message."[38]

So why not use the free surfer to disseminate this lifestyle message? The feminine ideal in surfing was built for this specific purpose. Leslie Heywood has argued that, as an iconographic figure in today's global economy, the "female surfer . . . is a carrier of the neoliberal ideologies of flexibility, do-it-yourself subjectivity, and possibility for all . . . complicit with neoliberalism and [serving to mark] the same erasures of structural inequality."[39] Heywood further explains that the female surfer, while not admitting to being an outright feminist, "reflects a representational nexus where the female body, instead of primarily signifying a dependent sexuality as in the second-wave feminist analyses that spoke of 'the objectification of women,' has come to signify an independent sexuality that reflects women's potential as 'self-determining' wage earners and consumers."[40] It is no coincidence that women also represent a growth market twice as big as China and India combined.[41]

The surf-derived idea of an independent femininity that is self-determined and confident, with a balance of beauty and individual achievement, is illusory, and "experienced primarily through consumer choices" made with capital increasingly generated by women in the Global North.[42] Describing monolithic representations of women's surfing engineered and broadcast by surf industry, media, and competitive governance as a stealth feminism might be overly generous. Surf industry's female surfing iconography is rather the definition of a commodity feminism—"feminist ideas and icons . . . appropriated for commercial purposes, emptied of their political significance and offered back to the public in a commodified form—usually in advertising"—whose main function is the proselytizing of a gospel of fun (noncompetition), while paving the way for the neoliberal practices of surf sportization (competition).[43]

Toward a Surfeminism

"Surfing . . . take[s] the form of entering into an existing wave. There's no longer an origin as starting point, but a sort of putting-into-orbit. The key thing is how to get taken up in the motion of a big wave . . . to 'get into something' instead of being the origin of an effort." —GILLES DELEUZE, "MEDIATORS" IN *Negotiations* (1995)

Women surfers, professional or otherwise, prove more varied and complex than dominant media representations, competitive surfing governance, or currently deployed surf scholarship are yet willing to admit.[44] The iconography of the female surfer, defined as it is by its relationship to heteronormative desire and commodification, has not succeeded in erasing female surfers' subjectivities, only in fracturing, then repressing, confounding desires and behaviors. The repressed deviations are abject: flowing multiplicities, queerly expressing the biological desires of an immersing and immersed porous body, ocean water spilling into and out of every intimate space, dissolving the illusion that the ocean and the female surfer do not share a material, even ontological, intimacy distinct from biological males and dissolving the boundaries of a female-subject and ocean-object. Writes Julia Kristeva, "It is thus not lack of cleanliness or health that causes abjection but what disturbs identity, system, order. What does not respect borders, positions, rules. The in-between, the ambiguous, the composite."[45] And so it is specifically in female surfers' repressed deviant desires, among her invisible nomadic tribes, within the untold oral histories, ensconced in masculine femininities, in her overlooked corporeal poetries, her strange haptic appetites, explosive affective states, emotionally destructive forces, all of which are rippling just below the visible surface of the vigilantly maintained surfer girl image, that we find the potential to resist the total infringements of the neoliberal surfer girl image, and what it attempts to instill through surf culture. The separation of female surfer subjectivities from the pervasive surfer girl image—a function of surfeminism—creates the possibility of manifesting abjection. For female surfers tired of the prevalent surfer girl image, "the abject [repressed] simultaneously beseeches and pulverizes the subject . . . experienced at the peak of its strength when that subject, weary of fruitless attempts to identify with something on the outside, finds the impossible within; when it finds that the impossible constitutes its very being, that it is none other than abject."[46]

When international furor exploded as a result of Quiksilver affiliate Roxy's "all sex, no surf" trailer for the 2013 Roxy Pro women's surfing contest in Biarritz, a rupture in the fabric of the surfer girl image occurred. The trailer—featuring consecutive takes of an anonymous team rider (later revealed to be Roxy team rider and six-time World Champion Stephanie "Happy" Gilmore) in various states of undress in her bedroom, the shower, and on the street prior to driving a luxury SUV to the beach and donning a competition jersey—united scholars, activists, and members of the surfing community to demand a response from the company and reforms to media portrayals of women's surfing. This constituted an international surfeminist revolt facilitated by a viral online petition that I spearheaded and the power of social media to bypass traditional surf media. Under a paradoxical set of circumstances, official WSL market research and grassroots activism intersected in reforming and revamping women's professional surfing for the first time since the competitive era of Zamba, Andersen, and Botha.

Not coincidentally, it was a year after this event that mermaid iconography and lingo began flooding female surfers' blogs, social media, and independent business ventures, from the Oʻahu Surfing Experience's video "Mermaids Learn to Surf," to mermaids used for reporting on surf expos and creating their own surf media, like The Mermaid Society, which launched in May 2014.[47] Even ex-Roxy riders are jumping on board. Kassia Meador's first visible project after separating from long-time sponsor Roxy is littered with mermaid references: "A long time mermaid," "Made by mermaids, for mermaids."[48]

The increasingly visible trend of women and girls self-identifying as mermaids in the wider culture collided with the rupture in women's surfing of the

Roxy feminine ideal, and a shift in perspectives on homosexuality in the wider culture.[49] The mermaid, in the context of women's surfing, represents the particular shape being given to the abject emerging from the rupture: a hybrid representing the limit of heterosexual desire as well as an ontological experiment whose "transgressive nature . . . is here located in her monstrosity, her threat embedded in her ambiguous, liminal morphology, part flesh, part fish."[50] This trend has no mirror image in men's surf culture, and might easily be dismissed were it not for the clear ontological repositioning of women's surfing, once defined solely by heterosexual desire and commodification, toward an environmental and (necessarily) mythical ontology. Indeed, the very identity of the surfer girl, reliant as it has always been upon immersion with the ocean environment, the struggle with the male gaze, and its prevailing use as a symbol of environmentalist activism is here writ large.

The mermaid is both sexually amorphous and undeniably, dauntingly female: her identity demands a reimagining of her purpose, her sexuality, and male desire. Her form complicates the fantasy of her sexual availability, the male gaze, even the heteronormative construct through aesthetically problematizing an imagining of sexual penetration. The fishy, scaly region of the mermaid, what once held the promise of heteronormative, androcentric sexual fulfillment, becomes the specific embodiment of her interaction and identification with the ocean.

The emergence of the self-identification of female surfers with mermaids signals a demand to self-narrate the identity and experience of women's surfing by female surfers, as much as it is an expression of their *transcorporeality,* "the time-space where human corporeality, in all its material fleshiness, is inseparable from 'nature' or 'environment.' Transcorporeality, as a theoretical site, is a place where corporeal theories and environmental theories meet and mingle in productive ways."[51] Female surfers, then, are embracing a hybrid metaphor of a distinct becoming, an expression of their potential as nomadic, embodied, overlapping sites of political, ecological, and economic subversion of the rhizomatic forces of neoliberal globalization.[52]

Surf industry, surf media, and competitive organizations have done the work of globally disseminating an image of women's surfing that is aligned with their neoliberal agenda. The mermaid exploits this agenda and other gender scripts in surfing, such as the reification and anthropomorphizing of the ocean as an Othered *She,* in order to radically personalize the effects of neoliberal modes of production, like climate change and ocean pollution: "what is done to the ocean and its creatures is done to me." By accepting that the iconography of the female surfer has effectively captured and been centralized in the neoliberal imagination, female surfers can actively utilize their centrality in order to subvert the ecologically damaging paradigm that exploits their image. And while the mermaid doesn't yet function to thoroughly disrupt the master narrative of surfing (in its heteronormative, white supremacist, Global North articulation), or its neoliberal vent, manifest in the sportization of surfing, she does have the potential to do the work contained in the very fabric of her making. The mermaid, in women's surfing, is one of the transitory identities bubbling up through the rupture created in 2013, a surfer-girl-becoming-mermaid-becoming-surfeminist.

To more thoroughly engage the potential theoretical and philosophical fecundity presented by a transcorporeal female surfer subjectivity (her way of knowing, being, and acting), new ontological formulations of female surfers, and the female surfer as a site of emerging environmental and social justice activisms will require the deployment of a transcorporeal feminism that pushes beyond representationalism, and instead merges female surfing history (and its many waves of feminist activisms) with a critically engaged material-discursive feminist practice grounded in the primacy of the intra-action of ocean ecology and the embodied experiences of female surfers as unique, nomadic agents: a queer surfeminism.[53]

NOTES

Epigraph: Faulkner, *As I Lay Dying*, 84. Faulkner's novel captures the journey of a poor family carting their mother's dead body back to her hometown for burial. While the novel is often narrated by the dead mother herself, in the five words contained in chapter 19, Vardaman, one of the children, expresses simply: "My mother is a fish." Stacy Alaimo ("States of Suspension," 478) explains: "Vardaman caught a big fish the same day his mother died and he saw his sister cutting up and frying the fish for dinner. This grotesque transference or conflation of the deaths of the mother and the fish is part of the black comedy of the novel, which exposes human irrationality, psychological defense mechanisms, and the characters' pathetic, tragic, comic, and confused attempts to make sense of their painful and chaotic world." Alaimo argues that "transcorporeal subjects are always themselves part of global networks of responsibility" (477). She expresses the "need to foster posthumanist—and postterrestrial—modes of knowing, being, and acting" (489). Through the title and epigraph of this chapter, I propose the emerging *surfeminist* as one such mode of knowing, being, and acting, but not before her tragic predecessor becomes a fish of sorts.

1. All three women are four-time world champions. Frieda Zamba, from Flagler Beach, Florida, won world titles in 1984, 1985, 1986, and 1988. Wendy Botha was born in East London, South Africa, and became an Australian citizen in 1989, winning world titles in 1987, 1989, 1991, and 1992. Lisa Andersen, arguably female professional surfing's most well-known icon, rose to prominence along with Quiksilver's Roxy brand in the mid-1990s. She began surfing at thirteen years old when her family moved to Ormond Beach, Florida.

She moved to Orange County, California, at sixteen to pursue her dream of becoming a women's world champion. She won four consecutive world titles from 1994 to 1997.

2. Bhabha, *The Location of Culture*, 44.

3. Leslie Heywood suggests that surfing might be a "stealth feminism" of the same ilk as women's sports in general. She argues that "stealth feminism, ... while being complicit with the dominant values of the global economy... nonetheless involve[s] ... the rene-gotiation of gender and its relation to core cultural values such as independence, personal competency, and strength." The female surfer in this mode is both an "ideal neoliberal sub-ject" and a cultural signifier occupying a "'third-wave,' signal-crossed space." See Heywood, "Third Wave Feminism," 63–64.

Surfeminism is a term that emerged through conversations I had with Krista Comer while we were working together on the Institute for Women Surfers, an ongoing public humanities project. While our understanding of surfeminism overlaps (rooted in intersec-tionality, local/global female surfing activist networks, social and environmental justice), in this work I articulate the need for a surfeminism that engages new feminist materialisms in order to imagine and deploy a transcorporeal feminism uniquely situated in the embodied experience and emerging subjectivities of female surfers.

4. Cohen, "Monster Culture," 13.

5. Surfing in the United States, however, has an unexamined first wave of female surf-ers that coincided with women winning the vote in the United States (1920). Posters and advertisements used by tourism promoters in Hawai'i at the time (i.e., the late 1920s and the 1930s) widely featured the newly liberated "flapper girl" surfing in Hawai'i to appeal to independent white women of means. See DeLaVega, *200 Years of Surfing Literature*. It is from the co-emergence of an iconography of carefree travel to Hawai'i and the newly liberated American female—not from *Gidget*—that we first encounter a Global North representation of the female surfer as autonomous, happy-go-lucky, and fully at ease on her surfboard in the ocean.

6. The formation of the Women's International Surfing Association (WISA) set off a chain reaction in women's competitive and noncompetitive surfing around the world. The founders of WISA, which was formed in 1975, would not, perhaps, use the term "femi-nist" themselves, but each of the founding members of WISA has described how she was inspired by the concurrent shifts in the larger culture because of the "women's movement," and how that was instigating changes in women's tennis. Billie Jean King's exploits and achievements (e.g., the Battle of the Sexes between King and Bobby Riggs, 1973) consis-tently stand out in these conversations.

In the spring of 2000, Rochelle Ballard, Kate Skarratt, Layne Beachley, Megan Abubo, and Prue Jeffries (all top competitors on the elite ASP world championship tour) formed the International Women's Surfing organization "with the goals of increasing the value of the women's pro tour, specifically by creating a series of women's-only events that could secure their own sponsorship dollars and media coverage." See Holly Beck, "Update: In-ternational Women's Surfing," *SurfLife for Women* 20 (Summer 2002), 20; https://issuu .com/historyofwomensurfing/docs/premierissue?e=14142323/9989637, accessed March 1 2017. Here, WISA is recognized as the forerunner of the International Women's Surfing organization.

7. The International Professional Surfers (formed in 1976 to organize events around the world under one umbrella) added women's events in 1977 because of the proven success of WISA. See Warshaw, *Encyclopedia of Surfing* (2003), 705–706.

8. During this time, "serious competitor[s]" who wished to qualify for the US Team were forced to focus on a single amateur series: that of the United States Surfing Federation. Jay Boldt, "WSA Allstar Team," 1992/93 WISA Newsletters, Historyofwomensurfing .com, https://issuu.com/historyofwomensurfing/docs/1992–93newsletters?e=14142323 /10500754, accessed March 1, 2017.

9. Gender-based disparities continue for female surfing competitors in every genre of wave-riding at both amateur and professional levels around the world today, the one exception being the 2014 World Surf League (WSL) commitment to equal opportunity for elite female surfers to ride top quality waves on the Championship Tour (CT). However, executing this commitment has varied with location, ostensibly with direct input from the female surfers through their WSL representative, Jessi Miley-Dyer.

10. Heywood, "Third-Wave Feminism," 66. Also see Stedman, "From *Gidget* to Gonad Man," 83. Consolidated in the surf media of the era, "femininity" was marked by long hair, bikinis, flirtatious behavior toward men, ever-present smiles (even while surfing, and especially for surf-action photos), easy-going attitudes, and a "fun" disposition. "Feminine" and "straight" were largely conflated, and continue to be today.

11. Reggae Ellis, "Jodie Cooper: Big Wave Trailblazer, Stunt Woman, Crowd Favourite," *Surfing World Magazine,* July 1, 2014, 83.

12. Warshaw, *Encyclopedia of Surfing* (2003), 198.

13. Stedman, "From *Gidget* to Gonad Man," 82.

14. Comer's work illustrates how the post–World War II subcultural alternative masculinity in surfing emerged simultaneously and in tension with early, atypical femininities in surfing. See Comer, *Surfer Girls,* 37, 49–53.

15. See *Tracks,* February 1983, 2; July 1994, 61; and April 1995, 139. See also Stedman, "From *Gidget* to Gonad Man," 81.

16. Roxy continues to highlight the support they give to female surfing athletes to this day: "At Roxy, we will never stop celebrating female athletes. That's our brand promise." See "What Roxy Stands For," Roxy.com, October 8, 2013, http://roxy.com/blog/surf /20131008230609BLOG989744155272.html.

17. "Surf Girls 2003 Preview w/ Donnas," Youtube.com, March 7, 2011, https://www .youtube.com/watch?v=HhN18ksPLcU. *Surf Girls* first aired on MTV on May 12, 2003; it lasted one season. It featured a group of fourteen female surfers hand-picked by Roxy employees.

18. From the late 1990s to the early 2000s, the "slim" ideal drove so many Roxy-sponsored surfers to eating disorders that the neologism "Roxy-rexia" was frequently used to describe the extreme weight loss exhibited by Roxy-sponsored riders. See "Cori Schumacher: Ser lésbica é um beijo da morte para os patrocínios," Woohoo.com.br, October 6, 2014, http:// www.woohoo.com.br/noticia/cori-schumacher. The Roxy ideal revolves around an essentialist notion of "feminine energy," which includes smiling all the time (especially while surfing), and being fun and graceful.

19. Writes Pat Griffin, "The lesbian label is a political weapon that can be used against any woman who steps out of line. Any woman who defies traditional gender roles is called

a lesbian. . . . Any woman who speaks out against sexism is called a lesbian. As long as women are afraid to be called lesbians, this label is an effective tool to control all women and limit women's challenges to sexism." See Griffin, "Changing the Game," 259.

20. During an interview with *Surfing* magazine, Coco Ho, a highly visible, top-ranking professional surfer who appeared surfing nude in *ESPN* magazine's 2014 "Body Issue," argued *for* prize money and salary inequality based on a facile merit-based metric that revolves around the performance level of top male professional surfers. See "The Mason and Coco Ho Interviews," Surfingmagazine.com, January 6, 2015, http://www.surfingmagazine.com/from-the-mag/mason-coco-ho-interview/#Zgeb88BuioguVJlF.97. The racism faced by black surfers is explored in Woods, *White Wash*.

21. This number is based on my own calculations for the 2014 QS, using Southern California as the place of origin, and my own accounting from my past travels with the tour (plus inflation). This number assumes excellent competition results in the top-rated events and does not include all events on the QS tour.

22. Philippa Anderson, "Get Philippa Anderson on the World Tour," indiegogo.com, June 2015, accessed August 31, 2015.

23. Darlene Conolly, Surfline.com writer and former WQS surfer, relates how "the infighting, eating disorders, and competing to be 'the whole package' has created this horrible, insular environment in the competitive scene. It is much worse than it used to be." See Cori Schumacher, "Cori Schumacher: Quintessential Girl," Huckmagazine.com, June 28, 2012, http://www.huckmagazine.com/perspectives/opinion-perspectives/cori-schumacher/, accessed March 1, 2017.

24. Cori Schumacher, "And What of the Current State of Women's Pro Surfing?," Cori Schumacher: State of Flux, March 19, 2014, http://www.corischumacher.com/2014/03/19/current-state-womens-pro-surfing/. Lima's comment was first published on Silvanafree.com, the site Lima used for her crowdfunding campaign (the website is no longer online).

25. "Perfect 10 for Silvana Lima at the Roxy Pro," Surfgirlmag.com, March 6, 2015, http://www.surfgirlmag.com/2015/03/06/silvana-lima-scores-roxy-pro/#.WE110PkrKyI.

26. The most well-known former CT competitor to turn to modeling for her sponsors is Alana Blanchard, who is no longer on the WCT tour after lackluster results in 2014.

27. Derek Rielly, "She Looked at Me with an Absolute Smirk on Her Pretty Face," Stabmag.com, December 31, 2010, http://stabmag.com/girls/laura-enever/.

28. Despite the fact that there are women on tour who range in age from nineteen to thirty years old, they are most often referred to as "girls" during the WSL webcasts, though this does vary by commentator.

29. Janet Fink confirms that "any study of women's sport is indelibly linked to hegemonic masculinity, heteronormativity, and homophobia—all of which serve to coerce female athletes to adhere to heterosexual, hyper-feminine 'scripts' or encounter the severe negative consequences that tend to follow when confronting the status quo." Fink, "Homophobia and Marketing," 50.

30. The use of Mark Stranger's notion of "sportization" emphasizes the inclusion of not only the simple structuring of competitions, but also the key roles of the extended bureaucracy and a particular cultural surfing identity fostered by surf industry (surfing as a selfish endeavor driven by competition for a limited resource, which drives the surfari and exclusionary practices). See Stranger, *Surfing Life*, 215–226.

31. Industry Spy, "ASP Women's World Longboard Tour Breaks Ground with Historic Event in China," Surfermag.com, August 9, 2011, http://www.surfermag.com/blogs/contest-wire/asp-women%E2%80%99s-world-longboard-tour-breaks-ground-with-historic-event-in-china/#wDUOp0GCK61rPWIf.97.

32. Kassia Meador is an iconic female longboarder who gained popularity and visibility not through competitive success, but through photo shoots and films. She rode for Roxy for fourteen years and was also sponsored by Swatch in 2011.

33. "Ambassadors of good will": personal correspondence with Brodie Carr.

34. In 2003, Quiksilver CEO Bob McKnight stated: "We believe the time is right for our lifestyle message, and are confident that it will resonate strongly with young consumers in this strong and fast-growing market. . . . We are excited to begin to capitalize on what we believe is a range of growth opportunities that exist for Quiksilver throughout Southeast Asia and the Pacific Rim." See Thorpe, "China: The New Frontier for the Action Sport Industry," in *Transnational Mobilities in Action Sport Cultures,* 44–45.

35. At the time of writing, I am aware of one other WSL women's event that will be used in much the same way in Melanesia. The surf adage "Fun *is* Freedom" erases systemic oppression completely and reorients liberation problematically as simply a state of mind. For a more detailed discussion of this idea and its origins, see Laderman, *Empire in Waves,* 136–142.

36. Stylish Southern Californian surfer Rob Machado is considered the world's first free surfer. He is a Surfing Walk of Fame inductee (2011) and was a solid performer on the ASP world tour until 2001. See Rob Machado, "The Day I Was Voted Off Tour," TheInertia.com, April 1, 2014, http://www.theinertia.com/surf/the-day-rob-machado-was-voted-off-tour/.

37. Though it is outside of the scope of this chapter, it is worth noting that "authenticity" is a gendered concept in surfing.

38. Matt Warshaw notes that a 2001 survey by market research firm Label Network found that surfing was the sport that women in North America most wanted to learn, women and girls' surf lines made up nearly 50 percent of total surfwear sales in 2001, and *Blue Crush* (2002), a Hollywood film about young women surfing, became the most expensive surf film made to date. Despite this, gender inequities on the professional tour "were nearly as significant as they had been in the early '60s." See Warshaw, *Encyclopedia* (2003), 705.

39. Heywood, "Third-Wave Feminism," 79.

40. Heywood, "Third-Wave Feminism," 64

41. Michael Silverstein and Kate Sayre, "The Female Economy," *Harvard Business Review,* September 2009, https://hbr.org/2009/09/the-female-economy.

42. Heywood, "Third-Wave Feminism," 80.

43. Gill, "Commodity Feminism."

44. The majority of surf scholarship that has attended to women's surfing centers on constructivist epistemology while addressing surfer girl representations (film, literature, marketing) and gender inequality in the surf space, competition, sponsorships, and media, using content analysis and ethnography as its two main methodologies. One notable exception is Georgina Roy, who treads deeper into ontological and materialist surfing territories, using a theoretical approach that incorporates the work of Deleuze and Guattari, post-structural and postmodern feminisms, along with aspects of queer theory. I would argue that Georgina Roy was the first to articulate the kind of surfeminist scholarship that I am advocating

for here, most notably in her *Feminism in New Sporting Spaces* and "Taking Emotions Seriously."

45. Kristeva, *Powers of Horror*, 4.

46. Kristeva, *Powers of Horror*, 5.

47. See David Moye, "Surfing Mermaids: The Newest Wave? (Video)," Huffington-Post.com, September 9, 2014, http://www.huffingtonpost.com/2014/09/09/surfing -mermaids_n_5793004.html; Jodelle Fitzwater, "Surf Expo 2014—A Mermaid's Top 15 Favorite 'Finds,'" StandupJournal.com, January 14, 2014, http://standupjournal.com/surf -expo-2014-mermaids-top-15-favorite-finds/; and "About," TheMermaidSociety.com.au, http://themermaidsociety.com.au/about/.

48. Original website contained these references. Kassia + Surf, "Who Is Kassia Meador?," KassiaSurf.com, accessed September 3, 2015. Reference to "Made by mermaids, for mermaids," can also be found at "Meet Kassia Meador of KASSIA SURF!," Free People Blog, accessed March 1, 2017, http://blog.freepeople.com/2015/04/kassia-surf-free-people/.

49. Brenda Peterson, "The New Wave for Women and Girls: IN Mermaids, OUT Vampires," HuffingtonPost.com, January 23, 2013, http://www.huffingtonpost.com/brenda -peterson/mermaids_b_2535367.html. It should also be noted that in 2014, *Out in the Lineup*, the first documentary to delve into homophobia in surfing, was released to wide acclaim.

50. Robertson, "Where Skin Meets Fin," 303–323.

51. Alaimo, "Trans-Corporeal Feminisms," 238.

52. Informing my thinking of female surfer's nomadic potential is Rosi Braidotti: "Nomadic shifts designate therefore a creative sort of becoming; a performative metaphor that allows for otherwise unlikely encounters and unsuspected sources of interaction of experience and of knowledge." See Braidotti, *Nomadic Subjects*, 6. "Nomadism . . . is not fluidity without borders, but rather an acute awareness of the nonfixity of boundaries. It is the intense desire to go on trespassing, transgressing. As a figuration of contemporary subjectivity . . . she cannot be reduced to a linear, teleological form of subjectivity, but rather the site of multiple connections" (66). One example of female surfers embracing a hybrid metaphor is the 2015 Surf+Social Good Summit, organized and founded by female surfers to support and connect environmental and social organizations in surfing with critical perspectives from academia. There are great research opportunities surrounding the growing number of female surfers involved with social and environmental justice organizations globally.

53. "Intra-action" is a neologism introduced by Karan Barad to highlight the ontological primacy of relations. The female surfer, for example, is a subjectivity defined by, and inseparable from, her corporeal (material) relation to the totality of the ocean environment, including sand, rocks, reef, marine flora, sea foam, sea spray, nonhuman animals, weather patterns, surface tensions, wave formations, toxins, and climate change.

Part IV / Capitalism, Economics, and the
Commodification of Surf Culture

14 / Free Ride: The Food Stamp Surfer, American Counterculture, and the Refusal of Work

KRISTIN LAWLER

In a 1978 interview with *Surfer* magazine, Timothy Leary called surfing "the spiritual aesthetic style of the liberated self," and went on to say, "I've been doing a lot of lecturing, and I've picked out as my symbol, surf. . . . I want to have film of a surfer right at that point moving along constantly right at the edge of the tube. That position is the metaphor of life to me, the highly conscious life." Leary, icon of the 1960s US counterculture, identifies surfing with a time-orientation that exists fully in the present, spontaneous and free. And he identifies the material conditions that make such a present-oriented spontaneity possible: "You have to be self-defined elite, not in any aristocratic sense, but in being a free person that can take the time off to actualize yourself this way. And only a very proud, independent, affluent, successful species can do that, you need leisure time . . . so it is a sign of a very advanced species. These are the future people being thrown forward by our species."[1]

As we will see, not everyone is quite so celebratory about the idea of a leisure-centered life in the moment. Still, Leary understood what over a century of tourism and beach promoters, journalists, advertisers, and filmmakers have known and put to profitable use: the surfer is American culture's most prominent and most consistent archetype of freedom—freedom *from* alienated work and the clocked time, repressed libido, and material scarcity that this work depends on, and freedom *to* live spontaneously, within a pleasurable ecological and subcultural connection. And the surfer image has always signified the transcendence of the imperatives of modern instrumental rationality in favor of a more "primitive," libidinal relationship to the world, a relationship that psychoanalytic theorists, significantly, refer to as "oceanic."

Since the late nineteenth century, in every era the image of the surfer has signified an opposition to and transcendence of contemporary repression in all its forms: the cold, productivist logic of capital as Marx lays it out; the Protestant work ethic and instrumental attitude to the lifeworld, including nature, that Weber describes as capital's cultural essence; the clock time that E. P. Thompson sees as central to, and contemporaneous with, the rise of capitalism; and the regime of rigid, system-supporting gender roles criticized by feminist and queer authors.[2] And what unites all of these is the question of work: where capital demands it, the surf image enacts a refusal of it. Thus, its every iteration bears some key insights about the status and meaning of work and its refusal in American society.

But there is another aspect of the surfer's significance to consider: its historical significance. Like the oceanic unconscious into which the image taps, it produces action that attempts to reproduce it, to bring it back into the present. This accounts for its persistent ubiquity; commercial forces see that the image of freedom—from work and from scarcity—inspires people to act. They buy movie tickets, cars, records, deodorant, you name it, because ads with the surfer have inspired them to.

The surfer in commercially disseminated popular culture, then, is an instance of what Daniel Bell calls the cultural contradictions of capitalism, the way in which capitalism inevitably generates opposition to the very Protestant work ethic at its heart. According to Bell, a "new capitalism of abundance" emerged in the 1920s with the advent of mass advertising. Preaching an "ethic of consumption—of hedonism, pleasure, and play," this new capitalism transformed the American social structure such that by the 1950s, "the culture was no longer concerned with how to work and achieve, but with how to spend and enjoy."

But capitalism still needed work from people, in addition to consumption, so the "new capitalism continued to demand a Protestant ethic in the area of production—that is, in the realm of work—but to stimulate a demand for pleasure and play in the area of consumption.... On the one hand, the business corporation wants an individual to work hard, pursue a career, accept delayed gratification—to be, in the crude sense, an organization man. And yet, in its products and its advertisements, the corporation promotes pleasure, instant joy, relaxing, and letting go. One is to be 'straight' by day and a 'swinger' by night."[3]

But people did not so easily compartmentalize their lives this way; the swinging night was a whole lot more compelling than the straight day. Capitalism had sold Americans an image of leisure and pleasure, and the people responded by taking the offer seriously. In the case of surfing, just as in the case of rock and roll and other commercially disseminated countercultural forms, this mass broadcasting of the pleasures of leisure and play had been productive not only of commercial behavior—buying stuff—but also of the growth of surfing itself. In fact, every amplification of the surf image contributed to a corresponding growth of surf culture, a defining feature of which has always been the placing of work at the margins of life and a compelling leisure pursuit at the center. So by the 1960s, when figures like Leary articulated a more and more widespread feeling about the possibility of new lifestyles and new desires, elites began to panic about what was coming to be called "the crisis of the work ethic."

During the height of this "crisis"—in which the American working class, from the factories to the universities to women in the home and soldiers in Vietnam, refused the Keynesian wages-for-productivity deal that had made industrial capitalism stable during the mid-twentieth century, and nearly ground productivity to a halt—the figure of the surfer was so fully identified with carefree leisure and the refusal of work that among philosophers and economists, a discussion emerged that centered on what political philosopher John Rawls in 1971 was the first to call "the Malibu surfer problem."

That year, Rawls published his epic *A Theory of Justice*, which makes a case for a conception of justice as "fairness," a conception he claims can form an alternative to utilitarianism as the philosophical basis of liberal constitutional democracies.[4] In Rawls's theory, the most just distribution of wealth is the one that is most fair to the least advantaged member of society. In a capitalist society, which Rawls assumes, the condition of fairness would be a guaranteed annual income for each member of society, regardless of the person's talents or the work the person performed. But this principle of fairness doesn't apply to lazy Malibu surfers, who would "unjustly" take their share without pulling their weight by contributing.

According to Rawls, "those who surf all day off Malibu must find a way to support themselves and would not be entitled to public funds."[5] And in all the many discussions around Rawls's theory that have, for decades now, riffed on this question, the "Malibu surfer problem" has continued to refer to the "issue" that if income were unconditionally guaranteed, some members of society would steadfastly refuse to work, and instead would "free ride" (no pun acknowledged) on the fairness generated by the existence of a guaranteed income in the context of a society in which the majority still works productively, thereby "earning" their share of the negative tax.

Given the close association between the image of the surfer and the refusal of work and of scarcity, and its relation to the question of welfare policy, I was not surprised when I saw that in August 2013, Fox News ran a story on a lively, Spicoli-esque character who, in right-wing circles, has come to be called the "Food Stamp Surfer." This new iteration of the surfer sheds light, I think, on what is again today's most pressing economic and cultural question, one laid out fifty years ago by Wilhelm Reich in *The Mass Psychology of Fascism*: what are the cultural and libidinal politics that explain whether the downwardly mobile will turn to the resentment of the right or to the potentially more liberatory vision of the left?

The Food Stamp Surfer first materialized in a series entitled "When the Safety Net Becomes a Hammock," which concerned President Obama's 2009 stimulus plan, especially the part of the legislation that removed some of the 1996 welfare reform law's restrictions on the receipts of food stamps. The central piece, entitled "Unabashed Surfer Receiving Food Stamps to Buy Sushi and Avoid Work," features Greenslate, a twenty-nine-year-old Southern California surfer and musician, who "unapologetically" receives $200 in food stamps per month.[6] Asked by the reporter about his everyday life, Greenslate says he rises in the afternoon, then goes to the beach, starts drinking, hits on some girls, plays rock and roll in his band, and catches some waves. What about work? Greenslate's quips are classic surf bum: standing on the beach, he says with a smirk, "This is my job . . . make sure the waves are rolling smoothly, the sun is up and the girls are out." As he is planning a party with his surf buddies for later that day, he says, "Another day in paradise."

According to the report, this "unemployed musician and surfer" has "chosen the life of a beach bum in the seaside paradise" of La Jolla and "doesn't want to take a regular job with a regular boss . . . he gets by with a little help from his friends, and you, the American taxpayer." The piece is set up so that the viewer's subject position, the "you," is a taxpayer, resentful of—rather than seduced by—the images of rock and roll, collective surfing and drinking, sunshine, and endless waves that largely constitute the visual piece of the report. Along with the images of fun in the sun, a picture of Greenslate's Electronic Benefits Transfer, or EBT, card comes up quickly—his ticket to free food, courtesy of the government.

The interviewer, John Roberts, can barely suppress his rage as he listens to Greenslate talk about the importance of surfing and rock and roll to his everyday life while he continuously mocks the idea of having a "real job" outside of practicing with his band. Most egregious from the perspective of the Fox piece is the fact that the unemployed surfer refuses the austerity implied in a $200 monthly food allowance. Eschewing a hair shirt, the surf bum blows his food stamps on the best that the gourmet section of his local supermarket has to offer: sushi and lobster. The camera follows Greenslate from the grocery store to the backyard party where he and his (clearly working-class) male friends grill and share the lobster, play guitar, laugh. Next, the interview commences with Roberts asking the key question: "So is it safe to say that this notion of holding down a steady job, it's just not in your wheelhouse?" Greenslate answers: "That's not really the direction I'm going right now." According to him, you can't really have a job and pursue the dream of rock stardom seriously. The lyrics he sings back this up: "I don't want a motherfuckin' job, I'd rather be broke, steal and rob."

Roberts admits that he "was really taken aback that he [Greenslate] seemed completely unembarrassed about sponging off the rest of us in this manner." Greenslate is, indeed, unashamed. He discusses his dreams of being a rock star, and insists on making his work on a record with his band the center of his life. Roberts is relentless: "So, tell me what's behind the lyric 'no job.'" Greenslate responds: "No job, living the dream, doing your thing." Roberts asks: "Living the dream is having no job?" When Greenslate responds, "Yeah," Roberts inquires, "And how is that going for you?" Greenslate breaks out into a wide stoner grin-laugh and responds, "Great, man. It's going great."

Roberts again presses the idea that Greenslate should be ashamed of himself. "It used to be," he says, "that people would feel like, oh, I'm on food stamps, I'm a loser." Greenslate responds: "Why would it be bad in any way? It's free food." "Do you feel guilty at all about doing this?" "Fuck no." A few weeks later, Fox's Sean Hannity had Greenslate as a guest on his show, and continued with the ideological work of creating the American public who could never be anything but resentful of the surf bum. The dynamic continued; the viewer was interpellated as one who shares the nearly sadistic rage of the anchor and the assumed resentment against the welfare sponger. Greenslate never conceded; when Hannity said he could get him a job making $80,000 a year driving a truck in North Dakota and asked if he'd take it, the surfer looks aghast and says dismissively, "No way."

Greenslate quite masterfully performs his slacker role for the camera, probably in an attempt to gain publicity for his band, and we, the viewer, are supposed to identify as "the public" off whom he is sponging, and who thus ought to oppose welfare benefits for slackers. To underline the ideological hailing of the piece and the subject position that the viewer is supposed to occupy within it, Fox polls its viewers, this time specifically on the question of how they feel about supporting the Food Stamp Surfer himself. A whopping 91 percent of respondents say they "have a problem with it." As the piece hammers home again and again, *you*, the viewer, have a problem with it.

Anchor Brett Baier ends the piece with a clear assertion of who "we"—the public both addressed and molded by Fox—really are, and "our" embrace of the work ethic is central to this. "Rugged individualism. It's a term that attempts to capture the American values of hard work, self-reliance, and pride in pulling your own weight. Those values, and a system that rewards them, help explain why America has prospered like no other nation." He ends the piece with an implicit warning that if we don't change the policies that reward sloth, "we" will be in danger of losing "all that has made America great."

Now, of course, the uncompromising anti-work stance taken by the surfer is, to say the least, unrepresentative of either food stamp recipients or the unemployed in the United States. But the reality is not at all what's interesting about the piece. Truth frequently doesn't drive politics nearly as much as the imaginary does. Fox hopes to use the image of the work-shirking wave-rider to create a certain kind of imagined "public" to which they can sell their message. But Fox, like the huckster capitalists of which Daniel Bell spoke, can't help but send contradictory messages, ones that ultimately subvert the reactionary project.

Fox is trying to both appeal to and create a familiar, and politically very productive, notion of the public: white, working class and middle class, whose attitudes toward work and responsibility define them, as they have for decades, against the black ghetto inhabitants and white countercultural types, coded as "lazy." But this subjunctive creative work of discursively appealing to and creating an anti-welfare public may be more complicated, even contradictory, than the writers at Fox News could ever imagine.

This work, to create and appeal to a public, is best understood in the sense in which Michael Warner discusses it in *Publics and Counterpublics*. The author lays out the idea of a public as a social formation both formed and assumed by its discursive hailing; in his words, "It exists by virtue of being addressed." Thus, it's the circulation of texts that both creates and addresses a scene: "Circulation accounts for the way a public seems both internal and external to discourse, both notional and material. From the concrete experience of a world in which available forms circulate, one projects a public. And both the known and the unknown are essential to the process. The known element in the addressee enables a scene of practical possibility; the unknown, a hope of transformation. Writing to a public helps to make a world insofar as the object of address is brought into being partly by postulating and characterizing it. This performative ability depends, however, on that object's being not entirely fictitious—not postulated merely, but recognized as a real path for the circulation of discourse. The path is then treated as a social entity."[7]

Warner could be talking about surfers when he says that "counterpublics tend to be those in which this ideology of reading does not have the same privilege. It might be that embodied sociability is too important to them; they might not be organized by the hierarchy of faculties that elevates rational-critical reflection as the self-image of humanity; they might depend more heavily on performance spaces than on print; it might be that they cannot so easily suppress from consciousness their own creative-expressive function. *How then, might they imagine their agency?*"[8]

The image of Greenslate and his friends can be seen as a counterpublic, but one without much agency at all. Their image is simply being used in the service of the creation of a reactionary public. Fox distributed copies of the "news" piece on Capitol Hill, and Republicans used it in their ultimately successful attempt to cut food stamp benefits (President Obama's 2014 farm bill included an $8.7 billion food stamp cut). In the debate before an earlier congressional vote to cut food stamps in the House of Representatives, Rep. Tim Huelskamp (R-Kan.) said, "You can no longer sit on your couch or ride a surfboard like Jason in California and expect the federal taxpayer to feed you." And at this writing, Republican lawmakers in Kansas have introduced legislation restricting how those receiving Temporary Assistance for Needy Families (TANF) can spend their money: no pools, tattoo parlors, psychics, or movies. Another measure, introduced by the House GOP in Missouri, aims to ban the use of food stamps for "steak, seafood, soda, cookies, chips, and energy drinks." Numerous commentators have pointed out the origin of these new proposals in the discourse on the Food Stamp Surfer; a recent feature on the bills on CNN didn't mention Greenslate but showed video of him scanning his lobster at the checkout behind the voiceover.

The Democrats, too, saw the Food Stamp Surfer as an irresponsible jerk jeopardizing the benefits of the working poor. "I don't give a damn about Surfer Dude," Democrat Jim McGovern, a member of the committee that oversees nutrition assistance, said, "As far as I'm concerned, he can walk off the nearest pier. To suggest that he's the face of SNAP [the Supplemental Nutrition Assistance Program, as the former Food Stamp program was designated by Congress in

2008] is offensive." Of course, McGovern is right about the true face of SNAP. But in the creation of a resentful public, the truth doesn't really matter. And either way, both sides agree on two things: the work ethic as the measure of a deserving person, and the power that the image of the slacker can have in (and on) public discourse.

However, Fox News's instrumentalization of the shameless surfers may just undermine its ideological intention: to create and recreate a resentful public. In doing its ideological work, Fox can't help but broadcast a subversive image, one that enrages but also seems to fascinate the reporters. Classic images of garage rock, golden sunsets, rolling waves, and beach parties are signifiers that are not necessarily so easy to control. And as labor historians like David Roediger and Jonathan Cutler assert, working-class fascination with and rage about perceived freedom are not unrelated to one another. For most American workers, Cutler says, "the desire for less work was first disavowed, then pathologized, and finally projected onto Others."[9] Discussing the racial politics of this dynamic, both writers quote George Rawick, author of the classic on American slavery, *From Sundown to Sunup*, at length to understand how this operates: "The Englishman met the West African as a reformed sinner meets a comrade of his previous debaucheries. The reformed sinner very often creates a pornography of his former life. He must suppress even his knowledge that he had acted that way or even wanted to act that way. Prompted by his uneasiness at this great act of repression, he cannot leave alone those who live as he once did or as he still unconsciously desires to live. He must devote himself to their conversion or repression."[10] This is applicable to the discourse around all "welfare cheats": living the repressed fantasy of the mainstream worker, these "cheats" can never be left alone.

Precisely because there is a hidden desire just under the surface of the able-bodied welfare cheat discourse, resentment is far more volatile and potentially subversive than those who would work to play it up imagine. This resentment is, counter to the angry, punishing, authoritative Fox discourse, simply not an affirmation of the Protestant work ethic that "we" are all supposed to share. In fact, the anchors at one point mention the folks "working their fingers to the bone" so that slackers like Greenslate can be supported. The key moment in the Hannity interview comes when Hannity, in the middle of recounting all the manual and service jobs he's had over the years, bursts out angrily, "If I had it my way, I wouldn't work either!" The resentment toward the imaginary figure of the slacker, on the beach or in the ghetto, is actually resentment against work itself. If we *did* all share Fox's idea of the hard workers that "we" are, folks would whistle while they worked and happily hand over the money to the sinful unfortunates who are missing out on all the inherent value of hard work and, as Baer puts it, the "pride in self-reliance" that characterizes American culture.

But we don't. Americans resent the welfare cheats of reactionary discourse precisely because we don't value work in itself. We know that it's a sacrifice necessary to get the money we need to get by. As is so often the case, just beneath the resentment lies desire. In order to create and appeal to a resentful, reactionary public that blames "the lazy" rather than, for instance, finance capital, for today's overwork and austerity, Fox News and other ideologues must broadcast a countercultural image that has the potential to overflow, and subvert, its intended significance. The rage that is so clearly on display in the visages of the reporters, as well as in the discourse of politicians going forward, is clear evidence of the fear of the powerful countercultural figure of the slacker betrayed by this resentful discourse.

Greenslate is a classic image of what remains of the counterculture, most of which was effectively destroyed by the oil shocks, union busting, and public sector austerity that began in the 1970s—largely, I argue, as capital's response to the countercultural refusal of work discipline that characterized the two and a half decades after the close of World War II. I see the counterculture as one with what Antonio Negri calls the essence of the working class under capitalism: the refusal of work. The counterculture embraced what Jock Young, following Herbert Marcuse, called the subterranean values of freedom and pleasure as against the ethos of productivity.

Young, whose work echoes that of Marcuse in many ways, lays out the difference between the formal values of the workaday world and what he calls the subterranean values—pleasure, play, instant gratification—that inherently oppose them and that characterize, for him, the cultures of both the "ghetto poor" and bohemian young people (surfers among them).

For Young, as for Marcuse, "formal values—the ethos of productivity—still rule the roost over the subterranean values of freedom." The transformation from pleasure to reality principle effected by socialization is what has driven these subterranean principles underground. The work ethic still rules supreme, and the desire for freedom in the moment gets marginalized. However, there are "two possible ways in which the socialization into the work ethic can break down and prove unsuccessful." The first, reminiscent of Robert Merton's work on deviance, occurs if the means of obtaining the culturally approved goals is blocked for certain groups. The second breakdown happens "if the material rewards or goals are not valued by the individuals, sections of the community which are *beyond the work ethos*." Young identifies the first tendency with "the ghetto black community" and the second with "the bohemian young," who disdain the rewards offered by the system for conformity with formal work values.[11]

The ethos of productivity, or work ethic, "attempts to legitimize and encompass the world of subterranean values" like pleasure, play, and instant gratification, but Young says that the attempt at co-optation fails in the case of groups, like surfers, that embrace the values of play and pleasure as central. How is it that some groups come to reject the ethos of productivity? In a 1973 essay entitled "The Hippie Solution: An Essay in the Politics of Leisure," he lays out precisely the problem for which a countercultural lifestyle provides a solution: work and artificially perpetuated material scarcity.[12]

The baby boomers were the first American generation to grow up in affluence, and for them the ethos of productivity seemed inapplicable to the new age of leisure, in which work was supposedly about to be automated out of existence. Young asserts that "the widespread occurrence of hippie cultures represents a tentative solution to emerging problems of work and leisure in the advanced industrial countries of the west. . . . The hippies are already rehearsing in vivo a number of possible cultural solutions to central life problems posed by the emerging society of the future." For Young as for Leary, surfers are the future.

These central life problems are related to the realization, articulated by Marcuse and felt deeply among the counterculture, that the abundance made possible by automation for the first time makes the ethos of productivity an anachronistic way to organize human life. For Young, the political significance of bohemians and hippies is that they are potentially prefigurative of a new world, a postindustrial utopia, in which the leisure time and abundance that modern technology makes possible becomes a lived reality. Again, there is no question that, because capital profits only through the exploitation of labor, capital pushed back, hard, against the refusal of labor that the hippies, surfers, and slackers of the sixties and seventies represented. The American workers of today work a full month per year more than their 1973 counterparts did, for the same or declining wages. And it's been a long time since people talked much about a "post-work" society.[13]

And still, the agents of capitalist reaction never rest. They must, and do, constantly work to create a "public" of people who share the "common sense" that it's morally wrong not to work. In this subjunctive/creative work, they can't help but broadcast the Other of this public, potentially generating a subversive counterpublic. The hardworking American public that Fox News is attempting to create, to appeal to, and to mobilize is defined only in opposition to what it is not. In order to do the ideological work of crafting this public, Fox must broadcast its Other—with what effects, it remains to be seen. Perhaps Fox, in its relentless attack on characters who refuse work, understands the latent power of this refusal better even than most of those who side with labor against capital.

Given the contemporary relationship between labor and capital, in which capital seems to be definitively winning, why would Fox News and the interests it represents be so worried about some SoCal slacker, remnant of the now-defeated bohemian uprising? Beyond the immediate impacts on food stamp benefit policy, I propose that it's because they understand something that the labor side of the class struggle has largely forgotten: when masses of people refuse work discipline, refuse the "common sense" that says endless work for low and declining wages is the best we can do, this radically transforms the power relations between labor and capital. Fox would do best to stay silent about this subterranean desire, but they (and the politicians and corporate types on their side) just can't stop talking about it. It is the inevitable return of the repressed in capitalist society, and it just won't be silenced.

The bumper-sticker version of the relationship between the refusal of work and the labor movement puts it well: "The Labor Movement: the folks who brought you the weekend." It is a reminder that the labor movement and the question of leisure and freedom were, at least at one point, one and the same. As the labor movement has declined in power, American leisure has been closed out. And to the extent that American labor has abandoned its most powerful tradition—the push for shorter hours—its fortunes have declined. Not surprisingly, as the American worker has, over the last several decades, been flooding the market with labor—hours keep going up—wages have declined or remained stagnant. It's a vicious cycle, but there is a tradition in the labor movement that appeals not to divide-and-conquer resentment or to some fantasy about how great it is to go to work, but to something inherently solidaristic: the desire to enjoy life. Labor strategy based on this concept would work to restrict the overall supply of labor to employers, thus driving up both wages and fun.

According to David Roediger and Philip Foner's *Our Own Time*, the seminal study of the movement for shorter hours within American labor, "the length of the workday has historically been the central issue raised by the American labor movement during its most dynamic periods of organization."[14] That is, the demand for shorter hours, both as a means to share the work during times of high unemployment and as a means to appropriate the enjoyable life that capitalist "progress" can technically make possible with a minimum of toil, has been the most inspirational undertaking that the labor movement has ever put forth.

Key for the discussion here, the essentially solidaristic nature of the demand for reduced hours has been another source of its great power: "Reduction of hours became an explosive demand partly because of its unique capacity to unify workers across the lines of craft, race, sex, skill, age, and ethnicity. Attempts by the employing classes to divide labor could be implemented with relative ease where wage rates were concerned. . . . With regard to hours, the situation was different . . . thus the shorter working day was an issue that could mitigate, though not completely overcome, the deep racial and ethnic divisions that complicated class organization in the United States."[15] Fox News broadcasts an image of a gleeful refusal of work, but frames it as unrealistic because Jason Greenslate's freedom comes at the expense of the taxpaying public. But the divisive class politics employed in this framing is far from the only political possibility that emerges from this image. It is potentially fuel for labor's most inspirational and solidaristic strategy: the push for a shorter workday and workweek. This project is, I think, best organized not through the institutional structure of a union or of a new government welfare policy, but through the cultivation of a culture of freedom that *inspires* workers to resist work. A culture of slowing down, enjoying life, and resisting work is perhaps easier to pump up and to mobilize than we are often led to believe. The raw material is everywhere in the popular culture that is so much the texture of our lives—a popular culture that consistently foregrounds the surfer image of the refusal of work precisely because it is so powerful. Advertisers use the image of the surfer to sell their product. Fox wants the Food Stamp Surfer to inspire divisiveness and resentment. But this iteration of the surfer image, like those that came before it, is, as Timothy Leary understood, potentially inspirational of much, much more liberating things than that.

NOTES

1. Pezman, "The Evolutionary Surfer."

2. Lawler, *The American Surfer.*

3. Bell, *The Cultural Contradictions of Capitalism*, 75.

4. Rawls, *Theory of Justice.*

5. Rawls, "Priority of the Right," 275, note.

6. "Unabashed Surfer Receiving Food Stamps to Buy Sushi and Avoid Work," FoxNews .com, August 12, 2013, http://nation.foxnews.com/2013/08/12/watch-unabashed-surfer -receiving-food-stamps-buy-sushi-and-avoid-work.

7. Warner, *Publics and Counterpublics*, 67, 92.

8. Warner, *Publics and Counterpublics*, 124.

9. Cutler, *Labor's Time*, 9.

10. Rawick, *From Sundown to Sunup*, quoted in Cutler, *Labor's Time,* 8.

11. Young, *The Drugtakers*.

12. Young, "The Hippie Solution."

13. Richards, ed., *Why Work?*

14. Roediger and Foner, *Our Own Time*, x.

15. Roediger and Foner, *Our Own Time*, xi.

15 / The Political Economy of Surfing Culture: Production, Profit, and Representation

DOUGLAS BOOTH

For many people, surfing defines their way of life, their manner of living—in short, their culture.[1] Surfers organize their lives around the rhythms of the tides and the seasons that determine when, and where, the surf runs; they follow their own fashions, and speak their own language.[2] Yet, irrespective of its social, artistic, or spiritual content, surfing, like all cultures, contains material content. As David Harvey notes, cultures involve separating, combining, transforming, and presenting material objects; they involve technologies of reproduction and circulation, the organization of markets for trading, expansion, and profit; and they involve a range of social relations between those who give and those who receive, between those who produce and those who consume, and between those for whom the culture is their livelihood and those for whom it is a spiritual experience.[3] Invariably, tensions arise in these social relations as different groups compete for ownership of, and access to, resources, or as they seek to control technologies or the diffusion of ideas.

In this chapter I analyze the material content of surfing culture within a historical materialist framework. The material content of surfing includes boards, wetsuits, clothing, accessories, magazines, books, memorabilia, videos, competitions, tourism, and surfing schools, and is worth an estimated $10 billion per annum.[4] I place this material content in the capitalist mode of production, a dynamic system that highlights economic growth; the quest for accumulation by the owners of the means of production (capitalists) who seek to extract maximum surplus value from those who own only their labor power (workers); and competition between capitalists who, in their attempts to accumulate capital, continually engage new technologies and new ways of organizing and controlling labor.[5] The precise form that the capitalist mode of production takes at any one time is never predetermined. Rather, capitalism develops and unfolds within constantly changing relationships and circumstances. This is especially true of relationships which, like those in surfing, tend to exist more on the periphery of mainstream capitalism. Many relationships in surfing coalesce around a cultural paradox. On the one hand, surfers celebrate irreverence, escape from drudgery, and harmony with the natural world; on the other, they compete with and socially rank each other while striving to accumulate various forms of cultural and economic capital.

The chapter comprises three substantive sections. I begin by tracing the development of the surf industry from backyard operations in the 1950s to global surf corporations in the 1980s; I also discuss some of the crises that the global industry has confronted in recent times. In the second section I look at different types of workers within surfing: shapers, who primarily rely on their labor; free surfers, whose riding skills and lifestyles embody the apparent ideals of surfing culture; and surfers who compete on the professional tour. The third section focuses on two issues at the heart of material relationships and the paradox in surfing culture: commercialization of surfing culture and its codification into a sport. In concluding the chapter, I point to demographic and social changes and trends that are further fragmenting surfing culture, introducing new lifestyles, tourist destinations, and fashions, as well as marketing, communication, and sporting opportunities (e.g., the World Surf League–sponsored Big Wave Tour). Fragmentation raises new questions about material relationships in contemporary surfing. For example, what constitutes authenticity in surfing culture, and how will surf companies reproduce authenticity under conditions of fragmentation?

The most substantial growth in the surf industry occurred during a thirty-year period beginning in the early 1950s.[6] Initially the industry consisted of backyard operations and small-scale businesses that arose with the invention of lightweight fiberglass Malibu surfboards. Jack O'Neill, the founder of O'Neill Wetsuits, conducted a surf business from his San Francisco garage where he shaped surfboards and glued strips of neoprene rubber into wetsuit vests to insulate surfers against extreme water and air temperatures.[7] When Brian Singer and Doug Warbrick decided to manufacture Rip Curl surfboards, they converted a home garage in Torquay (Victoria, Australia) into a shaping bay and glassing room.[8]

Some surfers stumbled into the industry. Greg Noll, a member of the American lifeguard team that introduced Malibu surfboards to Australia during a tour in 1956, took a movie camera on the trip "to show everybody back home what Australian surf looked like."[9] Returning to California, he discovered eager viewers willing to pay a dollar each to watch his film, and Noll earned enough money to finance further travel. In 1958 he spent several months at Mazatlán (Mexico) and repeated the filming exercise.[10] John Severson began his career as a surf film cinematographer in the late 1950s when the army posted him to Hawai'i. He made 16-mm movies with a Keystone camera and spliced several bits of film together under the title *Surf.* In 1960 Severson produced a black-and-white booklet, *The Surfer*, to promote the films he was by then regularly producing. It proved so popular that Severson developed the booklet into a quarterly magazine; a decade later, *Surfer* was a monthly magazine with a circulation of 100,000.[11]

Early technology was simple, often crude. Film enthusiasts, for example, watched the movies produced by Noll, Severson, and others in church, school, and public halls. The producers had little equipment. Bud Browne introduced his films from the stage, rushed "to the projection room to join the operator of an arc projector," and watched the screen holding a microphone over the tape machine that played music.[12] Surfboard and wetsuit manufacturing technologies were equally primitive. Brian Singer said that Rip Curl's "first boards were pretty rough. We didn't have a room clean enough for finish coating, so we used marine varnish and told everyone it was the new thing."[13] Alan Green, who made wetsuits in Australia under the Rip Curl label in the late 1960s, admitted that the first batches were "a fucking disaster": most fell apart and were replaced at the company's expense.[14]

Backyard industries fed the growth and diffusion of surfing culture. The surfboard-riding population of Southern California grew from some five thousand in 1956 to around 100,000 in 1962.[15] Manufacturers opened retail shops to sell their boards; films and magazines directed riders to new wave locations, board designs, riding styles, and general trends in fashion and taste. Cultural diffusion and expansion opened new doors for budding entrepreneurs. In Australia, Bob Evans followed a path similar to that of John Severson, showing imported surf films before producing his own and then launching *Surfing World* magazine.[16] Wetsuit pioneer Alan Green diversified into sheepskin boots and board shorts, and Rip Curl began mass-producing wetsuits. Brian Singer recalls his "defining moment": "We had one hundred orders to meet one week with ten bucks profit in every suit . . . I suddenly thought, shit, we could make a bit of money out of this."[17]

Mainstream industries, motivated by profit, appropriated surfing. In so doing they helped popularize the sport. Hollywood was the classic example. Columbia Pictures initiated a genre of beach film when it recreated Frederick Kohner's stories of Gidget. Columbia's *Gidget* (1959) reproduced the idyllic fantasy lifestyle of California surfers, and Columbia followed with three more beach films, including two *Gidget* sequels. Other production houses followed suit; the Hollywood beach film was a commercial success.

In order to ensure financial viability, Hollywood, with its elaborate sets, specialized labor systems, multiple cameras, expensive developing techniques, sophisticated advertising, and complex distribution networks, appealed to universal audiences. Hollywood beach films focused on beach life that the industry correctly saw as more encompassing, including women as well as men, and more accessible to a wider age range. But in broadening the appeal of its films, Hollywood alienated surfing aficionados who spurned the genre. Screen writer Marc Rubel, for example, denounced Hollywood's philosophy, which he said reduced surfing to a "total adolescent pastime." Among the stalwart "older generation," Rubel said, surfing was a vital activity that "kept us sane."[18]

On the other hand, while surfers recoiled at Hollywood's interpretations of their pastime, cinematographers from within surfing culture sought access to the distribution networks of the established industry. *The Endless Summer* enjoyed enormous popularity among surfers, and its producer Bruce Brown approached several Hollywood companies with a view to distributing it on the commercial circuit. They refused. Brown enlarged the film to 35 mm and sold it worldwide. It grossed $8 million.[19]

The commercial cinemas learned their lesson. Thirty years later they snatched up Brown's *The Endless Summer II* (1994)—which audiences, ironically, deemed a "mild disappointment." Hollywood nonetheless persisted with surfing, presenting it as sport based on contests in deadly waves.[20] Historian of surfing Matt

Warshaw believes that Hollywood films such as *North Shore* (1987), *In God's Hands* (1998), and *Blue Crush* (2002) well represented surfing action but that they parodied the pastime.[21]

Surfing became a multibillion-dollar industry in the 1980s and '90s, dominated by three Australian companies: Rip Curl, Quiksilver, and Billabong. They expanded the production of hardware and clothing for surfing and its first cousins, snowboarding and skateboarding; turned from an exclusively male clientele to include women; and sold surfing-influenced designs in traditionally nonsurfing areas.[22] Quiksilver led the way on the female front in the 1990s, launching the Roxy label.[23] After entering the market, Roxy diversified into fragrances, bedroom accessories, luggage, and books.[24]

Quiksilver charged into Western Europe in the mid-1980s, pushing far beyond the established surf culture of southwest France. Outwardly there seemed little prospect of developing a market for T-shirts and board shorts in continental Europe, but Harry Hodge, a former surf film cinematographer, saw the potential. Hodge, who headed the consortium that bought Quiksilver's Western Europe license, "realized that the difference between a small company selling surf products to parts of Europe and a big company supplying the lifestyle needs of the entire region, was simply a matter of lateral thinking." Hodge and his senior partner, pioneer professional surfer Jeff Hakman, headed to the mountains: "We looked at what [people] were wearing, and we saw how we could make Europe work for us. We would take surf clothes to the mountains."[25] Within two years of arriving in France, Quiksilver's net sales rose to $6 million; within six years they reached $26 million, and within a decade over $70 million. In 1998 net sales exceeded $113 million.[26]

The surfing media—videos (and DVDs from the early 2000s) and magazines—provided key marketing tools for the industry. Videos and DVDs are the "primary cinematic medium" of surfing.[27] Surf corporations flooded the culture with videos and DVDs, giving them away through their stores or including them with magazines.[28] Videos and DVDs became integral elements of the multimillion-dollar marketing campaigns launched by surf corporations, especially those focusing on exotic surfing locations (e.g., Rip Curl's *The Search*, Quiksilver's *The Crossing*, Billabong's *Odyssey*).

The big surf corporations wield immense influence through the magazines, which are "completely indentured to the surf brands."[29] "Revenue from subscriptions barely covers printing costs," explains surf journalist Chas Smith, which means that surf magazines depend on brand advertising.[30] They will not hesitate to withdraw advertising if they find objectionable content. Magazine editors grumble about manufacturers influencing editorial policy and effectively silencing criticism. Sociologist Mark Stranger observed an unusual silence in the surfing media after the courts convicted Quiksilver for false labeling by placing "made-in-Australia" labels on wetsuits manufactured in China. The editor of one magazine said that Quiksilver told him "there was nothing to be gained by publicizing the case." The editor admitted that he "agreed with their request," adding that "we walk a fine line between . . . our independence and not upsetting these companies."[31]

Cultural hegemony and industrial imperialism, of course, extend beyond videos and magazines. Small surf shops complain that Rip Curl, Quiksilver, and Billabong "bully" them into stocking their products, force them to "lift sales by an average of 10 percent every year to qualify for volume discounts," and threaten them with removing their accounts if they "discount outside traditional end-of-season sales."[32]

As the surf industry grew, its corporate leaders became wealthy moguls. Billabong's Gordon Merchant, Quiksilver's Alan Green and John Law, and Rip Curl's Doug Warbrick and Brian Singer entered the Australian *Business Review Weekly*'s list of the country's top 200 richest people.[33] In 1990, Quiksilver USA bought 100 percent of Quicksilver Europe, and Hodge and Hakman became multimillionaires.[34] Bob Hurley, who began shaping surfboards under his own name at Huntington Beach (California) in the late 1970s, bought the license for Billabong USA in 1983. Hurley left Billabong fifteen years later in 1998 and began trading under his own name; "four years later . . . he sold to Nike for an estimated $120 million."[35]

Diversification into products tangentially related to riding waves (e.g., jewelry, perfume, watches), and the actions of surfing capitalists such as Bob Hurley, lend weight to Marx's contention that bourgeois ambition rests on "accumulation for the sake of accumulation" and "production for the sake of production."[36] In contradistinction, Stranger draws attention to historical contingency when he argues that the image industry leaders "create for themselves as authentic insiders protecting surfing culture from mainstream rape and pillage is not all spin, but it is more of happy coincidence than corporate mission."[37] Yet irrespective of the precise and complex relationships between the surf industry, the general surfing population, and mainstream capital, accumulation and production contain their own seeds of crisis.

As a mode of production, capitalism confronts perpetual crises. Failed companies, many of which simply could not secure finance to ensure production, litter the surfing industry and illustrate the dynamic and competitive nature of capitalism and historical materialism. One collapse rocked the surfing industry. Clark Foam, which had been in business since the early 1960s, and which had a near monopoly over polyurethane foam surfboard blanks, producing some 90 percent of supplies in the United States and 60 percent of world supplies, abruptly closed down in 2005. Gordon Clark, the owner, claimed that state agencies wanted him for environmental violations.[38] The fallout was immediate, with prices for remaining supplies doubling, and new board prices increasing by up to $250.[39] Yet within two years, new companies had arisen, and manufacturers had introduced a range of new materials and new building methods (see "Workers and Aristocrats" below), although polyurethane remains the most popular and preferred core. Surftech, which manufactures nonpolyurethane boards, had already attained the position of the biggest surfboard manufacturer in 2004, before Clark Foam ceased production.[40] Following the demise of Clark Foam, Surftech expanded by subcontracting to Cobra International, a Thailand-based manufacturer specializing in composite products for recreational and industrial applications.

Competitors in the industry responded to Surftech's increased production with talk of lost local jobs, exploitation of Third World labor, and inferior products. While conceding some truth to these claims, Warshaw observed that they also contained an element of "propaganda." He cited one respected surf journalist who found Cobra International's Bangkok factory "clean," "efficient" and "well-run," and its workers "fully insured" and "making above-average laborer's pay." On the subject of exploitation, Warshaw commented that surfers had long been buying wetsuits and clothing made in Asia without any qualms.[41]

Capitalism demands growth, and the big surf corporations expanded into retail and acquired new brands at a rapid pace in the first decade of the new century. Quiksilver, for example, bought Hawk and D C (skateboarding), Raisin and Leilani (swimwear), Lib Technologies, Gnu and Bent Metal (snowboarding), and Rossignol (skiing). Not all these acquisitions were successful. Rossignol cost $550 million and increased Quiksilver's revenue over the next twelve months from $1.3 billion to $1.8 billion. But it also loaded debt, which rose to almost $1 billion, up from under $200 million, and reduced profitability. News of the purchase thus saw Quiksilver's share price plummet almost 20 percent.[42] Quiksilver's board quickly realized that Rossignol undermined the company and agreed to sell the ski brand. But the global financial crisis limited potential buyers, and the final sale achieved a mere $37.5 million. Quicksilver's shares tumbled from $8.66 to $1.10 on news of the sale.[43] In 2009 Quiksilver restructured, retrenching over 500 staff, reducing salaries, and closing nonperforming stores.[44]

An internal contradiction in the culture compounds the current crisis in the surf industry. In "Unresolved—and Unresolvable?—Tensions" (below), I describe surfing companies nurturing irreverence and antiestablishment sentiments (as evident in advertising campaigns such as Gotcha's "Don't Surf" in the 1980s and Volcom's "Youth Against Establishment" in the 1990s). Such sentiments are unsustainable in dynamic social environments and in economic systems that demand perpetual economic growth. For example, it is difficult to see how Volcom could keep its "Youth Against Establishment" slogan after being bought by Kering, a French-owned and establishment women's fashion company.[45] Against this background, Warren and Gibson propose that "the commercialization of surfing [has] perhaps reached its limits."[46]

Workers and Aristocrats

Fashion, style, taste, language, and localism contribute to cultural identity, and it is not unreasonable to expect cultural practices to conjoin producers and consumers and workers and capitalists in a relatively passive form of symbolic order.[47] At least one cultural insider believes that wealth generated by surfing has not changed social relationships: "If you go down to the pub [at Torquay], you'll still see [Quiksilver's Alan Green] having a beer with the plumber, or [Rip Curl's] Brian [Singer] having one with the gardener, who probably used to be the dope dealer ten years ago. We're like family."[48] Nonetheless, even outwardly harmonious personal relationships cannot conceal material realities. Workers and capitalists in the surf industry may ride the same waves, but few of the former enjoy material prosperity and real independence. In this section I highlight the conditions faced by three classes of workers in the surf industry: shapers, free surfers, and professional riders.

SHAPERS

Carcinogenic dust, chemicals, and glues make the production of surfboards and wetsuits dangerous occupations.[49] Occupational safety legislation may remove some risks, but ultimately the health of workers depends on the relations of production—and these are purely capitalist. Although the surfboard is the most "essential" piece of equipment, historically it has always been "the least profitable" and has been traditionally manufactured locally to meet local demands and conditions.[50] Today, surfboard manufacturing is virtually the last vestige of the early backyard operations, and survives in a "state of precariousness."[51] According to Warren and Gibson, local surfboard manufacturers confront numerous issues, including competition from mass production in Thailand and China, a transition from slow, labor-intensive, hand-crafted (shaped) boards to computer-aided design, and concentrated power in the hands of discount retailers and surf superstores.[52]

FIG. 15.1 Paul Zarifeh, Seventh Wave Wetsuits: "You can't take on $400 [million] companies; our focus is performance wetsuits, and we have one shop, one factory, and [we] sell online." Credit Derek Morrison.

Shapers traditionally cut and sanded boards to form from polyurethane foam blanks, which they covered with fiberglass and resin to given the board strength and make it waterproof. Manufacturers began experimenting with automated assembly-line production in the 1960s, employing molds, shaping machines, chopped-glass appliers, and other techniques to mass-produce so-called pop-out surfboards. However, limited technology and the social relations of production between shapers and riders initially undermined automation. Describing the surfboard as "part of the shaper's soul," master craftsman Maurice Cole refers to the highly "personal" properties of boards which draw riders and shapers into intimate relationships where the former "trusts" the latter to produce a highly "functional piece of art."[53] Warren and Gibson classify the traditional relations of surfboard production as "a tightly constrained form of bespoke manufacturing" in which workshops produce "small volumes (often between 300 and 600 boards per year), employ few people (or are sole traders/partnerships) and invest time and energy into maintaining strong relationships with loyal local surfers." Reinforcing the "family" relationships described above, Warren and Gibson stress that the surfing industry places a premium on "individual reputation."[54]

Notwithstanding these relationships, competition and the opportunity to produce for a mass market, especially "beginners and tourists" in the major surf centers who wanted a "user-friendly" board that they can ride immediately, encouraged surfboard manufacturers to develop technology.[55] In the 1990s new materials, notably polystyrene, and new technology based on computer-assisted design programs, combined with computer numerical control machines, finally allowed automated production.[56] Advanced manufacturing processes forced down the cost of entry-level boards to a point where they are now little more than disposable items.[57]

Shapers also have to negotiate with the larger corporations for access to retail space under conditions in which surfboard sales are of minor importance compared to surf clothing that provides the big retailers with most of their income.[58] Not surprisingly, the complaints are long and steady. One manufacturer reports retailers offering a litany of excuses as to why they can't pay for boards already sold, including having to pay the big corporations first.[59] Some small producers responded by organizing into collective-type arrangements. In the early 2000s, leading Australian shapers, including Darren Handley, Maurice Cole, Simon Anderson, and Murray Bourton, formed BASE as a strategy to achieve economies of scale and efficiencies, and to counter cheap imports. In 2012, the Australian Taxation Office closed the company's doors: BASE had debts of over $5 million.[60] In addition, some shapers complain that the big corporations prevent them from displaying their logos on surfboards. "We make the boards for [professional] surfers, pay them to ride our boards," says Maurice Cole, "and then clothing companies won't even let us put our stickers [logos] on the board."[61]

The automation of board production forced hand shapers into "a more peripheral role in many workshops."[62] Shapers "negotiate insecure working conditions (seasonality and long periods of no work are common), fluctuating wages and uncertain futures." In the words of one, the once forty-hour-week norm "now . . . might only be twenty hours," and "it's almost unheard of to find a permanent hand-shaping job."[63] Surf and weather conditions also determine labor demands. One shaper refers to "nervous November" and the anxious wait for orders in the lead-up to summer.[64]

Shapers have no industry association to organize training or professional qualifications, to ensure workplace safety, or to forge career pathways.[65] Flexible work practices in the surf industry may give workers access to the surf and, by extension, a semblance of command over the conditions of work, but shapers reject any notion of "lifestyle time" associated with casual work.[66] As one shaper put it, the idea that down time allows surfing is "a joke"; down time means no income.[67]

Like most industries, surfing supports an aristocratic class of worker. Surfing's aristocrats are free surfers who travel to the best and most exotic breaks, where they are variously photographed or filmed wearing, riding, or using sponsors' products. Free surfers illustrate a key feature of the political economy of surfing: wealth does not derive solely from ownership of the means of production and control over wage labor. Ownership of aesthetic ingenuity and the ability to create and mobilize cultural authenticity is a critical source of wealth. As Hollywood's failure to penetrate surf culture illustrates, the market within surfing culture is sophisticated and discerning. The ability to read the market is a prerequisite for financial success. In the late 1960s, most observers predicted that the commercial value of Jeff Hakman would plummet following his arrest for illegally importing marijuana into Hawai'i. But Duke Boyd recognized Hakman's real aesthetic worth: his uniquely smooth surfing. He recruited Hakman into the Golden Breed stable to give the fledgling company credibility. The strategy worked. Irrespective of his social standing in the wider community, Hakman remained a respected cult figure.[68]

Many free surfers begin their careers on the professional circuit that remains the principal means of exposure to potential sponsors. (Paradoxically, the surfers most in demand for editorial work are the top echelon of professional competitors, but scheduling conflicts, exclusive contracts, and high asking prices often preclude them from participating in pure photographic or filming trips.) Once recruited, and having established the "right image," often countercultural (see below) or retro, free surfers lead charmed lives. In 2011, Red Bull sponsored Ian Walsh to surf in Indonesia (twice), Fiji (twice), Mexico (three times), South Africa, Namibia, and the northeast coast of the United States. None of these surfaris involved competing. He also traveled to Bulgaria to work on a documentary about surfing in the Caspian Sea.[69] Little wonder that Walsh is "stoked."[70] Presumably, so too is free surfer Dane Reynolds. In 2013 he reportedly earned $3.5 million, making him the second-highest remunerated surfer that year.[71]

PRO SURFERS

In the 1970s a group of sports-minded surfers established a professional tour in the belief that it would offer them an economic avenue to eternal hedonism.[72] The reality was somewhat different, as surfing icon Mickey Dora predicted at the dawn of the professional era when he warned that "Wall Street flesh merchants" will "call the shots, collect the profits," and force surfers into "total subservience."[73] A plethora of cases confirm Dora's prognosis. For example, a few months after finishing second on the 1983 tour, Wayne Batholomew's principal sponsor demanded he retire, relocate to the company's headquarters in Torquay, and contribute to the company's corporate development. He refused, and Quiksilver withdrew his AU$25,000 annual sponsorship.[74]

Professional surfers earn a mere fraction of the money commanded by professional golfers, boxers, and tennis players. In 2014, contest earnings on the Association of Surfing Professionals (ASP) Men's World Championship Tour ranged from $90,500 for twenty-ninth place to $431,500 for first place.[75] Corporate sponsorships swell the earnings of the top echelon to over $1 million, and a few in this group constitute their own "brands" that are "more potent than the companies they represent."[76] But for those outside the regular place-getters, or those who compete on the second-tier World Qualification Series, the circuit means hard labor and perpetual struggle.[77] Surfing journalist Tim Baker likens professional surfers to "logs . . . on the furnace of surf commerce" whose role is to "keep the tills ringing." And there is "no shortage of hungry workers to stoke the furnace."[78] With regard to sponsorships, surfing journalist Nick Carroll defines surfers as "contractors rather than company employees," and notes that their "contracts rarely if ever include any health insurance," and leave surfers to "organise their own superannuation, income insurance and other financially protective measures."[79]

It is not uncommon for surfers to lose sponsors and compete without financial support. Bede Durbidge competed without a sponsor for most of 2007 after Billabong dropped him from its team. Durbidge took out a second mortgage on his home, and estimated that it cost $80,000 to compete on the tour. He won the last event in 2007 and finished the year fifth, which secured him another sponsor, MADA (a clothing company). But it was a short relationship: MADA went into liquidation during the global financial crisis and left Durbidge without a principal sponsor.[80] In 2013, Rip Curl dumped Ricardo Christie, and he turned to crowdfunding to finance participation in the Qualifying Series; he subsequently qualified for the elite World Surf League in 2015.[81]

Unresolved—and Unresolvable?—Tensions

Two enduring issues have shaped, and continue to shape, the material relationships of surfing: commercialization and codification. Many surfers regard their pastime as an alternative lifestyle and a way to commune with nature, and in these contexts commercialization and the codification of surfing into a competitive sport are the antitheses of the culture. In this section I analyze these two issues as a paradox in surfing culture.

COMMERCIALIZATION

In the 1950s, surfers were at the forefront of consumer reactions against the blandness and conformity of standardized mass production. Surfers forged new fashions, styles, and products that enabled them to express their individuality and distinctiveness. As noted above, small operators produced for this market, and some established themselves as credible surf brands. As they grew, a number of these brands—notably, the American labels Hang Ten and Ocean Pacific (better known as OP)—attempted "to break into the mainstream market" and sell surfing style to the mainstream culture via department stores. But such expansions proved to be short-term affairs: as soon as surfing brands became popular with nonsurfers, surfers stopped buying their products.[82] It was an important lesson in cultural authenticity and brand credibility for companies involved in producing for niche markets.

In the 1970s, the counterculture, an amalgam of alternate, typically utopian lifestyles and political activism, reinforced the lessons of cultural authenticity and brand credibility. Harvey describes the subcultures of this period as explorations into "individualized self-realization through a distinctive 'new left' politics, through the embrace of anti-authoritarian gestures, iconoclastic habits (in music, dress, language and lifestyle), and in the critique of everyday life."[83] Soul surfing—riding waves for "the good of one's soul"—articulated this new politics and social critique, and conjoined surfing with the counterculture.[84] Visual representations of soul surfing, and its associated "images of communal living, country farms, vegetarianism, ritualistic inhalation of the herb, yoga, meditation, and the majestic poetry of uncrowded light and space," appear in a number of period surf films, including *Hot Generation* (1967), *Evolution* (1969), *Pacific Vibrations* (1970), *Sea of Joy* (1971), and *The Morning of the Earth* (1972).[85]

Some scholars identify the counterculture as a turning point in capitalist modes of consumption, production, and distribution.[86] John Clarke and his colleagues note that "in many aspects, the revolutions in lifestyle were a pure, simple, raging, commercial success. In clothes, and styles, the counterculture explored shifts in taste which the mass consumption chain-stores were too cumbersome, inflexible and over-capitalised to exploit."[87] Meeting the demands of the emerging new consumers, with their insatiable appetites for novelty, perpetual stimulation, and authentic, sophisticated, and design-conscious products, meant continual innovation and fast production methods. Demands for novelty led producers to focus on aesthetic qualities and to constantly repackage and rename products. In the case of surfing this frequently leads to labels with an antisocial innuendo. Parawax, Waxmate, Mr. Zog's Sex Wax, Mrs Palmers Five Daughters, and Big Pecker Surf Wax are just some of the names given to the humble board wax. But consumer demands for instant satisfaction also created volatile markets and made planning for production exceedingly difficult.

In order to cope with volatile markets, advertisers changed their approaches to building their images and manipulating taste and opinion.[88] When Rip Curl put its first full-page advertisement—the dawning of Rip Curl surfboards—into *Surfing World* in 1969, the company's objective was simply to inform surfers of a new brand.[89] Today, "advertising is no longer built around the idea of informing or promoting in the ordinary sense"; instead, it is "geared to manipulating desires and tastes that may or may not have anything to do with the product to be sold."[90] "The Search," the fulcrum of Rip Curl's marketing strategy and a concept that the company tagged to its brand, offers a good example. According to the company's cofounder and co-owner Doug Warbrick, The Search articulates Rip Curl's broad philosophy of searching for "the uncrowded perfect wave, ... the perfect untracked powder bowl," and for the inner self— "what we're really achieving in life, and what our true values are."[91]

As well as a tool for producers and retailers to manipulate desire, advertising helps ensure company and brand recognition in competitive markets. Surfing advertisements highlight reputations for reliable and innovative products. Here, too, "The Search" is apposite: "If you're going to ... get into travel and adventure ... you need product that is functional. Stuff that really works. ... That is definitely one of our other quests—The Search for the best materials and technology to make products that really work when you're on the edge."[92]

Nonsurfing corporations were not shy in appropriating surfing images. Even at the height of soul surfing, capital boosted, incorporated, and exploited surfing's clean, refreshing, and sporting images.[93] From the 1950s, surfing complemented products concerned with body, health, and lifestyle, and became a highly visible signifier in twentieth-century promotional culture, appearing in magazines and newspapers, and on radio, television, neon signs, billboards, and posters.[94] In the soul-surfing era, advertising agencies inverted many negative images, such as the casual indifference associated with soul surfing. Surfer "Jimmy Peterson" (Bio-Clear medicated cream) symbolized the ideal middle-class Australian youth of the early 1970s. His tanned skin, lengthy blond-streaked hair, and casual form (nestling with his girlfriend) conveyed an image of simplicity and innocence rather than the scruffy, untidy indifference of the nomadic soul surfer.

But attempts by nonsurfing corporations to seize parts of the niche surfing market have invariably been short lived, as the experience of Hollister demonstrates. Hollister proceeded on the erroneous assumption that it could manufacture cultural authenticity. Abercrombie and Fitch launched Hollister—named after the fictitious merchant J. M. Hollister, who allegedly founded the company in 1922—as a strategy to sell "the sun-drenched spirit of California and the surf and soul of the Pacific Ocean" to a mainstream youth market living in the Midwest of the United States. Hollister surf shops sit at the center of this strategy. From the outside they look like beach shacks; inside, flat screens play live feeds of the surf at Huntington Beach, and potted palm trees, chairs, and surf magazines furnish lounge areas.[95] Tom Holbrook, from rival Quiksilver, gives Hollister stores an "A [for] . . . romance," and concedes that they convey authenticity even if that "is based on 'invented' history."[96] Yet in the notoriously fickle world of youth culture, not even Hollister could survive indefinitely. In 2014, Abercrombie and Fitch announced that in the wake of recession, and with a shift away from clothes emblazoned with logos and a new preference for disposable fashion among youth, it had decided to close dozens of surfer-themed Hollister stores and "reposition" the chain as "a fast-fashion brand."[97]

Even established sporting corporations struggled to sell surfing. Nike, the footwear and apparel company, for example, purchased Hurley in 2002 and launched Nike Surfing to sell board shorts, T-shirts, hoodies, and sweatshirts. The company opened three action sports stores in Southern California. A decade later, however, Nike returned surf products to its Hurley division. Like Hang Ten and OP in earlier generations, Nike belatedly recognized the "difficulties of entering into the realm of authentic surf brand."[98]

The commercialization of surfing has led some surfers to shun surf labels, in particular those of Rip Curl, Billabong, and Quiksilver.[99] After leaving his long-time sponsor Quiksilver in 2014, eleven-time world champion Kelly Slater blamed the recent financial declines of Quiksilver and Billabong on their decisions to publicly list, which he said had cost them credibility. Rather than tracking cultural trends, Slater said, Quiksilver and Billabong are more concerned about meeting financial targets than about their "DNA"—where and why they started, and their prime purpose.[100] Slater subsequently launched his own label, Outerknown, with designer and fellow surfer John Moore and investment from French conglomerate Kering. Discussing the new label, Moore offered some perceptive insights into the emerging market: "The surfing community . . . has evolved over the past few years and [is] looking for something [new]. Men and women . . . have grown up with surf brands, but the key is that they've *grown up* and their interests have evolved. Everyone dreams of a coastal lifestyle—what that surfing lifestyle represents—but they don't necessarily want to dress head to a toe like a surfer."[101] Perhaps not surprisingly, the pricing of the Outerknown range immediately drew strong criticism on Instagram where it was first publicized. One correspondent, who lamented that "my idol since childhood has now been tainted with these INSANE Louis Vuitton pricing[s]," asked "what surfer in his right mind would pay for this besides Beverly Hills poser clowns."[102]

Like commercialization, the codification of surfing into sport is an ongoing issue among surfers for whom the competition ethic, in the words of Australian pioneer surfer Bob Pike, creates "jealousies" and removes the "pleasure" from a pastime that should celebrate "communion with nature."[103]

SURFING SPORT

In the 1960s, surfers began forming new regional and national associations to endear them to the broader public; they also organized competitions to take their activity into the mainstream sporting world and as a means to bestow formal peer recognition and status. Initially, they appeared to have succeeded. Big capital and vested political interests flocked to the sport. Sponsors of the first official world surfing championships at Manly Beach, Sydney, in May 1964 included Manly Council, Ampol (Petroleum), and Trans Australian Airlines (TAA). In the mid-1970s a group of professional aspirants formed International Professional Surfers, the predecessor of the ASP, which governed the professional wing of the sport until recently, when it sold the elite men's and women's professional circuits to ZoSea Media, which rebranded itself as the World Surf League.[104]

Apathy, skepticism, doubt, and opposition greeted professional surfing. Even Graham Cassidy, a leading figure in the formation of the ASP, expressed doubts: "Deep in my subconscious I have this reluctance to be part of competitive surfing. I'm racked with these fears . . . that what I'm doing is going to take away from surfing the virtues that first attracted me."[105] Sections of the surfing press were equally unenthusiastic. *Tracks* editor Phil Jarratt admitted being "determinedly low key about pro surfing." While competitive surfing "gave us something to write about, . . . sucking up to sponsors didn't fit in with our image of the surfer as outlaw."[106] Certainly, the pro tour has not won the hearts and minds of grassroots surfers, who are not shy in voicing their opposition. "As soon as those assholes in the seventies tried to turn 'surfing the artform' into 'surfing the sport' surf culture suffered," complains Kit, a correspondent whose words echo the sentiments of thousands.[107] Correspondents Stuart Butler and David Shearer explain how contests have an impact on lifestyle and recreational surfers. Butler wrote after enduring a summer in which contests overran his local beaches. "All I gained from surf contests" this year, Butler protested, was "an increasing petrol bill, fewer places to surf, more crowds and more so called surf heroes dropping in on me."[108] Voicing his opposition to a proposed world tour event sponsored by Rip Curl in northern New South Wales, Shearer predicted "a month of total mayhem and disruption," and warned local surfers that they will wake up to find their beaches invaded by "dinky structures selling trinkets, loudspeakers, sirens and flabby music . . . , [and] the water filled with jetskis and cops clearing people out."[109]

Butler and Shearer articulate well the long-standing suspicion of, or outright enmity toward, commercialism and the mainstream within the surfing culture. As surf journalist Kirk Owers puts it, "Many [dedicated surfers] have an axe to grind with the surf industry, the pro tour, surf mags, surf schools or anyone else they feel is profiteering [sic] from surfing at the expense of their next wave."[110]

Conclusion: Surfing Culture in Transition?

By analyzing competition, economic growth, and the relations of production and consumption, a historical materialist approach to the political economy of surfing culture reveals complexity in a nondeterministic, dynamic capitalist social environment. While social complexity and dynamism are bulwarks against predeterminism and prognoses, demographic shifts and social trends alert us to potential changes in surf culture. A culture that previously cohered around specific ages, genders, and nationalities is now fragmenting.[111] Not so long ago, industry leaders believed that the surf would conjure an inexhaustible supply of consumers. Bob Hurley identified these consumers as "sixteen-year-old boys and girls who like surfing, skateboarding, snowboarding, punk-rock music [and] hip-hop music."[112] Bob McKnight, CEO of Quiksilver International, admitted that less than 10 percent of those who identify with surfing actually ride waves. Nonetheless, he insisted that the image is strong enough to capture millions: "[A] Generation Y customer might [only] go to the coast for a week during the year, [but] he wants to look like a surfer while he's there. And so he goes back to Des Moines [Iowa], and to him, he's a surfer—and you're not going to tell him any different."[113]

Today, cultural insiders observe both a proliferation of surfers—mothers, backpackers, middle-age riders of standup paddleboards—and a change in the lifestyles of the "obsessive 'core'" whose lives are becoming more diffuse with broader interests and greater options. Critically, few of these surfers are likely to "pin their image to a big brand."[114] Equally significant, official statistics show that not only has "participation in surfing dropped in the past 12 years," it has halved among youth in the important Australian market. Participation among the fifteen- to seventeen-year age group is the lowest of any age group—including the over-fifty-fives. The biggest single group of Australian surfers today is between the ages of thirty-five and forty-four.[115] Insiders predict that different companies will emerge in the future as the industry becomes "less identifiable, blurrier, more diffuse." These new companies will be "sleeker, more evasive," "able to hop across genres," and "have less interest in dominating surf culture."[116]

Recent debates over the respective lifestyles and performances of free surfers and professional surfers may also have implications for how surfing companies position themselves and how surfing culture develops. Traditionally, free surfers sold the most powerful images of lifestyle and progressive wave riding. Free surfers appeared in "tropical locales, only when the waves were right," and their lifestyle compared favorably to that of professionals who often competed in small, lousy waves and under judging regimes that rewarded robotic maneuvers.[117] Championing the influence of free surfing on performance, cult figure Craig Anderson ranks clips produced by free surfers far ahead of competition results. Anderson says that he "can't remember who won a couple of [world championship tour] events ago," but that he can always "get psyched" to surf by watching a DVD.[118] (Kelly Slater's recent 540-degree turn, of which 360 degrees were above the lip of the wave, performed during a lay day at a professional competition and disseminated via the Internet, further reinforces Anderson's view—as well as highlighting the importance, and the complexity, of digital communication in surfing culture.[119])

Yet free surfing lifestyle has not escaped critique. Many consumers well understand that "sporting companies, media and corporate sponsors carefully choreograph . . . images and narratives."[120] Moreover, the professional tour has proved adept at redefining progressive surfing by monitoring riding styles and trends, and adjusting judging criteria to reward critical maneuvers and radical styles. Even Anderson, who criticizes professional surfers for forcing moves on waves simply to earn points, concedes that occasionally a pro will find the perfect section on a contest wave and perform the most radical of maneuvers.[121] Of course, the emergence of progressive performances in contests is welcome news to surf corporations forced to reduce marketing budgets in the wake of the global financial crisis.

There will always be a surf industry. Surfers need boards, wax, leg ropes, board shorts, wetsuits, T-shirts, flip-flops, and shoes, and they want magazines and DVDs. Some nonsurfers will buy these products simply to "live the dream without getting wet."[122] And some surfers, caught by nostalgia, will support museums and books, DVDs, and magazines devoted to the past. David Harvey believes that the increasing pace of turnover in consumption and production, what he calls "the maelstrom of ephemerality," has had the unforeseen consequence of kindling "search[es] for historical roots" as individuals look for "more secure moorings and longer-lasting values in a shifting world."[123] It is fairly safe to say that relationships in the industry will remain capitalist for quite some time, but this in itself will neither reveal the precise shape of that industry nor resolve the struggle over cultural authenticity, which will forever endure.

NOTES

Many thanks to Rick Gruneau for his insightful thoughts and comments on an earlier draft of this chapter.

1. A vast literature defines and conceptualizes culture. Chris Jenks offers an accessible overview and introduction in *Culture*. See also Jenks, *Cultural Reproduction*, and Williams, *Sociology of Culture*.

2. "Career Opportunities," *Tracks*, February 2015, 54–70.

3. Harvey, *Condition of Postmodernity*, 346–347

4. Mark Stranger offers a particularly useful configuration of the surf culture industry as an inverse pyramid resting on the subjective experience of surfing. "The first level supplies functional commodities to surfers, such as surfboards, wetsuits, wax [and] legropes.... The next level up—one step removed from the experience—supplies ... lifestyle commodities such as travel packages, magazines and DVDs (which provide the means for communication with other surfers beyond the local community) and clothing, accessories and other tokens of identification. These signs are also marketed in the final level where the surfing image is sold to the mainstream as surf fashion." Stranger, *Surfing Life*, 196–197. Regarding surfing's worth, see Laderman, *Empire in Waves*, 134. Such figures "should be taken as a guide" (Stranger, *Surfing Life*, 188) given that only publicly listed surf companies open their financial accounts.

5. Marx, *Capital*.

6. Of course, there were industry antecedents. The Hawaiian surfer Duke Kahanamoku, widely regarded as the grandfather of modern surfing, is a good example. Kahanamoku's early travels effectively advertised the surfing lifestyle and drew attention to Waikīkī as an exotic tourist destination (Desmond, *Staging Tourism*). Later, Kahanamoku marketed surfing on billboards and in the cinema.

7. Kampion, *Jack O'Neill*.

8. Jarratt, *Salts and Suits*, 94.

9. Noll and Gabbard, *Da Bull*, 71. See also Jaggard, "Americans, Malibus, Torpedo Buoys."

10. Noll and Gabbard, *Da Bull*, 71, 85

11. John Severson, "In the Beginning," *Surfer*, January 1985, 110–113.

12. Gordon McClelland, "Scenes from the Life and Times of Bud Browne," *The Surfer's Journal*, Fall 1995, 30–51, 36.

13. Jarratt, *Salts and Suits*, 104.

14. Jarratt, *Salts and Suits*, 107.

15. Irwin, "Surfing," 144.

16. Jarratt, *Surfing Australia*, 92.

17. Jarratt, *Salts and Suits*, 110.

18. Brian Gillogly, "Surfing Sunset and Vine," *Surfer*, September 1982, 56–59, 58.

19. Wardlaw, *Cowabunga*, 45.

20. Warshaw, *History of Surfing*, 454, 456.

21. Warshaw identifies *Surf's Up* (2007) as the first culturally appropriate Hollywood surf film that "makes [surfers] want to go surfing." Warshaw, *History of Surfing*, 456.

22. In more recent times, many surf shops have become board shops, selling various combinations of skateboards, snowboards, wakeboards, standup paddle boards, and windsurfers—and associated accessories and fashions—depending on their geographical locations. Such cross-marketing is essential for economic survival.

23. Jarratt, *Salts and Suits*, 199–200.

24. Rose Jones, "Girls Surf Market Overview," *TransWorld Surf*, April 7, 1999, http://surf.transworld.net/1000003804/features/girls-surf-market-overview/.

25. Jarratt, *Mr Sunset*, 162.

26. Jarratt, *Mr Sunset*, 174.

27. Warshaw, *Encyclopedia of Surfing* (2004), 593.

28. Jarratt, *Salts and Suits*, 211.

29. Smith, *Welcome to Paradise*, 23.

30. Smith, *Welcome to Paradise*, 23.

31. Stranger, *Surfing Life*, 193.

32. Stranger, *Surfing Life*, 193; Joshua Gliddon, "Mad Wax," *Bulletin* (Australia), August 13, 2002, 20–24.

33. Gliddon, "Mad Wax."

34. Jarratt, *Mr Sunset*, 174.

35. Jarratt, *Salts and Suits*, 222.

36. Marx, *Capital*, 742.

37. Stranger, *Surfing Life*, 24.

38. William Finnegan, "Blank Monday," *The New Yorker*, August 21, 2006, 36–43.

39. Warshaw, *History of Surfing*, 467–468.

40. Surfboard shaper Randy French, who also manufactured sailboards (under the label SeaTrend), founded Surftech in 1992 in Santa Cruz.

41. Warshaw, *History of Surfing*, 468, 469.

42. Jarratt, *Salts and Suits*, 230–231.

43. Baker, *Australia's Century of Surf*, 252.

44. Eli Greenblat, "Quiksilver Still Riding the Downturn," *Sydney Morning Herald*, March 22, 2010, http://www.smh.com.au/business/quiksilver-still-riding-the-downturn-20100321-q03z.html. See also Andrew Warren and Chris Gibson, "All Washed Up: Have Surf Megabrands Forgotten Their Roots?," *The Conversation*, September 18, 2012, http://theconversation.com/all-washed-up-have-surf-megabrands-forgotten-their-roots-9620; and Warren and Gibson, *Surfing Places, Surfboard Makers*, 191.

45. Rebecca May Johnson, "Inside Outerknown, Kelly Slater's New Kering-backed Surf-lifestyle Brand," *Business of Fashion*, December 9, 2014, http://www.businessoffashion.com/articles/bof-exclusive/inside-kelly-slaters-new-kering-backed-surf-lifestyle-brand-outerknown.

46. Warren and Gibson, *Surfing Places, Surfboard Makers*, 191.

47. Harvey, *Condition of Postmodernity*, 347–348.

48. Butch Barr, quoted in Phil Jarratt, "Boys Town: Torquay," *The Australian Surfer's Journal*, Autumn 1998, 62–77, 76.

49. Warren and Gibson, *Surfing Places, Surfboard Makers*, 164–172.

50. Baker, *Australia's Century of Surf*, 233.

51. While international and national economic data pertaining to surfboard manufacturing do not exist, commentators generally agree that small to medium enterprises of less than five employees traditionally dominated board shaping and production. At a regional level, Warren and Gibson cite data from the Gold Coast, a surfing mecca in southern Queensland, which listed surfboard manufacturing as an AU$36 million industry. Warren and Gibson, "Making Things in a High Dollar Australia," 29.

52. Warren and Gibson, "Making Things," 29.

53. Regarding "master craftsman": Surfboard-making is highly gendered. See Warren and Gibson, *Surfing Places, Surfboard Makers*. Regarding the "personal" properties of boards, see Warren and Gibson, "Making Things," 34.

54. Warren and Gibson, "Making Things," 34.

55. Warren and Gibson, "Making Things," 36.

56. The new technology involves blowing polystyrene into preset molds and coating the emergent foam with polyvinyl chloride. See Warren and Gibson, *Surfing Places, Surfboard Makers*.

57. Warren and Gibson, "Making Things," 38–39.

58. Warren and Gibson, "Making Things," 40.

59. Warren and Gibson, *Surfing Places, Surfboard Makers*, 212.

60. "The Big Bang—or a Whimper?" *Surfing Life*, February 2012, 78–80.

61. Stranger, *Surfing Life*, 194. See also R. Dahlberg, "Industry Opinions," *Australia's Surfing Life*, June 2002, 104.

62. Warren and Gibson, "Making Things," 44.

63. Quoted in Warren and Gibson, "Making Things," 45.

64. Quoted in Warren and Gibson, "Making Things," 45.

65. Warren and Gibson, "Making Things," 43.

66. Evidence as to the existence of flexible work patterns in the surf industry is contradictory. Tak Kawahara, cofounder of T&C Surf Designs, reports that surfers "have to work" irrespective of surf conditions. Noll and Gabbard, *Da Bull*, 114. On the other hand, an employee of a surf company told Stranger that when he was hired, "the executive director [said] he expected to see me in the surf when it was good and not in the office." Stranger, *Surfing Life*, 195. Stranger interpreted this as part of the company's efforts to preserve its links with the foundational culture.

67. Quoted in Warren and Gibson, "Making Things," 46. See also Harvey, *Condition of Postmodernity*, 151.

68. Jarratt, *Mr Sunset*, 84.

69. Thorpe, *Transnational Mobilities*, 112.

70. Ian Walsh, "I'm Stoked to Be Doing What I'm Doing," 2014, Redbull.com, http://www.redbull.com/nz/en/surfing/athletes/1331575205471/ian-walsh.

71. Elliot Struck, "The 2013 *Stab* Rich List," *Stab Magazine*, October 2013, http://stabmag.com/news/the-2013-stab-rich-list/.

72. Booth, *Australian Beach Cultures*, 125–133.

73. Stecyk and Kampion, *Dora Lives*, 82.

74. Bartholomew, *Bustin' Down the Door*, 273–274. Professional surfing's governing body appointed Bartholomew CEO in 1999; he held the position for ten years.

75. Association of Surfing Professionals, "Men's World Championship Tour, Rankings," 2014, http://www.aspworldtour.com/athletes/tour/mct.

76. Nick Carroll, "The Questions We Face: Part Two," *Surfing Life*, June 24, 2011.

77. See the four-part series by directors Levy and Salomon on Redbull.com, *Qualifying: Road to the World Championship Tour* (2014/2015).

78. Baker, *Australia's Century of Surf*, 225.

79. Nick Carroll, "The Questions We Face: Part Two," *Surfing Life*, June 24, 2011.

80. "How Does the World #4 Pay His Bills?," *Surfing*, October 5, 2009, http://www.surfingmagazine.com/some-answers/how-does-the-world-4-pay-his-bills/. See also Luke Kennedy, "Off Contract," *Tracks*, March 2007, 29.

81. "Get Ricardo Christie Back on the World Tour," Sportfunder.com, April 20, 2013, http://sportfunder.com/projects/1346. Christie failed to requalify for 2016.

82. Stranger, *Surfing Life*, 192.

83. Harvey, *Condition of Postmodernity*, 38.

84. Warshaw, *History of Surfing*, 253–58.

85. Damien Lovelock, "Cult History," *Tracks*, April 1995, 114.

86. The counterculture coincided with what the regulationist school of political economy refers to as a crisis in the regime of accumulation and the transition from Fordism to flexible accumulation. Harvey, *The Condition of Postmodernity*, 125–172.

87. Clarke et al., "Subcultures, Cultures and Class," 67.

88. Harvey, *Condition of Postmodernity*, 287.

89. Jarratt, *Salts and Suits*, 104.

90. Harvey, *Condition of Postmodernity*, 287.

91. "Heli-Challenge," *Rip Curl*, August 10, 1999, http://www.helichallenge.co.nz/ripcurl.htm. Webpage no longer available; hard copy available from the author.

92. "Heli-Challenge," *Rip Curl*.

93. Booth, *Australian Beach Cultures*, 117.

94. Heimann, *Vintage Surfing Graphics*.

95. Josh Hunter, "How Hollister Co. Stole Surf," *Transworld Business*, August 8, 2008, http://www.grindtv.com/transworld-business/features/how-hollister-co-stole-surf-eight-years-after-abercrombie-fitch-invaded-the-surf-market-what-can-be-done-to-defend-against-them/#XJu9QE48OCAsQ4xl.97.

96. Hunter, "How Hollister Stole Surf."

97. Joann S. Lublin, "Abercrombie Plans to Remake Hollister Stores," *Wall Street Journal*, March 7, 2014.

98. Laylan Connelly and Lisa Liddane, "Nike Surf Products Folded into Hurley Brand," *Orange County Register*, November 27, 2012, updated August 21, 2013, http://www.ocregister.com/articles/nike-378933-hurley-surf.html.

99. Stranger, *Surfing Life*, 203.

100. Rebecca May Johnson, "Inside Outerknown, Kelly Slater's New Kering-backed Surf-lifestyle Brand," *Business of Fashion*, December 9, 2014.

101. Johnson, "Inside Outerknown."

102. Alex Workman, "Kelly Slater's Outerknown Has Landed," *Tracks*, July 16, 2015, http://www.tracksmag.com/kelly-slaters-outerknown-has-landed/.

103. Quoted in "Australia's Fifty Most Influential Surfers," *Australia's Surfing Life*, November 1992, 70–123, 88.

104. Tim Baker, "My Take on the New ASP/ZoSea Deal," bytimbaker.tumblr.com, October 7, 2012, http://bytimbaker.tumblr.com/post/33054943195/my-take-on-the-new-aspzosea-deal; and "RIP ASP, All Hail World Surf League," bytimbaker.tumblr.com, September 13, 2014, http://bytimbaker.tumblr.com/post/97335233755/rip-asp-all-hail-world-surf-league.

105. Phil Jarratt, "A Profile of Graham Cassidy," *Tracks*, December 1977, 16–17.

106. Phil Jarratt, "Reflections: Pro Surfing in the Olden Days," *Tracks*, May 1985, 12.

107. "DH's Tour (Forum)," *TransWorld Surf*, September 8, 1999, http://www.transworld.com/forums/Index.cfm?CFApp=10&message_ID=5166. See also "Surfers on Pro Surfing," *Tracks*, October 1991, 90–91. Webpage removed from TransWorld website; hard copy available from author.

108. Stuart Butler, "The Fear of Shame," *Tracks*, April 2011, 80. Nick Carroll observes that while there are more surfers than ever along Australia's east coast, high housing prices have forced many of the hardcore to vacate urban areas. There is now less fierce localism in the surf, which he describes as "strangely less intense" (Carroll, "Getting Richer, Getting Worse," *Surfing Life*, July 2015, 33–46, 42).

109. David Shearer, "David versus Rip Curl," *Kurungabaa* 2, no. 2 (2009): 81–83, 81, 83.

110. Kirk Owers, "Dangerous Ideas: Pro Surfing's Indy Future," *Tracks*, October 2014, 76.

111. Jack Tierney and Nick Carroll, "The Change You Won't Notice: What's Happening to the Surf Industry?," *Surfing Life*, December 2012, 37–38.

112. Ben Marcus, "Hurley Burly: Bob Hurley Looks Backward and Forward," *TransWorld Surf*, April 7, 1999.

113. Aaron Checkwood and John Stouffer, "Chairman of the Boards: Bob McKnight Believes in Surfing," *TransWorld Surf*, April 7, 1999, http://surf.transworld.net/1000003806/features/chairman-of-the-boards-bob-mcknight-believes-in-surfing/.

114. Tierney and Carroll, "The Change You Won't Notice." See also Emily Brugman, "Stop Ripping . . . Kook," *Tracks*, May 2016, 107.

115. Nick Carroll, "Lies, Damned Lies, and Statistics," *Surfing Life*, May 19, 2014, http://www.surfinglife.com.au/news/sl-news/11434-lies-damned-lies-and-statistics.

116. Tierney and Carroll, "The Change You Won't Notice."

117. Wade Davis, "Of Slackers and Shred-Borgs," *Surfing Life*, November 2014, 62–66.

118. Jed Smith, "Craig Anderson: The Inevitable Ascent of the Jesus Freak," *Surfing Life*, December 2012, 42–50.

119. Michael Roberts, "The Never Ending Ride of the World's Greatest Surfer," *Outside Magazine*, December 9, 2014, 60–63, 93.

120. Thorpe, *Transnational Mobilities*, 112.

121. Luke Kennedy, "Flight Facilities," *Tracks*, January 2015, 74–78.

122. Jarratt, *Salts and Suits*, 243.

123. Harvey, *Condition of Postmodernity*, 292.

16 / Soulful and Precarious:
The Working Experiences of Surfboard Makers

ANDREW WARREN AND CHRIS GIBSON

Surfboard manufacturing is an essential part of the multibillion-dollar global surf industry.[1] Not only do surfboard manufacturers supply consumers with the material means necessary for surfing, they provide subcultural capital to retailers and multinational surf brands that generate profit from surf-styled garments and apparel.[2] Initially drawing from centuries-old Hawaiian precedents, surfboard manufacturing only developed as a capitalist industry in the late 1950s.[3] Following convergence with Hollywood-inspired popular culture (film, television, and music) surfing became a fashionable leisure activity. A newfound popularity among Westerners produced a mass market for surfboard producers. Surfboard making, previously a do-it-yourself (DIY) hobbyist activity concentrated in backyard toolsheds, moved into factories and became full-time waged employment. Surfers found a way to sustain a living around pleasure.

In the early 1960s surfers scrounged enough financial investment, usually via social networks rather than banks, to fit out new commercial factories. A considerable number of ostensibly localized surfboard workshops were established in places where surfing was popular and increasingly a "way of life."[4] The production "hotbeds" were not the inner urban spaces of global cities, but rather prosaic suburban areas and coastal towns such as San Clemente and Santa Cruz, California; the North Shore of Oʻahu; and Sydney's Northern Beaches and the Gold Coast, Australia. From new workshops, board makers provided local surfers with customized, handcrafted products, tailored to prevailing marine environments. Shapers and glassers, performing the two primary labor tasks, used skills and techniques developed from a DIY scene. Close personal relationships were formed with surfing customers, who frequently returned to workshops for new orders.

Against the backdrop of industrial development, we explore the working conditions and wider social lives of surfboards makers. Rather than focusing on the contemporary situation in isolation, this chapter takes a historical approach. We draw out the significant features of the surfboard industry, tracing how these have been shaped, experienced, and contested by workers into the present. We are writing as geographers, and this chapter is conceptually animated by arguments emerging from two areas of our discipline—labor geography and cultural economy—and from the social sciences more broadly. Labor geography has its roots in Marxist political economy, but pivots against its perceived capital-centrism. Cultural economy theory is a reaction to orthodox approaches that studied economic phenomena in isolation from wider sociocultural forces.[5] Labor geography aims to scrutinize the changing nature of work, examining the capacity of working people to (re)shape economic landscapes and improve their material circumstances.[6] Meanwhile, cultural economy theory mobilizes ontological and epistemological questions about how to understand and conceptualize the relationship between culture and economy.[7] At a time when flexible labor markets and the terms and conditions of employment are fundamentally changing, our writing is thus part of a political maneuver to focus on the perspectives, values, and actions of workers rather than on firms, institutions, or the state. Of course, this does not preclude such important actors from analysis; it merely repositions them. The aim of this chapter is to contribute insights into how surfboard makers, a group of passionate craftsmen, balance work alongside lifestyle.

In the following section we elaborate our labor geography approach, situating its objectives against the realities of a growth in insecure, informal, and precarious work. A focus on surfboard makers as paid labor is then placed into dialogue with cultural economy theory. We conceptualize surfboard manufacturing as economic activity that is socially situated and culturally inflected. In the surfboard industry, meanings and motivations of work, spaces of production, and relations with customers are mediated by values, customs, and meanings attached to surfing culture.

After a brief overview of methodology, we present empirical results of research with surfboard makers, organized in two overarching sections. First we outline the craft-based systems of surfboard production around which an industry coalesced, and examine the working conditions engendered. Wages in surfboard manufacturing have always been paid by unit of production ("piecework"), not by the unit of time.[8] For many surfboard makers this mattered little, because work was plentiful and valued as a "soulful pursuit." After describing transformation in the surfboard industry, we analyze the pervasive systems of automated production. Representing a shift toward capital-intensive manufacturing, we discuss how working conditions have changed. In highlighting themes of subcontracting, dwindling working hours, rates of pay, and benefits, we argue that work in the surfboard industry increasingly constitutes precarious labor.[9] We also note countercurrents to the rise of standardized machine production, with a strong consumer movement returning to customized production and hand-shaping. Concluding the chapter, we consider several ongoing barriers facing surfboard makers. Traced to the "culture of the industry," such barriers include the absence of a centralized industry association to lobby retailers, suppliers, and governments on behalf of board makers; little provision of formal skills training; and a lack of succession planning.

Labor Geographies and Precarious Employment

A growing proportion of paid employment in advanced economies is demarcated by part-time or temporary contracts; weakened paid leave entitlements, health, and pension benefits; and declining levels of union coverage.[10] In Australia, an estimated 40 percent of the national workforce is now employed in insecure forms of casual, contracted, or project-based work, rising from just 15 percent in 1984.[11] The figures are closely echoed in the United States and the European Union. Precarious work has been precipitated by the evolution of economic globalization and neoliberal economic policies. Heightened working flexibility (hours, labor tasks, pay structures, mobility, and relations with employers), according to Jane Wills, is having "stark consequences for traditional models of trade union organization."[12] Collective bargaining is hampered by the spatial, emotional, and legal disconnection of employees from employers. For workers to challenge and contest the erosion of basic working entitlements, they need to focus on multiple and shifting targets. In this chapter we are interested in the experiences of a group of workers would do not exhibit solidarity or collective action via any trade union.

With cognizance of employment in other craft-based industries—from clothing and clocks to furniture and fashion—surfboard manufacturing is set against a backdrop of automation, standardization, and "global" geographies of (mass) production. Transformation to production has occurred in concert with moves to temporary, casual, and contract work. Precariousness denotes both the amplification of unstable, insecure employment, and new struggles and solidarities reaching beyond traditional models of trade unionism. According to Andrew Ross, the precarious nature of much paid work under contemporary capitalism offers a possible source of solidarity between disparate groups of workers.[13] Despite increases in precarious work, the lived experiences dealing with, and contesting against, short-term contracts, fluctuating wages, and uncertainty remain loosely implicated within labor studies.

Surfboard makers provide relevant insights into the experiences of workers as conditions of employment change and become less secure. Up until the 1950s, the labor of surfboard makers functioned outside the formal capitalist economy, highlighting the importance of feminist arguments that advance ontological understandings of labor as a dynamic social category, enrolling individuals, family, and communities in spaces of production/reproduction and paid/ unpaid human effort.[14] Surfboards were made in backyard sheds, DIY style, to enable surfing participation and enjoyment. Laboring in the contemporary industry for a wage remains an activity strongly influenced by cultural values and legacies established in a context of informal networks, backyard operations, and work structured around paid jobs. Culture powerfully shapes workplace relations in the surfboard industry.

Cultural Economy: Conceptualizing Work in the Surfboard Industry

Surfboard making has been strongly motivated by personal desires to create more functional products for surfing, rather than by financial incentives. Surfboard makers illustrate the relevance of engaging with workers beyond narrow identity categories such as wage laborer.[15] In this chapter, labor geography is placed in conversation with cultural economy to theorize the way cultural orientations of surfing feed into and shape surfboard manufacturing, labor processes, business practices, and industrial relations. The use of cultural economy

with developments from feminist economic geography that stress the
y of social constructions (of race, class, age, and gender) in configuring
g relations.

ause "the" cultural economy is most evident in certain sectors, such as
rts, entertainment, and tourism, it has become a general signifier of the
cultural and creative industries.[16] However, deploying cultural economy as a
narrow descriptor for the cultural and creative industries positions "culture"
as merely an economized component of post-industrial societies. In reality,
culture actively influences all economic activities, from decision-making about
work tasks to our consumption choices.[17] As traded products, surfboards en-
tangle regional identities, physical geography, leisure, creative design, and material production. Surfboard makers elucidate the synergies between so-called
cultural industries and manufacturing.[18] Indeed, manufacturing is an essential,
often ignored, element of cultural industries production, and surfboard makers
explicitly identify their work as being about "manufacturing things."

Our analysis in this chapter thus connects to the original theoretical thrust
of cultural economy: the understanding that economies are "neither separate
nor hermetically sealed away" from social, political, and cultural spheres.[19] Culture is not a passive reflection of material circumstances.[20] Shifts in economic
relations and making of new economic spaces never so much inculcate culture
anew as signal changing dynamics under a constellation of forces. Rather than
occupying abstract space somewhere "out there," economic activities, such as
surfboard manufacturing, are placed in their relevant contexts. Culture (like
history and politics) is acknowledged as a profound "shaper" of economic behavior, relations, and actions in the spaces of work.[21] We draw from cultural
economic thinking to trace the particular values, meanings, beliefs, and ethics
informing relations in commercial workshops and between surfboard makers.

In California and Australia, commercial surfboard manufacturing surfaced
within subcultural groups of surfers who, seeking legitimacy and a monetary
wage, began making and selling boards in local areas. Surfboard production
in Hawai'i has a much longer historical connection to traditional Polynesian
forms of crafting, dating back a thousand years.[22] In Hawai'i, too, capitalist
production only coalesced in the late 1950s, in a cultural setting where keen
surfers, often *haole* (foreign) immigrants, turned to making boards for others,
for cash.[23] Profit-driven production catalyzed as surfing converged with popular culture and a sufficient population took up the activity to create a viable
commercial market for surfboards. By this time, however, the approach, methods, and techniques related to surfboard manufacture were already in place,
instituted by surfers who had long made their own boards to enable personal

surfing participation. Personal passions, relationships, sporting competitiveness, and local waves define the profit-based capitalist version of surfboard making as much as prices, wages, and rents. Surfers pursued jobs in the industry as a way to maintain a particular lifestyle. Workers could put down their tools when waves were good and go surfing, because the culture of the industry made it acceptable to structure production around the rhythms of the ocean.

Economic matters such as profitability, rents, market share, and labor markets remain significant factors influencing working conditions in the surfboard industry. As Doreen Massey has urged, culturally informed analysis must not "float free of the [political] economic."[24] Rather, the argument is that the economic is socially situated and culturally inflected. The spheres of economy and culture maintain "specificities" but also intertwine.[25] Bringing labor geography and cultural economy into dialogue is an attempt to acknowledge the multiple identities of surfboard makers. Cultural economy encourages deeper thinking about the subjective positions of this group of workers, which is important in this chapter for conceptualizing worker's motivations and explaining why some self-exploit, do not see a need to collectivize, and endure precariously.

Research Methodology

Empirics for this chapter were taken from a broader research project examining the industrial development and contemporary conditions of the surfboard manufacturing industry. Between 2008 and 2015, thirty-eight commercial factories and 139 workers participated in the project. Research concentrated on the three main production hubs: Southern California (Los Angeles and San Diego), Oʻahu, Hawaiʻi, and Australia's east coast. In each of these locations surfing is highly popular and constitutes a substantial industry. Surfboard workshops across the three regions shared similarities in terms of commercial size, production levels, employees, and market geographies. The largest firms employed up to twenty workers, the smallest only two. A total of sixteen workshops (39 percent) exported internationally, with fourteen (37 percent) selling across national markets. Eight workshops (21 percent) serviced consumers within immediate regions. Workshops manufactured between two hundred and five thousand boards annually, with revenue ranging from approximately $145,000 to $3 million.

Research with individual workers commenced with guided "workshop tours." Designed as a form of participant observation, workshop tours were delivered by board makers and began with a walking tour through their workplace. Board makers explained production processes, use of tools and equipment, organization of space, divisions of labor, and personal aspects of work. Each workshop tour allowed us to meet individual workers, learn about their jobs, and establish a level of trust. Tours were initially led by a single worker, involving colleagues along the way. Depending on the physical size of factories, tours lasted between two and eight hours. Workshop tours were then supplemented with participation in surfboard making. Here the research adapted Michael Burawoy's extended case method, deploying participant observation alongside workers within and beyond the workplace.[26] Basic jobs (cleaning, sanding, unloading, carrying, storing, etc.) were completed collaboratively, with workers with technical tasks (designing, shaping, and glassing surfboards) closely observed so that workers could discuss the labor process in situ. Participant observation in workshops lasted more than a month in each region. Fieldwork diaries were used to document observations and preliminary findings. Contact was maintained with workers through return visits to factories and regular phone and email communication. Semistructured interviews with all thirty-eight workshop owners were also undertaken to provide additional information on workshop history, workforce, business challenges, and planning. While largely qualitative, the semistructured interviews posed questions that allowed quantitative sketching of a firm's production levels, marketing budgets, sales, turnover, and profitability. Interviews were recorded using a small handheld audio-recording device, with more than 650 hours of interview material captured.

An important final point: workers featured in this chapter are all men. While sharing diverse cultural and ethnic backgrounds, including Kanaka Maoli (native Hawaiians), the dominant male focus reflected the fact that not a single worker making surfboards across the workshops was female. Where women worked in factories, it was in administration and front office positions, reflecting (1) wider gendered discourses about the types of jobs suited to men and women, and (2) the gendered nature of Western surfing subculture more broadly.[27] Consequently, our empirical analysis relates to male workers, most from working-class backgrounds. Pseudonyms are used throughout to maintain the privacy of workers, their families, and workshop owners/managers.

A System of Craft-Based Customized Production

The labor process for hand-making surfboards has changed little since precontact Hawaiian times. In late Hawaiian society, specialized woodcrafters (*kālai papa heʻe nalu*) produced surfboards for *aliʻi* on a full-time basis. In a more contemporary context, shapers designed and planed surfboards from molded casts of foam, referred to as "blanks." Foam began to widely replace timber in surfboard construction in 1957 and dramatically reduced labor intensiveness.[28] Glassers (usually called laminators in California) covered finished foam shapes with fiberglass cloth (in sheets of varying density), then coated them in liquefied resin to achieve a watertight finish. Shaping and glassing were manual forms of labor involving highly attuned haptic skills: sense of feel and touch over foam and fiberglass, expert use of handheld tools (planers, sanders, surface form tools, and squeegees) and a sensitive eye for detail.[29]

In factories with higher production runs, additional jobs had devolved from shaping and glassing. Sanders performed the final stages of finishing work on shaped boards before they were glassed. Polishers cleaned glassed boards to ensure they were ready for collection. Sanders and polishers like Tony in Oʻahu commonly explained how they were "biding their time" performing more remedial jobs in anticipation of opportunities to shape or glass. Nonetheless, sanding and polishing were valued forms of labor in factories. Several busy workshops also employed full-time shop managers to ensure good customer service and organize business operations.

APPRENTICE, JOURNEYMAN, AND MASTER CRAFTSMAN

Occupational skills in surfboard making accrue gradually. No formal training environment or professional qualifications exist in the surfboard industry. New workers have traditionally been sourced from surfing communities, learning "the ropes with sanding or polishing duties," as described by Steve, a glasser in Southern California. Workplace hierarchies are based on experience, similar to a commercial kitchen. While not formally certified, board makers recognize different career stages: apprentices (0–4 years), early careers (5–9 years), mid-careers (10–15 years), and "journeyman" makers (15+ years). After some thirty years in the industry, personally making and supervising around 30,000 surfboards (shapers often number boards—meaning it is possible to quantify "expertise"), workers are recognized as "master craftsmen." In 2000, the International Surfboard Builders Hall of Fame was launched as a more formal approach to recognizing master craftsmen in the industry.

Handcrafted surfboards are labor-intensive products, usually personalized to individual customers. Customization is a ritualistic process tracing back to surfboard making's commercial beginnings. Mark, a journeyman shaper in Australia, explained:

> Customers come in . . . [we] talk with them about the style of board they're riding and what they are after. You develop an understanding of what sort of surfer they are. That's important. From this I design a board

using all the different elements that make it function: width, length, thickness, tail, fins, rocker. From those design features, when I get my hands on the blank I've got the board pictured in my mind. . . . Custom surfboards are the heart and soul of the surfboard industry because it's how you develop such great relationships with your customers.

Shapers, in particular, complete several different labor tasks: meeting with customers, designing new boards, and shaping the boards into material form. The same workers often exchange finished products with customers too.

The wider surfing identity of surfboard makers has commercial importance for workshops in two main ways. First, in craft-based production, board makers become intimately connected to final markets. Social interaction with customers in and out of the surf ensures regular feedback is provided on the performance of boards that need to match consumer expectations. Second, the personal surfing of makers helps ingrain and shape embodied knowledge on how various design elements complement certain waves. Physical geography seeps into custom surfboard making, and makers need an understanding of local surfing conditions. For instance, on Oʻahu's North Shore, where six participating factories were located, typical waves are large, hollow, and powerful. Hawaiian surfers require a unique design and style of board—longer, wider and more streamlined—compared to surfers riding smaller beach breaks in Australia or California.

For board builders, time invested in speaking with customers and personal surfing are important for both knowledge generation and the economic viability of factories aiming to produce high-quality cultural products. The subcultural credibility of "expert" shapers is attained over time. Overall, the subcultural credibility of board makers often translates into loyal commercial following. Local shapers become the symbolic craftsmen of the industry and custodians of surfing folklore. Board makers become deeply attached to their local surfing communities: members of board riding clubs, judges at surfing contests, and sources of information on new products and innovations.

Commercial viability of craft production was further supported by the high turnover of surfboards. In each region, avid surfers, who are in the water several times each week, commonly order two or three new custom boards a year. Surfboards cost between $500 and $1,200 depending on the design, size, and artwork. Custom board makers incentivize consumption by providing discounts for regular, return customers, often 10 to 20 percent over first-time customers.

In terms of output, experienced hand-shapers can complete four or five boards in an eight-hour working day. Such production numbers are rarely reached, however, owing to significant time investments required to talk over new orders with customers. Glassers can finish sealing a surfboard in under an hour, with preparation of materials and equipment adding additional time to the production process. Close relationship between workers and customers is what defines craft-based surfboard manufacturing as a distinctive form of commodity production.[30] In surfboard making, close, personal relations are a customary part of the industry.

WORK AND CRAFT-BASED PRODUCTION

Workers in craft-based workshops contested for (and maintained) suitable employment conditions by leveraging subcultural capital: attachments to customers, craft skills, surfing credibility, and expert knowledge. Wade, a shaper at a popular Australian label, described the agency created and maintained by workers in ostensibly small, endogenous firms: "No surfboard label has been able to monopolize the market. Waves break differently wherever you are in the world. It means you need a different design of board and different skills depending on where you are. For us [workers], we have the knowledge about waves, styles of boards and what our customers want. We come from that culture. It's a soulful process, hand-shaping, and the surfers who buy our boards absolutely get that. It's an art." Localized labor markets, slowly accrued haptic skills, and consumer preferences for "soulfully made" customized boards were important features of craft-based systems of surfboard production.

In surfboard workshops, wages were calculated based on the unit of production. The amount paid for each board shaped, glassed, sanded, or polished varied across the case study regions. Generally, hand shapers received $100 to $150 for a shortboard design (five to eight feet long), and $150 to $200 for a longboard. Glassers made around 75 percent of these amounts (on a per-board basis), but finished work in less time. Glassers then derived added income by completing colored resin tints, artwork, and decal work. Board makers had accurate information on the wages paid to fellow workers, including those employed in competing workshops. Historically, under craft-based systems of production, surfboard makers displayed an ability to directly and materially improve working conditions.[31] Specific tactics to affect change hinged on the size of the workshop and the seniority and expertise of individual workers. In most surfboard factories, workers could bargain directly with workshop owners. Actions were intended to achieve better terms of employment (permanency, longer contracts, or more hours) or working conditions (wage raises, health and safety improvements, or reconfigured divisions of labor).

A common strategy used in efforts to improve employment for surfboard makers was job-hopping (or the threat of job-hopping) between workshops. In popular surfing towns such as those on Australia's Gold Coast, San Clemente, Southern California, and O'ahu's North Shore, clusters of surfboard workshops were located in light industrial estates and beachside retail precincts.[32] Without use of signed contracts or agreements, workers had relative freedom to move workshops, particularly if they had gained a following for their designs and workmanship. Job-hopping in small workshops was an individual strategy for achieving personal aims. In larger workshops, a measure of informal collective bargaining was embraced by workers. Overall, more than two-thirds of shapers and three-quarters of glassers had changed workshops during the last five years, signifying a relatively high level of job mobility.

The most significant reasons for job-hopping were the chance to create working times more suitable to personal lifestyles, opportunities for a more senior role within a workshop (sanding to shaping for example), and ability to expand creativity, skills, and knowledge. Access to a pay increase ranked only fourth in importance, indicating the diverse motivations and high importance assigned to creative freedom that underpins surfboard makers' actions. Mitch, a shaper in his forties in Southern California, outlined the range of motivations informing his job mobility: "The first time [I moved] was about how I was valued. I was a junior shaper and the two older guys got all the creative freedom. I was doing stock boards. So I moved down the block and was second senior. But the factory was messy and disorganized. So this year [2012] I moved again. I'm going to be the lead shaper here when Bobby retires next year. Pay is really the same but I'm doing all different designs, which sparks the creative juices." In Australia, shapers also spoke about changing factories because, as articulated by Robert, a shaper in his sixties, they "wanted more creative freedom and time to surf." Board makers such as Joe in Hawai'i described job-hopping as a healthy practice because it stimulated creativity and helped to maintain a "passion and enjoyment" for the work. Most strongly associated with younger workers under forty, cross-firm mobility declined as workers aged and became more established.

Individual board makers from craft-based workshops also constructed working hours amenable to their personal lifestyles. For example, Chad in Australia and Dean in Southern California began work at 4:30 a.m., which allowed them to finish early and surf in the early afternoon when crowds were thinner. Jeremy and Pete in Hawai'i started work later, usually after 10:00 a.m., because it allowed them time to surf in the morning before taking their children to school. Such working times would be considered unusual for many occupations, but were standard in the surfboard industry.

The unique nature of the working day in the industry is a cultural legacy of surfboard making stretching back to the DIY era. When surfboard manufacturing became a profit-making enterprise, those employed in the industry continued to pursue time for personal surfing away from the workshop, often in the early morning or afternoon. Although factory owners and managers never considered this surfing activity by employees as part of the "real" job, the research and development accomplished during surfing resulted in innovative new designs, maintained interpersonal relationships with customers, and refined embodied knowledge, underscoring the financial viability of craft-based surfboard workshops. Such work (i.e., meeting with customers in the surf or trialing new designs), mostly performed outside the factory, is not incorporated into the sphere of waged labor.

Despite flexibility and freedom being "benefits" of the job, seasonality was a further test of stable, consistent wages. Quiet times for custom orders in California and Australia were during their respective winter periods. In Hawai'i, summer was slowest because waves were inconsistent then. During quiet periods, work declined to twenty or twenty-five hours per week. For six or so months of the year, weekly working hours could exceed forty-five hours. Shaping or glassing twelve to fifteen boards per week in busy times, workers earned more than $2,000. To counter seasonal fluctuations, some shapers also used their control over the custom labor process. Workers, particularly shapers, interacted with customers directly and provided the timeframes for the completion of boards. Customers were given standard delivery times of four to six weeks for handcrafted custom surfboards. To "smooth out" fluctuations in custom orders that corresponded to large wage variations, shapers adjusted the intensity of their labor. During a busy month in a large workshop in Southern California, lead shaper Dion had sixty custom boards on order, but he only shaped forty-eight of the sixty orders to leave himself a dozen as a "stockpile." The following month, when thirty-five new custom orders were received, Dion used boards he had stockpiled to maintain a consistent income. The cycle was often repeated to smooth out quieter periods of the year.

While shapers and glassers could regulate their labor, sanders and polishers had much less capacity to shift the speed of their work. They operated around the rhythms of the more prestigious shapers and glassers. Such workplace hierarchies illustrate the importance of intra-worker relations, as "senior" or high-ranking staff affect the employment conditions of the lower-ranked workers. Sanders and polishers illustrated how the performance of certain labor tasks positioned lower down a workplace hierarchy can constrain the agency of others.

Theorizing more broadly beyond the surfboard industry, scholars in labor studies and labor geography have consistently argued that one of the central benefits for union-represented workers is the ability to access information on employers.[33] Strategies for affecting change can then be tailored to combat management plans, such as proposed cutbacks, redundancies, restructures, wage freezes, and so on. Yet in craft-based custom surfboard workshops, the link between unionization and an informed labor force was compensated for by the nature of business operations. Employees had direct access to owners and shared respectful relationships. Individual workers had access to detailed information on sales volumes, income streams, and underlying profitability, which could be used to support individual claims for better conditions, working arrangements, or higher wages. In one example from a large factory in Southern California, three workers were able to use sales records over a three-year period to support a successful case for increased income.

The employment experiences and agency of surfboard makers was tied into the competitive dynamics of workshops. Under systems of craft-based production, commercial viability was maintained by producing high-quality, personalized products tuned to local waves, surfing styles, and consumer tastes. Workshops predominantly competed on the basis of specialized knowledge, customization, and quality, not over price and trying to achieve economies of scale.[34] In handmade, custom factories, workers' demands (for wage increases or unusual work times) weren't necessarily antithetical to the financial interests of the workshop. Board makers shared close relations with final consumers, helped attain customer loyalty, and became responsible and accountable for maintaining the profitability of the workshop. Generally, craft workers secured favorable flexibility matched to decent wages. Incomes were relatively stable and sufficient to support a family—as Tim, a shaper from Southern California put it, to "pay the mortgage and maintain the [surfer's] lifestyle." Nevertheless, in the last fifteen years, significant transformation has occurred in surfboard manufacturing.

A System of Automated, Standardized Surfboard Production

By the late 1990s an increasing number of "new" surfers mapped onto globalized surf retail networks. Encouraged by the economic success of the "big three" surf brands (Quiksilver, Billabong, and Rip Curl) surfboard manufacturers also pursued new growth opportunities beyond regional bases. By the early 2000s, computer-aided design (CAD) and computer numerical control (CNC) machines were being introduced to automate shaping. Under automated systems of production, designs were generated on CAD programs, which coordinated the movement of CNC cutting instruments. Widespread shifts to capital-intensive production boosted productivity and enabled precise design replication. The surfboard industry was transformed.

In total, thirty-two of the thirty-eight workshops across the three regions have switched to computerized shaping within the last fifteen years. In twenty-three factories, CAD/CNC technologies accounted for more than 90 percent of all shaping work. Jim, a workshop owner in Australia, described the logic behind workshop automation: "It became a business decision to expand my market. Customization is all very time consuming and with the average surfer I don't want all that time spent talking about a board. Things can be done more efficiently. Most surfers just need a standard design that will work in a variety of conditions. Automation and the computer open a lot more business opportunities." The motivations for shifting to capital-intensive, automated production were often financial. Workshop owners outlined ambitions to achieve international status for their firms, improving market share and profitability. The prevalence of automated production has caused the surfboard industry to become less like an artisanal craft-based industry and more like other mass-producing forms of capital-intensive manufacturing. Workshop owners seeking to access burgeoning beginner and tourist markets initially embraced automated technologies to upscale volume and deliver boards to retail stores in high-rent locations proximal to popular surfing beaches.

Comparative economic analysis between craft-based and automated production revealed only a slight (5 to 6 percent) increase in profit margins. Real benefits of automation were in the potential to capture greater market share and increase sales volumes via surf retail dealings. To improve retail exposure, workshop owners used loans to finance costly machinery. Marketing budgets expanded and workshops were refitted. Supply deals were also reached with corporate surf brands that aggressively expanded retail ownership in the mid-2000s. The place association of California, Hawai'i, and Australia in global surfing culture became helpful for selling surfboards into emerging markets such as France, Portugal, Spain, Brazil, Chile, Japan, and South Africa, among others.

Integration of automated systems of production in the form of CAD/CNC technologies allowed production to be streamlined, opening opportunities for accessing general mass markets. As articulated by an owner in Australia: "People that just want to get in touch with the culture, how are they going to get a surfboard for little Johnny? They don't necessarily need to take my time asking for measurements and designs. It's all very time-consuming. I've tried cutting that out and struck up a relationship with a local retail chain, which sells my boards in their shops off the shelf. I increase my market and generate more sales." Alteration of the labor process was predicated on changing relations between makers, customers, and local surfing breaks. Close interaction between shapers and customers directly at workshops was being replaced with online ordering and trade from retail outlets. Added to this was a select group of export-oriented factories in each of the three case-study regions that had begun subcontracting CNC operators in final markets. Rather than globally shipping finished surfboards to retailers at high cost, workshops emailed CAD files with generic designs manufactured on a CNC machine (in an agreed quantity) by the subcontractor. A wholesaler then delivered labeled boards to a network of local surf retail stores. While the technical, creative labor of designing surfboards was retained in Australian and American factories, the manufacturing was performed elsewhere, offering a financial saving on labor and transport.

While glassing could not yet be automated, these jobs were also transforming. In the last decade twenty-five of the thirty-eight workshops examined (66 percent) had outsourced their glassing to contracting firms in a classic example of flexible specialization.[35] Specialized glassing factories had become enrolled in competitive bids for work as shaping workshops no longer had to directly or continually support the wages and entitlements of glassers. A degree of financial risk was spread by disintegrating and subcontracting production tasks. Significantly for this chapter, transformation to surfboard manufacturing was altering employment conditions.

PRECARIOUS EMPLOYMENT: WORKING IN AUTOMATED
SURFBOARD WORKSHOPS

In workshops where automated systems of production had become dominant, new workers in the industry began careers learning CAD programming, machine shaping, and online ordering systems. In these cases, manual tools and development of embodied, haptic knowledge were not a priority. Shapers, in particular, had experienced the most acute changes to their employment conditions. Downsizing and reorganization of shaping labor were widespread. Craig, a shaper in Southern California, described the emerging situation: "The technology is quite advanced so they want workers who know how to program and operate it all. My job now is to make the odd custom board with my best designs handed over for replication. . . . They [owners] love it because it's a standard, generic thing coming out; 90% of our boards are computer shaped. It's really changed the job. I can see a time when shapers will be out of work." Turning shaping into a research and development (R&D) role was arguably one constructive adaptation to computerized production. While hand-shaping could be tiring, physical, and messy work, with long production cycles and high labor costs, for those who were not laid off, computerized shaping appeared to offer a more favorable experience for workers and workshops alike.

Indeed, several workers explained how they had assumed CAD/CNC would be used to meet the demands of entry-level and intermediate surfers for easy-to-ride designs, while hand-shaping would continue meeting the needs of the "core" surfing market for customized products. In reality, workers employed in factories using automated production quickly began experiencing undesirable changes to the tenure and conditions of their employment. At the forefront of concerns was the advance of subcontracted, casualized, irregular, and discontinuous work. Precarity was a consistent experience across automated workshops. As expressed by Peter, a shaper in Southern California: "Summer [June to August] and a month or so before Christmas are still busy. You'll work forty-five or fifty hours a week.... The rest of the year is slow now. I scrape together what I've saved. But employed casually I wait to get a call for work. I pick up a few weeks straight. Then it's a week without much work.... I do get worried. The shaping machine seems to mean less work for hand shapers. It's changed the work for everyone else too." Workers explicitly connected their precarious employment to the pervasiveness of automated systems of mass production. Precarity left board makers uncertain about when they were working, what their incomes would be, and how their lifestyles could be maintained.

Dean, working on O'ahu's North Shore, had twenty-four years' shaping experience and summarized his employment experiences through the recent era of automation: "You're permanently casual and have to subcontract yourself around. I have to get work from other factories and I don't have a good idea what my pay check will be this month or next. I wait for a call.... Last week I worked forty hours. This week it's Thursday afternoon and I'm at twelve hours.... Shaping machines get lots of work but we are running out of it.... I wouldn't suggest this [job] to anyone."

While the intensity and hours of work in the surfboard industry had always been seasonal, the casualized, contract, and irregular terms of employment—even within the busiest times of the year—were new experiences. In contrast to the cross-firm mobility uncovered in craft-based workshops, for shapers employed in automated firms job-hopping did not lead to a discernible improvement to working lives. For example, in "contracting around," Dean had accepted casual work in two other workshops where hourly pay was lower than at his primary job. The work was several steps down in seniority, and Dean considered it incommensurate with his levels of experience and skill.

In living with precarious jobs, shapers and glassers consistently expressed anxieties about meeting costs of living and planning lifestyles around fluctuating incomes. There were other noticeable conditions of precarity too: fears of losing jobs altogether and an absence of health care (especially for workers in California and Hawai'i). After many years in the industry, aging workers commonly suffered muscular and skeletal pain, and chronic respiratory illnesses.[36] In many workshops, employees were paid in cash, which had made it very difficult to apply for credit or a loan. Darren, a glasser in Australia, explained: "I was told I'm now going to be employed as a subcontractor . . . so it's my responsibility to pay taxes and my super [pension]." Precariousness was now part of the surfboard industry's employment terrain.

Incomes for workers in automated workshops had been stagnant for some time. As Michael, a shaper in Southern California, explained, "We've been paid about the same amount for the last decade. No increase." The sense of frustration arising from the casual, discontinuous nature of work was further described by Justin, an Australian shaper: "We call it fluffy talk. Hear it all the time now: 'Ah no work the next couple of days, might be Wednesday. Go surfing, or take the girlfriend for a trip.' It's bullshit, because that costs money. . . . I subcontract around now to pick up enough work. Honestly, I don't feel like my skills are valued much anymore." As workers increasingly contracted between factories, further complications arose when they committed to blocks of work with one workshop, only to be offered a longer stretch or better pay by another. Not wanting to "pack up and burn bridges," as articulated by Cameron, a shaper in Southern California, workers often met original obligations, only to miss out on longer stretches of work and a stable period of income.

For their part, sanders gained the most continuous work under automated systems of production. After CNC, shaping foam blanks required additional fine hand-sanding before boards were ready for glassing. Sanders completing this work were frequently discussed in derogatory terms, called "scrapers" and "production shapers" by conventional hand-shapers. Most sanders had begun careers in the industry after CNC/CAD production became common, and their labor was thus considered by older, more experienced shapers as being less skillful, uncreative, and of lower value. Production shapers usually could not perform the full range of tasks involved in surfboard making, from design through to shaping a finished board. Nonetheless, their work was important to the automated manufacturing process because the CNC cutting blades left irregular patterns, indentations, and imperfections on the foam that would adversely affect performance and appearance.

The widespread rollout of automated systems of production had left shapers most fearful for the future of their jobs. In popular coastal towns—Byron Bay in Australia, O'ahu's North Shore, San Clemente in Southern California—board makers were being priced out of local communities, unable to purchase a home or afford rent in suburbs proximal to work because property prices had become excessive while their income stagnated. The rollout of automated production systems influenced worker's personal lives in other unforeseen ways too. Several workers in the industry spoke of relationship breakups and financial hardships, which they blamed on the growing irregularity of work and future employment uncertainty. In several cases, anxieties were smoothed over by support from higher-earning partners. Most workers, however, were from working-class backgrounds and the major breadwinners in the household. Overall, CAD/CNC production was interpreted by workers as having negatively affected their livelihoods, limiting their power and ability to affect positive change.

WORK, AUTOMATED PRODUCTION, AND FUTURE PROSPECTS IN THE SURFBOARD INDUSTRY

Between the 1960s and early 1990s, an industrial context of highly endogenous, customized production provided a level of job security for surfboard makers. A laid-back, antithetical attitude toward workplace relations was not a significant problem. However, when automation arrived during the 1990s, informal working cultures exacerbated the insecurity of employment. The lack of workplace organization, legally binding agreements on job conditions, and formally recognized qualifications constrained the agency of craft-based surfboard makers. A path was smoothed to heightened precarity.

Despite the challenges facing workers under automated systems of production, there were attempts to effect affirmative change to employment conditions in the industry. In a large factory with twenty workers that machine-shaped 5,000 boards annually, two shapers and a glasser had secretly established a spinoff label as their work had become irregular. The three workers maintained casual employment while sourcing custom work "on the side" for their fledgling business, according to Mike, a shaper. The spinoff label helped successfully supplement the men's incomes for fourteen months. However, when the workshop owner uncovered its existence, the three lost their primary jobs. In another example, a shaper sabotaged a CNC machine. The factory owner had to rely on three shapers for a month while a cutting instrument was replaced, and a rare period of continuous work ensued. Such direct strategies by surfboard makers to contest the erosion of working conditions did have some success but represented temporary, fleeting victories.

Another strategy encountered among experienced shapers and glassers involved accessing high-paying, short-term contract work in emerging international surfing markets. During the slower Australian winter, Stu and Mike spent three months shaping and glassing in Indonesia, Japan, France, and the southwest of England. Several other workers based in California and Hawai'i also traveled from their home bases to work in Portugal, Spain, Japan, Peru, Chile, and South Africa. As commissioned fly-in "experts," workers were paid to design and craft boards to local specifications, also training inexperienced local makers. Guest shapers are often revered because of perceptions that their designs and workmanship are superior.

On the one hand, the emergence of international contract labor provided board makers with unique travel opportunities and a temporary income boost. On the other hand, short-term work overseas required turning over creative designs to foreign labels for standardized mass production. More worrying, work overseas was often illegally organized without appropriate working visas.[37] Subcontracting continues to be arranged using verbal "handshake" agreements. Yet again, the inherent informality of surfing subculture made it difficult for workers to legally challenge contracting workshops that frequently paid late or only a portion of amounts originally agreed. Rather than alleviating their problems, international contract work added new contours to the already-precarious labor conditions of board makers: precarity was exacerbated along new lines.

Ultimately, the surfboard industry is full of contradictions. Several owners spoke about the importance of hand-shaping and artistry in surfboard manufacturing, but were blasé when asked about worker's deteriorating employment conditions. Workshop owners praised hand-shaping as a soulful and creative form of work with important social and cultural value to surfing. Even so, during the research, eleven workshops had automated all of their shaping.

When workshop owners talked about employees, there was a sense of expectation that workers accept the tenuous nature of making surfboards for a living. As one owner said: "You know, you can't have too many expectations financially when you're coming into this. It has to start out as something you just want to do. It's a lifestyle. You should appreciate doing something you love. For me, there are a lot of people that come into the industry and need to be willing to take the vow of poverty [laughs], as we call it. Unless you get real lucky, you know, you should just follow your passion and enjoy the lifestyle." Interviews with workshop owners uncovered an unsympathetic view of worker's complaints about the nature of the work. Business owners circulated a discourse of board making as a "lifestyle choice" and "passion," consistently downplaying the legitimacy of workers' claims for improving job security and rates of pay.

A parallel exists between the experiences of work in surfboard manufacturing and other cultural industries such as tourism, media, entertainment, journalism, and academia.[38] Working in the surfboard industry was considered socially rewarding, but job insecurity and poor wages had become its darker side. Surfboard makers highlighted how technological change and cognizance of emerging global geographies of production generate different relations between workers, firms, tools, materials, products, and consumers.[39] Under automated systems of production, worker agency in the surfboard industry was disciplined, despite efforts to improve and reform employment conditions remaining visible.

There is, however, a bright spot for surfboard makers. Significantly, those six workshops resisting CAD/CNC automation and committing to hand-shaping custom products for more serious local surfing enthusiasts were financially outperforming most of the firms automating for general retail consumption. Craft-based workshops and workers differentiated themselves from standardized competitors. Reputations among core surfing consumers for producing well-made, customized products strengthened. Many local customers continued to value personalized products and close relationships shared with makers. Commercially, customized surfboards retain subcultural cachet, and this in turn relies on reputations associated with particular workshops, their skilled workers, and iconic surfing places (Snapper Rocks, Burleigh Heads, Trestles, Huntington Beach, O'ahu's North Shore, etc.).

Whether a return to customized production and revaluing of hand-shaping is substantial enough to provide workers with improved employment prospects is uncertain. Nevertheless, the trend shows the capacity for skilled, craft-based workers to help sustain market share and distinguish themselves and their wares from standardized, automated competitors. Surfboard makers emphasize the value of considering how cultural values, meanings, customs, and beliefs shape worker's experiences and capacities to achieve improved livelihoods.

Conclusions

This chapter has paired labor geography with cultural economy theory to examine the employment experiences of surfboard makers amidst industry transformation. Although affected by the dynamics of industrial change, surfboard makers have, to a certain extent, contested the reworking of employment conditions. Even so, workers' actions have not been universally effective or lastingly transformative. Agency fluctuates over time and space. Surfboard makers have both agency to reshape certain conditions of their work, but are also constrained in small workshop settings where production is increasingly automated and offshored, more work tasks are subcontracted, and close relations with customers have eroded. In consideration of the impacts of CAD/CNC automation on surfboard makers, we have advocated for a focus on understanding how such technologies alter relationships through the labor process, not just firm efficiency and profitability.

We have sought to go beyond narrow economistic visions of labor to analyze the experiences of workers in an industry continuing to undergo transformation. Changes in surfboard making are manifested in relationships between makers and customers, in the skills imparted through the labor process, in the integration of new technologies, and in the emergent global divisions of labor associated with offshoring.[40] Workers who participated in the research animate the conspicuous role surfing's subcultural legacies play in shaping industrial and workplace relations. In the surfboard industry, verbal "handshake" agreements remain the norm. The agency of board makers has been negatively affected by their own laid-back, antithetical attitude toward industry associations, formalization of skills training, and creation of a collective workers' union. Consequently, the working futures of surfboard makers are now precarious.

As more waged work in contemporary capitalist economies becomes casualized, contracted, and precarious, the job of labor studies and geography is to go beyond agency expressed in relations between unionized labor and management. Craft-based workers in the surfboard industry customizing products for primarily local markets demonstrate agency in relations with employers, fellow workers, tools, customers, and place. Subcultural capital, job-hopping, work slow-downs, and connections to consumers help leverage rewarding jobs anchored in iconic surfing locations. But equally, workers in the surfboard industry also face significant new obstacles to achieving materially rewarding employment now and into the future. Ultimately, we argue that analyzing the way culture shapes workplace relations provides valuable insights into the challenges and opportunities facing workers seeking to achieve positive change to livelihoods and lifestyles alike.

NOTES
1. Jarratt, *Salts and Suits.*
2. Warren and Gibson, *Surfing Places, Surfboard Makers.*

3. Surfboard makers explicitly identified their jobs as part of a manufacturing industry.

4. Waitt and Warren, "'Talking Shit over a Brew.'"

5. Barnes, "Retheorizing Economic Geography."

6. See, for example, Herod, "From a Geography of Labor"; Castree, "Labour Geography."

7. Lash and Urry, *Economies of Signs and Space*; Peet, "Culture, Imaginary, and Rationality."

8. Warren and Gibson, *Surfing Places, Surfboard Makers*.

9. Gill and Pratt, "In the Social Factory"; Kalleberg, "Precarious Work"; Warren, "Working Culture."

10. Ettlinger, "Precarity Unbound"; Wills, "Subcontracted Employment"; Peck and Theodore, "Labour Markets."

11. Wilson, "Precarious Work."

12. Wills, "Subcontracted Employment," 441.

13. Ross, "Life and Labour in Precarious Times."

14. McDowell, *Capital Culture*.

15. A similar argument is made by Rogaly, "Spaces of Work."

16. Scott, *Cultural Economy of Cities*.

17. Gibson, "Cultural Economy"; Warren, "Working Culture."

18. Pratt and Jeffcutt, *Creativity, Innovation and the Cultural Economy*.

19. Barnes, "Retheorizing Economic Geography," 558.

20. Amin and Thrift, "Cultural Economy."

21. Gibson, "Cultures at Work."

22. Finney and Houston, *Surfing: A History*.

23. Warren and Gibson, *Surfing Places, Surfboard Makers*.

24. Peck et al., "The Kilburn Manifesto," 2037

25. Sayer, "Critical Cultural Political Economy," 699.

26. Burawoy, "The Extended Case Method."

27. Warren, "Crafting Masculinities."

28. Warren and Gibson, *Surfing Places, Surfboard Makers*.

29. Paterson, "Haptic Geographies."

30. Fine and Leopold, *World of Consumption*.

31. Coe and Jordhus-Lier, "Constrained Agency."

32. Warren and Gibson, *Surfing Places, Surfboard Makers*.

33. Silver, *Forces of Labor*; Wills, "Subcontracted Employment."

34. Bryson, Taylor, and Cooper, "Competing by Design."

35. Scott, "US Recorded Music Industry."

36. Warren and Gibson, *Surfing Places, Surfboard Makers*.

37. For Australian and US surfboard makers, securing temporary work visas in foreign countries is a lengthy, complex process. Eligibility varies from country to country based on a range of factors, including age, qualifications, location, type of intended work, length of stay, and sponsoring employer. For US board makers traveling to Japan, the common approach was to apply for a work visa under the "Artist" category, which includes "craftspeople." For travel to the European Union (EU), US board makers need a written job offer by a registered firm, which is problematic in an informal industry. The company must prove

it had conducted a search of the EU labor market and had been unable to fill the vacant role. The EU work permit is also attached to the sponsoring firm and is not transferable to another employer. Thus, the majority of workers interviewed entered a foreign country on a tourist visa (staying less than three months) and did not indicate intentions to engage in paid work or declare income generated.

38. Kalleberg, "Precarious Work."

39. Kraft, *Stage to Studio*; Noble, *Forces of Production*.

40. Rogaly, "Spaces of Work"; Warren, "Working Culture."

17 / Branded Primitives

ROBIN CANNIFORD

The afternoon sun sinks, and I stand on the sand. There's no one out on the reef, but now and then waves approach and break. They peel right for 50 yards. It's [the surf] a little overhead, and the water is smooth. The tide is receding fast, though, revealing rubbery arms of kelp on the inside. I wade into the water and paddle out. As a smaller wave feels the peak, I see a familiar movement, like a bodysurfer. Then as another wave peaks, I see fins and I hear breath: two dolphins, three, more. They dive silently, then breach, all of them in the air. . . . I drop into a wave, and as I trim high I glance backwards to see them leap again. A surge of pleasure grips my body. . . . Between waves I watch them jump and jostle. I'm grinning. Then, as the warm spring breeze gently grooms another approaching set, they turn to face me and advance. I am still and silent. A few feet below the water, the dolphins slip beneath my outstretched toes. Light dapples their skins as they tilt their heads to eye me. As I get sucked over the falls, they take off. . . . End of day's effulgence fades from bright amber to dark red. The sea fades from blue to olive.

At face value, this diary extract from my field notes represents the idealized surfing experience: a magical encounter with "pure nature." Yet this encounter is as cultural as it is natural. This chapter questions how experiences of nature are constructed and harnessed to markets. Calling on archival, diary, and interview data, I argue that the iconicity enjoyed by the likes of Billabong, Quiksilver, and others is, in part, constructed through a branding phenomenon that connects nature to markets through the figure of "the primitive." This is a construction of nature that expresses the possibility of difference from modern cultures. Nevertheless, these narrative interventions that sustain brands harbor contradictions with ecological and political consequences. In particular, I suggest that contemporary deployments of the primitive as part of surfing's mythology illustrate a cultural inhibition of environmentally conscious marketing.

Nature and the Market

In this chapter, I take nature to be a construction of both physical geographies and cultural components as diverse as narratives, technologies, and value-making arrangements of all these multiple kinds of things—that is, markets. A useful way to consider how physical geographies are harnessed to those cultural components that constitute markets is through the concept of nature-culture assemblages.[1] Rather than carving up areas for knowledge creation where "natural things" and "economic things" are considered through different knowledge-making practices, this way of thinking about the world affords investigations of how nature and cultural economies are co-constituted through entanglements "of places, bodies, voices, skills, practices, technical devices, theories, social strategies," as well as the work of bringing these diverse kinds of things together.[2]

Market assemblages are characterized by fragility and contingency among their constituent elements. Put simply, linkages of technological things and linguistic acts, as well as natural features such as physical geographies and animals, are always subject to change and reconstitution into other forms.[3] It is here that the practices of marketing come into play. In short, the purpose of marketing, and branding, in particular, is to enhance stability and predictability within contingent market assemblages.[4] For the best part of the twentieth century, marketing was thought of as a subset of advertising practice, which claimed to enhance the desirability of products and services by establishing unique and consistent psychological associations as a way of firming up the position of products and services in the minds of target consumers.[5] Within a broader-reaching market-as-assemblage approach, however, the production of stability encompasses complex, nonlinear processes without starting or stopping points. More specifically, to enhance the functionality and stability of market assemblages, marketers build "allies," linkages between constituent things and institutions, that translate products and services within the practices of everyday life.[6]

This work encompasses multiple, divergent layers of activity that go beyond establishing psychological imprints on consumers' minds. Today, branding is a sociologically driven task of aligning a product within historical and material-cultural milieus. One practical approach to this task recommends instituting products and services as narrative stage props that allow people to live out fantasy lifestyles that attenuate their perceptions of social tensions and cultural failures.[7] Budweiser, for example, has been managed this way for some decades. Rather than seeking to install consistent psychological associations relative to its competitors, Budweiser's brand managers have manipulated the meaning of this product in order to appeal to waves of emergent crises in North American masculinity. During the industrial-economic downturn of the 1970s, Budweiser celebrated itself as the beer of the blue-collar worker. Once this tale became untenable, Budweiser subsequently latched onto 1990s slacker culture with its Frogs and Lizards campaign. Later, Budweiser celebrated performances of masculine mateship with its Whassup (1999) campaign.[8]

Over twenty years, Budweiser has radically altered its brand meanings, writing itself into American culture through narratives designed to salve emerging social issues, and rewriting when issues change or when consumers lose interest in the narrative on offer.[9] Underlying this position is the idea that people consume in manners that help them to live out particular narrative identities and lifestyles, and more specifically, that the narratives popularized at any particular moment are the ones that help to assuage cultural anxieties common to a target market.[10] This has led to the idea that marketing is not necessarily about competing in terms of product attributes, but in terms of the power of a particular narrative to maintain interest for consumers, and for this narrative to make a brand indispensable.[11] How does this assemblage perspective, and the narrative approach to marketing, play out in surfing culture?

There's always been plenty in surfing's favor as a marketing phenomenon. Combine the pleasure of the beach with minimal, mostly maintenance-free equipment, throw in some bushy-bushy-blonde hairdos, and there you have a recipe for simplicity and sexiness. Photographer Michael Dweck, who eyed Montauk, New York's, beachgoers for a summer, described surfers as "sexy and tribal," his photographs revealing surfing as a world within a world where pretty young people enjoy the beach as a place of embodied freedoms and group narcissism.[12] It would be fair to say that surfing has always been able to establish strong psychological imprints amongst consumers through these kinds of images and associations. Nonetheless, such straightforward sexiness has not been enough to secure the fortunes of the global surf industry.[13]

Perhaps the most interesting aspect of handling this work with surf brands is the unpredictability of the surfing experience. "Nature," by definition, acts according to principles that remind us how human intentions must be channeled through more or less cooperative material arrangements.[14] Unable to control nature itself, the surf industry has arranged "multiple and sometimes diverging layers" of nature and culture together in economically productive manners by tuning the narratives of surfing.[15] To be sure, prior work demonstrates that cultural interpretations of surfing and the beach have been manipulated via advertising images, film, music, and a variety of other material-cultural means.[16] This range of images, film, music, and material-cultural forms can be seen to be a market assemblage as described above. As we would expect, fragility and contingency feature here. In particular, cultural interpretations of surfing have never been entirely controlled by any particular cultural intermediary for two reasons.

First, as Doug Booth suggests, meanings are sited and negotiated within changing socioeconomic conditions.[17] As such, twentieth-century surfing was shaped by and expressive of various zeitgeists, such as emerging environmental concerns, or countercultural dissent in the 1960s, or by apolitical hedonism in the 1980s.[18] Surfing, in this case, is something of a rat that jumps aboard cultural vessels, travels the seas, and adapts to the politico-economic territory wherever it makes shore. Second, in place of the relatively top-down ordering influences of surfing magazines and videos of previous generations, the cultural flows that constitute contemporary surfing have been flattened (at least to some extent) by user-generated content of the Internet.[19] For these reasons, the current meanings of surfing are increasingly negotiable, a status that is borne out in the multinational, multiethnic, multitechnic cultural jumble of hard-core, soft-core and in-between-core surfers, stand-up paddle surfers, kite surfers, etc.

In this sense, therefore, the process of marketing surfing as a consistent set of ideas or ideals in the mind of "the consumer" has always been difficult, as new constructions of surfing culture constantly arise. Moreover, the potential for creating new narrative framings of surfing in ways that are inclusive for a variety of different groups is growing in force. A proliferating number of grassroots social movements, in which surfing features as a unifying activity in further-ing social and cultural causes, offer examples of such alternatives.[20] However, I wish to suggest that certain meanings of surfing have remained fairly stable over time, and that these reveal key aspects of how nature is treated in cultural economies, especially how nature is framed as escape from culture. I will pro-ceed toward this argument by interrogating the development of the narratives that have characterized the market assemblages of surfing over time, in partic-ular a theme that unites many of them, a Romantic conception of nature, and of humans in nature.

Waves of Primitivism

To consider these Romantic narratives in relation to surfing, it is instructive to consider cultural representations that resulted from European contact with in-digenous surfing cultures. The broader histories of these contacts are well de-scribed, but I wish to focus more specifically on how surfers were portrayed and stereotyped in popular media.[21] In so doing, I aim to reveal clues as to the man-ners in which surfing is established as a myth-market phenomenon. I will sug-gest that from the early nineteenth century to the present day, surfing has been associated with "the primitive." A technical and literary category that emerged within the general figuration of European colonialism, ideas of the primitive framed indigenous populations as geographically isolated and culturally retro-gressive. Yet equally, the primitive has and continues to be conceptualized as capable of breaking down schematic barriers between mind, body, and environ-ments, of restructuring thought and emotions as people become "one with na-ture."[22] Either way, conceptions of the primitive have performed a "cut" between colonizers and colonized cultures, as well as between culture and nature.[23]

Explicitly, in contrast to the increasingly differentiated social functions, centralized political structures, and personal foresight, rationality, and sexual repression exhibited in European nation-states during and after the commercial revolution, "primitive" societies were characterized as exhibiting circular con-ceptions of time, and a lack of cultural and psychological development.[24] These representations justified reformations of indigenous cultures; it became colo-nialists' *duty* to transform "savages" into docile, civilized subjects.[25] During the early nineteenth century, Hawaiian culture was transformed via institutions of education, religion, employment, and military service.[26] Increasingly interde-pendent with colonial economies, and disengaged from seasonal rhythms and traditional religions, one observer wrote in *Harper's New Monthly*, little more than fifty years after European contact with Hawai'i, that "missionaries have left an indelible mark upon these islands . . . they sought from the beginning to make New England men and women of these Hawaiians, and what is wonderful is that, to a large extent, they have succeeded."[27]

Representations of the primitive reflected not only the necessity for and celebration of colonial conquest, however, but also "repression at home."[28] Concurrent with enactments of the primitive as part of colonial projects, representations of primitive peoples, cultures, and artifacts became popular figures of contemplation. Literary accounts of Cooke, de Bougainville, and other eighteenth-century explorers' voyages had epitomized the South Seas as a place of indolent plenitude, sexual freedoms, and harmony with nature. Throughout the nineteenth century, these meanings were key aspects of desires for liberation from the constraints of modern rationalized cultures.[29] As Barkan spells out, "when it came to primitives, Victorians allowed themselves to transgress their own accepted morality."[30] In this way, indigenous societies became figures of desire for instinctual expression and kinship with natural environments, in which the psychic, material, and spiritual worlds were thought to coexist, and time had remained cyclical and sacred.[31] Constructions of the primitive that held up indigenous populations as figures that transgressed modernist barriers between reason and desire established the meaning of the primitive not only as a justification for cultural reform, but also as reflecting a "desire for cohesion and wholeness in simpler social structures than those of the West," and wishes for a future "more harmoniously fulfilling of the potencies of the human spirit."[32]

The power of these desires is evidenced by their emergence as popular cultural themes. Indeed, throughout the nineteenth century, ethnographic findings were transposed into cinematic and literary tracts for widespread consumption in manners that exploited notions of primitivism, both in terms of the power of colonialism to transform "backward" cultures into models of progress and as figures of excitement.[33] Moreover, in terms of the power to excite, the primitive Other could be framed as horrific—a genre gruesomely exemplified by ethnographer Eric Mjoberg's "skeleton hunts" in Australia's Kimberly region—or as erotic, embodying freedoms, carefree living, and magical vitality.[34] Common to both frames, the primitive becomes a discursive site around which boundaries of conduct are considered in popular media as diverse as film, photography, magazines, and pornography.[35] In other words, the cut between Euro-American and indigenous societies establishes principles for contemplation, and whether the primitive was a model through which to rediscover a classical golden age, or something subhuman to be "civilized off the face of the earth," popular culture tapped this discursive distinction between civility and savagery by reflecting the contested claims to either belief.[36]

There is, however, another layer to the use of the primitive that stems from this Janus-faced appeal. In the case of Hawai'i, throughout the late nineteenth century and into the twentieth century, surfers were framed by missionaries, travel writers, advertisers, and themselves as primitive, yet as indicated in the more general discussion above, the quality of this framing depends on the wider political-economic contexts in which surfing culture figures.[37] That Hawaiian culture was subject to general prohibitions by industrial and missionary institutions during the colonization and annexation of Hawai'i is well known. As Ishiwata illustrates, during this period, all that is considered to be primitive must be censured and reformed, including surfing.[38] However, despite ideological and financial investments in reforms to make Hawai'i more governable and appealing to American tourists, travel writer Charles Nordhoff's 1873 description of Hawai'i reveals an important impression, namely, that questions existed in terms of the perceived economic value of the islands: "What is certain is that these islands, aside from their fine climate, have absolutely nothing to tempt our own people to live on them, or to invest money in them. . . . More than one-half the surface of the island is lava, which may, I suppose in about three millions of years be worth perhaps a dollar and a quarter an acre."[39]

Perhaps this fear that nothing could tempt anyone to Hawai'i motivated a number of market-creation strategies that began in the late nineteenth and early twentieth centuries. Through this period, in addition to the growth of agriculture, tourism gained ground in the mainland United States through travel infrastructures, demand for which was driven by literary materials, travelogues, and advertising.[40] Many of these promotional materials featured photographs and editorials illustrating surf-bathing and surfing as activities of interest. Between 1910 and 1920, for instance, the *Mid-Pacific Magazine*, published by promoter Alexander Hume Ford, featured collections of photographs and editorial commentaries on Hawaiian pastimes, amongst which surfing became a regular feature.[41] Thereafter, through the 1920s and 1930s, *National Geographic* and *Popular Mechanics* illustrate a growing fascination with surfing.[42]

Shades of primitivism continued to be assigned to Hawaiian culture in these depictions. Rather than requiring censure, as had been the case in the nineteenth century, however, Douglas Booth has argued that the exotic, nostalgic, and authentic connotations of the Hawaiian beach were used to lure tourists with promises of harmony with nature, circular time, and simple living, as well as emotional and sexual freedoms uncommon in Euro-American societies.[43] In short, these promotional materials began to construct Hawai'i as a site for Romantic connection to nature, a subversion of cultural hierarchies established by Western modernity, and the reassertion of masculinity. Importantly, native

Hawaiians assumed ambivalent stances within the nascent tourism industry during the early decades of the twentieth century, physically seizing control of the beach and surf zone in ways that inverted Euro-American social and cultural hierarchies.[44] Arguably, this may have fueled the attractiveness of surfing culture. This is to say that just as Hawaiian surfers re-appropriated the territory of the beach, so too did marketers and tourists appropriate these meanings, in turn accruing prestige from contact with nature and with an activity with something of a hardball image. In this case, primitive tropes, with their heritage in colonialist anthropology and the contemplative forms of consumption that followed, began to be used as a means of self-Othering, where American tourists mimicked native Hawaiians by wrestling with the sea.[45]

This framing of surfing illustrates the potential for the primitive to reflect Romantic and utopian ideals against which the progress of European and American society could be criticized. Such critique tends to occur in response to breaches in the fabric of society, aspects of failed modernity. In this respect, Torgovnick explains the cultural articulations of primitivism in the early twentieth century as responses to the First World War.[46] In other words, other cultural solutions come into favor when the home system is thought to be failing. In many respects, this returns us to the idea of myth-markets, assemblages of markets stabilized via narrative interventions that offer solutions to cultural tensions of one kind or another. In the next section, I illustrate how this narrative lineage is written into surfing markets during the twentieth century.

Only a Surfer Knows the Feeling

How does the primitive play out in twentieth-century representations of surfing? Since their inception, surfing brands have drawn on and reconstructed many of the ideals and figures associated with primitive notions of man in nature. I wish to argue that these meanings are reproduced as part of the ordering of surfing cultures and surfing industries, between which surf brands are powerful mediators. With respect to primitivism emerging in response to cultural failure, the surfing and beach life in 1930s California might have developed partly in response to the anxieties that attended the improbabilities of employment and advancement in a widespread and extended period of economic depression.[47] It seems 1930s beach life was a simple affair, yet one that gained a toehold in popular US culture through various demonstrations, photographic exposes, and instructions for surfboard building.[48]

Though the popular progress of surfing slowed between 1939 and 1945, during the 1950s the boom in surfing culture and associated markets took place as part of a wider Hawaiian vogue in the United States.[49] The level of appeal created by this market is evident in the number and popularity of products associated with surfing during the 1950s.[50] The emergence of the surf industry at this time both responded to, and reaped the benefits of, this growing cultural demand, leading to further investment, growth, and sustained visibility of surfing in the mainstream media from the late 1950s through the 1960s.[51] Yet desires to avoid or eschew mainstream culture also motivated surfing entrepreneurs, some of whom had grown up among the prewar beach cultures of Southern California. A 2007 interview with Dick Metz, cofounder of *Surfline Hawaii* and instrumental in establishing Hobie Alter's business, is instructive in this respect:

> It was obvious to me from the beginning that we had a different attitude . . . you go to high school, you go to college, you find a husband, you get married, you have kids, your husband goes to work everyday, you live that kind of American dream, you buy a house. . . . We didn't want all that responsibility, we wanted to be more free to be able to do the things that you thought were more important like surfing and diving and . . . living that casual lifestyle and not being under the social gun to earn more money, to have a bigger house. . . . We didn't ever want to wear a coat or tie to work. We never wanted even to own a pair of hard, leather shoes. And we didn't want to work on the inland side of the coast highway.

Arguably, this lifestyle ethic was constructed into popular culture industries that installed primitive tropes in their various products.[52] For instance, *Gidget*'s characters, "fed up with too many rules and regulations," take to Malibu beach shacks, declaring themselves surf bums with not a care in the world. A fashion feature in a 1966 magazine targeted at teenagers also constructs this ideal as obviously as is possible. Parents also had the culture explained to them in newspaper features that again stressed the potential to step out of modern society through contact with nature:

> Surfing is a sport that is identified with the lifeguard image, the weather beaten fisherman (*The Old Man and the Sea*), the sailor, the skin diver. It is very masculine, yet the little guy can do it. And it doesn't take a lot of money: a beat up board, a pair of trunks and some enthusiasm. And if he can't do it, he can identify with those who can, especially those who ride the big surf. His dress, his language, his bleached blonde hair, all convince him that he is a surfer, that he is a man. Along with this goes what Grigg defines as "A release from the confining order of modern society."[53]

FIG. 17.1 *Teen Magazine* fashion feature, 1966.

Despite the sweetened form of the beach movies and the apparent harmlessness of bikini fashion shoots, these consumer-cultural forms imputed ideological difference.[54] Interestingly, the ambivalence and malleability of the primitive discourses witnessed during the development of early twentieth century tourism in Hawai'i return again during the 1950s and 1960s, when ideological otherness in youth culture was considered threatening.[55] The primitive beach is once again a place of eroticized freedoms and connection to nature, yet simultaneously it infers censure. Negative responses to surfing cultures abounded during the early 1960s, with many Californian beaches being closed to surfers entirely. Interestingly, many of these heaped primitive tropes of subhuman animality, and nomadism, onto surfing youths.[56]

Surfers who become one with nature, however, are seen as eschewing civilizations' discontents, a fantasy of being expelled from a diseased social body with which they no longer want to identify—"A release from the confining order of modern society," as Ricky Grigg put it.[57] As Booth spells out, these meanings are as affective as they are ideological.[58] This is to say, the search for oceanic feelings might reveal embodied themes similar to the embodied practices of modern primitives, notably, a master/slave relationship, and potential for fear, submission, and pain, all of which are seen as a means to intimately connect with the external cause of the sensation, in this case nature.[59] An ego with blurred boundaries—Phil Edwards, 1960s pop-culture ambassador of surfing, described the experience of surrender to a wave in this way:

> You lie there on your back—spread-eagled and heavy and helpless—and if you look you can see those spinning fingers of turbulence reaching down to get you . . . And for a few seconds you are spinning around crazily in a world that is neither land nor sea nor air. This is real back to the womb stuff, and this is how you get locked in on life. . . . There is a need in all of us for controlled danger; that is, a need for an activity that puts us—however briefly—on the edge of life. Civilization is breeding it out of us, this go-to-hell trait. There are uncounted millions of people right now who are going through life without any sort of real, vibrant kick. The legions of the unjazzed.[60]

Arguably, this affective sense of otherness is a powerful aspect of primitivism and, by association, surfing. Moreover, I would suggest that it is a feature that has recurred in surf culture and in surf marketing to the present day. The following introspection from a surfer's diary (Caroline, age twenty-three, California) collected in 2005 poetically describes another rendition of affective otherness:

> Intoxicating tendrils of moisture wind themselves around me, inviting me to dive down deep and immerse myself in coolness. . . . My lungs full of the briny sea vapors, and my body surrounded by the lavish liquid, I merged with the ocean in an intense marriage of flesh and saltwater. Cradled in the arms of my favorite lover, I swam to the harmony of the ocean's lullaby. I didn't care anymore about my life above the Ocean's face . . . the life I led imprisoned by insensate concrete, limited by unyielding obstacles. . . . There, blissfully surrounded by flowing, ethereal turquoise, I could hear the swish and gurgle of divine whisperings as she recounted timeless tales of human passions directed at her shores.

In some ways this passage harks back to Phil Edwards's words above: treading the territory of mystical desires, Caroline constructs surfing as a "primal harmony" and a "communion with nature," romantically stages her own death as a culturalized body, and rebirth through contact with the sea. Importantly, her oceanic feelings are afforded by the liquid materiality of the sea that—in contrast to "unyielding" or "insensate" objects—embraces her body.

These ideological and affective desires have been attached to surfing through expressions of primitive lifestyles in popular culture. At the beginning of the

1970s, Hollywood artist and author Eve Babitz refers to surfer David Nuuhiwa as possessing a face "abrupt in its savagery and its vestigial traces of paradise."[61] Australian surf cultures (increasingly connected to their US counterparts through the cultural exchanges of tourism, surf media, and the nascent international competition scene) also develop expressions of primitivism in the manner that surfing is used as a turn to nature against a broader Australian culture enmeshed in the Vietnam War. Early issues of *Tracks* featured "plenty of articles about surfing but just as many about environmental sustainability . . . and miscellaneous initiatives opposing conformist, competitive ways of living in a burgeoning capitalist country."[62] The "country soul" construction of surfing emphasizes the simple life in nature as a criticism of society and government: "By simply surfing we are supporting the revolution," said Nat Young.[63] In short, throughout the 1970s the popular cultural surfer is forged as a countercultural hero or heroine embedded in the spaces and rhythms of nature.[64]

During the 1980s, Billabong's marketing communications, epitomized in their surfing videos, stressed this same ideological point slightly differently: "The truth is only a surfer knows the feeling," exclaims Matt Warshaw at the beginning of Billabong's *Surf Into Summer* (1986), a tagline that has stood the test of time. Rip Curl's advertising and accompanying Search tagline have long emphasized empty lineup shots, save perhaps for a few "primitive" locals, fisherfolk, unconnected with surfing, or even with modernity, if their traditional clothes and lack of technology are any indication.[65] Through the 1990s, *Point Break*'s "Dead Presidents" represented the countercultural surfer, and Celtic tattoos became all the rage, both inferring surfers' sideways slide away from the modern world.

More recently, Electric Eyewear (Fig. 17.2) exemplifies a primitive theme. Carrying an *alaia*, hairy (just as nature intended) professional free surfer Dave Rastovich goes native with a companion, wearing shell bracelets and necklace.[66] So too do primitive themes abound in Taylor Steel's *The Drifter*, in which pro surfer Rob Machado is tired of the "cultural comfort zone" that follows him around the world.[67] "It is hard to evolve yourself as a person when your life is constantly under a microscope; it's important to disappear sometimes," drawls Machado. With only a single board, he sets out for the end of the world, where he finds his true nature. More recently still, we might think of the country soul throwback farm primitive constructed around Patagonia-brand ambassador surfers Chris, Dan, and Keith Malloy (similarly hirsute to Rastovich and Machado above). In all these cases, advertisers, filmmakers, and magazine editors seize upon and reproduce the cut between surfers and the rest of society as a means to construct marketing communications with powerful narrative

FIG. 17.2 Print advertisement for Electric Eyewear (part of the Volcom Group).

meanings. However, in constructing surfing as an escape from modern culture
by returning to primal nature, a variety of contradictions emerge.

Contradictions: The Trouble with Surf Brands

The instances considered above illustrate the power of the primitive in marketing representations. The primitive is a floating signifier, open to iterative constructions that serve purposes as diverse as a justification to reform indigenous
cultures according to the logics of colonial agendas; a model of excitement and
contemplation for wealthy tourists; and a means of self-Othering and empowerment against a variety of cultural events. In all cases, however, the primitive
infers a cut between nature and culture that underpins the construction of
Otherness, whether this is imposed on indigenous populations, or on oneself
as a way to declare difference from aspects of home culture that are perceived
as damaging.

   In terms of branding, the primitive offers a powerful narrative principle
that can be turned to solve changing social and political tensions. Indeed, this
potential to construct surfing as a form of otherness that responds to shifting
social conditions has been key to sustaining surfing over so many decades where
other youth cultures have dissipated. The Romantic, harmony-with-nature theme

attenuates the perception of failed cultural projects by constructing the possibility to quit the diseased social body. That the cultural effects against which surfing's primitivism is positioned alter through time returns us to Booth's consideration that surfing is interpreted according to changing cultural zeitgeists.[68] In line with Torgovnick's conception of primitivism emerging during periods when "modernities" are failing, I would like to extend Booth's account.[69] I agree that surfing is tailored to cultural conditions, but I suggest also that this is done in a predictable way, through the divergent possibilities of primitivism. As Tamplin observes, "the South Seas can be anything our psychologies demand," or, more generally, as Torgovnick explains, "the needs of the present determine the value and nature of the primitive."[70]

With respect to the power of primitivism as an ordering principle in the creation and re-creation of surfing brands, however, I now wish to illustrate contradictions that emerge within these narrative-led assemblages, especially in present times. If the malleable cultural category of "the primitive" has been so recurrent in the construction of surfing culture, then it clearly follows that surfing isn't exactly an escape from culture. When surfers go to "nature," they take with them all kinds of narrative forms, technological artifacts, and embodied habits, not least a category of knowledge-making connected with colonial histories—"the primitive." To this end, the back story to the Romantic vignette that opens this chapter is instructive:

This morning, buried in emails, I missed my train. Realizing the next one wouldn't arrive in time to get me to the faculty PhD conference, I take the better of our two vehicles, and drive to Melbourne, leaving Lu with the beach car, full of sand. Ninety minutes later, I discover the university parking lot is full, so I dip in and out of presentations, moving the car between one-hour meters. At lunchtime I attend a poorly-thought-out-policy-meeting, then move the car again. By four-o'clock the pollen count is sky-high, and I don't want to go to the conference dinner if I can't take advantage of the open bar. So I drive home. At this point I remember my standup paddleboard is still in the beach car . . . it's 96 [degrees Fahrenheit] in the shade and I assume the thing has exploded (poetic justice). Feeling glum, I stop home, collect the dog and a surfboard and then I head to the beach.

For most surfers, surfing is embedded in these kinds of everyday processes: the assemblages of commuting; the dispiriting qualities of organizations; undesirable responses of the body to nature (hay fever); the contradictions between nature and technology (the sun's heat that melts surfboards that are left in cars). Further still, a variety of specialist media are involved in the performance and construction of surfing.[71] If time commitment is any measure, then contemporary surfing is as much an online exercise as it is a seaborne one. Gone are the hours or days spent at the beach.[72] Today's surfer scours swell-models and subscribes to surf forecasts in order to stuff a few waves between other commitments. Moreover, as surfers take to the waves with GoPro point-of-view cameras, selfie sticks, and camera drones, the very practices of being on a wave are increasingly hybrid. The meanings of surfing, once transferred mainly by surf media, are now as likely to be (re)constructed by surfers themselves via the horizontal networks of social media that literally extend from the surf zone to the World Wide Web.[73]

Surfers scan online mags, stream World Surf League webcasts, and select from a range of surfing taste cultures under the broad beach-identity umbrella.[74] Surfing is a complex intersection where multiple cultural highways connect the material geographies of beaches not only to narrative and consumer technologies, but also to industry and management. The Save the Waves Coalition website (http://www.savethewaves.org/) illustrates the tentacles of business, politics, and planning that reach below high-tide marks and fix beaches to the marinas, jetties, and manufacturing plants of industrial or touristic assemblages.[75] Furthermore, prior work indicates how surfing has been harnessed to the extension of American lifestyle politics and colonialism.[76] As indicated at the beginning of this chapter, an approach to the assemblage of surf brands is helpful in that nature, culture, and economy are not treated as a priori different kinds, requiring different terms of method and analysis. The divide between nature and culture may seem self-evident at times, but these considerations of surfers' technologies and economic connections show that experiences of nature are always imbricated in hybrid, protean, and complex entanglements with culture.[77]

If surfing is a hybrid experience, however, this is not necessarily reflected in the manner in which surfing is represented by surf brands. The narrative of a return to nature offered in many of the instances above contradicts the hybrid status of surfing by inferring the possibility to step out of culture into this Other realm. By making the cut between modern and other societies, as well as a cut between cultures of modernity and natural premodernities, primitive representations are what Bruno Latour calls *purifications*, instances that overlook hybrid connections between nature and culture, modern and premodern worlds, colonized and colonial cultures.[78] Of course, these neat dualistic boundaries are fictions. Equally true, however, is that the authenticity of marketing communications or films is unimportant, since the categories put to use in marketing are valued not according to their hybrid truths, but according to capacities to produce compelling stories.[79] What is important here is the power of the man-in-nature theme, which depends on and reproduces ideals of nature as the opposite of culture.

This is where the problems of surfing brands emerge. Why and how do surfing brands sustain portrayals of a return to nature, when this possibility is contradicted by so many linkages to culture? The *why* question is easy to answer. As indicated previously, nature as the opposite of culture is a productive dualism that underpins narratives of primitivism, Romantic conceptions of the sublime, and the spiritually restorative power of the ocean. The possibility to escape culture by going to its supposed opposite—nature—and in the process to become more primitive is a narrative framing that sustains a gamut of outdoor leisure, tourism, and experiential markets. The *how* question is more interesting. If experiences of primitive nature are contradicted by wireless networks, transport infrastructures, and so on, then how do people direct their attention to the natural side of nature, hiding contradictory features?[80]

Despite the thoroughly hybrid status of surfing, a variety of strategies continue to perform the cut or purification of nature and culture so as to sustain the primitive fantasies of consumers and brand managers. Perhaps the simplest means of overcoming contradictions are the autotelic and oceanic blurring of self and environment that can emerge from embodied linkages with the material geographies in which subject and object are conjoined.[81] These intense embodied experiences focus surfers' attention away from logical contradictions within cultural and advertising discourses. Equally, magazines and videos have been slow to embrace the hybridities of surfing. Surfing's ideologies have until recently been guarded by editors and brand managers who managed meanings very carefully.[82] For many decades, surfing culture—shaped by its brands and the tropes that they recycle—has been rather like those expensive charter trips to the Maldives or the Mentawais, where wealthy white surfers sip beers on luxury boats, never making contact with island dwellers or the cultures behind the dim treelines of the beaches.

It is no wonder that marketing campaigns that offer escape and Other ways of living have been popular. Through the primitive themes investigated in the previous section, surfing can be seen to carry powerful narrative solutions to a variety of social tensions. Doubtless, many of us use surfing to heal ourselves by paddling into the breakers. However, while catching a wave does represent a human attachment to nature, the broader manner in which this is technically achieved and meaningfully framed is of vital importance, because this can be generalized beyond surfing to a host of other leisure and consumption forms. By masking the inconvenient or contradictory linkages between nature and culture, marketing encourages us to ignore hybrid status of fragile physical geographies as they are being degraded. Moreover, by purifying nature and culture—as is often practiced in order to build and sustain primitive meanings—we also risk reproducing categories of race and gender that are derived from troubled colonial histories. Hence, although "primitive" practices and meanings may be deployed earnestly by consumers, necessitating "cool readings," I would argue that marketing institutions have a more pressing responsibility to take care when drawing at the deep wells of Pacific cultures.[83]

Further still, and with respect to the current problematizations raised by pollution and climate change, it is clear that the use of marketing representations that portray nature as external draw attention away from the interconnections of nature and culture, economy and society. In short, narrative solutions might be effective in solving personally experienced tensions, but in so doing they potentially reduce the likelihood of more meaningful engagement in relation to the localized or global degeneration of natural environments. Similarly, brands that promise contact with nature are often imbricated in the processes by which physical geographies that we call "nature" are transformed into market entities, the process of which destroys that which we seek. Moreover, the more people feel alienated from nature, the more likely they are to seek out contact with nature. The potential impact of this is that the meanings offered by these consumer-cultural narratives become more sought after . . . and so on.

The picture I paint here is possibly more pessimistic than is necessary, however. At small-scale levels, some surfers seek to purge contradictions from their assemblages of nature. A sea change in surfing culture over the last decade has been the popularization of wooden boards and sailboat trips, or Chris Malloy's surfing documentaries, all of which, by promoting cleaner forms of travel and closer engagement with local culture, attempt to engender less contradictory versions of primitive encounters with nature.[84] This is to say that wooden boards (see fig. 17.2), or the apparently carbon-neutral option of traveling under wind power rather than via fossil fuel–hungry plane rides, allow surfers to enact the primitive fantasy by reducing potential contradictions to their back-to-nature fantasies. To be sure, such moves are largely aesthetic and practiced by a lucky or talented few. Nevertheless, as expressions of emergent meanings in surfing culture, these examples do perhaps speak of more general shifts. Indeed, change is more materially evident in the current proliferation of social movement–type entities that are beginning to deal with surfing natures as hybrid with all kinds of cultural effects, denying the necessity to purify nature away from culture, and instead connecting with culture, politics, and social media.[85] In these cases, organizations such as Save the Waves, Surf+Social Good, Waves of Freedom, SurfAid, and many others might retain Romantic conceptions of the sea as a restorative force. Equally, however, these organizations are using nature not to turn away from social ills, but rather to confront them head on.

In this respect, perhaps *The Drifter*, a film that preaches escape to nature, is not as guilty as I may have suggested above. Sure, Machado's return to nature in the film must have been accompanied by a media crew and their attendant technologies, yet they somehow vanish. Nor do we see the dolly track that Steele had built in the bush behind the beach to capture Machado on the high-speed Indonesian runways. Similarly, we see Machado in a tent rather than the very nice hotel on the beach at his final far-flung location. Observant viewers will also note that Machado's single board keeps changing color. These are the instances of purification where, by focusing the lens, as it were, surf cultures mask the contradictions to the narrative of man in nature, escaping modern living and attendant technologies. In this respect, the film is a crass contradiction.

Like Steele's other films, however, *The Drifter* does also involve and pull focus on the local cultures that surfers encounter, a welcome relief from the surfer-lifestyle or purely wave-focused videos of the 1990s in particular.[86] Perhaps, as the likes of Billabong and Quiksilver struggle to maintain their perceived authenticity in surfing culture, it will be the brands that follow this mode, and engage more closely with cultural aspects of surfing, that will develop credible values in the minds of customers over the coming decades. While contact with nature will doubtless continue to underpin the meaning of surfing brands, corporations that do business in ways that more carefully engage with nature-culture assemblages will likely enjoy iconic status, over and above those whose values are handled in such a way as to preclude engagement with the ecological, cultural, and social interconnections that contemporary surfers increasingly encounter.

NOTES

1. Latour, *We Have Never Been Modern*.
2. Watson-Veran and Turnbull, "Science and Other," 345–346.
3. Callon, "Some Elements" and *Laws of Markets*; Latour, *Reassembling the Social*.
4. Lury, "Brand as Assemblage."
5. Slater, "Marketing as a Monstrosity."
6. Moor, "Branding Consultants"; Latour, *Pasteurization of France*.
7. Thompson, "Marketplace Mythology."
8. Holt, *How Brands Become Icons*.
9. Holt, *How Brands Become Icons*.
10. See Warde, "Consumption, Identity-formation," and Thompson, "Marketplace Mythology."
11. Thompson, "Marketplace Mythology."

12. Dweck, *End: Montauk*, 1

13. At times, surfing has bobbed around in the troughs of the culture industries, becalmed in an ocean of other youth culture offerings. Even now, things aren't what they were less than a decade ago: Billabong's shares have sunk from a high of over AU$12 in June 2007, to AU$1.25 as of February 2017 (ASX.com.au).

14. Newton, *Nature and Sociology*.

15. Of course, the holy grail of surf marketing has always been to control the waves themselves, arguably a step closer with the Wavegarden wave pools (a test facility in the Basque Country and a commercial installation in Dolgarrog, Wales) and the Kelly Slater Wave Company's artificial wave in Lemoore, California.

16. Booth, "Paradoxes of Material Culture."

17. Booth, "Paradoxes of Material Culture."

18. Booth, *Australian Beach Cultures*.

19. Gilchrist and Wheaton, "New Media Technologies."

20. See, for example, Waves of Freedom (http://wavesoffreedom.org/) and The Lobitos Cinema Project (http://www.lobitoscinemaproject.com/).

21. The broader histories of these contacts are well described in Finney and Houston, *Surfing*; Laderman, *Empire in Waves*; and Walker, *Waves of Resistance*.

22. Arnould, Price, and Otnes, "Making Consumption Magic," 56.

23. Diamond, *In Search of the Primitive*.

24. Newton, "Credit Networks and Civilisation"; Oksiloff, *Picturing the Primitive*; Sweeney, *From Fetish to Subject*.

25. Diamond, *In Search of the Primitive*.

26. Benham and Heck, *Culture and Educational Policy*.

27. Charles Nordhoff, "Hawaii-Nei," *Harpers New Monthly Magazine* 27, no. 9 (August 1873), 382–402.

28. Diamond, *In Search of the Primitive*, 1.

29. Staszak, "Primitivism and the Other," 353–364.

30. Barkan, "Victorian Promiscuity."

31. Diamond, *In Search of the Primitive*; Staszak, "Primitivism and the Other."

32. Bell, "Primitivism"; Sweeney, *From Fetish to Subject*, 17; Stocking, "Ideas and Institutions," 31.

33. Oksiloff, *Picturing the Primitive*.

34. Hallgren, "Eric Mjöberg," 135–146; Torgovnick, *Gone Primitive*.

35. Roper, *Oedipus and the Devil*.

36. Dickens, "The Noble Savage," 337–339; Hallgren, "Eric Mjöberg."

37. Canniford and Karababa, "Partly Primitive."

38. Ishiwata, "Local Motions."

39. Charles Nordhoff, "Hawaii-Nei," *Harper's Monthly* 279 (August 1873): 402 [382–402].

40. Desmond, *Staging Tourism*.

41. Alexander Hume Ford, *Mid-Pacific Magazine* 1–4 (1911–1912). See also Castle, *Hawaiian Islands*. The University of Hawai'i has made every issue of *Mid-Pacific Magazine* publicly available through the Evols digital repository, https://evols.library.manoa.hawaii.edu/.

42. Castle, *Hawaiian Islands*; Faris, *Paradise of the Pacific*; Blake, "Waves and Thrills."

43. Booth, *Australian Beach Cultures.*

44. Walker, "Hui Nalu, Beachboys."

45. Willard, "Duke Kahanamoku's Body." See also, Desmond, *Staging Tourism.*

46. Torgovnick, *Gone Primitive*, 9.

47. Starr, *Endangered Dreams.*

48. See James, *Surfing San Onofre*; Lockwood, *Peanuts*; Blake, "Waves and Thrills," 597–604; Blake, "Riding the Breakers!," 114–115. Interestingly, surfing's primitivisms may not have been without their models. Many of the early Southern Californian surfers were living and working in Laguna, and socializing with artists through whom connections to other primitive expressions may have somehow flowed (personal correspondence with Craig Lockwood, 2015).

49. Irwin, "Surfing"; Schroeder and Borgerson, "Packaging Paradise," 32–53.

50. Booth, "Paradoxes of Material Culture."

51. Canniford and Karababa, "Partly Primitive."

52. Ormrod, "*Endless Summer* (1964)," 39–51.

53. Mitchell, "Fad and Fascination," 130.

54. Rutsky, "Surfing the Other."

55. May, *Golden State, Golden Youth.*

56. See Jim Murray, "Call of the Surf," *Los Angeles Times*, August 12, 1962; Mitchell, "Fad and Fascination."

57. Mitchell, "Fad and Fascination," 130.

58. Booth, "(Re-)reading the Surfers' Bible," 17–35.

59. Hewitt, *Mutilating the Body.*

60. Phil Edwards, "You Should Have Been Here an Hour Ago," *The Saturday Evening Post*, July 1, 1967, 32–39.

61. Babitz, *Eve's Hollywood.*

62. Engledown, "Arcadia, Sound of the Sea."

63. Booth, *Australian Beach Cultures.*

64. Booth, "Surfing Films and Videos," 313–325. See also Ormrod, "*Endless Summer* (1964)," and Laderman, *Empire in Waves.*

65. The Search, Rip Curl's tagline, expresses the surf-culture archetype of travel for the discovery of "virgin" territory: the terra nullius of Indonesian beaches where surfers have not yet set foot.

66. *Alaia* are wooden surfboards of a kind found in precontact Pacific cultures. A global resurgence in shaping and riding these craft (see http://www.tomwegenersurfboards.com) has arguably become one material and practical aspect of a new wave of surfing primitivism, an attempt to move beyond the petrochemical technologies of regular surfboards and the competitive expressions of surfing for which these are designed.

67. Steele, *The Drifter.*

68. Booth, *Australian Beach Cultures.*

69. Torgovnick, *Gone Primitive.*

70. Tamplin, "Noblemen and Noble Savages"; Torgovnick, *Gone Primitive.*

71. Gilchrist and Wheaton, "New Media Technologies."

72. Irwin, "Surfing."

73. Booth, *Australian Beach Cultures*; Booth, "Paradoxes of Material Culture"; Gilchrist and Wheaton, "New Media Technologies."

74. Compare with the simpler dichotomy drawn between "surfies" and "clubbies" in Australia and New Zealand (e.g., Pearson, *Surfing Subcultures*).

75. For example, New Zealand's Aramoana is entangled with the dredging practices of the Port of Otago harbor authority that threaten this popular surfing beach in order to sustain shipping channels; Madeira's Jardim do Mar and Lugar de Baixo became entangled with the island's cement industry and its cousin, the tourism industry. In both cases, surfers' assemblages have been superseded by seawalls designed to assemble touristic landscapes.

76. Canniford and Shankar, "Marketing the Savage"; Lawler, *American Surfer*; Laderman, *Empire in Waves*.

77. Castree and MacMillan, "Dissolving Dualisms," 208.

78. Latour, *We Have Never Been Modern*.

79. Jacobi et al., " 'Is There a Gap.' "

80. Canniford and Shankar, "Purifying Practices."

81. See Stranger, "Aesthetics of Risk"; Evers, "Becoming-Man, Becoming-Wave"; Kwinter, *Architectures of Time*.

82. Booth, "(Re-)reading the Surfers' Bible."

83. Turner, "Possibility of Primitiveness," 39.

84. See Beamish, *Voyage of the Cormorant*.

85. Castells, *Networks of Outrage*.

86. For a discussion of surfing films, see Booth, "Surfing Films and Videos."

18 / Surfing and Contemporary China

CLIFTON EVERS

To go surfing in China can mean traipsing along idyllic white sand beaches where palms trees tilt according to the commands of the wind. Alternately, it can involve a drive through vast agricultural fields, only to arrive at a beachfront path littered with construction detritus, paddling out in a thick wetsuit, and trying to ignore the oily surface sheen of the water and the gritty foam clinging to the wave faces.

It is not surprising that surfing has washed up on the shores of China. Surfing has long been part of the processes of globalization and transnationalism.[1] Krista Comer points out that surfing cultures are made and remade at the intersection of the global and local.[2] Globalization and transnationalism do not simply equate to imposition. There exist practical negotiations that can also lead to intensification of the local through resistance and hybridity.[3] Roland

Robertson uses the term *glocalization* to emphasize the "co-presence" of "universalizing and particularizing tendencies."[4] In this chapter, I argue that to understand the glocalization playing out around surfing in China, it is necessary to examine practical, everyday negotiations of these tendencies as industry, consumption, tourism, gender, and class come together.[5] It is this everydayness that matters, because it is where the variable agencies of people manifest and become measureable—that is, as problems occur and are dealt with, impositions are accepted or resisted, new hybrids are created, and domestic ways are exported.

Scholars to date have not given empirical attention to the increasing mobilization of surfing and its associated industry in China to see what the power effects are: realities (the organizing of practices, spaces, knowledge) and subjects.[6] This chapter is a "political anatomy of the detail" of everyday experiences to work out who and what benefits (or not) from surfing's rise in China, and how certain possibilities are coming about and limitations being imposed.[7] The task at hand obliges me to dig deeper into contemporary social, cultural, political, and economic processes in China.

This chapter challenges opinions and stereotypes in surfing's enthusiast media that inculcate and invoke colonialist Orientalism in affording surfing a capacity for salvation.[8] An example of such an opinion is that of Italian entrepreneur Francesco De Luca, who began the website ChinaSurfReport.com, when he writes that surfing will somehow "fix" and "better" the lives of the Chinese people: in light of the "Destruction of their [the Chinese people's] past, their cultural heritage, flattening of the entire society, loss of traditional values, and exploitation of natural resources, I realized China needed a new positive energy and positive creed. Things that could be conveyed by the stoke of surfing. That night, I decided to create the first surfing magazine in the history of China."[9] Putting aside the supposed essential positivity of surfing that De Luca assumes for the moment, this chapter shows that China's cultural heritage has not simply been destroyed, the society has not been flattened, and long-term belief systems and values are not lost but interwoven with contemporary sociopolitical-cultural life to form a unique Chinese form of modernity.[10]

The research I undertook to write this led to scrutinizing the hype and media spin of surfing's culture industry when it comes to China. By "surfing's culture industry," I am referring to the commodification of surfing experiences, practices, values, beliefs, spaces, materials, and images, which functions according to and naturalizes the capitalist principle of capital accumulation and associated modes of organizations, labor, and subject formation. This culture industry is made up of individuals, endemic and nonendemic businesses, and sanctioning organizations, such as the International Surfing Association (ISA) and World Surf League (WSL).[11] The media spin and hype of surfing's culture industry legitimizes, authorizes, and broadcasts a "manufactured stoke," selling some essential, if always indefinite, positivity of surfing.[12] This masks a capitalist fervor and accompanying endeavors, not to mention the consequences and everyday politics that these have for communities. One such effect is the overdetermining of all strata of social life that could work differently, such as generating more collective social, environmental, ecological, and equitably distributed economic benefits. Surfing's culture industry is now hard at work situating surfing in China, and the "manufacture of stoke" continues as a principle narrative aimed at turning communities into surf markets and individuals into surf lifestyle consumers. The thing is, in China evidence shows that this story is going to be amended in unique ways.

My methods to undertake this study were to analyze surfing-specific enthusiast media and wider print and online mass media, and cross-reference this with empirical engagements, such as personal communication with twenty-six surfing enthusiasts and people affected by surfing in China (some are not surfers) and participant observation undertaken since 2011.[13] While there is some reference to other Chinese surfing scenes, this archive is focused on the surfing scene on Hainan Island, because it is a particularly intense point of negotiation and therefore an instructive case study.

Background of Surfing in China

There is a documented history of celebrity surfers from various countries trying to introduce surfing to China as early as the 1960s.[14] There have also been undocumented expatriates surfing throughout China since the 1980s.[15] Yet foreign surfers aside, the Chinese have a long history with the sea. The nation's maritime history feeds into literature, philosophy, religion, governance, militarism, imperialism, consumption, and trade.[16] A vibrant Chinese history of beach leisure culture, including beach resorts and sea bathing, dates to the 1920s.[17] Given this backdrop, it makes sense that there is a contemporary beach culture in China, and that some people have taken to surfing.

Domestic surfers have been riding waves in Hong Kong for over two decades, expatriate surfers since the late 1970s.[18] After 2006, Chinese surfers including Dahai Zhang, Tie Zhuang, Huang Wen, Huang Ning, Liu Dan, Monica Guo, and Zhao Yuan Hong began surfing on Hainan Island. Post-2007, a surfing scene also emerged on the Dapeng peninsula near the city of Shenzhen in Guangdong Province. Dedicated and enthusiastic surfers Bin Lee and Song Ou began surfing at Bei'on, Changle, on the coastline near the city of Fuzhou in

Fujian Province in 2009, and a vibrant informal Typhoon Surf Club now operates out of a shipping container; there are no palm trees, the water is polluted, and conditions during winter are bitterly cold.[19] Ah Jian took to the waves in Xiamen (Fujian Province) and started a surf club at Taiyang Wan in 2010.[20] Chinese surfers also ride waves near the city of Qingdao (Shandong Province), and are members of the Qingdao Surfing Association, formed in 2014. Based upon personal interaction with surfers in China, interviews with entrepreneurs and surf club enthusiasts, participant observation, and survey of surfing media (domestic and international), I would estimate the numbers of Chinese nationals who regularly surf throughout China as of 2015 at approximately 800 people (in a nation of 1.3 billion people), the vast majority being in Hong Kong.[21]

The media like to claim that surfing is "catching on" in China. In an article in US-based *Surfer* magazine, Jeff Mull asks: "Will China Become Surfing's Next Frontier?"[22] Will Swanton writes that surfing is on the "crest of a wave in China."[23] ISA President Fernando Aguerre has declared that "the opportunities for the development of surfing in China are endless."[24] Aguerre has also proclaimed, "Without a doubt I can say that China has made a grand entrance into the surfing family."[25] Of course, the "development" and "entrance" that Aguerre cites refer to new marketplaces.[26] The World Surf Cities Network was attracted by the allure of access to "China's emerging middle class with cash and leisure time to burn."[27] A campaign in Australia was "launched to attract more Chinese board-riders to the Gold Coast [Australia]" because of "the potential to inject billions of dollars into the local economy."[28] In 2012, Dane Jordan, the Australasia General Manager of the Association of Surfing Professionals (ASP; now the WSL), declared, "There's probably a billion people in China who didn't know they had great waves on their doorstep."[29] The ISA and WSL now each sanction annual international surfing competitions on Hainan Island, which *Desillusion* magazine claims is "the beating heart of China's rapidly expanding surf industry."[30]

Surfing and China's Middle Class

The idea of a gold mine of Chinese middle-class citizens who would be attracted to surfing and consume its accoutrements is a popular discourse that the global surf culture industry has long liked to circulate. However, the dynamics of the Chinese middle class merit skepticism about whether this population will yield the profitability that surfing's culture industry hopes for. Who and what constitutes the middle class in China—interests, occupation, location, financial status, education level—remains contested among scholars, media, commercial observers, the public, and the Chinese government.[31]

A general definition of the Chinese middle class is households earning between 60,000 yuan to 229,000 yuan per year whose members are employed in certain types of professional occupations (e.g., entrepreneurs, managers, office workers, government officials), who engage in high levels of consumption, and who have a tertiary education level, leisure time, and access to financial and material resources.[32] There is disagreement about the size of the cohort. The Institute of Sociology of the Chinese Academy of Social Sciences explains the number of people who self-identify as middle class and lower middle class is low.[33] Many people classified as part of this stratum actually have to work long hours and have little to no disposable income as they feel the bite of increasing living costs such as education, property, food, and health care, particularly in cities where the majority of these people are located.[34] A higher number of college enrollments has also meant more white-collar workers putting downward pressure on the group's wages. Chinese scholars have found that, for the middle class, a key limitation in participation in extreme sports in China is cost and time.[35] China's middle class simply do not have "cash and leisure time to burn." Furthermore, the biggest beneficiaries of urban employment and wage growth in China have been rural-to-urban migrant-workers who begin at a low base wage, meaning that while they consume more, they, too, have little spare income, and their overall spending power is low.[36]

The hype of surfing's culture industry can be attributed to the seduction of China's much-heralded turn to a consumer-led economy as part of what Chinese authorities call "socialism with Chinese characteristics."[37] Efforts emerge to sell to the Chinese middle-class consumer surfing's manufactured stoke and concomitant beach lifestyle tropes—freedom, carefree fun, pristine nature, an all-welcoming, family-oriented activity, white sandy beaches, sun, and so forth. This is what David Lanagan calls "surfing capital," which is intended to facilitate consumption patterns through which the nonsurfer can "share in the surfing lifestyle, but not necessarily be identified as a surfer, by the purchase of a style of clothing and other products."[38] As Scott Laderman writes, surfing is "just another brand. Welcome to industrial surf culture."[39]

The Surfing Industry in China

Although, to date, Chinese consumers have not shown an inclination to launch a spending boom on surfing, Chinese businesses and various levels of government have caught on to the commercial possibilities of surfing. As a consequence, some Western surfing firms have been collaborating with Chinese manufacturers since the 1990s. For example, well-known surf company Rip

Curl set up part of its offshore production in China in the 1990s.[40] Throughout China, a massive surfing industrial complex—manufacturing apparel and surfing equipment such as surfboards, wetsuits, traction pads, wax, surfboard bags, leashes, and components—has been exporting to the global surf market for well over a decade. A survey I conducted of twenty Chinese mass-production surfboard company websites shows that they were established post-2004. If Chinese consumers do prove to be a gold mine, Chinese firms will be poised to innovate, to ensure that products fit local tastes and needs and that local enterprises become the market leaders. Ever since *gaige kaifang* (the opening up policy) in 1979, people have been rushing to *xiahai* (go into the sea), which connotes getting rich by working in the private and foreign sectors. In 2004, the Chinese government set up the Chinese Extreme Sports Association (CESA), and in 2008 the independent organization Surfing China was established. Both closely collaborate with the ISA to promote surfing, with the principle aim of further seducing the global surfing culture industry and fostering domestic commerce: retail, manufacturing, and tourism.[41]

The tourism industry in China—particularly the various levels of government and the tourism industry on Hainan Island—realized there were commercial possibilities if they collaborated with the global surfing culture industry. The government would like this island to be the "Hawai'i of the East."[42] It has luxury resorts, golf courses, marinas, theme parks, and apartment complexes. The surf breaks on the island fit the popularized mainstream marketing representations of surfing: surfable waves (particularly suitable for beginners given their gentle slope and low power), palm trees, a warm climate, and some white sandy beaches. This surfing capital is now used by various levels of government, property developers, and the tourism industry to enhance their beach lifestyle marketing to attract holiday travelers, conference-goers, and real estate consumers, as well as investors. On the island, the Wanning City government, in particular, invests in and co-organizes international surfing events with surfing's culture industry and its sanctioning organizations (ISA, WSL, CESA, and Surfing China). The government helped fund surfing-specific contest facilities at the popular surfing location of Riyuewan (Sun and Moon Bay), which falls within the city government's jurisdiction. In a study of surfing and tourism on Hainan Island, Christophe Guibert and Benjamin Taunay point out that the goal has been to "establish international exposure through surfing. . . . Surfing is perceived by the political authorities in charge of economic development and tourism more as a windfall for the development of the territory than as a new sport offered to local inhabitants."[43] Furthermore, officials are aware that announcements of support by the government for tourism improve the stocks of firms invested in Hainan, with which some officials have ties.[44] Relationships with the global surf culture industry and use of surfing capital helps Chinese politicians, bureaucrats, and property developers raise awareness of the area to profitably expand the built environment.

The surfing capital used in marketing hides how a consequence of the rapid expansion of the built environment has been the destruction of the coastal ecology of Hainan through real estate construction, reclaiming land from the sea, waste dumping, agricultural and industrial chemical runoff, and coastal infrastructure building.[45] There is no proof of anyone involved in the global surfing culture industry being concerned about this consequence and the role they now play in it. In fact, illegal dumping of waste has occurred following surfing competitions.[46] Current relationships among developers, government, business leaders, and surf industry representatives are toxic. It is clear that any potential for capital accumulation is not to be put in any jeopardy by choosing relationships more thoughtfully and being part of different power effects. It is much easier to participate in and help reproduce the hegemonic discourse rather than to become part of alternative discourses of those on Hainan Island resisting environmental destruction, such as local environmentalists, residents, and academics who study the environmental impact of Hainan's tourism industry and property development.[47]

Surfing's culture industry contributes precious little directly to the local Riyuewan community, aside from ceremonial photo shoots of companies associated with surfing (endemic and non-endemic) giving out a few trinkets and free surf lessons. Émilie Crossley points out that the patronizing approach of marketing poverty is used to transform "poverty into a source of moral redemption; by allowing poverty to become subsumed into a seductive, exotic landscape so that it can be admired and consumed; and by constructing impoverished communities as 'poor but happy.'"[48] This marketing of poverty papers over any problems and impositions born of industry presence and produces a palatable "happy local" subject position for sharing and use. However, as one resident puts it, a *dàngāo* (delicious cake) that all can supposedly share is promised, but residents know they aren't getting much of a bite.[49]

During the international competitions and festivals on Hainan Island there is only ever a smattering of spectators. Many competitors, visiting dignitaries, media, and various industry representatives stay at luxury five-star resorts surrounding Riyuewan and drive to and from the competition site. Representatives of multimillion dollar companies, media, competitors, and government dignitaries do business. Nearly all the capital generated leaves the island or doesn't even reach its shores, let alone Riyuewan. At the same time, local

inhabitants of the village filter through the trash behind the competition structure, pulling out plastics, banners, and other detritus that they may be able to
make use of. It is an elite few who benefit from the presence of surfing's culture
industry.

The village at Riyuewan remains poor. It can be argued that surfing's culture
industry indirectly leads to employment opportunities in the tourism industry.
Local residents are pragmatic but conflicted about such tourism work because
of environmental concerns and their limited access to economic gains.[50] The
few who do get employment in the tourism and construction industry find
that the labor is precarious because of its seasonal nature and sensitivity to
fluctuations in the global and national economy.[51] Furthermore, costs of living
on Hainan have increased because of the presence of tourism; housing affordability is increasingly out of reach, and communities have been cheated of land
with little to no compensation by property developers.[52] The arrival of tourism
and construction employment simply does not equate to an escape from poverty, and is no panacea for social inequities—in fact, they can generate inequities.[53] In a nutshell, any manufactured stoke about subject positions produced
by the coming together of surfing, tourism, and employment is not borne out by
the everyday realities of the average working person.

An example is a family that was foundational to the beginning of surfing at
Riyuewan (and Hainan Island more broadly) and initially saw promise for upward social mobility with the arrival of surfing at Riyuewan. The family was
squatting on beachfront land and set up an informal enterprise—a restaurant—
where surfers who lived on or visited Hainan would eat, hang out, sleep, and
leave their boards. The family also began renting out surfboards. In 2011 a property developer, the Nanshan Group, began collaborating with the Wanning City
government on ways to turn Riyuewan into a water sport destination and promote the surrounding region's beach lifestyle credentials. The family's restaurant
was torn down, a surf club and contest-dedicated building were constructed,
and a large paved car park was put in. Riyuewan was already partially developed,
and included hotels, a themed "folk village," and unfinished villas, which were
being squatted in by locals. However, development had stalled, and the arrival
of surfing's culture industry was coopted to fire it up again.

The family had no legal recourse or protections, as is the case for many
people in informal economies, despite their right to make a living.[54] The family
and other residents from the nearby village lack the adequate *guanxi* (personal,
social, government, and business relationships and networks) to push back
against the interests of powerful stakeholders.[55] The mother of the family
now operates a small shop and informal hostel out of one of the unfinished

villas—again, squatting. This family does not give up and is an example of how China's underclass repeatedly have to "eat bitterness" (*chiku*), which involves enduring hardships and difficulties and pressing ahead.[56]

Other people have fared a bit better than the family I have just described. A cottage industry of surfing—surf schools, surf shops, and surf guides and tourism—employs a small cohort of people throughout Hainan. There is a powerful presence of foreign expatriates in this cottage industry. A handful of Chinese surfers have also worked hard to convert their physical abilities, cultural know-how, and social contacts into economic capital through company sponsorship. They primarily receive goods for personal use rather than financial support. A China Surf Team now exists, and with the tutelage of representatives of the ISA, members of that team are to be ambassadors for surfing's culture industry in China. It's a precarious aspiration. Two local sponsored surfers (not part of the China Surf Team) explain how this way of life is stressful and difficult. Promises have been made to a couple of children about possible competitive and sponsored surfing futures. One parent argues that business people just want "to play with our children like toys," and a grandfather doesn't want his grandson "to get lost in surfing" as it could distract from his education and his future (and the family's future) social mobility.[57]

Arianne M. Gaetano points out that, in Confucian doctrine, manual labor (*wu*) has been separated from, but considered complementary to, mental labor (*wen*); however, in contemporary China, a competitive social and economic setting has led to a premium being placed on educational attainment for social mobility and family security.[58] The parent and grandfather have a healthy skepticism.

Neoliberalism, Exploitation, and Gender Issues

Sport sociologist Jay Coakley points out that we should think critically about contemporary sport sponsorship and how it is used to interpellate people into and reaffirm elite, organized, competitive, commercial forms of sports that prioritize marketization, commodification, and profit.[59] A form of neoliberal subject formation takes place that turns people into atomistic competitive individuals and "entrepreneurial selves" who should always be fearful or worried about their future. Neoliberal subjects are expected to undertake self-surveillance according to a marketized cost-benefit rationality, whereby their personal merit becomes based on market value and the ability to consume and generate consumption.[60] Self-care and social mobility become the moral responsibility of the individual rather than any shared social responsibility. Neoliberalism maintains a survival-of-the fittest ethic despite structural inequities based on class, race, ethnicity, religion, caste, sexuality, gender, and physicality, among other identifiers.

While China is "not an openly committed neoliberal capitalist social forma- tion," it now demonstrates neoliberal characteristics.[61] Sport sponsorship helps fertilize an extension to liberalism, which has been part of political, social, and economic thought in China for over a century.[62] The result of this model of neoliberal sponsorship is that when it comes to sport funding, only ambas- sadors for this ideology are supported, and there is increased difficulty (if not impossibility) for grassroots sporting communities that are geared toward col- lective outcomes to access funding. This bears out when we consider how the local Riyuewan youth surf team struggles to secure funding and has to rely on good will from the local surf shop and volunteers. According to the volunteer coach of the team, the emphasis is on fun, participation, and strengthening the cultural autonomy of the local surfing community.[63]

Those children on Hainan Island who go surfing express joy. One girl has told me about how she "just loves" Liu Dan (who also refers to herself as "Darci"), the first female and most prominent professional surfer in China.[64] Liu Dan is featured regularly in domestic and international media. The media have emphasized Liu Dan's history as a ballerina, and she has been dubbed "China's professional surfing queen."[65] She is predominantly represented wear- ing her bikini on the beach and in the waves, and has a social media account that highlights her gym-going fitness regime and beach lifestyle.[66]

The hetero-sexy surfer girl is a commoditized representation that has been widely exploited by surfing's culture industry to appeal to a heteronormative male gaze, generate consumer interest, promote consumer femininities, and initiate and widen the marketplace in new locations.[67] Surfing's culture industry has a long history of exploiting female athletes through sexualization.[68] This is despite the concern that sexualization trivializes women's sport and the evidence showing that competence is the "overwhelming choice for what best represents self/sport and increases respect" for and by women's sports fans and athletes.[69] It's been found that "sex sells sex" rather than women's sport.[70]

While exploitation exists, it is important to acknowledge the agency that some women such as Liu Dan can achieve by using this hetero-sexy surfer-girl representation to obtain a standard of living that may not otherwise be possi- ble. Liu Dan speaks about the sense of empowerment and happiness she feels because of surfing.[71] Such liberal self-fashioning by Liu Dan is a way some women express their agency by "making do" and practically negotiating the con- ditions of possibility they are confronted with.

However, it's worth being cautious about how it is possible for such agency, and corporate sponsorship framed as empowerment, to be coopted into a growing alliance of a form of feminism with neoliberalism.[72] The market supposedly provides new possibilities and opportunities for women to "get ahead"; however, this functions as interpellation into a neoliberal subjectivity that leaves structural factors that oppress women untouched. The choice, agency, economic independence, and consumption of a few privileged women are discursively celebrated as gains for all women in order to reproduce their subject position and the ideology, despite there being very different racial, economic, ethnic, class, sexual orientation, ability, religious, and caste intersectionalities.[73] Co-optation of feminism by neoliberalism won't occur without a fight within China. Throughout its history in China, feminism and feminists have had many ideological points of reference (e.g., state socialism, anarchism, liberalism).[74] No matter which ideological point of reference, feminism in China remains crucial because the society remains predominantly patriarchal and gendered inequality–prevalent.[75]

In a study of women and sport in China, Jinxia Dong points out that elite female athletes in China enjoy more support for sport participation than ever before.[76] However, barriers still exist for many women at the grassroots level of sport participation.[77] An affluent young woman told me that her parents' ongoing insistence on her getting married gets in the way of focusing on surfing. She invents stories so as to convince her parents she has a boyfriend and get them off her back. She says, "I feel so bad about doing this. I feel like I am not being a good daughter."[78] There is a stigma attached to "leftover women" (*sheng nu*), which is how unmarried women over the age of twenty-seven are pejoratively referred to and which affects their opportunities in life.[79] Filial piety is also paramount, with an emphasis on the responsibilities of wives and mothers and the pressure to put these first. One woman felt it necessary to ask for her husband's consent before going surfing: "I really like surfing. I wanted to take my husband along with me to learn after my lesson went so well but he never made time to go with me. I was told to wait for him to go with me before trying it again. I decided to wait for him although I know this is going to be forever. I am not satisfied with this but it's not right to go against him."[80] Daughters are not always afforded the same agency as sons, and are often expected to embody particular feminine traits and virtues (being gentle, compliant, humble, subservient, deferent, calm, quiet, moderate, demure, courteous, etc.). Such a mode of femininity is particularly valued in the upper strata of society (or by people seeking upward social mobility) and influences why some upper-class women are expected to intentionally avoid participating in sports requiring strength or considerable exertion.[81] This attitude affects how surfing manifests physiologically, highlighting other concerns. A young girl said that "it is better to be gentle and slender, not strong. Women are not supposed to be strong and have muscles."[82] Thinness and fragility are hegemonic traits of female body beauty in China. Pale skin also represents social status and a hegemonic feminine beauty. Chinese professional surfer Monica Guo explains: "At first my mom was worried I wouldn't get married because I was too tan. But my mom has come around, and she always wishes me good luck in my competitions."[83]

The labels used to represent Liu Dan—ballerina and surfing queen—go some way toward allaying patriarchal concern by others about her particular participation, because they serve to underscore her femininity despite her participation in surfing. Also, possibilities for women have diversified—for example, tanning as a sign of middle-class cultural capital and leisure, as well as a "fit" body (not too muscular) as a marker of modern beauty. Changes to femininities are being articulated by women in China who have had exposure to alternative possibilities because of critical reflection, migration (internal and external), feminisms, glocalization, and transnationalism.[84] There has been a noticeable growth in the numbers of women surfing in Hong Kong, in particular.[85]

Conclusion

What I have just described in this chapter is not the case for everyone in China. It's a complex society, with many crisscrossing cultures producing variations in meanings and practices. However, there are some hegemonic consistencies, and as a first step this chapter focuses on them. It examines how a quotidian cultural politics of surfing is now playing out across consumption, culture, tourism, industry, gender, class, bodies, space, and more. This practical negotiation means the production of very particular ways of knowing and subject positions—power effects—and reveals that the "manufactured stoke" story has shortcomings.

Surfing's culture industry would have us believe that China's middle class cannot wait to associate themselves with surfing capital and consume its lifestyle products. Yet, that middle class is not as big, willing, or able to embrace wave-riding culture as surfing's culture industry assumes. Furthermore, wage and consumption growth has occurred principally with rural-to-urban migrant workers. At Riyuewan, people who are not part of the middle class are struggling to deal with changes, because they are marginalized and excluded from decision-making networks that determine the elite few who will accrue benefits from contact with surfing. An example of this situation is the entanglement of the tourism industry, property development, and surfing's culture industry on Hainan Island. This relationship is also proving to be environmentally toxic.

Some individuals have managed to exert a degree of agency and derive some benefits from surfing, such as securing personal sport sponsorship to fulfill aspirations of being a professional surfer. However, this aspiration and involvement in surfing's culture industry is precarious, and involves interpellation into a problematic neoliberal subjectivity. Professional women's surfer Liu Dan has managed to achieve a degree of choice and economic independence through surfing, although structural societal barriers that remain for many women need to be dealt with as such. Participation is not simply about individual choice; this is especially true for children whose involvement in surfing is often weighed against countless social pressures.

My role here has been to examine surfing in China in an informed way so as to appreciate how some people are experiencing surfing as part of a very specific social-political-economic-cultural milieu, as well as to appreciate how the various agencies identified above are constituted and blocked. I have provided evidence of multiple factors affecting the dissemination of surfing culture in China—this, of course, indicative of an ongoing battle between an overdetermined cultural autonomy and the manufactured stoke of the global surf culture industry and its extended range of participants and advocates in China.[86]

NOTES

1. See Comer, *Surfer Girls*; Thorpe, *Transnational*. Being "transnational" refers to people who, as a result of late capitalism and globalization, take up their lives across national borders. See Ong, *Flexible Citizenship*.

2. Comer, *Surfer Girls*.

3. Appadurai, *Modernity at Large*.

4. Robertson, "Glocalization," 25.

5. This chapter is, of course, not exhaustive, and much lies outside its scope—for example, racialization, labor, and the surf product manufacturing industry in China; human rights issues; sexuality; environmentalism and sustainability; and much more.

6. This chapter expands upon the empirical studies conducted by Christophe Guibert and Benjamin Taunay. See Guibert and Taunay, "From Political Pressure to Cultural Constraints," 372.

7. "Political anatomy of the detail": Foucault, *Discipline and Punish*, 139.

8. Said, *Orientalism*.

9. Francesco De Luca, "Aloha China: China Surf Report Becomes First Chinese Surf Publication," TheInertia.com, January 10, 2014, http://www.theinertia.com/business-media

/aloha-china-china-surf-report-becomes-first-chinese-surf-publication/. The ChinaSurf-Report website no longer exists, but they still maintain a Facebook page at https://www.facebook.com/CsrChinaSurfReport.

10. See Yang, "The Modernity of Power."

11. Adorno and Horkheimer, *Dialectic of Enlightenment*.

12. Kavanagh, *Manufacturing Stoke*. The claim that surfing is implicitly "positive" ig-nores how it also involves selfishness, violent territorialism, gendered ostracism, sexism, racism, homophobia, ableism, exploitation of developing world labor, colonialism, and environmental destruction; note also the continued mainstream of the use of toxic petro-chemicals in the industry.

13. In order to protect interviewees, I have anonymized participant names.

14. For a summary of the publicized and documented efforts, see Laderman, *Empire in Waves*, 154–157; Warshaw, *Encyclopedia*, 120–121.

15. Expatriate Jon Sims has been surfing on Zhujiajian Island in Zhejiang Province since the 1990s, and expatriates have been traveling to Hainan Island to surf since the 1980s. Discussions with the author, October 2013.

16. Yangwen, *China on the Sea*.

17. Gao, "Beidaihe Beach."

18. Kenneth Howe, "Surf City, SAR," *South China Morning Post*, December 9, 2000, http://www.scmp.com/article/333546/surf-city-sar.

19. Song Ou, interview, November 13, 2014.

20. Ah Jian, discussion with the author, September 2013.

21. I am referring to people who surf regularly, not those who go surfing once or twice a year, or who try surfing at a surf school but never surf again. It is also worth bearing in mind how the semi-autonomous region of Hong Kong and the identity of its people, who call themselves "Hong Kongers," are unique in China for their values, orientations, and attitudes, given the region's and people's particular colonial, migrant, economic, and ethnic history.

22. Jeff Mull, "Will China Become Surfing's Next Frontier?," *Surfer Magazine*, October 4, 2012, http://www.surfermag.com/features/will-china-become-surfing%E2%80%99s-next-frontier/#1VJRlHGkMOmVmHiQ.97.

23. Will Swanton, "Surfing on the Crest of a Wave in China," *Reuters News Agency*, Decem-ber 3, 2012, http://www.reuters.com/article/uk-surfing-china-idUSLNE8B200U20121203.

24. "ISA China Cup," *Surfer Magazine*, November 13, 2012, http://www.surfermag.com/blogs/industry-news/isa-china-cup/#sJkRmODEV4D4y1fs.97.

25. "ISA to Announce ISA China Cup for 2013 & Hainan Classic ASP Men's 6-Star," *What's on Sanya*, March 22, 2012, http://www.whatsonsanya.com/news-20663-isa-to-announce-isa-china-cup-for-2013-hainan-classic-asp-men-s-6-star.html.

26. In an April 15, 2015, press release, the ISA wrote, "Providing access to Surfing for those in new Surfing markets has become a priority for the ISA." See "Surfing Extends Reach to New Markets as Scotland and Finland Become ISA Member Federations," April 15, 2015, https://www.isasurf.org/surfing-extends-reach-to-new-markets-as-scotland-and-finland-become-isa-member-federations/.

27. Justin Housman, "Surf City, China?," *Surfer Magazine*, April 24, 2013, http://www.surfermag.com/features/surf-city-china/#U1JozeJb34WkqE2g.97.

28. Nicole Rowles, "New Push to Get More Chinese Surfing on the Gold Coast," *NBN News*, November 18, 2014, http://www.nbnnews.com.au/2014/11/18/new-push-to-get-more-chinese-surfing-on-the-gold-coast/.

29. Swanton, "Surfing on the Crest."

30. "Be Water, My Friend," *Desillusion* 49, no. 1 (2015), http://dslmag.com/be-water-my-friend/ (accessed 29 February 2017). Such events include the Hainan Wanning Riyue Bay International Surfing Festival (also marketed as the ISA China Cup; 2011–ongoing) and the WSL men's QS Hainan Classic (2012–ongoing), respectively. There is also the WSL Swatch Girls Pro China longboard event (2011–ongoing) and Women's QS Hainan Pro (shortboard; 2015–ongoing), which are both sanctioned by the WSL. A one-off event, the Nixon Surf Challenge, took place on Hainan Island in 2015.

31. Chunling, *China's Emerging Middle Class*; Goodman, *Class in Contemporary China*.

32. Chunling, *China's Emerging Middle Class*; Goodman, *Class in Contemporary China*.

33. Xhang Yi, "New Changes in China's Social Class Structure," *Beijing Daily*, March 7, 2012, http://en.people.cn/102780/7750165.html .

34. National Bureau of Statistics of China, *China Statistical Yearbook 2014*, http://www.stats.gov.cn/tjsj/ndsj/2014/indexeh.htm; "Cost of Living Rises in Cities across China," *China Daily*, February 7, 2013, http://en.people.cn/90778/8125040.html.

35. Zhao, "On Limiting Factors," 53–54.

36. Dexter Roberts, "Why China's Middle Class Can't Flex Its Buying Power," *Bloomberg Business*, February 10, 2015, https://www.bloomberg.com/news/articles/2015-02-10/why-china-s-middle-class-can-t-find-its-buying-power.

37. Celine Sun, "Domestic Consumption Set to Become China's Main Economic Driver," *South China Morning Post*, January 21, 2015, http://www.scmp.com/business/economy/article/1683807/domestic-consumption-set-become-chinas-main-economic-driver; "Socialism with Chinese Characteristics," The 17th Congress of the Chinese Communist Party, September 30, 2007, http://en.people.cn/90002/92169/92211/6275043.html. The economy is claimed to be capitalist by some scholars; see Ho-fung Hung, "Labor Politics under Three Stages of Chinese Capitalism."

38. Lanagan, "Dropping In," 171, 173–174.

39. Laderman, *Empire in Waves*, 153.

40. Stewart, Skinner, and Edwards, "Cluster Theory."

41. SurfingChina.org, accessed March 1, 2017.

42. Minhui et al., "Research on Sports Tourism," 503.

43. Guibert and Taunay, "From Political Pressure," 372.

44. Jianjun, Zhang, and Yamori, *The Announcement Effects*.

45. Huang et al., "The Status of the Ecological Environment," 180–186.

46. Clifton Evers, "The Growth of Surfing in China: At What Cost?," Swellnet.com, February 7, 2012, http://www.swellnet.com/news/surfpolitik/2012/02/07/growth-surfing-china-what-cost?page=2.

47. Li Jing, "Environmentalist Liu Futang Fined for Exposing Hainan Pollution Scandals," *South China Morning Post*, December 6, 2012, http://www.scmp.com/news/china/article/1098532/environmentalist-liu-futang-fined-exposing-hainan-pollution-scandals; "Pollution, Tourism Put Coasts at Risk," *China Daily*, June 12, 2015, http://www.chinadaily

.com.cn/china/2015-06/12/content_20981638.htm; "Reclaiming Land from the Sea Evokes Environmental Concerns," China.org.cn, August 19, 2015, http://www.china.org .cn/environment/2011-07/03/content_22912102.htm.

48. Crossley, "Poor but Happy," 235.

49. "Yu," discussion with the author, January 2014.

50. "Huang" and "Xiong," discussion with the author, September 2013.

51. Lacher and Oh, "Is Tourism a Low-Income Industry?," 464–472.

52. Edward Hong, "On China's Hainan Island, the Boom Is Deafening," *New York Times*, March 30, 2010, http://www.nytimes.com/2010/03/31/world/asia/31hainan.html; Long, "The Social Impacts of Tourism."

53. Xuan et al., "Residents' Perception of Tourism," 741–46.

54. Evers and Seale, *Informal Urban Street Markets*.

55. *Guanxi*, used to obtain resources and opportunities, is tightly woven in with wealth, education, location (e.g., urban as opposed to rural), and government contacts. See Li, Kun, and Xuegang, "The Problem of 'Guanxi,'" 115–138.

56. Loyalka, *Eating Bitterness*.

57. "Zheng," discussion with the author, September 2014; "Bin," interview by Clifton Evers, November 12, 2013, transcript.

58. See Gaetano, *Out to Work*.

59. Coakley, "Ideology Doesn't Just Happen," 67–84.

60. Foucault, *Birth of Biopolitics*.

61. Zhao, "Neoliberal Strategies, Socialist Legacies," 26.

62. Jenco, "Chinese Liberalism," 164–168.

63. "Christophe," in discussion with the author, December 2013.

64. "Yuan," in discussion with the author, November 2013.

65. Will Swanton, "Ballerina Reveals Beauty of Surfing to China," *Reuters News Agency*, October 26, 2011, http://www.reuters.com/article/us-surfing-china-idUSTRE79P58 Y20111026; "Darcy Liu: China's Professional Surfing Queen," *CCTV News*, January 16, 2014, http://english.cntv.cn/program/sportsscene/20140116/104255.shtml.

66. See Darci Liu's website at http://www.darciliu.com/.

67. Comer, *Surfer Girls*; Heywood, "Third Wave Feminism."

68. Comer, *Surfer Girls*; Heywood, "Third Wave Feminism."

69. Kane, LaVoi, and Fink, "Exploring Elite Female Athletes," 269–298.

70. Mary Jo Kane, "Sex Sells Sex, and Not Women's Sport," *The Nation*, July 27, 2011, https://www.thenation.com/article/sex-sells-sex-not-womens-sports/.

71. Liu Dan, interview by Clifton Evers, November 8, 2014.

72. Chen, "Neoliberalism and Popular Women's Culture."

73. McCall, "Complexity of Intersectionality."

74. Liu, Karl, and Ko, *Birth of Chinese Feminism*.

75. Fincher, *Leftover Women*.

76. Dong, "The 'Long March.'"

77. Xiong, "Stratification of Women's Sport."

78. "Cai," interview by Clifton Evers, October 20, 2013, transcript.

79. Fincher, *Leftover Women*.

80. "Jie," interview by Clifton Evers, July 10, 2013, transcript.

81. Dong, "The 'Long March.'"

82. "Ning," interview by Clifton Evers, June 23, 2014, transcript.

83. "Q&A with Chinese Surfer Monica Guo," CRIEnglish.com, November 27, 2013, http://english.cri.cn/11354/2013/11/27/2982s800737.htm.

84. Farrer, *Opening Up.*

85. Kylie Knott, "How Surfing Suddenly Became Cool in Hong Kong, and Its '70s Expat Roots," *South China Morning Post*, updated May 25, 2016, http://www.scmp.com/lifestyle/travel-leisure/article/1946156/how-surfing-suddenly-became-cool-hong-kong-and-its-70s.

86. Waves serve as an apt metaphor to understand how I interpret this multiplicity. See Deleuze, *Difference and Repetition.*

Bibliography

Abu-Lughod, Lila. "Do Muslim Women Really Need Saving? Anthropological Reflections on Cultural Relativism and Its Others." *American Anthropologist* 104 (2002): 783–790.

Adorno, Theodor, and Max Horkheimer. *Dialectic of Enlightenment*. Palo Alto, CA: Stanford University Press, 2002.

Aeder, Erik. "The Southern Cone Expedition, Part III: Chile." *Surfer* 23, no. 11 (November 1982): 44–45.

Agrawal, Arun. "Common Property Institutions and Sustainable Governance of Resources." *World Development* 29 (2001): 1649–1672.

Agrawal, Arun. "Sustainable Governance of Common-pool Resources: Context, Methods, and Politics." *Annual Review of Anthropology* 32 (2003): 243–262.

Ahmed, Sara. *The Promise of Happiness*. Durham, NC: Duke University Press, 2010.

Aho, Paul. *Surfing Florida: A Photographic History*. Gainesville: University of Florida Press, 2014.

Ahorro, Joseph. *The Waves of Post-Development Theory and a Consideration of the Philippines*. Edmonton: University of Alberta, 2008.

Alaimo, Stacy. "States of Suspension: Trans-corporeality at Sea." *Interdisciplinary Studies in Literature and Environment* 19, no. 3 (2012): 476–493.

Alaimo, Stacy. "Trans-Corporeal Feminisms and the Ethical Space of Nature." In *Material Feminisms*, edited by Stacy Alaimo and Susan Hekman, 237–264. Bloomington: Indiana University Press, 2008.

Aldrich, Robert. *Colonialism and Homosexuality*. London: Routledge, 2002.

Alexander, James Edward. *Narrative of a Voyage of Observation among the Colonies of Western Africa*. 2 vol. London: H. Colburn, 1837.

Amin, Ash, and Nigel Thrift. "Cultural Economy and Cities." *Progress in Human Geography* 31, no. 2 (2007): 143–161.

Anderson, Benedict. *Imagined Communities: Reflection on the Origin and Spread of Nationalism* (revised and extended ed.). London: Verso, 1991.

Anderson, Eric. "Assessing the Sociology of Sport: On Changing Masculinities and Homophobia." *International Review for the Sociology of Sport* 50, no. 4–5 (2015): 363–367.

Anderson, Eric. *Inclusive Masculinity: The Changing Nature of Masculinities.* London: Routledge, 2009.

Anderson, Eric. *21st Century Jocks: Sporting Men and Contemporary Heterosexuality.* Basingstoke: Palgrave Macmillan, 2014.

Anderson, Eric. "Updating the Outcome: Gay Athletes, Straight Teams, and Coming Out in Educationally Based Sport Teams." *Gender & Society* 25, no. 2 (2011): 250–268.

Anderson, Eric, Adi Adams, and Ian Rivers. " 'I kiss them because I love them': The Emergence of Heterosexual Men Kissing in British Institutes of Education." *Archives of Sexual Behavior* 41, no. 2 (2012): 421–430.

Andrew, John A. III. *Rebuilding the Christian Commonwealth: New England Congregationalists and Foreign Missions, 1800–1830.* Lexington: University Press of Kentucky, 1976.

Angel-Ajani, Asale. "Expert Witness: Notes toward Revisiting the Politics of Listening." *Anthropology and Humanism* 29, no. 2 (2004): 133–144.

Antil, John, Rick Burton, and Matthew Robinson. "Exploring the Challenges Facing Female Athletes as Endorsers." *Journal of Brand Strategy* 1, no. 3 (2012): 292–307.

Anzaldúa, Gloria. *Borderlands/La Frontera: The New Mestiza.* San Francisco: Aunt Lute Books, 1987.

Appadurai, Arjun. *Modernity at Large: Cultural Dimensions of Globalization.* Minneapolis: University of Minnesota Press, 1996.

Archer, Robert, and Antoine Bouillon. *The South African Game: Sport and Racism.* London: Zed Press, 1982.

Arnould, Eric, Linda Price, and Cele Otnes, "Making Consumption Magic: A Study of White-Water River Rafting." *Journal of Contemporary Ethnography* 28, no. 1 (1999): 33–68.

Aronowitz, Stanley, Jonathan Cutler, and Michael Roberts, ed. *Class: An Anthology.* New York: Wiley-Blackwell, 2017.

Atencio, Matthew, Becky Beal, and Charlene Wilson. "The Distinction of Risk: Urban Skateboarding, Street Habitus and the Construction of Hierarchical Gender Relations." *Qualitative Research in Sport and Exercise* 1, no. 1 (2009): 3–20.

Atkinson, Michael. "Parkour, Anarcho-Environmentalism, and Poiesis." *Journal of Sport and Social Issues* 33, no. 2 (2009): 169–194.

Austen, Roger. "Stoddard's Little Tricks in *South Sea Idyls.*" In *Essays on Gay Literature,* edited by Stuart Kellogg, 73–82. New York: Routledge, 1985.

Aveling, Nado. "Critical Whiteness Studies and the Challenges of Learning to Be a 'White Ally.' " *Borderlands eJournal* 3, no. 2 (2004): n.p.

Babitz, Eve. *Eve's Hollywood.* Delacorte Press, 1974.

Bailyn, Bernard, and Patricia L. Denault, eds. *Soundings in Atlantic History: Latent Structures and Intellectual Currents, 1500–1830.* Cambridge, MA: Harvard University Press, 2009.

Baker, Bernie. "Perils of the Tropics." *Surfer* 11, no. 5 (November 1970).

Baker, Bernie. "Return to El Salvador." *Surfer* 28, no. 3 (March 1987).

Baker, Tim. *Australia's Century of Surf.* Sydney: Ebury Press, 2013.

Barclay, Ryan, and Peter West. "Racism or Patriotism? An Eyewitness Account of the Cronulla Demonstrations of 11 December 2005." *People and Place* 14, no. 1 (2006): 75–85.

Barilotti, Steve. "Lost Horizons: Surfer Colonialism in the 21st Century." *The Surfer's Journal* 3, no. 11 (2002): 88–97.

Barkan, Elazar. "Victorian Promiscuity: Greek Ethics and Primitive Exemplars." In *Prehistories of the Future: The Primitivist Project and the Culture of Modernism*, edited by Elazar Barkan and Ronald Bush, 56–92. Palo Alto, CA: Stanford University Press, 1995.

Barker, Joanne. *Native Acts: Laws, Recognition, and Cultural Authenticity.* Durham, NC: Duke University Press, 2011.

Barnes, Trevor J. "Retheorizing Economic Geography: From the Quantitative Revolution to the 'Cultural' Turn." *Annals of the Association of American Geographers* 91, no. 3 (2001): 546–565.

Barnett, Cornel. *Hitting the Lip: Surfing in South Africa.* Johannesburg: Macmillan South Africa, 1974.

Barrère, Dorothy, and Marshall Sahlins. "Tahitians in the Early History of Hawaiian Christianity: The Journal of Toketa." *Hawaiian Journal of History* 13 (1979): 19–35.

Barry, Boubacar. *Senegambia and the Slave Trade.* Cambridge: Cambridge University Press, 1998.

Bartholomew, Wayne, and Tim Baker. *Bustin' Down the Door.* Sydney: HarperSports, 1996.

Basson, Laura. *White Enough to Be American? Race Mixing, Indigenous People, and the Boundaries of State and Nation.* Chapel Hill: University of North Carolina Press, 2008.

Bates, George Washington. *Sandwich Islands Notes. By a Haole.* New York: Harper & Brothers, 1854.

Beaglehole, J. G., ed. *The Journals of Captain James Cook on His Voyages of Discovery: The Voyage of the Resolution and Discovery, 1776–1780.* 3 vols. Cambridge: Cambridge University Press, 1967.

Beamish, Christian. *Voyage of the Cormorant.* Ventura, CA: Patagonia Books, 2012.

Beattie, Keith. "Sick, Filthy, and Delirious: Surf Film and Video and the Documentary Mode." *Continuum* 15, no. 3 (2001): 333–348.

Beinart, William. *Twentieth-Century South Africa.* Oxford: Oxford University Press, 1994.

Bell, Daniel. *The Cultural Contradictions of Capitalism.* New York: Basic Books, 1976.

Bell, Michael. "Primitivism." In *The Critical Idiom.* New York: Barnes and Noble, 1972.

Benham, M. K. A., and R. H. Heck. *Culture and Educational Policy in Hawai'i: The Silencing of Native Voices.* New York: Routledge, 2013.

Bentley, Jerry H., Renate Bridenthal, and Kären Wigen, eds. *Seascapes: Maritime Histories, Littoral Cultures, and Transoceanic Exchanges.* Honolulu: University of Hawai'i Press, 2007.

Berkhofer Jr., Robert F. *The White Man's Indian: Images of the American Indian from Columbus to the Present.* New York: Vintage, 2011.

Bhabha, Homi. *The Location of Culture.* London: Routledge, 1994.

Bhabha, Homi, ed. *Nation and Narration*. New York: Routledge, 1990.

Billings, Andrew, and Marie Hardin, ed. *The Routledge Handbook of Sport and New Media*. New York: Routledge, 2014.

Bingham, Hiram. *A Residence of Twenty-One Years in the Sandwich Islands*. New York: Converse, 1847.

Blake, Tom Edward. *Hawaiian Surfriders, 1935*. Redondo Beach: Mountain and Sea, 2006 [1983].

Blake, Tom Edward. "Riding the Breakers! Hollow Hawaiian Surfboard." *Popular Mechanics Magazine* 68, no. 1 (1937): 114–115.

Blake, Tom Edward. "Waves and Thrills at Waikiki." *National Geographic* 67, no. 5 (May 1935): 597–604.

Bold, Harry. "Bruces Beauties." *South African Surfer* 3, no. 1 (January 1967).

Bold, Harry. "Editorial." *South African Surfer* 1, no. 1 (April 1965).

Bold, Harry. "Editorial." *South African Surfer* 3, no. 2 (1967).

Bold, Harry. "S.A. Titles 1966." *South African Surfer* 2, no. 4 (October 1966).

Bolster, W. Jeffrey. *The Mortal Sea: Fishing the Atlantic in the Age of Sail*. Cambridge, MA: Harvard University Press, 2012.

Bolster, W. Jeffrey. "Putting the Ocean in Atlantic History: Maritime Communities and Marine Ecology in the Northwest Atlantic, 1500–1800." *American Historical Review* 113 (2008): 19–47.

Bonilla-Silva, Eduardo. *Racism Without Racists: Color-Blind Racism and the Persistence of Racial Inequality in the United States*. Lanham, MD: Rowman & Littlefield, 2006.

Bonner, Frances, Susan McKay, and Alan McKee. "On the Beach." *Continuum: Journal of Media & Cultural Studies* 15, no. 3 (2001): 270–274.

Booth, Douglas. "Ambiguities in Pleasure and Discipline: The Development of Competitive Surfing." *Journal of Sport History* 22, no. 3 (1995): 189–206.

Booth, Douglas. *Australian Beach Cultures: The History of Sun, Sand and Surf*. London and Portland: F. Cass [Routledge], 2001.

Booth, Douglas. "Evidence Revisited: Interpreting Historical Materials in Sport History." *Rethinking History* 9, no. 4 (2005): 459–483.

Booth, Douglas. "From Bikinis to Boardshorts: Wahines and the Paradoxes of Surfing Culture." *Journal of Sport History* 28, no. 1 (2001): 3–22.

Booth, Douglas. "Paradoxes of Material Culture: The Political Economy of Surfing." In *The Political Economy of Sport*, edited by John Nauright and Kim Schimmel, 310–343. New York: Palgrave Macmillan, 2006.

Booth, Douglas. "(Re-)reading the Surfers' Bible: The Affects of Tracks." *Continuum* 22, no. 1 (2008): 17–35.

Booth, Douglas. "Surfing: The Cultural and Technological Determinants." *Culture, Sport, Society* 2, no. 1 (1999): 35–55.

Booth, Douglas. "Surfing Films and Videos: Adolescent Fun, Alternative Lifestyle, Adventure Industry." *Journal of Sport History* 23, no. 3 (1996): 313–327.

Booth, Douglas. "Surfing: From One (Cultural) Extreme to Another." In *Understanding Lifestyle Sports: Consumption, Identity and Difference*, edited by Belinda Wheaton, 94–109. London: Routledge, 2004.

Booth, Douglas. *Surfing: The Ultimate Guide.* Westport, CT: Greenwood Press, 2011.

Booth, Douglas. "War off the Water: The Australian Surf Lifesaving Association and the Beach." *Sporting Traditions* 7 (1991): 134–162.

Borgerson, Janet. "Judith Butler: On Organizing Subjectivities." *Sociological Review* 53, no. 1 (2005): 63–79.

Borne, Gregory. "Surfing and Sustainable Development." In *Sustainable Stoke: Transitions to Sustainability in the Surfing World*, edited by Gregory Borne and Jess Ponting, 18–27. Plymouth, UK: University of Plymouth Press, 2015.

Borne, Gregory, and Jess Ponting. *Sustainable Stoke: Transitions to Sustainability in the Surfing World.* Plymouth, UK: University of Plymouth Press, 2015.

Bosman, William. *A New and Accurate Description of the Coast of Guinea, Divided into the Gold, the Slave, and the Ivory Coasts.* New York: Knapton and Midwinter, 1705.

Bourdieu, Pierre. "Cultural Reproduction and Social Reproduction." In *Knowledge, Education, and Cultural Change: Papers in the Sociology of Education*, edited by Richard Brown, 71–112. London: Tavistock, 1973.

Bourdieu, Pierre. *Distinction: A Social Critique of the Judgement of Taste.* London: Routledge, 1984.

Bourdieu, Pierre. *Homo Academicus.* Oxford: Polity Press, 2001.

Bourdieu, Pierre. *The Logic of Practice.* Cambridge: Polity Press, 1990.

Bourdieu, Pierre. *Outline of a Theory of Practice.* Cambridge: Cambridge University Press, 1977.

Bourdieu, Pierre. *Practical Reason: On the Theory of Action.* Cambridge: Polity Press, 1998.

Bourdieu, Pierre. "Social Space and Symbolic Power." *Sociological Theory* 7, no. 1 (1989): 14–25.

Bourdieu, Pierre, and Loïc Wacquant. *An Invitation to Reflexive Sociology.* Chicago: University of Chicago Press, 1992.

Bradley, James. *The Imperial Cruise: A Secret History of Empire and War.* New York: Back Bay Books, 2009.

Braidotti, Rosi. *Nomadic Subjects: Embodiment and Sexual Difference in Contemporary Feminist Theory.* New York: Columbia University Press, 1994.

Brassey, Anna. *A Voyage in the "Sunbeam": Our Home on the Ocean for Eleven Months.* St. Louis, 1890.

Brennan, Teresa. *Globalization and Its Terrors: Daily Life in the West.* New York: Routledge, 2003.

Briassoulis, Helen. "Sustainable Tourism and the Question of the Commons." *Annals of Tourism Research* 29, no. 4 (2002): 1065–1085.

Bridge, Horatio. *Journal of an African Cruiser.* New York: G.P. Putnam & Co., 1853.

Briggs, Laura, "Activisms and Epistemologies: Problems for Transnationalisms." *Social Text* 26, no. 4 (2008): 79–95.

Broeze, Frank J. A., ed. *A Merchant's Perspective: Captain Jacobus Boelen's Narrative of His Visit to Hawai'i in 1828.* Honolulu: Hawaiian Historical Society, 1988.

Brooks, James. *Captives and Cousins: Slavery, Kinship, and Community in the Southwest Borderlands.* Chapel Hill: University of North Carolina Press, 2002.

Brownell, Susan, ed. *The 1904 Anthropology Days and Olympic Games: Sport, Race, and American Imperialism.* Lincoln: University of Nebraska Press, 2008.

Bruce, Toni. "Assessing the Sociology of Sport: On Media and Representations of Sportswomen." *International Review for the Sociology of Sport* 50, no. 4–5 (2015): 380–384.

Bruce, Toni. "Reflections on Communication and Sport: On Women and Femininities." *Communication & Sport* 1, no. 1–2 (2013): 125–137.

Bruce, Toni, and Marie Hardin. "Reclaiming Our Voices: Sportswomen and Social Media." In *Routledge Handbook of Sport and New Media*, edited by Andrew Billings and Marie Hardin, 311–319. New York: Routledge, 2014.

Bruce, William Straton. *Commentary on the Gospel According to St. Matthew.* Boston: H. H. & T. W. Carter, 1867.

Bryson, John, Michael Taylor, and Richard Cooper. "Competing by Design, Specialization and Customization: Manufacturing Locks in the West Midlands (UK)." *Geografiska Annaler* 90, no. 2 (2008): 173–186.

Bryson, Lois. "Sport and the Maintenance of Masculine Hegemony." *Women's Studies International Forum* 10, no. 4 (1987): 349–360.

Buckley, Ralf. *Adventure Tourism.* Oxford: CAB International, 2006.

Buckley, Ralf. "Surf Tourism and Sustainable Development in Indo-Pacific Islands. I. The Industry and the Islands." *Journal of Sustainable Tourism* 10, no. 5 (2002): 405–424.

Buckley, Ralf. "Surf Tourism and Sustainable Development in Indo-Pacific Islands: II. Recreational Capacity Management and Case Study." *Journal of Sustainable Tourism* 10, no. 5 (2002): 425–442.

Buckley, Ralf, and Claudia Ollenburg. "Tacit Knowledge Transfer: Cross-Cultural Adventure." *Annals of Tourism Research* 40 (2013): 419–422.

Burawoy, Michael. "The Extended Case Method." *Sociological Theory* 16, no. 1 (2002): 4–33.

Burdsey, Daniel. "'One of the Lads'? Dual Ethnicity and Assimilated Ethnicities in the Careers of British Asian Professional Footballers." *Ethnic and Racial Studies* 27, no. 5 (2004): 757–779.

Burdsey, Daniel. "That Joke Isn't Funny Anymore: Racial Microaggressions, Color-Blind Ideology and the Mitigation of Racism in English Men's First-Class Cricket." *Sociology of Sport* 28 (2011): 261–283.

Burns, Tim, dir., and Huey Benjamin, prod. *Surfing the Healing Wave.* Canberra: Ronin Films, 1999. DVD.

Burstyn, Varda. *The Rites of Men: Manhood, Politics, and the Culture of Sport.* Toronto: University of Toronto Press, 1999.

Butler, David. *The Adventures of a Reluctant Printer.* Cape Town: David Butler, 2010.

Butler, Judith. *Gender Trouble: Feminism and the Subversion of Identity.* New York: Routledge, 1999.

Butler, Judith, and Gayatri Chakravorty Spivak. *Who Sings the Nation-State? Language, Politics, Belonging.* Calcutta: Seagull Books, 2007.

Butler, R. W. "The Concept of a Tourist Area Cycle of Evolution Implications for Management of Resources." *Canadian Geographer* 24, no. 1 (1980): 5–12.

Butt, Tony. *Surf Science: An Introduction to Waves for Surfing*. Honolulu: University of Hawai'i Press, 2004.

Callon, Michel. "Some Elements of a Sociology of Translation: Domestication of the Scallops and the Fishermen of St. Brieuc Bay." In *Power, Action and Belief: A New Sociology of Knowledge*, edited by J. Law, 196–233. London: Routledge, 1986.

Callon, Michel, ed. *The Laws of the Markets*. Oxford: Blackwell, 1998.

Cameron, Jenny. "Collaborating with Communities: An Assets-Based Approach to Community and Economic Development." Paper presented to the Planning Institute of Australia, National Planning Congress 2003, Adelaide.

Cameron, Jenny, and Katherine Gibson. "Participatory Action Research in a Poststructuralist Vein." *Geoforum* 36, no. 3 (2005): 315–331.

Campbell, James. "The Americanization of South Africa." In *A South African and American Comparative Reader: The Best of Safundi and Other Selected Articles*, edited by Andrew Offenburger, Scott Rosenberg, and Christopher Saunders, 23–40. New Haven, CT: Safundi, 2002.

Camporesi, Piero. *Fear of Hell: Images of Damnation and Salvation in Early Modern Europe*. University Park: Pennsylvania State University Press, 1987.

Cañizares-Esguerra, Jorge. *Puritan Conquistadors: Iberianizing the Atlantic, 1550–1700*. Palo Alto: Stanford University Press, 2006.

Cañizares-Esguerra, Jorge, Matt Childs, and James Sidbury, eds. *The Black Urban Atlantic in the Age of the Slave Trade*. Philadelphia: University of Pennsylvania Press, 2013.

Canniford, Robin. "Culture Clash: Economic Reconstructions of Hawaiian Surfing." In *On the Edge: Leisure, Consumption, and the Representation of Adventure Sports*, edited by Joan Ormrod and Belinda Wheaton, 1–16. Eastbourne, UK: Leisure Studies Association, 2009.

Canniford, Robin. "Moving Shadows: Suggestions for Ethnography in Globalised Cultures." *Qualitative Market Research: An International Journal* 8, no. 2 (1998): 204–218.

Canniford, Robin, and Eminegül Karababa. "Partly Primitive: Discursive Constructions of the Domestic Surfer." *Consumption, Markets & Culture* 16, no. 2 (2013): 119–144.

Canniford, Robin, and Avi Shankar. "Marketing the Savage: Appropriating Tribal Tropes." In *Consumer Tribes*, edited by Bernard Cova, Robert Kozinets, and Avi Shankar, 35–48. Amsterdam: Butterworth-Heinemann, 2007.

Canniford, Robin, and Avi Shankar. "Purifying Practices: How Consumers Assemble Romantic Experiences of Nature." *Journal of Consumer Research* 39, no. 5 (2013): 1051–1069.

Carbery, Graham. *Towards Homosexual Equality in Australian Criminal Law—A Brief History*. Parkville, Victoria: Australian Lesbian and Gay Archives, 2014.

Carlson, Bronwyn. *The Politics of Identity: Who Counts as Aboriginal Today?* Canberra: Aboriginal Studies Press, 2016.

Carlson, Elof. *The 7 Sexes: Biology of Sex Determination*. Bloomington: Indiana University Press, 2013.

Carrington, Ben. "Double Consciousness and the Black British Athlete." In *Black British Culture and Society: A Text Reader*, edited by Kwesi Owusu, 133–156. London: Routledge, 2000.

Carrington, Ben. "Fear of a Black Athlete: Masculinity, Politics, and the Body." *New Formations* 45 (2001/2002): 91–110.

Carrington, Ben. "Leeds and the Topography of Race in Six Scenes." In *Sport, Leisure and Culture in the Postmodern City*, edited by Peter Bramham and Stephen Wagg, 99–128. Leeds: Ashgate, 2009.

Carrington, Ben. *Race, Sport, and Politics: The Sporting Black Diaspora.* London: Sage, 2010.

Castells, Manuel. *Networks of Outrage and Hope: Social Movements in the Internet Age.* Cambridge: Polity Press, 2013

Castle, William R. Jr. *Hawaiian Islands, Past and Present.* New York: Dodd Mead & Co., 1917.

Castree, Noel. "Labour Geography: A Work in Progress." *International Journal of Urban and Regional Research* 31, no. 4 (2007): 853–862.

Castree, Noel, and Thomas MacMillan. "Dissolving Dualisms: Actor-Networks and the Reimagination of Nature." In *Social Nature: Theory, Practice, and Politics*, edited by Noel Castree and Bruce Braun, 208–224. Malden, MA: Blackwell Publishers, 2001.

Caudwell, Jayne. *Sport, Sexualities and Queer/Theory.* Abingdon: Routledge, 2006.

Caudwell, Jayne. "Sporting Gender: Women's Footballing Bodies As Sites/Sights for the (Re)Articulation of Sex, Gender, and Desire." *Sociology of Sport Journal* 20 (2003): 371–386.

Charlesworth, Cecile. "Girls Overboard." *South African Surfer* 2, no. 3 (July 1966).

Cheever, Henry Theodore. *Life in the Sandwich Islands: or, The Heart of the Pacific, as It Was and Is.* New York: A. S. Barnes & Co., 1851.

Chen, Eva. "Neoliberalism and Popular Women's Culture: Rethinking Choice, Freedom and Agency." *European Journal of Cultural Studies* 16, no. 4 (2013): 440–452.

Chen, T. A. "The Chinese Guild." *Mid-Pacific Magazine* 23, no. 6 (1922): 529–533.

Chen, Xiaomei. *Occidentalism: A Theory of Counter-Discourse in Post-Mao China.* New York: Oxford, 1995.

Cheng, Tiejun, and Mark Selden. "The Origins and Social Consequences of China's Hukou System." *The China Quarterly* 139 (1994): 644–668.

Cheng, Tien-Ming, and Sheng-Hshiung Tsaur. "The Relationship between Serious Leisure Characteristics and Recreation Involvement: A Case Study of Taiwan's Surfing Activities." *Leisure Studies* 31, no. 1 (2012): 53–68.

Chivers-Yochim, Emily. *Skate Life: Re-imagining White Masculinity.* Ann Arbor: University of Michigan Press, 2010.

Christie, Ian, and Diane Warburton, eds. *From Here to Sustainability.* London: Earthscan.

Chunling, Li, ed. *China's Emerging Middle Class.* Washington: Brookings Institution Press, 2010.

Clark, John. *Hawaiian Surfing: Traditions from the Past.* Honolulu: University of Hawai'i Press, 2011.

Clarke, John, Stuart Hall, Tony Jefferson, and Brian Roberts. "Subcultures, Cultures and Class: A Theoretical Overview." In *Resistance through Rituals: Youth Subcultures in Post-War Britain*, edited by Stuart Hall and Tony Jefferson, 9–74. London: Hutchinson, 1976.

Cleary, Bill. "Through Arid Desert and Steaming Jungle, on the Trail of a Mexican Malibu." *Surfer Magazine* 6, no. 4 (September 1965): n.p.

Coakley, Jay. "Assessing the Sociology of Sport: On Cultural Sensibilities and the Great Sport Myth." *International Review for the Sociology of Sport* 50, no. 4–5 (2015): 402–406.

Coakley, Jay. "Ideology Doesn't Just Happen: Sports and Neoliberalism." *Revista da Associación Latinoamericana de Estudios Socioculturales del Deporte* 1, no. 1 (2011): 67–84.

Cock, Martin, and Bill Hopwood. *Global Warning: Socialism and the Environment.* London: Militant Labour, 1996.

Coe, Neil, and David Jordhus-Lier. "Constrained Agency? Re-evaluating the Geographies of Labour." *Progress in Human Geography* 35 (2011): 211–233.

Cohen, Jeffrey. "Monster Culture (Seven Theses)." In *Monster Theory: Reading Culture,* edited by Jeffrey Cohen, 3–25. Minneapolis: University of Minnesota Press, 1996.

Colás, Yago. *Ball Don't Lie! Myth, Genealogy and Invention in the Cultures of Basketball.* Philadelphia: Temple University Press, 2016.

Colás, Yago. "'Ball Don't Lie!': Rasheed Wallace and the Politics of Protest in the National Basketball Association." *Communication & Sport* (2015): 1–22.

Colás, Yago. "Getting Free: The Arts and Politics of Basketball Modernity." *Journal of Sport and Social Issues* 39, no. 4 (2015): 267–286.

Colás, Yago. "The Meanings of Manu: Style, Race, and Globalization in the Culture of Basketball." In *Sports and Nationalism in Latin/o America,* edited by Héctor Fernández L'Hoeste, Robert McKee Irwin, and Juan Poblete, 249–268. New York: Palgrave Macmillan, 2015.

Colás, Yago. "What We Mean When We Say 'Play the Right Way': Strategic Fundamentals, Morality, and Race in the Cultures of Basketball." *Journal of the Midwest MLA* 45, no. 2 (2012): 109–125.

Coleman, Stuart Holmes. *Eddie Would Go: The Story of Eddie Aikau, Hawaiian Hero and Pioneer of Big Wave Surfing.* New York: St. Martin's Griffin, 2001.

Colwin, Cecil. *Breakthrough Swimming.* Champaign: Human Kinetics, 2002.

Comer, Krista. *Surfer Girls in the New World Order.* Durham, NC: Duke University Press, 2010.

Comer, Krista. "Thinking Otherwise across Global Wests: Issues of Mobility and Feminist Critical Regionalism." *Occasion* 10 (December 7, 2016): 1–18. http://arcade.stanford.edu/occasion/thinking-otherwise-across-global-wests-issues-mobility-and-feminist-critical-regionalism.

Comer, Krista. "Wanting to Be Lisa: Generational Rifts, Girl Power, and the Globalization of Surf Culture." In *American Youth Cultures,* edited by Neil Campbell, 237–265. Edinburgh: Edinburgh University Press, 2004.

Comer, Krista. "'We're Blacksurfing': Public History and Liberation Politics in *White Wash.*" *Journal of American Ethnic History* 35, no. 2 (2016): 68–78.

Commission on the Truth for El Salvador. "From Madness to Hope: The 12-Year War in El Salvador: Report of the Commission on the Truth for El Salvador. 15 March 1993." In *The United Nations and El Salvador, 1990–1995,* 354–357. New York: UN Department of Public Information, 1995.

Connell, R. W. *Gender and Power: Society, the Person and Sexual Politics.* Sydney: Allen & Unwin, 1987.

Connell, R. W., and James Messerschimdt. "Hegemonic Masculinity: Rethinking the Concept." *Gender and Society* 9, no. 6 (December 2005): 829–859.

Conner, Clifford D. *A People's History of Science: Miners, Midwives, and "Low Mechanicks."* New York: Nation Books, 2005.

Connery, Christopher. "There Was No More Sea: The Suppression of the Oceans, from the Bible to Cyberspace." *Journal of Historical Geographic* 32 (2006): 494–511.

Conroy, Joel, dir. *Waveriders.* Dublin: Inis Films/Besom Productions, 2008. DVD.

Cooley, Timothy. *Surfing About Music.* Berkeley: University of California Press, 2014.

Corbin, Alain. *Lure of the Sea.* Berkeley: University of California Press, 1994.

Crais, Clifton C. *Pamela Scully Sara Baartman & the Hottentot Venus: A Ghost Story & a Biography.* Princeton: Princeton University Press, 2009.

Craven, Christa, and Dána-Ain Davis. *Feminist Activist Ethnography: Counterpoints to Neoliberalism in North America.* Lanham, MD: Lexington Books, 2013.

Cresswell, Time. *Place: A Short Introduction.* Oxford: Blackwell, 2004.

Crossley, Émilie. "Poor but Happy: Volunteer Tourists' Encounters with Poverty." *Tourism Geographies: An International Journal of Tourism Space, Place and Environment* 14, no. 2 (2012): 235–253.

Curthoys, Ann. "Identity Crisis, Colonialism, Nation, and Gender in Australian History." *Gender & History* 15, no. 2 (1993): 165–176.

Cutler, Jonathan. *Labor's Time: Shorter Hours, the UAW, and the Struggle for American Unionism.* Philadelphia: Temple University Press, 2004.

Daly, Herman. "Sustainable Growth: An Impossibility Theorem." *Development Rome* 40, no. 1 (January 1997): 121–125.

Daniel, G. Reginald. "Either Black or White: Race, Modernity, and the Law of the Excluded Middle." In *Racial Thinking in the United States*, edited by Paul Sprickard and G. Reginald Daniel, 21–59. Notre Dame, IN: University of Notre Dame Press, 2004.

Darnell, Simon C., and Lyndsay M. C. Hayhurst. "Sport for Decolonization: Exploring a New Praxis of Sport for Development." *Progress in Development Studies* 11, no. 3 (2011): 183–196.

Davis, Lynne, and Heather Yanique Shpuniarsky. "The Spirit of Relationships: What We Have Learned about Indigenous/Non-Indigenous Alliances and Coalitions." In *Alliances: Re/Envisioning Indigenous–Non-Indigenous Relationships*, edited by Lynne Davis, 334–348. Toronto: University of Toronto Press, 2010.

Daws, Gavan. *Shoal of Time: A History of the Hawaiian Islands.* Honolulu: University of Hawai'i Press, 1968.

Dawson, Kevin. "Enslaved Ship Pilots in the Age of Revolutions: Challenging Perceptions of Race and Slavery between the Boundaries of Maritime and Terrestrial Bondage." *Journal of Social History* 47, no. 1 (2013): 71–100.

Dawson, Kevin. "Enslaved Swimmers and Divers in the Atlantic World." *The Journal of American History* 92, no. 4 (2006): 1327–1355.

Dawson, Kevin. *Enslaved Water People in the Atlantic World, 1444–1888: The Cultural Meanings of Water, Swimming, Surfing, and Canoeing in Atlantic Africa and the African Diaspora.* Philadelphia: University of Pennsylvania Press, 2017.

Dawson, Kevin. "Swimming, Surfing, and Underwater Diving in Early Modern Atlantic Africa and the African Diaspora." In *Navigating African Maritime History*, edited by Carina Ray and Jeremy Rich, 81–116. Liverpool: Liverpool University Press, 2009.

Debelle, Rob. "El Salvador: Is Paradise Lost?" *Tracks* 128 (May 1981): 15.

DeLaVega, Timothy Tovar. *Surfing in Hawai'i: 1778–1930*. Charleston: Arcadia Publishing, 2011.

DeLaVega, Timothy Tovar. *200 Years of Surfing Literature: An Annotated Bibliography*. Hanapepe, HI: Timothy DeLaVega, 2004.

Deleuze, Gilles. *Difference and Repetition*. New York: Columbia University Press, 1994.

Deleuze, Gilles. *Negotiations*. New York: Columbia University Press, 1995.

Deleuze, Gilles, and Felix Guattari. *A Thousand Plateaus*. New York: Continuum, 2004.

Deloria, Phillip. *Playing Indian*. New Haven, CT: Yale University Press, 1998.

de Marees, Pieter. *Description and Historical Account of the Gold Kingdom of Guinea*. Translated by Albert Van Dantzig and Adam Jones. New York: British Academy, 1987.

Dening, Greg. "Deep Time, Deep Spaces: Civilizing the Sea." In *Sea Changes: Historicizing the Ocean*, edited by Bernhard Klein and Gesa Mackenthun, 13–36. London: Routledge, 2004.

Dening, Greg. *Mr. Bligh's Bad Language: Passion, Power, and Theater on the Bounty*. New York: Cambridge University Press, 1997.

Denzin, Norman, Yvonna Lincoln, and Linda Tuhiwai Smith, eds. *Handbook of Critical and Indigenous Methodologies*. London: Sage, 2008.

de Rosnay, Joel. "Discovery: Mauritius." *Surfer Bi-Monthly* 4, no. 3 (June–July 1963).

Desch Obi, T. J. *Fighting for Honor: The History of African Martial Art Traditions in the Atlantic World*. Columbia: University of South Carolina Press, 2008.

Desmond, Jane. *Staging Tourism: Bodies on Display from Waikiki to Sea World*. Chicago: University of Chicago Press, 1999.

Diamond, Stanley. *In Search of the Primitive: A Critique of Civilization*. New Brunswick, NJ: Transaction Books, 1974.

Dibble, Sheldon. *A History of the Sandwich Islands*. Honolulu: T. G. Thrum, 1909.

Dickens, Charles. "The Noble Savage." *Household Words* 11 (1853): 337–339.

Dillabough, Jo-Anne. "To Be or Not to Be (a Gendered Subject): Was That the Question?" *Gender and Education* 21, no. 4 (2009): 455–466.

Dolnicar, Sara, and Martin Fluker. "Who's Riding the Wave? An Investigation into Demographic and Psychographic Characteristics of Surf Tourists." In *Riding the Wave of Tourism and Hospitality Research*, edited by R. L. Braithwaite and R. W. Braithwaite, 313–327. Lismore: Southern Cross University, 2003.

Dong, Jinxia. "The 'Long March' of Women and Sport in Mainland China: Revolution, Resistance and Resilience." In *Routledge Handbook of Sport, Gender and Sexuality*, edited by Jennifer Hargreaves and Eric Anderson, 87–96. London: Routledge, 2014.

Dora, Mickey. "To Whom It May Underestimate." *Surfer* 12, no. 4 (October 1971): 53–63.

Douglas, Bronwen, and Chris Ballard, eds. *Foreign Bodies: Oceania and the Science of Race 1750–1940*. Canberra: The Australian National University Press, 2008.

Driscoll, Colin M. H. "Artificial Protection against Solar Radiation—Fabrics." *Sun Protection in Man*, edited by Paulo Giacomoni, 457–486. Amsterdam: Elsevier, 2001.

Duane, Daniel. *Caught Inside: A Surfer's Year on the California Coast.* New York: North Point Press, 1996.

Du Bois, W. E. B. "Of Our Spiritual Strivings." In *The Souls of Black Folk.* New York: Gramercy Books, 1994.

Dunbar-Ortiz, Roxanne, and Dina Gilio-Whitaker. *"All the Real Indians Died Off" and 20 Other Myths about Native Americans.* Boston: Beacon Press, 2016.

Durrheim, Kevin, and John Dixon. "The Role of Place and Metaphor in Racial Exclusion: South Africa's Beaches as Sites of Shifting Racialization." *Ethnic and Racial Studies* 24, no. 3 (2001): 433–540.

Dweck, Michael. *The End: Montauk, N.Y.* New York: Harry N. Abrams, 2004.

Dwight, E. W. *Memoirs of Henry Obookiah, a Native of Owhyhee, and a Member of the Foreign Mission School.* Philadelphia: American Sunday School Union, 1830.

Eagleton, Terry. *Literary Theory: An Introduction.* Oxford: Wiley-Blackwell, 1996.

Edwards, Justin D. *Exotic Journeys: Exploring the Erotics of U.S. Travel Literature, 1840–1930.* Hanover: University Press of New England, 2001.

Egan, Danielle, and Gail Hawkes. "Girls, Sexuality and the Strange Carnalities of Advertisements." *Australian Feminist Studies* 23, no. 57 (2008): 307–322.

Ellis, William. *Narrative of a Tour through Hawai'i.* London: Fisher, Son, and P. Jackson, 1826.

Ellis, William. *Polynesian Researches, During a Residence of Nearly Six Years in the South Sea Islands.* 2 vols. London: Fisher, Son, and P. Jackson, 1829.

Emerson, Nathaniel B. "Causes of Decline of Ancient Hawaiian Sports." *The Friend* 50, no. 8 (August 1, 1892): 57.

Endo, Tetsuhiko. "Crimes Committed in the Spirit of Play." In *Sustainable Stoke: Transitions to Sustainability in the Surfing World*, edited by Gregory Borne and Jess Ponting, 84–88. Plymouth, UK: University of Plymouth Press, 2015.

Engledown, Sarah, ed. "Arcadia, Sound of the Sea: Exhibition Introduction." Canberra: National Portrait Gallery, Australia, 2014. Published in conjunction with the exhibition "Arcadia, Sound of the Sea."

Eperjesi, John R. *Imperialist Imaginary: Visions of Asia and the Pacific in American Culture.* Lebanon, NH: University Press of New England, 2005.

Erickson, Beth, Cory Johnson, and B. Dana Kivel. "Rocky Mountain National Park: History and Culture as Factors in African-American Park Visitation." *Journal of Leisure Research* 41, no. 4 (2009): 529–545.

Escobar, Arturo. "Construction Nature: Elements for a Post-Structuralist Political Ecology." *Futures* 28, no. 4 (1996): 325–343.

Escobar, Arturo. *Encountering Development: The Making and Unmaking of the Third World.* Princeton: Princeton University Press, 1995.

Esteva, Gustavo. "Development." In *The Development Dictionary: A Guide to Knowledge as Power*, edited by Wolfgang Sachs, 6–25. London: Zed Books, 2009.

Ettlinger, Nancy. "Precarity Unbound." *Alternatives: Global, Local, Political* 32, no. 3 (2007): 319–340.

Evan, Dick. "Body Surfing." *South African Surfer* 1, no. 2 (July 1965).

Evans, Jeremy. *The Battle for Paradise: Surfing, Tuna, and One Town's Quest to Save a Wave.* Lincoln: University of Nebraska Press, 2015.

Evers, Clifton. "Becoming-Man, Becoming-Wave." PhD diss., University of Sydney, 2005.

Evers, Clifton. "The Cronulla Race Riots: Safety Maps on an Australian Beach." *South Atlantic Quarterly* 107, no. 2 (2008): 411–429.

Evers, Clifton. "How to Surf." *Journal of Sport and Social Issues* 30, no. 3 (2006): 229–243.

Evers, Clifton. "Men Who Surf." *Cultural Studies Review* 10, no. 1 (2004): 27–41

Evers, Clifton. *Notes for a Young Surfer*. Australia: Melbourne University Press, 2010.

Evers, Clifton. "The Point: Surfing, Geography, and a Sensual Life of Men and Masculinity on the Gold Coast, Australia." *Social & Cultural Geography* 10, no. 8 (2009): 893–908.

Evers, Clifton. "Queer Waves." *Kurungubaa* 1, no. 2 (2008): 1–5.

Evers, Clifton, and Kirsten Seale, eds. *Informal Urban Street Markets: International Perspectives*. London: Routledge, 2014.

Falola, Toyin, and Matt D. Childs, eds. *The Changing Worlds of Atlantic Africa: Essays in Honor of Robin Law*. Durham, NC: Duke University Press, 2009.

Faris, John T. *Paradise of the Pacific*. New York: Doubleday Doran, 1929.

Farrer, James. *Opening Up: Youth, Sex, Culture and Market Reform in Shanghai*. Chicago: University of Chicago Press, 2002.

Faulkner, William. *As I Lay Dying*. New York: Modern Library, 2000.

Fausto-Sterling, A. "The Five Sexes, Revisited." *Sciences* 40, no. 4 (2000): 18–23.

Fiebert, Martin, and Mark Meyer. "Gender Stereotypes: A Bias Against Men." *Journal of Psychology* 131, no. 4 (1997): 407–410.

Fincher, Leta Hong. *Leftover Women: The Resurgence of Gender Inequality in China*. London: Zed Books, 2014.

Fine, Ben, and Ellen Leopold. *The World of Consumption: The Material and Cultural Revisited*. London: Routledge, 1993.

Fink, Janet. "Homophobia and the Marketing of Female Athletes and Women's Sport." *Sexual Orientation and Gender Identity in Sport*, edited by G. B. Cunningham, 49–60. College Station, TX: Center for Sport Management Research and Education, 2012.

Fink, Janet, George Cunningham, and Linda Kensicki. "Using Athletes as Endorsers to Sell Women's Sport: Attractiveness Versus Expertise." *Journal of Sport Management* 18 (2004): 350–367.

Finnegan, William. *Barbarian Days: A Surfing Life*. New York: Penguin, 2015.

Finney, Ben. "The Development and Diffusion of Modern Hawaiian Surfing." *Journal of the Polynesian Society* 69 (1960): 315–331.

Finney, Ben. "Surf Boarding in Oceania: Its Pre-European Distribution." *Wiener Voelkerkundliche Mitteilungen* 2 (1959): 23–36.

Finney, Ben. "Surf Boarding in West Africa." *Wiener Voelkerkundliche Mitteilungen* 5 (1962): 41–42.

Finney, Ben. "Surfing in Ancient Hawaii." *Journal of the Polynesian Society* 68 (1959): 327–347.

Finney, Ben, and James Houston. *Surfing: A History of the Ancient Hawaiian Sport*. San Francisco: Pomegranate Artbooks, 1996.

Finney, Ben, and James Houston. *Surfing: The Sport of Hawaiian Kings*. Rutland, VT: C. E. Tuttle, 1966.

Firmin, Joseph-Anténor. *The Equality of the Human Races*. Urbana: University of Illinois Press, 2002.

Fisher, Kevin. "Economies of Loss and Questions of Style in Contemporary Surf Subcultures." *Junctures* 4 (2005): 13–21.

Fletcher, Robert. "Between the Cattle and the Deep Blue Sea: The Janus Face of the Ecotourism-Extraction Nexus in Costa Rica." In *The Ecotourism-Extraction Nexus: Political Economies and Rural Realities of (Un)comfortable Bedfellows*, edited by Bram Büscher and Veronica Davidov, 69–87. New York: Routledge, 2014.

Fletcher, Robert. "Bodies Do Matter: The Peculiar Persistence of Neoliberalism in Environmental Governance." *Human Geography* 6, no. 1 (2013): 29–45.

Fletcher, Robert. "Neoliberal Environmentality: Towards a Poststructuralist Political Ecology of the Conservation Debate." *Conservation and Society* 8, no. 3 (2010): 171–181.

Fletcher, Robert. *Romancing the Wild: Cultural Dimensions of Ecotourism*. Durham, NC: Duke University Press, 2014.

Fletcher, Robert. "Sustaining Tourism, Sustaining Capitalism? The Tourism Industry's Role in Global Capitalist Expansion." *Tourism Geographies* 13, no. 3 (2011): 443–461.

Fletcher, Robert. "Using the Master's Tools? Neoliberal Conservation and the Evasion of Inequality." *Development and Change* 43, no. 1 (2012): 295–317.

Flynn, Pierce Julius. "Waves of Semiosis: Surfing's Iconic Progression." *American Journal of Semiotics* 5 no. 3 (1987): 397–418.

Ford, Nick, and David Brown. *Surfing and Social Theory: Experience, Embodiment and Narrative of the Dream Glide*. Abingdon: Routledge, 2006.

Fornander, Abraham. *Fornander Collection of Hawaiian Antiquities and Folk-Lore*. 12 vols. Honolulu: Bishop Museum Press, 1916–1917.

Fortes, Rafael. "Making Surf Media in Brazil." *Journal of Sport History* 40, no. 3 (2013): 385–392.

Fosfuri, Andrea, Marco Giarratana, and Esther Roca. "Community-Focused Strategies." *Strategic Organization* 9, no. 3 (2011): 222–239.

Foucault, Michel. *The Archaeology of Knowledge*. Translated by A. M. Sheridan-Smith. London: Tavistock, 1977.

Foucault, Michel. *The Birth of Biopolitics: Lectures at the College de France 1978–79*. New York: Palgrave Macmillan, 2008.

Foucault, Michel. *Discipline and Punish: The Birth of the Prison*. New York: Vintage Books, 1979.

Foucault, Michel. *Truth and Power. Power/Knowledge: Selected Interviews and Other Writings 1972–1977*. New York: Pantheon Books, 1980.

Foucault, Michel, James D. Faubion, and Robert Hurley. *Power*. Vol. 3. New York: New Press, 2000.

Franklin, Roslyn. "Making Waves: Contesting the Lifestyle Marketing and Sponsorship of Female Surfers." PhD diss., Griffith University, 2013.

Fynn, Henry Francis. *The Diary of Henry Francis Fynn: Compiled from Original Sources*. Edited by James Stuart. Pietermaritzburg: Shuter & Shooter, 1950.

Gaetano, Arianne M. *Out to Work: Migration, Gender, and the Changing Lives of Rural Women in Contemporary China*. Honolulu: University of Hawai'i Press, 2015.

Games, Alison. "Atlantic History: Definitions, Challenges and Opportunities." *American Historical Review* 111, no. 3 (2006): 741–757.

Gao, Yunxiang. "Beidaihe Beach: Leisure Culture and Modernity in Republican China," *Sport in Society: Cultures, Commerce, Media, Politics* 15, no. 10 (2012): 1353–1380.

Garcia, Robert, and Erica Flores Baltodano. "Free the Beach! Public Access, Equal Justice, and the California Coast." *Stanford Journal of Civil Rights and Civil Liberties* 2, no. 1 (2005): 143–208.

Garroutte, Eva. *Real Indians: Identity and the Survival of Native America.* Berkeley: University of California Press, 2003.

George, Sam, dir. *Hawaiian: The Legend of Eddie Aikau.* ESPN 30-for-30, 2013. Film.

Gibson, Chris. "Cultural Economy: Achievements, Divergences, Future Prospects." *Geographical Research* 50, no. 3 (2012): 282–290.

Gibson, Chris. "Cultures at Work: Why Culture Matters in Research on the Cultural Industries." *Social and Cultural Geography* 4, no. 2 (2003): 201–215.

Gibson-Graham, J. K. *A Postcapitalist Politics.* Minneapolis: University of Minnesota Press, 2006.

Gibson-Graham, J. K. "Surplus Possibilities: Postdevelopment and Community Economies." *Singapore Journal of Tropical Geography* 26, no. 1 (2005): 4–26.

Gilchrist, Paul, and Belinda Wheaton. "New Media Technologies in Lifestyle Sport." In *Digital Media Sport: Technology, Power and Culture in the Network Society*, edited by Brett Hutchins and David Rowe, 169–185. Abingdon: Routledge, 2013.

Gilio-Whitaker, Dina. "Panhe at the Crossroads: Toward an Indigenized Environmental Justice Discourse." Master's thesis, University of New Mexico, 2011.

Gill, Rosalind. "Commodity Feminism." In *The International Encyclopedia of Communication*, edited by Wolfgang Donsbach, 583–585. Malden: Blackwell, 2008.

Gill, Rosalind, and Andy Pratt. "In the Social Factory? Immaterial Labour, Precariousness and Cultural Work." *Theory, Culture and Society* 25 (2008): 1–30.

Gillis, John. *The Human Shore: Seacoasts in History.* Chicago: The University of Chicago Press, 2012.

Gillis, John. *Islands of the Mind: How the Human Imagination Created the Atlantic World.* New York: Palgrave Macmillan, 2009.

Gilmore, David D. *Manhood in the Making: Cultural Concepts of Masculinity.* New Haven, CT: Yale University Press, 1990.

Giroux, Henry. *On Critical Pedagogy.* New York: Continuum International Publishing Group, 2011.

Giroux, Henry. *The Terror of Neoliberalism.* Boulder, CO: Paradigm Publishers, 2004.

Go, Julian. *American Empire and the Politics of Meaning: Elite Political Culture in the Philippines and Puerto Rico during U.S. Colonialism.* Durham, NC: Duke University Press, 2008.

Goldberg, David Theo. *The Threat of Race: Reflections on Racial Neoliberalism.* Oxford: Blackwell, 2009.

Goltz, Dustin. "Investigating Queer Future Meanings: Destructive Perceptions of 'The Harder Path.'" *Qualitative Inquiry* 15, no. 3 (2009): 561–586.

Goodman, David S. *Class in Contemporary China.* Cambridge: Polity Press, 2014.

Gordon, Lewis. "Shifting the Geography of Reason in an Age of Disciplinary Decadence." *Transmodernity: Journal of Peripheral Cultural Production of the Luso-Hispanic World* 1, no. 2 (2011): 95–103.

Gordon, Michael, and Layne Beachley. *Layne Beachley: Beneath the Waves.* Melbourne: Random House, 2008.

Gosch, Jeremy, dir. *Bustin' Down the Door.* DVD. Screen Media Films, 2009.

Greene, Charles S. *Talofa, Samoa: A Summer Sail to an Enchanted Island.* San Francisco: San Francisco News Company, 1900.

Griffin, Pat. "Changing the Game: Homophobia, Sexism, and Lesbians in Sport." *Quest* 44 (1992): 251–265.

Gross, Ariela. *What Blood Won't Tell: A History of Race on Trial in America.* Cambridge, MA: Harvard University Press, 2008.

Grossman, Greg M., and Alan B. Krueger. "Economic Growth and the Environment." *The Quarterly Journal of Economics* 110, no. 2 (1995): 353–377.

Grugel, Jean, and Pía Riggirozzi. "Post-neoliberalism in Latin America: Rebuilding and Reclaiming the State after Crisis." *Development and Change* 43, no. 1 (2012): 1–21.

Grundlingh, Albert. "'Are We Afrikaners Getting Too Rich?' Cornucopia and Change in Afrikanerdom in the 1960s." *Journal of Historical Sociology* 21, no. 2/3 (2008): 143–165.

Grundlingh, Albert. *Potent Pastimes: Sport and Leisure Practices in Modern Afrikaner History.* Pretoria: Protea Book House, 2013.

Guerrón-Montero, Carla. "Tourism and Afro-Antillean Identity in Panama." *Journal of Tourism and Cultural Change* 4, no. 2 (2006): 65–84.

Guibert, Christophe, and Benjamin Taunay. "From Political Pressure to Cultural Constraints: The Prime Dissemination of Surfing in Hainan." *Journal of China Tourism Research* 9, no. 3 (2013): 365–380.

Gumbrecht, Hans Ulrich. *In Praise of Athletic Beauty.* Cambridge, MA: Harvard University Press, 2006.

Gutkind, Peter C. W. "Trade and Labor in Early Precolonial African History: The Canoemen of Southern Ghana." In *The Workers of the African Trade*, edited by Catherine Coquery-Vidrovitch and Paul E. Lovejoy, 25–50. Beverly Hills: Sage Publications, 1985.

Hague, James D. "Our Equatorial Islands with an Account of Some Personal Experiences." *Century Magazine* 154, no. 5 (September 1902): 653–670.

Hair, P. E. H., Adam Jones, and Robin Law, eds., *Barbot on Guinea: The Writings of Jean Barbot on West Africa.* 2 vols. London: Hakluyt Society, 1992.

Hale, Charles R., ed. *Emerging Contradictions: Theory, Politics, and Methods of Activist Scholarship.* Berkeley: University of California Press, 2008.

Haleole, S. N. *The Hawaiian Romance of Laieikawai.* Washington, DC: US Government Printing Office, 1919.

Hall, Ann. "Knowledge and Gender: Epistemological Questions in the Social Analysis of Sport." *Sociology of Sport Journal* 2 (1985): 25–42.

Hall, Lisa Kahaleole. "Managing Our Own 'Sea of Islands': Remapping a Theoretical Space for Hawaiian Women and Indigenous Feminism." *Wicazo Sa Review* 24, no. 2 (2009): 15–38.

Hallgren, Claes. "Eric Mjöberg and the Rhetorics of Human Remains." In *The Long Way Home: The Meaning and Values of Repatriation*, edited by Paul Turnbull and Michael Pickering, 135–146. New York: Berghahn, 2010.

Harewood, Ian. "Mauritius: Surfing Paradise." *Surfer* 7, no. 4 (September 1966): 49.

Hargreaves, Jennifer, and Eric Anderson, eds. *Routledge Handbook of Sport, Gender and Sexuality*. Florence, KY: Taylor & Francis, 2014.

Harris, Cheryl. "Whiteness as Property." In *Critical Race Theory: The Key Writings That Formed the Movement*, edited by K. Crenshaw, N. Gotanda, G. Peller, and K. Thomas, 276–291. New York: The New Press, 1995.

Harris, Cheryl. "Whiteness as Property." *Harvard Law Review* 106 (1996): 1709–1791.

Harvey, David. *A Brief History of Neoliberalism*. Oxford: Oxford University Press, 2005.

Harvey, David. *The Condition of Postmodernity*. Oxford: Blackwell, 1990.

Hauʻofa, Epeli. "Our Sea of Islands." In *We Are the Ocean: Selected Works*, edited by Epeli Hauʻoa, 27–40. Honolulu: University of Hawaiʻi Press, 2008.

"The Hawaiian Islands." *National Geographic Magazine* 45, no. 2 (February 1924).

Hawkesworth, John, ed. *An Account of the Voyages Undertaken by the Order of His Present Majesty for Making Discoveries in the Southern Hemisphere: And Successively Performed by Commodore Byron, Captain Wallis, Captain Carteret, and Captain Cook, in the Dolphin, the Swallow, and the Endeavor*. 2 vols. London: Strahan and Cadell, 1773.

Haywood, Les, Francis Kew, Peter Bramham, John Spink, John Capenerhurst, and Ian Henry, eds. *Understanding Leisure*. 2nd ed. Cheltenham: Stanley Thornes Publishers, 1995.

Healy, Robert G. "The Common Pool Problem in Tourism Landscapes." *Annals of Tourism Research* 21, no. 3 (1995): 596–611.

Heard, Anthony. *The Cape of Storms: A Personal History of the Crisis in South Africa*. Johannesburg: Ravan Press, 1991.

Heimann, Jim. *Surfing: Vintage Surfing Graphics*. Cologne, Germany: Taschen, 2004.

Henderson, Margaret. "A Shifting Line Up: Men, Women, and *Tracks* Surfing Magazine." *Continuum* 15 (2001): 319–332.

Henry, Warren. *The Confessions of a Tenderfoot "Coaster": A Trader's Chronicle of Life on the West African Coast*. London: Witherby, 1927.

Herod, Andrew. "From a Geography of Labor to a Labor Geography: Labor's Spatial Fix and the Geography of Capitalism." *Antipode* 29, no. 1 (1997): 1–31.

Hewitt, Kim. *Mutilating the Body: Identity in Blood and Ink*. Madison: University of Wisconsin Press, 1997.

Heywood, Leslie. "Producing Girls and the Neoliberal Body." In *Physical Culture, Power, and the Body*, edited by Jennifer Hargreaves and Patricia Vertinsky, 101–120. Abingdon: Routledge, 2007.

Heywood, Leslie. "Third Wave Feminism, the Global Economy, and Women's Surfing: Sport as Stealth Feminism in Girls' Surf Culture." In *Next Wave Cultures: Feminism, Subcultures, Activism*, edited by Anita Harris, 63–82. London: Routledge, 2008.

Heywood, Leslie, and Shari Dworkin. *Built to Win: The Female Athlete as Cultural Icon*. Minneapolis: University of Minnesota Press, 2003.

Heywood, Leslie, and Mark Montgomery. "'Ambassadors of the Last Wilderness': Surfers, Environmental Ethics, and Activism in America." In *Tribal Play: Subcultural Journeys Through Sport*, edited by Michael Atkinson and Kevin Young, 153–172. Bingley, UK: Emerald Publishing, 2008.

Heywood, Leslie, and Mark Montgomery. "Economies of Surf: Evolution, Territorialism, and the Erosion of Localism." In *Sport and Neoliberalism: Politics, Consumption, and Culture*, edited by David Andrews and Michael Silk, 177–192. Philadelphia: Temple University Press, 2012.

Hift, Robbie. *Legends of Jeffreys Bay*. Jeffreys Bay, South Africa: Robbie Hift, 2003.

Hill, S. S. *Travels in the Sandwich and Society Islands*. London: Chapman and Hall, 1856.

Hodes, Martha. *White Women, Black Men: Illicit Sex in the Nineteenth-Century South*. New Haven, CT: Yale University Press, 1997.

Holden, Andrew. "Achieving a Sustainable Relationship between Common Pool Resources and Tourism: The Role of Environmental Ethics." *Journal of Sustainable Tourism* 13, no. 4 (2005): 339–352.

Holmes, Rachel. *The Hottentot Venus: The Life and Death of Saartjie Baartman: Born 1789–Buried 2002*. New York: Bloomsbury, 2008.

Holt, Douglas. *How Brands Become Icons*. Cambridge, MA: Harvard University Press, 2004.

Hopwood, Bill, Mary Mellor, and Geoff O'Brien. "Sustainable Development: Mapping Different Approaches." *Sustainable Development* 13, no. 1 (2005): 38–52.

Horne, Gerald. *White Pacific: U.S. Imperialism and Black Slavery in the South Seas after the Civil War*. Honolulu: University of Hawai'i Press, 2007.

Horrell, Muriel. *A Survey of Race Relations in South Africa 1965*. Johannesburg: South African Institute of Race Relations, 1966.

Horsman, Reginald. "Scientific Racism and the American Indian in the Mid-Nineteenth Century." *American Quarterly* 27, no. 2 (1975): 152–168.

Housman, Justin. "Rebel Whisper." *Surfer* 56, no. 4 (April 2015).

Huang, Liangmin, Yehui Tan, Xingyu Song, Xiaoping Huang, Hankui Wang, Si Zhang, Junde Dong, and Rongyu Chen. "The Status of the Ecological Environment and a Proposed Protection Strategy in Sanya Bay, Hainan Island, China." *Marine Pollution Bulletin* 46, no. 1 (2003): 180–186.

Hughes, Heather. "Struggling for a Day in the Sun: The Emergence of a Beach Culture among African People in Durban." In *Art and Identity at the Water's Edge*, edited by Tricia Cusack, 141–160. Burlington: Ashgate, 2012.

Hugues Dit Ciles, Emily Kate. "The Sustainability of Surfing Tourism at Remote Destinations." PhD diss., University of Plymouth, 2009.

Huhndorf, Shari. *Going Native: Indians in the American Cultural Imagination*. Ithaca: Cornell University Press, 2001.

Huizinga, J. *Homo Ludens: A Study of Play Element in Culture*. London: Routledge, 1998.

Hung, Ho-Fung. "Labor Politics under Three Stages of Chinese Capitalism." *South Atlantic Quarterly* 112, no. 1 (2013): 203–212.

Hynson, Michael, and Donna Jost. *Mike Hynson: Transcendental Memories of a Surf Rebel*. Dana Point: Endless Dreams, 2009.

Hyslop, Jonathan. "'Days of Miracle and Wonder?' Conformity and Revolt in *Searching for Sugarman.*" *Safundi: The Journal of South African and American Studies* 14, no. 4 (2013): 490–501.

Hyslop, Jonathan. "Why Did Apartheid's Supporters Capitulate? 'Whiteness,' Class and Consumption in Urban South Africa, 1985–1995." *Society in Transition* 31, no. 1 (2000): 36–44.

Igler, David. *The Great Ocean: Pacific Worlds from Captain Cook to the Gold Rush.* Oxford: Oxford University Press, 2013.

'Ī'ī, John Papa. *Fragments of Hawaiian History.* Translated by Mary Kawena Pukui. Edited by Dorothy B. Barrère. Honolulu: Bishop Museum, 1959.

Iliffe, John. *Honour in African History.* Cambridge: Cambridge University Press, 2005.

Irwin, John Keith. "Surfers: A Study of the Growth of a Deviant Subculture." Master's thesis, University of California, Berkeley, 1962.

Irwin, John Keith. "Surfing: The Natural History of an Urban Scene." *Journal of Contemporary Ethnography* (formerly *Urban Life and Culture*) 2, no. 2 (1973): 131–160.

Ishiwata, Eric. "Local Motions: Surfing and the Politics of Wave Sliding." *Cultural Values* 6, no. 3 (2002): 257–272.

Jacobi, Erik S., James Freund, and Luis Araujo. "'Is There a Gap in the Market, and Is There a Market in the Gap?' How Advertising Planning Performs Markets." *Journal of Marketing Management* 31, no. 1 (2015): 37–61.

Jaggard, Ed. "Americans, Malibus, Torpedo Buoys, and Australian Beach Culture." *Journal of Sport History* 41, no. 2 (2014): 269–286.

Jaggard, Ed. "Australian Surf Life-Saving and the 'Forgotten Members.'" *Australian Historical Studies* 29, no. 112 (1999): 23–43.

Jaggard, Ed. "Chameleons in the Surf." *Journal of Australian Studies* 21, no. 53 (1997): 183–191.

Jagose, Annamarie. *Queer Theory.* Melbourne: Melbourne University Press, 1996.

James, Don. *Surfing San Onofre to Point Dume: 1936–1942.* San Francisco: Chronicle, 1998.

Jarratt, Phil. *Mr Sunset: The Jeff Hakman Story.* London: Gen X Publishing, 1997.

Jarratt, Phil. *Salts and Suits.* Melbourne: Hardie Grant, 2010.

Jarratt, Phil. *Surfing Australia: A Complete History of Surfboard Riding in Australia.* Melbourne: Hardie Grant, 2012.

Jarvis, James J. *Scenes and Scenery in the Sandwich Islands.* London: Edward Moxon, 1844.

Jefferson, Alison Rose. "African American Leisure Space in Santa Monica: The Beach Sometimes Known as the 'Inkwell,' 1900s–1960s." *Southern California Quarterly* 91, no. 2 (2009): 155–189.

Jenco, Leigh. "Chinese Liberalism." In *Encyclopaedia of Political Theory*, edited by Mark Bevir, 164–168. Thousand Oaks, CA: Sage, 2010.

Jenks, Chris. *Culture.* London: Routledge, 2004.

Jenks, Chris, ed. *Cultural Reproduction.* London: Routlege, 1993.

Jianjun Sun, Su Zhang, and Nobuyoshi Yamori. "The Announcement Effects of Regional Tourism Industrial Policy." Discussion Paper, Research Institute for Economics and Business Administration, Kobe University, July 27, 2014.

Johnson, Pete. "Esta Na Onda." *International Surfing* 3, no. 3 (July 1967): 17–19.

Johnson, Susan Lee. *Roaring Camp: The Social World of the California Gold Rush.* New York: Norton, 2000.

Johnston, Anna. "Antipodean Heathens: The London Missionary Society in Polynesia and Australia, 1800–50." In *Colonial Frontiers: Indigenous-European Encounters in Settler Societies,* edited by Lynette Russell, 68–81. Manchester, UK: Manchester University Press, 2001.

Jones, Adam, ed. *German Sources for West African History.* Weisbaden, Germany: Coronet Books, 1983.

Kahanamoku, Duke, with Joe Brennan. *Duke Kahanamoku's World of Surfing.* New York: Grosset & Dunlap, 1968.

Kalakaua, David. *The Legends and Myths of Hawaii.* New York: C. L. Webster & Company, 1888.

Kalleberg, Arne L. "Precarious Work, Insecure Workers: Employment Relations in Transition." *American Sociological Review* 74, no. 1 (2009): 1–22.

Kamakau, Samuel M. *Ruling Chiefs of Hawaii.* Honolulu: Kamehameha, 1961.

Kamakau, Samuel M. *Tales and Traditions of the People of Old.* Honolulu: Bishop Museum Press, 1991.

Kampion, Drew. *Greg Noll: The Art of the Surfboard.* Layton, UT: Gibbs Smith, 2007.

Kampion, Drew. *Jack O'Neill: It's Always Summer on the Inside.* San Francisco: Chronicle Books, 2011.

Kampion, Drew. *Stoked! A History of Surf Culture.* Layton, UT: Gibbs Smith, 2003.

Kampion, Drew. *Waves: From Surfing to Tsunami.* Layton, UT: Gibbs Smith, 2005.

Kampion, Drew. *The Way of the Surfer: Living It, 1935 to Tomorrow.* New York: Harry N. Abrams, 2003.

Kampion, Drew, and Bruce Brown. *A History of Surf Culture.* Koln: Taschen, 2003.

Kanda, Baron N. "Japan at the Great Conference." *Mid-Pacific Magazine* 23, no. 5 (1922): 431–434.

Kane, Mary Jo. "The Better Sportwomen Get, the More the Media Ignore Them." *Communication & Sport* 1, no. 3 (2013): 231–236.

Kane, Mary Jo, Nicole LaVoi, and Janet Fink. "Exploring Elite Female Athletes' Interpretations of Sport Media Images: A Window Into the Construction of Social Identity and 'Selling Sex' in Women's Sports." *Communication & Sport* 1, no. 3 (2013): 269–298.

Kane, Mary Jo, and Helen Lenskyi. "Female Athletes: Issues of Gender and Sexualities." In *MediaSport,* edited by L. Wenner, 186–201. London: Routledge, 1998.

Kane, Mary Jo, and Heather Maxwell. "Expanding the Boundaries of Sport Media Research: Using Critical Theory to Explore Consumer Responses to Representations of Women's Sports." *Journal of Sport Management* 25 (2011): 202–216.

Karhl, Andrew W. *The Land Was Ours: African American Beaches from Jim Crow to the Sunbelt South.* Cambridge, MA: Harvard University Press, 2012.

Katsiaficas, Georgy. *The Subversion of Politics: European Autonomous Social Movements and the Decolonization of Everyday Life.* Edinburgh: AK Press, 2006.

Kauanui, J. Kehaulani. *Hawaiian Blood: Colonialism and the Politics of Sovereignty and Indigeneity.* Durham, NC: Duke University Press, 2008.

Kauanui, J. Kehaulani. "Precarious Positions: Native Hawaiian and US Federal Recognition." *The Contemporary Pacific* 17, no. 1 (2005): 1–27.

Kauer, Kerrie, and Vikki Krane. "'Scary Dykes and Feminine Queens': Stereotypes and Female Athletes." *Women in Sport and Physical Activity Journal* 15 (2006): 43–56.

Kavanagh, Pierce Michael, dir. *Manufacturing Stoke*. Misfit Pictures, 2011. DVD.

Kenvin, Richard, and Christine Knoke. *Surf Craft: Design and the Culture of Board Riding*. Boston: MIT Press, 2014.

Kimball, Taylor. "The Spot." *The Surfer's Journal* 15, no. 6 (2006): 108–119.

King, Wilma. *Stolen Childhood: Slave Youth in Nineteenth-Century America*. 2nd ed. Bloomington: Indiana University Press, 2011.

Kingsley, Mary H. *Travels in West Africa: Congo Français, Corisco and Cameroons*. London: Macmillan, 1897.

Klein, Bernhard, and Gesa Mackenthun, eds. *Sea Changes Historicizing the Ocean*. New York: Routledge, 2004.

Koenig, Bernard. "si Notes: From the Lost Island." *Surfing Illustrated* 3, no. 4 (August 1965).

Kohner, Frederick *Gidget: The Little Girl with Big Ideas*. New York: Penguin Publishing Group, 2001. First published 1957.

Komonor, Rabbi David. "M. S. D." *Surfer* 12, no. 5 (December 1971).

Korn, Alforns L., ed. *The Victorian Visitors*. Honolulu: University of Hawai'i Press, 1958.

Kraft, James P. *Stage to Studio: Musicians and the Sound Revolution, 1890–1950*. Baltimore: John Hopkins University Press, 1996.

Krane, Vikki. "We Can Be Athletic and Feminine, But Do We Want To? Challenging Hegemonic Femininity in Women's Sport." *Quest* 53 (2001): 115–133.

Kretzmann, John, and John McKnight. *Building Communities from the Inside Out: A Path Toward Finding and Mobilizing a Community's Assets*. Evanston, IL: ABCD Institute for Policy Research of Northwestern University, 1993.

Kristeva, Julia. *Powers of Horror: An Essay on Abjection*. New York: Columbia University Press, 1982.

Kusz, Kyle. "'Extreme America': The Cultural Politics of Extreme Sports in 1990s America." In *Understanding Lifestyle Sports: Consumption, Identity and Difference*, edited by Belinda Wheaton, 197–213. Abingdon: Routledge, 2004.

Kusz, Kyle. *Revolt of the White Athlete: Race, Media and the Emergence of Extreme Athletes in America*. New York: Peter Lang Publishing, 2007.

Kwinter, Sanford. *Architectures of Time: Toward a Theory of the Event in Modernist Culture*. Cambridge, MA: MIT Press, 2001.

Lacher, R. Geoffrey, and Chi-Ok Oh. "Is Tourism a Low-Income Industry? Evidence from Three Coastal Regions." *Journal of Travel Research* 51, no. 4 (2012): 464–472.

Laderman, Scott. *Empire in Waves: A Political History of Surfing*. Berkeley: University of California Press, 2014.

Laderman, Scott. "Reds, Revolutionaries, and Racists: Surfing, Travel, and Diplomacy in the Reagan Era." In *Diplomatic Games: Sport, Statecraft, and International Relations since 1945*, edited by Heather Dichter and Andrew Johns, 409–430. Lexington: University Press of Kentucky, 2014.

LaDow, Beth. *The Medicine Line: The Life and Death of a North American Borderland*. New York: Routledge, 2000.

Lamont, Chris B. "Viet Nam on Dora." *Surfer* 6, no. 6 (January 1966).

Lanagan, David. "Dropping In: Surfing, Identity, Community and Commodity." In *Some Like It Hot: The Beach as a Cultural Dimension*, edited by James Skinner, Keith Gilbert, and Allan Edwards, 169–184. Oxford: Meyer and Meyer Sport, 2003.

Langton, Macia, "Native Title, Poverty and Economic Development." Lecture at People, Place, Power: Native Title Conference, Canberra, June 3, 2010.

Lash, Scott, and John Urry. *Economies of Signs and Space (Theory, Culture & Society)*. Thousand Oaks: Sage Publications, 1994.

Latour, Bruno. *The Pasteurization of France*. Cambridge, MA: Harvard University Press, 1988.

Latour, Bruno. *Reassembling the Social: An Introduction to Actor-Network Theory*. Oxford: Oxford University Press, 2005.

Latour, Bruno. *We Have Never Been Modern*. Cambridge, MA: MIT Press, 1996.

LaTourrette, Dean. "Land Grab: Finding the Plot in Nicaragua." *The Surfer's Journal* 15, no. 2 (April 2006): 106–119.

Law, Robin, Hugh Campbell, and John Dolan, eds. *Masculinities in Aotearoa/New Zealand*. Auckland: Dunmore Press, 1999.

Lawler, Kristin. *The American Surfer: Radical Culture and Capitalism*. New York: Routledge, 2011.

Lazarow, Neil. "Using Observed Market Expenditure to Estimate the Economic Impact of Recreational Surfing to the Gold Coast, Australia." *Journal of Coastal Research* 56, no. 9 (2009): 1130–1134.

Lazarow, Neil. "The Value of Coastal Recreational Resources: A Case Study Approach to Examine the Value of Recreational Surfing to Specific Locales." *Journal of Coastal Research* 50 (2007): 12–20.

Ledesma, Antonio. *Landless Workers and Rice Farmers: Peasant Subclasses Under Agrarian Reform in Two Philippines Villages*. Los Baños, CA: International Rice Research Institute, 1982.

Ledward, Brandon C. "On Being Hawaiian Enough: Contesting American Racialization with Native Hybridity." *Hulili: Multidisciplinary Research on Hawaiian Well-Being* 4, no. 1 (2007): 107–140.

Leed, Eric. *The Mind of the Traveler: From Gilgamesh to Global Tourism*. New York: Basic Books, 1991.

Leimbach, Bill. *Wave of Change: Balinese Surfer II*. Avalon, NSW: Lucky Country Productions, 2002.

Lenskyj, Helen. " 'Inside Sport' or 'On the Margins'?: Australian Women and the Sport Media." *International Review for the Sociology of Sport* 33, no. 1 (1998): 19–32.

Leonard, Peter. *Records of a Voyage to the Western Coast of Africa*. Edinburgh: A. Shortrede, 1833.

Lewis, Jeff. "Between the Lines: Surf Texts, Prosthetics, and Everyday Theory." *Social Semiotics* 8, no. 1 (1998): 55–70.

Lewis, Jeff. "In Search of the Postmodern Surfer: Territory, Terror and Masculinity." In *Some Like It Hot: The Beach as a Cultural Dimension*, edited by James Skinner, Keith Gilbert, and Allan Edwards, 58–76. Oxford: Meyer and Meyer Sport, 2003.

Li, Yiping, Kun Lai, and Xuegang Feng. "The Problem of 'Guanxi' for Actualizing Community Tourism: A Case Study of Relationship Networking in China." *Tourism Ge-*

ographies: An International Journal of Tourism Space, Place and Environment 9, no. 2 (2007): 115–138.

Lindberg, Michael, and Daniel Todd. *Brown-, Green- and Blue-Water Fleets: The Influence of Geography on Naval Warfare, 1861 to the Present.* Westport, CT: Praeger, 2002.

Lindner, Evelin. *A Dignity Economy: Creating an Economy That Serves Human Dignity and Preserves Our Planet.* Oregon: World Dignity University Press, 2012.

Linebaugh, Peter, and Marcus Rediker. *The Many-Headed Hydra: Sailors, Slaves, Commoners, and the Hidden History of the Revolutionary Atlantic.* Boston: Beacon Press, 2000.

Linfors, Bernth, ed. *Africans on Stage: Studies in Ethnological Show Business.* Bloomington: Indiana University Press, 1999.

Lipsitz, George. "The Possessive Investment of Whiteness: Racialized Social Democracy and the 'White' Problem in American Studies." *American Studies Quarterly* 47, no. 3 (1995): 369–387.

lisahunter. "Becoming Visible. Visual Narratives of 'Female' as a Political Position: The History, Perpetuation, and Disruption of Patriocolonial Pedagogies?" In *Women in Action Sport Cultures: Identity, Politics, Experience and Pedagogy*, edited by Holly Thorpe and Rebecca Olive, 319–347. Basingstoke, UK: Palgrave Macmillan, 2016.

lisahunter. "Exploitation and (Unqueering) Public Pedagogy: Gender and Sex Parody in YouTube Surf Festival Promotion." Paper presented at the Gender and Education Conference, Melbourne, Australia, April 2014.

lisahunter. "Positioning Participation in the Field of Surfing: Sex, Equity, and Illusio." In *Bourdieu's Field Theory and the Social Sciences*, edited by James Albright, Deborah Hartman, and J. Wildin. Basingstoke, UK: Palgrave Macmillan, 2017.

lisahunter. "Sex(ed/y/uality) Positions in Surfing: Illusio, Equity, or Something Else?" Paper presented at the Sociological Association of Aotearoa (NZ), University of Waikato, Kirikiriroa, December 10, 2015.

lisahunter. "'Stop': 'No.' Exploring Social Suffering in Practices of Surfing as Opportunities for Change." In *Pierre Bourdieu and Physical Capital*, edited by lisahunter, Wayne Smith, and elke emerald, 47–56. Abingdon: Routledge, 2015.

lisahunter. "A Stranger Surfing Life: Surface, Substructure and the Commodification of the Sublime." *Sport, Education & Society* (2012): 1–4.

lisahunter. "What Did I Do-See-Learn at the Beach? Surfing Festival as a Cultural Pedagogical Sight/Site." In *Physical Culture, Pedagogies and Visual Methods*, edited by Laura Azzarito and David Kirk, 144–161. New York: Routledge, 2013.

lisahunter, and elke emerald. "(A)dressing the Long (Boardies) and Short (Bikinis) of Performance Surfing: A Posthumanist Tightening of Patriarchal Threads as Body Pedagogy." Paper presented at the Gender and Education Conference, Roehampton University, London, July 27, 2015.

lisahunter, elke emerald, and Martin Gregory. *Participatory Activist Research in the Globalised World: Social Change through the Cultural Professions.* New York: Springer, 2012.

Liu, Lydie, Rebecca Karl, and Dorothy Ko, eds. *Birth of Chinese Feminism: Essential Texts in Transnational Theory.* New York: Columbia University Press, 2013.

Lockwood, Craig. *Peanuts: An Oral Biography.* Newport Beach, CA: Croul Publications, 2009.

Lockwood, Craig. "Peru: Peru International Nets Doyle Thousand Dollars Cash Prize." *Surfing Action around the World* 2, no. 3 (June 1969).

Logue, David, Neil Argent, and Andrew Warren. "Wipeout? The Gold Coast and Tweed Surfboard Manufacturing Cluster and Local Economic Development." *Local Economy* 30, no. 1 (2015): 119–138.

London, Charmian. *Our Hawaii (Islands and Islanders)*. New York: Macmillan, 1922.

London, Jack. *The Cruise of the Snark*. New York: Macmillan, 1928.

Long, Yihe. "The Social Impacts of Tourism Development on Hainan Island." Master's thesis, Vaasa University of Applied Science, 2010.

Lopez, Gerry. "Aftermath Winter 1976: Attitude Dancing." *Surfer Magazine* 17, no. 2 (Jun/Jul 1976): 101–108.

Louie, Kam. *Theorising Chinese Masculinity: Society and Gender in China*. Cambridge: Cambridge University Press, 2009.

Loyalka, Michelle. *Eating Bitterness: Stories from the Front Lines of China's Great Urban Migration*. Berkeley: University of California Press, 2012.

Lueras, Leonard. *Surfing: The Ultimate Pleasure*. New York: Workman Publishing, 1984.

Lury, Celia. "Brand as Assemblage: Assembling Culture." *Journal of Cultural Economy* 2, no. 1 (2009): 67–82.

MacGinty, Roger, and Gurchathen Sanghera. "Hybridity in Peacebuilding and Development: An Introduction." *Journal of Peacebuilding & Development* 7, no. 2 (2012): 3–8.

Mach, Leon. "Finding Another Wave: The Need for Ecotourism Principles in International Surf Culture." Master's thesis, American University, 2009.

Mach, Leon. "From the Endless Summer to the Surf Spring: Technology and Governance in Development World Surf Tourism." PhD diss., University of Delaware, 2014.

Mack, John. *The Sea: A Cultural History*. London: Reaktion Books, 2013.

Mager, Anne. *Beer, Sociability, and Masculinity in South Africa*. Cape Town: Cape Town University Press, 2010.

Maguire, Pete, and Mike Ritter. *Thai Stick: Surfers, Scammers, and the Untold Story of the Marijuana Trade*. New York: Columbia University Press, 2015.

Maiava, S. "When Is Development Not Development? Recognizing Unofficial Development (or Practising Post-development)." Unpublished paper, Massey University, Auckland, New Zealand, 2002.

Malo, David. *Hawaiian Antiquities (Moolelo Hawaii)*. Honolulu: Hawaiian Gazette Company, 1903.

Malo, David. *Moʻolelo Hawaii*. Honolulu: Bishop Museum Press, 1951.

Manganaro, Christine. *Assimilating Hawaii: Racial Science in a Colonial Laboratory, 1919–1939*. PhD diss., University of Minnesota, 2012.

Marcus, Ben. *Surfing USA! An Illustrated History of the Coolest Sport of All Time*. Stillwater, Minnesota: Voyageur Press, 2005.

Marcuse, Herbert. *Negations: Essays in Critical Theory*. London: Free Association Books, 1988.

Martin, Steven Andrew, and Ilian Assenov. "Developing a Surf Resource Sustainability Index as a Global Model for Surf Beach Conservation and Tourism Research." *Asia Pacific Journal of Tourism Research* 4 (2013): 760–792.

Martin, Steven Andrew, and Ilian Assenov. "The Genesis of a New Body of Sport Tourism Literature: A Systematic Review of Surf Tourism Research (1997–2011)." *Journal of Sport and Tourism* 17, no. 4 (2012): 257–287.

Martin, Steven, and Ilian Assenov. "Measuring the Conservation Aptitude of Surf Beaches in Phuket, Thailand: An Application of the Surf Resource Sustainability Index." *International Journal of Tourism Research* 17, no. 2 (2015): 105–117.

Marx, Karl. *Capital.* Vol. 1. Harmondsworth: Penguin, 1976.

Masterson, Miles. "Well Connected: The Parallel Universe of South Africa's 'Godfather' of Surfing, John 'Oom' Whitmore." *The Surfer's Journal* 20, no. 3 (June–July 2011).

Matsuda, Matt K. "The Pacific." *American Historical Review* 111, no. 3 (2006): 758–780.

Mauro, Chris, and Steve Hawk, eds. *The Best of Surfer Magazine.* San Francisco: Chronicle Books, 2007.

Maxton, Donald A., ed. *After the Bounty: A Sailor's Account of the Mutiny and Life in the South Seas.* Washington, DC: Potomac Books, 2010.

May, Kirse Granat. *Golden State, Golden Youth: The California Image in Popular Culture, 1955–1966.* Chapel Hill: University of North Carolina Press, 2002.

McCall, Leslie. "The Complexity of Intersectionality." *Signs: Journal of Women in Culture and Society* 30, no. 3 (2005): 1771–1800.

McCormack, Mark. *The Declining Significance of Homophobia: How Teenage Boys Are Redefining Masculinity and Heterosexuality.* New York: Oxford University Press, 2012.

McDowell, Linda. *Capital Culture: Gender at Work in the City.* Revised edition. London: Wiley-Blackwell, 2011.

McElveen, James, and James Siekmeier, eds. *Foreign Relations of the United States, 1969–1976, Volume XXI: Chile, 1969–1973.* Washington, DC: US Government Printing Office, 2014.

McGloin, Colleen. "Aboriginal Surfing: Reinstating Culture and Country." *International Journal of Humanities* 4, no. 1 (2007): 93–110.

McGloin, Colleen. "Considering the Work of Martin Nakata's 'Cultural Interface': A Reflection on Theory and Practice by a Non-Indigenous Academic." *Australian Journal of Indigenous Education* 38 (2009): 36–41.

McGloin, Colleen. "Listening to Hear: Dialogic Pedagogy and Critical Allies in Indigenous Studies." *Australian Journal of Adult Learning* 55, no. 2 (2015): 267–282.

McGloin, Colleen. "Reviving Eva in Tim Winton's Breath." *The Journal of Commonwealth Literature* 47, no. 1 (2012): 109–120.

McGloin, Colleen. "Surfing Nation(s) Surfing Country(s)." PhD diss., University of Wollongong, 2005.

McGloin, Colleen. *Surfing Nation(s) Surfing Country(s).* Saarbrucken: VDM Verlag, 2008.

McGovern, George. "Foreword." In *Western Sahara: War, Nationalism, and Conflict Irresolution,* edited by Stephen Zunes and Jacob Mundy, xiii–xvi. Syracuse, NY: Syracuse University Press, 2010.

McShane, Thomas O., Paul D. Hirsch, Tran Chi Trung, Alexander N. Songorwa, Ann Kinzig, Bruno Monteferri, David Mutekanga, et al. "Hard Choices: Making Trade-Offs Between Biodiversity Conservation and Human Well-Being." *Biological Conservation* 144, no. 3 (2011): 966–972.

Meân, Lindsey, and Jeffrey Kassing. "'I Would Just Like to Be Known as an Athlete': Managing Hegemony, Femininity, and Heterosexuality in Female Sport." *Western Journal of Communication* 72 (2008): 126–144.

Melville, Herman. *Mardi and a Voyage Thither.* New York: St. Botolph Society, 1932.

Mergen, Bernard. *Play and Playthings: A Reference Guide.* Westport: Greenwood, 1982.

Messner, Michael. "Gender Ideologies, Youth Sports, and the Production of Soft Essentialism." *Sociology of Sport Journal* 28 (2011): 151–170.

Messner, Michael. *Power at Play: Sports and the Problem of Masculinity.* Boston: Beacon Press, 1992.

Messner, Michael, and Jeffrey Montez de Oca. "The Male Consumer as Loser: Beer and Liquor Ads in Mega Sports Media Events." *Signs: A Journal of Women in Culture and Society* 30, no. 3 (2005): 1879–1909.

"Mickey Chapin Dora: Surf Stuntman." *Surfer* 6, no. 3 (July 1965).

Mignolo, Walter D. "Epistemic Disobedience, Independent Thought and De-Colonial Freedom." *Theory Culture and Society* 26, no. 7–8 (2009): 1–23.

Mikosza, Janine. *Inching Forward: Newspaper Coverage and Portrayal of Women's Sport in Australia: A Quantitative and Qualitative Analysis, 1996–1997.* Canberra: Womensport Australia, 1997.

Minhui, Xia, Wang Hui, Wang Xiaolin, and Su You. "A Research on the Sports Tourism Special Project in Hainan International Tourism Island." In *Advances in Sport Science and Computer Science,* edited by Mark Zhou, 501–509. Southampton, UK: WIT Press, 2014.

Mintz, Steven. *Huck's Raft: A History of American Childhood.* Cambridge, MA: Harvard University Press, 2004.

Mitchell, Carleton. "The Fad and Fascination of Surfing." *Holiday* 35 (1964): 122–130.

Mohanty, Chandra Talpade. "Under Western Eyes: Feminist Scholarship and Colonial Discourses." *Feminist Review* 30 (1988): 61–88.

Mookini, Esther T. "Keōpuōlani: Sacred Wife, Queen Mother, 1778–1823." *The Hawaiian Journal of History* 32 (1998): 1–24.

Moor, Liz. "Branding Consultants as Cultural Intermediaries." *The Sociological Review* 56, no. 3 (2008): 408–428.

Morrell, Robert. "The Times of Change: Men and Masculinity in South Africa." In *Changing Men in Southern Africa,* edited by Robert Morrell. London: Zed Books, 2001.

Moser, Patrick. "The Endurance of Surfing in 19th-Century Hawai'i." *Journal of the Polynesian Society* 125, no. 4 (2016): 411–432.

Moser, Patrick. "The Reports of Surfing's Demise Have Been Greatly Exaggerated." *Bamboo Ridge* 98 (2011): 195–204.

Moser, Patrick, ed. *Pacific Passages: An Anthology of Surf Writing.* Honolulu: University of Hawai'i Press, 2008.

Mowforth, Martin, and Ian Munt. *Tourism and Sustainability: New Tourism in the Third World.* London: Routledge, 1998.

Musick, John R. *Hawaii: Our New Possessions.* New York: Funk, 1898.

Myrdahl, Tiffany. "Lesbian Visibility and the Politics of Covering in Women's Basketball Game Spaces." *Leisure Studies* 30, no. 2 (2013): 139–156.

Nakata, Martin. *Disciplining the Savages, Savaging the Disciplines.* Canberra: Aboriginal Studies Press, 2007.

Naples, Nancy. *Feminism and Method: Ethnography, Discourse Analysis, and Activist Research.* New York: Routledge, 2003.

Naughton, Kevin. "A Feel for the Road: Thoughts on the Zen, Luck, Conscience, and Timing of World Travel." *Surfer* 31, no. 7 (July 1990).

Nayak, Anoop. "After Race: Ethnography, Race and Post-Racial Theory." *Ethnic and Racial Studies* 29, no. 3 (2006): 411–430.

Nayak, Anoop. "Race, Affect, and Emotion: Young People, Racism, and Graffiti in the Postcolonial English Suburbs." *Environment and Planning* 42, no. 10 (2010): 2370–2392.

Nayak, Anoop. *Race, Place, and Globalization: Youth Cultures in a Changing World.* Oxford: Berg, 2003.

Neal, Sarah. "Rural Landscapes, Representations and Racism: Examining Multicultural Citizenship and Policy-Making in the English Countryside." *Ethnic and Racial Studies* 25, no. 3 (2002): 442–461.

Nellist, George F. "The Story of Hawaii and Its Builders." *Honolulu Star Bulletin,* 1925. http://files.usgwarchives.net/hi/statewide/bios/green25bs.txt.

Nemani, Mihi. "Being a Brown Bodyboarder." In *Seascapes: Shaped by the Sea,* edited by Barbara Humberstone and Mike Brown, 83–100. Farnham, Surrey: Ashgate, 2015.

Nemani, Mihi. "Getting Deep: Experiences of New Zealand Bodyboarders." Master's thesis, University of Waikato, 2013.

Nendel, James D. "Duke Kahanamoku, Twentieth Century Monarch: The Values and Contributions to Hawaiian Culture from Hawaii's Sporting Legend." PhD diss., Pennsylvania State University, 2006.

Nendel, Jim. "Surfing in Early Twentieth-Century Hawai'i: The Appropriation of a Transcendent Experience to Competitive Sport." *The International Journal of the History of Sport* 26, no. 16 (December 2009): 2432–2446.

Newell, Stephanie. "Postcolonial Masculinities and the Politics of Visibility." *Journal of Postcolonial Writing* 45, no. 3 (2009): 243–250.

Newton, Tim. "Credit Networks and Civilisation." *British Journal of Sociology* 54, no. 3 (2003): 347–372.

Newton, Tim. *Nature and Sociology.* New York: Routledge, 2007.

Noble, David F. *Forces of Production: A Social History of Industrial Automation.* Revised edition. New Jersey: Transaction Publishers, 2011.

Nodaway, Max. *Rollo in Hawaii.* Chicago: Thompson & Thomas, 1908.

Noll, Greg, and Andrea Gabbard. *Da Bull: Life Over the Edge.* Berkeley: North Atlantic Books, 1989.

Norling, Lisa. *Captain Ahab Had a Wife: New England Women and the Whalefishery, 1720–1870.* Chapel Hill: University of North Carolina Press, 2000.

O'Brien, Danny, and I. Eddie, "Benchmarking Global Best Practice: Innovation and Leadership in Surf City Tourism and Industry Development." Paper presented at the Global Surf Cities Conference, Kirra Community and Cultural Centre, 2013.

O'Brien, Danny, and Jess Ponting. "Sustainable Surf Tourism: A Community Centered Approach in Papua New Guinea." *Journal of Sports Management* 27, no. 2 (2013): 158–172.

O'Brien, Jean. *Firsting and Lasting: Writing Indians Out of Existence in New England.* Minneapolis: University of Minnesota Press, 2010.

O'Connor, James. "Capitalism, Nature, Socialism: A Theoretical Introduction." *Capitalism, Nature, Socialism* 1, no. 1 (1988): 11–38.

O'Connor, James. "Uneven and Combined Development and Ecological Crisis: A Theoretical Introduction." *Race and Class* 30, no. 3 (1989): 1–11.

Ogden, John. *Saltwater People of the Broken Bays: Sydney's Northern Beaches.* North Sydney: Cyclops Press, 2011.

Okihiro, Gary. *Island World: A History of Hawai'i and the United States.* Berkeley: University of California Press, 2008.

Oksiloff, Assenka. *Picturing the Primitive: Visual Culture, Ethnography, and Early German Cinema.* New York: Palgrave, 2001.

Olive, Rebecca. "Going Surfing/Doing Research: Learning How to Negotiate Cultural Politics from Women Who Surf." *Continuum* 30, no. 2 (2006). doi:10.1080.10304312.2016.1143199.

Olive, Rebecca. "Making Friends with the Neighbours: Blogging as a Research Method." *International Journal of Cultural Studies* 16, no. 1 (2013): 71–84.

Olive, Rebecca. "Reframing Surfing: Physical Culture in Online Spaces." *Media International Australia, Incorporating Culture & Policy* 155 (June 2015): 99–107.

Olive, Rebecca. "Surfing, Localism, Place-based Pedagogies, and Ecological Sensibilities in Australia." In *International Handbook of Outdoor Studies*, edited by Barbara Humberstone, Heather Prince, and Karla Henderson, 501–510. London: Routledge, 2015.

Olive, Rebecca. "Women Who Surf: Female Difference, Intersecting Subjectivities and Cultural Pedagogies." In *The Pedagogies of Cultural Studies*, edited by Andrew Hickey, 179–195. New York: Routledge, 2016.

Olive, Rebecca, Louise McCuaig, and Murray Phillips. "Women's Recreational Surfing: A Patronising Experience." *Sport, Education and Society* 20, no. 2 (2015): 258–276.

Olkowski, Dorothea. *Gilles Deleuze and the Ruin of Representation.* Berkeley: University of California Press, 1999.

Omi, Michael, and Howard Winant. *Racial Formation in the United States: From the 1960s to the 1990s.* 2nd ed. New York: Routledge, 1994.

Ong, Aihwa. *Flexible Citizenship: The Cultural Logics of Transnationality.* Durham, NC: Duke University Press, 1999.

Orme, Nicholas. *Early British Swimming, 55 B.C.–A.D. 1719: With the First Swimming Treatise in English, 1595.* Exeter: University of Exeter Press, 1983.

Ormrod, Joan. "*Endless Summer* (1964): Consuming Waves and Surfing the Frontier." *Film & History* 35, no. 1 (2005): 39–51.

Ormrod, Joan. "*Endless Summer*: Consuming Waves and Surfing the Frontier." In *All Stars and Movie Stars: Sports in Film and History*, edited by Ron Briley, Michael Schoenecke, and Deborah Carmichael, 17–39. Lexington: University Press of Kentucky, 2008.

Ormrod, Joan. "Issues of Gender in *Muscle Beach Party* (1964)." *ScopeOnline* (2003).

Ormrod, Joan. "Representing 'Authentic' Surfers Identities in 'Pure' Surf Films." In *"On the Edge": Leisure, Consumption and the Representation of Adventure Sport*, edited by Joan Ormrod and Belinda Wheaton, 17–42. Eastbourne: Leisure Studies Association, 2009.

Ormrod, Joan. "Surf Rhetoric in American and British Surfing Magazines between 1965 and 1976." *Sport in History* 27, no. 1 (March 2007): 88–109.

Ormrod, Joan, and Belinda Wheaton, eds. *On the Edge: Leisure, Consumption, and the Representation of Adventure Sports*. Eastbourne, UK: Leisure Studies Association, 2009.

Osgerby, Bill. *Playboys in Paradise: Masculinity, Youth and Leisure-Style in Modern America*. Oxford: Berg, 2001.

Osmond, Gary. "The Duke Paoa Kahanamoku Statue at Freshwater: Motivations, Memory, and Identity." *Sporting Traditions* 33, no. 1 (2016): 67–92.

Osmond, Gary. " 'Modest Monuments'? Postage Stamps, Duke Kahanamoku, and Hierarchies of Social Memory." *The Journal of Pacific History* 43, no. 3 (2008): 313–329.

Osmond, Gary. "Myth-making in Australian Sport History: Re-evaluating Duke Kahanamoku's Contribution to Surfing." *Australian Historical Studies* 42, no. 2 (2011): 260–176.

Osmond, Gary. "Racial Dimensions of Duke Kahanamoku's Tour of Australia and New Zealand, 1914–1915." *New Zealand Journal of History* 44, no. 1 (2010): 22–34.

Osmond, Gary. "The Surfing Tommy Tanna." *The Journal of Pacific History* 46, no. 2 (2011): 177–195.

Osmond, Gary, and Murray Phillips. "Australia's Women Surfers: History, Methodology, and the Digital Humanities." *Australian Historical Studies* 46, no. 2 (2015): 285–303.

Osmond, Gary, and Murray Phillips. " 'The Bloke with a Stroke': Alan Wickham, the Crawl and Social Memory." *The Journal of Pacific History* 39, no. 3 (2004): 309–324.

Osmond, Gary, Murray Philips, and Mark O'Neill. " 'Putting Up Your Dukes': Statues, Social Memory and Duke Paoa Kahanamoku." *International Journal of the History of Sport* 23, no. 1 (2006): 82–103.

Osorio, Jonathan Kay Kamakawiwo'ole. *Dismembering Lāhui: A History of the Hawaiian Nation to 1887*. Honolulu: University of Hawai'i Press, 2002.

Ostrom, Elinor. *Governing the Commons: The Evolution of Institutions for Collective Action*. Cambridge: Cambridge University Press, 1990.

Paarman, Donald. *Lunatic Surfer or Destiny? Autobiography of a Springbok . . . Whaaat!* Wilderness, South Africa: Donald Paarman, 2008.

Packard, Vance. *Our Endangered Children: Growing up in a Changing World*. Boston: Little, Brown & Company, 1983.

Paoa, Duke. "Riding the Surfboard." *The Mid-Pacific Magazine* 1, no. 1 (January 1911): 3–10, and 1, no. 2 (February 1911): 152–158.

Parkin, Shawn. "Points of Common Desire." *The Surfer's Journal* 23, no. 1 (2014): 62–71.

Paskowitz, Abraham. "Israel: Surfing in the Land of King David." *Surfer* 28, no. 9 (September 1987).

Paterson, Mark. "Haptic Geographies: Ethnography, Haptic Knowledge and Sensuous Dispositions." *Progress in Human Geography* 33, no. 6 (2009): 766–788.

Pearson, Kent. "Conflict, Stereotypes, and Masculinity in Australian and New Zealand Surfing." *Journal of Sociology* 18, no. 2 (1982): 117–135.

Pearson, Kent. "Surfies and Clubbies in Australia and New Zealand." *Journal of Sociology* 18, no. 1 (1982): 5–15.

Pearson, Kent. *Surfing Subcultures of Australia and New Zealand*. St. Lucia: University of Queensland Press, 1979.

Peck, Jamie, Doreen Massey, Katherine Gibson, and Victoria Lawson. "Symposium: The Kilburn Manifesto: After Neoliberalism?" *Environment and Planning A* 46, no. 9 (2014): 2033–2049.

Peck, Jamie, and Nik Theodore. "Labour Markets from the Bottom-Up." In *Working Space: Handbook of Employment and Society*, edited by Susan McGrath-Champ, Andrew Herod, and Al Rainnie, 87–105. Cheltenham: Edward Elgar, 2010.

Peck, Sam. "What Is a Real Indian? The Interminable Question of Cultural Authenticity." *AlterNative: An International Journal of Indigenous Scholarship* 8, no. 2 (2012): 176–188.

Peet, Richard. "Culture, Imaginary, and Rationality in Regional Economic Development." *Environment and Planning A* 32, no. 7 (2000): 1215–1234.

Pensky, Max. *Ends of Solidarity: Discourse Theory in Ethics and Politics.* Ithaca: State University of New York Press, 2008.

Pepper, David. *Eco-Socialism: From Deep Ecology to Social Justice.* London: Routledge, 1993.

Peralta, Stacy, dir. *Riding Giants.* Sony Pictures Classic, 2004. DVD.

Peralta, Stacy, dir., and Paul Taublieb, prod. *Hawaiian: The Legend of Eddie Aikau.* ESPN Films, 2013. DVD.

Perrott, Ron. " 'Crocodiles,' Zulus, and Surf Suid Afrika." *Surfer* 7, no. 2 (May 1966).

Peterson, Craig. "Sojourn into the Western Sahara." *Surfer* 17, no. 6 (March 1977).

Pezman, Steve. "The Evolutionary Surfer: Interview with Timothy Leary." *Surfer* 20, no. 8 (January 1978).

Phillips, Murray. *An Illusory Image: A Report on the Media Coverage and Portrayal of Women's Sport in Australia, 1996.* Canberra: Australian Sports Commission, 1997.

Poignant, Rolyn. *Professional Savages: Captive Lives and Western Spectacles.* New Haven, CT: Yale University Press, 2004.

Ponting, Jess. "Consuming Nirvana: An Exploration of Surfing Tourist Space." PhD diss., University of Technology, Sydney, Australia, 2008.

Ponting, Jess. "The Endless Bummer? The Past, Present and Future of Surfing Tourism Management in the Pacific." Proceedings of the Council of Australian University Tourism and Hospitality Educators (CAUTHE) Conference, Coffs Harbour, Australia, 2007.

Ponting, Jess. "Projecting Paradise: The Surf Media and the Hermeneutic Circle in Surfing Tourism." *Tourism Analysis* 14, no. 2 (2009): 175–185.

Ponting, Jess, and Mathew G. McDonald. "Performance, Agency, and Change in Surfing Tourist Space." *Annals of Tourism Research* 43 (2013): 414–434.

Ponting, Jess, Mathew McDonald, and Stephen Wearing. (2005). "De-constructing Wonderland: Surfing Tourism in the Mentawai Islands, Indonesia." *Society and Leisure* 28, no. 1 (2005): 141–162.

Ponting, Jess, and Danny O'Brien. "Liberalizing Nirvana: An Analysis of the Consequences of Common Pool Resource Deregulation for the Sustainability of Fiji's Surf Tourism Industry." *Journal of Sustainable Tourism* 22, no. 3 (2013): 384–402.

Poole, Ralph. "Cannibal Cruising, or, 'to the Careful Student of the Unnatural History of Civilization.' " *Amerikastudien/American Studies* 46, no. 1 (2001): 71–86.

Posel, Deborah. "Races to Consume: Revisiting South Africa's History of Race, Consumption and the Struggle for Freedom." *Ethnic and Racial Studies* 33, no. 2 (2010): 157–175.

Pratt, Andy C., and Paul Jeffcutt, eds. *Creativity, Innovation and the Cultural Economy.* London: Routledge, 2009.

Priestly, M. "An Early Strike in Ghana." *Historical Society of Ghana* 7 (1965): 25.

Puwar, Nirmal. *Space Invaders: Race, Gender and Bodies Out of Place.* Oxford: Berg, 2004.

Qureshi, Sadiah. *Peoples on Parade: Exhibitions, Empire, and Anthropology in Nineteenth-Century Britain.* Chicago: The University of Chicago Press, 2011.

Rattray, Robert Sutherland. *Ashanti.* Oxford: Clarendon Press, 1923.

Rawick, George. *From Sundown to Sunup: The Making of the Black Community.* Westwood, CT: Greenwood Press, 1972.

Rawls, John. "The Priority of the Right and Ideas of the Good." *Philosophy and Public Affairs* 17, no. 4 (1988): 251–276.

Rawls, John. *A Theory of Justice.* Cambridge, MA: Harvard University Press, 1971.

Reinier, Jacqueline. *From Virtue to Character: American Childhood, 1775–1850.* London: Twayne Publishers, 1996.

Rensin, David. *All for a Few Perfect Waves: The Audacious Life and Legend of Rebel Surfer Miki Dora.* New York: Harper Entertainment, 2008.

Rich, Adrienne. "Compulsory Heterosexuality and Lesbian Existence." *Signs: Journal of Women in Culture and Society* 5 (1980): 631–660.

Richards, Vernon, ed. *Why Work? Arguments for the Leisure Society.* London: Freedom Press, 1983.

Richards, William. *Memoir.* Boston, MA: Crocker & Brewster, 1825.

Rinehart, Robert. "Surf Film, Then & Now: The Endless Summer Meets Slow Dance." *Journal of Sport & Social Issues* 39, no. 6 (2015), 545–561.

Rinehart, Robert, and Sydny Sydnor, eds. *To the Extreme: Alternative Sports, Inside Out.* Albany: SUNY Press, 2003.

"Rio: City of Love . . . and Surf." *Surfer* 8, no. 6 (January 1968): 50.

Robert, Anne. "Paradigm Shift: New Perspectives, Changing Relationships." Lecture delivered at the University for Peace, San José, Costa Rica, January 28, 2013.

Roberts, Michael. "Occupy the Hammock." In *Class: An Anthology*, edited by Stanley Aronowitz and Michael Roberts. New York: Wiley-Blackwell, 2017.

Robertson, Roland. "Glocalization: Time-Space and Homogeneity-Heterogeneity." In *Global Modernities*, edited by Mike Featherstone, Scott Lash, and Roland Robertson, 25–44. London: Sage, 1995.

Robertson, Venetia Laura Delano. "Where Skin Meets Fin: The Mermaid as Myth, Monster and Other-Than-Human Identity." *Journal for the Academic Study of Religion* 26, no. 3 (2013): 303–323.

Roediger, David R., and Philip Sheldon Foner. *Our Own Time: A History of American Labor and the Working Day.* New York: Greenwood Press, 1989.

Rogaly, Ben. "Spaces of Work and Everyday Life: Labour Geographies and the Agency of Unorganized Temporary Migrant Workers." *Geography Compass* 3, no. 6 (2009): 1975–1987.

Roper, Lyndall. *Oedipus and the Devil: Witchcraft, Sexuality and Religion in Early Modern Europe.* London: Routledge, 1994.

Rorvick, Honor. "A Certain Kind of Madness." *South African Surfer* 1, no. 2 (July 1965).

Ross, Andrew. *"Nice Work If You Can Get It": Life and Labor in Precarious Times.* New York: New York University Press, 2009.

Roy, Georgina. "Feminism in New Sporting Spaces: Gender, Subjectivity and the Female Surfer in Britain." PhD diss., University of Brighton, 2013.

Roy, Georgina. "'Taking Emotions Seriously': Feeling Female and Becoming-Surfer through UK Surf Space." *Emotion, Space, and Society* 12 (2014): 41–48.

Roy, Georgina, and Jayne Caudwell. "Women and Surfing Spaces in Newquay, UK." In *Routledge Handbook of Sport, Gender, and Sexuality*, edited by Jennifer Hargreaves and Eric Anderson, 235–245. London: Routledge 2014.

Rubin, Gayle. "Thinking Sex: Notes for a Radical Theory of the Politics of Sexuality." In *Pleasure and Danger: Exploring Female Sexuality*, edited by Carol S. Vance. Boston: Routledge & Kegan Paul, 1984.

Ruschenberger, W. S. W. *Narrative of a Voyage Round the World, during the Years 1835, 36, and 37; Including a Narrative of an Embassy to the Sultan of Muscat and King of Siam.* 2 vols. Folkestone: Dawsons of Pall Mall, 1970.

Rutsky, Robert L. "Surfing the Other: Ideology on the Beach." *Film Quarterly* 52, no. 4 (1999): 12–23.

Ruttenberg, Tara. "Economic and Social Policy in Post-Neoliberal Latin America: Analyzing Impact on Poverty, Inequality and Social Wellbeing." *Ciência & Trópico* 35, no. 1 (2013): 279–325.

Ruttenberg, Tara. "Wellbeing Economics and Buen Vivir: Development Alternatives for Inclusive Human Security." *PRAXIS: The Fletcher Journal of Human Security* 28 (2013): 68–93.

Ruuska, T. "Ideological Transformation and Influences of Neoliberalism on Academic Work." Public lecture presented at the University for Peace, San José, Costa Rica, March 6, 2015.

Sachs, Wolfgang. "Preface to the New Edition." *The Development Dictionary: A Guide to Knowledge as Power*, edited by Wolfgang Sachs, 1–6. London: Zed Books, 2009.

Sai, David Keanu. "The American Occupation of the Hawaiian Kingdom: Beginning the Transition from Occupied to Restored State." PhD diss., University of Hawai'i, 2008.

Sai, David Keanu. "A Slippery Path towards Hawaiian Indigeneity: An Analysis and Comparison between Hawaiian State Sovereignty and Hawaiian Indigeneity and Its Use and Practice in Hawai'i Today." *Journal of Law and Social Challenges* 10 (2008): 68–133.

Sai, David Keanu. *Ua Mau Ke Ea, Sovereignty Endures: An Overview of the Political and Legal History of the Hawaiian Islands.* Honolulu: Pua'a Foundation, 2011.

Said, Edward. *Culture and Imperialism.* London: Vintage, 1994.

Said, Edward. *Orientalism.* New York: Vintage Books, 1978.

Samuelson, Meg. "Re-telling Freedom in Otelo Burning: The Beach, Surf Noir, and Bildung at the Lamontville Pool." *Journal of African Cultural Studies* 26, no. 3 (2014): 307–323.

Samuelson, Meg, and Glen Thompson. "Interview with Sara Blecher and Sihle Xaba: The Making and Meanings of *Otelo Burning*." *Journal of African Cultural Studies* 26, no. 3 (2014): 352–361.

Samuelson, Meg, and Glen Thompson. "Introduction." *Journal of African Cultural Studies* 26, no. 3 (2014): 303–306.

Santa Maria, Pete, dir. *Mixed Tape.* Reef Entertainment, 2007. DVD.

Santos, Boaventura de Sousa. "The WSF: Toward a Counter-Hegemonic Globalization." In *World Social Forum: Challenging Empires*, edited by Jai Sen, Anita Anand, Arturo Escobar, and Peter Waterman, 235–245. New Delhi: The Viveka Foundation, 2004.

Saranillo, Dean. "Why Asian Settler Colonialism Matters: A Thought Piece on Critiques, Debates, and Indigenous Difference." *Settler Colonial Studies* 3, no. 3–4 (2013): 280–294.

Sayer, Andrew. "For a Critical Cultural Political Economy." *Antipode* 33, no. 4 (2001): 687–708.

Scheibel, Dean. "'Making Waves' with Burke: Surf Nazi Culture and the Rhetoric of Localism." *Western Journal of Communication* 59, no. 4 (1995): 253–269.

Schroeder, Jonathan, and Janet Borgerson. "Packaging Paradise: Organizing Representations of Hawaii." In *Against the Grain: Advances in Postcolonial Organization Studies*, edited by Anshuman Prasad, 32–53. Copenhagen: Copenhagen University Business School Press, 2012.

Schumacher, Cori. (2012). "Women in the Sub-Culture of Surfing." *Gender across Borders*. February 7, 2012. http://www.genderacrossborders.com/2012/02/07/women-in-the-sub-culture-of-surfing/.

Scott, A. J. *The Cultural Economy of Cities*. London: Sage, 2000.

Scott, A. J. "The US Recorded Music Industry: On the Relations between Organization, Location, and Creativity in the Cultural Economy." *Environment and Planning A* 31, no. 11 (1999): 1965–1984.

Seed, Patricia. *Ceremonies of Possession in Europe's Conquest of the New World, 1492–1640*. Cambridge: Cambridge University Press, 1995.

Sefa Dei, George. "Revisiting the Question of the Indigenous." In *Indigenous Philosophies and Critical Education: A Reader*, edited by George Sefa Dei, 21–33. New York: Peter Lang Publishing, 2011.

Shaath, Nadim, ed. *Sunscreens: Regulations and Commercial Development*. New York: CRC Press, 2005.

Sidbury, James, and Jorge Cañizares-Esguerra. "Mapping Ethnogenesis in the Early Modern Atlantic." *William and Mary Quarterly* 68, no. 2 (2011): 181–208.

Sigrid, Paul. "The Wrestling Tradition and Its Social Function." *Sport in Africa: Essays in Social History*, edited by William J. Baker and James A. Mangan, 23–46. New York: Routledge, 1987.

Silva, Noenoe K. *Aloha Betrayed: Native Hawaiian Resistance to American Colonialism*. Durham, NC: Duke University Press, 2004.

Silver, Beverly J. *Forces of Labor: Workers' Movements and Globalization since 1870*. Cambridge: Cambridge University Press, 2003.

Silverman, Jane L. *Kaahumanu, Molder of Changer*. Honolulu: Friends of the Judiciary History Center, 1987.

Silvers, Ash. *Land of the O-O. Facts, Figures, Fables, and Fancies*. Cleveland: The Cleveland Printing and Publishing Co., 1892.

Slater, Don. "Marketing as a Monstrosity: The Impossible Place between Culture and Economy." In *Inside Marketing: Practices, Ideologies, Devices*, edited by Detlev Zwick and Julien Cayla, n.p. Oxford and New York: Oxford University Press, 2011.

Smith, Andrea, and J. Kēhaulani Kauanui. "Native Feminisms Engage American Studies." *American Quarterly* 60, no. 2 (2008): 241–249.

Smith, Charles. *Welcome to Paradise, Now Go to Hell.* Nero: Melbourne, 2013.

Smith, Linda Tuhiwai. *Decolonizing Methodologies: Research and Indigenous Peoples.* London: Zed Books, 1999.

Smith, Mark. *How Race Is Made: Slavery, Segregation, and the Senses.* Chapel Hill: University of North Carolina Press, 2006.

Smith, William. *A New Voyage to Guinea.* London: J. Nourse, 1774.

Spivak, Gayatri Chakravorty. "Can the Subaltern Speak?" In *Marxism and the Interpretation of Culture,* edited by Cary Nelson and Lawrence Grossberg, 271–316. London: Macmillan, 1988.

Spivak, Gayatri Chakravorty. *Other Asias.* Oxford: Blackwell, 2008.

Starr, Kevin. *California: A History.* New York: Modern Library, 2007.

Starr, Kevin. *Endangered Dreams: The Great Depression in California.* New York: Oxford University Press, 1997.

Staszak, Jean. "Primitivism and the Other: History of Art and Cultural Geography." *GeoJournal* 60, no. 1 (2004): 353–364.

Stecyk, C. R. III, and Drew Kampion. *Dora Lives: The Authorized Story of Miki Dora.* Santa Barbara, CA: T. Adler Books, 2005.

Stedman, Leanne. "From Gidget to Gonad Man: Surfers, Feminists and Postmodernisation." *The Australian and New Zealand Journal of Statistics* 33, no. 1 (1997): 75–90.

Steele, Taylor, dir. *The Drifter.* San Diego, CA: Sipping Jetstreams Media, 2009. DVD.

Steinberg, Philip. *The Social Construction of the Ocean.* Cambridge: Cambridge University Press, 2001.

Stell, Marion. *Pam Burridge.* Sydney: Angus & Robertson, 1992.

Stenger, Josh. "Mapping the Beach: Beach Movies, Exploitation Film and Geographies of Whiteness." In *The Persistence of Whiteness: Race and Contemporary Hollywood Cinema,* edited by Daniel Bernardi, 28–50. Abingdon: Routledge, 2008.

Stewart, Bob, James Skinner, and Allan Edwards. "Cluster Theory and Competitive Advantage: The Torquay Surfing Experience." *International Journal of Sport Management and Marketing* 3, no. 3 (2008): 201–220.

Stewart, C. S. *A Residence in the Sandwich Islands.* New York: John P. Haven, 1828.

Stewart, C. S. *A Visit to the South Seas, in the U.S. Ship Vincennes, during the Years 1829 and 1830.* 2 vols. New York: John P. Haven, 1831.

Stewart, Frank Henderson. *Honor.* Chicago: The University of Chicago Press, 1994.

Stocking, George W. Jr. "Ideas and Institutions in American Anthropology: Toward a History of the Interwar Period." In *Selected Papers from the American Anthropologist, 1921–1945,* edited by George W. Stocking Jr. Washington, DC: American Anthropological Association, 1976.

Stoddard, B. *Invisible Games: A Report on the Media Coverage of Women's Sports, 1992.* Canberra: Australian Sports Commission, 1994.

Stoddard, Charles Warren. *Summer Cruising in the South Seas.* London: Chatto and Windus, 1881.

Stoler, Ann Laura. *Carnal Knowledge and Imperial Power: Race and the Intimate in Colonial Rule*. Berkeley: University of California Press, 2002.

Stranger, Mark. "The Aesthetics of Risk: A Study of Surfing." *International Review for the Sociology of Sport* 34, no. 3 (1999): 265–276.

Stranger, Mark. "Surface and Substructure: Beneath Surfing's Commodified Surface." *Sport in Society* 13, no. 7–8 (2010): 1117–1134.

Stranger, Mark. *Surfing Life: Surface, Substructure and the Commodification of the Sublime*. Farnham: Ashgate, 2011.

Stuart, Ossie. "The Lions Stir: Football in African Society." In *Giving the Game Away: Football, Politics and Culture on Five Continents*, edited by Stephen Waggs, 24–51. London: Leicester University Press, 1995.

Sturm, Circe. *Blood Politics: Race, Culture, and Identity in the Cherokee Nation of Oklahoma*. Berkeley: University of California Press, 2002.

Surfing Heritage and Cultural Centre, dir. *Travel Adventures with Dick Metz*. 2015. DVD.

Sweeney, Carole. *From Fetish to Subject: Race, Modernism, and Primitivism, 1919–1935*. Westport, CT: Praeger, 2004.

Sweet, James H. *Domingos Álvares, African Healing, and the Intellectual History of the Atlantic World*. Chapel Hill: University of North Carolina Press, 2011.

Tamas, Peter. "Misrecognitions and Missed Opportunities: Post-Structuralism and the Practice of Development." *Third World Quarterly* 25, no. 4 (2004): 649–660.

Tamplin, Ron. "Noblemen and Noble Savages." In *Representing Others: White Views of Indigenous Peoples*, edited by Mick. Gidley, 60–83. Exeter, UK: Exeter University Press, 1992.

Tengan, Ty Kāwika. "(En)gendering Colonialism: Masculinities in Hawai'i and Aotearoa." *Cultural Values* 6, no. 3 (2002): 239–256.

Tengan, Ty Kāwika. *Native Men Remade: Gender and Nation in Contemporary Hawai'i*. Durham, NC: Duke University Press, 2008.

Te Punga Somerville, Alice. *Once Were Pacific: Māori Connections to Oceania*. Minneapolis: University of Minnesota Press, 2012.

Thomas, Charles W. *Adventures and Observations on the West Coast of Africa*. Baltimore: Derby & Jackson, 1860.

Thomas, Nicholas. *Islanders: The Pacific in the Age of Empire*. New Haven, CT: Yale University Press, 2010.

Thompson, Craig J. "Marketplace Mythology and Discourses of Power." *Journal of Consumer Research* 31, no. 1 (2004): 162–180.

Thompson, Glen. "'Certain Political Considerations': South African Competitive Surfing During the International Sports Boycott." *The International Journal of the History of Sport* 28, no. 1 (2011): 32–46.

Thompson, Glen. "'Certain Political Considerations': South African Competitive Surfing During the International Sports Boycott." In *Sport Past and Present in South Africa: (Trans)forming the Nation*, edited by Scarlett Cornelissen and Albert Grundlingh, 31–45. Abingdon: Routledge, 2012.

Thompson, Glen. "Disturbed Waters: New Currents in the History of Water Sport." *Radical History Review*, no. 125 (2016): 199–205.

Thompson, Glen. "Judging Surf Culture: The Making of a White Exemplar Masculinity During the 1966 Natal and South African Surf Riding Championships Held in Durban." *Journal of Natal and Zulu History* 26 (2008): 81–109.

Thompson, Glen. "*Otelo Burning* and Zulu Surfing Histories." *Journal of African Cultural Studies* 26, no. 3 (2014): 324–340.

Thompson, Glen. "Reimagining Surf City: Surfing and the Making of the Post-Apartheid Beach in South Africa." *The International Journal of the History of Sport* 28, no. 15 (2011): 2115–2129.

Thompson, Glen. "Surfing, Gender and Politics: Identity and Society in the History of South African Surfing Culture." PhD diss., Stellenbosch University, 2014.

Thorne, Tanis. "Legends of the Surfer Subculture: Part One." *Western Folklore* 35, no. 3 (1976): 209–217.

Thorne, Tanis. "Legends of the Surfer Subculture: Part Two." *Western Folklore* 35, no. 4 (1976): 270–280.

Thornton, John K. *Warfare in Atlantic Africa, 1500–1800*. London: Routledge, 1999.

Thorpe, Holly. "Action Sports for Youth Development: Critical Insights for the SDP Community." *International Journal of Sport Policy and Politics* 8 (2016): 91–116.

Thorpe, Holly. "Boarders, Babes and Bad-asses: Theories of a Female Physical Youth Culture." PhD diss., University of Waikato, 2007.

Thorpe, Holly. "Bourdieu, Feminism and Female Physical Culture: Gender Reflexivity and the Habitus-Field Complex." *Sociology of Sport Journal* 26 (2009): 491–516.

Thorpe, Holly. "Bourdieu, Gender Reflexivity and Physical Culture: A Case of Masculinities in the Snowboarding Field." *Journal of Sport and Social Issues* 34, no. 2 (2010): 176–214.

Thorpe, Holly. *Transnational Mobilities in Action Sport Cultures: Migration, Diasporas and Citizenship*. Hampshire, UK: Palgrave, 2014.

Thorpe, Holly, and Rebecca Olive. "The Power, Politics, and Potential of Feminist Sports History: A Multigenerational Dialogue." *Journal of Sport History* 39, no. 3 (2012): 379–394.

Thorpe, Holly, and R. Rinehart. "Alternative Sport and Affect: Non-representational Theory Examined." *Sport and Society* 14, no. 7/8 (2010): 1268–1291.

Thorpe, Holly, and Belinda Wheaton. "Dissecting Action Sports Studies: Past, Present, and Beyond." In *A Companion to Sport*, edited by Dave Andrews and Ben Carrington, 341–356. Malden, MA: Blackwell, 2013

Timmons, Grady. *Waikiki Beachboy*. Honolulu: Editions, 1989.

Tobin, Jeffrey. "Cultural Construction and Native Nationalism: A Report from the Hawaiian Front." *Boundary 2* 21, no. 1 (1994): 111–133.

Tom, Walter Blair. "Surfer Exploration and Migration: North American Surfers in Mexico, El Salvador and Nicaragua." Master's thesis, Sonoma State University, Sonoma, California, 2013.

Tomson, Shaun. *Bustin' Down the Door: The Surf Revolution of '75*. New York: Abrams, 2008.

Tomson, Shaun, with Patrick Moser. *The Code: The Power of I Will*. Salt Lake City: Gibbs Smith, 2013.

Tomson, Shaun, with Patrick Moser. *Surfer's Code: 12 Simple Lessons for Riding through Life*. Salt Lake City: Gibbs Smith, 2006.

Torgovnick, Marianna. *Gone Primitive: Savage Intellects, Modern Lives.* Chicago: University of Chicago Press, 1991.

Trachtenberg, Alan. *Shades of Hiawatha: Staging Indians, Making Americans, 1880–1930.* New York: Hill and Wang, 2004.

Trask, Haunani-Kay. *From a Native Daughter: Colonialism and Sovereignty in Hawai'i.* Monroe, ME: Common Courage Press, 1993.

Turner, Bryan. "The Possibility of Primitiveness: Towards a Sociology of Body Marks in Cool Societies." *Body Modification* 5, no. 2–3 (2000): 39–50.

Turner, Timmy, dir. *Second Thoughts.* Timmy Turner Films, 2004. DVD.

Twain, Mark. *Roughing It.* Hartford: American Publishing Company, 1872.

United Nations World Commission on Environment and Development (UNWCED). Brundtland Report, *Our Common Future*, 1987.

Usher, Lindsay, and Deborah Kerstetter. "'Surfistas Locales': Transnationalism and the Construction of Surfer Identity in Nicaragua." *Journal of Sport & Social Issues* 4, no. 3 (2015): 286–302.

Van Oordt, Melissa Joyce. "A Historical Overview of the Origins of Anti-Shark Measures in Natal, 1940–1980." Master's thesis, University of KwaZulu-Natal, 2006.

Van Veldhuizen, Laurens, and COMPAS. *Learning Endogenous Development: Building on Biocultural Diversity.* Warwickshire, UK: Practical Action Publishing, 2007.

Verge, Arthur. "George Freeth: King of the Surfers and California's Forgotten Hero." *California History* 80, no. 2–3 (2001): 82–105.

Vickers, Daniel, with Vince Walsh. *Young Men and the Sea: Yankee Seafarers in the Age of Sail.* New Haven, CT: Yale University Press, 2005.

Visvanathan, Shiv. "Mrs. Bruntland's Disenchanted Cosmos." *Alternatives: Global, Local, Political* 16, no. 3 (1991): 377–384.

Wagner-Wright, Sandra. *The Structure of the Missionary Call to the Sandwich Islands, 1790–1830.* San Francisco: Mellen University Press, 1990.

Waitt, Gordon. "'Killing Waves': Surfing, Space, and Gender." *Social and Cultural Geography* 9, no. 1 (2008): 75–94.

Waitt, Gordon, and Andrew Warren. "'Talking Shit over a Brew after a Good Session with Your Mates': Surfing, Space, and Masculinity." *Australian Geographer* 39, no. 3 (2008): 353–365.

Walker, Isaiah Helekunihi. "Hui Nalu, Beachboys, and the Surfing Boarder-Lands of Hawai'i." *The Contemporary Pacific* 20, no. 1 (2008): 89–113.

Walker, Isaiah Helekunihi. "North Shore Reign: The Hui 'O He 'e Nalu and the Surfing Borderlands of Hawai'i." PhD diss., University of California, Santa Barbara, 2006.

Walker, Isaiah Helekunihi. "Review: *Empire in Waves: A Political History of Surfing.*" *The Journal of Pacific History* 50, no. 1 (2015). http://www.tandfonline.com/doi/full/10.1080/00223344.2015.1079937.

Walker, Isaiah Helekunihi. "Terrorism or Native Protest? The Hui 'O He'e Nalu and Hawaiian Resistance to Colonialism." *Pacific Historical Review* 74, no. 4 (2005): 575–601.

Walker, Isaiah Helekunihi. *Waves of Resistance: Surfing and History in Twentieth-Century Hawai'i.* Honolulu: University of Hawai'i Press, 2011.

Walker, M. "El Confessor: Atoning for Surfer's Sins in Nicaragua." *The Surfer's Path* (Jan/Feb 2006): 64–75.

Wallace, Rick. "Grassroots Community-Based Peacebuilding: Critical Narratives on Peacebuilding and Collaboration from the Locality of Indigenous and Non-Indigenous Activists in Canada." PhD diss., University of Bradford, 2010.

Warde, Alan. "Consumption, Identity-formation and Uncertainty." *Sociology* 28, no. 4 (1994): 877–898.

Wardlaw, Lee. *Cowabunga*. New York: Avon Books, 1991.

Warner, Michael. "Introduction: Fear of a Queer Planet." *Social Text* 9, no. 4 (1991): 3–17.

Warner, Michael. *Publics and Counterpublics*. Cambridge, MA: Zone Books, 2002.

Warren, Andrew. "Crafting Masculinities: Gender, Culture and Emotion at Work in the Surfboard Industry." *Gender, Place and Culture: A Journal of Feminist Geography* 23, no. 1 (2016): 36–54.

Warren, Andrew. "Working Culture: The Agency and Employment Experiences of Non-unionized Workers in the Surfboard Industry." *Environment and Planning A* 46, no. 10 (2014): 2300–2316.

Warren, Andrew, and Chris Gibson. "Making Things in a High Dollar Australia: The Case of the Surfboard Industry." *Journal of Australian Political Economy* 71, no. 1 (2013): 26–50.

Warren, Andrew, and Chris Gibson. *Surfing Places, Surfboard Makers: Craft, Creativity, and Cultural Heritage in Hawaii, California, and Australia*. Honolulu: University of Hawai'i Press, 2014.

Warshaw, Matt. "Articles of Faith. 35 Years of Surf Magazines: An Insider's View," *The Surfer's Journal* 5, no. 1 (1996), 86–103.

Warshaw, Matt. *The Encyclopedia of Surfing*. Orlando, FL: Harcourt, 2003.

Warshaw, Matt. *The Encyclopedia of Surfing*. 2nd ed. San Diego, CA: Harcourt, 2005.

Warshaw, Matt. "Foreword." In *The Perfect Day: Forty Years of Surfer Magazine* by Sam George. San Francisco: Chronicle Books, 2003.

Warshaw, Matt. *The History of Surfing*. San Francisco: Chronicle Books, 2010.

Warshaw, Matt. *Photo/Stoner: The Rise, Fall, and Mysterious Disappearance of Surfing's Greatest Photographer*. San Francisco: Chronicle Books, 2006.

Warshaw, Matt. *Surf Movie Tonite!: Surf Movie Poster Art, 1957–2004*. San Francisco: Chronicle Books, 2005.

Warshaw, Matt. *Surf Riders: In Search of the Perfect Wave*. New York: Harper Collins, 1997.

Warshaw, Matt. *Zero Break: An Illustrated Collection of Surf Writing: 1777–2004*. Orlando: Harcourt, 2004.

Watson-Veran, Helen, and David Turnbull. "Science and Other Indigenous Knowledge Systems." In *Knowledge: Critical Concepts*, edited by Nico Stehr and Reiner Grundmann, 345–369. Abingdon and New York: Routledge, 2005.

Weeks, Kathi. *The Problem with Work: Feminism, Marxism, Antiwork Politics, and Postwork Imaginaries*. Durham, NC: Duke University Press, 2011.

Wensing, Emma, and Bruce, Toni. "Bending the Rules: Media Representations of Gender during an International Sporting Event." *International Review for the Sociology of Sport* 38, no. 4 (2003): 387–396.

Westervelt, W. D. *Legends of Old Honolulu*. Boston: Press of Geo. H. Ellis, 1915.

Westwick, Peter, and Peter Neushul. *The World in the Curl: An Unconventional History of Surfing*. New York: Crown Publishers, 2013.

Wheaton, Belinda. *The Cultural Politics of Lifestyle Sports*. Abingdon: Routledge, 2013.

Wheaton, Belinda. "From the Pavement to the Beach: Politics and Identity in Surfers Against Sewage." In *Tribal Play: Subcultural Journeys through Sport*, edited by Michael Atkinson and Kevin Young, 113–134. Bingley, UK: Emerald Publishing, 2008.

Wheaton, Belinda. "Habitus." In *Key Concepts in Sport Studies*, edited by Stephen Wagg, Carlton Brick, Belinda Wheaton, and Jayne Caudwell, 102–108. London: Sage, 2009.

Wheaton, Belinda. "Identity, Politics, and the Beach: Environmental Activism in Surfers Against Sewage." *Leisure Studies* 26, no. 3 (2007): 279–302.

Whitmore, John. "Surfing Around the Cape." *South African Surfer* 1, no. 1 (April 1965): 5.

Willard, Michael. "Duke Kahanamoku's Body: Biography of Hawai'i." In *Sports Matters: Race, Recreation, and Culture*, edited by John Bloom and Michael Willard, 13–38. New York: New York University Press, 2002.

Willett, Graham. *Living out Loud: A History of Gay and Lesbian Activism in Australia*. Crows Nest, NSW: Allen & Unwin, 2000.

Williams, Raymond. *The Sociology of Culture*. Chicago: University of Chicago Press, 1995.

Wills, Jane. "Subcontracted Employment and Its Challenge to Labor." *Labor Studies Journal* 34, no. 4 (2009): 441–460.

Wilson, Brian. "Cape St. Francis: South Africa's Premier Surf Spot." *South African Surfer* 1, no. 2 (July 1965).

Wilson, Margaret. "Precarious Work: The Need for a New Policy Framework." In *The Whitlam Institute Perspectives*, 1–12. Rydalmere, NSW: University of Western Sydney, 2013.

Wolch, Jennifer, and Jin Zhang. "Beach Recreation, Cultural Diversity and Attitudes to Nature." *Journal of Leisure Research* 36, no. 3 (2004): 414–443.

Wolfe, Patrick. "Settler Colonialism and the Elimination of the Native." *Journal of Genocide Research* 8, no. 4 (2006): 387–409.

Wood, David. "On the Crest of a Wave: Surfing and Literature in Peru." *Sport in History* 29, no. 2 (2009): 226–242.

Wood, David. "Representing Peru: Seeing the Female Sporting Body." *Journal of Latin American Cultural Studies* 21, no. 3 (2012): 417–436.

Woods, Ted. *White Wash*. Trespass Productions, 2011. Documentary film.

Woodward, Keith, Deborah Dixon, and John Paul Jones. "Poststructuralism/Poststructuralist Geographies." *International Encyclopedia of Human Geography*, edited by Rob Kitchin and Nigel Thrift, 396–407. Oxford: Elsevier, 2009.

Xiong, Huan. "Stratification of Women's Sport in Contemporary China." *International Journal of the History of Sport* 28, no. 7 (2011): 990–1015.

Xuan, Guo-Fu, Lin Lu, Hin-He Zhang, and Xiao-Zhong Yang. "Residents' Perception of Tourism Impacts in Coast Resorts: The Case Study of Haikou and Sanya Cities, Hainan Province." *Scientia Geographica Sinica* 22, no. 6 (2002): 741–746.

Yang, Mei-hui. "The Modernity of Power in the Chinese Socialist Order." *Cultural Anthropology* 3, no. 4 (1988): 408–427.

Yangwen, Zheng. *China on the Sea: How the Maritime World Shaped Modern China*. Boston: Brill Academic Publishing, 2011.

Young, Jock. *The Drugtakers*. London: MacGibbon and Kee, 1971.

Young, Jock. "The Hippie Solution: An Essay in the Politics of Leisure." In *Politics and Deviance*, edited by Ian Taylor and Laurie Taylor. Baltimore: Penguin Books, 1973.

Young, Nat, and Craig McGregor. *The History of Surfing*. Palm Beach, NSW: Palm Beach Press, 1983.

Zavalza Hough-Snee, Dexter. "You Have the Right to Surf: Riding Waves of Decolonization, Modernity, and Nationalism in Peru." In *Sports and Nationalism in Latin/o America*, edited by Hector Fernández L'Hoeste, Robert McKee Irwin, and Juan Poblete, 201–223. New York: Palgrave Macmillan, 2015.

Zhang, Li, and Aihwa Ong, eds. *Privatizing China: Socialism from Afar*. Ithaca, NY: Cornell University Press, 2008.

Zhao, Yin. "On Limiting Factors of Developing Stage of Extreme Sport Behavior." *Shandong Sport Science & Technology* 32, no. 1 (2010): 53–54.

Zhao, Yuezhi. "Neoliberal Strategies, Socialist Legacies: Communication and State Transformation in China." In *Global Communications: Toward a Transcultural Political Economy*, edited by Paula Chakravartty and Yuezhi Zhao, 23–49. Lanham, MD: Rowman & Littlefield, 2008.

Zwiep, Mary. *Pilgrim Path: The First Company of Women Missionaries to Hawaii*. Madison: University of Wisconsin Press, 1991.

Contributors

DOUGLAS BOOTH is professor of sport studies and dean of the School of Physical Education and Sport and Exercise Sciences at the University of Otago, New Zealand. He is the author of *The Race Game* (1998), *Australian Beach Cultures* (2001), and *The Field* (2005). Douglas serves on the editorial boards of *Rethinking History* and the *Journal of Sport History* and is an executive member of the Australian Society for Sport History.

PETER BROSIUS is distinguished research professor of anthropology at the University of Georgia and a surfer since 1969. He is widely recognized for his work with Penan hunter-gatherers in Sarawak (Malaysian Borneo), where he has recently been involved in court testimony in support of Penan land claims against oil palm companies. Brosius's work focuses on the political ecology of conservation, with a particular interest in the impact of environmental degradation on local and indigenous communities. He is also the founding director of UGA's Center for Integrative Conservation Research. Brosius teaches a study abroad program called Surfing & Sustainability: Political Ecology in Costa Rica, and is currently developing a comparative research project on sustainable surf tourism in Bali, Fiji, and Costa Rica.

ROBIN CANNIFORD is co-director of the Cluster for Organisation, Society and Markets and senior lecturer in management and marketing at the University of Melbourne. The author of multiple book chapters and articles, his work on surfing as an example of nature/culture entanglements has been published in *The Journal of Consumer Research*, as well as in the journals *Consumption Markets and Culture* and *Marketing Theory*. More recent work on sport and social movements is forthcoming in *Sociology*. He co-edited *Assembling Consumption* (2015, with Domen Bajde). His most recent research project investigates the intersections of sport and sound.

KRISTA COMER is professor of English and associate director of the Center for the Study of Women, Gender, and Sexuality at Rice University in Houston, Texas. She is interested in interdisciplinary approaches to problems of place and space, and their theorization. Her books include *Landscapes of the New West: Gender and Geography in Contemporary Women's Writing* (1999) and *Surfer Girls in the New World Order* (2010). In 2014, she co-founded the Institute for Women Surfers, a grassroots educational initiative in the public humanities. Her current project, *Feminist States of Critical Regionalism*, synthesizes public humanities activism with studies in contemporary literature and film to investigate new democratic geographies and state imaginaries.

KEVIN DAWSON is assistant professor of history at the University of California, Merced. His research is situated at the historiographic crossroads of Atlantic history and the African diaspora, examining swimming, underwater diving, surfing, canoe-making, canoeing, and fishing to consider how Atlantic Africans and members of the African diaspora used water as a cultural space. He is completing a book titled *Enslaved Water People in the Atlantic World, 1444–1888: The Cultural Meanings of Water, Swimming, Surfing, and Canoeing in Atlantic Africa and the African Diaspora* (forthcoming). His publications include "Enslaved Ship Pilots in the Age of Revolutions: Challenging Perceptions of Race and Slavery Between the Boundaries of Maritime and Terrestrial Bondage" in *The Journal of Social History* and "Enslaved Swimmers and Divers in the Atlantic World" in *The Journal of American History*, which was awarded the Louis Pelzer Memorial Award from the Organization of American Historians.

CLIFTON EVERS is lecturer in gender and cultural studies at Newcastle University, UK. His research explores gender (particularly masculinity) and media, and he has an interest in critically examining surfing. Clifton has conducted research for government departments, elite sporting organizations, community groups, media outlets, and private industry. He is an editor of the *Journal of Sport & Social Issues* and the *International Journal of Cultural Studies*. He is currently researching surfing in northeast Asia, the labor of surfing, as well as thinking about the interfacing of digital media and surfing.

CHRIS GIBSON is professor of human geography at the University of Wollongong, Australia, and currently editor-in-chief of the journal *Australian Geographer*. His research explores cultural economies of creative, manufacturing, and rural industries, ranging from festivals to surfboards and musical instruments. He is the author of several books, including *Sound Tracks: Popular Music, Identity and Space* (2003), *Music Festivals and Regional Development in Australia* (2013), and *Surfing Places, Surfboard Makers* (2014, with Andrew Warren). He is also a keen bodysurfer and guitar player.

DINA GILIO-WHITAKER (Colville Confederated Tribes) is policy director and senior research associate at the Center for World Indigenous Studies. An award-winning journalist at Indian Country Today Media Network, she has contributed to *Native People's Magazine* and numerous other online outlets, and she has been involved with Indigenous peoples' participation in the United Nations. Dina's research focuses on Indigenous nationalism, self-determination, environmental justice, and education. She also works within the field of critical sports studies, examining the intersections of indigeneity and surfing. She is coauthor with Roxanne Dunbar-Ortiz of *"All the Real Indians Died Off" and 20 Other Myths About Native Americans* (2016). She is working on a new book, *Embodied Resistance: Indigenous Peoples and Environmental Justice in the United States*.

SCOTT LADERMAN teaches history at the University of Minnesota, Duluth. He is the author of *Empire in Waves: A Political History of Surfing* (2014) and *Tours of Vietnam:*

War, Travel Guides, and Memory (2009). A Californian by birth, he now regularly surfs Lake Superior.

KRISTIN LAWLER is associate professor and chair of the sociology department at the College of Mount Saint Vincent in Bronx, New York. Her first book, *The American Surfer: Radical Culture and Capitalism* (2011), examined the politics of American surf culture during the twentieth century. She is a member of the editorial collective of the journal *Situations: Project of the Radical Imagination*; her work has been published there and in several edited collections, in *Z Magazine*, and in the digital forum of the Social Science Research Council. She is currently at work on her new book, *Shanty Irish: The Roots of American Syndicalism*.

LISAHUNTER was previously a senior lecturer in the Te Oranga School of Human Development and Movement Studies at the University of Waikato, New Zealand. Organizer of the 2016 international conference Surfing Social in Aotearoa/New Zealand, she is the author of dozens of articles and chapters. Most recently she co-edited *Pierre Bourdieu and Physical Culture* (2015, with Wayne Smith and elke emerald). Select recent works on surfing include "Seaspaces: Surfing the Sea as Pedagogy of Self" (in *Seascapes: Shaped by the Sea*, 2015); "'Stop': 'No.' Exploring Social Suffering in Practices of Surfing as Opportunities for Change" (in *Bourdieu and Physical Culture*, 2015); and "Visual Narratives of 'Female' as a Political Position: Pedagogies of Surfing Events and their Media" (in *Women in Action Sport Cultures: Identity, Politics, and Experience*, 2016). She is currently coordinating the volume *Surfing, Sex, Genders, and Sexualities* (forthcoming).

COLLEEN MCGLOIN is honorary senior fellow in the faculty of law at the University of Wollongong, Australia. Her background is in cultural studies and literature with a focus on issues of race, gender, and culture. Colleen's research interests are in pedagogical practices in higher education as these inform and construct subjectivities for academics and for students, specifically in relation to race and gender. Colleen has published on issues of critical pedagogy in indigenous contexts. She is the author of *Surfing Nation(s) Surfing Country(s)*, a study of Australian national identity through surf and beach culture that proposes a counter-discourse of nation through an examination of indigenous concepts of nation and country.

PATRICK MOSER is professor of French at Drury University. He is the editor of *Pacific Passages: An Anthology of Surf Writing* (2008). His essays on surfing have appeared in *Surfer* magazine, *The Surfer's Journal, Gingko Tree Review, Sport Literate, Kurungabaa*, and *Bamboo Ridge*. He has collaborated with former surfing world champion Shaun Tomson on *The Code* (2013) and *Surfer's Code: 12 Simple Lessons for Riding through Life* (2006). His current research focuses on how period newspaper reports are changing our understanding of surf history. Recent and forthcoming publications include "The Endurance of Surfing in 19th-Century Hawai'i" in *The Journal of the Polynesian Society* and "The Hawai'i Promotion Committee and the Revival of Surfing" in *Pacific Historical Review*.

TARA RUTTENBERG is a doctoral candidate in development studies at Wageningen University. At the University for Peace in Costa Rica, she has taught on alternatives to development and well-being economics. Centering a decolonizing, participatory-action approach to sustainable surf tourism, Tara created SUSPIRO: Sustainable Tourism Solutions for Communities in Surf Tourism Destinations. Tara works as teaching assistant for the University of Georgia's study abroad program, Surfing & Sustainability: Political Ecology in Costa Rica, and she created Tarantula Surf (www.tarantulasurf.com) as an online platform for authentic story-sharing and engaging with new social paradigms and enacting post-capitalist futures in surfing communities and beyond.

CORI SCHUMACHER is a three-time ASP/WSL Women's Longboard World Champion (2000, 2001, 2010), activist, writer, and cofounder of The Inspire Initiative. She is currently exploring how diverse female surfing bodies serve as unique sites from which to birth cogent, effective, and intimate environmental justice activisms and surprising political will in the twenty-first century. She has written for diverse publications, including *The Guardian* and *The Surfer's Journal*.

ALEXANDER SOTELO EASTMAN is postdoctoral fellow of the Society of Fellows at Dartmouth College, where he teaches and researches the African diaspora in Latin America and the Caribbean. He has published articles on the black press, abolitionism, and Cuba's wars of independence in journals such as the *Afro-Hispanic Review*, *Bulletin of Spanish Studies*, and *Siglo diecinueve*. He is currently preparing a manuscript about the history of black intellectual thought and the cultural, social, and political associations linked to the civil rights movement in nineteenth- and early twentieth-century Cuba. His interest in print culture and the formation of collective identities bridges his scholarship on surfing, where he focuses on travel writing and the social history of international surf tourism.

GLEN THOMPSON is a research associate in the Department of History at Stellenbosch University. He writes on gender, race, and politics in the history of South African surfing culture. His publications include chapters in Robert Morrell's *Changing Men in South Africa* (2001) and Scarlett Cornelissen and Albert Grundlingh's *Sport Past and Present in South Africa: (Trans)forming the Nation* (2012), and articles in the *Journal of Natal and Zulu History*, *The International Journal of the History of Sport*, *Journal of African Cultural Studies*, and *Radical History Review*. His work has also appeared as an art installation in Paul Weinberg's *Beyond the Beach* exhibition. He is currently completing a book about South African surfing histories.

ISAIAH HELEKUNIHI WALKER is department chair and professor of history at Brigham Young University, Hawai'i, located on O'ahu's North Shore. The author of *Waves of Resistance: Surfing and History in Twentieth-Century Hawai'i* (2011), Isaiah has also published about surfing in *The Contemporary Pacific and Pacific Historical Review*. At BYUH, he teaches world, Hawaiian, and Pacific Islands history and actively participates in the Hawaiian surfing community.

ANDREW WARREN is lecturer in economic geography at the University of Wollongong, Australia. His research interests span labor, class, and cultural political economy. Andrew completed a doctoral thesis on the surfboard manufacturing industry in 2011 and, with Chris Gibson, authored *Surfing Places, Surfboard Makers* (2014). The book was shortlisted for the 2015 Ka Palapala Po'okela Hawai'i Book of the Year Award (Excellence in Nonfiction category) and won the 2015 Australian Society for Sports History Book Prize. Andrew is a lifelong surfer and is based on the New South Wales south coast.

BELINDA WHEATON is associate professor in sport and leisure studies in the Department of Te Oranga at the University of Waikato, New Zealand. Previously, she was reader in sport and leisure cultures at the University of Brighton, UK, where she taught sociology, sport and leisure studies, and sport journalism. She is best known for her research on the politics of identity in lifestyle sport, including the monograph *The Cultural Politics of Lifestyle Sports* (2013) and several edited collections, including *Understanding Lifestyle Sports: Consumption, Identity, and Difference* (2004).

DEXTER ZAVALZA HOUGH-SNEE is a doctoral candidate in the Department of Spanish and Portuguese at the University of California, Berkeley. A specialist in colonial Latin American literatures and culture, he is co-editor of *Estudios de sátira hispanoamericana colonial: "De estranhos casos que jamais pintaram" a "despoblados extensos"* (2015) and has written much about colonial satire, economic philosophy, and visual culture. Dexter has also published extensively about surfing's relationship to national identity, indigeneity, coloniality, and environmental protest in South America. He is currently preparing two book manuscripts, the first theorizing alienation in the colonial Andes in 1570–1640, and the other examining surfing's role in nation-building, indigenous identity formation, and political protest in contemporary Peru.

Index

CPSIA information can be obtained
at www.ICGtesting.com
Printed in the USA
LVHW080137301120
672984LV00068B/4756